A History of
Russian and Soviet
Sea Power

A HISTORY OF RUSSIAN AND SOVIET SEA POWER

Donald W. Mitchell

MACMILLAN PUBLISHING CO., INC.

NEW YORK

Maps and charts drawn by Rafael D. Palacios

Macmillan Publishing Co., Inc.
866 Third Avenue, New York, N.Y. 10022
Collier-Macmillan Canada Ltd.

Library of Congress Catalog Card Number: 72–93629

First Printing 1974

Printed in the United States of America

TO *Scotty, Bonnie, David, Samy,*

Mike, Sonya, AND *Robin,*

AND TO

their new grandmother,

Helen

Contents

Contents

Illustrations

Maps

Tables

Foreword

Adm. George W. Anderson
U.S. NAVY (RET.)

IN THE MONTH of April 1970, the Soviet navy conducted the largest naval exercise in the long history of Russia. Most significant is the fact that this group of naval operations was the widest in scope ever conducted by any navy in peacetime. Soviet units were operating simultaneously in the Atlantic, Pacific, and Indian oceans, in the Black, Baltic, and Mediterranean seas, and in the Sea of Japan, the Norwegian Sea, and the Philippine Sea, as well as the Sea of Okhotsk and the Barents Sea. The waters contiguous to the shores of the Soviet Union probably were covered at the same time by coastal craft. It is very clear that under the direction of the commanders in chief of all of the Soviet fleets there were more than 200 Soviet naval units deployed on the high seas. We do not know, of course, exactly how many submarines were active in the operations, but it is reasonable to believe that there must have been between 50 and 100 modern undersea vessels involved. Furthermore, Soviet naval aviation actively participated, with long-range aircraft extending their flights not only into the seas close around Russia but far into the reaches of the open oceans.

Public press releases from Moscow concerning this massive exercise emphasized the many phases of simulated naval warfare that were under survey—including even such sophisticated and modern activities as the launching of ballistic missiles on command from national headquarters. We Americans know that an exercise of such size and scope requires a high degree of planning, training, and logistic support involving officers and men of all ranks and rates, both in higher command headquarters and in the ships themselves. The benefits from such an exercise are far-reaching: it serves to demonstrate both capabilities and limitations, and detected limitations normally are subjected to subsequent corrective action. Following the practice of most of the navies of the free world, on completion of the exercise at sea, Soviet ships visited ports around the world, fulfilling political and psychological missions and at the same time according their crews the opportunity "to see the world through a porthole."

Each year we have observed an increasing capability on the part of the Soviet navy, reflecting a growing official appreciation of the importance of naval power both in peace and in war. In some of its aspects, particularly with respect to its submarine force, the Soviet navy today is much larger than its U.S. counterpart and in fact has a capability significantly greater than that maintained by any navy during peacetime. What the future holds regarding further expansion, greater sophistication, and modernization remains to be seen.

In September 1969 a coup was carried out in Libya when King Idris, temporarily absent from the country, was deposed by a group of relatively unknown young military officers. Shortly thereafter the new rulers of the country terminated British military agreements and informed the United States government that Wheelus Air Force Base near Tripoli would have to be vacated. These developments gave rise to serious apprehension as to the continuing validity of American and European oil concessions in Libya. Concern was evident in Tunisia and as far to the west as Morocco that subversive efforts would be made to overthrow the pro-Western governments of those countries. Since the coup the new government has formed increasingly close ties with the United Arab Republic and Syria, two nations which have become dependent on the Soviet Union for military and economic support, and which in turn both provide operating facilities for Soviet naval forces in the Mediterranean.

It is uncertain in the light of prevailing information whether the coup in Libya was stimulated by or with the knowledge of clandestine agencies of the U.S.S.R. There is no question, however, that at the time of the coup large naval forces of the Soviet Union were strategically deployed in the eastern Mediterranean Sea in a manner that could have been related to developments in Libya. Specifically, the U.S.S.R. had in the Mediterranean at that time some 65 ships, of which about half were surface combat types, including the new helicopter carrier *Moskva*. There were about a dozen Soviet submarines operating in the sea in positions perhaps calculated to be most effective against the U. S. Sixth Fleet; Russian-built aircraft and ships, especially configured for electronic intelligence collection activity, contributed to the Soviet naval posture. Moreover, along with their provision of surface ships, submarines, and aircraft to the United Arab Republic and Syria, the Soviets have sent large numbers of naval technicians to assist in a buildup of base facilities which they have been able to use themselves.

Although Soviet naval strength in the Mediterranean at the time of the coup in Libya was probably greater than it had been at any time to that date, it occasioned no great surprise among informed observers. They realized it was just a new peak in a progression of naval deployments which had begun in the Mediterranean more than a decade earlier and which had been steadily increasing not only there but worldwide. By now there should be no doubt in anyone's mind that the U.S.S.R. is determined to be a major maritime power and to maintain, in the words of Admiral Gorshkov, commander in chief of the Soviet navy, "a completely modern ocean-going navy fully responding to the requirements of missile-nuclear warfare."

In this volume, the story of Russian sea power is told in the context of eleven centuries of Russian history. Most of that story is not one of great naval glory, for predominantly land-oriented Russia has traditionally allocated a great share of her talents, finances, and resources to the expansion and defense of land frontiers and has utilized her navy primarily in a subservient role to support her army. There have been some notable exceptions to this generalization—under Peter the Great, Catherine the Great, and the Alexanders II and III—when the importance of sea power was recognized and naval strength was emphasized. Such recognition was rarely sustained, however, and even emphasized goals often suffered from inadequacy of means. Industrial weakness, technological deficiencies, uninspiring leadership, and a weak educational base were the principal adverse factors which negated the vision of

the more enlightened tsars. Aspirations to naval dominance beyond
coastal seas and territorial waters were thwarted not only by domestic failures but by external opposition frequently involving coalitions
of powers. What is more, geographical separation of the obvious
areas of Russian operation—the Black, the Baltic, and the Barents
seas and the Pacific Ocean—forced dispersion of effort and complicated the problems of logistical support.

In the early Soviet period it was beyond the capacity of the
government to reestablish the naval forces which were destroyed in
World War I and during the revolution. Then time ran out before
Stalin could build up his navy sufficiently to mount a successful
defense against German attack, and base areas in the Baltic and on
the Black Sea were overrun. Murmansk became an active area
of operations as the major terminal for military aid supplied to
the Soviet Union by the United States and Great Britain. Since
Stalin was faced with a struggle for survival in the west, the Pacific
was relegated to secondary importance and priority. In broad terms,
the performance of the Soviet navy in World War II was poor. Its
weakness is attributable to (a) a leadership failure to understand
sea power and its capabilities in time to provide adequately trained
and properly equipped forces; (b) the early loss of base and industrial areas to German attack; and (c) a preoccupation of the entire
Soviet Union with the strength of ground operations, so that air
and naval forces were kept in supporting roles.

World War II took a terrible toll in the Soviet Union, and the
immediate postwar years were necessarily occupied in recuperation,
rehabilitation, and reconstruction. It is clear, however, that during
those years there was much reflection over the wartime experiences
and the lessons to be learned from them. As the Western allies set
about rapidly demobilizing the greatest naval armadas the world
had ever seen, the Soviet Union began a long process of building
balanced naval forces capable of carrying out both defensive tasks
for offshore defense of the homeland, and offensive operations on
the high seas.

The initial stages of such a program are never ostentatious, particularly when conducted by a government dedicated to secrecy
and internal security. Hence it is understandable, though perhaps
not excusable, that many Western strategists and political authori-

ties failed initially to perceive Soviet plans for naval construction as a prelude to sea power—the first steps in a program of vast maritime expansion. After all, Western attention by then was focused on nuclear weapons, on the new range of missiles and rockets, on measures to constitute allied ground and tactical air strength to counter the proven threat of Soviet armies. Meanwhile, Soviet naval strength was reconstituted, and it was increasing in size, variety, and proficiency.

In retrospect there is little doubt that the Cuban missile crisis of 1962 came as both a shock and a stimulant to the Soviet leaders. As is pointed out in some detail in chapter 23 of this volume, in a crisis situation of their own creation the Soviets found themselves critically short of usable forces and clearly obliged to retreat. The need to prevent the recurrence of such a situation compelled them to revise their programs.

Developments in the past seven years obviously reflect decisions taken in the highest councils of the U.S.S.R. following the Cuban missile crisis. Production of intercontinental and intermediate range ballistic missiles has increased in quality, quantity, and warhead yield. Construction of nuclear-powered ballistic missile submarines has accelerated. New missile-firing surface ships and attack submarines have been programmed; training has been augmented; out-of-area operations have expanded; deployments to the Mediterranean proceed on a continuing basis. Concurrent emphasis has been placed on the buildup of the Soviet merchant marine and on activities in oceanic research. A new sophistication is noted in the employment of all maritime and naval forces to achieve maximum political and psychological impact.

And so it should not be surprising that the Soviet naval forces in the Mediterranean were deployed in opportune positions and in strength at the time of the Libyan coup in 1969. Nor would it be prudent to conclude from the large Soviet naval construction programs currently under way that the U.S.S.R. will stop short of achieving that level of sea power which in its view constitutes clear-cut superiority over any potential combination of opponents.

The Western world, and the United States in particular, naturally hopes that the buildup of such strategic and maritime strength by the U.S.S.R. will be accompanied by a growing Soviet awareness of the folly of using it. We hope most sincerely that Soviet intentions are and will continue to be to avoid hostilities—to resolve differences justly, peacefully, and on mutually acceptable terms. But unfortunately, in the light of past experiences and with the stakes of national security so high, there can be no sound alternative to realistic assessment of the capabilities of Soviet sea power. It therefore behooves the United States *and its allies* to maintain balanced forces of such size, composition, and state of readiness as to constitute a positive deterrent to any hostile use by the U.S.S.R. of the sea power she is building.

A unified deterrent posture at sea by the United States and its allies east and west, each in its own enlightened self-interest, is of vital security importance to all. If such a posture is taken, then there can indeed be hope that in time and under proper circumstances the U.S.S.R. will recognize with us the wisdom of mutual reduction of armaments at sea.

If there is any doubt concerning the ability and determination of the United States and its allies to meet the challenge of the growing naval and maritime strength of the Soviet Union, it must rise out of a fundamental question: Are these allies, as sovereign democratic nations acting in concert, stronger for the long pull than the Soviet Union with its communist system?

We all profess the faith that we are actually stronger. However, that faith can be justified only if we are unified, prudent, wise, and disciplined. Unified if each "pulls his weight in the boat." Prudent if we take timely actions in our own self-interest. Wise if we are properly selective in the allocation of our efforts and resources. Disciplined if we impose necessary restraints on our appetites for affluence.

Certainly the knowledge of the history of Russian sea power is a matter of importance to those who are—or should be—involved in the security of the United States and its allies. Nowhere can that knowledge be acquired more graphically than from the comprehensive story set forth in the chapters that follow. From these pages can be derived an important lesson—that sea power is essential to a nation that aspires to expanded world influence and, conversely, that adequate sea power is essential to a nation that seeks to preserve a prestige and position it has already attained.

Preface

In *A History of Russian and Soviet Sea Power* I have attempted to present a compact but complete account of the attempts of first the Russian and later the Soviet state to achieve naval strength. Beginning with the first efforts of Varangian pirates to attack Byzantium in the ninth century, the story ends with the year 1972, at which time a very substantial Soviet naval presence in almost every sea and ocean, a growing Soviet development of merchant ships, fishing fleets, and oceanography, and an increasingly sophisticated Soviet submarine threat were all combining to arouse the concern of American admirals.

The story of Russian sea power has so far never been written by an American, nor have Americans until very recently shown any interest in this direction. Consequently there has been a very general tendency in this country to underrate the Russians at sea. This is unfortunate. For aside from some mediocre performances—a phenomenon common to all military services with long histories—Russian seamen have established an imposing record of victories, explorations, inventions, and generally constructive achievements. Further, since World War II general naval strength and effectiveness have made a quantum jump. For possibly the first time in her history Russia has achieved sea power.

Though I have been a student of naval affairs in general since the age of seven years, I did not become interested in Russian naval history specifically until 1955. At that time the idea entered my thinking as a result of a seminar conducted for students of military affairs by Col. (now Brig. Gen.) James D. Hittle, Jr., USMC (ret.) (General Hittle is currently Undersecretary of Defense). The realization came to me that no American had written a Russian naval history and that there was no modern work in English whatever. Secondly, in view of the extremely limited sources available in English the project appeared to be so difficult as to constitute a major challenge. Further, a modern evaluation of the development of a rival military force, regarding which little was generally known, could prove an extremely useful addition to military information. Finally, as the story developed and the challenges were met, the subject itself became of primary interest.

The first draft, completed in 1961, was based on available English and American sources. This draft revealed immense gaps and the necessity of working in other languages. From 1961 to the summer of 1972 the manuscript was in process of continual change as new information was uncovered, mainly through research in French, German, and Russian sources. The present volume is, in fact, the sixth draft. The extensive use of foreign sources eventually enabled me to fill most of the gaps, though not equally satisfactorily for all periods. The sources of Russian naval history for the eighteenth century were found to be virtually complete and of excellent quality. They were much less authoritative and complete but still relatively reliable for the period between 1801 and 1917. However, for the early Soviet period they were exceedingly scanty and unreliable. Though in recent years they have shown improvement, there are still many deficiencies.

To cover the immense eleven-century scope of this history I have used the works of other writers where they were available. Thus two books of R. C. Anderson dealing with naval wars in the Levant and Baltic, as well as the excellent multi-volume *Seekriegsgeschichte* by Alfred von Stenzel, have been used as the main sources on sea battles in the eighteenth and early nineteenth century. But in most areas such assistance from high-grade secondary sources was unavailable.

The nature of the subject made advisable the adoption of certain special techniques. Thus in the matter of dates the Western calendar rather than the pre-1917 Russian calendar has been used. This accounts for the eleven-day discrepancy between the dates here and those cited in certain other studies. I have attempted, so far as possible, to supply first names for all persons named in the text of the manuscript. Unfortunately, the habit of Continental naval writers of omitting first names in their accounts defeated this effort on numerous occasions, and the number of officers bearing the same family name at times made identification difficult. In the further interests of accuracy, I also attempted to locate all place names mentioned on modern maps of the areas concerned; usually this could be done, but in a few instances a complete change in name or the disappearance of a town thwarted this attempt. Again, frequent inconsistencies as to names of ships, guns carried, details of battles, etc., have been resolved on the basis of which of several differing accounts appeared to be most plausible. In areas where the documentation itself is nonexistent, incomplete, or violently prejudiced, I have found it necessary to use my best judgment. For these and other reasons a completely definitive history on this topic is not possible at the present time, or perhaps ever.

That as close an approach to exactitude has been reached is due to prolonged and careful study aided by a long list of assistants whose generous and unselfish expenditure of time can never be repaid. Those who participated regarded their work as being in the national interest and gave unstintingly of their time and skills. They include many members of the library staffs of the Library of Congress, the New York Public Library, the Navy Department Library, the Washington, D.C., Public Library, Oxford University and the British Museum, the libraries of the National War College and the Industrial College of the Armed Forces, the Stanford University and Hoover Institution libraries, the Library of the University of Edinburgh (which used its archives to provide information on professors from that institution who founded the first Russian naval academy under Peter the Great), Universities of Iowa and Missouri, Parsons College, and Northeast Missouri State University. Information regarding the Bauer submarine was obtained through the Technical Museum of Munich, Germany. The State Department and Navy Department sections of the National Archives were consulted for certain purposes, as were the Archives of Former Russian

Imperial Naval Officers in America in New York City. The latter was, indeed, one of the most valuable single sources. Members of several branches of the Navy Department, especially the Office of Naval Intelligence, proved very helpful, as did individuals in the Central Intelligence Agency and the Historical Branch of the British Admiralty. Various types of assistance were also received from fellow faculty members, staff, and students of the Industrial College and the National War College. On various matters of specialized information the Smithsonian Institution gave assistance as did the naval attaché's offices of the British, French, Swedish, German, Soviet, Finnish, and Japanese embassies in Washington. Finally, in the summers of 1966, 1969, and 1971, the writer spent some four months visiting the Baltic, the Gulf of Finland, the Black Sea and the Mediterranean, the Volga and Dnieper rivers, and the few Soviet naval installations not off limits to an American. Throughout these journeys, unfortunately, assistance from Soviet authorities was so limited as to be nonexistent; in fact, in 1969 a diary and all other materials in the author's possession were searched and scrutinized before he was allowed to leave Soviet territory.

More than sixty persons have rendered direct assistance in the researching or writing of this volume. While mentioning everyone by name is not possible, a long list of acknowledgments is in order.

Reviewers and critics have included Rear Adms. E. M. Eller and F. Kent Loomis and Dr. William Morgan of the Office of Naval History, Brig. Gen. James D. Hittle, Jr., USMC (ret.), Cmdr. Robert Herrick, USN (ret.), Brig. Gen. and Mrs. Donald Armstrong, USA (ret.), Dr. Philip Lundeberg of the Smithsonian Institution, Dr. Paul Lindeman, and Mr. Sam Smiley of the Office of Naval Intelligence. Among the former Russian naval officers now resident in this country who assisted in the project were Messrs. Serge Glad (deceased), George Taube, I. V. Mishtowt, George Dvorjitsky, and Serge Kostenko of New York, and Victor Kamkin of Washington, D.C. Each of these men held naval rank and in most instances titles of nobility prior to the Russian Revolution. Lt. Cmdr. P. K. Kemp, O.B.E., R. N., editor of the *Royal United Service Institution Journal*, was helpful in locating some minor errors in the World War II chapters. Cols. K. J. Mikola and V. Tervasmäki of the Institute of Military History in Finland read chapters eighteen and nineteen and offered several factual corrections concerning Finland's World War II role. Mme Maroussia Krchivitsky of Washington, D.C., daughter of a Russian admiral and in her youth a personal acquaintance of many leading Russian naval figures, has aided in clearing up certain points.

Translation from foreign sources constituted the greatest single research problem. In translating I covered all of the French sources, most of the German, and a portion of the Russian. Assistance was received in German translations from Prof. Frederic Kirchberger of the Northeast Missouri State University faculty, Mrs. Helga Wood of the Industrial College staff, and Mr. C. Paul Koines of the Office of Naval Intelligence. My principal Russian language assistant, the magnitude and excellence of whose work was beyond praise, was Mr. Constantin Feodoroff of New York City. Considerable assistance was also received from Lt. Cmdr. Sumner Shapiro, USN, Mr. Herman Dworkin of the Office of Naval Intelligence, Mr. George Taube of New York, and a former Soviet naval officer who must remain anonymous.

Library and archival assistance was rendered by a very long list of persons, including Drs. Sergius Yakobson, "Fritz" Epstein, and Nicholas Gregg of the Library of Congress, Mr. George Stansfield of the National War College, and Miss Clara Widger and Mrs. Mary Stuart Terres of the Industrial College Library.

Typists are again too numerous for complete listing but included Mesdames Richard Heston, Goldie Benda, and Ginger Rust of Fairfield, Iowa, and Sergeant Johnston, USA, Mrs. Debby Livingston of Kirksville, Missouri, and Mrs. Mary McNab, Mrs. Marie de Toto, and Mary Schmitt of Washington, D.C.

Miscellaneous forms of assistance were given by many persons, including Rear Adm. Rufus Taylor of the Office of Naval Intelligence and later of the Central Intelligence Agency, Vice Adm. Edwin Hooper of the U.S. Navy History Office, fellow Industrial College faculty members Capt. Ben Worcester, USN, and Cols. Omar Knox and Sam Leocha, USAF, Rear Adm. D. W. Knoll who supplied information on Russian contributions to oceanography, Mr. Pablo Alemar of the Industrial College staff, Mr. Edward Freers of the Department of State. Among Hoover Institution people, Mrs. Mariam Hopiak and Mrs. Carole Norton both proved efficient and cooperative editors with whom it was a pleasure to work. Mr. Brien Benson, Head of Publications, was also most cooperative. Mr. Fred Honig of Macmillan proved very helpful. The form of transliteration of Russian into English employed was chosen by the publisher. My late wife, Mrs. Louise Mitchell, aided greatly as an editor, typist, literary critic, and cheerleader.

One further individual deserves special credit in connection with this book. My 1969 visit to the Soviet Union as well as publication delays suggested the need for some further changes, especially since considerable new Soviet material was becoming available. New data included the first-class report on an investigation of Soviet sea power which was conducted by an eminent panel of experts working at the Institute for Strategic Studies of Georgetown University during the summer of 1969. While this investigation covered much of the same ground as my own much larger study, it was more specifically directed toward strategic evaluation and an assessment of the implications of Soviet naval growth for American policy. One of the distinguished panel members, Adm. George W. Anderson, a former Chief of Naval Operations under President Kennedy, kindly accepted my invitation to write the introduction to this volume. In doing so he has brought a fresh and highly professional point of view into the study.

The majority of the illustrations used have come from the archives of the Former Imperial Russian Naval Officers in America. The remainder are from U.S. Navy or Soviet sources. Indebtedness is acknowledged for their use. The United States Naval Institute and Dr. Philip Lundeberg are thanked for permission to use a chart and a map respectively.

As the writer has previously stated, the unavailability of Russian naval archives since 1801, plus the vast informational gaps since 1917, make the writing of a completely accurate history on this subject a present impossibility. As a result absolute authenticity in some instances may never be attained. An author can only hope to illuminate an area previously dark, while reducing inaccuracies to the lowest possible level.

DONALD W. MITCHELL

A History of
Russian and Soviet
Sea Power

CHAPTER 1

Beginnings

THE SETTING

THE BEGINNING of the Russian state is shrouded in uncertainty and myth, for it was not until the ninth century A.D. that legendary Russia began to yield to historic Russia. Early records show a country of a few million people, pagan in religion and largely primitive in culture, who occupied only a small part of what later became European Russia. Lacking national unity and without fixed boundaries, they were divided into numerous feudal states, incessantly at war with one another as well as with the Poles, Turks, Swedes, Mongols, and other neighbors.

Perhaps the most important geographic feature of the normally flat Russian prairie land, ranging from the unproductive southern salt plains through the rich steppes and the woodlands of the central plains to the frozen tundras and swamplands of the Arctic, are the rivers flowing mainly from north to south. The sources of the Volga, Dnieper, Niemen, Dvina, and Neva—all the main rivers of European Russia except the Don—lie close together in the Valdai Hills, an upland region in northwest European Russia less than 100 miles square and about 1,000 feet above sea level. From this small area arise the wide, slow-moving rivers which either flow through most of two continents or permit easy portage to other rivers which do, thus bringing the Caspian, Black, Baltic, and White seas of Russia into relatively easy contact by water. A comparable situation obtains in Asiatic Russia. There the Ob, Yenesei, and Lena lose much of their value by emptying into the Arctic, but their numerous east-west tributaries permit movement with but few portages wherever their sources close together. There, through much of Russia's history boats and barges have crowded the river roads and served as the main means of transportation during the summer months, and hard-frozen ice has provided surface for sledges in winter. Commerce, transportation, fishing, war, and pioneer settlement have all followed the rivers.

Appropriately enough, the first outstanding Russian ruler was a navigator of the Russian rivers: Riurik of Jutland, who in 1862 was invited to assume the rule of the trading city of Novgorod on Lake Ilmen. Riuyik's companions and immediate followers, Danes, Frisians, and Swedes, known historically as Vikings or Varangians, were pirates by choice but also traders by necessity. Hardy, adventurous, and cruel, they were probably the best fighters of their age. They wandered widely along the sea coasts and up the rivers of medieval Europe from Sicily to England and from Normandy to Russia and Byzantium, frequently settling and being absorbed by the local population.

The Varangians were thus Russia's first seamen. Though they did not encounter much open sea, they explored widely, penetrating at least as far as the Murmansk Coast, the Caspian, and the Pechora Coast of the Arctic. The ships used by these chieftains were probably about 60 feet long and rose possibly 12 feet above the water, employing both sails and oars. They carried arms, a water supply, and primitive rations (mainly salt fish). Crews numbered (according to Gibbon) 40 to 70 men.

As soon as Riurik had established his power in Novgorod he turned his attention to the city's most pressing problem: the restoration of trade relations to the south. The Khazars, in establishing a kingdom north of the Black Sea, had subjugated the city of Kiev, thereby blocking commerce. Riurik sent two of his lieutenants, Askold and Dir, southward by water with the mission of chasing out the Khazars and reestablishing commerce. Both objectives were successfully accomplished.

THE ATTACKS ON BYZANTIUM

The Kiev venture was only the prelude to a far more ambitious undertaking. In 865 Askold and Dir with some 200 small ships descended the Russian rivers to the Black Sea, secured the support of tribes around the Sea of Azov, and attacked Byzantium, then the principal city of Europe. The appearance of these pirates in the Sea of Marmora surprised and greatly alarmed the Byzantines, whose emperor was away fighting the Saracens. Indeed, had the invaders attacked at once instead of pausing to plunder rich residences and monasteries outside the walls, they might well have succeeded in taking the city. As it was, their delayed approach enabled the Greeks to make preparations to withstand attack, and a tempest wrecked part of the pirate fleet, enabling the Greeks to resist until the return of their emperor with his much larger ships. The Russians were defeated.

The first attack on Byzantium by Russian pirates was destined to have far-reaching results. In the first place, it brought the Russians within the influence of what was then the most advanced culture and civilization in Europe. In the second place, it was the beginning of the irresistible attraction which the city by the Bosphorus was to hold for ambitious Russian leaders for more than a thousand years. Finally, the very fact that such an expedition could be undertaken seriously speaks volumes for the strength and ambition of these earliest of Russian sailors. In fact, such maritime enterprise so impressed the Byzantines themselves that by 900 A.D. a considerable number of Russian mercenaries were serving aboard the Byzantine emperor's ships, where their reputation for maritime skill and fighting ability was excellent.

Nearly a generation after the first Russian defeat a second and much larger amphibious expedition, reportedly including 2,000 ships, was sent south under Oleg, the son of Riurik. Despite losses in the cataracts of the Dnieper, about 80,000 men arrived before Byzantium. Though this force proved as unable to take the city by storm as had the earlier expedition, the Greek emperor was unable or unwilling to risk battle. By portaging their boats the Russians bypassed the forts that commanded the Bosphorus, crossed the isthmus, and launched their ships on the Sea of Marmora. Oleg's followers then ravaged the countryside for four years with little or no opposition until they were bought off by the emperor and retired with vast booty.

In 941 the Russians were back at Byzantium again, this time under their Grand Duke Igor. External conditions were apparently propitious: the Byzantine emperor this time was away in Italy with most of his fleet; the forces remaining were too weak to fight the Russians with much chance of success. Igor established a blockade and rejected efforts to buy him off, a decision which was to prove unfortunate from a Russian standpoint. The Byzantines had been quietly experimenting with an incendiary of great power, known historically as "Greek fire," whose exact ingredients are still a mystery and were then of course utterly unknown to the Russians. With the utmost secrecy the Greeks equipped fifteen old galleys with tubes for projecting this fire. When all was in readiness, the few Byzantine ships sallied forth. The Russians attacked vigorously and immediately were met with Greek fire. Recoiling in terror from this awesome new weapon, the Russian fleet speedily became disorganized, flames spread, and virtually the whole fleet was destroyed.

The Russians made two further attempts to take Byzantium. The first, led in 967 by the able Sviatoslav who reigned in Kiev, resulted in a Russian defeat, due partly to Greek fire and partly to a storm which destroyed a portion of the fleet. A second attack was made in 1043 by another Russian army and fleet under Grand Prince Yaroslav, great-grandson of Igor. The Byzantine Emperor Constantine IX offered compensation which the invaders refused to accept, and two sea battles ensued. In the second battle the Russians destroyed 24 enemy galleys but were again defeated by the devastating effects of Greek fire and the superiority of the Byzantine force.

The repeated attacks on Byzantium were not, of course, the only naval projects to engage the attention of the Varangian leaders of Russia; extensive commerce was conducted with the Byzantine Empire via the river highways. The principal trade route ran from the Baltic to the Bosphorus by way of Lake Ladoga, the western Dvina, and the Dnieper to the Black Sea, a river road which for a time offered few difficulties save for the waterfalls on one section of the Dnieper which made a portage necessary. Russian ships from Novgorod, Kiev, Smolensk, and other towns brought cargoes of furs, tallow, amber, and slaves to exchange for gold, wine, and fine fabrics. To the southeast, Russian vessels pushed down the Volga as far as the Caspian Sea, where they plundered Baku without, however, establishing any firm control. On this route Astrakhan was the principal trade center, where Persian and Indian goods were exchanged for the products of the north. In the north, Novgorod carried on trade through the White Sea by way of the Pechora and other rivers. For a time during the thirteenth century Novgorod was a member of the Hanseatic League.

Piratical raids constituted yet another aspect of maritime activity. As early as 840 there was a reported Russian amphibious raid on Amastris in Asia Minor, and between 880 and 1041 Russian expeditions raided and looted northern Persia five times. To the south the Russians obtained an outlet on the Black Sea.

Meantime the Viking character of the Russian leadership was changing. Partly through intermarriage with the more numerous Slavs and partly through borrowings from the Byzantines in religion, art, and culture, the descendants of the Varangians were gradually coming to bear less resemblance to their fathers.

Between the death of Sviatoslav (972) and the Mongol conquests of the mid-thirteenth century, there was a definite recession of maritime enterprise as the Russians gradually lost access to the Baltic in the north and the Black Sea in the south. Their weakened pressure in the south resulted from internal dissension owing to a lack of strong leadership, together with the westward push of various warlike tribes along the northern shores of the Black Sea. And while the rulers of Novgorod were able to establish trading settlements on the White Sea and in the Urals in the north as they continued their search for furs, somewhat less success attended their military exploits. In 1188 and 1191 Russian river fleets prevailed against the Swedes, and the Russians even annexed Finland, but their conquests were of brief duration. The Swedes recaptured Finland and established Vyborg as a fortress against the Russians. They also barred the Russians from the Baltic Coast and from Lake Ladoga and, in fact, at one time held nearly every important strategic or commercial point in northern Russia.

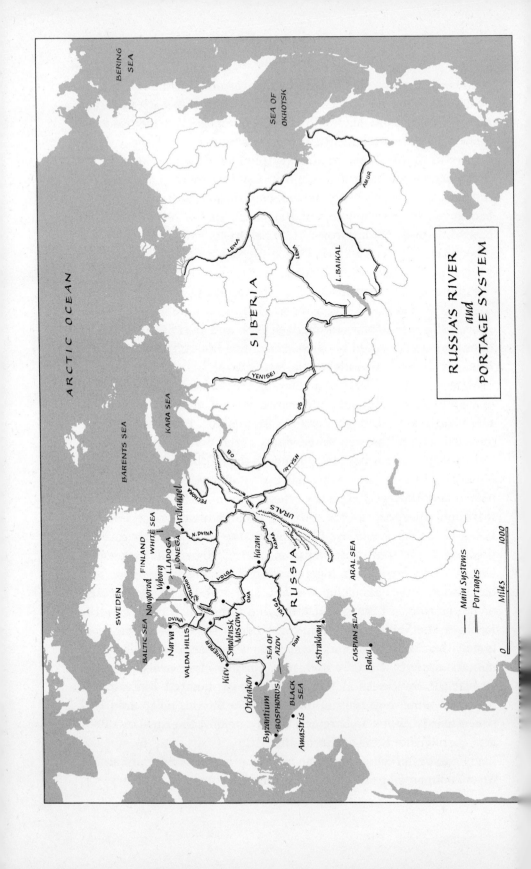

RUSSIA'S RIVER
and
PORTAGE SYSTEM

ARCTIC OCEAN

BERING
SEA

SEA OF
OKHOTSK

SIBERIA

AMUR

LENA

LENA

L. BAIKAL

YENISEI

OB

IRTYSH

OB

PECHORA

URALS

BARENTS SEA

KARA SEA

WHITE SEA

Archangel

N. DVINA

KAMA

ARAL SEA

Kazan

VOLGA

OKA

VOLGA

CASPIAN SEA

Baku

Astrakhan

DON

SEA OF
AZOV

Moscow

Smolensk

DNIEPER

Kiev

Otchakov

BLACK
SEA

Byzantium

BOSPHORUS

Amastris

FINLAND

L. LADOGA
L. ONEGA

Novgorod

Viborg

VOLKHOV

DVINA

Narva

VALDAI HILLS

BALTIC SEA

SWEDEN

RUSSIA

——— Main Systems
═══ Portages

Miles

0   1000

Nevertheless, despite these setbacks, Russian beginnings in European civilization showed decided promise when the thirteenth century began. Russian leaders had made progress in exploration and maritime enterprise and had been deeply influenced by one of the greatest civilizations of the time. The city of Kiev, unofficial capital of Russia for three and a half centuries, had become a center of religious and artistic life. And though all the attacks on Byzantium had failed, Russian sailors had given evidence of real ability combined with an ambitious and determined spirit.

THE MONGOL PERIOD

That this promising beginning came to naught was owing to one of the great disasters in the history of the civilized world. The Mongols were by far the most formidable barbarian invaders ever to pour out of Central Asia, and in fact the most successful conquerors of all times. Under the leadership of Genghis Khan and his successors, they marched east, west, and south, overcoming all resistance from the Baltic to the Adriatic, and ultimately to the Indian Ocean. Of all the peoples of Europe who fell victim to their onslaught, the Russians were the most thoroughly and disastrously conquered: Kiev and other Russian cities were destroyed; much of the population was slaughtered; the land was laid waste. The two hundred and forty years Russia spent under Mongol and Tatar domination had a basic and far-reaching effect, turning the country eastward and away from a Europe just beginning to blossom with the Renaissance. The Mongol political example of pure autocracy, or the ruler in a position of absolute power, was imitated by the Russians. As the land slowly recovered from the invasion, the leading city was neither Kiev the enlightened nor the democratic commercial center of Novgorod; it was Moscow. This town profited by its particularly slavish submission to the conquerors, and under a series of able and unscrupulous princes it gradually extended power, partly by taking over neighboring states and partly by establishing colonies.

The period of Mongol control had the further effect of turning Russians away from the sea. The ambitious campaigns and explorations conducted by the Varangians were no more; and the Varangians themselves disappeared, absorbed into the native population. The Russians lost their foothold in the Black Sea region to new Tatar states and were prevented from reaching the Baltic by other peoples, especially the Teutonic knights. Without direct contact with Byzantium, the internal trade routes along the Russian rivers fell into decline. In 1419 the Swedes even captured Arkhangelsk on the White Sea, though they were unable to hold it.

MARITIME INTERESTS 1450–1700

The decline in maritime achievements under Mongol conquest, though extensive, was by no means total. As the Russian state gradually took form under absolute monarchs, there were indications of reviving efforts to reach the sea.

Ivan the Terrible, or the Dread (1533–84), was unquestionably the most naval-minded Russian monarch prior to Peter the Great. Though best known in the West for his immorality and spectacular cruelty, he was a hard worker and a ruler of ambition and force, with a notable record of primarily constructive achievements. His grandfather, Ivan the Great (1462–1505), who had broken the Tatar yoke and conquered for Moscow all the dominions of Novgorod, had sought to turn Russia toward the West. Ivan the Terrible continued these policies, striving to strengthen the royal power and to change the landward orientation of his country by reaching toward the sea. Aware of the limitations of his own people, he imported instructors from England, France, Spain, and Holland to teach the Russians the more practical aspects of warfare and maritime industry. Early in his reign he opened commercial relations with England, sought a matrimonial alliance with an English princess, and requested Queen Elizabeth to send naval engineers and shipbuilders. The English queen was clever enough to evade all commitments while still preserving amicable relations. On one occasion she assisted Russian commerce in the Baltic by sending in a fleet which captured and turned over to Ivan some Polish pirates who had been particularly troublesome; she also sent the tsar as a gift a small sailing vessel which was carefully preserved for centuries. In return Ivan threw open the port of Arkhangelsk, first to British trade and later to the trade of all nations.

The central theme of Ivan's reign was expansion, especially in the direction of water outlets. During the months in which Arkhangelsk was open, fishing boats and coastal craft navigated in the White Sea and Ivan attempted to guard this trade from piracy by building a small fleet. Later, when his own force proved ineffective, he encouraged a fleet of privateers to attack the pirates.

The Baltic Sea, at that time being contested by Sweden, Denmark, and the Hanseatic League (all naval powers), was the scene of Ivan's greatest failure. He was able to carry on a limited trade through Narva and had hoped to establish a port bearing his name (Ivangorod) near the mouth of the Narva, but his efforts to seize Livonian territory resulted only in the extremely long Livonian war, which Russia lost.

Ivan's efforts in the south were somewhat more successful. In 1552, using a river fleet to supplement his large army, he captured Kazan on the Volga. Two years later he captured Astrakhan, thus providing his country with a second water outlet—though it opened only on northern Persia.

Because of Turkish strength, Ivan's efforts to find a larger outlet on the Black Sea met with more limited success. One Russian expedition descended the Don to Azov, which it occupied temporarily. Another force, 8,000 men under Alachev, followed the Dnieper to the Black Sea, freed Russian prisoners and captured Turks, and finally found itself in the Crimea fighting Tatars. But as in the Livonian war, a lack of naval strength weakened the Russian effort so that it attained no lasting results.

One other maritime development of the period should be noted —expansion eastward. Lured on by the fur trade, Russian adventurers, mainly hardy Cossacks who were explorers, traders, or soldiers as occasion demanded, greatly extended their sphere of activity. An eastward movement which ultimately was to lead through Siberia to the Pacific had gotten under way as early as the thirteenth century. As fur-bearing animals became scarce in Europe, Russian traders and trappers turned to Siberia, crossing the low Urals and reaching their destination by the Pechora, Ural, and Ob portages. The lower Ob was exploited during the fourteenth century but did

FINLAND

GULF OF FINLAND

LAKE LADO

Kronstadt

Noteburg

St. Petersburg

Narva

NARVA R.

LUGA R.

L.PEIPUS

Novgoro

L.VYRTS

SHELON R.

L.ILMEN

GULF
OF RIGA

Pskov

VELIKAYA R.

LIVONIA

Riga

DVINA R.

COURLAND

VELIKAYA R.

LOVAT R.

KUNYA R.

L.NESHCHERDO

L.D

DRISSA R.

USVIAT R.

N

Polotsk

KASP

OBOL R.

DVINA R.

Vitebsk

Portages

LUCHESA R.

0   Miles   100

DNIEPER

TO BLACK SEA

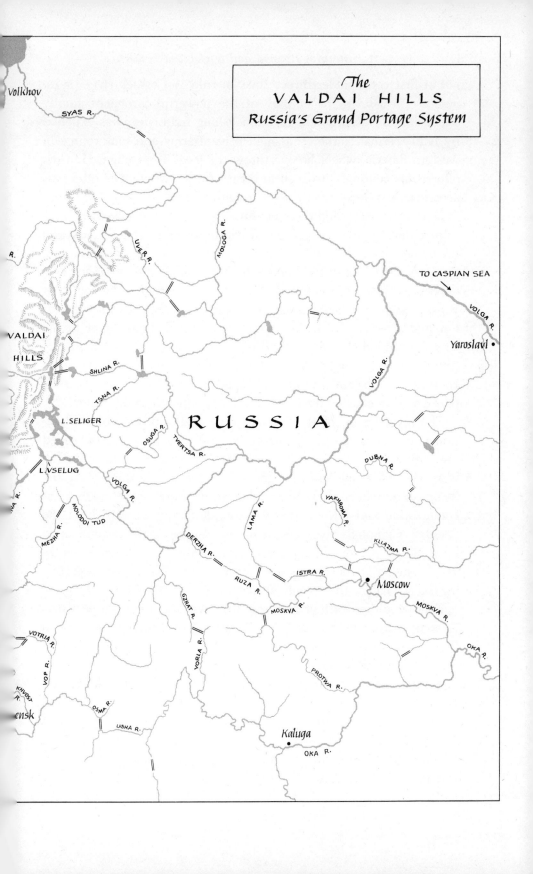

not at first come under direct Russian rule. A Cossack river pirate named Yermak, in the employ of the powerful Stroganov family which had developed salt, fur, and fishing industries, was expelled by Ivan. Yermak gathered a small private army and took refuge in western Siberia, where he overthrew the local Tatar chief. He then offered his conquests to Ivan in return for a pardon. The offer was accepted, and thus began Russian rule in Siberia.

During the following three centuries the eastward movement continued, led mainly by private adventurers in search of furs and unclaimed lands as well. As furs decreased in the Yenisei basin, trappers moved on to the Lena, which was discovered in 1630. Two years later Yakutsk was founded and speedily became the center of Russian activity in eastern Siberia. As early as 1648 Semen I. Dezhnev and others sailed in five boats down the Kolyma River to the Arctic, rounded the eastern end of Siberia, and then sailed up the Anadyr River, proving the separation of Asia and North America. In the same decade (1644) an expedition under Vasily Poiarkov penetrated uncharted territory to reach the mouth of the Amur.

The involvement of the Russian state in the process of exploration and conquest was not extensive; only in instances of armed opposition, such as the resistance of the Buriats around Lake Baikal, were the tsar's soldiers sent in. When the Russians reached the Amur in numbers they found that raids were not enough, that colonization and farming were required if they were to hold the country. Complete involvement of the Russian state, accompanied by diplomacy and military force, came only when Russia's southward-ranging adventurers came into contact with the Chinese during the last half of the seventeenth century.

Following the death of Ivan the Terrible came the grim period in Russian history known as "The Time of Troubles," during which Russian power declined. Boris Godunov (1598–1605), who succeeded Ivan following a term as regent, recognized the importance of naval power; but he was so beset with conspiracies, wars, and famines as to be unable to make any progress, naval or otherwise. Michael Romanov (1613–45), his successor following a period of rebellion and conflict, was compelled to abandon a contest for Karelia and Livonia and to grant many commercial concessions to foreign countries. Through much of his reign the Dutch held a monopoly over the trade from Arkhangelsk. Although during this period the *Fredrick*, a 120-foot three-masted warship with 24 oars, was constructed for the Russians at Nizhni Novgorod under Dutch direction, the vessel was soon lost in the Caspian Sea.

During the reign of Michael Romanov there was a great deal of small-scale naval activity in the south, where Cossacks in large or small bands navigated the rivers and penetrated into the Black Sea for purposes of pillage. These pirates, tactical descendants of the Varangians, used small (40- to 50-foot) galleys which occasionally employed a small sail but were propelled mainly by oars. Each vessel carried 50 to 70 men. The Cossack admiral held absolute command while the ships were at sea, and discipline prevailed to the extent that no drinking of vodka was permitted. To check the Cossack raids the Turks strengthened Azov on the Don and built Ochakov on the Dnieper, but such steps proved only partially effective. The Cossacks avoided daylight conflict with the Turks (whose vessels were qualitatively superior), and concentrated instead on surprise night raids on towns and commercial vessels. Such tactics were employed against Turkish cities of the Caucasus and Anatolia, and in 1624 a Cossack band even pillaged homes in the suburbs of Constantinople. These seagoing guerrilla fighters rarely embarked on large campaigns, and their connection with the Russian government in Moscow was slight or nonexistent.

The Russian ships employed during the early post-Mongol period were for the most part little more than large boats. Many a boat had a bottom fashioned from a single hollowed-out willow or linden tree with boards nailed along the sides. Normally there was no deck. Oars furnished the principal means of propulsion, although some also carried a small square sail. A boat might have a belt of reeds as a kind of bustle around the hull to prevent damage by chafing with other vessels. Length ranged from 40 to 100 feet. On the White Sea were to be found several types of large boats known as ketches, ladyas, kerbasses, bus's, and shiskas. Early accounts credit these vessels with the virtues of seaworthiness and lightness. They could be pulled overland for considerable distances by their crews, so that when the Turks "closed" the Dnieper the Cossack pirates merely dragged their boats around enemy fortifications and launched them in the river below.

The second Romanov, Alexis (1645–76), the father of Peter the Great, came to the throne at the age of sixteen. As soon as the domestic problems which beset the first decade of his reign were solved, he turned with the aid of his able adviser, A. L. Ordin-Nashchokin, to possible foreign adventure. Like Ivan the Terrible, he recognized the need for a navy and for securing outlets on the Baltic and Black seas; he, too, was unable to carry his plans to fruition. In a brief war with Sweden he made some use of a large galley flotilla which sailed down the Neva, surprised and defeated a Swedish force, and took the important island of Kotlin (later the site of Kronstadt). Alexis even considered using his galleys against the much better warships of the Swedes in an attempt to take Stockholm. Ordin-Nashchokin had a number of larger warships built on the Upper Dvina for use in a planned attempt to capture Riga, but unfortunately the Polish entrance into the war on the side of Sweden tipped the scales against the Russians, who ultimately were forced to give up even Kotlin.

Soon thereafter Alexis lost interest in the war with Sweden and negotiated a peace. He next turned his attention to the south, where Poles, Turks, and the Cossack rebel Stenka Razin were all potential foes. The difficulty of dealing with Stenka Razin, who maintained his camp on a fortified island in the Caspian Sea, demonstrated anew the need for a Russian fleet. In 1658 Ordin-Nashchokin induced Alexis to accept a program of shipbuilding under Dutch direction. Johann Sveden, the first shipyard director for the new program, soon died and was replaced by Cornelius Bucksgoven and his son Isaac. In spite of many other interruptions, the year 1668 saw the completion of the *Orel* 22, a three-masted ship 80 feet in length by 21 feet in width with eagles carved on poop and prow. A number of small gunboats also were built, and the entire squadron, based at Astrakhan on the Caspian, may be considered the first Russian national fleet. Shortly thereafter a set of naval regulations, modeled after those of the Dutch, was issued by Ordin-Nashchokin.

This second attempt to build and use warships proved no more successful than the first, however. Manned by Dutch sailors who were little interested in the tsar's quarrels, the *Orel* and her consorts were abandoned at Astrakhan by their crews (who departed for Persia and later got back to Holland) and were then captured and burned by the forces of Stenka Razin.

As this brief survey of early beginnings indicates, Russia had maritime interests of importance long before the time of Peter the Great, interests which in early times were largely connected with navigation on the inland seas and lakes. Promising Varangian maritime exploits never reached fruition. The Mongol period proved catastrophic to the Russians in every respect, maritime interests included. Yet even during the last years of this era the Russians were expanding toward the sea by following their matchless system of inland waterways. Both Ivan the Terrible and Ordin-Nashchokin clearly perceived the importance to Russia of a navy and access to the sea. Yet they were unable to overcome the enormous difficulties of updating a largely landlocked and extremely backward state to the extent necessary for carrying out maritime objectives.

CHAPTER 2

Peter the Great:
Father of the Russian Navy
(1689-1725)

CHARACTER OF PETER THE GREAT

As an institution is but the lengthened shadow of a man, so the Russian navy shows the imprint of Peter the Great's strong hand in many ways even to this day.

Peter the Great (1672–1725) would have been a remarkable man in any age or in any nation. Born in the most backward country in Europe during a period of strife and violence, he was in his own time more than remarkable. His father, Tsar Alexis, died while Peter was still a child. His half sister Sophia served as regent from 1682 to 1689 following the brief reign (1676–82) of an older brother, Fedor II. Between 1682 and 1696 Peter was co-tsar with a feeble-minded half brother, Ivan, both under the de facto domination of Peter's mother. During the period of his co-regency Peter was acquiring an education, largely under the tutelage of a Dutchman named Franz Timmerman and a Swiss adventurer and boon companion, François Lefort. His studies were at times interrupted, once by a conspiracy aimed at murdering him and nominally conferring full leadership to Ivan, under whom Sophia herself hoped to rule as regent. Lefort and Gen. Patrick Gordon played an active role in assisting Peter, who suppressed the rebellious Streltsy, confined Sophia to a convent, and returned to his studies.

Peter early showed an insatiable curiosity and a determination to learn first-hand, as well as limitless energy, dedication, restlessness, and an imperious temper. Physically, he was nearly seven feet tall and possessed of gigantic strength. In 1688 he discovered in an abandoned shed at Izmailov a small English-built sailing vessel which had belonged to his grandfather. He at once had the ship repaired (by Karshden Brandt, the Dutch carpenter who had largely built the *Orel*), fitted it with sails, and learned to navigate it. Later he referred to it as the "little grandfather of the Russian navy." Technical and mechanical arts and their application to military and naval affairs early fascinated him and continued to be a lifelong interest. During his lifetime he learned more than twenty trades, mostly trades with direct military or naval applications. In 1693 he saw the ocean for the first time at Arkhangelsk. At this village, then the only Russian port, he eagerly questioned the English and Dutch seamen whose ships occasionally stopped to trade. At a banquet he gave for the foreigners he seated himself among the common seamen, thus indicating a humble desire to acquire learning at all levels.

Peter was quick to recognize the educational limitations in his own country; he went abroad in order to learn first-hand the bases of Western superiority. He worked on the wharves at Arkhangelsk, served as a cabin boy and common seaman, labored with his hands as a carpenter and shipwright at Amsterdam, learned ordnance in Germany and naval science in Holland and England. He sent nobles to England, Holland, and Italy for nautical training and enlisted numerous foreigners into his own service. Peter's projects were rarely original, but he pursued them with an energy and persistence that brought success, and though he made many mistakes he learned from experience and never made the same blunder twice. Able, cruel to his enemies, imperious, he was yet entirely teachable and humbly respectful before the demonstrated capacity or knowledge of others. He attempted to force rather than lead the backward, semi-Oriental Russia of his day to a westward orientation and turn it overnight into a modern, powerful, European state with a strong navy and a merchant marine, a nation with clear access to the sea.

Peter held the view, as expressed to his confidant, Prince Aleksandr Menshikov, as well as to his favorite foreign adviser, English Gen. Patrick Gordon, that the mouths of the Don, the Neva, and the Amur were of primary importance to Russia as outlets to the sea.

This view foreshadowed the direction of Russian naval policy for the next two centuries. During the first year of his reign (1689) Russia lost access to the mouth of the Amur to China by the Treaty of Nerchinsk, a development which Peter regarded as catastrophic. Since the mouths of the Don and the Neva were at that time in the firm possession of Turkey and Sweden respectively, Russia's only realistic hope of gaining access to the oceans, and thereby communication with the West, was through successful military campaigns.

Before starting the wars that were to run continuously for most of his reign, Peter appears to have weighed the possibilities of turning Arkhangelsk into a major center of maritime activity. On his 1693 visit he expressed irritation at the many limitations of the port and the few Russian vessels trading there. He also started a limited shipbuilding program under Count (later Adm. Fedor Matveevich Apraksin, which quickly resulted in the completion of the *Apostol Pavel* 24, the *St. Pierre et Von* 12, and finally the 44-gun *Sainte Prophetie*. These ships, which Peter tested in person when he returned a year later, became his White Sea fleet and were placed under the command of Vice Admiral Buturlin. Some of his biographers claim that Peter also considered a possible sea route north of Siberia. Such a route was never developed during his reign, however, and now, apparently satisfied that he had given the White Sea all the attention it deserved, he turned his attention southward.

THE TURKISH CAMPAIGNS

In the late 1600s, Russian access to the Black Sea was blocked by Tatars who were somewhat loosely allied to Turkey. In his first military expedition, undertaken in 1695, Peter attacked Azov with some 30,000 men. This attempt fared no better than had Russian attacks in 1687 and 1689: the garrison, strengthened by sea communications, suffered little damage and in a return sortie badly defeated the besiegers.

This defeat lent confirmation to Peter's estimation of the importance of sea power, and he set out to repair the deficiencies of his forces in that area. He established shipyards at Voronezh on the

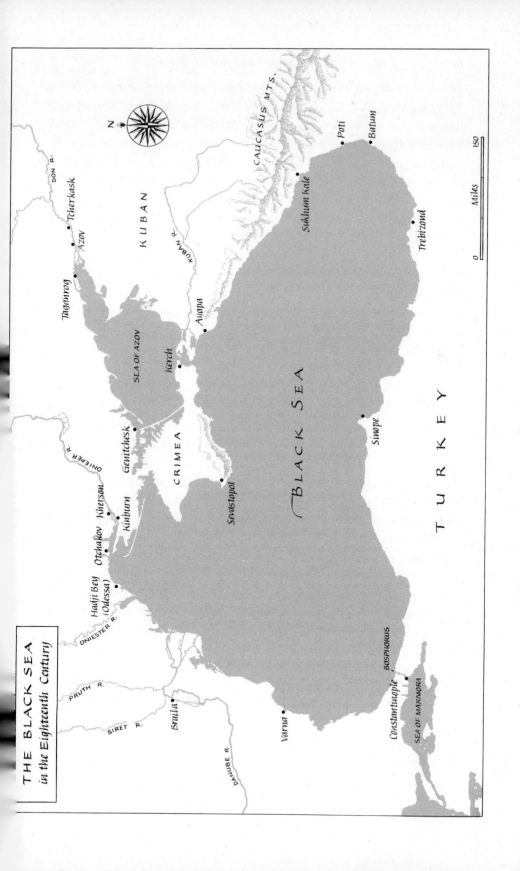

THE BLACK SEA
in the Eighteenth Century

N

DON R.

Tcherkask
Azov
Taganrog

KUBAN

KUBAN R.

Poti
Batum

Sukhum Kale

CAUCASUS MTS.

Trebizond

SEA OF AZOV

Kerch

Anapa

CRIMEA

Genitchesk

DNIEPER R.

Kherson

Otchakov
Kinburn

Hadji Bey
(Odessa)

Sevastopol

BLACK SEA

Sinope

TURKEY

DNIESTER R.

PRUTH R.

SIRET R.

Braila

DANUBE R.

Varna

BOSPHORUS

Constantinople

SEA OF MARMORA

0   150

Miles

upper Don and at Briansk on the Desna, a tributary of the Dnieper. By June 22, 1696, the Russians had completed 22 galleys and 24 fireships, as well as some larger craft and approximately 1,500 barges, rafts, and small boats. Peter placed François Lefort in command of sea forces while he himself served as captain of a division of galleys. Troops were under command of a Russian noble named Aleksei Shein. In late June the siege of Azov began. Though a small Turkish fleet appeared, it made no move to fight the Russians. Attempts of Turkish commercial vessels to bring in supplies were defeated by the Russians, who either captured or burned the supply ships. On land Peter's Cossack allies successfully raided supplies intended for the garrison. After a month of siege and a decisive storming, Azov surrendered. On the Dnieper a Russian force of 118 small craft operated less decisively against the Turks but did succeed in capturing a number of Turkish merchantmen and storeships.

The logistic effort behind the first defeat of the Tatars was a far greater achievement than the victory itself. The building of a fleet meant obtaining engineers, shipwrights, and artillerists abroad, for Russia had no shipbuilding resources. A working force of 30,000 men had to be gathered, trained, and provisioned. The small craft were built at Briansk. The larger vessels were built at Voronezh under the direction of Dutch, Italian, and English engineers. Galleys were constructed from a Dutch model and under Dutch direction. A Dutchman, Jan Eric, directed the building of korobels, craft 126 feet long by 35 wide and capable of mounting up to 60 guns. An Englishman, Baldwin Andrews, superintended the building of ships 115 feet long, 27 feet wide, and seven feet deep, capable of carrying 46 guns. Giacomo Moro, a Venetian, supervised construction of a 50-foot boat, ten feet wide and propelled by oars. Ironically, the fleet was armed with cannon made in Sweden, which was to be Russia's next foe. Some of the crews were Don Cossacks; others were sailors from the White Sea, brought south in forced marches. The cost of the effort was defrayed by a new *corvée maritime*, an exceedingly unpopular measure by which towns, large landlords, the clergy, merchants, and other elements were forced to contribute to shipbuilding. The minimum time estimated to create this fleet was two years. Yet Peter, at the cost of heavy losses of manpower from disease and fatigue and a great deal of suffering from cold on the part of everyone including himself, got the job done in about six months of the Russian winter.

The war between Turkey and Russia lasted for several years. In the meantime Russian shipbuilding continued on the Don and its tributaries with larger vessels being turned out, including line-of-battle ships. A naval base was set up at Taganrog on the Sea of Azov, and in 1698 an elementary naval establishment was opened. In order to Russianize a predominantly Tatar area Peter brought in 15,000 colonists. Turkish attacks to interrupt these preparations were defeated. In the winter of 1697 the Russians repelled a Tatar attack on the Russian galleys, and during June of the same year a Turkish assault on Azov was successfully resisted. The next summer the port was blockaded by Turkish galleys. Peter returned to the south in 1699, and with his presence a more aggressive spirit was introduced. Despite a shortage of crews he oversaw the fitting out of a fleet consisting of 11 ships of 36 to 52 guns, a bomb vessel, and four galleys. On July 3 most of this fleet, with Adm. T. A. Golovin in command and Peter serving as senior captain, exercised in the Sea of Azov. Impressed by such a display of power, the Turks agreed to a truce which left Azov in Russian hands.

The new territorial gains proved disappointing for several reasons. Not only were the Sea of Azov and the Black Sea into which it emptied almost completely enclosed by land, but in both instances the Turks controlled the outlets. Unable to enlist the aid of other European powers in a major war of conquest against Turkey, Peter had to be satisfied with an incomplete victory. Furthermore, the upkeep of a naval force posed new problems. Galleys were badly damaged by ice during the frozen-in periods of the Russian winter. Since many of the ships were of pine and fir rather than oak and all had been built hastily, they deteriorated rapidly. The upkeep of a naval force under such conditions required constant effort which was in fact sustained only when Peter was present. But for a decade following 1699 Peter was elsewhere, and the Black Sea establishment was permitted to decay.

In 1710 Turkey declared war. The Russian fleet was then in bad condition and put up no resistance when a Turkish fleet appeared before Taganrog. On land Peter's army suffered decisive defeat along the Prut River. In the Peace of Prut, Peter gave up all of his south-

ern conquests, thus putting an end to the first Russian Black Sea
Fleet. Some ships were surrendered to the Turks, others proceeded
up the rivers, and still others were destroyed by their own crews.
During the 16 years of this fleet's existence, the Russians had put
forth a shipbuilding effort which produced no less than 58 battleships besides smaller vessels. As they gained experience their production improved, and by the end of the period Russian builders
were launching vessels (bearing such colorful names as *Scorpion*,
Tortoise, *War Flower*, and *Sleeping Lion*) which were at least no
worse than those built by other nations.

THE SWEDISH WAR: EARLY PHASES

Long before his efforts in the Black Sea met with failure, Peter's
main interest had turned in another direction. By 1700 the Baltic
was largely a Swedish lake, for under a series of able rulers Sweden
had become one of the principal naval and military powers of
Europe. She controlled most of the Baltic coastline, including both
sides of the Gulf of Finland, all of the Gulf of Bothnia, the eastern
coast of the Baltic, and the mouths of several German rivers (e.g.,
the Peene and the Oder). Also in Swedish control was most of the
coast of Lake Ladoga and Lake Peipus (Chudskoe). These conditions presented formidable difficulties and complications to the task
of establishing effective Russian naval power. After 1700 Peter's
Swedish policy aimed at four objectives: (1) the occupation of the
Baltic Coast, (2) the destruction of Sweden's grip on the Russian
rivers and lakes, (3) the creation of a strong Russian Baltic fleet,
and (4) the engagement and destruction of the Swedish fleet.

To all appearances fate played into Russian hands in 1697 when
Charles XI, King of Sweden, died, leaving his throne to a boy of
fifteen years. Resolved to take prompt advantage of this supposed
weakening of Swedish power, Frederick IV of Denmark, Augustus
II of Poland and Saxony, and Peter I of Russia concluded an alliance and declared war on Sweden. They agreed that Poland was to
receive Livonia and Estonia, Russia to get Ingria and Karelia, and
Denmark to annex Holstein and the mouths of the Elbe and Weser.

The disillusionment of the allies was rude and swift. Charles XII was a boy in years, but he was also a lover of war and one of the greatest military commanders of his time. He readily defeated the western half of the alliance and forced Denmark (then also being coerced by British and Dutch naval power) to withdraw from the war. He then turned against the Russians. On November 19, 1700, at the village of Narva in Estonia, his army of 8,000 Swedes attacked 40,000 entrenched Russians in a snowstorm, capturing all the Russian artillery and killing or capturing a sizable portion of the Russian Army. In this decisive engagement the older Russian cavalry and irregulars fled, the new infantry proved untrained, and the foreign advisers proved incompetent.

Unfortunately for the Swedes, Charles failed to follow up this brilliant victory and instead turned southward against his other foe. Though he speedily and soundly defeated Augustus II, he was unable to knock Poland out of the war until 1706.

Meantime, Peter had shown brilliance of his own in recovering from disaster. Peter used the breathing space his enemy had given him to excellent advantage in reorganizing and improving his army. Duke Kroa, who had lost at Narva, was replaced by the able B. P. Sheremetev. By melting church bells the Russians produced 255 new cannon. Peter also introduced reforms in training, arming, and organization of his troops; within a year of his defeat he had a new and far stronger army to which he applied the lessons learned from his Swedish "teachers."

As the Russian forces recovered, Peter used them to conquer territory around the eastern end of the Gulf of Finland, clearing Swedish garrisons from the shores of Lake Peipus and Lake Ladoga and the banks of the Neva River. By now the task was not difficult, for Charles, greatly underrating his northern foe, had left only 15,000 men to defend the Baltic provinces.

The Russian conquests paved the way for sea power, and in this setting of constant war Peter proceeded to the appointed task of creating a Russian navy. His first ships were small boats, and the first naval battles were fought on Lakes Ladoga and Peipus and on the Neva River.

The first naval action of the Great Northern War came in 1701 when the Swedes sent seven ships to the White Sea to attack Arkhangelsk. Although the Russians at the time had nothing afloat that could offer opposition, the Swedes lost two six-gun ships on the banks of the Dvina: Russian prisoners, impressed into duty as pilots, deliberately ran the ships aground under the guns of a Russian fort, where they were captured in a night attack by two Russian boats loaded with soldiers. The remainder of the Swedish squadron cruised the White Sea, capturing fishing smacks and burning coastal villages until July 21, when it returned to Sweden. This encounter attracted Peter's attention; the next summer he resumed shipbuilding and developed shore defenses at Arkhangelsk, though in his planning he always kept the White Sea subordinate to the Baltic.

Peter's first offensive move against Sweden following his Estonian defeat and the departure of Charles XII was an attempt to capture the town of Narva, which lay only 15 miles from the Gulf of Finland on the Narova River. This initial move foiled, Peter turned in another direction. He moved ships built on the White Sea from Arkhangelsk to Lake Onega, portaged his fleet to the Svir River and then entered Lake Ladoga from the east.

In several actions between small ship squadrons the Russians (commanded at various times by Colonels Ostrovsky, Tyrtov, and Tolbukhin) were victorious over Swedish flotillas under Admiral Nummers. On June 27 a force of 700 Russian soldiers in 18 unarmed boats attacked a Swedish force of three brigantines, three galleys, and two boats at a time when most of their crews were ashore, and scored a definite victory. Again, on September 7 near Kexholm, 20 Russian boats attacked and defeated the same squadron. On October 12, 1702, the fortress of Noteburg, located at the source of the Neva, fell to a combined assault by army troops and 50 Russian boats hauled overland, and was renamed Schlüsselburg (Key City). Thus Peter blocked Swedish access to northern Russia and Lake Ladoga, and to discourage a possible Swedish return he also promptly built a dockyard to provide ships.

The next step involved the Neva River and direct access to the Gulf of Finland. Early in 1703 Russian forces took Nyenskans, a fort at the mouth of the Neva. In May a boarding party in small boats captured Swedish *Astrel* 14 and *Hayden* 10 in the Neva, and in the autumn the Russians were able to take the important island at the mouth of the river which they named Kotlin (for a kettle of cooking fish the Swedes had left in their flight). Thus before the end of 1703 Peter had gained a narrow outlet on the Baltic.

To protect and widen this corridor it was necessary to capture Lake Peipus. This struggle consumed more time. In 1702 a Swedish squadron of four small ships seized control of the entire lake and beat off an attack by 100 Russian boats. Later, however, the Swedes lost first the *Flundra* 4, which the Russians took after her crew had run her aground in an attempt to escape capture, and then the *Vivat* 12 when she was attacked by 100 Russian boats while on a reconnaissance mission. The Russians did not capture the *Vivat*, however; Capt. Jonas Hokeflycht, the Swedish commander, chose to blow up his vessel rather than surrender. The Swedes then retreated up the Embach River with their remaining ships.

During the winter the Swedes reinforced their fleet, and in the spring of 1703 it numbered 13 sail. On August 7 this reinforced fleet beat off a Russian attack with a loss to the Russians of 20 boats. The next year a Russian army of 9,000 men landed at the mouth of the Embach, constructed a boom across the river and waited. When the Swedish commander Löschern arrived on May 17 with all his 13 ships, the Russian batteries opened fire. Unable to deal with the boom, the Swedish ships drifted against it and were either captured or destroyed. The battle ended Swedish sea power on Lake Peipus and left the Russian troops, under Sheremetev and a Scotch soldier named Ogilvie, free to take Derpt, Ivangorod, and Narva. Thus, by the end of 1704 Peter had eliminated the Swedes from Lake Ladoga and Lake Peipus and was in control of a narrow corridor to the Baltic along both sides of the Neva River.

THE FOUNDING OF THE BALTIC FLEET

Decisive differences between Charles XII of Sweden and Peter the Great lay in the latter's superior strategic sense and in his promptness to exploit success. These gifts were never more in evidence than in the use he made of the land conquered at the head of the Baltic. Though much of it was thinly settled swamp, its location held for Peter a supreme attraction. In 1703 he started work on a new capital, St. Petersburg, which would lie directly on the sea and

THE BALTIC at the time of Peter the Great

WHITE SEA

Archangel

N

NORWAY

SWEDEN

GULF OF BOTHNIA

Gotborg

Stockholm

Karlskrona

DENMARK

Copenhagen

BORNHOLM

Kolberg

Danzig

Königsberg

BALTIC SEA

COURLAND

Memel

Libau

GULF OF RIGA

ÖSEL

DAGÖ

Riga

LIVONIA

Revel

Baltic Port

Hangö

Porkkala

Borga

Helsinfors

Abo (Turku)

Nystadt

FINLAND

KARELIA

Vyborg

Kexholm

LAKE LADOGA

Olonets

LAKE ONEGA

SVIR R.

GULF OF FINLAND

NEVA R.

Schlüsselburg

St. Petersburg

Kronstadt

Ivangorod

Narva

LAKE PEIPUS

L. ILMEN

Novgorod

VOLKHOV R.

VALDAI HILLS

RUSSIA

MSTA R.

EMBACH R.

DVINA R.

VOLGA R.

Moscow

Smolensk

Palaeies

0   200
Miles

face westward. Almost simultaneously he established a dockyard and began building seagoing warships. During the winter of 1703–1704 he fortified the island of Kotlin, establishing the naval base of Kronstadt. The fortresses of Olonets on Lake Ladoga and of Peter-and-Paul at the mouth of the Neva were other bastions in his system of defenses.

A less resolute and resourceful man than Peter would have shrunk from the costs and risks involved in a huge building project under such adverse conditions. St. Petersburg was then remote from the centers of Russian strength, and all supplies had to be brought through the wilderness. A determined Swedish attack could have destroyed most of Peter's handiwork. On two occasions the Swedes did launch attacks. The first was so light it was easily repelled with heavy Swedish loss; the second found the Russian forces weak but was countered by a ruse when Peter dispatched a swarm of messengers with letters directing officials to send to his assistance regiments which were either nonexistent or elsewhere. When several of the messengers were captured, the Swedish commander concluded the Russians were in far greater strength than he had anticipated and ordered a hasty retreat. But the Swedes were not the Russians' only peril: losses of men from exposure and disease were burdensome and the financial cost almost prohibitive.

While Peter was founding his new capital and setting up its defenses, he was simultaneously building ships. Because the resources available to him inside Russia did not include shipbuilders, he secured the services of two British master builders, Messrs. Richard Brown and Peter Bent, and later additional British, Danish, and Dutch experts. The first vessels built were galleys, but Peter soon ordered the construction of 52-gun line-of-battle ships as well. By 1705 the Russian fleet consisted of nine ships of the line and 36 smaller craft, some built in Russia and some purchased abroad, principally in England and Holland. In June 1705 the young Russian fleet was challenged by a Swedish squadron of seven battleships and five frigates. It is significant that Peter refused the challenge. Though fond of conflict, he was not foolhardy, and he realized that the new fleet could not risk battle with an able and determined enemy without a few years of development to produce efficiency. Even in later years Peter was so convinced of Swedish qualitative superiority that he ordered his commanders to avoid battle unless they had a one-third superiority of force.

Naval development proceeded rapidly. Further conquests along the Baltic widened the narrow corridor to the sea and provided a more secure base. At the same time, Peter was expanding Russian shipbuilding and base facilities and strengthening shore defenses at Kronstadt. He succeeded in importing skilled foreigners who set up and ran important auxiliary industries, such as iron works, cannon foundries, and woodworking establishments. By funneling all foreign trade through St. Petersburg he assured the commercial future of his new capital. On November 16, 1705, Peter founded a naval marine force to guard ships and ports ashore, and to lead boarding parties and head landing operations at sea.

His most difficult problems, however, concerned personnel. Since Russia was without a merchant marine and had very few fishing boats, she had no large reservoir of potential seamen. In later days the people of the Baltic provinces were able to help offset this deficiency, but in Peter's time that resource was under the Swedish flag. Hence peasants and soldiers had to be employed and taught the rudiments of their trade aboard ship. The task of training was never well performed. Long-service seamen were a rarity and never constituted more than ten percent of the crews. Although the pay scale provided greater compensation than could be obtained ashore and Peter took great pains to make life aboard his ships tolerable, few Russians liked the sea and they avoided it whenever possible. Conditions aboard ship in *any* navy during the eighteenth century would seem intolerable by today's standards. Inferior and inadequate clothing, lack of ventilation below decks, poor water, wormy and monotonous food, and frequent and severe punishments were the common lot of Russian sailors. Peter's insistence on sanitation was never fully implemented, with the result that Russian ships usually had long sick lists—at times so long as to interfere with their deployment in battle. Certain other handicaps, such as the long winters and the frequency of religious fasts, also interfered with the training of crews.

The procurement of first-class officers was also difficult. A certain number of Russian officers were, like Peter himself, self-taught. Apraksin, Naum and Ivan Seniavin, Konon Zotov, Muklinov, M.

Golitsyn, Zakharia Mishukov, and Menshikov all turned to the sea in mature years and established creditable records. Unfortunately most of the young nobles sent to learn in foreign navies or in schools abroad were not genuinely interested in learning. Many apparently devoted themselves principally to riotous living and when examined on their return "were found instead of attaining the rudiments of a seaman, to have acquired only the insignificant accomplishments of fine gentlemen."[1] These youths Peter promptly demoted to the rank of common seaman.

The only other alternative to meet immediate needs was the employment of foreign officers. These Peter recruited in large numbers, principally from England but also from Holland, Norway, Denmark, the German states, Scotland, Ireland, and even the American colonies.[2] A few of these foreigners, among them Cornelius Cruys, Thomas Gordon, Charles von Werden, Peter Sievers, P. Bredal, and Peter Lacy, attained flag rank; a much larger number were captains. Gen. Patrick Gordon, an Englishman loyal to the Stuarts, was probably Peter's principal foreign adviser. He kept Peter abreast of literary and scientific developments in Europe, assisted in the birth of Russian sea power, and even served as acting ruler of the country during the young tsar's visits in western Europe.

On the whole, however, Peter's naval officers were not of high caliber. Few of the Russian officers truly knew their business, and the foreigners, many of whom had been dismissed from their own navies, tended to be quarrelsome and were often incompetent as well. Little love was lost between the two groups. On the other hand, all of these men had many valid complaints. Pay was low, and so uncertain that one officer complained he had been paid only one year out of thirteen served. Further, because the restrictions incidental to living in Russia made many regard it as a prison, foreigners were reluctant to stay permanently. Petty officers and warrant officers, themselves few and poor in quality, were subjected to abuse by lieutenants who had full authority over them and were often brutal.

Peter did all he could to emphasize efficiency and merit as a basis for advancement, setting a personal example by going through the several grades of high command and promoting himself only after service and achievement. The man under whom Peter served most frequently was a Russian of remarkable abilities. Count Fedor

Apraksin (1671–1728) was a soldier before he turned to the sea and developed a high degree of aptitude and talent. He was the first Russian admiral, and as general-admiral he became the highest ranking officer in the Russian navy. Equally at home on land and at sea, Apraksin was the one Russian officer other than Peter to command the respect of all foreigners. Peter often served as his second in command, a situation so rare for an able absolute monarch of imperious disposition and strong will as to be virtually without precedent. Although financial rectitude was apparently not one of Apraksin's qualities (he was charged with misapplication of public moneys), he seems to have demonstrated a degree of sincerity and faithfulness to his work all too rare in his age and country.

Two other naval men very close to Peter were a Norwegian with long Dutch service, Cornelius Cruys (or Kruys), and Prince Aleksandr Menshikov. Cruys was crusty and unsociable but of unquestioned honesty and great capability in shore administration. Menshikov was not primarily a sailor but attained the rank of vice admiral mainly on the strength of his individual exploits and charming (though unscrupulous) character.

The practice of recruitment abroad and reliance on luck at home could be acceptable only as it met immediate needs. In order to assure a dependable future source of Russian personnel Peter attacked the problem of education with immense zeal. In January 1701 he opened the School of Mathematical and Navigational Sciences and Naval Academy with Prof. Henry Farquharson from the University of Edinburgh in charge of instruction under the supervision of Apraksin. Two other Edinburgh teachers, Richard Grice and Steven Gegn, taught navigation. Between 1709 and 1715 all three became full professors. The new institution was the first nonreligious school in Russia, and for two centuries it played a key role in the training of civil servants as well as seamen. The curriculum embraced Russian, arithmetic, geography, geometry, trigonometry, spherical trigonometry, gunnery, fortifications, seamanship, navigation, fencing, astronomy, and art. This training was followed by practical application ashore or at sea. The tsar encouraged the writing of books on naval subjects and collected foreign texts dealing with sea power to enrich and advance the school's resources. He also dispatched hydrographic expeditions to the Caspian and

Pacific and procured charts of all Russian seas. By 1715 all of his crews and about half of his officers were Russians; by 1725, Peter's educational system provided an adequate number of junior officers.

In the development of material Peter was more successful than he had been in procuring personnel, though here again quality was quite uneven. His ships were well built from the standpoint of speed, and the best material was made available for their anchors, masts, cables, and other equipment. However, as in the case of the Sea of Azov most of the Baltic vessels were built of fir, which rotted after eight years though the Russians tried to double or triple the lifetime of fir-built ships. Peter finally recognized the weakness of fir as a material for construction and went to considerable trouble to get oak from Kazan by way of the Russian rivers and canals. But even oak ships were affected by the severe winters and required repair and refitting after about eight years, and their hasty construction, often with raw wood, resulted in other weaknesses. The Russian Baltic ships were abnormally short in relation to their beam, rolled heavily, and were often weak in hulls, masts, and rigging.

Russian names for various types of ships differ so greatly from those in the West that comparisons are difficult. Line-of-battle ships and frigates were in many respects similar to their Western prototypes, though the frigates were at times smaller, built with only one deck and usually equipped with no more than 30 guns. But the smaller types of vessels and the galleys are less readily identifiable. To some degree bombs and mortar boats were similar to those in Western Europe. Prams were of shallow draft but carried a strong armament. Shniavas had two masts, 16 or 18 guns, and resembled brigs. Large galleys were up to 150 feet in length and could carry as many as 260 men plus large guns fore and aft and lighter guns amidships. But most galleys were much smaller. Other Russian types resembled pinks, brigantines, and yachts. Gekboats and gukers resembled corvettes in Western navies—smaller than frigates but larger than brigs.

Almost all Russian ships were weak in their ordnance. Cannon often burst, powder was poor, and shooting was inaccurate. Peter tried to correct this by sending youths to gunnery schools abroad, but the attempt never fully succeeded.

From a quantitative standpoint Peter's efforts at shipbuilding were truly impressive. Of the very large total of 1,024 vessels, 686 were built between 1701 and 1714. The first Russian dockyard in the Baltic area opened in 1703 and by 1710 had produced 66 armed galleys and 50 warships, the first of any size being the 28-gun frigate *Shtandart*, built in 1703. In the St. Petersburg area several yards were established, the most important being the Admiralty Yard in 1705. In 1712 this yard completed the *Poltava*, the first Russian battleship. Other yards started by Peter were at Arkhangelsk, Vyborg, and Abo (Turku). These turned out ships up to 2,000 tons, armed with 50 to 100 guns that fired cannonballs weighing from six to 20 pounds. A yard at Kazan supplied the ships for the Caspian flotilla while, after 1708, the Solombola shipyard at Arkhangelsk turned out ships for the White Sea.

Work in the Russian naval bases, though at times directed by Peter himself, was rarely of high quality. Experienced marine engineers were few, organization ashore was often inadequate, repair facilities were poor, and there was no systematic procedure of overhaul. Consequently, even after the fleet was well established the naval base at Kronstadt (and later at Revel) invariably contained reserve ships in various states of decay.

Naval administration had to be developed from the ground up. In 1703 the Admiralty was established to handle naval affairs. The main fleets (Baltic and Sea of Azov) and two flotillas (White Sea and Caspian) were organized to operate under this body. In 1712 Peter created a dual administration consisting of a Navy Office in St. Petersburg and the Admiralty Department in Moscow, renamed the Navy Commissariat and the Moscow Admiralty Bureau in 1715. When the functions of the two offices were found to be overlapping, Peter in 1718 combined them into the Admiralty College in St. Petersburg. Under this body were ten bureaus dealing with such matters as ships, bases, training, and coast defense.

Naval regulations developed between 1696 and 1722 received the close and continued attention of Peter as well as of General Gordon and such Russian advisers as Zotov, Captain Gesler (or Gosler), and Baron P. P. Shafirov. The Russians borrowed freely from the laws of the Danish, French, Dutch, Swedish, and British navies. The principle that even the highest officers are answerable for bad conduct had been established in the winter of 1713–14 when Vice

Admiral Cruys and two associates were courtmartialed (and convicted) for conduct approaching cowardice during a skirmish with the Swedes. (Peter commuted Cruys' death sentence to banishment to Kazan and later issued a pardon.)

The rank and pay structure created by the regulations placed the greatest responsibilities and rewards at the top, though not to a greater degree than was common in other navies of the period. Ten officer ranks were established, plus two grades corresponding to noncommissioned officers (michmen and midshipmen) and several levels among seamen. Roughly two-thirds of the crews were either sailors or gunners and the remainder sea soldiers or marines. Annual pay ranged from two rubles and 40 kopecks for a second-rank seaman to 7,000 rubles for a general-admiral. Captain's pay was 400 rubles per year. Pay of foreign officers was determined by contract but was invariably higher than that of Russian officers of corresponding rank.

Three naval flags of red, white, and blue, all bearing the St. Andrew cross, were adopted in 1701 with the color denoting the rank of the admiral concerned.

In general, Peter's efforts produced two types of naval forces. The larger vessels were placed in the Baltic Fleet, which might operate in one, two, or three squadrons. The smaller craft were confined to the galley fleet, an organization employed mainly in ravaging the enemy's coast. Galleys, largely built and commanded by Italians and Greeks, were propelled by oars rather than sails and could be constructed in about three months. Usually the Russians had about 200 galleys, but the size of this fleet was easily varied. The first galley crews were composed of criminals (later soldiers were used), and since they had a record of conduct that was considered shockingly barbarous even by the standards of the eighteenth century, a social distinction existed between this fleet and the regular navy.

THE SWEDISH WAR 1705–22

While he was engaged in establishing the Baltic Fleet, Peter continued his war with Sweden in order to secure and enlarge the Russian outlet on the Baltic.

By 1705 Charles XII, still engaged primarily in Poland, became sufficiently concerned with the Russian threat to attempt to dislodge Peter from his Baltic foothold. In June 1705, when a Swedish fleet of seven battleships plus lesser vessels attacked Kotlin, the Russians were well prepared to defend. A line of eight anchored frigates ran between Kronslot and a new battery on Kotlin. Behind them were two lines of smaller craft. Across the front of the line of frigates ran a boom. Two attacks on June 26 were repulsed, and a bombardment the next day by the entire Swedish fleet ended indecisively. A second bombardment six days later brought no results. The Swedes then left, only to return on August 1 with a landing force. Their attempt to land was repulsed on August 2, and the Swedish fleet had to content itself with blockading the Neva.

Throughout 1706 and 1707 the picture was much the same. The Swedes held superiority at sea but were unable to turn it to account. The Russians carried on small operations which took a few Swedish prizes, but an attempt to capture Vyborg on the Finnish coast failed.

By 1708 Augustus II was forced to sue for peace and the Swedes were able to inject greater life into their campaign against Russia. Two armies were landed on Russian soil in the fall of 1708, one consisting of 13,000 men under Gen. K. E. Leuwenhaupt and the other of 43,000 men under Charles himself. The first disembarked near St. Petersburg and marched into Ingria. It left a month later, and when Apraksin arrived in time to cut off the Swedish rear guard the Swedes lost 1,100 men.

The larger Swedish army had better luck—for the moment. It crossed the Vistula on January 7, 1708 and advanced on Moscow, defeating Peter in a hard-fought battle at Smolensk. Then, instead of continuing toward Moscow or seizing the Baltic provinces, Charles XII turned south toward the Ukraine. Here he expected to be joined by 30,000 Cossacks under Ivan Mazepa, and also by Poles (under Stanislaus, a Swedish puppet) and Tatars. These hopes were not wholly unreasonable in light of the two important rebellions which had recently broken out in Russia: Sheremetev had put down a revolt in Astrakhan, and the Don Cossacks had been vanquished in 1708 after a major rebellion. Excellent countermeasures by Menshikov had kept the Ukraine loyal, however. Hence only 4,000 Cossacks supported Mazepa when he joined Charles, and neither Poles nor Tatars gave any assistance. Meanwhile Peter devastated the country and kept the Swedes on edge by continual minor attacks. At Lesnaia on October 9, 1708, the Russians destroyed a Swedish army of 15,000 intended to reinforce Charles, and captured intact its huge supply dumps. The Swedes were forced to winter in the Ukraine, where their army was weakened by the most severe season in a century. Cold, hunger, and constant attacks reduced the Swedish army to slightly over 20,000 men, and most of their gunpowder was ruined. In 1709 Peter with an army of more than 40,000 defeated Charles decisively at Poltava in a campaign that saw the Russian land forces perform well from every standpoint. Charles and a few followers escaped into the Turkish domains, but most of the Swedish army surrendered. And even though Charles succeeded in bringing Turkey into the war (with results that have been noted) his own country had to continue fighting without the direction only he could supply.

Poltava brought Peter immediate and important dividends. Denmark and Poland hastened to rejoin their earlier alliance, and Sweden found herself fighting Russia, Prussia, Hanover, Saxony, Poland, and Denmark.

The Swedes, now badly outmatched on land, could have expected less unequal odds at sea, where their only strong foe was Denmark. That one foe proved foe enough, however: the Danes forced the main Swedish fleet to withdraw from the Gulf of Finland, and during its absence Peter continued, with few interruptions, to build up the Baltic Fleet and to train officers and men. He also pushed a successful campaign to further widen his outlet on the Baltic, at the same time keeping his sea forces busy in a series of small actions, cruising as far afield as the North Sea in pursuit of Swedish prizes.

Peter was never a man to overlook obvious opportunity. In the years following 1709 he took the fullest possible advantage of Swedish preoccupation with his allies. Operations on the north coast of the Gulf of Finland were pushed with vigor, and in 1710 Russian land and sea forces under Apraksin succeeded in capturing the important fortress of Vyborg on the Finnish coast. Elbing, Riga, and Revel (Tallin) on the south coast of the Gulf of Finland also fell. The next year Borgå (Porvoo) and Abo were taken, and in 1713 a fleet of 200 small craft assisted in the capture of Helsinki.

The conquest of the last-named town was marred by an act of singular barbarity on the part of the commander of the Russian galley fleet, who ordered the slaughter of the crews of five Dutch merchant vessels. It should be noted, however, that Apraksin promptly condemned the action and reprimanded the commander.

The successes on land were accompanied by several skirmishes at sea. In July 1712 a Russian fleet under Cruys fell in with a smaller Swedish force but performed badly. Two years later a fleet of five Russian battleships and six smaller craft pursued a smaller Swedish force of three battleships. The Swedes escaped and the Russians lost the *Vyborg* 50, which ran aground and had to be burned.

Meanwhile, in their continuing effort to improve and strengthen their Baltic Fleet the Russians constructed a second main base at Revel. Ships purchased in England and three warships constructed in the White Sea all became part of the Baltic Fleet. By 1714 the Russian navy list bore the names of ten battleships and seven frigates. That year was climaxed by a Russian victory at Gangut, or Hangö Head, as it is more commonly known, where most of the Russian galley fleet under Apraksin destroyed a weaker Swedish detachment numbering some 28 units under S. Nils Ehrensköld. After a determined, courageous, and skilled but futile show of Swedish resistance, the Russian loss stood at one galley and 466 men killed and wounded; that of the Swedes was ten galleys of 116 guns captured, 361 men killed, and 941 taken prisoner.[3] The Russian victory, based as it was on weight of numbers and accompanied by a number of mistakes traceable to inexperience, would not have received much notice in a country noted for its naval power, but as their first naval victory of any size Gangut has long been hailed by the Russians. Indeed, Peter made its anniversary a national holiday. It was at this time that he promoted himself to the rank of vice admiral.

After 1715 there were several years during which the Swedes were largely outclassed at sea but in which the Russians took no part in any decisive naval action. In the spring of 1715 16 Swedish battleships entered the harbor of Revel and bombarded a Russian fleet lying under the protection of shore batteries. Neither side incurred much damage. This was almost the last offensive gesture by the Swedes, whose enemies now included the British Navy. In

June the Russian Kronstadt fleet of 17 battleships, four frigates, and two snows[4] under General Admiral Apraksin with Vice Adm. Petr Alekseevich (Peter's naval name and title) second in command, left port and joined the Revel squadron. The combined fleet, cruising during the summer months, met a British and Dutch fleet under Sir John Norris. Courtesy visits were exchanged.[5]

In the winter of 1715–16 ambitious plans were formulated for a joint Russian-Danish landing on the Skåne section of the Swedish coast. With the breaking up of Baltic ice in late April the Russian fleets, now stronger by seven British-built ships and one from the White Sea, proceeded toward Copenhagen. Here Peter the Great commanded a Russian-Danish-English-Dutch fleet which greatly outnumbered the Swedish force. However, the allied commanders were so divided by jealousies and misunderstandings that the projected attack on the Swedish coast never materialized. The next year a Russian squadron under Apraksin landed soldiers on the coast of Gotland at Östergarn. The Russians departed after pillaging movable property, mainly cattle.

There followed a protracted period in which no naval actions of importance occurred in North European waters. The outnumbered Swedish fleets stayed in port while the Russian, Danish, and at times British, squadrons sailed about very much at will. When Swedish commercial vessels did venture out of port in an attempt to run the blockade, many were lost to Russian cruisers. Meantime, shipbuilding in Russian, Dutch, and British yards steadily strengthened the Baltic Fleet to the point where it was superior to the Swedish navy without any assistance from allies. To be sure, there were setbacks in the form of occasional wrecks and a certain number of vessels with rotted timbers had to be condemned, but on the whole the Russian naval picture was one of continued progress.

In 1718 and subsequent years naval activity increased. On May 24, 1719, three Russian 50-gun ships under Naum Seniavin encountered a small Swedish squadron consisting of the *Wachmeister* 48, a 24-gun frigate, a 16-gun brig, and a schooner. The Russians easily captured the small craft, but the *Wachmeister* put up a fight until two more Russian 50's appeared, whereupon she gave up the uneven struggle. This action, fought northwest of Gotland, and known to

Russian historians as the Battle of Ösel Island, was the first victory of Russian battleships.

Pleasing as this was from the standpoint of prestige, other Russian successes of the period were more important. In 1719 and 1721 Russian galley fleets under the successive leadership of Apraksin, Lacy, and Gen. Mikhail M. Golitsyn conducted a number of highly destructive plunder raids on the Swedish coast. These raids were conducted in the face of superior opposition, for the British had changed sides and in 1719 and 1720 sent fleets under Admiral Norris to support the Swedes against the Russians. The Russians managed to avoid battle with a superior enemy and still exact a heavy toll of the Swedish coastal towns and countryside.

Meanwhile, conditions were tending to bring the long war to a close. Peter had on several earlier occasions been ready to negotiate but had been defeated by Charles's unrealistic unwillingness to surrender territory. Now Sweden was militarily and economically exhausted, her population diminished, her commerce reduced, her coastal villages burned. In 1718 Charles XII was killed in Norway, and with his death the will to fight went out of the Swedes. In 1721, by the Treaty of Nystadt, Russia acquired Livonia, Estonia, Ingria, part of Kurland, and eastern Finland including Vyborg. These gains, far more than Peter had hoped for early in the war, laid deeply and firmly the foundations of Russian maritime power. The outlet on the Baltic had become a wide open door. Many ports were now available and one of them, Riga, was shortly handling twice the commerce of St. Petersburg, though to Peter's regret most of the commerce was still carried on by foreign vessels.

The territorial changes were accompanied by a startling growth of Russian naval power. As late as 1710 the Swedish navy had possessed 43 line-of-battle ships as compared to 41 for Denmark and none for Russia. At the end of the war the Swedes possessed only 24 such vessels and the Danes 25. During the war the Russians had acquired no less than 53 battleships. Of these, 24 had been built in the Baltic, seven at Arkhangelsk, and 22 abroad. One had been taken from the Swedes. During 11 years of war a total of 19 Russian ships had been lost. Of these, six were wrecked, one blown up, one destroyed the enemy, one captured, three sold, four cut down, and three broken up. Five more were condemned in 1722;

but the Russians had remaining 29 serviceable ships, besides a great many smaller vessels. Personnel numbered approximately 18,000. During the war years Peter had fashioned from very unpromising materials a navy which had become the strongest in the Baltic. Moreover, this had been achieved against a Swedish fleet which until near the end of the war was superior to the Russian fleet from every standpoint. There are in all history few greater maritime achievements than this accomplishment of Peter the Great.

OTHER PROJECTS UNDERTAKEN BY PETER

During the long war with Sweden Peter's alert mind turned in many directions. He recognized the disadvantages of widely scattered points of access to the sea, but his plans for minimizing this handicap by building canals between the larger Russian rivers were largely unsuccessful. He had ordered the construction of canals between the Neva and the Volkhov in the north and between the Volga and the Don in southeastern Russia, but both of these projects were abandoned when engineering techniques of the day proved inadequate. He was successful, however, in uniting the Volga with the Baltic by way of two canals and a portage, and his remarkably sound recommendations for other waterways were carried through centuries later.

Peter also managed to expand Russian interests to the south and east. As early as 1693 he had planned to extend Russian influence to the Caspian and Central Asia. During the middle years of his reign he had sent two caravans to trade with India by way of Bukhara. In 1713 an interest in India as well as a desire to outflank and defeat the Turks prompted him to construct a large flotilla at Astrakhan on the Volga with a view to sending an expedition to the Caspian Sea, then somewhat weakly held by the shah of Persia. This first effort ended in failure. In 1716 he sent Artemy Volynsky, the governor of Astrakhan, to study commercial possibilities in Persia and to discover whether certain rivers flowing into the Caspian had their start in India. The following year he sent Capt. Charles von Werden down the Volga to the Caspian to explore and map the area. Volynsky secured a trade agreement from the shah, whom he found fearful of a possible Russian attack; von Werden also completed his mission. Armed with this new information, Peter next collected timber at Kazan and built some 20 transports and other vessels. In 1721 the Persians, whose country was then in a state of disorder, provided him a *casus belli* by attacking Russian merchants. With Apraksin in command Russian forces moved toward Astrakhan by way of the Oka and Volga rivers. The campaign itself was brief. An army marched along the west shore while transports and supply ships sailed south through the Caspian. Owing to damage and delays caused by storms, the transports failed to keep up with the troops on land. But though the campaign was thus curtailed, Peter had no difficulty in concluding an advantageous peace. The shah gave up Baku, Derbent, and territory which included the south shore of the Caspian. Most of the Persian princes submitted, and those who did not were put down by the army.

The southern outlet secured in the Persian campaign was, however, even less satisfactory than that in the Sea of Azov, and far more limited. Between 1722 and 1725 Peter ordered large fleets built at Voronezh on the Don and at Tavrov on the Dnieper in preparation for renewed war with the Turks. Vice Admiral Zmaevich was placed in charge of this operation, which was abandoned at Peter's death.

Shortly after the conclusion of the war with Sweden the two powers reached a naval agreement (1724) by which either could call on the other in case of war; the Russians being bound to furnish in such case nine battleships and three frigates, and the Swedes six battleships and two frigates.

Peter at one time had a minor interest in Madagascar. Pirates from the West Indies had established themselves on the island and in 1717 sought the protection of Charles XII, who sent the 30-gun frigate *Jairamas* to take possession in 1721. Meantime a former buccaneer named Narcross, who had been in the Swedish service, joined the Russian navy and persuaded Peter of the desirability of annexation. In January 1724 Vice Admiral Wilater was sent out with two frigates on an expedition which Peter hoped might pave the way for Russian trade with the East Indies. The enterprise failed because of hurried and incomplete preparations; one of the two ships sprang a serious leak and both returned to port. Peter subsequently learned that the Swedes were in fact less interested in Madagascar than he had supposed, and the expedition was canceled.

As another of his minor projects, Peter underwrote an attempt to produce a working submarine. A Russian peasant, Yefim Nikonov, who had also invented a diving suit, proposed to build an underwater craft "by which at sea in calm weather it would be possible to destroy ships by projectiles."[6] Peter gave the project his blessing in 1720, but after the tsar's death Nikonov's work was hampered by the interference and delays of unimaginative officials. In 1727 his boat failed at her trials, whereupon Nikonov was demoted and exiled to Astrakhan.

One last facet of Peter's diverse interests deserves more than casual mention. As a result of forays by early Russian explorers in the Far East who had conducted themselves with ill-considered brutality, plundering and betraying the natives and burning alive their hostages, the natives had appealed for help to the Manchus in China. A Chinese force of about 10,000 men had marched north, accompanied along the coast by a fleet of junks. Surprised and greatly outnumbered, the Russians had agreed to the territorial settlement that was concluded in the Treaty of Nerchinsk (1689). This settlement shut off from Russia the mouth of the Amur, severely damaged dawning Russian interests in the Pacific, and even threatened the food supply of eastern Siberia. It also interfered with a possible Russian opening of Japan, prevented any strong commercial relations with China, weakened Russia's military position in Siberia (since it left her no advantageous site for a naval base), and greatly decreased the profits of Alaskan fur traders who subsequently were obliged to ship over hazardous land routes. Peter for some time had encouraged exploration in both eastern Asia and the Arctic, and Japan, the Kurile Islands, and the Amur had been explored during his reign by Fedor Luzhin, Ivan Yevremov, and Ivan Kazirevsky. In 1725 he dispatched Vitus Bering to the Far East, ostensibly on a geographic survey expedition, but actually to reopen the Amur question and to examine the possibilities of trade with Japan. Peter's death in 1725 ended both projects—at least for the time.[7]

CHAPTER 3

Successors to Peter
(1725-62)

THE DECLINE OF PETER'S NAVY

FROM THE REIGN of Peter the Great to that of Catherine the Great a period of 37 years, or a little more than a generation, elapsed. During this period Russia participated in five wars while six rulers—Catherine I, Peter II, Anne I, Ivan VI, Elizabeth I, and Peter III—occupied the throne in fairly rapid succession. Only Anne I (1730–40) and Elizabeth I (1741–61) reigned for any appreciable length of time. Several attained power through palace revolutions and then in turn died violent deaths. None possessed outstanding ability or was responsible for great achievements. None evidenced any strong interest in or understanding of naval affairs.

In such hands it is not surprising that the navy which Peter had labored so long and zealously to create should deteriorate. For years after Peter's death the naval tradition he had built lived on, but the force's reputation came to be increasingly at variance with reality.

As far as administration was concerned, there was an immediate decline from the intelligent and energetic direction of affairs which Peter had provided. Peter's unfinished projects, such as the proposed war with Turkey and the building of canals, stopped abruptly.

The effect of his death also was felt almost immediately in the naval officer corps. Of the 243 top officers of the navy in 1725, at least 75 were foreigners. These men had greatly respected Peter, but their loyalty was personal and did not extend to his successors or to the Russian state. Many therefore left the service or, if they remained, lapsed into an attitude of indifference. The practice of employing foreign officers and of sending young Russian officers to serve in the navies of friendly powers was not entirely abandoned, although it became decreasingly effective. A large proportion of the higher Russian officers stayed with the navy, but their performance suffered in the absence of a vigorous leader who demanded—and rewarded—competence. Menshikov, Apraksin, and others became concerned with other matters and ceased devoting their major interest to the navy. Admiral Cruys, vice president of the Admiralty College, grew senile and hampered more than he aided. He died in 1727 and Apraksin the year following. Shortly after Peter's death favoritism and venality made an appearance and continued to spread.

At Peter's death in 1725 the Baltic Fleet consisted of 34 battleships, nine frigates, and numerous lesser craft operating in three divisions and manned by some 25,000 officers and men. In the Caspian were 17 sailing and 38 rowing vessels based at Astrakhan, Derbent, and Baku. The White Sea also had a small fleet which included several larger vessels. For seven years no new ships were built, while those in service, especially those constructed of fir, rapidly rotted. When building was resumed it was at a much slower tempo.

Despite the weakening of naval power under inferior leadership, however, a great deal of Peter's work survived. A number of the abler admirals, loyal to the service, managed to keep the fleet going. No important territory was lost and the outlet to the Baltic remained unobstructed. Russia continued to participate in the affairs of Europe. The fleet, even though in very poor condition, retained considerable military importance abroad and performed reasonably well in the limited and indecisive wars in which it participated.

EXPLORATIONS

The rapid succession of monarchs had comparatively little effect on one activity of considerable maritime significance: exploration. Along the distant frontiers of the North Pacific and the Arctic, Russian seamen continued their search. In 1728 Vitus Bering in the *Sviatoi Gavriil* sailed along the northeastern coasts of Asia and discovered the strait which bears his name today, thus proving a division between North America and Asia. In a later (1734) expedition, undertaken in two ships, Sv. Petr and Sv. Pavel, Bering failed to find a northeastern passage from the White Sea to the Pacific. In a final 1741 voyage, undertaken in company with Lt. Petr Chirikov, he crossed the North Pacific from Kamchatka to North America, where he touched the northwest coast but was prevented by sickness and storms from pursuing his explorations. Chirikov explored the Alaskan coast in the neighborhood of Sitka and on his return discovered several of the Aleutian Islands.

During the same years a group of younger men, mainly navy lieutenants—the brothers Khariton and Dmitry Laptev, A. Spuratov (or Skuratov), Stefan G. Malgin, Muravev, Pavlov, Ovtsin, Fedor A. Minin, V. Prontishev, Lasinius, Chekin, Martin Shpanberg, Walton, Semen I. Cheliuskin, and others—were actively exploring the coast of Northern Siberia and the northern reaches of the Dvina, Lena, Yenisei, and Ob, the Kurile Islands, and the Okhotsk Sea and Peninsula.[1] Though no one of these men could be termed a major explorer, their collective efforts added greatly to geographical knowledge. The northern coast was explored along 120 degrees of longitude and the coastline of Kamchatka was demarcated. The whole chain of the Kuriles was examined as well as some of the Aleutians. The Sea of Okhotsk and the extreme Northern Pacific was navigated, and ways were found of reaching both North America and Japan. Novaia Zemlia was demonstrated to be two islands and not a peninsula. Several islands shown on maps were found to be nonexistent. The separation of North America from Asia was demonstrated. All these explorations were endorsed and encouraged by the Admiralty College despite great human costs; most of the explorers died in service, and those who returned to European Russia were broken in health.

THE NAVY UNDER CATHERINE I (1725–27) AND PETER II (1727–30)

Catherine I, widow of Peter, reigned for only two years after she secured the throne with the aid of the powerful Prince Menshikov. Though she was a woman of considerable general ability, her inept administration of the navy nearly brought on complete disaster.

In 1726 a British fleet entered the Baltic and the Gulf of Finland for a visit which was based on a British desire to preserve the balance of power, and which was correctly perceived by the Russians as a threat. The Russian leaders in previous years had carefully avoided conflict in similar instances by keeping their ships in port whenever it seemed expedient to do so. Catherine, however, met the encroachment with a request that the British fleet leave Russian waters, and thereby precipitated a crisis as perilous as it was unnecessary. Through some clever diplomatic maneuvers, Menshikov and Apraksin were able to smooth over her blunder, but the British fleet of 22 battleships (accompanied by seven Danish ships) remained in Russian waters for four months. The following year a second British fleet, under Admiral Norris, entered the Baltic but this time remained in Danish waters.

More commonly, however, Catherine's naval policy was one of almost complete neglect. She laid down no new ships, completed only five battleships and 80 galleys which were building at Peter's death, failed to authorize repairs and upkeep, and demanded very little in the furtherance of efficient performance. There were few changes in administration other than the setting up in 1726 of a Supreme Secret Council which was superior to the Admiralty. In 1725 the navy sent a battleship and two frigates on a voyage to Spain, but Apraksin the same year noted that the Baltic Fleet ships were unable to keep in formation, that some men were naked and unshaved, and that officers had no uniforms. In a desperate effort to keep the fleet going, Apraksin donated 2,000 rubles of his own money for cleaning the bottoms of the ships. Such exemplary personal effort, however, was not widespread and could not check the downward trend.

Catherine's brief rule was followed by the almost equally brief reign of Peter's grandson, Peter II (1727–30), who came to the throne at the age of twelve years and died three years later of smallpox. During his reign the country was ruled by a reactionary regency which moved the capital back to Moscow and in effect concentrated on undoing the work of Peter the Great. All shipbuilding ceased, and naval funds were slashed by 50 percent. Shore administration was in complete disorder; ships were greatly undermanned and rotting. Admiral Zmaevich, caught stealing, was demoted in rank only one grade. In 1728 an order was promulgated forbidding warships to put to sea save for the movement of royalty (probably no more than five or six vessels could have gotten to sea in any case). In the Caspian there was some replacement of older vessels and a survey of the sea was made under Semenov; nevertheless, the general Russian position there was felt to be so weak that Russian land forces were ordered to stay out of Maganderan and Astrabad, which had been ceded by Persia several years earlier.

ANNE I (1730–40)

Anne Ivanovna, niece of Peter the Great, succeeded to the throne following the death of Peter II. Though a number of unpopular court favorites, mainly of German derivation, were responsible for some cruel and stupid policies during her reign, Anne was by no means all bad. She was a conscientious and moderately able monarch who sought to improve the efficiency of the fleet. Her principal naval advisers were Admirals Naum Seniavin and Dmitrev-Mamonov (Russian), Saunders (British), and Bredal (Norwegian). Acting through Count Andrei Ivanovich Ostermann, her chancellor of the empire, Anne reestablished the naval and military college and replaced the Supreme Secret Council with a cabinet. In 1732 she named a royal commission to examine the state of the navy. The commission correctly reported that the condition of the navy was deplorable; unfortunately it failed to go sufficiently far in urging reforms and those it did recommend were accepted slowly. Admiral Sievers retired during Anne's reign, and Adm. N. F. Golovin was found guilty of misappropriating funds.

Despite her inability to reverse the general downward drift, Anne did effect a number of reforms. Naval bureaus were reorganized and reduced in number from ten to five. A Bureau of Ports was created, as was a commission to check on the materials used in shipbuilding. In 1734 the fleet marine force was reorganized into regiments containing 1,800 and 2,000 men, each regiment consisting of three battalions made up of four companies each. Because the wars of Anne, and of Elizabeth who followed, involved many landing operations, the marines became probably the most efficient part of the navy. Anne or her naval advisers instituted a budget for the navy, organized a course in navigation, simplified the accounting system, and in general put more order into administration.[2]

Considering its decrepit condition the Baltic Fleet was reasonably successful in the War of the Polish Succession (1733–35), which involved a contest between France on the one hand and Austria and Russia on the other, the issue being whether Augustus, the son of the Polish King Augustus II, or Stanislas Leszczyński should occupy the throne. Russia supported Augustus; France sent a fleet in the Baltic to support the claims of Leszczyński. In an ensuing battle the French *Fleuron* 60 and *Gloire* 46 captured the Russian *Mitau* 32. A landing of 4,200 troops from the French fleet to attack Russian entrenchments at the mouth of the Vistula eventuated in a French defeat. The French landing parties were presently reembarked, and the fleet returned to Brest.

Russia's main effort in the war took place on land and involved a siege of Danzig. Assistance by sea was provided by a fleet of 14 battleships, five frigates, and two bombs under Adm. M. Gordon. This squadron, aided by flotilla craft, bombarded Weichselmünde and forced its surrender, and captured the French frigate *Brilliant* 30 and three smaller vessels in the harbor; it then blockaded Danzig and furnished support for the land forces. Leszczyński fled. On July 9 Danzig surrendered and Augustus III ascended the Polish throne.

Simultaneously with the successful conclusion of the War of the Polish Succession, Russia reopened its duel with Turkey. During the last years of his reign Peter the Great had prepared for this by resuming shipbuilding at Tavrov on the Don and Briansk on the Dnieper, though his death had put a stop to the program before many ships were finished. In 1735 Russia concluded an alliance with Austria against the Turks, who in turn were supported by France. In an effort to obtain Persian support as well, Anne returned part of the territory taken by Peter. She was unable to secure an alliance, however, and had to be content with an assurance of Persian neutrality. Russia then precipitated hostilities by an attack on the Tatars of the Ukraine.

Though Anne did not make the mistake of attacking Turkey entirely without naval support, the Second Black Sea Fleet, which was to aid in transporting the Russian army, consisted mainly of small boats armed with two- and three-pounder cannon that had been built in very large numbers, mainly at Briansk and Tavrov. There were some larger craft, including galleys and prams (shallow-draft flat-bottomed boats with two masts and pointed stem), a few of which carried as many as 44 guns.[3] Qualitatively the fleet was hopelessly defective; its individual units were incapable of navigating safely in any but the calmest seas, much less of fighting the Turks on even terms. One of the first lessons learned by Peter—that even for successful coastal operations ships must meet certain minimum standards of stability and size—had been forgotten a decade after his death.

Despite Russia's naval weakness the first season of fighting was comparatively successful, since the army left by Peter had declined less than had his navy. The ultimate Russian objective was, of course, Constantinople, but the more immediate aim was to gain an opening on the Black Sea. To accomplish this a Russian army under Field Marshal M. Lacy and the Don Flotilla under Rear Admiral Bredal attacked Azov. The river fleet consisted of nine large and six small prams, 35 galleys, and 29 kaiks. The Russians easily prevailed: Azov surrendered on June 30, 1736. The fleet was put up for the winter at Azov and Cherkassy while the Russians busied themselves in building some 900 boats for service on the Don and the Dnieper. Farther west Gen. Burkhard von Münnich's army, with the support of the Dnieper Flotilla, had pushed the Turks south along the Dnieper.

Had the Turks operated with greater skill during 1737, they could have inflicted a decisive defeat on the Russians that year. When the fighting season opened Rear Admiral Bredal used 217 boats to form a floating bridge by which Lacy's army entered the Crimea from the north. The Russian vessels proved too weak to protect the Russian troops from bombardment by Turkish warships, and on July 9 a gale wrecked 170 of Bredal's boats. The next two days the Turks attacked with a force that should have been able to destroy the remnants of the Russian fleet, but they failed to push home their attack and the encounter was indecisive. A storm then caused the loss of additional Russian ships and Bredal, with six-sevenths of his fleet destroyed, had to fall back on Genichesk to await reinforcements. The Turkish army remained intact, forcing Lacy's army, with its line of communications threatened, to retreat to Genichesk as well. In two subsequent naval actions, during August, the greatly superior but poorly directed Turkish forces were unable to achieve decisive success over Bredal's boats. When the Russian base at Azov sent in 140 boats as reinforcements, Bredal, despite his staggering losses, was able to finish the summer with a force of 15 prams, five lighters, 20 galleys, and 220 boats.

The two succeeding summers showed almost the same pattern, with Russian land forces superior to those of the Turks but badly handicapped by the weakness of their naval support. The Turks in turn continued to be unable to win decisively because their own sea forces were badly directed. Several Turkish naval attacks at or near Genichesk failed. On the Dnieper, the Russian river fleet aided General Münnich's army in the capture of Ochakov, which fell on July 13, 1738.

On land Russia's ally, Austria, had been forced to sue for a separate peace. This action threw the tsarina into such a panic that she was willing to make peace on unfavorable terms. By the Treaty of Belgrade Russia retained Azov but gave up all her other conquests and agreed to maintain no warships either there or in the Black Sea. Thus the Second Russian Black Sea Fleet came to an end. Though much weaker than the first, it had from first to last contained 13 44-gun prams, nine small prams, 92 galleys, and well over 1,000 boats, double sloops, and other small craft.

ELIZABETH I (1741–61)

Anne was succeeded in October 1740 by a two-month-old grand-nephew who was proclaimed tsar as Ivan VI under the regency first of the Duke of Kurland and then of the boy's mother, also named Anne. Late the following year a coup d'état brought Elizabeth to the throne and sent the baby tsar into more than twenty years of solitary confinement, an imprisonment that ended only with his murder in 1764 by officers determined to prevent his liberation.

Elizabeth I, daughter of Peter the Great and Catherine, was beautiful, tyrannical, licentious, and intelligent. As a patron of the arts she founded the University of Moscow and corresponded with Voltaire, but she allowed favorites to conduct her government. She chose Count A. Mishukov, a man of moderate leadership ability, to head the Admiralty College, and she restored Peter's naval regulations. The Naval Academy was moved from Moscow to St. Petersburg and given some able faculty members, including A. I. Nagaev, Grigory Spiridov, Khariton Laptev, and Ivan Golenishchev-Kutuzov. Elizabeth also finished the Peter the Great Canal at Kronstadt, started by her father. In two other respects she resembled her great father: she recognized the need for shipbuilding, and she was prepared to do something about it. She named a royal commission to strengthen her fleet. Despite precarious finances, 36 new battleships and eight frigates as well as many smaller vessels were built during her reign. Yet she never understood the importance of quality and was only mildly interested in internal improvements within the navy. As a result, most of the strengthening of the fleet was done on paper. Ships showed weak rigging and a proneness to leak and were often short-handed. Further, for all the favors she extended to such men as Ostermann, Mishukov, Golovin, and Mikhail Golitsyn, Elizabeth never selected a truly able admiral.

Russian involvement in the War of the Austrian Succession began during the brief reign of Ivan VI when on July 24, 1741, Sweden declared war; but the war was actually fought during the reign of Elizabeth. On land the Russian armies under Lacy held an edge over the Swedes and in two years of war were able to capture 17,000 men at Helsinki and drive the Swedes out of nearly all of Finland. At sea the two powers were approximately equal, each being weaker than at the time of the Great Northern War between Peter and Charles XII, and here the conflict ended in a nearly bloodless draw. The Baltic Fleet of 14 battleships and 11 frigates, based at Kronstadt and commanded by Admiral Mishukov, was so badly disorganized that Admiral Bredal was ordered to bring the small White Sea Fleet to the Baltic in a fruitless effort at reinforcement. On the other hand, when Adm. Charles E. Leuwenhaupt, the Swedish commander, ordered a naval attack on Vyborg, the Swedish fleet of 12 battleships and 11 frigates proved too weak for that attempt since the Swedish fleet was in at least as poor shape as the Baltic Fleet. Crews in both navies were short-handed and untrained; food and other necessities were in short supply; and in course of the war an epidemic of dysentery which killed Swedish Adm. Tomas von Rajalin also took the lives of at least 700 other men. Hence, each commander made every effort to avoid battle.

On only one occasion was there even a threat of a major naval engagement. This occurred in 1743 when Lacy, having collected a fleet of 17 battleships and 48 galleys, ordered Admiral Golovin to attack a Swedish fleet of 16 battleships, five frigates, and some small craft off Hangö Point (Gangut). The battle was never joined, for the Swedes retreated and Golovin, instead of pursuing, retired to Revel. Because of her victories on land, Russia was able to conclude the Swedish war with a favorable treaty giving her part of Finland, signed in 1743 while most of the other participants were still fighting. The Baltic Fleet, however, under the direction of Golovin, never gave the Russian army effective cooperation, nor did it play any important role of its own.

Two other wars—a dispute with Persia and the Seven Years' War—occurred during the reign of Elizabeth. The Persian conflict was of brief duration and was somewhat in the nature of a modern-day police action. With the aid of British agents the Persians had built several warships at the port of Enzeli on the Caspian. Moreover, Persian officials had often attacked and despoiled Russian merchants who conceivably were also acting as spies. In retaliation the tsarina ordered the seizure of all Persian goods in the port of Astrakhan and the destruction of the Persian navy in the Caspian, actions which were successfully carried out.

The Seven Years' War, in which nearly every European power participated, began in May 1756 with England and Prussia arrayed against France, Russia, Austria, and Sweden. While Russia and her allies were greatly superior on land, they faced in the Prussian Frederick the Great one of the ablest commanders of the age. In the Baltic both Sweden (with 26 battleships) and Denmark (with 27) opened the war with stronger fleets than that of Russia (20 battleships), the naval predominance gained by Peter having disappeared under his successors; indeed, between 1750 and 1756 no less than 21 Russian battleships, mainly built of fir, had been scrapped. However, since Russia and Sweden, and also for a time Denmark, were on the same side during the Seven Years' War, their relative strength was not of great importance. Prussia had no true navy; and as it happened England, which had by then achieved overall naval superiority, never sent her fleet into the Baltic. But though there was very little fighting at sea during the war, the poor condition of the Russian Baltic Fleet was demonstrated by the number of vessels lost from other than military causes.

When in 1757 both Sweden and Russia opened hostilities against Prussia, the Kronstadt squadron (under Rear Admiral Lewis) and the Revel fleet (under Admiral Mishukov), numbering 22 battle-ships in all, united in front of Memel, which the Russians were attacking from both land and sea. Leaving the prams and bomb vessels to aid the army in its siege, Mishukov blockaded the Danish Straits and remained alert against approach of a British fleet. The Russians did well on land, capturing Memel and defeating the Prussian army at Wahlau, but apart from coastal bombardments at Memel and Danzig and injury to ships in heavy seas, there was little naval action. When it became evident that no British fleet was likely to appear, Mishukov sent some of his ships home. He followed them himself in late August. The Russian galley fleet, which had been highly effective under Peter and could have been used to harry the enemy's coast, remained inactive. Most of the gains on land were nullified when Count Aleksei Bestuzhev-Riumin, chancellor of the then ailing Empress Elizabeth, withdrew the Russian army in the hope of currying favor with Elizabeth's heir, Peter, who was an admirer of Frederick the Great.

The year 1758 was entirely uneventful, save for some joint cruising on the part of the Russian and Swedish squadrons under Mishukov and the wreck of the battleship *Moskva* 66 near Libau. During the following summer small Russian squadrons blockaded Danzig. The Russian army continued its successes, capturing Königsberg and, with Austrian help, beating the Prussians at Kunersdorf near Frankfurt on the Oder. As in 1757, however, Russian failure to follow up military victory enabled Frederick to recover.

During 1761–62 the Russian fleet was somewhat more active but failed to achieve any telling victories. A halfhearted two-year siege of Kolberg, assisted by fleet bombardments and the landing of troops, was poorly conducted at many points by both the Russians and their Swedish allies. During December 1762 Kolberg surrendered, primarily in response to military rather than naval pressure, though during 1762 Admiral Poliansky (who replaced Mishukov) had performed ably.

Finally, with Prussia worn out and all but bled white, fortune played into the hands of Frederick the Great. Tsarina Elizabeth died and was succeeded by Peter III, who at once allied himself with Frederick. Sweden was thereby induced to make a separate peace with Prussia. Peter's reign proved brief: he was deposed by a conspiracy of nobles who on July 28, 1762, replaced him with his wife, the vigorous and able Catherine II (the Great).

Had Peter lived he might well have proved even more naval-minded than his grandfather. As it was he set to work with feverish zeal to improve Russia's maritime condition. Golitsyn and Mishukov were speedily displaced and an immediate move was made to build nine new battleships. Steps were taken to process timber and other needed supplies. Peter also proposed to start a war against Denmark to regain some of the lands taken from his family. When he died in prison a week after he was deposed, Catherine recalled the Russian troops from Germany and announced a policy of neutrality. In 1763 the Treaty of Paris ended the Seven Years' War, and a peace which was to last for a generation settled over the Baltic.

It is a high tribute to Peter the Great that much of the work he had done in establishing Russian sea power survived the reigns of the six mediocrities who followed him to the throne. When Catherine the Great came to power the fleet was, of course, weakened in both size and quality, but there had been no eclipse of Russian sea power nor had there been any disastrous defeats. The outlet to the West remained open. Russia continued to be a part of the European scene, with diplomatic and commercial relations with all other European powers. The Russian army continued to give a good account of itself. The Baltic Fleet retained both its identity and much of the international prestige it had earned so painfully under Peter. That it also retained the capability to influence decisively the course of history was soon to be demonstrated.

CHAPTER 4

Catherine the Great:
The Turkish Wars

NAVAL POLICY OF CATHERINE THE GREAT

CATHERINE II is generally regarded as one of the most outstanding rulers in the history of Imperial Russia. Through a long (1762–96) and brilliant reign punctuated with romances and intrigues, she conducted affairs of state with great ability and marked success.

Catherine's concern with naval matters proved her a worthy successor to Peter the Great, for she carried out many of his plans and followed many of his general policies. Her aims included gaining a new outlet to the south; further exploration of the northern coasts and large Siberian rivers; construction of fortifications to protect naval bases; promotion of commerce; and continuation of learning from foreigners. She took great interest in the naval school as a source of officers but also sent many young nobles to serve abroad, especially in the British navy, in quest of further education.

Much could be written of Catherine's talent hunt for foreign officers. Samuel Karlovich Greig, her ablest admiral, was only a master's mate in the British navy when he entered the Russian service in 1764. His rise in rank was rapid and in 1782, six years before his death, he became a full admiral (Greig's son and his grandson also were to attain high rank in the Russian navy). In 1770 Catherine secured the services of British Adm. Sir Charles

Knowles, and there were a number of other Englishmen who served the navy ashore—notably Lt. A. Mackenzie and Col. Samuel Bentham, who played prominent roles in the south; the former in founding the naval base at Sevastopol; the latter in building the Black Sea Fleet. Also among her foreign-born assistants was Charles Gascoigne, who set up the main Russian cannon foundry at Olonets on the shore of Lake Ladoga. A. Kruse and J. H. Kingsbergen (Dutch), John Paul Jones (American), Prince Charles of Nassau-Siegen (Prussian), Arf (Norwegian), and Jacob Travenine, Roman V. Crown, and G. K. Elphinstone (British), were all leading admirals during Catherine's rule. While as a group these men were superior in ability to the foreigners who served Peter, not all had happy experiences in a service in which favoritism and intrigue played a definite role. Nor should all their experiences have been happy; many were arrogant and tended to hold all Russians in contempt. The American John Paul Jones, for one, at least, became thoroughly disenchanted with a career under Catherine.

Although Catherine lacked Peter's first-hand acquaintance with the tools of sea power and never understood the importance of quality—Russian ships in her time were frequently in very bad condition, with weak hulls and masts, unreliable guns, and a general lack of stability—her strategic sense was excellent. She had an almost infallible sense of timing and knew exactly how far she could exert pressure without provoking hostilities. She made continuous and effective use of sea power both in peacetime diplomacy and in war, and she understood perfectly the importance of a naval force that could strike at a distance.

Shortly after her accession to power she became aware that if the Baltic Fleet was to serve as an effective arm of diplomacy and foreign policy it would have to be rehabilitated. The team of officers chosen to study the problem consisted of Vice Adm. S. I. Mordvinov (who had served six years in the French navy), Count I. G. Chernyshev, Commo. Grigory I. Spiridov, and Capt. I. L. Golenishchev-Kutuzov. In 1774, acting on their recommendations, she set the strength of the Baltic Fleet at 21 battleships in time of peace, 32 in time of war, and 40 in case of an emergency war situation. During the 1770s she also launched an ambitious program of naval building. For the first time Russia had sufficient shipbuilders and naval architects of her own, though Catherine employed talented foreigners in addition. In all, approximately 89 battleships and 40 frigates were built in the Baltic and the White Sea during Catherine's reign, and 14 battleships and 50 frigates were built in the Black Sea.

The objectives of Catherine's initial foreign policy were relatively simple. Though she encouraged exploration in the Pacific, urging Grigory Shelekhov to explore and set up commercial enterprises in Alaska and sending Adam Laxman to Japan for permission to trade, her primary interest lay to the south. She was as devoted to gaining access to the Black Sea as Peter had been in obtaining an outlet on the Baltic. As in Peter's day, a powerful Turkish state stood in the way of realizing this ambition. In order to gain time for the thorough diplomatic, military, and naval preparations needed to crush the Turks, Catherine kept Russia out of the Seven Years' War, then nearing its end, and was able in three seizures of territory to absorb most of Poland—all without recourse to a general war. Good relations with England were essential for Russia's long-range plans, so that although Catherine frowned upon high-handed British interference with neutral commerce, she did not allow her feelings to go beyond occasional protests. As a result relations remained cordial, and the British in 1769–70 permitted the Russians to repair and dock in their harbors and to hire British naval vessels as transports.

Catherine's hostile intentions were not unknown to the Turks. Encouraged by the French, who hoped to protect Poland by diverting Catherine's attention elsewhere, they were openly belligerent. In 1768, well before the tsarina's war preparations were complete, Turkey declared war. Turkish plans included the raising of an army of 400,000 men who were to capture Warsaw and subsequently to move against Smolensk and Kiev, there to unite with 100,000 troops of the Crimean khan and take Astrakhan. Catherine successfully countered this strategy by (1) a two-pronged army attack from the north against the Crimea and to the west along the Dniester River; (2) a naval attack through the Mediterranean; and (3) the encouragement of revolt among Turkey's subject populations—in the Balkans, in the Kuban and Georgia, and especially among the Greeks in the Aegean.

THE MEDITERRANEAN EXPEDITION

The attack through the Mediterranean against Turkey, the first naval venture of Catherine the Great, showed great originality and daring. The idea occurred initially to Count Aleksei Orlov. He and his brother Grigory, who was then stationed in Leghorn, apparently proposed the dispatch of eight or ten warships from the Baltic to the Aegean, and Catherine at once gave her approval.[1] The plan was at that time without precedent and, considering the limited experience of the Russians in long ocean voyages and the poor condition of their vessels, also quite risky. Nevertheless on August 23, 1769, nine battleships and several lesser vessels of the Baltic Fleet, with Rear Admiral Spiridov in command, left the Baltic and were followed shortly by a second Mediterranean squadron under Rear Admiral Elphinstone. The long voyage to the Mediterranean was indeed a triumph over danger and hardship. One ship, the *Lapomnik* 22, was wrecked in the Skaw off Jutland, and the crews of all ships, unused to navigation in the late fall and winter, suffered severely and would have suffered far more had not the British permitted them a short rest stop in English ports. As it was, 332 men had died and 600 were sick by the time the squadrons reached England. Eventually the two Russian squadrons struggled separately into the eastern Mediterranean. The first few vessels arrived at the Morea (Peloponnesus) in March 1770, two battleships and a frigate of Spiridov's squadron bombarded Navarino. Considerably aided by the fact that the Greeks were then in rebellion against the Turks, the Russians were able to make a landing and capture the city. On May 20 they were reinforced by Elphinstone's arrival at Cape Matapan with three battleships and five smaller vessels.

The Turkish navy, which the venturesome Russian squadrons had yet to meet, held a paper superiority of at least two to one over the invaders. It was reported to have Black Sea and Aegean forces each totaling at least 40 battleships and frigates, besides smaller craft manned by 60,000 men from Greece, Rumania, and the Barbary States. Main bases and arsenals were maintained at Mytilene, Constantinople, and Sinope. Finally, there was a Danube flotilla of about 200 small craft, each carrying two light cannon firing three-to eight-pound balls. Since the Turks regarded as impracticable Catherine's project of circumnavigating Europe to bring a fleet to the eastern Mediterranean, however, they had made no special preparations to meet attack and were both psychologically and militarily unprepared. Hence, once the Russians had arrived in the Aegean the hardest part of their mission lay behind them.

The Russians were particularly weak in certain respects. Not only was their organization for supply and replenishment inadequate, but the marine landing forces carried aboard ship, even when aided by Greek partisans, were insufficient to hold captured towns and islands. The Greeks also fell short of being ideal allies. They were undisciplined and unwilling to take orders, and their propensity to attack and kill Turkish prisoners of the Russians whenever they had an opportunity had the effect of encouraging the Turks to fight to the last.

The first brush with the Turkish fleet occurred on May 27: Rear Admiral Elphinstone's force (three battleships and five smaller vessels) sighted a much larger Turkish force consisting of 13 battleships of 50 to 84 guns each and some smaller vessels. Despite the disparity of forces, Elphinstone ordered an attack. His own ship, *Sviatoslav* 80, and the *Afrika* 32 were slow getting into action. On this occasion, however, the Turks showed little enthusiasm for a fight, even with the advantages in their favor, and retired before either side incurred serious damage. During the night both fleets moved north, and the Turks anchored under the batteries of Nauplia. A Russian attempt to attack on May 28 failed because (1) the wind died down, and (2) some of Elphinstone's captains objected that an offensive action would be foolhardy considering the additional aid shore batteries could give to an enemy of already greatly superior strength.

On June 2 Admiral Spiridov joined Admiral Elphinstone and the combined fleets stood at seven battleships, three frigates, and two storeships. From the first, command relations between the two men were strained because of decided differences in personality. Spiridov, whose record during the Seven Years' War had been excellent, was fifty-four years old and in poor health. His lethargic and somewhat overcautious nature tended both to hold back and to irritate his more energetic but frequently rash colleague. Both moved their

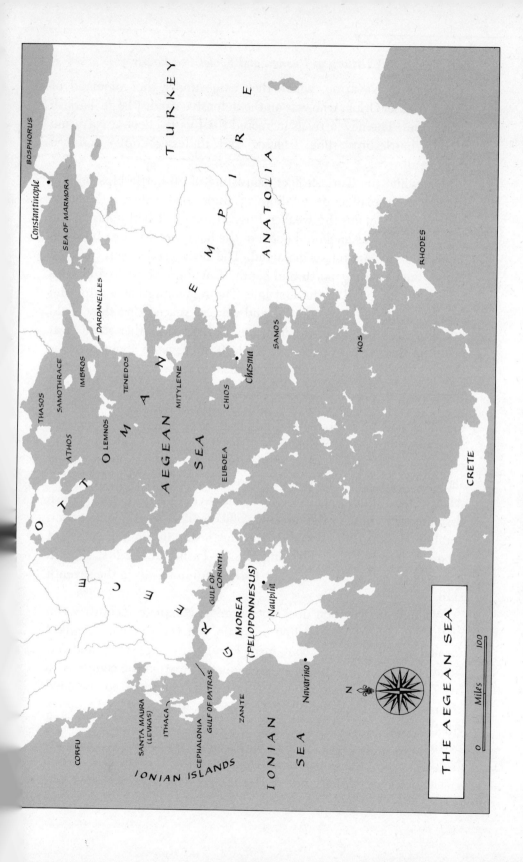

THE AEGEAN SEA

squadrons to Navarino, where they came under the command of Count Aleksei Orlov, who was on the defensive against large Turkish land forces. The new arrivals increased the Russian fleet at Navarino to nine battleships, three frigates, and 18 lesser craft—some 30 ships in all.

Meanwhile the Turkish fleet, consisting of 16 battleships besides frigates and small craft totaling 73 ships, had entered the area. Instead of attacking the weaker Russian forces, it had gone on the defensive and was anchored north of the harbor of Chesma between Chios and the Anatolian mainland. The heavy ships were moored in two lines running north and south. Ten ships of 70 to 100 guns each were stationed in the first line. The remaining battleships and frigates composed a second line and were so spaced that they could fire through intervals in the first line. Galleys and other small craft made up the rear. On paper the Turkish forces were about twice as strong as the Russian, numbering at least 20 vessels (battleships and frigates) carrying about 1,300 heavy guns compared with the Russians' 12 heavy ships with 710 guns. But these figures are misleading. The Turkish captains and admirals were mainly incompetents who knew little about their jobs. The Turkish enlisted men were courageous but poor sailors while the Greek sailors among them, though thoroughly competent, were not eager to die for either Allah or the sultan. The first, fourth, and seventh ships in the Turkish first line were those of the three flag officers. The overall commander, Ibrahim Hosemeddin, occupied the fourth ship in the line and went ashore before the battle, leaving Hassan Pasha, in the first ship, in command. Djaffer Bey, the other Turkish admiral, was in the seventh ship.

Available information does not permit a complete reconstruction of the Turkish forces and line of battle, but the Russian vanguard formed under Spiridov contained *Evropa*, *Sv. Yevstafy*, and *Tri Sviatitelia*. Orlov had under his immediate direction the center, with *Sv. Yanuary*, *Tri Yerarkha*, and *Rostislav*. Elphinstone commanded the rear, which consisted of *Ne Tron Menia*, *Sviatoslav*, and *Saratov*. All the Russian battleships were 66's except the *Sviatoslav*, which carried 80 guns. The frigates *Afrika* 32, *Nadezhda* 32, and *Sv. Nikolai* 26, and the bomb *Grom* completed the Russian fleet.

The battle of Chesma, one of Russia's greatest naval victories, was fought in two stages. In the first stage, starting at about 11:30 A.M. on July 5, Count Orlov brought his vessels into action in a long, irregular line with each ship moving to her station independently between 11:45 A.M. and 12:50 P.M. The main action came at the head of the line, where Spiridov's *Sv. Yevstafy* closed with Hassan Pasha's *Real Mustafa* 84. In the ensuing contest both ships caught fire and blew up, killing all but 63 of the crew of the *Sv. Yevstafy*. Aboard the *Mustafa* the loss of life must have been equally high. Surprisingly, both admirals escaped. The Turks, disconcerted, cut their cables and fled into the Bay of Chesma, though not before the 100-gun *Capudan Pasha* was badly damaged by *Tri Yerarkha's* fire. By 2:00 P.M. the day's fighting was over. The Russians had lost 636 men in the *Sv. Yevstafy* but their other casualties were low, with only 14 killed and 30 wounded in the remainder of the fleet. This small loss of life doubtless was due to the poor gunnery of the Turks, who aimed much too high and damaged the masts and the rigging but not the hulls or the crews of the Russian ships. Turkish losses were almost certainly higher but are not accurately known.

On the night of July 5 the Russian fleet adopted blockade formation before the harbor of Chesma. The *Grom*, a Russian bomb vessel, bombarded the Turks within the harbor for the next two nights.

A large fleet anchored under friendly shore batteries generally discourages direct attack. Fortunately for the Russians, however, some of the British officers serving Catherine had had experience with fireships (called "branders" in Russian accounts), and an attack was planned for the night of July 6. Four fireships were to be towed by ten-oared boats alongside four Turkish ships, skeleton crews were to set the enemy ships afire and then escape in rowboats. The attack, an elaborate and well conducted affair, was carried out against a demoralized foe as innocent of the knowledge of the proper defense measures as had been the Russians when subjected to Greek fire at Byzantium—and it achieved similar results.

At 11:30 on the night of July 6 the preliminary Russian moves got under way. The *Evropa*, *Grom*, *Rostislav*, and *Ne Tron Menia* entered the harbor of Chesma while the *Nadezhda* attacked the northern and the *Afrika* the southern batteries. Rear Admiral Elphinstone and the remaining ships of the fleet stationed themselves to cover the mouth of the harbor lest the Turks seek to escape.

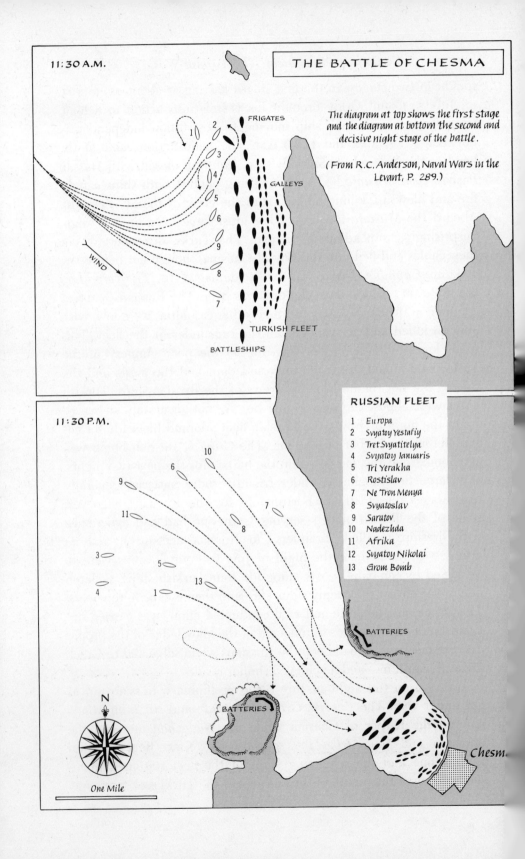

11:30 A.M.

FRIGATES

GALLEYS

WIND

TURKISH FLEET

BATTLESHIPS

THE BATTLE OF CHESMA

The diagram at top shows the first stage
and the diagram at bottom the second and
decisive night stage of the battle.

(From R.C. Anderson, Naval Wars in the
Levant, P. 289.)

11:30 P.M.

RUSSIAN FLEET

1	Europa
2	Svyatoy Yestafiy
3	Tret Svyatitelya
4	Svyatoy Ianuaris
5	Tri Yerakha
6	Rostislav
7	Ne Tron Menya
8	Svyatoslav
9	Saratov
10	Nadezhda
11	Afrika
12	Svyatoy Nikolai
13	Grom Bomb

BATTERIES

BATTERIES

Chesm.

N

One Mile

Then night artillery practice began. At about 1:30 A.M. on July 7 one of the shells from the *Grom* set fire to the main topsail of a Turkish ship. The whole vessel was soon in flames, and by two o'clock two Turkish ships had blown up and others were burning. Admiral Greig then sent in four fireships commanded by Lieutenant Dugdale with Lieutenant Mackenzie second in command. The first fireship was intercepted and sunk by two Turkish galleys. The second reached a ship already on fire. The third, under Dmitry Illin, fired a Turkish ship, and the wind rapidly spread the flames down the Turkish line. The fourth never went in because there was no need: the demoralization of the Turks was complete. The flames spread from ship to ship, with each vessel exploding as the fire reached its powder magazine. The destruction continued for many hours. At 4:00 A.M. Russian landing parties attempted to capture two battleships and some smaller craft not yet afire and succeeded in saving the *Rodos* 60 and five galleys.

At 8:00 A.M. on July 8, the Russians, at the cost of 11 men killed, had won victory at Chesma. The Turkish fleet had been annihilated in the greatest naval defeat suffered by the Turks since the Battle of Lepanto in 1571. Loss figures are uncertain, but indicated casualties included 11 battleships burned and one captured, probably six frigates and six shebeks burned, eight galleys burned and five captured, and 32 small craft burned. The Turkish loss of life must have been enormous. One writer estimates it at 8,000 men. E. V. Tarle, one of the most reliable Soviet historians, puts it at a minimum of 11,000. Numerous wounded men were rescued from the water by the Russians, given medical treatment, and later freed. This show of humanity impressed the Turks and was in contrast to their own conduct at nearby Smyrna, where news of the Russian victory triggered a Turkish massacre of Greek Christians.

There has been considerable dispute over responsibility for the victory of Chesma, with English writers claiming credit for their own countrymen because of the prominent position of British officers in the Russian service.[2] While the role played by the British is undeniable, the fact remains that the victory was achieved by a Russian fleet under Russian command. Greig in particular performed well; so did many Russian officers, including Admiral Spiridov and Captains Khmetevsky, Klokachev, and Lupandin, and

Lieutenant Illin. The gunner on the *Grom* whose shot started the first fire may well have been the real hero. The Russian sailors showed courage, intelligence, and skill throughout.

After Chesma the Russians occupied a paradoxical position. Their achievement was justly applauded throughout Europe, their international prestige was high, and they were still supreme at sea. There remained, however, many unsolved problems. The Russians were far from their base of operations and lacked the necessary land forces to follow up the achievements of their fleet. Upkeep was a serious problem, and the accidents inevitable to ships kept constantly at sea invited losses. Even their naval superiority in the area was subject to challenge, for the Turks were soon feverishly building a new fleet. There were also fears of French intervention on the side of the Turks, though this possibility was reduced by the friendly attitude of England toward Catherine.

A new offensive appeared advisable before the Turkish fleet could be completed. Elphinstone proposed that the Russians force passage of the Dardanelles, but Orlov hesitated and permitted only a blockade. This delay proved costly. The Turks, though unprepared initially, gained time to refurbish their old forts and build new ones under the direction of Baron de Tott, their French military adviser. When Orlov halfheartedly attacked one of the new forts, he was repulsed. About the same time an attack on two Turkish battleships anchored under the protection of shore batteries likewise failed. The golden moment had been lost. Orlov abandoned the attempt and sailed away to attack Lemnos. One of the greatest ironies in Russian naval history may well be that it was a Russian commander who held back when a British admiral urged the attack that would probably have achieved Russia's age-old objective in the Black Sea.

Between Chesma and the Treaty of Kuchuk-Kainardzhi, which closed the war in 1774, approximately three years elapsed during which the Russians were involved in many spheres of activity. In January 1771 Admiral Spiridov accepted the surrender of 18 islands and proclaimed them part of the Russian empire as the Grand Duchy of the Archipelago Islands. The fleet established bases in the Aegean at Auza, Trio, and Port Maria. These did not serve for all purposes, and the Russian fleet required constant reinforcement. A third Mediterranean squadron of three 66's and 16 transports under Admiral Arf left Revel on July 11, 1770, but did not arrive in the eastern Mediterranean until January 1771. The next year, in October, a fourth squadron reached the Levant. These reinforcements were by no means simply additions to Russian strength, for ships were being lost during the same period. But they did serve to prevent any diminution of the Russian fleet. At the beginning of 1771 the Russian Mediterranean fleet numbered ten battleships, nine frigates, a bomb, and five small craft. A year later there were ten battleships, 24 frigates, three bombs, and a few small craft. By early 1773 the number of battleships had been raised to 12. During the long period of activity in the Mediterranean there was also a considerable turnover in officers and crews; most of the British admirals had been recalled to Russia by early 1771. At that time the flag officers were Admiral Spiridov, Vice Admiral Ylmanov (Elphinstone left on January 12, 1771), and Rear Admiral Arf.[3]

During the remainder of the war the Russian navy was consistently victorious. Late in December 1771 the *Saratov* discovered and destroyed a Turkish 66 ashore on the island of Kos. On June 18, 1772, a detachment of Russian small craft forced a Turkish frigate ashore near Ture and burned her. In October 1772 after a three-month lull, one Lieutenant Aleksianov, in command of the frigate *Sv. Pavel* and two polaccas, discovered a small squadron of Barbary ships anchored at Damietta on the coast of Egypt. His frigate sailed between the two largest ships—each of which carried 20 guns—and engaged on each broadside. The ensuing artillery duel lasted for two hours, after which both Barbary ships were abandoned by their crews, so badly damaged that they had to be destroyed. However, the Russians managed to capture a number of smaller vessels.

The largest of several minor naval actions occurred in early November in the Gulf of Patras and was fought between a small Russian squadron of two battleships and five smaller craft under Captain Koniaev, and a Turkish fleet comprising eight frigates and 14 shebeks each carrying 26 to 30 guns. This Turkish force was part of a much larger concentration of ships from outlying areas (such as the Bosphorus, the Adriatic, and North Africa) with which the Turks hoped to surprise and destroy Orlov's squadron. In the first fight the Turks lost a frigate and two shebeks, but the remainder of the fleet took refuge under the guns of a nearby fort. Two further Russian attacks were made. The first, on November 7, was indecisive. The second, by gunfire and with boarding parties in small boats, took place the next day and achieved decisive results. Six shebeks escaped but eight frigates were destroyed and one run aground. Russian losses amounted to one man killed and seven wounded. This victory effectively ended the Turkish plan of concentrating naval forces for a surprise attack.

Russian landing operations were usually successful, but they did not secure lasting results. One of the few failures came immediately after Chesma in the town of Pelari, which Orlov besieged until its garrison was reinforced. Better luck attended him on the island of Mitylene. Here the Russians made a successful landing, overran the dockyard, burned two 74's and a shebek on the stocks, captured some 20 small vessels, and then retired. On November 4, 1772, an attack by Greig on the town of Chesma was similarly successful. Part of the town was burned, and ships in the harbor were captured. On October 10, 1773, following a siege, Russian land and sea forces captured the port of Beirut.

Russian losses during this war were due more to natural causes than to the Turks. As already noted Elphinstone lost the *Sviatoslav*, which grounded between Imbros and Tenedos. Later the *Rodos* 60 was wrecked on the Morean coast. Late in the war the *Aziia* 54 foundered with her entire crew in a severe storm.

During 1773 there was comparatively little fighting, and in 1774 there were no hostilities of any importance. The Russian squadrons gradually returned to the Baltic. The battleships were in such poor condition that of the 13 in the first three Mediterranean squadrons only six got back to Russia. Several were lost and three were sold for firewood. In all, the Russians had sent 20 battleships, five frigates, and eight lesser vessels to the Aegean, and bought 11 frigates and two bombs. Of these, 13 battleships and all the frigates returned to Russia. Of some 12,200 men sent to the Aegean, 4,516 did not return. Considering the achievements of the Russian fleets, these costs were extremely modest.

BLACK SEA OPERATIONS

In the Black Sea the Russians faced even heavier odds than they had encountered in the Aegean: here they started the war with no sea coast and, of course, no fleet. Russian land forces under Gen. Petr Aleksandrovich Rumiantsev were ordered to seize the coastline and to capture the mouth of the Don. Under the direction of Vice Adm. Aleksei Seniavin (son of Adm. Naum Seniavin) a fleet was to be constructed from scratch on the upper Don. Seniavin did remarkably well with the modest resources available, and in less than a year he had produced several ships armed with 12 to 15 medium-size guns and propelled by both oars and sails to ensure mobility, besides some special landing craft for amphibious operations. By May 28, 1771, Seniavin had put to sea with seven small vessels, most of which carried 14 to 16 guns.

The Turkish Black Sea Fleet, which had forty large ships, could have crushed the venturesome Russians had it demonstrated any initiative. As it was, Turkish lethargy allowed Seniavin's forces to take the offensive, leaving the latter in temporary control of the Sea of Azov and in a position to lend support to two Russian armies then entering the Crimea. Patrolling the central and eastern Black Sea respectively were task forces commanded by Capt. H. Kinsbergen (a Dutch officer who in 1791 wrote the first Russian book on tactics) and Capt. M. Sukhotin.

Although the Russian Black Sea Fleet was augmented by the addition of two 32-gun frigates in 1772 and two 58-gun battleships the following year, it remained numerically inferior to the Turkish fleet. This inferiority mattered little, for the Turks never did undertake offensive action or interfere with the naval operations conducted in cooperation with the successful Russian land campaign.

The years 1773 and 1774 saw a considerable intensification of the war at sea, with a number of minor encounters between the small squadrons of Sukhotin and Kinsbergen and the much larger Turkish forces. On June 9, 1773, five vessels under Captain Sukhotin destroyed six ships off the Kuban delta and the following day claimed two others. Ten days later the same squadron attacked 20 Turkish transports in the same area, burning two and driving the rest ashore.

On July 4, 1773, Captain Kinsbergen, in the *Karron* 16, and the *Taganrog* 16 fought a Turkish force of three 52's and a 24-gun shebek for six hours—but without serious damage to either side. This was the first deep-water action of the Black Sea Fleet and demonstrated Russian aggressiveness and willingness to attack superior forces; it also pointed up poor gunnery on both sides. Two months later, on September 3, Kinsbergen with a 32-gun frigate, three 16's, a fireship, and a gunboat fought three Turkish battleships, four frigates, and three shebeks for two hours south of the Kerch Strait, but with indecisive results. A little later Vice Admiral Seniavin with two frigates, five 16's, and three smaller craft attacked five Turkish battleships, two frigates, two shebeks, and two small craft. As usual the vastly outnumbered Russians pushed the attack; but the faster Turkish ships retreated.

In two larger brushes in 1774 the Turks showed a more aggressive spirit. In the first, on June 20, Rear Adm. Pavel V. Chichagov, with a 58, two 32's, and two 16's, was surprised and attacked south of Kerch by five battleships, nine frigates, and 26 smaller craft whose superior speed was used in an attempt to cut off the Russian forces. Outnumbered eight to one, the Russians retreated, and the Turks were not sufficiently skillful to prevent their escape. Then on July 9 a Turkish squadron of six battleships, seven frigates, and 18 smaller craft attacked the Russian squadron (now under Seniavin) which included three frigates, four 16's, two bombs, and three small craft. The Russians' only advantage was the greater range of their bomb vessels; when they demonstrated this range the Turks retreated.

By 1774 both Catherine and the Sublime Porte were tired of fighting and ready to conclude the war. The Russian armies had done well, and since no third power was prepared to intervene to aid the Turks, the terms of peace reflected a definitive victory for Russian arms. The tsarina received Kinburn (a fortress near the mouth of the Dnieper), Azov, Taganrog, and Kerch; a protectorate over the Crimea; and the right to maintain a fleet with secure access to the Black Sea. Peter the Great's ambition for an outlet to the south was thus fulfilled by Catherine the Great.

From a Russian standpoint the war had been deeply satisfying. The Turks, though not lacking in courage, were poorly trained and unimaginative, and they never demonstrated the aggressiveness that should have accompanied their overwhelming superiority in ships, men, and gun power. By contrast, the strategic conceptions of the Russians had been not only original but brilliantly executed. While Catherine's admirals did not always possess all the tools needed, they invariably made good use of what they had. Only in Orlov's vacillation about attacking the Dardanelles had there been a major sin of omission.

THE PERIOD OF TRUCE (1774–87)

The next period of Russian peace with Turkey lasted for 13 years, during which Catherine was involved in other areas but not in a manner that led to war. Russia participated with Austria and Prussia in the successive partitions of Poland, and in 1781 she conducted minor sorties against Persia.

The major diplomatic question affecting seapower at this time, a question which resulted largely from international conflicts following the American Revolution, concerned freedom of the seas. Russia remained officially neutral during this period, though she maintained small patrol squadrons at the North Cape and the Straits of Gibraltar as protection against American corsairs and Spanish privateers. To the intense chagrin of the British, who complained that the small Russian merchant marine suffered no real injury as a result of British blockade measures, Catherine adopted a liberal viewpoint concerning freedom of the seas. This she applied to both neutral ships and their cargoes except for genuine contraband of war—actual arms and munitions. Furthermore, from the Russian standpoint an acceptable blockade had to be near shore and maintained by adequate force. Ships seized as prizes were to be judged promptly and by regular methods.

This liberal attitude stemmed partly from economic considerations and partly from a desire to assert Russian power. Timber for ship masts came mainly from North America, a source blocked by war, and from the Baltic. Russia had a profitable trade with France and Spain in ship timber which would have been interrupted if timber were declared contraband. By exerting pressure Catherine was able to prevent British seizures of Russian ships carrying timber to France, though Britain seized the ships of all other powers.

Russian views regarding blockade, considered reasonable by other neutrals and in fact frequently supported by the United States in the earlier years of its national existence, were given only lip service by the British. Catherine's irritation at what most neutrals regarded as high-handed British conduct was contained short of actual war, however, probably because Russian use of British ports and naval officers limited the extent to which she could afford to pursue an anti-British policy.

Catherine made full use of her years of peace to strengthen her naval forces, particularly in the Black Sea. The initial administrative step was the establishment of the Don River Flotilla in 1768. After the capture of Azov this force became the Azov Fleet, with bases on Azov, Kerch, and Taganrog. Also dating from the war was the Danube River Flotilla, which by 1771 numbered 30 small craft. In 1778 the port city of Kherson was established and shipyards constructed for both naval and maritime vessels. Though this proved a difficult location because all supplies of lumber and iron had to be imported and stockpiled, within a year Kherson had launched its first battleship, *Slava Yekaterine*, and thereafter maintained a building rate of one battleship a year until 1787, when output was raised to two a year. During the 1780's the new Black Sea Fleet gradually took shape with its own shore-based admiralty. By 1786 it comprised six battleships, 19 frigates, and many small craft. A second major base, named Sevastopol, was started at the site of the village of Akhtier, and in 1787 when Catherine entertained Joseph II of Austria at the Black Sea she was able to show him a 46-unit fleet. The Turks attempted to delay the progress of Russian aggression by fomenting a revolt among the Crimean Tatars, but this was easily suppressed; it was followed (in 1783) by outright Russian annexation of the Crimea. Catherine then appointed Prince Grigory Potemkin governor. Although Potemkin's subsequent reports of progress in his new capacity at times greatly exceeded the truth, his actual achievements were notable and included the building of forts, the opening at Kherson of a naval school (later moved to Nikolaev), and the procurement of an able corps of officers.

In 1781 the Caspian Fleet was reestablished with bases at Astrakhan and Sara Island. This force was always kept small; but by 1794 it numbered three frigates and 24 small craft. Ships for the Caspian were turned out from yards on the Volga.

Because the lack of sufficient troops afloat had clearly been a weakness during the first Turkish war, Catherine now lent some attention to the reorganization of the marines, or naval infantry. Each ship was given a complement of naval infantry determined by the size of the ship and its campaign objective. Thus an 80-gun battleship carried 160 to 165 marines, while frigates had 54 to 56. As of 1777, eight battalions were carried afloat. The marine complement was raised in 1782 so that the 40 battleships of the Baltic Fleet carried 8,208 marines in time of peace and 9,416 in time of war.

Catherine gave great encouragement to naval shipbuilding. Between 1760 and 1780 no less than 90 battleships, 40 large and 18 small frigates, and smaller craft in large number were built for the Baltic Fleet. The Black Sea Fleet building included only 15 battleships and 50 frigates. Thus, though the Black Sea Fleet played the greater role in Catherine's plans for the expansion, the Baltic Fleet continued to be the nation's main naval force.

While Catherine's naval efforts impressed most of Europe, a somewhat contrary feeling was expressed in 1774 by one John Blackett, an Englishman who visited Russia. He pointed out many factors which he judged would prevent Russia from becoming a great maritime power; the lack of merchant marine and seamen forced the navy to rely on raw levies who were discharged after each campaign; the officers disliked the sea, partly because of poor pay and partly because of incomplete knowledge of their jobs; long-drawn-out procedures dictated that everything be reported to the Admiralty College, where the heads of the naval bureaus were incompetent and tended to cling to precedent; major ports were blocked by ice for seven months of the year.[4]

THE SECOND TURKISH WAR

Turkey also made use of the years following Chesma to rebuild her fleet, and in 1787, under the encouragement of other powers, especially France, she again declared war. Russia at first considered repeating her earlier strategy of sending a squadron to the Mediterranean, but Swedish action in the renewed conflict made this impossible: Gustav III, concluding that Russia's involvement with Turkey had created a situation favorable for recouping Sweden's earlier losses, attacked Russia without a declaration of war. Catherine found herself, with few allies except Austria and Denmark, unwillingly fighting two full-scale wars at the same time, each with an ancient foe. Officially neutral, Great Britain tended to sympathize with Sweden, and a number of British officers fought for the Swedes. Most of the British officers employed by the Russians remained in their positions.

On Russia's southern boundaries the Turks were once more nominally superior so far as naval strength was concerned, especially since the war with Sweden prevented Catherine from sending squadrons to the Mediterranean. Although accounts of the forces available to both the Russians and the Turks vary widely depending on the authority used, it seems that the Russian Black Sea Fleet consisted of squadrons on the Don and the Dnieper, and at Sevastopol, totaling five battleships and 20 frigates of 1,134 guns. The Turks had available 22 battleships (some of the Turkish battleships were actually too small to merit such a classification) and eight frigates with a total of 1,700 guns.

The command arrangements of the Russians had some serious drawbacks. Prince Grigory Potemkin, who though competent owed his job mainly to royal favoritism, was in supreme command; below him the chain of authority was obscure. Commanding land forces under Potemkin was the extremely able Count Aleksandr Suvorov, who apparently also directed the local naval forces in his vicinity. Two other squadrons started the war under Adm. Count M. Voinovich (Sevastopol) and Rear Admiral Mordvinov (Dnieper). A galley fleet under Brig. O. de Ribas aided in sieges and assisted the army on the Danube. At the beginning of the war these detachments were united neither in theory nor in fact, and Suvorov was at times greatly handicapped by lack of dependable naval aid. Among those who played important roles in the conflict were two foreigners—the Prussian Rear Admiral Nassau-Siegen (Prince Charles of Nassau-Siegen) and the American naval hero Rear Adm. John Paul Jones. The later years of the war brought forward Adm. Fedor Ushakov, who was to become one of Russia's greatest naval heroes.

During the first year of the war much of the fighting was ineffective. On September 11 the Turks started a land and sea offensive against Kinburn with a squadron of three battleships, a frigate, a bomb, and about 30 small vessels bombarding the fort in cooperation with the Turkish army. Though clearly superior in numbers, the Turks again failed to make adequate use of their strength. At one point the Russian galley *Desna* under Lieutenant Lombard attacked the entire Turkish fleet and with the fire of one 36-pound carronade forced it to retire. On this occasion the *Desna* was able to move between two columns of the Turkish fleet with little injury, since most of the Turkish guns were overcharged and firing high. The *Desna* then fired into Ochakov but was disabled two days later while fighting 17 gunboats and three bombs. Attempts to land Turkish forces at Kinburn proved a dismal failure, with the Turks losing two gunboats and two shebeks from the naval support force and all but about 500 men from the landing force. When the battle ended, Suvorov had won despite Turkish naval strength.

While the few Russian ships at Kinburn performed heroically in the early days of the war, the same cannot be said for the main fleets. Mordvinov's squadron of two battleships, three frigates, five galleys, two floating batteries, and two gunboats did not leave the Dnieper until October 24, and arrived at the scene of action only after Suvorov's great victory. Mordvinov's force did encounter a slightly superior Turkish fleet of three battleships, five frigates, seven shebeks, four bombs, 12 gunboats, and 30 small craft east of the fortress. From October 25 to 27, just before the Turks retired to winter quarters, the two fleets fought several indecisive engagements during which a Russian floating battery ran aground. The Sevastopol squadron under Admiral Voinovich was even less successful. For a time it allowed itself to be blockaded in Kherson. When it left port on imperative orders from Potemkin, it promptly ran into a heavy storm in which a battleship and a frigate were lost and eight other ships damaged, several seriously. Catherine's response to these reverses was to order the galleys to fight harder while the sailing fleet was being rebuilt for the following year's action.

In 1788 Potemkin made changes in leadership but still failed to establish a clear chain of command. Suvorov, whose abilities had held off defeat the preceding year, continued to exercise command on land. The gunboat and galley fleet was under Rear Admiral Nassau-Siegen, and the main sailing fleet of four battleships, six frigates, two fireships, and 23 small craft was under Rear Admiral Jones. The latter's appointment so antagonized the numerous British officers in Russian service that they considered protesting to Catherine. They were strongly advised not to do so, however, and were partly mollified on learning that Jones would serve in the Black Sea rather than in the Baltic. Both Mordvinov and Voinovich remained in service, but it is not clear what their positions were.

The details of the 1788 campaign, which saw far more decisive action than the previous year, are obscured by contradictory accounts from different sources. On paper the Turks retained their superiority, but their actual strength is in doubt: some of their "battleships" may have been merely converted merchantmen.

The theater of battle in 1788 was the mouth of the Dnieper, where the Russians now launched an offensive against the Turkish fortress of Ochakov. In early June Suvorov began a slow advance along the north shore of the Dnieper, using both galley and sailing fleets to guard his seaward flank. Early on the morning of June 13, five Turkish galleys and 36 small craft attacked the inshore end of the Russian line. The Russians were temporarily outnumbered, but their main fleets came to join the fight, as did other Turkish vessels. However, the engagement never became more than a skirmish; at 11:00 A.M., after losing two or three ships, the Turks retreated.

Two weeks later a more decisive battle took place. At noon on June 27 the Turkish fleet steered toward the left flank of the Russian Dnieper line. The Turkish flagship, a 64, ran aground in shallow water, and the rest of the Turkish ships anchored in confusion. At about 5:15 P.M. the Russian fleets attacked. The main sailing fleet came into action against the Turks' offshore line, while Nassau-Siegen struck the Turkish left wing, which was inshore from the ships being attacked by Jones. On the Turkish right some small craft, unengaged, sank the *Maly Aleksandr* 34. The Turks incurred less damage from Russian attacks in this phase of the action than from their own uninformed and careless navigation; two of their battleships were lost from grounding. At 9:30 P.M. they retreated under the guns of Fort Ochakov.

But the Turks' misfortunes were not ended. When their fleet sought to escape during the night it steered too far to the north in an attempt to avoid the powerful Russian batteries on the south shore, with the result that no less than nine vessels grounded. At daybreak the Russians attacked and scored a complete victory, which was subsequently claimed by both Jones and Nassau-Siegen. One Turkish battleship was captured; seven battleships, two 34-gun frigates, a bomb, two shebeks, a galley, and a transport were destroyed. The Turkish loss in personnel is unknown but must have been large. The Russians lost only 18 killed and 67 wounded.

On July 12 Russian land and sea forces aimed a sharp blow at Ochakov. Only nine Turkish vessels of various types were still defending the fortress, and these the Russians promptly attacked. For once they were numerically superior, with about 50 small craft. The battle proved very one-sided; Jones captured two galleys and two gunboats, and the rest of the Turkish fleet went up in flames. The Russians lost no ships and sustained casualties of 24 killed and 80 wounded.

Following this Turkish defeat the Russians held both moral and numerical superiority. Jones was able to capture several Turkish gunboats and to establish a close blockade. The Turks turned to blockade-running but paid with heavy losses for limited successes. Strained relations between Nassau-Siegen and Jones finally led to the transfer of Nassau-Siegen to the Baltic and the replacement of Jones by Mordvinov. Jones protested, obtained no redress, and in fact left Russia under a cloud.[5] However, both officers had made important contributions.

With the siege of Ochakov continued, some action was taking place on other fronts. The main Turkish fleet, consisting of 17 battleships, eight frigates, three bombs, and 21 shebeks, pursued the Sevastopol squadron of Count Voinovich, which comprised four battleships, eight frigates, and 24 small craft. Though they had a better than two-to-one superiority in the ensuing action, the Turks sustained a slight tactical defeat, losing a shebek in a two-hour action on July 25. The Russians lost no ships and had only seven men killed or wounded. The two fleets maneuvered in the same area for several days with neither commander anxious to engage after their initial rather brief encounter.

On one occasion a Russian galley fell in with 11 Turkish vessels. After a brave but futile resistance, Capt. R. von Saken ordered his crew to save themselves while he remained aboard and fired the magazines, destroying himself, his ship, and four Turkish ships which tried to board.

Ochakov was taken by Suvorov in December 1788, though fighting erupted there again in 1789 when the Turks sought to recapture the fort with the aid of a fleet of 57 sail (17 battleships, 10 frigates, 30 small craft) on June 23. The Russian sea forces were completely outclassed in the June battle, but as before, the Turkish commander failed to make full use of his strength; he contented himself with ending the Russian blockade and with separating the two main Russian squadrons, which were based at Kherson and Sevastopol. By taking Hadji Bey (Odessa) on September 25, Suvorov forced the Turkish fleet to move and at the same time succeeded in rejoining the separated Russian squadrons. The combined Russian fleet of 11 battleships, nine frigates, and lesser vessels was then smaller than the Turkish force. Neither side sought battle.

While most of the fighting in Catherine's Second Turkish war took place in the Black Sea, the Russians by 1789 had succeeded in creating a secondary front in the Aegean and the Adriatic. Three privateering squadrons were created under the Greek Lombros Katzones, who had formerly held a commission in the Russian navy; a mercenary named de Chapelet; and a Maltese pirate, Guglielmo Lorenzi. All of these operated under the Russian flag and were based (after Austria joined the war) on Trieste. The Katzones squadron took several prizes, beat off an attack by a vastly superior Turkish force, and for a time operated with marked success. Chapelet was less successful. But Lorenzi, whose squadron had originally been organized by Rear Adm. Samuel Gibbs (a British officer serving Catherine), did quite well. Failure of overall Russian leadership, the inability of the squadron commanders to cooperate with one another, and the piratical tendencies of all these squadrons were limiting factors.

On land during 1789 the struggle continued to favor the Russians, who gained several key towns, including Akkerman on the Dniester estuary and Bendari. At the end of the year only Izmail remained in Turkish hands. Building even as they fought, the Russians established a port and arsenal at Nikolaev at the junction of the Bug and Ingul rivers.

Before the 1790 fighting season was under way, the Russians made a vital change in command. Admiral Ushakov was moved to the top post at sea to secure what had been signally lacking: a unified direction of the naval war by an aggressive and able admiral.

In terms of family background and education Fedor Ushakov would seem to have been a highly unlikely individual to attain glory at sea. He came from a poor but noble family of Mongol origin living in the interior of Russia. His early education had been solely under the tutelage of a village priest. Yet when he entered the naval school in 1766 his brilliance amazed all of his professors and comrades. When pressures of his new responsibilities led him to devote considerable thought to the method of conducting war, he arrived at conclusions not dissimilar to those of his British contemporary, Lord Nelson. Key points in his naval doctrine were (1) good care of material was essential; (2) it was excellent strategy to concentrate all of one's strength on a portion of the enemy's forces; (3) the unexpected action was of inestimable value in breaking the enemy's formation; (4) faithful support of injured Russian ships was a necessity; (5) avid exploitation of enemy weaknesses was essential to victory. He was opposed to extremely long lines of battle, believing them to be difficult to maintain and not conducive to decisive victories. Like Nelson, he left considerable initiative to his captains once he had trained them in his own philosophy of naval warfare. In the Black Sea he had been second in command to Voinovich, and had observed at first hand the timid ineffectiveness of his own chief, the unedifying quarrels between Jones and Nassau-Siegen, and the failure of officers to use naval power in a unified manner. Though still in his thirties when he assumed his command, Ushakov was approximately as able at sea as was Suvorov on land.

Because of this important change the Russian position in the Black Sea was greatly enhanced. On May 27, 1790, Ushakov left Sevastopol with a light squadron of eight frigates and 11 privateers to carry the fight to the enemy. After sailing to the area of Sinope, he released the privateers—which promptly captured eight Turkish ships and forced the beaching of four others. Ushakov continued with the rest of his force to Anapa, where his bombardment was relatively ineffective, then returned to port.

On July 13 Ushakov put to sea with the main Russian fleet, which now consisted of 16 battleships and frigates and 17 small vessels and privateers. On July 19 at the Kerch Strait the Russians sighted the main Turkish fleet of Hussein Pasha, a force consisting of ten battleships, eight frigates, and 36 small craft. The two fleets were not greatly unequal in strength, though the Turks possessed— at least on paper—a superiority of about 20 percent. The day was foggy and visibility limited. At 11:00 A.M. the first Turkish ships appeared in parallel lines. Ushakov gave orders to attack. From noon to 3:00 P.M. an indecisive artillery duel took place in which the Russians, with 29 killed and 68 wounded, had somewhat the better of the exchange. The Turks had two ships damaged and suffered an indeterminate loss of life before they sailed out of range and broke off the engagement. The battle checked Turkish plans to attack the Crimea, which by this time was largely in Russian hands.

On September 5, after six weeks in port, Ushakov sailed again with nearly the same fleet as before. On September 8 he sighted the Turks off the island of Tendra. Several hours of complicated maneuvers followed as each commander sought an advantageous position. By 2:00 P.M. the two fleets were disposed on parallel courses. The Turks were superior to about the same degree as in the previous battle. They had 14 battleships and eight frigates against the Russians' ten battleships and six frigates. Firing commenced about 3:00 P.M. The Turks speedily got the worst of the exchange and retreated in disorder. Because their sailing qualities were superior to those of Ushakov's ships, most of them made good their escape to the Bosphorus. However, seven of their ships were lost, including two cripples which were picked up the following day by the Russians. The *Melik Bahri* surrendered to the *Mariia Magdalena* 66 without resistance, but the *Kapitania* 74, flagship of Adm. Said Bey, put up a tremendous fight against heavy odds, and only 81 of the crew of 800 were rescued before the ship blew up. The Turks lost 1,500 men taken prisoner, while the Russians lost only 46 men in all. The day after the battle four frigates and 17 rowing vessels reinforced Ushakov for a cruise that continued for some time.

The Battle of Tendra was a clear-cut and important Russian victory, and its effects were felt on many fronts. With its conclusion the Russian galley fleet under Brigadier de Ribas, which had been giving support to the army on the Danube, was freed from the threat of the Turkish sailing fleet and was able to aid the army in taking

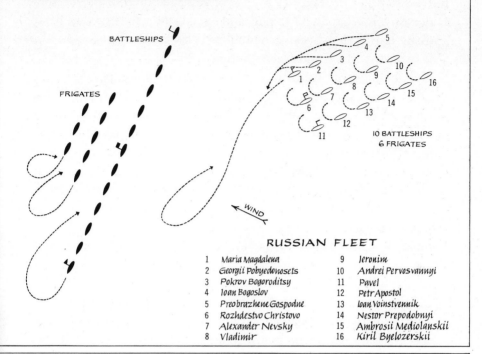

THE BATTLE OF TENDRA

BATTLESHIPS

FRIGATES

WIND

5
4
3
2
1
9
10
16
15
8
14
6
7
13
12
11

10 BATTLESHIPS
6 FRIGATES

RUSSIAN FLEET

1	Maria Magdalena	9	Ieronim
2	Georgii Pobyedonosets	10	Andrei Pervosvannyi
3	Pokrov Bogoroditsy	11	Pavel
4	Ioan Bogoslov	12	Petr Apostol
5	Preobrazhene Gospodne	13	Ioan Voinstvennik
6	Rozhdestvo Christovo	14	Nestor Prepodobnyi
7	Alexander Nevsky	15	Ambrosii Mediolanskii
8	Vladimir	16	Kiril Byelozerskii

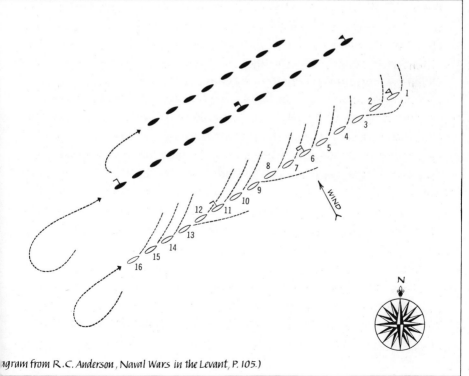

WIND

N

…gram from R.C. Anderson, Naval Wars in the Levant, P. 105.)

fortresses. On Christmas Day 1790 a Russian force of 20,000 men under Suvorov captured Izmail and 30,000 of its defenders in an 18-hour battle that became a military classic. De Ribas was also able to destroy the Turkish river flotilla.

Both belligerents were now prepared to treat for peace—Catherine because she had gained all she really expected, the Turks because of ill fortune. Negotiations were begun at Galatz; but the Turks, hoping to obtain better terms by a naval demonstration, called to Varna all their ships from as far away as Tripoli and Algeria in a last-stand hope of defeating the Russian fleet. This hope was not to be realized: on April 11, 1791, before the naval concentration became effective, the Turks surrendered the key fortress of Brăila on the Danube after a siege which cost them 11 gunboats and four bombs. By early August, Hussein Pasha had assembled 18 battleships, 17 frigates, and more than 40 smaller vessels as against Ushakov's six battleships, 12 frigates, and some small craft. On August 8, with seven of the Turkish ships elsewhere and the Russians at full strength, the two fleets came together in the Battle of Cape Kaliakra —the Russians with 990 guns compared to 1600 for the Turks. Ushakov attacked the head of the enemy line with his entire force and threw the Turkish fleet into confusion and disorder. According to some accounts the Turks lost several ships; according to others they lost no vessels but escaped only by flight. The fact of Russian victory over a superior enemy was conceded by all.

Peace was concluded on Jassy (Iassi) early the next year. Because of the influence of England and Prussia, who were supporting Turkey, Russia failed to reap the reward that might have been expected from the excellent work of her admirals and generals. Her real gains, however, were greater than the addition of the territory between the Bug and Dniester rivers would indicate. In 1787 the Black Sea Fleet had contained seven battleships; in 1792 it had 21. The long list of victories achieved against superior odds went far toward establishing a respectable naval tradition.

From the perspective of history neither opponent appears to have been lacking in bravery, but the direction of Russian naval affairs, especially in the latter part of the war, was far superior to that of the Turks. If the Turks had superior sailing ships, the Russian crews were better trained for both fighting and maneuvering, and the

Russians' constructive use of privateers was not imitated by the Turks. In the coordination of land and sea campaigns the Russians were far more successful, though none of the Russian admirals, except possibly Jones and Nassau-Siegen, made anything like continuous use of sea power; naval operations could ordinarily have been started much earlier and continued far longer. Notwithstanding, the overall Russian achievement was genuinely impressive. Always outnumbered, they still had the better of every sea fight and finished the war with a fleet in excellent condition and under able command.

CHAPTER 5

Catherine the Great:
War with Sweden

1788: THE OPENING MOVES

THOUGH THE WAR with Sweden (1788–90) was Russia's principal naval conflict under Catherine the Great, it owed its origin not to the Russians but to Gustav III of Sweden, who believed that the time was propitious for settling old scores. He hoped, by a surprise attack without declaration of war, to destroy the Russian fleet and retake Finland, and to capture St. Petersburg after landing an army of 30,000 men at Oranienburg. From a naval standpoint such hopes had some possibility of fulfillment. Sweden had 20 ships of the line in reasonably good condition, and her flotilla strength was clearly superior to that of the Russians. The Russians could claim a total of 54 battleships, but this figure was subject to heavy discount since six of those ships were in the Black Sea and five were at Arkhangelsk. In addition, Catherine had already planned to send 15 battleships to the Mediterranean. Of the remaining 28, no fewer than 19 were in poor repair and scarely fit to go to sea.

Unfortunately for his country, Gustav III ordered his forces to strike when only three of the 15 Russian battleships had left for the Mediterranean and before all of his own ships were ready. Carl, Duke of Södermanland, began commissioning ships in April 1788 and on June 9 his fleet left Karlskrona, moving east and north toward Hangö, sighting various Russian naval forces en route. Meanwhile 8,000 troops, in the Swedish flotilla of 28 galleys and 30 gunboats, left port on June 24. They passed the sailing fleet at Hangö on July 1. Diplomatic relations between the two countries were severed, and the Russian ambassador in Sweden was sent home.

The next day the Swedes landed at Helsinki, and on July 3 they bombarded the Russian fortress at Nyslott. Although Duke Carl did not receive orders to start hostilities until July 7, he captured two Russian frigates, *Yaroslavets* 36 and *Gektor* 26, north of Revel on July 4. He then retired with his prizes to Mjolo, where he was reinforced by four ships and 3,000 troops. Until this date, with the Swedes initiating all of the naval activity, they reaped some of the advantages to be expected from an unforeseen attack.

The Russians, however, though taken by surprise, did not remain entirely idle. Most of the ships intended for the Mediterranean had been ordered retained in the Baltic, and on July 3 Admiral Greig, probably the most proficient of Catherine's admirals, put to sea with 17 battleships and eight frigates. His fleet moved slowly westward, sailing in three squadrons, the first under Rear Admiral von Dessen, the second under Greig himself (with Spiridov second in command), and the third under Rear Admiral Koslianinov. On the morning of July 17 the Swedes were sighted to the northwest off the island of Hogland. After early maneuvers, the two fleets came together. The Swedish fleet was well organized, the Russian fleet poorly arranged and in an order other than that which Greig had intended. In number of vessels and in weight of metal the two fleets were remarkably well matched, the Swedes having in the line 20 ships carrying 1,180 guns, the Russians 17 ships with 1,220 guns. Out of the line the Swedes had five frigates and a sloop, the Russians seven frigates. Total guns favored the Russians by 1,450 compared to 1,299.

The battle that followed was a fair reflection of the even strength of the contestants. Admiral Greig, in the *Rostislav* 100, attacked the lighter Swedish flagship *Gustav III* and the *Fadernesland*. In the van, seven Russian battleships were matched against ten Swedish battleships, but the greater weight of the Russian ships enabled them to more than hold their own. Farther back, the Russians did poorly. In the center the Swedes were able to concentrate the fire of six ships on three Russian vessels while the Russian vessels in the rear got into action only at long range. In fighting ability there was

little to choose between the two fleets. The conflict began about
3:00 P.M. and ended several hours later with each side having captured one battleship: the Swedes took the *Vladislav* 74, the Russians the *Prins Gustaf* 70. Manpower losses favored the Swedes, with
the Russians losing 321 killed, 702 wounded, and 783 captured in
the *Vladislov*; the Swedes had 130 killed, 334 wounded, and 687
captured in the *Gustaf*. Both fleets were badly battered, and neither
tried to renew the battle. Among the Russians the *Mstislav, Rostislav,* and *Iziaslav* had been hit more than 100 times each. Strategically, however, the fight was a Russian victory, since it defeated the
planned attack on the capital.

The Russian fleet worked to the island of Seskar, 40 miles from
Kronstadt, where Admiral Greig sent home his most heavily damaged ships and was reinforced by four others. In moving toward
Sveaborg on August 5, Admiral Greig met with some unexpected
good fortune. The Russian fleet was able because of a dense fog to
move very close to a small Swedish detachment of three battleships
and four frigates. Upon discovering their peril, the Swedish ships
cut their cables and sought to escape, but the *Prins Gustav Adolf*
62 ran aground and surrendered. After failing to refloat her on the
following day, Greig ordered the ship burned.

The Battle of Hogland was the main naval engagement of the
year, but there was some activity elsewhere as well. The Swedish
galley fleet made gestures toward Fredrikshamn on the coast of Finland, but the Finns proved unfriendly. Moreover, Admiral Greig's
fleet threatened to cut Swedish communications along the coast.

Russian activities were interrupted on October 16 by the death
of Admiral Greig. Admiral Koslianinov, who succeeded to the command, accomplished little before departing to winter at Revel on October 31. Duke Carl, who had to collect ships from various locations,
was almost a month later in going into winter quarters at Karlskrona.

In the meantime—and before the death of Admiral Greig—Russian Admiral von Dessen had been active with a small squadron in
the western Baltic and North Sea. He reached Copenhagen on July
8 and was joined there by two battleships purchased in England, by
the frigate *Nadezhda* 32 from Revel, and by two storeships laden
with ordnance and provisions for Arkhangelsk. In addition to pro-

tecting the storeships while they were in Swedish waters, he was assigned the destruction of three 40-gun Swedish frigates reported to be at Gothenburg. He failed in both missions, losing the storeships (one was recaptured later) to the Swedes and failing to bring the enemy frigates to action. However, there were gains in other respects. Four battleships and two frigates from Arkhangelsk joined von Dessen's force, as did three Danish battleships and nine frigates under Adm. Petr V. Povalishin, Denmark having decided to join the war on the Russian side. With this greatly reinforced fleet, Admiral von Dessen was ordered by Admiral Greig to blockade Karlskrona with a view to intercepting the returning Swedish fleet. After staying for a month at Karlskrona, von Dessen left for Copenhagen, missing Duke Carl by a wide margin. Had an encounter taken place, von Dessen would have had 12 battleships with 856 guns to pit against a Swedish fleet of 18 ships and 1,082 guns, a margin of difference not sufficient to preclude a Russian victory.

Pressure from England, Prussia, and Holland soon forced the Danes to agree to an inconclusive armistice. Though they were then unable to provide their increment for von Dessen's fleet, they permitted him to winter at Copenhagen—to his detriment, as it happened, since the Russians were not prepared to care for their needs so far from home bases.

1789 CAMPAIGN

Both sides made much more careful preparations for the 1789 campaign, each in the hope of achieving a definitive victory that year. Catherine II ordered the commissioning of 35 of the 41 battleships she had available; Gustav III ordered the preparation of 21 of his 25 battleships. Thus when the campaign began the Russians possessed a margin of at least 40 percent in total force (probably 70 percent if the larger size of the Russian ships is kept in mind). Of the Russian squadrons, ten battleships were stationed at Revel under Admiral Chichagov, 14 were at Kronstadt under Admiral Spiridov, and 11 were at Copenhagen under Admiral Koslianinov, who had succeeded Von Dessen. In case of a union between the Kronstadt and Revel squadrons, Admiral Chichagov was to command. The Swedes' position was superior, for all of their fleet was concentrated at Karlskrona, where the prospect of an earlier ice breakup afforded them a likely chance of getting to sea sooner than two of the three Russian squadrons.

Despite the fact that both belligerents were intent on bringing hostilities to a conclusion, neither the Russians nor the Swedes acted to exploit their respective advantages. The ice broke up at Karlskrona late in April, but Duke Carl did not put to sea until July 6, when he left port with a fleet of 21 battleships, 13 frigates, and eight smaller craft manned by 16,000 men. A week later Russia's combined Revel and Kronstadt squadrons, comprising 20 battleships, six frigates, and 19 small craft, left Revel. Far to the west and south was Koslianinov with 11 battleships, four frigates, and three smaller ships. Cruising with him to protect the Russian vessels while in Danish waters, but not to take offensive action, was a sizable Danish fleet of 11 battleships, three frigates, and other small vessels.

Duke Carl, occupying a central position between the two Russian squadrons, apparently was unable to decide what to do. For several days he cruised near the Danish coast, then turned eastward and cruised at random. On July 24 he found Admiral Chichagov's fleet. At about the same time, Admiral Chichagov became aware of the presence of the Swedish fleet and sent a dispatch to Koslianinov suggesting a meeting at the nearby island of Åland. There followed a full day of maneuvering before the two opposing fleets came together.

The Battle of Åland on July 26 proved to be little more than a long-range skirmish. The fleets were again quite evenly matched, though the Swedes held numerical superiority in both vessels and guns. That Russian casualties exceeded those of the Swedes was due merely to the fact that a greater number of guns burst among the Russian forces. Several days of jockeying for superior position followed during which neither commander appeared eager to engage. Finally Duke Carl's withdrawal to Karlskrona permitted Admirals Koslianinov and Chichagov to join forces on the night of August 1. One day later the now vastly superior Russian fleet of 33 battleships, 13 frigates, and seven smaller vessels had arrived in front of Karlskrona, in time to prevent the departure of a small Swedish squadron. But here it was Admiral Chichagov who failed to show enterprise; after cruising in the neighborhood for several days he returned to Russia.

The year 1789 saw more action by the flotillas of small craft than by the larger vessels. Numerous tiny islands lie off the southern coast of Finland. Inside this skargaard it is possible for small craft to work along the Finnish coast secure from attack by larger vessels. At only two points, Hangö and Porkkala, is the water deep enough to permit large vessels to get close to the coast. Late in May Admiral Chichagov had sent out detachments to investigate the Finnish coast at these points. His scouts reported that the Swedish fortifications at Hangö protected coastal traffic from interruption by big ships, but that Porkkala was relatively open. Acting on this information, Admiral Chichagov on June 12 dispatched a battleship and three frigates under Capt. B. Y. Sheshukov to occupy a position near Porkkala. This force soon succeeded in disrupting enemy coastal communications by holding a point between two Swedish forces. On June 14–15 Captain Sheshukov repulsed an attack by 17 Swedish rowing craft, and on July 2 three Russian ships carrying 60 guns repulsed a second attack by eight Swedish vessels with 30 guns. Immediately thereafter, Captain Sheshukov left to join Admiral Chichagov and was replaced at Porkkala by one Captain Glebov.

The two Swedish forces now consisted of a western detachment of 62 small vessels (turumas, gunboats, galleys, etc.) stationed at Sveaborg, east of Porkkala, and 65 similar vessels at Svensksund. During June the flotillas at Sveaborg succeeded in taking prizes among Russian storeships in the Gulf of Finland as well as in interfering with the communications of Russian troops in Finland.[1]

These activities of the Swedish galleys did not go unchallenged. During 1788 the Swedish flotilla had been vastly stronger than the Russian force, but extensive Russian building during the winter had brought the two much closer to equality. Now Vice Admiral Nassau-Siegen, recalled from the Black Sea, took command of the Russian flotillas and occupied Fredrickshamn, ten miles northeast of the Swedish eastern flotilla which was then based on Svensksund. The Russians were still holding back the Swedish western flotilla at Porkkala. In addition to the flotillas there was a small Russian sailing ship squadron operating in the Gulf of Finland under Rear Adm. A. Kruse. This squadron, which varied somewhat in strength from

time to time, moved south of Svensksund on August 7. It consisted
of two battleships—*Sv. Nikolai* 100 and *Ne Tron Menia* 66 (which
did not move to Svensksund at the time)—the 38-gun frigates
Patriky and *Simeon,* two transports, and two bomb vessels. Rear
Admiral Kruse joined and took command of the southern Russian
flotilla based south of Svensksund.

Reinforcements having arrived in the meantime, Nassau-Siegen
decided to launch a Russian attack from two directions. The Swedes,
under Admiral Ehrensvärd, had 49 ships with 686 guns. The Russian northern squadron was stronger at about 60 ships with 879
guns. With the addition of Rear Admiral Kruse's southern squadron
of 21 vessels with 404 guns, the Russians, if they could coordinate
their attack, held almost a two-to-one superiority. However, the
Swedes enjoyed the advantage of a central and naturally strong
position, since Svensksund is a circular harbor bounded by islands,
rocks, and shoals. Admiral Ehrensvärd sank vessels in the narrow
channels to the north to prevent the approach of Nassau-Siegen and
left two galleys and 11 gunboats to protect the obstructions. He
anchored the remainder of his fleet in a curved line between two
islets. Nassau-Siegen proposed that the southern Russian squadron
strike first and be supported by the northern squadron. When Kruse
opposed this plan, Nassau-Siegen replaced him on the eve of attack,
with General Major Balle.

The outcome of the battle fully justified Kruse's doubts. Balle
began his advance at 6:30 in the morning; Nassau-Siegen started
moving more than three hours later, and then obstructions and the
fire of the gunboats delayed him until seven in the evening. When
Balle's forces reached the Swedes and started their attack, they
were greeted with a heavy concentrated fire. By 2:00 P.M. a few
Russian ships had run aground, two had been captured, the rest
repulsed.

Meantime Nassau-Siegen's flotilla was beset by difficulties as it
sought to reach Svensksund through obstructed and well-defended
passages where there was constant danger of going aground. As the
Russian flotilla gradually cleared a way through the obstacles, the
defending Swedish galleys and gunboats fell back on their main
fleet. Ehrensvärd was not only short of ammunition to deal with a
new foe; he was also overmatched by about the same margin as

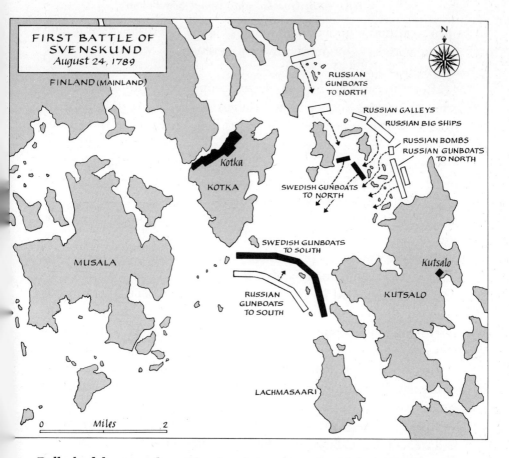

FIRST BATTLE OF
SVENSKUND
August 24, 1789

FINLAND (MAINLAND)

N

RUSSIAN
GUNBOATS
TO NORTH

RUSSIAN GALLEYS

RUSSIAN BIG SHIPS

RUSSIAN BOMBS
RUSSIAN GUNBOATS
TO NORTH

Kotka

KOTKA

SWEDISH GUNBOATS
TO NORTH

SWEDISH GUNBOATS
TO SOUTH

MUSALA

Kutsalo

KUTSALO

RUSSIAN
GUNBOATS
TO SOUTH

LACHMASAARI

0   Miles   2

Balle had been earlier. The Swedes retreated and a scattered running battle ensued. Now the Russians, in addition to recapturing the
two ships they had lost earlier, took or sank three 48-gun turumas
(*Sallan Varre*, *Rogvald*, and *Bjorn Jernsida*), the frigate *af Trolle*
24, the hemmema *Oden* 26, a galley, and two gunboats. Among
smaller vessels, the Swedes lost one galley, two gunboats, 14 transports (burned to prevent capture), and two hospital ships (captured). The Russians lost a gunboat and a galley and had several
other ships badly damaged. Personnel losses were 1,345 for the
Swedes, 1,035 for the Russians. The Battle of Svensksund was thus a
Russian victory, though not as decisive as should have been achieved
in view of the much greater Russian strength. Ehrensvärd was able
to escape with most of his flotilla to Svartholm, a strongly fortified
coastal town twenty miles to the south. Nassau-Siegen's strategy in
forcing the weaker Russian force to bear the burden of attack is

open to criticism on many grounds, as is the Swedish action in failing to withdraw promptly from a position in which they were heavily overmatched.

After this victory Nassau-Siegen cooperated with the Russian army by making attacks and landings farther down the coast—a strategy which forced the Swedish army to retreat even though the landings themselves were unsuccessful.

Several other naval actions, all relatively minor, took place during the fighting season. The first occurred on May 1 in the vicinity of the Kattegat, when the Swedish frigate *Venus* 40 fell in with part of the western Russian squadron under Captain Lezhnev. The *Venus* retreated up Christiania Fjord but was followed by the *Merkury* 22 (under Capt. Roman V. Crown) which, by pretending to be a merchantman, was able to get close to the Swedish ship. Though outmatched in gunpower at least two to one, the *Merkury* engaged the *Venus* closely on both quarters, bringing down the foretopmast and capturing her—a sparkling action for which Crown was promoted.

The Russian detachment at Porkkala was involved in several minor naval actions, especially with a small Swedish squadron under Tomas von Rajalin at Barosund. On August 26 Rajalin made the strongest of several unsuccessful attacks on the Russians when about a dozen of his galleys and gunboats attacked two battleships, a frigate, and two cutters. On September 18 a reinforced Russian squadron from Porkkala comprising four battleships, a frigate, and three small vessels mounting 374 guns attacked the Swedes in Barosund. The latter, badly outnumbered, had only a turuma, five galleys, and two gunboats with 152 guns, plus the coastal batteries. The outcome of the battle was a nominal Russian victory which was in fact a defeat. The Swedes retreated after a short fight in which they lost a galley which ran aground, but the Russian *Severny Orel* 66 also ran aground. Both ships had to be burned. The Russians failed in attempts to follow up this doubtful victory by coastal landings.

Late in October three Russian ships, *Aleksandr Nevsky* 74, *Rodislav* 66, and *Gavriil* 38, grounded. Of these, the *Rodislav* could not be refloated and had to be burned. Shortly thereafter both Swedes and Russians retired to winter quarters. During this period each lost a ship, the Russians the *Viacheslav* 66 by grounding, the Swedes the *Minerva* by an accidental burning in Karlskrona harbor.

1790 CAMPAIGN

At the conclusion of two years the conflict remained undecided. The Swedes had lost two battleships and the Russians four, with each belligerent taking one vessel from the other. The two fleet actions had been comparatively even but quite barren of results for either side, and the only clear-cut victory at sea had been that at Svensksund. Determined to bring the war to a successful conclusion, Gustav III ordered that a supreme effort be made in 1790. Every one of the 25 Swedish battleships was commissioned, along with 16 frigates and 16 smaller vessels. Swedish flotilla craft numbered 349.

The Russian mobilization was less complete. Catherine ordered the preparation of 29 battleships (nine in the Reserve) in three squadrons, together with 13 frigates and some smaller craft. The Russian flotillas numbered 201 vessels. Thus though the sailing fleets were about equal in strength, flotilla strength definitely favored the Swedes. In dividing their ships into squadrons, each smaller than the Swedish units, the Russians continued their mistake of the two previous years. No important command changes were made by either side: for the Swedes, Gustav III led the flotillas and Carl, Duke of Södermanland, the sailing fleets; their Russian counterparts were Admirals Nassau-Siegen and Chichagov.

The Swedes continued to pursue their main objective, the advance on and capture of St. Petersburg. This time they got a head start on the Russians. On March 17 four small Swedish vessels commanded by Captain Cederstrom were completely successful in a surprise raid on the town of Ragervik. There the fort and military stores were destroyed by a commando-type landing party, which left the next day.

The main Swedish fleet of 22 battleships, 12 frigates, and 13 small craft with 18,800 men left Karlskrona on April 30 with the strategic objective of destroying the Russian squadron at Revel before it

could join the larger fleet from Kronstadt. Had this been the first
move of the Swedish campaign, it might easily have succeeded. As
it was, the attack on Ragervik had alarmed the Russians so that they
prepared earlier than usual, and Admiral Chichagov left the dockyard for the outer harbor three days before Duke Carl left Karlskrona. On May 11 Russian scouts sighted the Swedish fleet beyond
Nargen. Admiral Chichagov promptly recalled his cruisers and stationed his ships in a defensive formation of three lines. The first-line
ships carried 804 guns, but even counting ships in the third line the
Russian fleet mounted a total of only 1,083 guns. Against this force
the Swedes could bring a very large superiority in both ships and
guns, for Duke Carl had at his disposal 26 line-of-battleships and
large frigates which collectively carried 1,580 guns. This gave him an
almost two-to-one advantage if first-line ships alone are taken into
consideration.

With such odds in strength, the Battle of Revel, fought from
6:30 A.M. to 1:00 P.M., May 13, 1790, should have resulted in a
decisive Swedish victory. However, partly due to their own mistakes
and partly because of unfavorable weather conditions, the Swedes
instead sustained a defeat. Duke Carl had decided on a scheme of
close action recommended by his chief of staff, Admiral Nordenskjöld. The scheme involved "doubling" and "tripling" on the principal Russian ships—in short, it was much the same strategy Lord
Nelson used at Aboukir. But very heavy winds made delicate maneuvers impossible and the tactics actually employed by the Swedes
involved a rapid run past the Russian line by all the Swedish ships
in a manner similar to that ordered much later by Dewey at Manila.
From the first, things went wrong. The *Tapperheten* grounded; some
12 of the Swedish ships never got into action save at long range;
ships that did see closer action were subjected to heavy and damaging fire from the tightly bunched Russians. The *Adolf Frederik* 70,
Forsightigheten 64, *Prins Carl* 64, and *Sophia Magdalena* 74 all sustained serious damage. *Prins Carl* was unable to get away and surrendered. The *Riksens Ständer* 60 grounded on the way out, could
not be moved, and had to be burned. The *Tapperheten* was finally
floated. The Swedes lost two battleships, the Russians none. Casualties included 51 Swedes killed and 81 wounded, plus 100 taken
prisoner. For the Russians the comparable figures were eight and

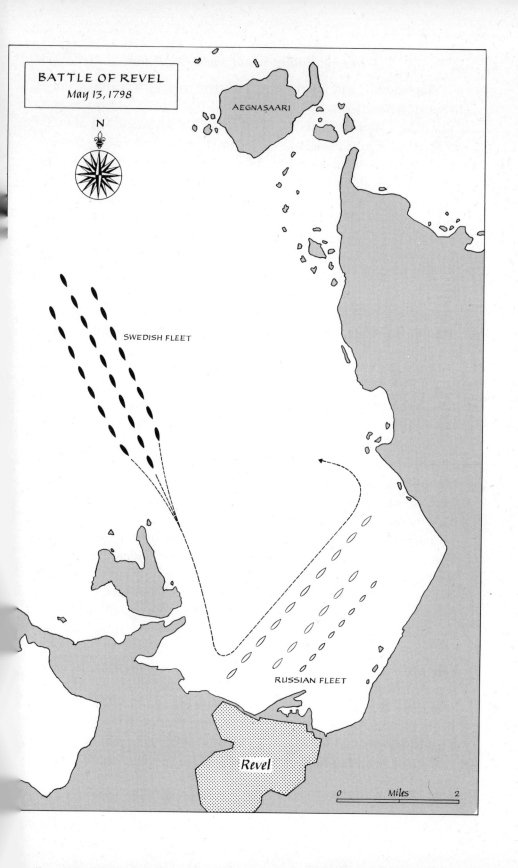

BATTLE OF REVEL
May 13, 1798

N

AEGNASAARI

SWEDISH FLEET

RUSSIAN FLEET

Revel

0   Miles   2

27. The Russians had fought well, but their victory was due mainly to Swedish mistakes.

Two days later the Swedish flotilla achieved a victory. On May 8, 70 Swedish gunboats left Sveaborg and worked eastward for an attack on the Russians in Frederikshamn. King Gustav III had taken personal command on June 30 and brought in reinforcements. When the Swedes attacked, the Russians at Frederikshamn, led by Captain Slysov, were barely ready. Slysov had under his command 63 ships, of which the captured turuma (or shebek) *Sallen Varre* 48 and the two half prams, *Leppard* 28 and *Bars*, were the largest. The remaining vessels were small kaiks, double sloops, and gunboats. In all they carried 2,205 men and 408 guns. Gustav had one turuma, two udemas, eight bombs, some small sailing vessels, 20 galleys, and about 70 gunboats, besides transports and storeships—in all roughly 110 ships with about 1,000 guns and 10,000 men.

Faced with so large a Swedish superiority, Captain Slysov could have little hope of victory; however, he did conduct a skillful delaying action. When the Swedes opened fire in the early morning of May 15, they were met by an effective counterfire from close range, which continued until the Russian ammunition supply ran out. Then and only then were the Swedes able to gain a victory. They captured the three larger vessels and seven smaller craft, while 16 were sunk or burned by the Russians. Manpower losses numbered 60 Swedes and 242 Russians.

Considering all factors, Slysov's showing had been highly creditable. Most of his flotilla escaped to take refuge under the guns of the fort, and when Gustav renewed the attack in the afternoon he met heavy fire. Meanwhile, the town prepared for resistance. When a regiment of Russian troops arrived in the evening, all chance of the Swedes' winning a cheap victory disappeared. Three landing attempts, made from May 16 to May 18 by Captain Virgin (who had under his command seven bombs and 18 gunboats), were repelled with heavy losses. When a final naval attack on May 20 was ineffective, the Swedes were compelled to abandon for the time being their hopes of taking Fredrikshamn. Gustav III then turned his attention to easier objectives. On May 27 he made two minor but successful troop landings to destroy Russian artillery and a supply depot.

Attention now shifted to the land armies and the sailing fleets. The Swedish advance on St. Petersburg enjoyed the support of its own flotilla, which was superior to the Russian, but it also needed effective assistance from a sailing fleet in the eastern part of the Gulf of Finland. Both Sweden and Russia therefore took steps to acquire control over the eastern gulf area.

As soon as the Swedish battleship fleet had recovered from its defeat at Revel and had been reinforced from Karlskrona (*Hertig Ferdinand* 62, *Finland* 56, *Illerin* 32), it moved to the vicinity of Hogland. This close approach brought a change in Russian plans, which had originally contemplated uniting the active Kronstadt fleet and the Revel squadron. With this union now unlikely and a Swedish attack apparently imminent, the Russians commissioned six of the eight ships of their reserve fleet and joined them to the active Kronstadt squadron. Kruse then left Kronstadt on May 23 with 17 battleships, pursuing a very slow westward course, and for the next ten days the two fleets gradually drew together, each avid for attack. On June 3, some four miles south of the point known as Styrsudd on the Gulf of Finland about midway between St. Petersburg and Vyborg, the enemies came within sighting distance of each other. The Swedes held a slight edge in total force, with 23 ships of 1,470 guns plus 6 frigates of 252, compared to 17 Russian battleships of 1,256 guns and 9 frigates of 358 guns, for a grand total of 1,722 guns for the Swedes and 1,614 for the Russians.

The Battle of Styrsudd was not a single action. It was rather a series of short engagements fought on June 3–4, 1790, between the Russian and Swedish fleets. The fleet actions were general, but never close or decisive. Duke Carl, who logically ought to have tried to cripple the Russian Kronstadt fleet before a union with the fleet of Admiral Chichagov could give it superiority, never sought to force a decision; and of course Kruse, whose forces would be superior only when joined by the Revel squadron, can hardly be criticized for failing to act more aggressively. Tactically, the two commanders were about on a par; each was able to frustrate the more threatening moves of the other. Attempts of Swedish gunboats to join the fray or of Swedish ships to "double" on the Russians were defeated by the prompt action of Rear Adm. A. K. Denisov's squadron of 38-gun "rowing frigates" which, with light winds prevailing, were con-

siderably more mobile than the sailing vessels. While exact losses
are uncertain, they were apparently even, each side suffering casualties of about 350 killed and wounded. Two Russian ships which left
the line for repairs could probably have remained in the fray in the
case of necessity. One notable feature of the battle was the very
large number of gunbursts on Russian vessels: the *Konstantin* 74
alone had eleven.

After his victory at Revel, Chichagov had waited there until June
3 before putting to sea—ten days after Duke Carl's departure. Now,
within a matter of hours after the fighting ended off Styrsudd, Duke
Carl learned that the Revel squadron was on its way. He knew he
must reckon with combined Russian forces. On June 6 Chichagov
added a force of 11 battleships and five frigates, carrying respectively 824 and 200 guns, to that of Kruse, giving the Russians a
decisive superiority. Duke Carl sought refuge in Vyborg Bay, and
the enlarged Russian fleet waited outside until increasing shortages
compelled the Swedes to accept battle.

Actually the Russian battle fleet before Vyborg was blockading
more than the Swedish battle fleet. Most of the Swedish flotilla,
consisting of about 175 galleys, bombs, and small sailing vessels,
was in nearby Björkö Sund, where it had also been cut off from
supplies and reinforcements. In addition, 40 Swedish gunboats were
moving east along the Finnish coast. The Russian flotilla was less
concentrated: in Vyborg under Koslianinov were 42 relatively large
ships; at Fredrikshamn was the defeated but still strong squadron
of 59 boats under Slysov; ten gunboats were at Revel. North of the
Swedish position, in Trangsund, Nassau-Siegen commanded a miscellaneous force of three battleships, two frigates, six rowing frigates,
six shebeks, two half shebeks, a pram, a bomb, four cutters, 11
schooners, four half prams, two galiots, three floating batteries, two
fireships, 46 gunboats, and 20 transports—113 vessels in all.

The next four weeks were spent in preparations and skirmishes.
The Russians were reinforced by their Frederikshamn flotilla, while
40 Swedish flotilla boats from the west reached Svensksund. Koslianinov, defending the approaches to Vyborg harbor with his 42
ships, was separated from Chichagov and hence in apparent danger.
He deployed his forces, however, in the narrow waters of Trangsund
between two islands, both of which he fortified heavily. From this

position he was able to discourage Swedish attacks with great effectiveness. Heavy weather caused abandonment of a general Swedish
attack planned for June 17, and a flanking attempt by Swedish forces
landing on the neighboring islands was repulsed with heavy loss.
Faced with these reverses and fearing a direct Russian attack, the
king gave up further offensive moves against Koslianinov.

Actually, although they had preparations for a combined attack
under way, the Russians had no need of offensive moves. Time was
on their side as the Swedish supply shortage grew more critical. An
effort to reinforce Vyborg from Svensksund was repelled by Crown
(now a commodore), whose two frigates and four cutters were at
first repulsed but after receiving reinforcements drove the Swedes
back to port on July 1. Nassau-Siegen then arrived with the Kronstadt flotilla, which anchored just south of Björkö Sund. At length
the Swedes decided to attempt a break through the Russian blockade
and retreat westward.

The Russian hope was for Nassau-Siegen to force the Björkö Sund
passage and join Koslianinov. Their flotilla would then attack the
Swedish battle fleet from one direction while the Russian battle
fleet attacked it from the other. Swedish strategy was simply to
escape via the Krysserort Channel to the north of Admiral Chichagov's ships. The time for this attempt was set for early morning on
July 3. Six sailing ships, 20 galleys, ten gun vessels and 50 gunboats
under Viktor von Stedingk were left at Koivisto to contain Vice
Admiral Nassau-Siegen's force. The transports and 15 gunboats
moved north of the Swedish battleships, while 65 gunboats and
eight bombs under Hemming Törning advanced between the
islands of Biskopso and Toisari to attack the eastern end of the Russian line. Nassau-Siegen pressed forward with his smaller vessels
against the now greatly weakened Swedish flotilla. The Swedes
resisted for three hours and then retired in good order with a loss
of four ships as compared to one for the Russians. Shortly after midnight, the main force of Swedish gunboats attacked, suffered their
expected repulse, and retired behind their own battleships. At 6:00
A.M. the entire Swedish fleet, both flotillas and sailing ships, got
under way. Admiral Chichagov signaled to prepare for action but
failed to do much else. One Swedish ship, *Finland* 56, grounded
almost at once, but the other Swedish battleships, led by *Dris-*

tigheten 64, passed directly through the Russian line between *Sv. Petr* 74 and *Vseslav* 74, raking the Russian ships as they passed and inflicting (and incurring) considerable damage. By 8:30 A.M. over half the Swedish fleet had escaped, and still the Russians had not moved. The Swedish plan appeared to be successful.

Then good fortune deserted the Swedes. A fireship intended for a Russian target collided with *Enigheten* 70, which in turn ran into *Zemire* 42. All three blew up with crews on board, and most of the men were lost. In the ensuing smoke and confusion, several Swedish ships at the rear lost their bearings and grounded on neighboring shoals. These included *Hedvig Elisabeth Charlotta* 64, *Omheten* 62, *Louise Ulrika* 70, the frigates *Uppland* 44 and *Jarislavits* 32, a schooner, and three galleys. By 10:00 A.M. the remainder of the Swedish forces had escaped.

Had Admiral Chichagov been a seaman of the caliber of Farragut or Nelson, had he seized the moment, he could probably have destroyed most of the Swedish fleet as it left Vyborg. But he vacillated, waiting several hours to start pursuit. Finally, an hour before the Swedish flotilla entered the inner belt of islands, leaving the sailing fleet in the open sea, 17 of Chichagov's battleships set off. Because the Swedes had a good start, there was no immediate action; but by eight o'clock in the evening the slowest Swedish ships were within Russian range. The *Sophia Magdalena* 74 was overtaken by *Mstislav* 74. In the action that followed both ships were damaged, but the Swedish battleship suffered the greater harm and struck her flag at 10:30 P.M. During the night most of the Swedes got away in the direction of Sveaborg, but on the morning of July 4 two battleships, *Rattvisa* 62 and *Gotha Lejon* 70, were discovered apart from the Swedish fleet. The *Iziaslav* 66 and *Venus* 44 attacked and captured the *Rattvisa*; the *Gotha Lejon* escaped.

The Battle of Vyborg was one of the greatest disasters in the history of the Swedish navy. Seven battleships and three frigates were lost and 5,000 men taken prisoner—with no significant corresponding loss to the Russians. Moreover, the Swedes had not yet made good their escape. Admiral Chichagov next quickly set up a blockade of Sveaborg with 17 battleships and four frigates, a force superior to the 14 battleships and six frigates remaining to Duke Carl. At the same time Russian reinforcements arrived from Vyborg.

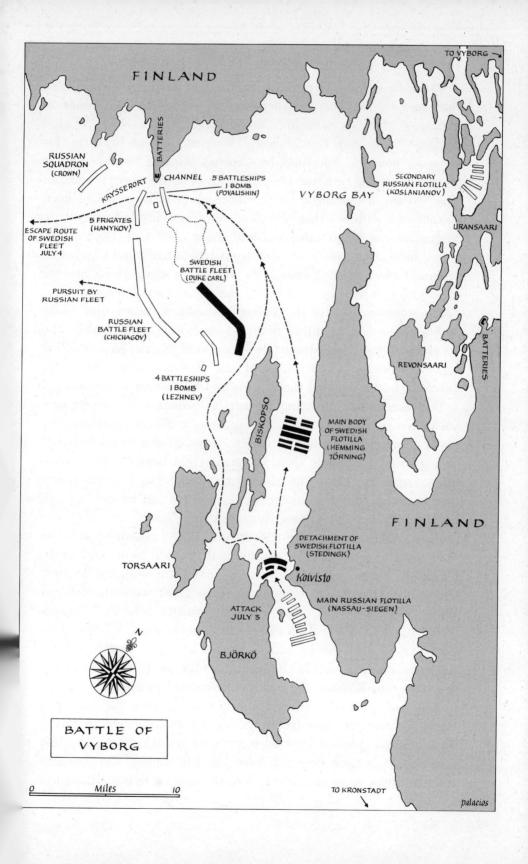

FINLAND

RUSSIAN
SQUADRON
(CROWN)

BATTERIES

KRYSSERORT

CHANNEL   5 BATTLESHIPS
1 BOMB
(POVALISHIN)

VYBORG BAY

TO VYBORG

SECONDARY
RUSSIAN FLOTILLA
(KOSLANIANOV)

URANSAARI

ESCAPE ROUTE
OF SWEDISH
FLEET
JULY 4

5 FRIGATES
(HANYKOV)

SWEDISH
BATTLE FLEET
(DUKE CARL)

PURSUIT BY
RUSSIAN FLEET

RUSSIAN
BATTLE FLEET
(CHICHAGOV)

BATTERIES

REVONSAARI

4 BATTLESHIPS
1 BOMB
(LEZHNEV)

BISKOPSO

MAIN BODY
OF SWEDISH
FLOTILLA
(HEMMING
TÖRNING)

FINLAND

TORSAARI

DETACHMENT OF
SWEDISH FLOTILLA
(STEDINGK)

Koivisto

ATTACK
JULY 3

MAIN RUSSIAN FLOTILLA
(NASSAU-SIEGEN)

N

BJÖRKÖ

BATTLE OF
VYBORG

0   Miles   10

TO KRONSTADT

palacios

In the meantime, the Swedish flotillas had fared somewhat better than had the battleships. They had suffered little loss either in clearing Vyborg or in fleeing the Russian flotillas of Vice Admiral Nassau-Siegen, and Rear Admiral Koslianinov had been too far away for concern. An attack by Crown's ships at Pitkopas on the afternoon of July 4, however, proved to be a more serious matter. The Swedes, demoralized by the destruction in their sailing fleet, surrendered with less than the usual resistance, losing four galleys, 11 gunboats, some 30 transports, and about 1,000 men. Their defeat would have been even more disastrous had not Admiral Chichagov ordered Crown in the *Venus* 42 to join him, a move which enabled the Swedes to recapture several of their surrendered vessels.

For a few days after the Vyborg encounters, heavy seas inhibited much action by either flotilla. During this period, while the Swedish rowing fleet gathered at Svensksund, Nassau-Siegen pulled together the various divisions of the Russian rowing fleet. By July 7 he had completed the process and was prepared to attack.

The Swedes had six sailing vessels, 18 galleys, eight bombs, one yacht, ten gun vessels, and 153 gunboats—in all 196 ships carrying about 1,200 guns. Against this fleet Nassau-Siegen could bring 30 sailing ships, 23 galleys, three batteries, eight bombs, and 77 gunboats—some 141 ships with about 1,500 guns.[2] The Russians therefore possessed about a 20-percent superiority, and on the basis of the statistics they should have won a victory.

They suffered a stunning defeat. With the northern approaches once more blocked and the obstructions guarded by a small craft, Gustav had arranged his forces in a curved line with the greatest strength on the flanks. Only along their front were the Swedes easily open to attack, and a force pressing into their center would subject itself to flank attacks from both wings. Whether Gustav realized it or not, he had set up for his naval warfare exactly the same position used by Hannibal at Cannae in his greatest triumph over the Romans: the classic double envelopment.

The analogy can be carried a step farther, since the moves in the battle also corresponded to moves at Cannae. Early on July 9 Nassau-Siegen pressed forward in a direct frontal attack. The first elements to become engaged were the left wing of the Russians and the right wing of the Swedes. Because of heavy winds and

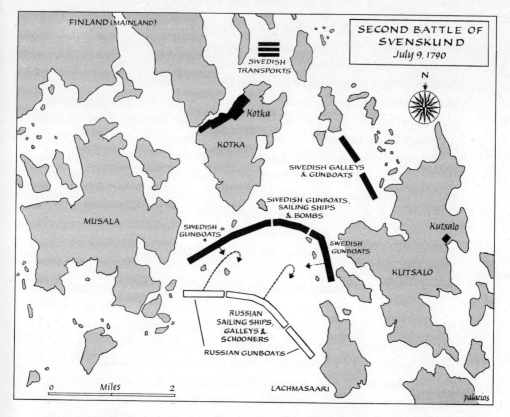

FINLAND (MAINLAND)

SECOND BATTLE OF
SVENSKUND
July 9, 1790

N

SWEDISH
TRANSPORTS

Kotka

KOTKA

SWEDISH GALLEYS
& GUNBOATS

SWEDISH GUNBOATS,
SAILING SHIPS
& BOMBS

SWEDISH
GUNBOATS

SWEDISH
GUNBOATS

MUSALA

Kutsalo

KUTSALO

RUSSIAN
SAILING SHIPS,
GALLEYS &
SCHOONERS

RUSSIAN GUNBOATS

0   Miles   2

LACHMASAARI

palacios

seas, as well as Swedish resistance, the Russians were pushed back, especially when Gustav threw in his reserve gunboats. As the Russians advanced in the center, a steady raking from the Swedish right wing threw them into a state of confusion. Meanwhile the gunboats on the Swedish left also outflanked the Russians, forcing them back. The Russian center, attacked from the front and both flanks, soon suffered heavily. At seven o'clock in the evening Nassau-Siegen ordered a retreat, but his ships could not at once extricate themselves and firing continued until ten. Early the next day the Russians were attacked again and driven to their base at nearby Aspo.

The Second Battle of Svensksund was a decisive Swedish victory. Russian losses in destroyed or captured ships amounted to about 64 with personnel losses of 7,369, as compared to Swedish losses of four vessels and about 300 men. One account lists Russian losses as 9,500 men or more than 50 percent, plus 53 vessels sunk and 34 captured.

This battle came near the end of the war. Both sides were thoroughly tired of the fight; and Catherine, since her ally Austria had recently withdrawn from the war with Turkey, was disposed to liquidate the unwanted war with Sweden. She therefore offered generous terms: complete restoration of the territorial and political status prior to the war. Gustav, who had lost at least 50,000 men and been defeated on sea and land, thankfully accepted.

Despite its barrenness so far as political changes were concerned, the 1790 Treaty of Werela was important. At the end of the war the Russians possessed 46 battleships in the Baltic, while losses had reduced the Swedish navy to 16 battleships. From 1790 until the rise of the new German navy more than a century later, Russian sea superiority among the Baltic maritime powers would be unquestioned.

The general performance of the Russian navy during the Swedish war had been extremely creditable. Catherine's admirals, both foreign and Russian, were a distinct improvement over those of Peter the Great. While not all of the Russian direction of the war could be termed brilliant, it at least considerably outshone that of the Swedes. Moreover, Russian officers and men as well as Russian ships, if not topnotch, were of high enough quality that it was now possible for them to win without possessing an overwhelming superiority. Indeed, in most of the naval battles against both Turkey and Sweden the Russians were overmatched—on paper. Yet they consistently defeated the Turks and achieved a better than even record against the Swedes. In retrospect, then, the reign of Catherine II was a Golden Age of Russian sea power.

CHAPTER 6

The Napoleonic Wars
(1789-1815)

RUSSIAN INVOLVEMENT UNDER CATHERINE

FROM A MILITARY STANDPOINT, the Napoleonic wars were essentially a long and involved struggle between the land power of France and the sea power of Great Britain. From an ideological standpoint they represented a confrontation between the European Old Order and the newer ideals of liberty, equality, and fraternity proclaimed by the French Revolution. The Old Order emphasized hereditary monarchy, the established aristocracy and church, and a fixed class structure. The French rejected the Old Order, proclaimed the rule of reason, became a nation at arms, and brought forth the military and political genius of Napoleon Bonaparte.

In common with every nation in Europe, Russia was deeply involved in the struggle, participating in both diplomatic and military activities. But her national interests were not always directly concerned, and she pursued as well designs that were unrelated to the main struggle, designs related, for example, to the absorption of Georgia and the partitioning of Poland. At the outset of the Napoleonic wars Catherine, still distracted by her quarrels with Turkey and Sweden, remained aloof from extended involvement. Nevertheless she was ever alert to Russian interests—and mobilized her naval forces to the extent that these interests were affected.

As an absolute monarch who had outlasted the apparent liberalism of her earlier years, Catherine was no friend of the French

Revolution. She detested its extremes, not only on ideological grounds but because they tended to upset plans of her own and to interfere with the European balance of power. In 1789 she showed her displeasure by terminating diplomatic relations with France and decreeing a day of mourning following the execution of Louis XVI. She also adopted repressive and reactionary measures at home to prevent the spread of the French contagion. In 1793, after the return of some Russian vessels seized by British privateers, she agreed to a treaty with Great Britain whereby Russian ports would be closed to French ships and their seizure on the high seas authorized. However, when the British sought the aid of a Russian army corps on the Rhine in their own campaign, Catherine sidestepped the request. She did not wish to be diverted from the approaching Third Partition of Poland.

Catherine's naval policy during the years of noninvolvement varied according to the nature of the threats that appeared on the horizon. In 1791 she commissioned 32 battleships against a threat of war with Prussia and England. A war failed to materialize, and the next year only five battleships were manned. In 1793, fearing possible foreign intervention before she could complete the Second Partition of Poland, the tsarina ordered 26 battleships fitted out as additional protective insurance. At this time the Revel and Kronstadt squadrons, united under Admiral Chichagov, cruised for several weeks in the Baltic and North Seas.

In the last full year of her reign (1795), with the Third Partition of Poland accomplished, Catherine took more direct notice of the growing power of France: she moved toward a limited support of the First Coalition just as that alliance against France was on the verge of collapse. At this time 21 battleships were commissioned. The following year she ordered a full war-emergency mobilization of 40 battleships.

Russia's first military action in the Napoleonic wars took the form of naval cooperation with England against the French and Dutch. A fleet of 12 battleships and eight frigates, initially commanded by Rear Admiral Khanykov, cruised in the North Sea as part of an allied fleet under British Adm. Adam Duncan. The ships wintered in English ports. The following year two smaller squadrons under Rear Adm. S. O. Makarov were sent out, and again served under Admiral Duncan.

Naval cooperation with the English in the North Sea continued for several years; the Russian squadrons were periodically reinforced from the White Sea and the Baltic and wintered in England rather than returning to Russia. In a bloody joint attack on the Dutch fleet in the Texel on August 30, 1798, the Russians captured two Dutch battleships while the British took six. Soon thereafter, on September 16, 1798, a Russian fleet of five battleships and five frigates landed 17,000 troops on the Dutch coast. This invasion attempt not only failed but led to the capture of the Russian Gen. I. I. Herman, a reverse which the new Tsar Paul blamed on insufficient support by the British.

NAVAL POLICY OF PAUL I

Paul I (1796–1801), who succeeded Catherine, was morose, unstable, erratic, and given to making sudden changes in policy. Impulsive, cruel, suspicious and at times self-contradictory, he was "difficult" for both his advisers and his allies. These qualities, combined with certain physical characteristics (a catlike face and uncoordinated limbs), led some to state that the new tsar was mad; others more charitably declared him merely half-mad. Peter III had refused to recognize him as a legitimate son, and Catherine, his mother, had tried to exclude him from the throne.

On his accession, Paul at first embarked on a peaceful policy which included putting an end to the war with Persia. Though opposed to nearly everything for which Catherine had stood, Paul shared his mother's views concerning the French Revolution, the necessity of repressive laws to shut out Jacobinism, and the navy, for which he felt a deep affection.

One of Paul's peculiarities which affected naval policy was his extraordinary regard for the Grand Order of the Knights of St. John of Malta. Paul may have seen in this order of ancient chivalry a means of fighting the teachings of the French Revolution; at any rate, his favor exceeded all bounds. He paid the debts of the order, opened new chapters in Russia, sought to place Malta, where the order was headquartered, under the Russian flag, and assumed for himself the title of Grand Master. In a move widely resented by Russian naval officers (who felt the flag of St. Andrew had been insulted) he finally placed the fleet under Admiral Kuchelev, who next became Grand Admiral of the Order of Malta.

On the whole, however, Paul's naval policy was in no sense unbalanced. He continued to develop the Black Sea Fleet and sent Admiral Kartsev to turn Odessa into a naval base. Because he wished to centralize power in the admiralty in St. Petersburg, where he could exercise control more easily, the separate admiralty for the Black Sea Fleet was abolished. He took such a deep interest in maritime affairs that he even passed personally on the promotion of officers. He also supervised other details of naval administration which were customarily neglected in times of peace. For example, he prescribed a green uniform for officers, similar in appearance to the green and white selected earlier by Empress Elizabeth. In 1797 a new "Law of the Fleet of War" was issued which, though based on Peter's work, was more humane and up to date. His efforts to improve Russian shipbuilding resulted in some new types which were used as models by the British.[1] A Baltic Fleet of 390 vessels, 45 of which were battleships, and a Black Sea Fleet of 115 sail including 15 battleships, were indications of Paul's strong interest in an effective navy, as was the development of smaller flotillas on the Caspian, the Volga, and the Sea of Okhotsk. Two schools were opened for the training of officers in mechanics and ships' architecture. Concern with naval matters was extended to include both hydrographic expeditions and the promotion of commerce.

To the great dismay of the British, Paul reversed Catherine's policy of support in the North Sea. Admiral Makarov's fleet of 17 battleships and seven frigates, which had served in the North Sea for two years and had even assisted in suppressing a mutiny among British seamen, was recalled to the Baltic. As a parting gesture to an ally, the British showered Makarov with praise and decorations.

THE IONIAN CAMPAIGN

Though he was not interested in continuing the somewhat fruitless North Sea campaign, Paul was very much alert to possible extension of Russian interests in the Mediterranean, his attention having been aroused by the French expeditions to Malta and Egypt. The Second Coalition (England, Austria, Turkey, Naples, Portugal, and Russia) was speedily formed, and after Nelson annihilated the French fleet at the Battle of the Nile, the Turks and Russians joined actively in the Mediterranean war. Desiring to reverse the French Revolution, the allies undertook to force a royalist restoration in Italy. Count A. V. Suvorov, in charge of an army of 18,000 Russians and 44,000 Austrians and with a supporting fleet, was to occupy northern Italy. Plans to use the Black Sea Fleet to aid the Turks in holding the Straits were altered; Vice Adm. Fedor Ushakov was ordered to the Eastern Mediterranean to pick up French-garrisoned islands in the Aegean and to support a royalist restoration in southern Italy. In addition, attempts were to be made to bombard the French in Alexandria and to capture Malta.

These plans actually involved two campaigns, interrelated, to be sure, but also differing in objectives, time spent, and forces employed. Consequently, the Ionian and Italian campaigns will be considered separately.

The Greek population of the three major islands of Corfu, Cephalonia, and Zante and the four smaller islands of the Ionian Archipelago had long suffered under the selfish domination of the Republic of Venice, and was quite willing to see a change in rule. Following conquest by France, the new status of the islands had been recognized by the October 1797 Treaty of Campo Formio, between France and Austria. However, though they were somewhat stirred by the ideology of the French Revolution, the islanders felt far stronger ethnic and religious ties to the Russians; it is therefore not surprising that they were soon disappointed in the reality of French rule.

Naval support for the Ionian campaign was furnished by a Black Sea fleet that had been comparatively inactive, save on the one occasion when Catherine had ordered its full commissioning in a move to assure Turkish neutrality during the partitions of Poland. The force of four frigates and six battleships with which Vice Admiral Ushakov left Sevastopol on August 24, 1798, was thus largely untrained. Four weeks thereafter it was united with a Turkish contingent of four battleships and six frigates, which also served under Ushakov. From this force two Russian and two Turkish frigates and ten Turkish gunboats were detached to join British forces at Alexandria. Here they bombarded shore targets and otherwise sought to add to the miseries of a French army left unsupported following the destruction of its fleet.

However, Russia's main interest was the capture of the Aegean islands. Ushakov's marine landing force of 1,700 men was large enough for most of the task, since generally the islands proved to be lightly garrisoned. On Cerigo, one of the smaller islands and the first to be attacked, the French garrison surrendered after a ten-hour naval bombardment. On Zante an already pro-Russian population revolted in response to a religious appeal, and a 700-man landing force completed the conquest. The capture of Cephalonia was almost identical. The French garrison on Ithaca escaped in a boat flying the Turkish flag. On the island of Santa Maura (Leukas), where French prisoners were divided between the Turks and the Russians, those assigned to the Russians received by far the more humane treatment.

Corfu, however, was defended by about 3,000 men, 600 cannon, and 60 ships, mostly small, and its conquest proved far more difficult. On January 1, 1799, Ushakov instituted a blockade. It was challenged on several occasions by the French battleship *Generaux* 74, an escapee from the Battle of the Nile, but by making use of 4,250 Albanians who were supporting the Slavs, together with 1,500 Turkish troops, Ushakov managed to scrape together a sufficiently large landing force to defeat the garrison. On March 3 the French surrendered their land forces and 15 small naval craft.

After the surrender of Corfu Ushakov announced the creation of a Greek-governed Ionian Republic under a joint Turkish-Russian protectorate. The government thus established was so successful that Ushakov's popularity as an administrator became known throughout the Balkans. Indeed, the anomaly of a Russian admiral who represented an absolute monarch setting up a liberal and even a democratic republic is one of the minor ironies of the period. Russian garrisons proved highly effective at preventing looting by Turks and Albanians, and when the Russians departed in July 1801, there ensued such a period of terror and anarchy that a task force of five

Russian ships and 1,600 men had to return to Corfu to reestablish peace.

Both the Aegean and the Italian campaigns which followed were beset by problems for the Russians. Logistics were at best uncertain, and while Russian reinforcements arrived from time to time, the shipment of supplies was not only inadequate but irregular. Moreover, Russia's coalition allies gave no help, and attempts to secure supplies and manpower from the Greeks and Albanians usually failed. Hence Ushakov's fleet was constantly plagued with shortages of supplies and equipment.

THE ITALIAN CAMPAIGN

The Italian campaign had first been projected under Catherine the Great, but it was slower in getting under way than the Ionian venture. Primarily intended to benefit Austria by undoing Napoleon's conquests in Italy and elsewhere, the Italian campaign also involved Russian military forces and British financial support. Russia's brilliant Gen. A. V. Suvorov, then nearing seventy, was designated supreme commander in charge of both Russian and Austrian forces. However, he was never actually in direct command of more than about 60,000 men.

From a military standpoint, Suvorov's campaign in northern Italy was itself a classic, despite the fact that it was so marred by lack of support from Vienna as to render its results fruitless. Entering Italy from the north, Suvorov in five months won three major victories. The French were speedily cleared out of the country, and the Russians took some 80,000 prisoners and 25 fortresses in the process. Suvorov then planned to invade France, but when lack of Austrian support made this clearly impossible he turned instead to the north and crossed the Alps into Switzerland in the teeth of French resistance. Here he expected to join his forces to those of the Archduke Charles and Gen. L. P. Rimsky-Korsakov and chase the French out of Switzerland. But Rimsky-Korsakov had been defeated, Charles for reasons best known to himself had decided to leave Switzerland, and the logistic aid promised by the Austrians was not forthcoming. Tired, vastly outnumbered, and out of supplies, the Russians by all the rules of warfare should have surrendered. But Suvorov succeeded in eluding the traps set by the French, departed Switzerland from the east, and marched his troops through Europe back to Russia.

During his land campaign Suvorov had received both indirect and direct support from the Russian Navy. The first naval move took the form of indirect support to a native rebellion in Apulia in southern Italy: two frigates and four corvettes under Commo. A. Sorokin were sent to the aid of the natives. Sorokin and his successor, Capt. N. Belli, were for a time highly successful. A small Russian force marching along the coast toward Naples defeated the French amid the plaudits of natives who were otherwise of limited value as allies. Thereafter, aided by other small Russian landing parties, the rebellion spread as town after town joined the royalists.

Meanwhile Suvorov arrived in Verona in April 1799 to ask naval assistance in taking Ancona, a step which would sever communications between the northern and southern French armies. Ushakov sent into the Adriatic a small squadron under Adm. P. Pustoshkin (who was later succeeded by Voinovich) to aid Suvorov. He then sailed to Naples with the remainder of his fleet. Both ventures succeeded. A naval bombardment of Naples on May 18 was followed by a lengthy siege. The city was taken, and Russian landing parties assisted in the elimination of pro-French holdouts. Ushakov and his subordinates granted generous terms to prisoners—terms which were later violated by Lord Nelson when he seized the prisoners and turned them over to the king of Naples, who publicly tortured and executed the vast majority. On December 5, 1799, Ancona also surrendered, but only to the Austrians, who thus gained three French battleships. The ships were given to Venice despite Russian efforts to gain their possession.

COLLAPSE OF THE SECOND COALITION

The Russian attempts to seize ships surrendered earlier to the Austrians could be regarded as justifiable under any laws of retaliation. Indeed, by that time relations between the Russians and Austrians had become almost as hostile as those between the Russians and the French. The Austrians had hampered Suvorov in nearly every way possible. They resented his liberal attitude toward native Italians and his restoration of royal families in Italy to territories which Austria had hoped to annex. They had countermanded his orders, denied him promised logistic and military support, and in effect sabotaged his brilliant victories. In brief, if Paul I felt greatly aggrieved toward this ally, he had ample provocation.

Russian relations with England were scarcely better than with Austria. A small British-Russian landing in Holland had been quickly repelled by the French, amid allegations by both Russians and British of mutual lack of support. Finally the allied armies had to be evacuated by sea, leaving the French in complete control.

Relations had also become strained in the Mediterranean, where Admiral Nelson took few pains to conceal his strong dislike for his Turkish and Russian allies. While he could not refuse them recognition he made no effort to serve their interests. Ushakov in particular was an object of his disesteem: this extremely capable officer was referred to in Nelson's correspondence as a "blackguard."

Nelson's attitude had made little difference during the Ionian campaign, but it affected the Italian campaign in a manner that greatly hurt the tsar. Paul I was particularly anxious to see Russian forces capture Malta from the French, since the Knights of St. John (the favored order which he headed) had previously ruled the island under a shadowy suzerainty from the kingdom of Naples. That wish Admiral Nelson, who held naval superiority and was then blockading the island, refused to gratify. When this became clear to him, Paul resentfully issued an order to Ushakov on December 22, 1799, directing his return to the Black Sea; by October 1800 the Russian fleet had been pulled out of the active military theater and returned to Sevastopol. Thus, though both Ushakov and Suvorov had commanded with great effectiveness, Russia reaped no permanent advantages. And although Ushakov was advanced to the rank of admiral he was to receive little acclaim from the next tsar, Alexander I, who disliked him.

Largely as a result of the deterioration of Russian relations with Austria and England, the Second Coalition ended in 1800. The French, unable to continue their hold on Malta in the face of the British blockade, presented it as a gift to the tsar. It was a gift that

cost the French nothing, but it mollified Paul. The tsar then signaled his growing hostility toward the British by ordering the seizure of all British shipping in Russian ports, and by joining with
Prussia, Sweden, and Denmark in the Armed Neutrality to protest
British interference with neutral shipping, especially their exercise
of the "right of search." Though this was not a declaration of war,
it was a very forceful protest. But Paul had even more forceful
measures in mind: he ordered 22,000 Cossacks to start an advance
on India—a genuinely hopeless and harebrained scheme that meant
almost certain death for those engaged in it.

The British answer to the Armed Neutrality and the seizure of
300 British ships was an immediate embargo on all Russian, Swedish, and Danish shipping, together with the issuance of letters of
marque for the capture of the ships of these nations. A fleet of 18
battleships and 35 smaller vessels under Sir Hyde Parker, with
Nelson second in command, was sent to the Baltic.

This move caught the Baltic nations napping. Had the navies of
the three powers been prepared and united, the British would
surely have been decisively outnumbered; Russia alone had 47 of her
82 battleships in the Baltic. However, inasmuch as only 15 Russian
battleships were in fighting condition and no move was made to
unite the three navies, the British were able to deal with each in
turn. Nelson, who favored an attack on Revel, was overruled by his
chief, who chose instead to move against Denmark. The result was
the morally indefensible but highly successful Battle of Copenhagen,
which destroyed Denmark as a sea power. Parker then entered the
Baltic and proceeded to Revel. En route he learned that Tsar Paul
had been assassinated, and that his successor, Alexander, had
ordered the Baltic Fleet to abstain from hostilities. On May 5, 1801,
Parker gave up his command to Nelson and returned home with five
battleships and a frigate. At Karlskrona, where he stopped briefly,
he informed the Swedes that their fleet would be attacked if it put
to sea.

On May 14 Nelson, with 12 battleships and some smaller vessels,
reached Revel. Knowing the usual disposition of Russian sea power,
he had hoped to arrive before the Revel squadron could join the
squadron at Kronstadt. But he was too late; the Revel fleet had left
on May 2. Nelson's instructions were to engage in warlike opera-

tions only if the Russians continued to hold British ships, and then only if the Revel and Kronstadt squadrons could be encountered separately. His visit therefore assumed a diplomatic character. He explained that his mission was a friendly one, but Alexander replied that the mere presence of the British was a threat. Three days after his arrival Nelson put to sea en route to England, and shortly thereafter the tsar lifted the embargo on British ships and signed a convention ending hostilities. The other allies, Sweden and Denmark, had little choice but to do the same. England in turn released certain Russian ships she had seized.

ALEXANDER I AND THE THIRD COALITION

Alexander I (1801–25) came to the throne as a young man, impressionable and relatively liberal. He had been educated under the direction of Catherine the Great and disliked his father; in some quarters he was even suspected of responsibility for Paul's assassination. He speedily reversed Paul's anti-British policy, canceled the proposed march of Cossacks to India, and adopted a Near Eastern policy which followed that of Catherine.

In 1805 a Russian Caspian flotilla comprised of a frigate and four galiots warred successfully against the Persians, and Engeli was taken by a joint fleet and marine attack. Baku proved too strong for capture by the 700 marines available, but it was blockaded until the end of the war.

Eastern Georgia had joined the tsarist empire in 1801. Now all of Georgia, an Orthodox Christian country which had long wanted Russian protection against her Moslem neighbors, was annexed to Russia as a result of the terms of peace. And in Western Europe, after a brief period of accommodation with England, Alexander became an admirer of Napoleon. Their later break, which led to Napoleon's ill-fated invasion of Russia and his subsequent downfall, is well-known history.

Although his record in strictly naval matters was mixed, Alexander must be seen in this sphere as something of a disappointment. Lack of understanding of sea power led him to feel little appreciation for the outstanding services rendered by some of his admirals.

Unconcerned with the importance of freedom of the seas, he quite willingly agreed to a convention granting the British extreme rights to visit and search, something neither Catherine nor Paul would ever have accepted. He was not interested in developing naval administration. He concentrated on cutting costs while at the same time demanding an efficient and modern service and sponsoring maritime exploration. His naval advisers also were men of varied quality: Adm. I. I. Traverse, minister of marine, and Admiral Mordvinov were of poor caliber, but Adm. Pavel V. Chichagov, who headed the admiralty college, was competent; Rear Adm. Aleksei Greig, a shore administrator of bases and ports, was a brilliant and energetic administrator whose improvements extended even as far as the port of Okhotsk on the Pacific (lighthouses, the substitution of machinery for manpower in new and improved naval establishments, hydrographic activities, the creation of naval libraries, and the improvement in all types of personnel facilities were among Greig's accomplishments). With this admixture of the able and indifferent in personnel, it is not surprising that Alexander never got as much out of the Russian navy as had his two predecessors.

In May 1803 the duel between France and England was reopened, although it did not at once involve other countries. By this time Alexander's admiration for Napoleon was waning, for French military victories appeared to threaten both Germany and Turkey, countries in which the Russians had an interest. Alexander's personality had won over Friedrich Wilhelm, the emperor of Prussia, who had made his country a near satellite. As for Turkey, the perennial "sick man of Europe," it was as usual regarded as a possible area for later Russian aggrandizement—and Napoleon's control over Naples brought French power very close to the Turks as well as to Russia's base at Corfu. The French thus threatened to preempt the Russians and preside over the dismemberment of Turkey themselves. Though the issues of Malta and neutral rights at sea had not been resolved to the satisfaction of Alexander, Napoleon's aggressiveness brought about a Russian agreement in April 1805 with the British. When some months later they were joined by first the Austrians and then the Prussians, the Third Coalition was completed.

The main campaign of the war which followed was soon finished. Before Russian reinforcements could arrive, Napoleon swiftly attacked the Austrians, secured the surrender of one Austrian army under Gen. Mack von Leiberich, and then advanced on Vienna. An army predominantly Russian but including Austrian forces was encountered at Austerlitz. Because Alexander chose to disregard the advice of his ablest general, Mikhail I. Kutuzov, this army was outmaneuvered and thoroughly beaten by Napoleon, a defeat which caused Austria to accept a disastrous separate peace. In addition, an allied expedition then operating in Holland and northwest Germany was forced to disband.

On March 17, 1805, Napoleon proclaimed himself king of Italy, annexing first Genoa and then other states north of Rome. Though Russia remained in the conflict and in fact was shortly joined by Prussia, the fortunes of war still continued to favor Napoleon. He annihilated the luckless Prussians at Jena and Auerstadt, imposing on them a peace so punitive that Prussia was virtually robbed of its rank as a major power. Russia herself was more fortunate. Though vastly superior in numbers, Napoleon's armies were successful in inflicting a major defeat on the Russians only at the Battle of Friedland, June 14, 1807, where the Russian commander was forced to alter his normal style of campaign because of an obligation to protect the Prussian royal family in Königsberg. Yet even Friedland failed to bring about a decisive Russian defeat; the Peace of Tilsit of July 7, 1807, gave tactical recognition to this fact. Although Russia had to accept some territorial arrangements that were not entirely favorable, she emerged as the leading power in Eastern Europe, and the only important power in Continental Europe apart from France. Further, the cessation of hostilities freed her to pursue other designs with respect to Turkey, Sweden, and Persia. Despite these advantages, however, the treaty as a whole was unpopular inside Russia with nearly everyone except Alexander and a few court officials. It would have been even more unpopular had not a British expeditionary force under Admiral of the Fleet Lord James Gambier on September 1 made an unprovoked attack on Denmark, a weak neutral state, and reduced the Danish capital at Copenhagen to ashes. This move was odious enough in Russian eyes to make Napoleon appear a degree less objectionable in comparison.

THE DALMATIAN CAMPAIGN (1805–1807)

Though the Dalmatian campaign was but a secondary phase of the War of the Third Coalition, it embraced events of considerable importance to Russian naval history. Austria, in the Treaty of Pressburg of December 26, 1805, had been forced to cede Dalmatia, the Republic of Ragusa, and Cattaro (Kotor)—roughly half of the eastern coast of the Adriatic—to France. Russia, still at war with France, was greatly interested in holding this area, and to this end she made use of both her own naval and land forces and the support of friendly natives—mainly Albanians and Montenegrins.

The Russians undertook their first action in the campaign well in advance of the Austrian defeat. Earlier in 1805 the king of Naples had joined the anti-French forces, and small Russian squadrons under Sorokin and Aleksei Greig had proceeded to Naples, where some 13,000 troops were landed to assist in opposing the French.

This move was the preliminary to a major Russian effort. In October 1805 Adm. Dmitry N. Seniavin was dispatched from the Baltic with five battleships and various lesser vessels, bringing the strength of the Russian Mediterranean fleet to nine battleships, eight frigates, six corvettes, seven brigs, a schooner, 12 gunboats, two transports, and a hospital ship—46 sail in all. After a stop at Portsmouth for supplies and repairs, this fleet reached the central Mediterranean in February 1806. Admiral Seniavin's immediate mission was to prevent Austrian territory in the vicinity of Cattaro from being given to France in accord with the terms of the Pressburg Treaty. A more general Russian objective was to keep Napoleon out of the Balkans and prevent his concluding an alliance with the Turks. The selection of Dmitry Seniavin for this important mission turned out to be a good one, although the choice was in some respects unnatural. Seniavin, born to the great Russian naval family of that name, had been so unpromising a naval student that he had spent three years in the same class. Once settled into a career, however, he displayed surprising abilities, and had compiled a good record as an officer in the Black Sea Fleet during the wars against the Turks.

During most of 1806 the Russian Mediterranean fleet was kept busy in the Adriatic, where France held most of the eastern shore.

Here the inhabitants, unhappy over the change to French rule, had requested Russian protection. With the aid of Montenegrins, Seniavin first occupied most ungarrisoned cities and then attacked those manned by French. Under the command of Captain Belli the battleship *Aziia*, two frigates and a schooner, plus a small landing force, proceeded to Cattaro, where the Austrians commanding the port of Castelnuovo were quite willing to surrender to them rather than to the French who were scheduled to take possession. Seniavin's ships evacuated 2,500 prisoners to Trieste. The island of Curzola changed hands several times before it was finally taken firmly by the Russians. On March 19 a Russian ship took the island of Lissa, but on Lesina the French garrison resisted successfully. Seniavin then moved to Trieste and on threat of bombardment secured the release of 20 Russian merchantmen who had been captured eight days earlier. Following this success he attacked Ragusa, only to find the town already occupied by the French in sufficient force to repel his onslaught. Meanwhile, the two Russian frigates *Venus* and *Avtrail* were set upon by 11 French small craft and succeeded in capturing and destroying five of their attackers.

The superior land strength of the French and Austrians would seem to have doomed Seniavin to almost certain failure from the outset. Yet it was not his enemies who brought about his defeat. Alexander I became annoyed with England, and on September 4, 1806, he ordered Seniavin to surrender his conquests to the French and return to the Black Sea. Seniavin reluctantly complied, giving up all but the Bay of Cattaro, which he continued to hold for the time being. Under the terms of the Treaty of Tilsit in July 1807, the liquidation of Russian interests in the Mediterranean was completed with the surrender of the Ionian islands to the French and the withdrawal of 4,740 men in six battleships and three brigs to Trieste. These ships were turned over to the French; the crews went home through Austria.

THE TURKISH WAR (1806–12)

Well before the end of the Dalmatian campaign the Russians had resumed a conflict with Turkey which, except for a peaceful interval from 1807 to 1809, was to last for six years. Hostilities were started on September 30, 1806, by a Turkish declaration of war undertaken at the urging of Napoleon. At that time Turkey was allied with France while Russia still supported Great Britain, a situation which was not destined to last. The Turkish navy then comprised 15 battleships, ten frigates, 18 corvettes, and 100 smaller ships—a fleet slightly larger than Seniavin's forces in the Mediterranean. Russian plans called for the Black Sea Fleet to blockade the Bosphorus, while Seniavin was to occupy the Aegean Islands and attack Constantinople in cooperation with the British.

Admiral Seniavin left his base at Corfu with eight battleships and some lesser craft, and reached the Dardanelles on March 7, 1807. There he found that a British fleet under Adm. Sir John Duckworth had already entered the straits, only to be beaten back by the Turks. After declining Seniavin's invitation to join in a combined attack, Duckworth sailed away on March 13.

Seniavin was thus left to his own devices in a situation that appeared unpromising. The Turks had available a fleet of possibly a dozen battleships, which could be easily protected in harbor while officials pondered the advisability of accepting or declining action. The Black Sea Fleet, which had been completely unsuccessful in a series of small operations during the first two months of the war, consisted of six battleships, five frigates, and some brigantines and gunboats. The Turkish fleet, clearly superior and able to attack at will, thus occupied a central position between two Russian forces.

Admiral Seniavin decided to blockade the Dardanelles. Seizing the island of Tenedos as a base for his fleet, he stationed two battleships before the entrance to the straits. On April 22 a Turkish fleet of nine battleships and a frigate appeared at the mouth of the Dardanelles, but made no move to attack.

For about a month the Russians, in a cat-and-mouse game, attempted to entice the Turkish fleet to leave the straits. Greek privateers were dispatched to cruise close to the Asiatic mainland, where they threatened to make a landing in the rear of the Dardanelles defenders. Finally, on May 19, a Turkish fleet of eight battleships, six frigates, four sloops, a brig, and 50 gunboats commanded by Seid Ali, the Kapudan Pasha, ventured outside the straits. Seniavin retreated from Tenedos to attack Imbros in the hope of luring the Turks farther out and then cutting off their retreat. Contrary winds, however, defeated this plan. Though the Turks were able to land troops on Tenedos, they were not able to hold their beachhead and were finally driven off with heavy loss. On May 22 the wind favored the Russians, who were able to get within firing distance with ten battleships and a frigate. The Turks promptly headed for the Dardanelles. There followed a confused night action, fought at the mouth of the straits between six and nine o'clock. Though neither foe lost a ship in this engagement, the Turks paid more heavily than the Russians. At dawn on May 23 three Turkish cripples were discerned making their way to safety behind the main Turkish fleet as it proceeded up the straits. Admiral Seniavin ordered Rear Admiral Greig, in command of the *Retvizan* 64, *Salafail* 74, *Skory* 64, *Yaroslav* 74, and frigate *Venus* 50, to capture them. When the Turkish ships ran aground under the guns of the shore forts Seniavin refused further pursuit and returned his ships to Tenedos.

While the outcome of this battle was clearly favorable to the Russians, it was at the same time not decisive, nor did it inflict vital injuries on the Turks. For the next month Seniavin continued his blockade tactics while attempting to lure the Turks out of the Dardanelles. Eventually the Russian blockade began to have some effect: with Constantinople afflicted by a growing shortage of food, a revolt of the Janissaries brought about the succession of Selim II. On June 22 the Turkish fleet again left the Dardanelles, but contrary winds and currents prevented a Russian interception. Seniavin then sent Greig to Lemnos in the hope of luring the Turks into an attack on a portion of his fleet. He was aided in the attempt when the sultan, responding to effects of the blockade, ordered his fleet to retake Tenedos. On June 27 the entire Turkish fleet of ten battleships, nine frigates, a sloop, a brig, and about 70 gunboats laid siege to the island. In the ensuing heavy bombardment the Turks sank a Russian brig and some very small vessels but had a frigate disabled by the fire of the shore batteries. Troops numbering 10,000 were landed to fight the Russian shore garrison.

On June 29, however, when the Turks sighted the Russian fleet, they immediately abandoned their siege and sailed westward. The Russians, after landing supplies for their beleaguered garrison, set out in search of the enemy, Admiral Seniavin steering northward in the hope of placing himself between the enemy fleet and the Dardanelles. On the morning of July 1 he sighted the Turks near the western end of Lemnos, well to leeward. Circumstances had at last provided the desired chance for a decisive engagement.

In the Battle of Athos, which followed, the Turks held their usual superiority. Each fleet had ten battleships, with the Russians carrying 750 guns as compared to the 850 of the Turks (one Turkish battleship, however, would fail to get into action). In addition, the Turks had five heavy frigates and five smaller ships which brought the total of Turkish guns to 1,200. The *Venus* 50, together with the smaller Russian ships, had been left at Tenedos.

There are some discrepancies between Russian and Turkish descriptions of the two fleet dispositions. According to Russian accounts, the three Turkish flagships were in the center of the line, with an uncertain number of frigates in a second line. Seniavin's plan of attack, which was very similar to that of Nelson at Trafalgar, called for an approach in two lines, each consisting of five ships. The northernmost line was commanded by Seniavin, the other by Rear Admiral Greig. The plan of action called for the first six ships to "pair off" so that two Russian vessels would be brought against each Turkish flagship, while those in the Russian rear would also "double" against the ships in the Turkish van. If the plan worked, the forward part of the Turkish line would be greatly outnumbered and the ships in the rear would not get into action. Seniavin's final orders to his fleet, similar to those earlier used by Nelson, ended with "I hope that every son of his country will try to do his duty in a glorious way."[2]

The Russians were able to operate much as they had intended. Between eight and nine o'clock they drove through the Turkish line between two forward flagships. In this phase of the action *Rafail* was badly damaged aloft by the fire of the Turkish fleet. But because the other Russian battleships were able to come into action according to plan, the forward part of the Turkish fleet was outmatched six ships against nine. Admiral Seniavin's flagship, in the lead, soon scored damaging hits on the foremost Turkish frigate. The battleship following immediately hove to, throwing the entire Turkish line into a confusion that enabled *Rafail* to escape from a concentration of enemy fire and get to the head of the Russian

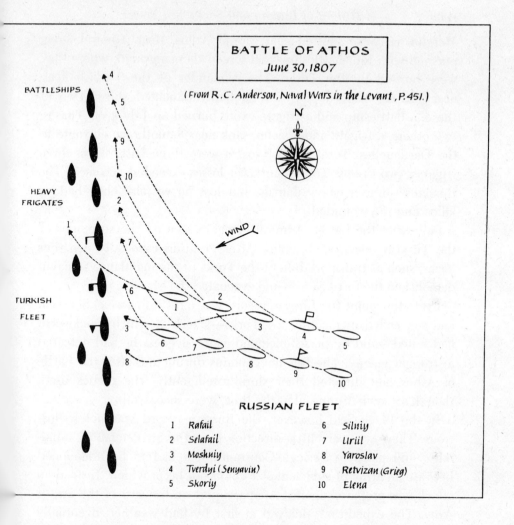

BATTLE OF ATHOS
June 30, 1807

(*From R.C. Anderson, Naval Wars in the Levant, P.451.*)

N

WIND

BATTLESHIPS

HEAVY
FRIGATES

TURKISH

FLEET

RUSSIAN FLEET

1	*Rafail*	6	*Silniy*
2	*Selafail*	7	*Uriil*
3	*Moshniy*	8	*Yaroslav*
4	*Tverdyi (Senyavin)*	9	*Retvizan (Grieg)*
5	*Skoriy*	10	*Elena*

line, where she made needed repairs. Meantime the leading Turkish ships, suffering severely, had started to fall back. By ten o'clock the Turks were in full retreat with two Russian ships, *Skory* and *Moshchny,* pressing them very closely and the other Russian vessels not far behind.

At that point the wind dropped and Admiral Seniavin temporarily halted action to allow time for repairs. When the breeze freshened and the Turks continued to fall back, two Turkish battleships, a frigate, and a sloop dropped behind. *Sv. Yelena, Salafail,* and *Silny* pursued, and during the night they overhauled and captured *Sadd al-Bahr* 84, flagship of Bechir Bey, the Turkish second-in-command. The next morning three stragglers, *Biafaret* 84, *Nessim* 50, and

Metelin 32, were spotted near Mount Athos. Rear Admiral Greig pursued with four battleships and forced them aground, where they were burned by the Turks. The remainder of the Turkish fleet, near Thasos, also counted several badly damaged ships. Two of these, a battleship and a frigate, were burned on July 4 off Thasos; two others, a frigate and a sloop, sank near Samothrace en route to the Dardanelles. Total Turkish losses were three battleships, three frigates, two sloops. Total manpower losses exceeded 500 men. The Russians suffered heavy damage but lost no vessels. They had 79 killed and 189 wounded.

Following the battle, Admiral Seniavin secured the surrender of the Turkish force on Tenedos. After granting especially generous terms, such as transportation of the Turks to the mainland, Seniavin demolished the fortifications and evacuated the island.

Up to this point the Russian record was most impressive. Seniavin had succeeded in meeting the Turks—a task at which Duckworth had failed—and by persistence and aggressiveness he had defeated a stronger enemy. The Russian captains during and after the Battle of Athos had directed their ships intelligently; the tactics used, though somewhat unusual at the time, were successful.

In the Black Sea, however, the Russian record was not so lustrous. There was very little direction from the St. Petersburg admiralty, and plans to besiege Constantinople had to be abandoned because an army of sufficient size could not be provided. Instead an attack was prepared against Anapa, a port on the east of the Sea of Azov. The expedition, delayed at first by bad weather, eventually mounted a combined land-sea attack which on May 11, 1807, resulted in the capture of the town together with the large stores of supplies. For this action, Rear Adm. Pavel V. Pustoshkin had under his command six battleships (*Ratny* 110, *Yegudiil* 110, *Pravy* 74, *Isidor* 74, *Pobeda* 66, *Varakhail* 66), five frigates (*Krepky* 54, *Nazaret* 44, *Pospeshny* 36, *Voin* 32, *Ioann Zlatoust* 32), and some smaller vessels. Following his minor success at Anapa, Pustoshkin returned to Sevastopol on May 24. He sailed again on June 12 for an attack on Trebizond, an expedition which consumed more than a month and was so poorly managed that it accomplished exactly nothing.

Meanwhile, events elsewhere in Europe were moving rapidly. While Russian armies had been beaten by Napoleon, Admiral

Seniavin's position in the Aegean had, as previously described, been made completely untenable by the Treaty of Tilsit, by which Russia again changed sides and became an ally of Napoleon.

An order to return his fleet to the Baltic proved impossible for Seniavin to execute successfully. Cooperation between Adm. Cuthbert Collingwood (who succeeded the inept Admiral Duckworth) and Admiral Seniavin had been cordial, but the new alliance with Napoleon brought this to an end. The Russian ships could doubtless have proceeded to the Black Sea with little difficulty, but to pass through British-dominated waters to the Baltic was a different matter entirely. On September 7 Admiral Seniavin left Tenedos on his return trip; bad weather, the need of repairs, and the lack of the naval bases already surrendered to the French—many of them blockaded by the British—all led to delays. On November 6 the fleet suffered damage in a violent gale and put into the Tagus River at Lisbon to refit. Before the ships could be made ready for sea, war broke out between England and Russia, and a British blockade of Lisbon forced Gen. Andoche Junot, the French commander there, to vacate. In September 1808 in an agreement with Sir Charles Cotton, the British commander in Portuguese waters, Admiral Seniavin surrendered his ships on condition that they be returned to Russia when peace was established and that his men be transported to Russia. The surrendered fleet consisted of nine battleships and a frigate. The British allowed this fleet to sail to Portsmouth under Seniavin's command. Crews were gradually returned to Russia during 1808 and 1809. Two of the warships were returned to Russia in 1813; the others were scrapped before then as unseaworthy. On their return to Russia, Seniavin and his men were poorly received by Tsar Alexander, and this insult to a successful leader undoubtedly injured the navy's morale for the remainder of the war.

There were other Russian vessels in the Mediterranean besides those under Admiral Seniavin's direct command. A few of them were originally from the Black Sea, and returned there. One or two were interned in Spanish ports. One squadron of four battleships, three frigates, and four brigs under Commo. Ivan O. Saltenov went to Trieste, where they were interned and later surrendered to the French. Other vessels in Venice and Corfu were given to the French, although in some cases they continued to fly the Russian flag and were served by Russian crews. In one odd instance the tiny brig

Spitsberg, commanded by Lt. Ivan Kochelev, put into Vigo, where she was for four years protected by the Spaniards from the British, who demanded her surrender.

In early 1809 there was a renewal of hostilities between Russia and Turkey. But since Russia no longer had a Mediterranean fleet, naval activities in the new war were confined to the Black Sea, and though the fighting went well for Russia on land there were no significant naval engagements. In April and May a few cruisers were sent out from Sevastopol. They captured a number of prizes and undertook some minor bombardments of coastal towns but obtained no news of the main Turkish fleet. A small squadron of two battleships, two frigates, a bomb and a transport occupied Anapa on June 27, then returned to port—still without doing battle. On the west coast of the Black Sea some 30 Russian gunboats stationed on the Danube engaged in a successful ten-day bombardment of Dobrudja and later aided the army in its gradual capture. Several frigates blockaded the port of Varna, but were driven off by a stronger Turkish force.

Hostilities during 1810 were similarly indecisive. The gunboats on the Danube continued to aid the army in capturing Turkish fortresses. On July 23 a small squadron took Sukhum Kale near the eastern end of the Black Sea. All the while the main fleet of each power was seeking to engage the other, but neither could ascertain the enemy's location. Rear Adm. A. Sarychev's fleet of seven battleships, two frigates, and three brigs left Sevastopol on July 12 to search for the Turks along the southern coast of the Black Sea. At the same time a Turkish squadron of nine battleships, six frigates, and three lesser vessels, seeking the Russians in the neighborhood of the Crimea, came in sight of Sevastopol. When this news reached Sarychev, he ordered a return to Sevastopol; however, by the time he arrived on August 7 the Turkish fleet had departed. He waited long enough to be joined by the small squadron from Sukhum Kale, and on August 21 the combined fleet of eight battleships, five frigates, and four smaller vessels proceeded toward Varna with the intention of supporting the army.

Annoying delays occurred as several unseaworthy ships were tossed about by contrary winds. Then, very early on the morning of September 29 a lookout reported the presence of the Turkish fleet. As dawn broke, the Turkish vessels could be seen in a state of considerable disorder toward the south-southeast. The Russians were held back in their pursuit by their slower ships, whereupon Sarychev detached, in the command of Captain Klokachev, his three fastest battleships and a frigate. At 5:00 P.M., after an all-day chase, the *Anapa* 74 came within range of a Turkish battleship and a frigate. The other Turkish battleship then put about to support these ships, and the *Anapa* had either to avoid action or to attack a very strong enemy force. A more vigorous Russian commander would have risked an engagement, but Sarychev regarded a night action as too dangerous: he recalled his detachment. During the night the Russians lost contact with the Turks, and on September 8 they returned to port. About a month later Sarychev was out again—this time to attack Trebizond. Once more the mission failed, as did a later attempted amphibious landing at Platona, ten miles to the west.

Fighting during the next year was halfhearted. The tsar was becoming disaffected with his French alliance. With a war with France a possibility, it was to Russia's advantage to liquidate its smaller dispute with Turkey in order to free its Balkan army. This the Russians did skillfully, using smaller forces to hold conquests in the face of Turkish pressure. However, as the danger from France accelerated, the tsar had to give up hope of a boundary on the Danube and settle for one on the Prut (the Treaty of Bucharest, May 28, 1812).

With a Russo-Turkish peace in prospect, the 1811 naval war was comparatively uneventful. A few Russian scouts were sent out in April and May, but the main Russian fleet of ten battleships and five smaller craft under Vice Adm. Robert Hall, an Englishman in the Russian service, did not get under way until the end of June, when it left Sevastopol for Varna. Aside from the capture of a Turkish frigate and a sloop, and some commerce raiding by Russian cruisers, the summer was entirely lacking in action.

BALTIC OPERATIONS (1807–1809)

Alexander's agreement with Napoleon at Tilsit in 1807 led to the renewal of the long duel with Sweden. War was declared on February 22, 1808, after the Swedes had made clear their disinclination to join the Continental System. Denmark, thirsting for revenge against England, permitted the passage of French troops on their way to attack Sweden from the west. The tsar's armies, now greatly superior to those of Sweden in both quality and quantity, promptly invaded Finland and in nearly every encounter defeated the Swedes. The Swedish fleet of 12 battleships, eight frigates, and 190 small craft was weaker than usual. However, most of the Russian navy was not in the Baltic, and the force afloat—nine battleships, seven frigates, ten small craft, and a galley fleet of 170 units—was of about the same strength as that of the Swedes. Supplemental British ships in the Baltic provided naval superiority for Sweden. British vessels participated in some attacks on the Russian coast, the capture of a few small Russian warships, and the ravaging of Kola and some small fishing settlements on the White Sea—all minor blows that had little effect on the outcome of the war. Nor did the fact that the Swedish coastal flotillas were superior in size to their own unduly handicap the Russians.

The war at sea was less of a general success for the Russians than was the conflict on land; nevertheless, victorious naval encounters were numerous and often followed military triumphs. On one occasion at least 71 Swedish vessels had to be burned to prevent Russian seizure. On another (May 5, 1807), Sveaborg surrendered with a loss for the Swedes of three hemmemas, seven turumas, a brig, 25 gun sloops, 51 gun yawls, and four gunboats. Since most of these vessels were in good condition, they were immediately put to use by the Russians. Balancing the major victories were Russian failures at Gotland and the Åland Islands, together with a few setbacks at the hands of the Swedes in minor small-craft actions. In the largest of several such battles which were fought during the summer months of 1808, the Swedes lost 12 gun sloops and 173 men, as compared to a Russian loss of 22 gun sloops and 330 men. However, at the same time the Swedes suffered serious defeat on land and had to retreat westward some twenty miles from Halmo to Korpo Strom.

The two main fleets went into action quite slowly. The Swedes moved first, shifting their fleet of 11 battleships and five frigates eastward, first to cover Stockholm and later to redress the balance of naval power which had been upset by the flotilla disasters. The Russian Kronstadt fleet, of nine battleships, 11 frigates, and 11 lesser craft led by Admiral Khanykov, did not leave port until July 20. When it arrived at Hängo it made no attempt to engage the

Swedes. The delay proved costly: Adm. Sir James Saumarez, whose fleet had been operating in Danish waters, had dispatched two of his battleships, the 74's *Implacable* and *Centaur*, to reinforce the Swedes, and on August 20 these vessels, after pursuing three Russian frigates, joined the Swedes in Oro Roads. The reinforcement was important both quantitatively and qualitatively, in that the British ships were fast and well-handled and gave the Swedish fleet a definite margin of superiority. On August 25 the combined fleet put to sea to attack the Russians, who had taken up a position nearby.

The events that followed illustrate the immense moral superiority which English ships held over all others in the Napoleonic wars. In numbers and gunpower the two fleets were not greatly unequal, the Russians having nine battleships and five big frigates carrying a total of 962 guns, as compared to 12 British and Swedish battleships and four big frigates with 966 guns in all. Further, the Russians were accustomed in contests with both Turks and Swedes to fighting against (or in spite of) unfavorable odds and yet winning. But on this occasion Khanykov retreated as soon as he saw his enemy, and the pursuit lasted all day, with the English ships sailing beautifully, the Swedes badly, and the Russians very badly. By evening the two English ships were five miles ahead of any Swedish vessel and had nearly caught up with the rearmost Russian ship, *Vsevolod* 74. A brief action between this ship and the *Implacable* was won by the latter, which outmaneuvered the Russian and forced her to strike her colors following losses of 32 men by the English ship and 128 by the *Vsevolod*. Other Russian ships coming to her rescue prevented the English from removing their prize, and the *Vsevolod* was taken in tow by a Russian frigate. As the Russian ships neared refuge at Port Baltic, the frigate cast off the tow. This forced the *Vsevolod* to anchor outside rather than inside the harbor, and when boats appeared to tow her in, the *Centaur* drove them off and attacked at close range. Both ships grounded in the fight, which again resulted in about four-to-one losses, with the *Centaur* losing 30 men compared to 124 by the *Vsevolod*. When the *Implacable* joined the fight, the Russian ship surrendered. The *Implacable* was able to tow off her consort, but the *Vsevolod* was burned.

Several hours after the Russian ships took refuge, the Swedish fleet caught up with its English allies. Three days later Admiral

Saumarez also put in an appearance—with four more ships of the line and various lesser vessels. These arrivals gave the allied forces such decisive superiority that Saumarez had very nearly decided to attack. Then a wind shift caused a further delay of a week. In the meantime the Russians had steadily strengthened their shore defenses. As a consequence, when Saumarez was able to attack, the Russian position had become so strong he had to content himself with a month-long blockade.

While the main Russian fleet was blockaded, considerable flotilla action took place along the Finnish coast. On August 30, 35 Swedish sloops under Brandt attacked a Russian flotilla of about 30 gun sloops and gun yawls commanded by Selivanov. The Russians finally broke off the engagement, quite an even match wherein each side lost two vessels; both contestants suffered many damaged ships.

The Russians fell back on their base at Åbo for repairs, and as soon as he received reinforcements Brandt launched a campaign against this base that was to be continued fruitlessly even after his replacement by Admiral Rajalin. A landing attempt on September 17 proved a failure. The next day a naval battle was fought at Palmosund, west of Åbo, between about 70 Swedish craft and a slightly larger Russian force under Miasoedov. The Russians had slightly heavier losses in the encounter, but this time it was the Swedes who retreated. Gustav IV then attempted a large landing at Helsinge, six miles north of the Swedish base at Grovikssund. This move coincided with and largely neutralized a Russian naval attack on the Swedish base. Neither side made much headway, and early in October the 1808 campaign ended.

On September 30 the allies ended their blockade of Port Baltic. The Swedes retreated to Karlskrona while the British proceeded into the western Baltic for convoy duty. The Russian fleet lost two of its frigates en route to its base at Kronstadt.

Although there were fewer battles in 1809 than during the previous year, the fighting on land was decisive. A winter invasion of Sweden was launched by the Russians. One army crossed the ice to the Åland Islands and was stranded there when the ice broke up. Two other ventures were more successful: a second army marched around the north of the Gulf of Bothnia and captured the remnants of Sweden's Finland Army, and a third crossed the ice and captured

Umeå. All together, these military expeditions had the effect of eliminating Finland as an area of conflict.

Very little happened at sea during 1809. Only three Swedish battleships were put into service, and the thirteen Russian battleships commissioned never left Kronstadt. Thirteen Swedish gunboats were burned to prevent their capture. Both Swedes and Russians had reinforced their flotillas during the winter, but there were few encounters between the two. A few small-scale naval actions were fought between the Russians and portions of the sizable British fleet in the eastern Baltic. On the night of July 7–8 boats from several British ships successfully attacked eight Russian gunboats and 14 merchantmen with a casualty loss of about 50 British and 190 Russians. In another action two weeks later the British captured three gunboats and a storeship at a cost of 150 Russian and 60 British casualties.

Allied naval superiority enabled the Swedes on August 17 to land 6,300 men 30 miles north of the Russian army at Umeå, but their battle plan promptly miscarried when the Swedish army was beaten by the Russians and forced to re-embark. Another Swedish army, advancing from the south with naval support, failed in an attempt to trap the Russians by using a landing force to destroy a bridge in their rear. Sweden was clearly defeated, and the Treaty of Fredrikshamn ended the Russian phase of the war on September 17, 1809. All of Finland, the Åland Islands, and all Swedish territory east of the Gulf of Bothnia were ceded to Russia. Sweden also announced her adherence to the Continental System and the closing of certain ports to British vessels.

THE ALLIANCE WITH ENGLAND (1810–15)

Though England and Russia remained legally at war from 1809 to 1812, there was little action during those years. Hoping to conciliate the Russians, whom they had regarded throughout the Napoleonic wars as their natural allies, the British now withheld their fleets from the eastern Baltic.

Meanwhile, British faith in a possible change in Russia's political orientation was on the way to fulfillment. Though the Continental System proved beneficial to the development of Russian manufacturing because it eliminated British competition, its operation was in other respects vexatious. Napoleon's steady annexation of new territories to aid in the enforcement of the Continental System appeared highly threatening, and after a short time the Russians paid it no more than lip service. When Austria declared war on France in 1809, Russian assistance to Napoleon was less than minimal. Moreover, the Grand Duchy of Warsaw, which Napoleon had created, seemed to menace Russia's Polish territories, while the French, distrustful of Russian activities in the Mediterranean and Balkans, refused to give Russia a free hand in dealing with Turkey. To Russian military men, Russian defeats by France following a century of victories called for reversal. And to the religiously inclined, Napoleon with his atheistic followers was not far removed from the Anti-Christ.

Nor was Napoleon altogether pleased with his ally. For one thing, Russia remained unbowed, the last obstacle to his complete military domination of Europe. Also, Russian failures after 1810 to enforce the Continental System had encouraged similar attitudes elsewhere and meant the defeat of the weapon by which the French emperor had hoped to vanquish the English. Further, when his courtship of a Russian princess, the younger sister of Alexander, was refused, he was greatly chagrined.

The result of such constant friction was a mutual agreement separation. By 1811 both France and Russia were preparing for a decisive military showdown. The French decision to attack Russia appears to have been made on August 16, 1811. Soon thereafter, extensive military and logistic preparations were under way.

At first glance the advantages appear to have been entirely with Napoleon. By manpower drafts on nearly all the countries of Europe except Spain, Portugal, Turkey, England, and Sweden, he was able to raise an army of 1,300,000 men. This provided an immense four-to-one superiority over the 250-300,000 men the Russians could muster, what with the demands of their wars with Persia and Turkey and their garrison of Finland. The closing of the Turkish war released General Kutuzov and some troops in the south, but did not redress the balance.

On June 24, 1812, when the Grand Army started its campaign, Napoleon had under his direct command some 220,000 men, with 80,000 on the right flank under the viceroy of Italy and 40,000 on the left under Jacques Macdonald. Some 200-250,000 additional troops were stationed nearby or in strategic reserve. Against these forces stood the Russian First Army of 90,000 men under Barclay de Tolly; the Second Army of 60,000 men under Count Petr I. Bagration, which was stationed several hundred miles south; and much farther to the south, the Third Army or Army of Reserve (45,000 men) under Tormasov.

In view of the overwhelming numerical superiority of the French, the Russians retreated for several hundred miles. These retreats were made in excellent order, and were attended, despite Napoleon's efforts to prevent it, by a junction of the two main Russian armies at Smolensk. Aside from an indecisive engagement fought at Smolensk on August 16, there were few battles—a feature which greatly disconcerted Napoleon. In the meantime, the French supply system proved inadequate to the strain, with the result that widespread looting and poor discipline prevailed. Disease, death, desertions, and detachment to supply duty thinned the French ranks.

On August 29 Kutuzov was named to command all Russian forces. The Russian retreat continued, but with a series of rearguard actions. As the numbers of the two armies approached equality, Kutuzov prepared for a stand 70 miles before Moscow near the small village of Borodino. Here on September 5–6 the two armies clashed in one of the bloodiest and most desperately fought battles of the nineteenth century. The contest was a near draw—despite the fact that it was Kutuzov rather than Napoleon who retired.

The road to Moscow was now open, and Napoleon did in fact enter the city on September 15. But it was to prove a hollow triumph. The all-but-deserted city was soon destroyed by fire, and with it the large supplies of food so needed by the French. Napoleon's expectations of Russian surrender were not realized, and five weeks later he began a retreat from the city. Meanwhile Kutuzov had given his army a rest, and reinforcements had given him military strength that was now superior to that of Napoleon.

The story of the French retreat from Moscow has been told many times, but often in a fashion that is misleading. The French were steadily harried and weakened by rearguard actions, by attacks from partisans and from Cossack cavalry, by disease and privation. It was not until November 15, when they were more than halfway back to the Niemen River, that the first snowfall of the winter arrived. At that time Napoleon had 42,000 men left. Winter weather therefore had little effect on the final outcome; it only served at the very end of the campaign to reduce the number of survivors of an army already decimated. Napoleon was not defeated, as some of his admirers are wont to claim, by General Winter, but rather by his own mistakes in dealing with an opponent that out-thought and out-fought him throughout the entire campaign, an opponent that also demonstrated better morale and enjoyed undivided public support.

The naval war which accompanied Napoleon's invasion of Russia has been almost completely overlooked by historians, yet it was an important factor in the defeat of the Grand Army. Its contribution was made possible by a very rapid courtship, which in a period of about three months turned a nominal war with England first into peace and then into firm alliance.

The French in 1812 had hoped to use a vast fleet of coastal gunboats to ease their problem of land transport, though they had taken no steps to secure a local control of the sea. In order to attain such control it was necessary that they either eliminate Russian—and possibly British—sea power along the Russian coast, or occupy the coastline and gain control of bases from which the Russian vessels might operate. They opted for the latter. With Macdonald's army of 40,000 on the left flank, Napoleon detached 40,000 more men under Nicolas Oudinot (later replaced by Marshal Laurent St. Cyr) to march north along the coast to St. Petersburg. Barclay de Tolly, though outnumbered by about four to one, dispatched 25,000 men under General Prince Wittgenstein.

But in spite of all French efforts, the Russians were able to hold sufficient coastline to operate at sea. A British fleet under Rear Adm. Sir George Martin arrived in the Baltic near Riga on July 16, and its crews assisted Admiral Chichagov in setting up a gunboat defense of the city. The successful Russian defense denied the French a supply terminal that would have greatly relieved the pressure on the Grand Army.

British and Russian sea power accomplished even more. About the time of the Battle of Borodino, Admiral Martin escorted 13 Russian transports to Danzig in order to land Russian and Swedish forces in the rear of the French. This threat ultimately caused the French to abandon the siege of Riga; Napoleon even detached men from his own front lines to defend the rear.

The Russian Baltic forces operated mainly in the southern Baltic, where they held control in cooperation with a British blockading squadron commanded by Adm. George Tate. The British force consisted of several battleships based on Gothenburg. Wisely or not, Alexander sent the Baltic Fleet under Admiral Greig and the White Sea Fleet under Vice Admiral Crown into English waters, a move which had no effect on the British squadron's command of the sea.

The Russian flotillas remained very active in defending the coastline and the larger rivers. Russian and British small craft also interfered with French crossings of the major rivers while giving aid to the Russian Army.

Several military critics have observed that one of Napoleon's major shortcomings as a general was his lack of understanding of sea power. The 1812 campaign in Russia provides excellent support for this contention.

END OF THE NAPOLEONIC WARS

Though the defeat of Napoleon in Russia in 1812 was to prove his undoing, more than two and a half years of fighting lay ahead before his departure for St. Helena. On December 5 Napoleon left the remnants of the Grand Army with Marshal Joachim Murat in command, and on December 18 he was in Paris. By his nationwide system of conscription—one of his major contributions to the art of warfare—he quickly raised a new (though inexperienced) army of 350,000 men. Once more he held numerical superiority over his opposition, which now included Prussia with its greatly improved and reorganized army. Spain and Austria were to array forces against him later.

Despite the greenness of his troops and a woeful lack of cavalry, Napoleon fought for several months more with his old fire and genius, and for a while he was everywhere victorious. The allies, suffering from lack of a unified command, were beaten at Lützen on May 2, 1813, and at Bautzen three weeks later. Then a six weeks' armistice which gave Napoleon a breathing space at the same time allowed his opponents to gather the forces to outnumber him. Though victorious at the Battle of Dresden, August 26–27, he had to fall back on Leipzig, where on October 16–19 he was soundly defeated in the Battle of the Nations and forced to make a disastrous retreat across the Rhine. Another conscription of 300,000 men allowed him to raise new armies speedily, and once more he fought brilliantly for a time—but now on French soil and against great odds. On March 31, 1814, Alexander and Arthur Wellesley, Duke of Wellington, entered Paris together, and on April 6 Napoleon abdicated at Fontainebleau in favor of his son. He was then removed to the island of Elba aboard a British frigate. After ten months spent in plotting, he escaped and made his way to France. Three weeks after his arrival on March 1, 1815, Louis XVIII had fled; most of the French army had joined Napoleon; once more Napoleon was in power in Paris.

But he reckoned without the allies. Though separated by numerous differences, they saw eye-to-eye where Napoleon was concerned. In his final campaign Bonaparte fought again with brilliance, but it was not enough. In the Battle of Waterloo on June 18, 1815, he was defeated by Wellington with some assistance from Prussian Marshal Gebhard von Blücher. When Napoleon's life appeared to be in danger in France, he surrendered to the captain of a British battleship. It was the *Northumberland*, another British battleship, which bore him to St. Helena and final exile.

For the men of the Russian navy the last two years of the war were uneventful. Seven new battleships were built in the Baltic, and the 19 battleships serving with the British returned to the Baltic in 1815. The fleet of 26 battleships was one-third smaller than before the Napoleonic wars. But its international ranking was high and its record had been entirely creditable. When the fighting ended Sweden had only 13 battleships left in the Baltic, and Denmark but one.

Unhappily, because Alexander I was not naval-minded the sizable contributions of his fleet commanders were never fully appreciated. Despite the fact that Ushakov and Seniavin had played roughly the same role in Russian naval history that Nelson and Rodney played in that of Great Britain, they were all but ignored completely. When Nicholas I came to the throne a belated effort was made to repair the neglect. In 1831, when Seniavin died following a long physical and mental illness, he was given the simple funeral he had requested; but the tsar himself took command of the single squad of sailors chosen as honor guard for the occasion.

CHAPTER 7

The Last Years of the Sailing Navy

(1815-53)

AFTER THE NAPOLEONIC WARS

THOUGH THE Russian navy lost rather than gained ships during the Napoleonic wars, it was powerfully strengthened in other respects by the course of events. During a quarter-century of conflict it had met the Turks, the Swedes, the French, and the English —and only against the last had its record been poor. In the Baltic, the Swedish navy was no longer a serious rival and the Danish fleet had not recovered from its losses at Copenhagen. In the Black Sea and the eastern Mediterranean, the Turks had been seriously weakened by Russian successes. Beyond Russian waters, the French and Spanish navies had been all but annihilated. Hence in 1815 the Russian navy stood supreme in its own waters, while elsewhere its strength was second only to that of England. But between the English and Russian fleets there lay a wide gap in both quantity and quality; and because they were well aware of this gap Russian authorities continued for a generation after 1815 the practice of sending senior-class midshipmen as "volunteers" for short terms of duty in the British navy.

During the first half of the eighteenth century only two men sat on the Russian throne. The wartime naval policies of Alexander I (1801–25) have already been considered. During the decade of peace before his death Alexander encouraged exploration and permitted some shipbuilding, but from most other standpoints he

neglected the fleet and took little interest in it.[1] Though total
expenditures were not curtailed, naval activities were so reduced
that the fleets became almost wholly inactive. Neither Adm. Pavel
Chichagov nor his successor, the Marquis of Traverse, did much as
navy minister to improve the fleet. Ships rotted; admirals were often
ignorant, aged, and ailing; most of the men were virtually untrained
peasants whose lives were made miserable by continuous beatings
and the misdeeds of their superiors. Revolutionary organizations
were forming aboard many vessels, the beginnings of groups
destined to destroy the tsarist navy a century later.

Adm. Vasily Golovnin, in a pamphlet describing the navy at the
end of Alexander's reign, wrote:

> If the rotten, badly, and poorly equipped vessels, [the] aged, ailing,
> ignorant, and confused at sea admirals of the fleet, [the] inexperienced
> captains and officers and farmers under the name of sailors, enrolled
> for ship's crews, could make a navy, then we have it.[2]

This view of the fleet was probably justified. In 1818, when Alexander agreed to send a fleet to help Spain regain its American colonies, the condition of the ships prevented any getting farther than
Spain. Some could not make even that distance.

At the end of Alexander's reign the bulk of Russian sea power
was concentrated in the Baltic Fleet, whose 28 battleships, 17 frigates, and 35 lesser vessels constituted the nucleus of the nation's
navy. The Black Sea Fleet comprised 11 battleships, eight frigates,
and some lesser vessels; two battleships and a frigate were in the
White Sea.

The Russian battleships of the period were of eight general types
with armament ranging from 60 to 120 guns and displacement
varying from 1,800 to nearly 4,900 tons. The largest single class was
represented by the *Varshava* 120, which measured 206 feet in length
by 55 feet in beam and 22 feet in depth, and which displaced 4,587
tons. In one phase of shipbuilding the Russians showed they had
learned little from experience: ships were still made of fir rather
than oak, a construction which committed them to a short average
lifetime.

Nicholas I (1825–55), the fairly able but unbending autocrat
who succeeded Alexander I, made all decisions himself and ruth-

lessly suppressed dissent. Unlike his brother, who at times had displayed some liberality, Nicholas constantly decided even the smallest details himself, interfered with everything, and devoted his life to the suppression of change, not only in Russia but elsewhere in Europe. For a brief period he encouraged science and education—in the mistaken belief that it would inculcate loyalty to the throne; later he sent spies into the universities and had his political police survey all intellectual activities. In successful pursuit of a policy of territorial expansion he supported both army and navy, especially the former.

His first two important naval appointments brought Adm. A. V. von Muller to the head of the navy ministry and Prince Aleksandr S. Menshikov to the position of chief of the naval staff. The latter appointment, made because Menshikov as an outsider would be free of the intrigues of those close to the navy, proved a bad mistake. In a long period in power Menshikov failed to display notable qualities of any kind; during his tenure any improvements in the navy came as a result of either the personal interest of the tsar or the efforts of a small group of distinguished and dedicated admirals, many of whom served on the prestigious Committee on the Organization of the Navy, appointed by Nicholas.

As a breakdown of disbursements reveals (see table 1), Nicholas' naval interests were far from constant. Though over a 30-year period he was responsible for the construction of 69 battleships, 47 frigates, ten steam frigates, 43 steamers, and some 600 small and very small craft, expenditures which had been high during the 1830s thereafter declined sharply. This reflects a naval building program which for a time increased the fleet by as much as seven to ten battleships a year but later provided for only two battleships, a frigate, and three lesser vessels annually. The sharp reduction in expenditure after 1840 was also a reflection of the fact that Nicholas was a good deal more land-minded than sea-minded. English observers reported that after reviewing naval personnel he would frequently draft the most promising sailors for service in the army. The reduction in support coincided with a decline in Russian naval ranking, and during the 1840s the French navy again replaced the Russian as the second in strength.

Despite handicaps, there was considerable improvement in the

TABLE 1

Expenditures of Naval Ministry, 1805–56°

(IN MILLIONS OF RUBLES)

1805	12.4	1833	30.5	1845	14.5
1812	18.6	1834	30.2	1846	10.7
1815	15.0	1835	37.5	1847	11.3
1818	22.7	1836	35.9	1848	11.4
1822	25.4	1837	36.4	1849	15.4
1825	20.7	1838	35.6	1850	12.4
1826	21.9	1839	37.7	1851	14.6
1827	24.1	1840	11.6	1852	17.9
1828	27.5	1841	11.6	1853	20.7
1829	31.3	1842	12.3	1854	14.4
1830	31.6	1843	11.0	1855	19.1
1831	30.9	1844	10.7	1856	18.2

° SOURCE: S. F. Ogorodnikov, *Istorichesky obzor razvitiia i deiatelnosti Morskago Ministerstva za sto let ego sushchestvovaniia: 1802–1902* (St. Petersburg, 1902), p. 130.

Black Sea Fleet, which increased in both quantity and quality largely as the result of the exertions of Adm. Mikhail P. Lazarev, who served as its commander from 1833 to 1851. This remarkable man, at once an explorer, a scientist, an inventor, and a first-class administrator, ran an effective school of sea power which emphasized thorough training and sent its students on frequent cruises. He was responsible for the first ironclad in the Russian navy, the *Inkerman* of 1838; he was interested in steam navigation; he promoted the development of Sevastopol as the main naval arsenal. During his administration new forts and docks were built under the supervision of British engineers.

The last years of the sailing navy were years that brought many innovations forecasting the direction of future progress. In ordnance the 48-pound "unicorn" cannonballs and 24-pound carronades were added to the 36-pounder ammunition carried by most of the battleships. Later the Russians led in introducing shell-firing guns. In 1846 chain was substituted for hemp in cables used on anchors. The first Baltic steamer of war was built in 1817 at the Izhora works and named *Skory*. Three years later the *Vezuvy* was finished on the Black Sea. Half a dozen other vessels followed, most of them small, with engines under 100 horsepower. The first steam vessel of any size was a frigate built in 1836. The first propeller-driven frigate, *Arkhimed*, was finished at St. Petersburg in 1838.

About the same time that the steamer ceased to be a novelty, the Russians began experimenting with submarines. In 1829 Kazimir Chernovsky, an imprisoned nobleman, devised a plan for a submarine to be made of iron and propelled by 28 oars which passed through special leather-sewn ports intended to be waterproof. Air was to be pumped to the interior from 28 air bags. Other features were a movable conning tower with a periscope, and a "torpedo" that could be fastened to the bottom of an enemy ship and then ignited by chemical action of sea water on calcium. The tsar was interested enough in this project to submit it to study by a naval engineer, who reported unfavorably. Two years later the shipbuilding committee of the navy rejected another design calling for a small double-hulled boat.

Gen. K. A. Shidner, a distinguished inventor of mines and torpedoes, fared somewhat better. In May 1834 his submarine prototype, a small boat less than 20 feet in length, was finished. It included a periscope equipped with reflecting mirrors, a 50-pound barrel of powder attached to a harpoon at the end of a bowsprit, and two side rockets in tubes. Motive power was furnished by two pairs of oars with folding blades which closed in forward strokes and opened, fanlike, with backward strokes. At trials in September 1834 this ship demonstrated an ability to submerge, and it was otherwise sufficiently successful to be copied in a more advanced model which was tried out at Kronstadt four years later. However, the later model, though it demonstrated its main weapon successfully against a schooner, proved so weak in locomotion as to be virtually at the mercy of any strong current.

EXPLORATION AND EXPANSION

Geography had tended to discourage Russian maritime development, but it exerted no such limitation on Russian land expansion. On the contrary, the extension of Russian frontiers to the east and to a lesser degree to the south had been relatively easy. By 1815, following several centuries of expansion, the Russians had established a somewhat loose control over an empire that included all of northern Asia and Alaska, and extended even to Fort Ross, north of San Francisco Bay in California.

Throughout most of the early nineteenth century the Russian tsars actively favored this policy of exploration and expansion, and to implement it they used the navy predominantly for the first and the army primarily for the second. Motives for exploration were partly scientific, partly commercial.

The first Russian seamen in the North Pacific were the daring and venturesome but (in a maritime sense) completely unskilled Cossacks, whose boats and ships were by most standards poorly built and unseaworthy. Since these seamen, who knew little of navigation, left neither reliable observations nor maps and normally kept no journals of their voyages, little was known of the Russian areas of the North Pacific. The principal motivation for the Cossacks' presence was not discovery but rather the profit to be obtained from the pelts of millions of sea otters and fur seals. With the help of the natives of the Aleutians, the Russians hunted these animals so intensely over a period of several decades as to bring about their near extinction.

Because of inhospitable climate and lack of agricultural skills, the Cossacks in both Alaska and Siberia were often close to starvation; indeed, the establishment of the Russian settlement at Fort Ross was a none-too-successful attempt to provide food. As the fur-bearing animals were exterminated the Russians gradually lost interest in Fort Ross, and in 1841 they sold the settlement to Capt. John Sutter, a Swiss-American pioneer in California.

Russian explorations in the Pacific were only partly connected with the fur trade, however; other motives played a role. Among these was the desire to open trade relations with Japan and China and to gain unfettered access to the Pacific. More farsighted in this one respect than most of his naval advisers, Alexander I saw the value of long voyages, not only to gain skill in navigation but also to obtain information concerning the Russian domain and its surrounding seas.

As early as 1786 Capt. G. I. Mulovsky had urged that four ships be sent on a circumnavigation of the globe. Catherine II viewed the proposal with favor, as she was particularly interested in sea communications in the North Pacific. Unhappily, with the outbreak of the Swedish war the project was shelved and no action was taken for twenty years. Then it was revived by a former ensign under

Mulovsky, Capt. Adam Johann von Kruzhenstern. Alexander I was attracted to the proposal; he gave his consent.

The expedition which was destined to accomplish the first Russian circumnavigation of the globe consisted of two small ships, both purchased in England. The *Nadezhda* under Kruzhenstern was of 450 tons and carried a crew of 58. Her consort was the 375-ton *Neva*, which carried a crew of 47 men and was commanded by Capt. Yury Lysiansky. The two vessels carried in addition to their regular crews a number of scientists and passengers.

The tiny fleet left Kronstadt in June 1803. While its main purpose, opening up trade with Japan, was not achieved, the expedition, as the first definitely long-range exploit attempted by the Russians, proved notable in many ways. The ships sailed southward through the Atlantic, entered the Pacific by way of Cape Horn, and then moved west and north, eventually reaching the North Pacific. There the explorers made the first thorough investigation of the northern Kuriles, and assisted the Russians in Alaska in a war against the natives. The expedition next turned south along the coast of eastern Asia, studied the west coast of Japan, entered the Indian Ocean, and finally reached the Atlantic by way of the Cape of Good Hope. In 1806 it returned to Russia. The voyage marked a great many "firsts," including the first time a Russian ship had crossed the equator and entered the Southern Hemisphere. The ethnographic and social studies of island peoples had been extremely thorough, though it is only fair to note that a wholly German scientific staff was largely responsible. Later Kruzhenstern claimed that the study of oceanography began with his observations at that time of sea currents, tides, and the density and temperature of sea water.

An even more impressive circumnavigation was carried out from 1819 to 1821 by Capt. Fabian von Bellingshausen in the sloop *Vostok* and Lt. M. P. Lazarev in the *Mirny*. The object of their venture was to follow up Captain Cook's voyage by circumnavigating the Antarctic as far south as ice conditions would permit. The ships sailed from the Baltic and stopped in London for charts, chronometers, and a visit with the eminent English explorer Sir Joseph Banks, who had sailed with Cook. They then sailed to Rio de Janeiro by way of Teneriffe, stopped briefly, and turned again southward. Though they were an ill-assorted pair, the *Vostok* being fast and the *Mirny* a slow and beamy ex-freighter, they managed to keep together for most of the voyage. By December 1819 they had arrived at South Georgia, whence they proceeded east, moving well south of the latitudes reached by Captain Cook. Though stopped from time to time by the ice pack, the Russian vessels cruised between 60° and 70° south latitude. On January 22, 1821, they sighted the first land within the Antarctic Circle and named it after Peter I. In course of their continued navigation, which was interrupted only by a journey to Sydney, Australia, for supplies, they discovered many islands in the Antarctic, and before sailing for Russia they had reached the South Shetlands. This expedition not only afforded valuable experience in navigation; it also yielded important scientific findings. Moreover, it furnished the basis for the Russian claim to discovery of the Antarctic Continent.

Probably no other Russian voyage quite equals either of these two in terms of discovery and distance. However, other exploratory expeditions were numerous. In 1806 the *Neva*, under Capt. Lt. L. A. Hagemeister had made the first Russian visit to Australia. Two voyages around the world were completed by Lieutenant Lazarev in the *Suvorov* (from 1814 to 1816 when he explored the coast of Alaska, among other accomplishments) and in the *Kreyser* (1822–25).

Lt. Otto von Kotzebue in the *Riurik* also made a voyage around the world (1815–18) in search of a northeast passage around Asia and also to gain knowledge of the North Pacific and the Arctic. He crossed through the Bering Strait and discovered many islands in the Arctic as well as numerous atolls in the Carolines. His explorations were rich in botanical, zoological, geographical, and oceanographic discovery.

Adm. Fedor Litke in the years after 1821 made several voyages during which he charted the coasts of Kamchatka and Siberia along the Bering Sea and attempted, unsuccessfully, to pass around northern Novaia Zemlia. On the voyage undertaken in 1826 in the *Seniavin*, Litke sailed around Cape Horn, north to Sitka, then south to the Marshalls and Carolines, where he discovered new islands. He then returned to the North Pacific and finally reached home via the Indian Ocean. He left excellent accounts of his journeys.

In 1805 Lt. G. Davydov in the *Yunona* and Lt. I. M. Khvostov in the *Avos*, both ships of the Russian-American Fur Company, established the first settlement of any importance on the island of Sakhalin. In 1819 Capt. Lt. G. Vasilev led an expedition with two sloops to explore the Arctic Ocean. Lt. Aleksandr von Wrangel, in the course of Siberian explorations, surveyed the northern coast between the Yana and Kolyma rivers and confirmed the separation of North America from Asia. Capt. (later Adm.) Vasily M. Golovnin made many voyages in the North Pacific; in the sloop of war *Diana* he charted the Kuriles and established the fact that Sakhalin was an island and not a peninsula—a discovery confirmed in 1848 by Capt. K. I. Nevelsky in the transport *Baikal*. Golovnin failed in his attempt to open Japan to trade but left excellent accounts of his explorations. During 1817–19 he also circumnavigated the globe. Between 1849 and 1855 Captain Nevelsky led several expeditions to Sakhalin and eastern Siberia preparatory to establishing posts at Petrovsk and Nikolaevsk. Lt. Petr F. Gavrilov in the *Konstantin* thoroughly explored the mouth of the Amur. M. F. Reynske in 1827 examined the Kola Gulf and western Lapland. Lieutenant Paktusov explored the eastern coast of Novaia Zemlia. Vice Adm. E. V. Putiatin followed closely on the heels of Commo. Matthew G. Perry, USN, in opening Japan; his work led to the conclusion of a commercial treaty in 1858. Other explorations resulting in discoveries in the Pacific and the Arctic involved Pansfidine, Klochkov, Schantz, Gaguemeister, Unkovsky, Moller, Khrushchev, Lulabrev, Dakturov, Khromchenko, Staniukovich, and other naval officers. Between 1803 and 1849 there were 36 round-the-world voyages by Russian expeditions.

Such were the Russian sea explorers. Originally unskilled, they attained a considerable measure of competence in their trade, added appreciably to the store of geographic and scientific knowledge possessed by their countrymen, and in many instances paved the way for the commercial and military penetration that followed. Astronomy, meteorology, geography, ethnography, oceanography are merely a few of the fields of study enriched by their efforts. So far as the Russian navy was concerned, the long voyages into unknown seas under varied conditions provided a top-notch education in both diplomacy and seamanship. Further, many of the explorers themselves later advanced to high positions whence they sought to modernize the navy and build up its cadres. Kruzhenstern was for 16 years director of the Naval Cadet School, into which he introduced many reforms. Litke, Golovnin, and Lysiansky all achieved success as scientific writers, and Litke also served as president of the Russian Academy of Science for the last 18 years of his life. Though personally loyal to the tsar, most of the explorers were also scholars and humanitarian reformers who urged more education for their crews, less brutal discipline, better treatment of natives, and more intelligent economic development of Siberia and Alaska.

The reformer is ever without honor in his own country. These men were hardly exceptions to the rule. M. A. Sergeev has concluded:

> They had to wage a constant and stubborn struggle against the ignorance and routine incompetencé of the high command. Their discoveries were distrusted, the value of their scientific research was depreciated, and the significance of their work was systematically underrated. The attitude of the ruling circles toward them was one of deep suspicion. At best, they were just tolerated. In their own naval circles they met very strong opposition. Their "undue" humane attitude towards their crews was generally condemned; stick-in-the-mud officers considered it "an undermining of the traditional discipline of the rod in the navy."[3]

Russian expansion meantime kept peace with Russian exploration. In 1811, by the Treaty of Gulistan, Persia was forced to cede the Persian Caucasus and five years later to give up Baku. In 1828 another small war with Persia was ended by the Treaty of Turkmanchai, under which Persia ceded territory to the Araks River and granted Russia the sole right to keep naval vessels on the Caspian. Thereafter the Russians established naval stations on Sara Island and, east of Engeli, at Ashurada on the Gulf of Astrabad. Ordinarily they kept few vessels in the Caspian, but in 1852 steamers were transported in sections from Sweden to St. Petersburg for river transport to the Caspian, where they were reassembled.

The campaigns in central Asia by which Russia steadily established suzerainty over various Asiatic peoples were fought principally on land. However, some use was made of river and lake fleets. In 1847 an Aral Sea Flotilla was established, and about the same time small fleets were created on several of the great rivers.

In the Far East, Russian expansion was in the hands of Gen. Nikolai Muravev, whose choice by Tsar Nicholas I proved to be an unusually brilliant one. Though many disliked Muravev and others considered him a visionary, he was nevertheless an explorer, pioneer, and statesman of the very first rank. In a long career he established a firm Russian hold on eastern Siberia, explored the coasts of the Sea of Okhotsk, opened Japan, brought in settlers, founded Khabarovsk and Petropavlovsk, created industries, and (as will be seen in chapter 7) defended the area from superior British and French forces with great ingenuity and success. By a combination of diplomacy and force he persuaded the Chinese to recognize, in the 1858 Treaty of Aigun, Russian suzerainty over both banks of the Amur and the coastal region north of what was to be the city of Vladivostok (founded 1860).

North America was another area of Russian interest. Here the Russian-American Fur Company operated virtually as a government in itself. The founding of Sitka in 1804 and Fort Ross in 1812 was followed by the establishment of eleven other settlements. Yet Russia did not thrive in the New World. Brutal exploitation of the natives led to repeated uprisings, and unrestrained hunting methods depleted the supply of the fur-bearing animals on which the colony depended. Further, Alaska suffered from being at the end of a very long supply line that could be maintained only with great difficulty.

An area of expansion in which the Black Sea Fleet aided the Russian army was the Caucasus, where constant minor wars and insurrections erupted as Russia extended her sway over hardy and independent mountaineers. For many years small vessels of the Black Sea Fleet provided land forces with seaborne transport and supply, as well as with occasional artillery support and reinforcement.

In expanding east and south the Russians met with very little opposition. The British were sensitive to any expansion in the direction of India but could do little about Russian moves in central Asia. Neither Japan nor China was in a position to oppose Russian expansion in the Far East. However, Alexander's unrealistic hope of consolidating an empire extending down the North American coast as far as Vancouver Island was discouraged by the Monroe Doctrine.

RUSSIAN SEA POWER IN WAR WITH TURKEY 1829–32

The principal area for the employment of Russian sea power during the expansion period was the Middle East, where the moribund Turkish Empire continued to pose many problems for the European powers. Here the first naval actions were occasioned by the Greek War of Independence, in which other powers took both senti-mental and practical interest. This war, which broke out in 1821, created a dilemma for Nicholas, who disapproved of all revolutions on principle but at the same time favored a chance to extend Russian interests. Other foreigners were more actively sympathetic (Lord Byron, Adm. Thomas Cochrane, and numerous other promi-nent western figures actively joined the Greek cause), and for purely sentimental reasons the European powers were inclined to favor the Greeks. Their sympathy was heightened by the tactics of the Turkish army, which uprooted olive trees—the only major agri-cultural food resource—and massacred thousands of men, older women, and children while saving young girls for Turkish harems. Fearing Russian motives, however, both Britain and France opposed any singlehanded Russian action against the Turks and for this reason sought to sustain the sultan.

The Greeks proved no match for the Turks on land, but being a maritime people, they established a navy. To command it they sum-moned Lord Cochrane, a man of unusual talent who had been dis-missed from the British navy and then gone on to become a hero in South America's (especially Chile's) struggle for independence. Because the revolutionary government could rarely pay its sailors they operated largely as pirates, plundering not only Turkish ships but those of neutrals as well. Nominally the Turkish navy was greatly superior, but the far greater aptitude of the Greeks for the sea made such calculations worthless. Meanwhile, the piratical habits of the Greek captains persuaded most maritime nations to station warships in the Aegean to guard their shipping.

In 1826 Russian pressure forced the sultan to sign the Treaty of Akkerman, by which he agreed to evacuate Moldavia and Walla-chia. But when Russia, England, and France all urged him to grant self-government to the Greeks also, he refused to yield further. Early in 1827 the three powers held a conference which resulted in a deci-sion on a joint "pacific blockade" of the Turkish army in Greece in order to force the sultan to grant autonomy.

Because of the sultan's weakness in naval power, no one of the three countries was obliged to detail a strong naval force to Turkish waters. On June 29, 1827, a Russian fleet of nine battleships, six frigates, and six corvettes under Adm. Dmitry Seniavin left Revel, spent a few days at Copenhagen, and then proceeded to Spithead on the southern coast of England, where it arrived August 7. Two weeks later there sailed under Rear Adm. Count Login P. Geyden a squadron comprised of the *Gangut* 84, *Azov* 74, *Yezekiil* 74, *Aleksandr Nevsky* 74, *Provorny* 44, *Konstantin* 44, *Kastor* 36, *Yelena* 36, and *Gremiashchy* 24. This fleet entered the Straits of Gibraltar and proceeded to the Aegean, making stops at Palermo and Messina en route. On October 13 the Russian squadron joined that of Adm. Sir Edward Codrington, the commander of a joint fleet. The British and Russian contingents proceeded to Navarino on October 14 and were joined there by the French two days later. The combined fleet comprised 11 battleships, eight frigates, and eight smaller craft—27 ships in all carrying 1,298 guns and manned by 17,500 men.

Inside the bay of Navarino lay a joint Turkish-Egyptian-Tunisian fleet. Accounts differ as to its strength, but it probably consisted of three battleships, 20 frigates, 32 corvettes, seven brigs, and five brulots or fireships, besides some miscellaneous smaller craft. Crews numbered about 22,000 and the guns are put by one authority at 2,224, but of these only about 1,150 were carried by ships in the line.[4] The general commander was Ibrahim, son of Mehemet Ali, ruler of Egypt, who had enlisted French officers to create a modern fleet. Ibrahim was in most respects able, but he knew little about maritime matters. Hence, although he strongly disliked a situation in which Egypt and Turkey were opposing the great powers he did not feel able to alter the situation.

The transition from "pacific blockade" to actual battle came about inevitably. A British frigate delivered a dispatch from Codrington charging the Turkish commander with devastation of the Morea in violation of an armistice. Simultaneously, French Adm. Count G. de Rigny addressed a letter to the French commissioned officers aboard the Egyptian ships warning them to leave the Egyptian service (most of them had already taken this step). When the letter from Codrington was not delivered—allegedly because no one knew the whereabouts of Ibrahim, who was in fact absent—the allied commanders took their ships inside the harbor at about 1:00 P.M., advancing in a double line with the French and British ships to starboard, the Russians to port. The Russian ships proceeded in the

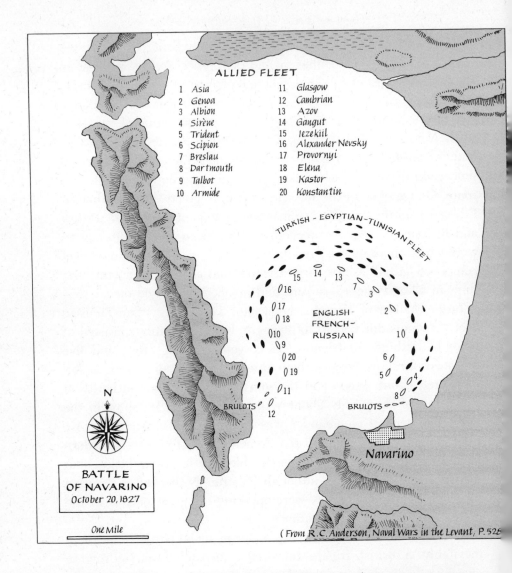

ALLIED FLEET

1	Asia	11	Glasgow
2	Genoa	12	Cambrian
3	Albion	13	Azov
4	Sirène	14	Gangut
5	Trident	15	Iezekiil
6	Scipion	16	Alexander Nevsky
7	Breslau	17	Provornyi
8	Dartmouth	18	Elena
9	Talbot	19	Kastor
10	Armide	20	Konstantin

TURKISH - EGYPTIAN - TUNISIAN FLEET

ENGLISH -
FRENCH -
RUSSIAN

BRULOTS

BRULOTS

Navarino

N

BATTLE
OF NAVARINO
October 20, 1827

One Mile

(From R.C. Anderson, Naval Wars in the Levant, P. 526)

following order: *Azov, Gangut, Yezekiil, Aleksandr Nevsky, Yelena,*
and *Kastor*. The allies found the Turkish-Egyptian fleet ranged in
three lines in crescent formation, with the brulots (fireships) on the
flanks ready to employ incendiaries.

At this point a boat approached from the shore with a message
ordering the allies to leave the harbor. Admiral Codrington replied
that if the enemy ships fired they would be destroyed.

Events proved him prophetic. The Turks opened fire on the
French *Sirène*, and the action quickly became general. Admiral
Codrington had planned that the French should attack the first

Egyptian ships, on the assumption that the French officers on board would refuse to fire on their own flag whereas they might be entirely willing to fight the Russians or British. The British battleships in turn were to attack the next three Turkish vessels. Then the Russians would turn their guns on the eight or nine succeeding enemy ships. The last allied ships, three British frigates and the French *Armide*, were to fire on the remaining enemy vessels and in addition deal with the brulots at both ends of the Turkish line. Of the national contingents, the Russians were the last to come into action and were given the largest group of enemy ships to fight.

Because the Turkish-Egyptian fleet was outmatched enormously in quality of men and materiel and in leadership, there was little doubt of the outcome, but at the beginning of the engagement a few allied ships found themselves overmatched. The *Azov*, for example, was at one time opposed to five enemy ships and lost 91 men. This condition did not last, however. The *Azov* was first given support by the French *Breslau* and then by the other Russian ships. The three other Russian battleships, though temporarily delayed in finding their way in the smoke of battle, entered the fray and opposed the five enemy frigates. The *Gangut* sank one Turkish frigate and a fireship. The *Azov* sank two large frigates and a corvette and wrecked a 60-gun ship which ran aground. A Turkish frigate fighting the *Nevsky* ran up a white flag and then exploded. A second enemy frigate also blew up. The Russian *Konstantin*, arriving late, supported the British *Talbot* and the *Kastor*. Later the *Azov* aided the British *Asia* while the *Konstantin* took in tow a British brig which had lost all anchors.

By 4:00 P.M. signs of the allied victory were clear. The first-line Turkish ships were destroyed, and the second- and third-line ships were on fire or had run ashore. Firing continued for several hours, but by 6:00 P.M. the enemy fleet had ceased to exist and even the shore batteries were no longer firing. Many of the Turkish ships, as they became disabled, had been destroyed by their own crews. A last threat to the Russians came at midnight, when a fireship drifted toward the *Azov* and *Gangut*. The latter ship was endangered but escaped.

Only one Turkish frigate and 14 or 15 of the smaller vessels escaped. Turkish losses of manpower are not known but probably numbered about 7,000 dead and wounded. Allied casualties amounted to 182 killed and 789 wounded, of which Russian losses numbered 59 and 139 respectively. No allied ships were sunk, though the *Azov* was badly damaged—with 153 holes in the hull and masts so weakened they would barely support sails. Relations between Count Geyden and his two colleagues had been excellent, and Codrington in particular was loud in his praise of the Russian leader. Count Geyden was promoted to the rank of vice admiral, and in remembrance of the *Azov* Tsar Nicholas decreed that the Black Sea Fleet should always contain a ship named *Pamiat Azova*.

After Navarino there was a noticeable change in allied policy. The British hope had been to preserve the balance of power, not to destroy the Turkish navy or to secure Greek independence. As a result of the clear naval victory, Codrington for the rest of his life found himself defending his actions. Moreover, the British and French were becoming less eager to continue the war while the tsar's enthusiasm was growing. By December 1828 Nicholas had succeeded in involving his two allies to the extent that they withdrew their ambassadors from Constantinople, at which time he announced an intention of campaigning by land the following spring.

With a state of formal war existing, Geyden's position as squadron leader in the Mediterranean became somewhat anomalous. Though his country was at war, he felt obliged to continue cooperating with two allies who were not at war and were therefore less interested in defeating the Turks. For a time all three powers participated in a blockade of Turkish ports in the Morea, and by a combination of force and diplomacy succeeded in getting the sultan's ally, Mehemet Ali, to withdraw the troops in this area, thus virtually assuring Greek independence. This accomplished, the British and French squadrons withdrew.

But the Russo-Turkish war continued; and in late September and October 1829 a second Russian squadron under Rear Adm. P. Rickard arrived to reinforce Count Geyden. This squadron included three 74's *Fershampenuoz*, *Kniaz Vladimir*, and *Konstantin;* the *Emanuil* 64; and four 50-gun frigates, *Olga*, *Aleksandra*, *Mariia*, and *Kniazinia Lovich.*

The Russian Mediterranean Fleet for most of the war numbered eight battleships, seven frigates, and about 20 small craft. In the Black Sea were 11 battleships, eight frigates, and 12 smaller vessels. In between these forces the Turks, with eight battleships, two frigates, and eight smaller vessels based on Constantinople, were far weaker than usual. The Russians in the Aegean, operating from Tenedos, established a blockade of the Dardanelles. In one of the few naval actions there, the Russian frigate *Kastor* captured the Egyptian brig *Candia* and the corvette *Navarin* after a bloody fight.

The first action of the war in the Black Sea occurred on May 18, 1828, when the Russian army was supported in an attack on Anapa by Vice Adm. Aleksei Greig, son of the British admiral who served Catherine II, with his *Panteleimon* 80; the 74's *Ioann Zlatoust*, *Pimen, Nord-Adler*, and *Parmen*; the 44-gun frigates *Flora, Yevstafy, Shtandart, Pospeshny;* two bombs; and some smaller craft. On July 5, after more than a month of bombardment, the port surrendered to the Russian army. Then on August 7, following a six-week lull, a land assault was begun on Varna. Greig by this time had been reinforced by two 110's (*Imperator Frantz* and *Parizh*), the 84-gun *Imperatritsa Mariia*, and the frigate *Rafail*. The siege proceeded uneventfully with usually no more than one battleship firing at a time until October 11, when the Turkish garrison surrendered.

The Russian gunboat flotillas saw action on the Danube. On June 9, 1828, 16 Russian gunboats passed the fort of Brăila and attacked 23 Turkish gunboats, capturing twelve and destroying two. Between August and November, 50 gunboats aided the army in the siege of Silistria; then winter weather brought action to a temporary halt. In mid-May of the next year the siege was resumed with a somewhat smaller gunboat flotilla supporting, and the city surrendered on July 2, 1829.

Early in 1829 the Black Sea Fleet was again active. On February 27 a squadron led by Rear Adm. Nikolai P. Kumani and comprising the *Imperatritsa Mariia* 84, *Panteleimon* 80, *Parmen* 74, *Rafail* 44, *Yevstafy* 44, and three gunboats bombarded the coastal town of Sozopol, 50 miles south of Varna on the southern coast of Bulgaria. The next day the Turkish garrison surrendered. On March 23 much the same squadron bombarded Inobolu. This time the attack failed since the Russians, fighting under adverse weather conditions, found themselves under attack by Turkish shore batteries.

A lull of two months followed. In May the entire Black Sea Fleet of nine battleships, five frigates, and 13 smaller craft made an appearance off Sizoboli. On May 16 a strong detachment comprising three 74's, two frigates, and a brig attacked Pendraklia on the Anatolian coast. Under cover of bombardment, a landing party set fire to a 50-gun Turkish ship. The flames spread and burned other shipping. The next day the Russians destroyed a 26-gun corvette on the building ways.

Early in June 1829 the Turkish fleet (six battleships, two frigates, five corvettes, and two brigs) made its only appearance in force of the entire war. Approaching off the Anatolian coast it captured the *Rafail* 44, which surrendered without fighting.[5] On June 6 three other Russian ships, the frigate *Shtandart* 44 and the brigs *Osfer* and *Merkury* 18, fell in with the Turks but retreated independently. This retreat gave rise to one of the most famous actions in Russian naval history when two Turkish battleships—one a 110 and the other a 74—overtook the tiny *Merkury* under Lt. A. I. Kazarsky. The brig refused to surrender: all officers were determined to resist and agreed that if necessary the last survivor should blow up the ship. In a four-hour action the *Merkury* damaged the rigging of her two huge antagonists while sustaining only 22 hits in the hull and seven casualties. When the wind freshened, she escaped. Greatly pleased, Nicholas ordered that thenceforth one ship of the Black Sea Fleet would always bear the name *Pamiat Merkuriia.*

During July and August detachments of the Russian fleet were active at several points in support of the army. On July 21 three battleships and two bombs bombarded Mesambria, which surrendered two days later, as did Inebolu. Following a bombardment on August 19, Iniada was taken. Cape Midia, on the Black Sea coast of Rumania, fell ten days later.

By August 1829 a vigorous and successful summer campaign had carried the Russian armies to Adrianople. These gains occasioned anxiety among the French and British, who felt that the time had come to contain Russian ambition. Accordingly, they brought enough pressure to induce Nicholas to accept a peace less favorable than the course of the war justified. By the September 14, 1829, Treaty of Adrianople, Turkey ceded to Russia the frontier towns of Anapa and Poti on the northeast shore of the Black Sea and granted near independence to the Danubian Principalities (Rumania and Bulgaria).

The obvious lack of strength which Turkey had displayed against the Russians invited aggression from another quarter. Mehemet Ali, viceroy of Egypt and nominally tributary to the sultan, had become both independent and extremely powerful. Able and unscrupulous, he was not the man to overlook another nation's weakness. In November 1831 he sent the Egyptian army under Ibrahim into Syria, where its defeat of the sultan's troops was crushing.

In his extremity the sultan then called for aid from his hereditary enemy Russia. Nothing loath to fish in troubled waters, the tsar promptly dispatched Rear Admiral Lazarev with four 84-gun battleships (*Pamiat Yevstafiia, Chesma, Anapa,* and *Imperatritsa Yekaterina II*), three 60-gun frigates (*Yerevan, Arkhipelag,* and *Voin*), a corvette, and a brig. Lazarev's fleet arrived at Constantinople on March 3. Meanwhile the British and French had managed by strenuous diplomatic efforts to patch up a peace between the two contending powers which they hoped would forestall further Russian intervention: Turkey gained peace, but at the cost of ceding Syria, Damascus, Aleppo, and Adana to Egypt.

The agreement came too late to serve its intended purpose, since before matters could be settled two additional Russian squadrons arrived. The first, under Rear Admiral Kumani, appeared on April 5 and consisted of the *Imperatritsa Mariia* 84, *Adrianopol* 84, *Parmen* 74, *Tenedos* 60, four transports loaded with 5,000 troops, and a steamer. On April 23, Rear Adm. Aleksandr Stozhevsky arrived with a squadron which comprised the *Parizh* 110, *Pimen* 74, *Ioann Zlatoust* 74, two bombs, and a transport, and carried nearly 5,000 troops. The Russians used these forces as a lever, to induce the sultan to conclude an alliance on terms highly advantageous to themselves, continuing a prohibition on the use of the Turkish Straits by all foreign (except Russian) men of war.

Seven years later Turkey and Egypt were again fighting, but that time the other powers imposed a settlement which included a prohibition on the navigation of the straits by any warship in time of peace. The Middle East then settled down to an uneasy peace.

CHAPTER 8

The Crimean War and Its Lessons

(1853-77)

ORIGINS OF THE WAR

THE 1839 RESTORATION of peace in the Middle East had no possibility of permanence as long as the sultan demonstrated neither the ability to manage his own affairs nor the strength to repel outside interference. Tsar Nicholas proved as determined as any of his predecessors to acquire the Turkish Straits and Constantinople. In 1853 a small dispute over the guardianship of the holy places in Jerusalem furnished an excuse for war when the sultan, on British advice, refused a Russian demand that the Greek Church in Turkey be placed under Russian protection. In late July 1853 Nicholas ordered his troops into the Danubian Principalities, which he proposed to occupy until such time as the Turks accepted his demands.

In taking this high-handed action Nicholas assumed that the principal European powers would be sympathetic to his cause or at any rate that none of them, with the possible exception of Great Britain, would interfere actively before he was able to achieve his aims. It was tantamount to an assumption that he would be left undisturbed to upset the balance of power. He was speedily proven incorrect. The Turks declared war on Russia on October 4, 1853, while Britain and France, acting in concert for almost the first time in two centuries, moved large fleets to the vicinity of Constantinople. Russia had a certain amount of sympathetic support from Prussia and Austria, but it was passive in nature and did not deter the other two great powers from taking action.[1]

Had the French and British failed to intervene there could have been no doubt as to the outcome of a Russo-Turkish war: the Russians were overwhelmingly stronger both on sea and land. In 1853 the Turks had about a dozen battleships, a number of smaller vessels, and a few steamers, and their shore establishment was in poor condition. The Russians had about 130 ships carrying 2,600 guns and manned by 1,450 officers and 33,000 men; manning the coast defenses were an additional 20,000 marines. Russian naval administration was excellent. The great Lazarev had left two worthy pupils when he died—Vice Adm. Pavel S. Nakhimov, commander of the Black Sea Fleet, and Vice Adm. Vladimir Kornilov, commandant of the Naval Staff. These men directed the well-prepared Black Sea Fleet. As early as December 10, 1852, Nicholas had ordered his naval commanders in the area to seize the Bosphorus in the event of war, but this plan was later abandoned on the advice of Prince Menshikov, who advocated instead an army advance through the Balkans.

The war at sea opened in November 1853 with a series of sharp skirmishes between steamers, a most significant development since it presaged the end of the sailing fleets. On November 16 the Russian steamer *Bessarabiia* captured the Turkish steamer *Medzhire Tadzhiret*. The next day the steam frigate *Vladimir II*, under Capt. Grigory Butakov, took the Egyptian steamer *Pervaz Bahri* 10 following a brisk action in which the ships circled each other as in the later *Alabama-Kearsarge* duel. Two days later a Russian squadron of four steamers, two corvettes, and two frigates bombarded the Turkish forts near Batum but were repulsed with losses. On November 20 the *Flora* 44 fought an indecisive night engagement with three Turkish steamers that carried 62 guns in all.

FROM SINOPE TO THE CRIMEAN WAR

The November skirmishes proved to be the prelude to a major engagement. Land fighting in the Caucasus had started in October, with the Russians supporting their forces by sea. The Sublime

Porte also decided to send supplies by sea to Turkish troops in Asia Minor. He entrusted the detail to Vice Adm. Osman Pasha, whose sailing fleet consisted mainly of frigates (seven in all, plus three corvettes and small craft). The Turkish squadron put to sea in November and soon thereafter anchored off Sinope, the best harbor on the south coast of the Black Sea, some 350 miles from Constantinople. In this position the force was in a situation of maximum danger. It was beyond any support from the British and French, whose objectives at this time involved no more than the defense of Constantinople from seaward attack; and the Russian admirals had been specifically directed to prevent the shipment of supplies to the Turkish Caucasus forces.

The Russians at this point showed great alertness. Having learned from prisoners that the Turks were at Sinope, Admiral Nakhimov blockaded the port with a small task force of only three ships, meantime requesting reinforcements from Sevastopol. Had the Turks chosen to make an early departure they would have been opposed by relatively weak Russian forces. Instead of leaving, however, they anchored their ships under the cover of nine shore batteries and disembarked guns for further protection from the landward sides of their ships. This delay gave the Russians ample time to build up an overpowering force. Nakhimov then demanded that the Turkish fleet surrender. When he was answered by a broadside, the Russians swiftly prepared for battle.

The Battle of Sinope was in no respect an even contest. There is some uncertainty as to the armaments of the Turkish ships, but there is no doubt of a decisive Russian superiority in artillery—perhaps as great as two to one. Further, 76 of the Russian guns fired shells as compared to only two for the Turks, and the Russian guns had a greater range. The unmeasurable factors of training, morale, and leadership also favored the Russians. Osman Pasha, the Turkish admiral, was merely a brave man. Nakhimov, his Russian counterpart, was a brilliant and dedicated officer who had received combat experience under both Lazarev and Bellingshausen, and who had well-trained captains and crews serving under him. Though a severe disciplinarian, he cared for his men as if they were his children, and in return was well liked by them. Since Turkish inactivity had given him a choice of both time and method of attack, he elected

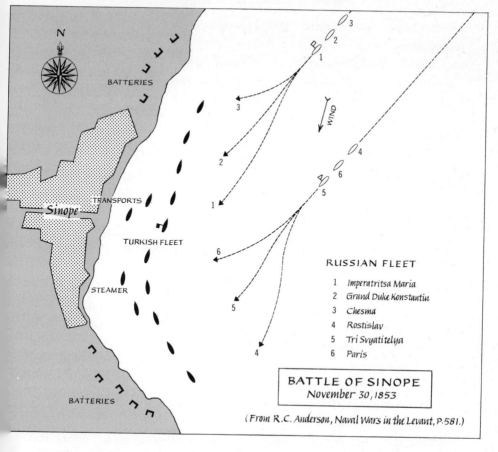

BATTLE OF SINOPE
November 30, 1853

RUSSIAN FLEET

1 *Imperatritsa Maria*
2 *Grand Duke Konstantin*
3 *Chesma*
4 *Rostislav*
5 *Tri Svyatitelya*
6 *Paris*

(From R.C. Anderson, Naval Wars in the Levant, p. 581.)

to strike at about 12:30 P.M. on November 30, in two columns with three battleships heading each column and lesser vessels in the rear. One column was led by his flagship, *Imperatritsa Mariia*, together with the *Chesma* and *Rostislav* (all 84's), and the other by the *Parizh*, flagship of Rear Admiral Novosilsky, followed by the *Veliky Kniaz Konstantin* and the *Tri Sviatitelia* (all 120's).

The Russians entered the harbor at good speed, aided by a stiff breeze. They found the seven Turkish frigates drawn up in a semicircle with strong shore batteries at each end of the line. A second line consisted of two small steamers and two transports. The Turkish flagship *Avni Illah* opened fire and was joined by the other Turkish ships, all aiming high in the hope of dismasting the attackers. The Russians waited until they were at close range before replying with a murderous bombardment. In half an hour the *Illah* cut her moorings to escape the cannonade of the *Mariia*, which then turned her fire against and speedily destroyed the *Fazl Illah* (ex-*Rafail*).

The Turks fought with their usual bravery but with complete futility; in a little more than two hours their fleet had ceased to exist. The only escapee was the steamer *Taif* which, ably commanded by an English officer, outran two frigates and the Russian steamers *Odessa, Krym,* and *Khersones* (reinforcements under Vice Adm. Vladimir Kornilov which arrived just as the battle ended). The Turkish admiral, mortally wounded, was abandoned by his men and captured by the Russians. Turkish losses totaled about 3,000 men, or some 75 percent of all engaged. The Russians lost no ships but incurred casualties totaling 37 killed and 229 wounded. The *Tri Sviatitelia* was hard hit in masts and rigging, mainly by fire from the shore batteries, but survived.

The British referred to Sinope as a "butchery" and a "massacre." That judgment seems undeservedly harsh, since the conflict took place in circumstances of openly declared war. The Russians had simply fought well, the Turks poorly. Further, the Russian superiority, while certainly overwhelming, was hardly greater than the Turks had enjoyed in numerous past battles.

The one-sided Battle of Sinope, one of the most important naval battles in Russian history, proved to be the last fleet victory achieved by the Russian navy. Commonly referred to as one of the last large fleet actions of the sailing-ship era, it was also one of the first which involved steam vessels and shell-firing guns, and as such it marked the beginning of modern sea power in action.

Its political significance was equally great, for it was the Battle of Sinope that made inevitable the Crimean War. As soon as the *Taif* carried news of the disaster back to Constantinople, the Turks sought British protection. On January 3, 1854, the French and British fleets entered the Black Sea to convoy to the eastern Black Sea Turkish steamers loaded with troops and supplies for the Ottoman garrisons. The allied commanders had been ordered to employ force if hostile Russian ships were encountered. Following this undertaking the allied fleets returned to the Bosphorus.

Meanwhile, the Russian armies on the Danube had been making steady progress. On February 27 the British and French demanded on pain of war that the Russians evacuate their conquests. When the demand was refused, the allies ordered their fleets to Varna on the Bulgarian coast. On March 27–28 they declared war. Austria mobilized an army of 150,000 men, and with this threat of a land attack from the rear the tsar decided to abandon his land campaign in the Balkans.

Russia's position as a naval power was now completely reversed. Not only were both the French and the British fleets far stronger than the Russian; they were also more modern and included a greater proportion of steam vessels. Further, they were supported by greatly superior industrial economies. While the Russians had scarcely been affected by the Industrial Revolution, both Great Britain and France were greatly advanced as a result of its influence. There was therefore a wide quantitative and qualitative gap between the navies of the belligerents. In the Black Sea the Russians had only two steam corvettes to supplement a sailing navy that was itself impressive only on paper. The apparent strength of its 21 battleships, seven frigates, 25 corvettes, and various brigs and lesser vessels was subject to heavy discount because, as has been previously noted, most of the ships were fir-built and therefore unseaworthy. Stationed in the Baltic were 25 Russian ships of the line, 18 frigates, 40 corvettes, and smaller vessels. The best ship in this fleet was the American-built steam frigate *Kamchatka*. Also in the Baltic were 23 steam corvettes, 20 of which were propelled by paddle wheels.[2] Morale was probably low, for the Russian sailors were too preoccupied with their immediate grievances to be impressed by the deeds of former heroes like Admiral Ushakov and General Suvorov.

The Russians, nevertheless, did hold certain advantages. They were fighting in their own territory, and their overall leadership was at least as good as that of the allies. Admiral Greig was now suspect because of his British background, but both Kornilov and Nakhimov in the Black Sea were rightly considered first-class leaders. Even from a technical standpoint the Russians could claim certain advantages. They had pioneered in developing both shell-firing artillery and mines, experiments for the latter having been conducted under the direction of Moritz Jacobi, a German physicist, and Emanuel Nobel (father of the dynamite king), a Swedish engineer who had established his factory in Russia ten years earlier.[3] Though the mines were primitive by modern standards and were not always correctly planted (nervous sailors sometimes failed to remove the safety clip which controlled their activation), they nevertheless constituted a new threat. The Russians also lay claim to having developed, in 1853, the first minelayer.

From the command standpoint the Russians may have had another advantage. Most of the British officers were in their late sixties or seventies, survivors of the Napoleonic Wars. Many commanders and lieutenants had served a quarter of a century in grade. The French leaders on the whole were younger.

However, British and French materiel was far superior. The French flagship *Napoleon* 92, built by Dupuy de Lome, had engines of 500 horsepower which could propel her at 11 knots against a stiff wind and at 14 knots under ordinary conditions. She was nearly as fast when using only sails. The British ships carried shrapnel shells and Congreve rockets. Far more ships in both fleets were large steamers than in the case of the Russians.

Allied strategy in the Crimean War was never very clearly developed. Originally the allied objective was the removal of Russian armies from the Balkans. Later, attacks were extended to counter the Russians in the White Sea, Pacific, Baltic, and of course the Black Sea, which area ultimately became the center of the main allied effort. Here allied naval superiority was employed to transport the expeditionary force that was to besiege Sevastopol, the main Russian naval base, by both sea and land. All other allied operations became strictly subordinate to the attempt to capture the base and to destroy the Black Sea Fleet.

From the standpoint of early Russian strategy, general preparedness suffered seriously from the limitations of Prince Aleksandr Sergeevich Menshikov, the tsar's minister of naval affairs. While shortly before the war he had been replaced by the Grand Duke Konstantin, an able and highly progressive student of naval affairs then in his twenties, the change was to prove too little and too late. Conversion of the Russian navy to steam, and the improvement in materiel and port organization so urgently needed could not be accomplished overnight. Moreover, the removal of Menshikov only meant a kick upstairs: he was assigned command in the important Black Sea area. With two exceedingly able naval officers directly under him he should still have succeeded. Instead, being land-minded and having no conception of the possible services and values of an active fleet, he vetoed virtually all suggestions made by Nakhimov and Kornilov, who were eager to measure their abilities against the allies. An inactive policy was therefore decreed for the fleet, which was ordered to remain in port under the protection of shore batteries.

THE WAR IN THE BLACK SEA

The months that passed between the declarations of war and the first large-scale offensive gestures by the allies gave the Russians time to make advance preparations. In April the allies conducted a halfhearted and none-too-successful bombardment of Odessa. Two months later squadrons of allied warships indicated the probable direction of attack by appearing before Sevastopol. During the same period the Russian steam frigate *Vladimir* successfully raided the Turkish coast, capturing two prizes and sinking others. In August the Black Sea Fleet moved troops and supplies to the Caucasus front to oppose the Turks. Unfortunately, however, the Russians did not make full use of their available time, nor did Prince Menshikov attempt to strengthen Sevastopol's defenses.

On September 7 the allied campaign finally got under way as the fleets left Varna for Sevastopol. The British contingent comprised 150 ships sailing to five columns of 30 ships each. The naval escort, commanded by Adm. Sir Edmund Lyons in the *Agamemnon*, listed ten battleships, one screw steamer, and two 50-gun frigates. The French fleet comprised 15 battleships and about 25 steamers. The Turks had eight battleships and three steamers. Since the French and the Turks lacked transports, they carried their troops aboard the warships.

Despite the fact that the allied force was superior to the Black Sea Fleet, a Russian attack on the transports and on the crowded French and Turkish warships might have done vast damage, a possibility that has been acknowledged by several British writers. Acting individually the Russian ships might also have had considerable success in raiding allied lines of communication. Admiral Kornilov, who favored an aggressive role, had in fact prepared such an attack, but fortunately for the allies Menshikov refused Kornilov permission to carry it out.

The allies, without immediate opposition, were able to make a landing of more than 62,000 men at Yevpatoriia, about 30 miles south of Sevastopol, completing disembarkation on September 16 (a request by Nakhimov for orders to attack the landing was also refused by Menshikov). As they moved inland, the allies encountered and defeated a small Russian army under Menshikov on the banks of the Alma. At this point, however, with everything in their favor, the allied commanders made a thoroughly unwise decision. Instead of proceeding to attack the port of Sevastopol from the almost undefended northern side, where the Russian line of communications lay, they elected to attack the city from the seaward side to the south, where Russian fortifications were considered invulnerable. This not only brought their armies into very barren country but materially lengthened the time and effort of the siege. Meanwhile, on October 25 the Russians were defeated at the well-known Battle of Balaklava, and on November 5 at Inkerman the allies beat off a Russian attack, winning a third victory on land. Even before the last-named battle took place the siege of Sevastopol was under way.

Prince Menshikov had left the defense of the port city to reserve battalions numbering at their greatest strength about 49,000 men, about half of them sailors. To prevent a direct naval attack he ordered the sinking of seven warships at the narrow entrance of the harbor, after first removing their guns to add to the shore defenses. When Kornilov protested the weakening of fleet power by these actions, he was told bluntly to comply or resign. With Menshikov commanding the army in the field, the defense of Sevastopol fell mainly to the personnel of the Black Sea Fleet, with Kornilov in command. In actual operations he commanded the forces on the north side of the city and Nakhimov the remainder of the fleet and the defenses on the south side.

The fiery Kornilov had announced when he took command: "We shall fight to the end. . . . There is nowhere to retreat. . . . Behind us is the sea. . . . Comrades, if I should sound a retreat do not obey, for a villain will be he who does not shoot me."[4] He was as good as his

River warship of about 1151 of the general type used by the
Varangians.

Peter I (Peter the Great).

БОТИКЪ

„ДѢДУШКА РУССКАГО ФЛОТА".

Design plan of the *Botik*, the "grandfather of the Russian navy." At the stern is Peter the Great's naval jack.

General Adm. Fedor Apraksin.

Building warships early in the eighteenth century.

Catherine II (Catherine the Great).

Adm. Aleksei S. Greig, one of three generations of the Greig family (of British origin) to become admirals of the Russian navy.

Adm. Grigory I. Spiridov.

A Russian artist's concept of the Battle of Chesma, probably Russia's single greatest naval victory, which has long been a contributor to the Russian naval tradition.

Adm. Fedor Ushakov, one of the greatest naval heroes Imperial Russia produced, was easily the most successful commander during Catherine's second Turkish war. He was the "opposite number" of Britain's Admiral Lord Nelson.

Adm. Dmitry N. Seniavin. A "late bloomer," Seniavin proved to be one of the two most successful admirals Russia produced during the Napoleonic wars.

Adm. Mikhail P. Lazarev.

Adm. A. J. von Kruzhenstern, one of the leading Russian explorers of the early nineteenth century.

Adm. Fabian von Bellingshausen, leading naval explorer.

The heroic battle of the *Merkury* against two Turkish battleships, 1829.

Adm. Count L. P. Geyden, the Russian commander at Navarino.

Adm. G. I. Butakov.

Grand Duke Konstantin.

Adm. Pavel S. Nakhimov.

The *Petr Veliky*, Russia's first large ironclad.

A very early Russian submarine prototype.

Russian torpedo boats attacking a Turkish warship in one of the first flotilla attacks in history.

The corvette *Vitiaz* at Nagasaki.

The *Yermak*, the world's first icebreaker.

The *Novgorod* and *Admiral Popov*, circular ironclads, were possibly the most remarkable ships ever built.

Vice Adm. Stefan O. Makarov, entist, inventor, writer, Arctic plorer, tactical innovator, leader. One of the most versa admirals in history.

Mutiny on the *Potemkin*.

The 22,500-ton *Imperatritsa Mariia* (1915), a top-
notch battleship in her day, equipped with the
longest-range main battery guns afloat.

Adm. Ivan Konstantinovich Grigorovich.

Adm. N. O. von Essen, the ablest Russian
naval leader of World War I.

word. At no time did he sound a retreat; indeed he scarcely had the chance. He was severely wounded during the first bombardment of the allied fleet on October 17, and three days later he was dead. Nakhimov then moved into supreme command. He had two capable assistants in Rear Adm. V. I. Istomin and a military engineer, Col. Count Edward Todtleben, who erected a series of virtually impregnable earthworks against which allied bombardments made little impression.

On the south side of Sevastopol were Quariantin Fort with 60 cannon; Fort Alexander, 90; Artillery Fort and Fort Nicholas, 96; and Fort Paul, 86. On the north side were Battery No. 4 with 35 guns; Battery Michael, 90; Fort Konstantin, 110; Telegraph Battery, 20; and Volokhov Battery, 40. Also, although the Russians found their wooden sailing ships useless, some ten small shallow-draft steamers proved very useful in bombarding allied camps and in aiding Russian land forces by conducting scouting forays and furnishing gunfire support. Since the allies had failed at the outset to sever the Russian supply lines into Sevastopol, it is not hard to understand why they found the siege unusually difficult or why for six months they realized no appreciable gains. They were also plagued with heavy losses from disease, but were able to bring in enough reinforcements to raise their ground strength to 117,000.

On March 17, 1855, the allied fleets renewed their bombardment of the forts, inflicting some damage but accepting punishment in return. Nakhimov ordered additional ships to be sunk in the harbor in the hope of preventing allied warships from entering. April 9 marked the opening of a heavy ten-day bombardment which killed many defenders (including Admiral Istomin, who was decapitated by a cannonball). At length the tsar, nettled by continued bad news from the south, replaced Count Menshikov with Count A. M. Gorchakov who, however, did not and perhaps could not alter Russian strategy. In June approximately 40,000 additional allied troops were landed. By this time the defenders were suffering severely, for allied operations in the Sea of Azov and on the Kerch Peninsula had finally partially severed the lines of supply. Another bombardment June 7–12 was followed by an allied land assault. When the land attack failed, the bombardment was resumed. On June 27 Nakhimov fell wounded. He died the following day. To indicate their respect for him as a military leader, the British and French withheld their fire during his funeral.

There followed a period of relative quiet, which lasted for about a month; then bombardments accompanied by assaults were resumed. On September 8 French troops successfully stormed the Malakhov, a hill overlooking the Russian position. When attempts to dislodge them failed, the Russians abandoned the southern sector of Sevastopol and moved north after setting fires in the city that burned for two days and two nights. The allies entered on September 11. The Russian garrisons moved north and joined the army of General Gorchakov.

The year-long siege of Sevastopol occupies a unique place in Russian naval tradition. The deaths of three admirals while directing its defense, each a born leader of men and a disciple of Lazarev and each a progressive who had sought to improve conditions within the navy, appealed to the Russian mind. The remains of all three were ultimately interred side by side with the body of Lazarev in the Cathedral of Saint Vladimir in Sevastopol, which was renamed "The Cathedral of the Four Admirals."[5]

With the fall of Sevastopol the Russian Black Sea Fleet ceased to exist except for some small steamers at Odessa. In accord with military orders all other vessels had been sunk or burned. The principal losses to the fleet had been sustained on three occasions: (1) early in the siege seven warships were sunk to block the narrow mouth of the harbor of Sevastopol; (2) 14 Russian warships were destroyed or burned in the Sea of Azov when a successful allied expedition cut Russian supply lines via the Straits of Kerch; (3) the remainder of the vessels in Sevastopol were sunk on September 12 after the French succeeded in taking the Malakhov. The total Russian loss at Sevastopol, according to British sources, was 14 sailing battleships, four sailing frigates, five corvettes and brigs, 82 miscellaneous, and five steam vessels.[6]

During and immediately after the siege of Sevastopol certain auxiliary operations took place which deserve some mention. The old fortress of Kinburn on October 17, 1855, fell to a naval bombardment which featured the 1,600-ton French armored floating batteries *Tonnante*, *Lave*, and *Devastation*, the first ironclads used in sea warfare. These ships had been ordered, constructed, and moved into action in a little over a year, a remarkable achievement. Of 1,400 tons displacement, they measured 55 meters in length by 28 in width and 13 in depth and carried armor 35 centimeters thick. They sailed low in the water and carried 18 50-pound guns in broadside. In the Kinburn fight *Lave* was hit 64 times and *Tonnante* 70 times without serious injury. Casualties were two killed and 22 wounded for the French, and 45 and 130 for the Russians.

Meanwhile Russian seaborne trade was badly interrupted though not completely stopped, and many captures of small coastal vessels were made. In the Sea of Azov 14 British and four French warships were able to destroy 14 Russian warships, 50 merchant ships, 340 cannon, and vast stores of food, munitions, and weapons, and to bombard Kerch, Taganrog, Taman, and Mariupol. Though the Russians had attempted to block access with 53 sunken ships, booms, and more than 100 mines, the allies succeeded in passing these obstructions without loss. At the same time they gave support to the Turkish armies fighting the Russians at the eastern end of the Black Sea.

THE WAR IN THE BALTIC

Allied naval forces sent into the Baltic were almost as powerful as those assigned to the Black Sea—far too strong for the Russian Baltic Fleet to engage with any hope of success. As a consequence the Russians kept their principal warships in port behind strong defenses, laid minefields, and confined their naval operations largely to shallow-draft gunboats which operated in coastal waters where the British and French, who had deep-draft ships and moreover lacked reliable maps, dared not venture. Russian Baltic forces, though theoretically directed by the Grand Duke Konstantin, were in fact led by Tsar Nicholas, who personally decided all key matters and often without recourse to any intermediary.

During 1854 Great Britain's Adm. Sir Charles Napier's Baltic fleet consisted of nine screw and six sailing battleships, four screw frigates, and some nine paddlewheel small craft; French Rear Adm. Alexandre Ferdinand Parseval-Deschenes commanded eight sailing battleships, six sailing frigates, and three steamers. These fleets at first accomplished nothing. Admiral Napier was too old (sixty-eight years) and too timid to be an effective commander and rightly did not enjoy the confidence of the British admiralty. Further, the large and cumbersome British and French ships were not fitted to sail in shallow waters. The main allied achievement of an almost totally barren year was the capture on August 16 of Bomarsund, principal fortress in the Åland Islands. Though Russia had taken these islands from Sweden in 1809, the Swedes now refused to accept them from the allies as a gift, possibly because of the probable difficulty of holding them later in the face of greater Russian strength. Other allied efforts at sea amounted to no more than a few landings and the capture of a number of Russian commercial vessels. Efforts at blockade were almost totally ineffective. On land the Russians carried on a brisk trade with Prussia, while at sea small light-draft craft were able to continue an active coastal trade that the enemy blockade was never able to intercept, much less stop. When the British and French fleets left the Baltic before the winter freeze, it was with a general feeling of dissatisfaction over their performance.

The 1855 fighting season opened with two new commanders, Rear Adm. Richard S. Dundas for the British and Rear Admiral Penaud for the French. This time the British admiralty had ordered all sailing vessels left at home, did not insist on conducting every operation in close (and difficult to achieve) coordination with the French, and supplied the British Baltic Fleet with many and varied small craft capable of operating in narrow waters.

Though the allies were better equipped to carry on a campaign than they had been during the preceding year, their achievements were still far from impressive. The French were relatively inactive, while the British, despite the fact that they made an earlier start than in 1854, spent their energies in small coastal landings of little strategic importance. Though the majority of these resulted in some injury to the Russians, there were several instances in which landing parties were roughly handled by Russian troops ashore. British ships reconnoitered Kronstadt, but their commanders decided it was too strong to be attacked.

Their only operation of more than minor importance was a bombardment of Sveaborg on the north coast of the Gulf of Finland near Helsinki by small craft armed with mortars. This took place

August 9–13 and did a certain amount of damage, with about two dozen Russian vessels being sunk and 2,000 men killed or wounded. In the absence of any kind of follow-up action the entire episode could be regarded as pointless. The British blockading squadron, which was equipped with small steam gunboats, was probably somewhat more effective than during the preceding year, but fear of Russian minefields in shallow waters limited its usefulness. The Russian mines were actually too weak to be more than moderately effective, but they did damage several British warships and were one of the factors that greatly discouraged an attack on Kronstadt. They were not used offensively but merely as an adjunct to coastal defense. The British, to their credit, evolved a method of sweeping —by employing small boats, the first countermeasures to mine warfare.

The outcome of the Baltic campaign was in a sense favorable to the Russians, whose fleet suffered very little damage in port. The greatly superior enemy fleets accomplished little; not even their commanders claimed that they had done any real damage to the enemy, though for the two years the British claimed a Russian loss of shipping of about 80,000 tons.

THE PACIFIC

At the beginning of the Crimean War French and British forces in the Pacific were enormously superior to those of the Russians. A French squadron, commanded by Rear Admiral Febvrier-Despointes and consisting of the frigate *Forte* 60 and five lesser vessels carrying 190 guns and 2,000 men, was stationed at Callao, Peru. A somewhat larger British Pacific fleet under Rear Adm. David Price was composed of two frigates and seven smaller vessels carrying 300 guns. In addition the British China Squadron, under Rear Adm. James Stirling, was available. Had the British viewed the war in the Far East as a land conflict, they could also have made use of British troops in Australia, India, and other colonies.

Against these forces the Russians had three frigates of which only one, the *Avrora* 44, was available. The *Diana* 44, under Rear Adm. E. V. Putiatin, had been sent to Japan to carry on diplomatic negoti-

ations and to secure supplies (it was soon to be wrecked in an earth-
quake); the *Pallas* 60, judged unseaworthy, had been sent to Port
Imperial to serve as a hulk. In addition three corvettes and some
very small naval craft, as well as other private vessels belonging to
the Russian-American Fur Company, could be counted. As a possible protection to these private ships and to shore installations, Alaska
was declared neutral, a declaration that was respected by the British and the French. On land the Russians had slightly more than
1,000 troops.

Yet the Russians held a great advantage in quality of leadership.
The French and British commanders were either mediocre or over-
aged, while Count Nikolai N. Muravev, the governor general of eastern Siberia, was one of the great empire builders of the nineteenth
century and his army and navy subordinates demonstrated excellent
qualities throughout. E. H. Nolan, the British historian of the war,
rightly observed of the Russian leadership:

> All the Russian authorities, whether acting on the shores or water,
> showed the utmost zeal for their country's service, the most untiring
> vigilance, the quickest celerity and promptitude, a sagacious foresight,
> and careful precaution.[7]

Allied moves in the Pacific were disorganized and improvised.
The Russians, faced with the impossibility of defending a vast area
with slender resources, concentrated on holding Kamchatka, the
mouth of the Amur River, and Sakhalin. ,

News of the war reached the British and French squadrons at
Callao on May 7, 1854. Several British ships were then elsewhere on
the Pacific station, but Admiral Price decided to cross the Pacific to
attack the Russian base at Petropavlovsk with the ships at hand.
Four British and two French ships, acting as an international task
force, sailed west; on August 29 they reached Kamchatka and
entered the bay.

In the meantime the Russians had learned of impending attack
from two sources: their transport *Dvina* had brought news of the
war, and some American ships had reached Petropavlovsk after
encountering the allied squadron en route and learning of its destination. Under the direction of Rear Adm. V. S. Zavoiko they prepared with speed and efficiency. The *Avrora* 44 was anchored

behind a sand spit with land batteries in front of her, while smaller Russian vessels ascended the Amur River. Though Muravev had hauled in cannon from as far away as Tobolsk, he was outnumbered by 236 guns to 101 and even more in terms of men. Yet the allies failed to bombard at once; and the bombardment that started August 30 was discontinued after Admiral Price committed suicide. The French officer who replaced him was far too old and incompetent to be an effective commander. Though a second bombardment on August 31 temporarily silenced most of the defending guns, the Russians, by working at top speed all night, were able to make repairs and were prepared for the next attack, which came four days later.

The British had received information from three Americans who had deserted a whaler that Petropavlovsk could be better attacked by land. Hence after silencing several Russian batteries by bombardment the allies landed 700 men, only to discover that the route recommended by the Americans was rough and exposed—and led directly into an ambush. Some 330 well-concealed Russians poured in a withering fire, and an allied retreat quickly became a rout. The British lost 107 men and the French 101 killed or wounded in the rush back to their ships.[8] The allied fleet then left for North America to await replacements and orders, the British at Vancouver and the French at San Francisco. During this retreat the allies captured the Russian transport *Sitka* 10 and a small supply ship.

Count Muravev, though gratified by the victory at Petropavlovsk, was too much of a realist to believe he could hold the port for very long against the much larger forces the allies could mobilize. Accordingly, he appealed for additional troops and equipment. He did not receive them, and when he learned of the wreck of the *Diana*, from whose voyage he had expected to receive supplies, he decided to evacuate Petropavlovsk and move his forces to a less exposed position. To insure that the mouth of the Amur would remain in Russian hands, he moved in as colonists hardy Cossack frontiersmen accustomed to conflict. The continued absence of Admiral Putiatin dictated the appointment of Rear Admiral Zavoyko, a former general who, like Apraksin, had turned to the navy in his mature years.

Muravev's anticipation of allied plans proved correct: the Pacific squadrons were again ordered to attack Petropavlovsk. Changes in command had brought in two new admirals but very little increase in competence. In 1855 Rear Adm. William H. Bruce directed the British fleet and Rear Adm. Martin Fourichon the French squadron. The combined forces, totaling 13 ships, arrived off Kamchatka in April but did not then attack. Instead, two sentry ships were selected to stand guard over Petropavlovsk—at a distance of 80 miles. Under such circumstances the Russians experienced no difficulty in loading their men and equipment onto two small naval vessels and four merchant ships which on April 17 slipped past the enemy cruisers in a fog.

When the allies began their bombardment the following month they soon discovered they were cannonading an empty port. Disdaining to occupy the abandoned quarters, they razed several buildings and then reembarked. The fleet then moved about in a somewhat meaningless manner. It paid a visit to Sitka in Alaska, detached four vessels to serve with Admiral Stirling's China Squadron, and finally crossed the Pacific to return to bases in San Francisco and Vancouver.

British Commodore Elliott, whose task force of the China Squadron included the four detached ships, somehow proved even more inept than the other allied commanders. On one occasion he chased two Russian ships north along the coast between Sakhalin and the mainland. When fog closed in, unaware that Sakhalin was an island and not part of a bay, he waited for clearing skies in the belief that he had the Russians trapped. When at last he discovered his error his ships moved north, and in Castries Bay on May 18, 1855, they came upon all the Russian naval forces from Petropavlovsk. These consisted of the frigate *Avrora* 44, the corvette *Olivutsu* 22, the three lightly armed transports *Baikal* 6, *Irtysh* 6, *Dvina* 10, and the cutter *Kodiak*. Elliott had with him the *Sybilla* 40, *Hornet* 17, and *Bittern* 12, with additional ships farther south. Instead of attacking the Russian forces he fired one shot at long range. The Russians replied with one shot. Elliott then left the harbor, sending the *Bittern* south for reinforcements. When the reinforcements arrived and Elliott returned, the Russians had departed. A Russian ruse failed (some "important" papers were left behind to mislead the British, but nobody could be found among the allies who could read Russian), and the British departed. Aided to some extent by two French ships, they searched for the Russian fleet all through the summer months. In the Sea of Okhotsk the allies took one of the Kurile Islands (Uruppu) and captured a few small boats and some furs. In October the allied squadron discovered the concentration of Russian forces at the mouth of the Amur River, where a landing party was soundly beaten by the Cossack settlers. Though the Keystone Cops performance of the British and French in the Pacific was never well enough reported to produce a demand for an official investigation, it has been treated briefly and with obvious distaste by British naval historians and with much more attention by the Russians.

Highly creditable as was the Russian performance during the same period, it is not the end of the story. Early in 1855 Admiral Putiatin, following lengthy negotiations and the wrecking of his ship *Diana*, concluded a treaty with Japan similar to that concluded by Commodore Perry, though the Russian treaty was somewhat more favorable. The next year Muravev opened negotiations with China to gain territory in the Pacific coastal region. Between 1857 and 1860 he was able to strengthen the Russian hold on the Amur valley after obtaining additional men and money in St. Petersburg. In 14 years as diplomat, administrator, and military leader Count Muravev-Amursky (as he came to be known) added 400,000 square miles to the Russian Empire.

THE WHITE SEA

Very little naval action took place in the White Sea during the Crimean War, although the allies sent small squadrons there in the summer months of 1854 and 1855. Late in 1854 the allies proclaimed a blockade in the area. Minor activities included small gunnery duels with troops ashore, bombardment of the famous Solovetsky monastery, destruction of public buildings and coastal batteries, a few landings at small towns, and some insignificant captures of merchant and small fishing vessels. The allies destroyed the town of Kola in Russian Lapland but failed in an attempt to reach Arkhangelsk.

ENDING THE WAR

The Crimean War had never had much meaning, and its conclusion with the Treaty of Paris of March 1856 reflected even less purpose, beyond the fact that the belligerents were tired of the war. In one theater at least, the Black Sea, the Russians had clearly lost and this fact was reflected in the terms of the treaty—in its provisions that navigation of the Danube be thrown open to all states and that the Black Sea be neutralized. Russia also agreed to give up all naval forces in that area except for some small coast guard vessels. The Danubian Principalities, together with a small strip of Bessarabia, were granted self-government under Turkish rule. Turkish and Russian boundaries were restored to their prewar positions, and all the powers agreed to respect the integrity and independence of the Turkish empire. The sultan in turn agreed to grant religious liberty and equality to his Christian subjects—a promise he never kept. In fact it should be stated that all the treaty arrangements proved to be of a very temporary nature.

From a strategic standpoint one fact stood out clearly. While the allies had won, both on sea and land, the war had demonstrated conclusively the difficulty of seriously hurting Russia. For the land operations the allies had had the good judgment or good luck to choose a theater of very limited size and one whose configuration made their logistics problem relatively easy, since they commanded the sea. Outside this limited area, however, they had achieved no more than a draw in the struggle.

The war was highly significant from a technological standpoint. It involved the first extensive use of steamships in battle and demonstrated finally that the day of the sailing warship was past. The Battle of Sinope showed what rifled guns could do to wooden ships, while the defense against such guns as well as the shape of naval development in the future was clearly foretold by the armored floating batteries used by the French at Kinburn. The Russians had a submarine building in the Baltic, though it was not used. Also, they made the first extensive use of mines in warfare, and the British before the end of hostilities had discovered possible countermeasures.

RUSSIAN NAVAL DEVELOPMENT 1855–77

All through the Crimean War portents of the future were clearly visible. A host of new developments in naval technology—steam propulsion, improved ordnance, the replacement of wooden hulls with iron and later with steel, the development of armor plate, early improvements in mines, torpedoes, and submarines—were introduced into the world's navies within the brief period of a few decades.

The Russian position between the old and the new was particularly difficult, for Russia lacked the technological and industrial base to support a modern fleet. There was no lack of leaders capable of perceiving the need for change, and several men had made gestures in the direction of progress. For instance, long before the Crimean War Admiral Lazarev had tried to bring in steam propulsion and iron-built warships. Other naval and industrial leaders had sent observers to the United States, and the steam frigate *Kamchatka*, which became the pride of the Baltic Fleet and was unquestionably one of the best of her day, was built to Russian order in an American shipyard. However, these and other efforts toward modernity were little more than isolated gestures.

During much of the painful period of modernization following the Crimean War the Russian navy was dominated by one personality, the Grand Duke Konstantin, great-grandfather of the present Prince Philip of England. Though less than twenty-five years old at the time, Konstantin had become minister of marine in 1853, just prior to the outbreak of war. He quickly perceived some of the fleet's weaknesses, but was at first deterred from accomplishing much by the imminence of war and the domineering personality of Nicholas I. With the accession in 1855 of his older brother, Alexander II (1855–81), a well-meaning and relatively liberal monarch who was not particularly interested in the navy, Konstantin came into effective control.

Konstantin's achievements as navy minister were always limited somewhat by the amount of money and support he could get for the navy as well as by his brother's penchant for sending him on important missions which bore no relation to his naval interests.

Even so, and in spite of marked opposition to his urgings for a strong fleet, he finally succeeded in converting the tsar to a policy of maintaining the third strongest navy. Though a good deal of money went for coast-defense gunboats, Konstantin showed his progressivism by fighting for the introduction of armored and steam-propelled ships, and by financing out of his own pocket experimentation which led to the building during the Crimean War of Russia's first successful submarine.

The majority of the reforms which Konstantin achieved occurred in the field of administration. During his tenure the Russian fleet was reorganized into three divisions: (1) the active fleet; (2) a reserve in waiting; (3) a general reserve. In 1862 the naval cadet corps was reoriented along Western lines, and most of the incompetent instructors were replaced. Changes within the naval ministry included the creation of powerful departments to deal with construction and artillery, a special ministry to handle technical changes and to administer naval hospitals, and the reorganization of the hydrographic department. Port administration unfortunately was left needlessly complicated, in that St. Petersburg, Kronstadt, and Nikolaev were directed by one department, and the other bases (Sveaborg, Revel, Arkhangelsk, Baku, Nikolaevsk on the Amur, and Vladivostok) by another. However, port facilities were increased and improved generally.

Reforms dealing with personnel included raising the standards of *Morskoi sbornik* and requiring that this journal carry articles reporting progress in Western fleets. Naval laws were rewritten and improved, and court procedures were changed to assure a defense for seamen accused of crimes and to separate the posts of judge and prosecutor, previously often held by the same man. A great deal of effort was expended in advancing living and working conditions. A drive to educate personnel had succeeded in 1881 in reducing the illiteracy rate to less than 50 percent. Wardrooms and ships' libraries were bettered. Annual foreign cruises which tended to improve education and restore morale were encouraged. Raises in pay, and even subventions for the education of children and pensions for widows and orphans, were not neglected.

As assistants to Konstantin in reforming the Russian fleet, three admirals should be noted. Adm. I. F. Likhachev, as an adjutant to the minister of marine, was largely responsible for the creation of the Pacific Fleet. Convinced that only on the Pacific did his country have unfettered access to the sea, he argued that Russia should control the three exits to the Sea of Japan. As commander of the Pacific Fleet he at one time occupied Tsushima Island, which controlled the best exit, and set up a naval station there. Though Konstantin supported this move, the tsar did not; Likhachev was ordered to evacuate the island. He then turned his energy to studying new types of ironclads and urged the creation of a naval chief of staff post.

Adm. G. I. Butakov was both a naval officer and a scholar. A leader in the transformation of the navy to steam, he stressed the need for technical knowledge, organized around-the-world cruises, wrote the first book on the naval tactics of steam warships, and for ten years (1867–77) headed the new armored squadron. He was a kindly man, adored by younger officers and men.

The third leader was the "terrible Admiral Popov," a fine technician and drillmaster, long-term commander of the Pacific Fleet, a man whose unreasonable demands were legendary. His ships were taut rather than happy, but by demanding the impossible he actually obtained a high measure of smartness and efficiency. Successful diplomacy and original but generally unsuccessful ship design were Popov's other achievements.

Under these leaders efforts were made to learn and to implement the lessons taught by the Crimean War. One of these, the superiority of steam over sail propulsion, was extremely clear, and the Russians wasted no time in applying it. Even during the Crimean War the Russians built about 75 screw gunboats, plus smaller numbers of corvettes, clippers, and frigates. Between 1855 and 1863 no less than 130 additional steam warships were built under the direction of Admirals Likhachev and Butakov, and though by 1863 there still remained many sailing vessels on the navy list the majority were steam propelled. The vast bulk of this steam-powered navy was in the Baltic; the other four squadrons were relatively minor.

The lessons of the Crimean War regarding the use of ironclads were far less clear, and for more than a decade after 1855 no one naval policy proved completely dominant. Ironclads for coast defense, seagoing ironclads, ironclads converted from wooden ships, all received some attention.

Before considering the makeup of the new ironclad fleet it is important that we turn briefly to a conflict apparently remote from Russia—the American Civil War. This struggle, which opened five years after the Crimean War, lasted long enough and involved sufficient naval action to be of considerable interest to all maritime powers. Yet it is doubtful that any other European power experienced anything resembling Russia's keen interest in the tactical lessons taught by that war. The tsar's government was then on excellent terms with the North—in fact its friendship was closer than that of any other major European power.

In 1863 there occurred an event which has been greatly misinterpreted by some Americans. The Russian Baltic Fleet, or rather its better non-sailing ships, left home waters in great secrecy, crossed the Atlantic, and in September docked at New York. The ships involved were the screw frigates *Aleksandr Nevsky* 51 (4,500 tons), *Peresvet* 48 (3,800 tons), *Osliabia* 33 (3,800 tons); and two screw sloops, *Vitiaz* 17 (2,100 tons) and *Variag* 17 (2,100 tons). The *Osliabia*, first to arrive, was visited on September 16 by President Lincoln, and the Russian officers were enthusiastically entertained by Americans who saw in the call a gesture of support at a time when England and France were sympathetic toward the Confederacy.

At about the same time the Russian Pacific squadron also left port for an American visit. The corvette *Novik*, first to reach this country, was wrecked off the Pacific coast in late September. Other arrivals at San Francisco were the steam corvette *Bogatyr* (with Admiral Popov in command) on October 11, the steam frigate *Gaidamak* on October 16, the corvette *Kalevala* two days later, the steam corvette *Abrek* on October 28, and the corvette *Rynda* on November 7. The Russians were welcomed as warmly in San Francisco as in New York, and their visit received much the same interpretation. Admiral Popov had made two earlier trips and was especially well liked. On November 23 he landed 200 men to help fight one of the big fires in San Francisco. At a civic banquet he even indiscreetly pledged Russian aid in defending the city from the *Alabama* and the *Sumter*.

These naval visits probably served several purposes other than the one of mere sympathy for the North generally attributed by the Americans. The tsar was then pursuing a policy of ruthless Russification in Poland and feared the sort of intervention by other powers which had occurred in the Crimean War. In that war, as has been shown, Russian naval vessels had been uselessly bottled up within closed seas. To the Russian mind, the *Alabama* and other Confederate cruisers were at the time demonstrating how useful the warships of a weaker power might be on the high seas if able to move about freely. By visiting American waters the Russian warships not only were able to pose the threat of serving as possible commerce destroyers should France and England again declare war; they also acquired a mobility that would not have been possible had they remained in their home ports. In addition, they were in a position to learn of any outbreak of war involving Russia and would therefore not be caught unprepared. As it happened the Polish insurrection was crushed; Britain was unwilling to go to war; and Napoleon III refused to act alone.

In all probability the visits served the further purpose of apprising the Russians of what progress the Americans were making in naval affairs and how to profit by their example. It is difficult to determine with certainty if this was the case, but both internal and external evidence is fairly strong. In Russian eyes the United States was a friendly power which, though industrially more advanced, occupied a naval position vis-à-vis Britain and France not unlike that of Russia. American naval development was consequently of the greatest interest. During the 1860s *Morskoi sbornik* was filled with articles dealing with American naval technology, and when the ordnance committee of the ministry of marine began an extensive study of mine warfare in 1864, it started by using American reports.

It should be noted that the American naval thinking which prevailed during most of the nineteenth century was not that of Mahan. Instead it laid great stress on coastal defense and commerce destruction and hence was thoroughly understandable to the Russians, whose naval history had emphasized the coast-defense use of naval forces as a mobile flank of the army. The main tactical developments of the Civil War had been the use of monitors, fast commerce-destroying cruisers, primitive torpedo craft, and submarines. The Russians showed in subsequent years an appreciation of the use of all four.

Russia started the building of ironclads in 1863. In that year she secured from Great Britain the *Pervenets*, a ship of some 3,280 tons, 200 feet in length, 52-½ feet in beam, and covered with 4-½-inch iron plating. This ship carried a battery of 68-pound guns, made nine knots on her trials, and was basically a floating battery. Two sister ships, *Ne Tron Menia* and *Kreml*, were then built in the Baltic together with two wooden battleships, the *Sevastopol* and the *Petropavlovsk*, which were cut down and armored with 4-½-inch steel plate. The latter were larger vessels of more than 6,000 tons, which after conversion were able to make 11 knots.

The next step, which shortly followed the return of the Baltic Fleet, was the building of monitors. Ten were launched in 1864 and finished in later years. These were assigned primarily for the defense of Kronstadt. Their tonnage ranged from 1,400 to 1,800 tons. Five 1-inch plates of armor were carried on the sides, while turret armor was 11 inches thick. Two big guns were placed in the revolving turret. Aside from armament, these ships almost duplicated the American Civil War monitors. This one difference was typical of the Russian navy. Whereas the successors of the *Monitor* carried either 11-inch or 15-inch guns, the Russians adopted a 9-inch piece. This fondness for light artillery has many examples in later Russian naval construction.

Like the United States, the Russians did some developing of the *Monitor* type, especially after they had seen the *Miantanomoh*, an excellent double-turret monitor which Washington sent on a friendly visit to the Baltic shortly after the Civil War.[9] Double-turret monitors were designed in 1867 and triple-turret monitors of about 3,500 tons a year later—though each turret carried only one gun.

Then in 1873–75 Admiral Popov designed two of the most remarkable vessels ever built, the circular ironclads *Novgorod* and *Admiral Popov*. The *Novgorod* had a hull diameter of 121 feet and 2,500 tons displacement. She carried two 11-inch guns and 7 to 9 inches of side armor. Designed speed was six knots on six screws. The *Popov* was 1,000 tons larger, carried 12-inch guns and 16-inch armor and made eight and a half knots on her trial. *Popov* and *Novgorod* were both complete failures. On a trip up the Dnieper the ships were caught by the currents and whirled helplessly around until they were carried out to sea, their crews prostrated by seasickness. Thereafter the only use made of the *Popovkas* was as floating forts.

By no means all Russian effort was devoted to perpetuating the *Monitor*: a number of British-type ironclads were built. The largest of these, the *Petr Veliky*, launched in 1872, might fairly be described as a battleship. She was of 9,000 tons displacement, made 14 knots, and carried four 12-inch guns. Armor amidships was 8-10 inches thick with 12-inch armor over the turrets. For her time the *Petr Veliky* was an extremely powerful vessel and one of the most formidable warships in the world. However, the type was not repeated and she had no sisters. Although the change from wooden to iron ships was somewhat slower in the Russian navy than was that from sail to steam, some results were visible after the late 1860s.

In addition to battleships or monitors, the Russians, like certain other Europeans, had become interested in the fast commerce-destroyer types of ironclad. One reason the *Petr Veliky* was not repeated was that interest shifted to a class of small armorclads carrying three 6-inch guns. Eight of these were built during the 1870s, but these so-called clippers were felt to be of too limited range, so that, about 1870, the Naval Ministry requested Admiral Popov to draw up plans for oceangoing cruisers. As a result the *General Admiral* and the *Duke of Edinburgh* were built. These were of 4,600 tons, carried ten 6-inch guns, and were designed to make 13-¼ knots, a speed which the *Duke of Edinburgh* actually exceeded by nearly two knots. The type was regarded as successful, and two earlier ironclad frigates, the *Pozharsky* and the *Minin*, were rebuilt as cruisers. These early ships might well be regarded as ancestors of the armored cruiser class.

Although Russian surface warships were not, on the whole, superior to those of other powers during the same period, their construction necessitated many changes in the shore establishments. In the Black Sea the shore establishments at Nikolaev and Sevastopol required much modernization and expansion and gave rise to whole new industries in some cases. Workmen at the Izhora Works in the Baltic learned first to roll strips of armor plate which were fastened together, and later to roll armor plate from six to 15 inches thick. The Obukhov Steel Works developed the capacity to build ships' guns of up to 12-inch caliber, and to manufacture shells weighing 736 pounds for these same guns to fire. In 1856 the Russian Society of Steamships and Commerce was established under government subsidy to promote commercial shipbuilding and foreign trade.

The Russian interest in mines, torpedo craft (see chapter 9), and submarines continued after the Crimean War and was heightened by the American Civil War. The mines used during the Crimean War were of a primitive type. Fuses consisting of glass tubes filled with sulphuric acid and embedded in a mixture of chlorate of potassium and sugar were encased in an outer tube of lead. When a ship's hull bent the lead shell, the inner glass tube broke, releasing the acid which contacted the chemicals, thus firing the main charge. This charge, sometimes as small as eight pounds and usually not larger than 25 pounds of gun cotton, generally did no great damage; nevertheless, the British ships *Merlin* and *Firefly* were badly damaged off Kronstadt after striking such mines. Another type of mine, used rather sparingly by the Russians but far more powerful, was placed on the sea bed and fired electrically from shore. Encouraged by their wartime achievements with mines, the Russians continued work. In 1875 they established a school of mine warfare, and in 1877 the naval academy at Nikolaev instituted courses in mine strategy and warfare.

Before 1850 the Russians had taken only occasional notice of the possibility of developing undersea craft. But the Crimean War pointed up a need for coast-defense forces more mobile than coastal artillery or mines. Since the submarine promised to fill such a role, the Russian navy for the next half century provided alert audience to scores of inventors or would-be inventors of underseas craft. While the Crimean War was still in progress two submarine developers, the German Wilhelm Bauer and the Russian I. F. Aleksandrovsky, were busily at work. Bauer had built his first submarine at Kiel and thereafter moved to Russia, where in May 1855 he completed at the Leuchtenberg Works the *Sea Devil*, a dolphin-shaped boat 52 feet long, 12 feet wide, with an 11-foot draft. The iron hull was built to withstand a 150-foot submersion. Entrance was by hatch in the bow. Propulsion was furnished by a stern propeller consisting of four large wheels driven manually. Bauer completed 133 dives with the boat, but on its trial in November 1855 with a Russian crew the propeller became entangled with seaweed and the craft was nearly lost. Bauer refloated the boat, but it later sank again. Since no love was lost between Bauer and his Russian associates, he shortly left.

About the time of the Crimean War other submarine projects were suggested by N. Polway, A. Sprindov, and A. Litkov, but none ever went beyond the planning stage. In 1863 I. F. Aleksandrovsky developed a 360-ton all-metal submarine which worked on compressed air with two screws in tandem. It was completed in 1866 and was used for several years despite several near disasters attributable to an insufficiently trained crew. In testing this boat Aleksandrovsky found answers to several of the questions connected with undersea navigation, but he failed to develop an effective torpedo. Though the boat was in most respects a success, no new units were built and the original was finally crushed in 1870 when it submerged to too great a depth. Aleksandrovsky also presented plans for a torpedo propelled by compressed air which reached a speed during tests in 1869 of over nine knots. Later development brought it to ten knots in 1875 and 18 knots in 1879. Viktor von Schelika, a Prussian ordnance expert who had participated in the American Civil War on the Confederate side and who was familiar with the defenses of Charleston Harbor, also served the Russians in the development of automotive torpedoes. However, the Whitehead torpedo was finally adopted despite the fact that its performance was only marginally better than that of the Russian models.

Besides the inventors of submarines and the naval administrators, mention should be made of several other key Russians who helped to modernize the fleet. A talented shipbuilder was P. A. Titov. In the important field of ordnance development the leading Russian figure was undoubtedly N. I. Putilov.

Some indication of the degree of interest in Russian naval development after the Crimean War is furnished by the figures for naval expenditures between 1856 and 1878 (see table 2).

It is clear that in the next decades the Russian effort to establish a modern fleet of steam-powered, iron warships persisted and, over the years, increased. There remains to be answered a key question: How effective was this effort?

The first step, conversion of the navy from sail to steam, was

TABLE 2

Expenditures of Naval Ministry, 1856–78*

(IN MILLIONS OF RUBLES)

1856	18.2	1864	20.1	1872	22.3
1857	19.0	1865	21.1	1873	22.8
1858	18.7	1866	24.1	1874	25.4
1859	18.3	1867	17.5	1875	25.8
1860	21.4	1868	18.1	1876	27.1
1861	21.4	1869	18.8	1877	32.4
1862	19.6	1870	20.1	1878	32.7

* SOURCE: S. F. Ogorodnikov, Istorichesky obzor razvitiia i deiatelnosti Morskago Ministerstva za sto let ego sushchestvovaniia: 1802–1902 (St. Petersburg, 1902), pp. 215–16.

accomplished with fair speed. By 1859 nearly half of the fleet was propelled by steam. The navy list of that year cited 73 steam vessels and 85 sailing ships. The steamers included seven screw battleships, 11 screw frigates, 12 screw corvettes, and 43 miscellaneous. During the next two decades the sailing vessels were steadily replaced by steam ships. The success of the conversion to ironclads, including armor protection, ordnance, and torpedoes, is far harder to gauge.

A quarter of a century after the start of the Crimean War the Russian navy presented a spotty appearance. It had not regained its position in the Black Sea, and its other fleets had not attained any great power or efficiency. The 223 ships then on the navy list were divided into six fleets. The Baltic Fleet, with 137 vessels, was the strongest single force. The Black Sea Fleet contained 31 small vessels. There were 27 ships in Siberian waters, where Russia had by now largely consolidated her control of areas very lightly held in 1853. A White Sea Fleet of three units, and flotillas on the Caspian and Aral seas numbering 19 and six respectively, completed the distribution of naval forces. Qualitatively, these forces no longer measured up to the fleets of other great powers.

CHAPTER 9

Naval Development
(1877 - 1904)

GENERAL NAVAL POLICY

FROM 1877 TO 1904 Russia experienced a period of rapid naval development. During those years no one personage completely dominated the stage; there were several leaders in naval thinking who at various times left their imprints on progress. Three tsars ruled during the period. Alexander II (1855–81), who exhibited a mixture of humane and reactionary traits, was aware that Russia was failing to match Western progress in government and showed some willingness to weigh reforms. In 1861 he freed the serfs, though two years later he imposed repressive measures in Poland. By 1881, at the time of his assassination by a nihilist bomber, he was on the verge of granting a constitution. He was not an enthusiastic supporter of his brother Konstantin's attempts at naval reforms, but he was at least open to conviction and at times could be persuaded to change his mind.

Alexander II's son and successor, Alexander III (1881–93), was a strong and efficient autocrat who used every possible means to centralize the government and increase his own power, meantime savagely repressing liberals and subject nationalities. His reign was a nightmare of reaction. His son, Nicholas II (1893–1917), was equally autocratic by nature but far weaker and less capable. Under him graft reached new heights and tsarism achieved its own destruction.

Both Alexander III and Nicholas II favored a large army and navy, but both were incompletely informed on naval matters. Neither insisted on getting his money's worth in shipbuilding, and both failed to perceive the importance of well trained personnel; as a result they paid well for new ships but economized on crews. Training, officer selection, experimentation, foreign cruises, marksmanship—virtually everything that contributes to a smart, alert navy—was neglected. Ships and crews spent more and more time in port, where some of the men and even a few of the officers listened to revolutionaries and joined their organizations. So little time was passed at sea that both ships and men became "rusty." The reputation for smartness which the Russian navy had enjoyed early in the nineteenth century gradually diminished until finally the fleet became known as the least efficient maintained by any great power.

The degree of financial support furnished the navy by these three rulers is indicated in the following table:

TABLE 3

Russian Naval Expenditures, 1879–1902[*]

(IN MILLIONS OF RUBLES)

1879	31.0	1885	38.5	1891	45.5	1897	59.9
1880	29.4	1886	44.6	1892	48.2	1898	67.1
1881	30.7	1887	40.0	1893	50.4	1899	83.1
1882	30.7	1888	40.9	1894	51.2	1900	86.6
1883	34.0	1889	40.8	1895	54.9	1901	95.6
1884	34.2	1890	40.9	1896	58.0	1902	98.3

[*] SOURCE: S. F. Ogorodnikov, *Istorichesky óbzor razvitiia i deiatelnosti Morskago Ministerstva za sto let ego sushchestvovaniia: 1802–1902* (St. Petersburg, 1902), pp. 216, 243–44, 259.

THE TURKISH WAR 1877–78

Russian hopes to secure the Turkish Straits still had not been abandoned. In 1877 Tsar Alexander II decided on a renewed effort to seize the prize. Contributing to his advantage were the weakness of France, following her defeat by Prussia in the Franco-Prussian War, and the decadent nature of the Ottoman Empire, which was ruled at that time by Abdul Hamid II. This sultan had become extremely unpopular in Europe because of his repudiation of finan-

cial obligations and his massacres of Christians. Using Turkish perse-
cutions of Orthodox Christians as an excuse, Russia declared war
on April 24, 1877.

At the outset of hostilities Russia was far stronger on land than
at sea, as had been the case in most of her previous wars with Turkey. Though she had in 1870 denounced the provisions of the Treaty
of Paris, by which she was limited to ten small police vessels in the
Black Sea, the penurious policies of Tsar Alexander II had since
prevented any genuine naval buildup. In the spring of 1877 only
seven Russian seagoing battleships existed, and six of them were in
the Baltic. The other, the old *Petropavlovsk*, was to remain inactive
at Spezia throughout the war. In the Black Sea there were only the
two worthless *Popovkas* and a small assortment of old tubs and small
craft. These were supplemented by about twenty merchant steamers which were purchased from other nations and armed, and by a
number of primitive torpedo launches shipped by rail from St.
Petersburg. Coast defenses, manned in Russia by the navy rather
than the army, included seven batteries at Ochakov, nine at Sevastopol, three at Odessa, and one at Kerch.

In sharp contrast to the Russian naval weakness, the Turks had a
powerful and reasonably modern fleet that included one ironclad
of 9,000 tons, four of about 6,000 tons, one of 4,000 tons, and seven
of 2,000 tons, besides a number of monitors and armored gunboats
and a sizable aggregation of small craft. Turkish naval personnel
numbered 23,000 men as compared to a total of 25,076 for the Russians. Since the entire Turkish force could be used in the battle area
but Russian strength could not be moved about, it would probably
be correct to say that the Turkish superiority at sea was nearly ten
to one. Yet as is often the case strengths proved deceptive.

The Turkish navy reflected in its chaotic and corrupt administration and in its low morale the general backwardness of the Turkish
government. Hobart Pasha, the English officer in command, was a
sailor of fortune who, as one "Captain Roberts," had served the
Confederacy as a blockade runner in the American Civil War.
Though this officer was himself capable of demonstrating a measure
of ability, his orders were continually overruled.

At the beginning of the war the Turks hoped to blockade Russian
ports to prevent the Russians from moving troops by sea. The Rus-

sians, for their part, were anxious to confine the conflict to a simple war with Turkey. As they visualized it, the Russian navy would serve simply as an adjunct to the army, its principal duty being to neutralize the mouth of the Danube. In order to discourage possible British intervention, the Russians laid mines in the Baltic, but this early precaution proved unnecessary, as the British were not then ready to intervene.

The story of the brief Turko-Russian war well demonstrates the uselessness of inactive seapower. The Turks did very little to capitalize on their overwhelming naval superiority, either in support of land warfare or in independent operations. The Russians, on the other hand, employed all the weapons available to them—coastal batteries, mines, and primitive torpedo craft—and waged a campaign of attrition that was nothing short of brilliant.

Most of the fighting in the early period of the war was an outgrowth of the Russian land campaign and occurred near the mouth of the Danube. Here the only rail line running into Rumania from Russia was within reach of gunboats at both Brăila and Galatz. In an attempt to interfere with Russian river crossings, the Turks lost one of their ironclads, the *Lufti Djel*, with her entire crew, to a Russian coastal battery. This loss, combined with a fear of torpedo attacks, produced in the Turks an attitude of such extreme caution that they anchored their ironclads behind booms and other defenses. The Russian river fleet, manned by 160 officers and 2,423 seamen and comprising eight steamers, three schooners, three ironclads, two mortar boats, a gunboat, seven ironclad sloops, and about 30 small mining craft, was then free to move around at will. It aided the army in crossing the lower Danube near Galatz, and later in making a second crossing near Nikopol on the middle Danube. Navy boats also planted river mines carrying 35 to 50 pounds of powder to protect the Russian crossings from Turkish interference. At the fall of Nikopol the Russians captured two Turkish monitors. On October 9 Sulina was taken by army forces aided by 12 small craft under Lt. I. M. Dikov. At Silistria a schooner and two vedettes under Lt. F. V. Dubasov attacked and heavily damaged a Turkish monitor.

In the Black Sea, as on the Danube, the Turks had far greater naval power than the Russians, whose fighting force consisted of about 30 steam vessels, most of which were floating batteries. Yet here the sole Turkish offensive gesture came very early in the war, when Turkish armorclads bombarded and forced the Russians to give up the port of Sukhumi. Again the Russian campaign of mine laying and torpedo attacks had the effect of immobilizing the Turks. As a result, the Russians were able despite their naval inferiority to transport food and supplies to their Caucasus armies, to lay mines, to make torpedo attacks, and to interfere with Turkish sea transport. Russian armed merchant ships also sank or captured several Turkish vessels. One of the few ship duels occurred near Constantsa on July 23, 1877, when the 1,880-ton *Vesta* under Captain Baranov, carrying five 6-inch guns and with a speed of 12 knots, fought and escaped from the 2,760-ton *Feth-I-Bulend* of five 11-inch guns and 13 knots.

In late May the Russians started the main action of their naval war: torpedo attacks which resembled somewhat those of the American Civil War, but which were carried out with larger forces and with greater intensity. At this period mobile torpedoes had not yet become tactically usable, and torpedoes had to be either carried at the end of spars or towed through the water.

The first torpedo attack of the war was attempted at Batum by forces under the command of Lt. Stepan O. Makarov, a brilliant young officer whose plan had won the approval of the Grand Duke Konstantin. In his attempt the 1,500-ton steamer *Veliky Kniaz Konstantin* was used to transport six fast steam launches on davits to within six or seven miles of the target. The *Veliky Kniaz Konstantin* used Welsh coal, which gave off almost no smoke, and Makarov had painted the launches to harmonize with the ocean background. Four of the launches then undertook to tow a torpedo under a Turkish ironclad. On this first occasion the Turks awoke before the attack could be carried out.

A few days later, on the night of May 25, four torpedo launches under Lieutenant Dubasov (*Tsesarevich, Kseniia, Dzhigit,* and *Tsarevna*) made a successful attack on two river monitors, *Seife* and *Feth-ul-Islam*, and a gunboat. The four relatively primitive Russian boats, each carrying a spar torpedo, set out in a rainstorm, in inky darkness. Capable of a speed of only five knots, they succeeded in escaping detection until they were within 70 yards of their target. Then they were hailed by the Turks, who opened a highly inaccurate fire. The torpedo boats pressed forward, and both *Tsesarevich* and *Kseniia* scored hits. The *Tsesarevich's* torpedo did little damage, but the *Kseniia's* torpedo struck the *Seife* under its turret and produced ·an explosion. At about daybreak the Turkish monitor sank. The Russian boats retired following the first successful flotilla attack in history.

The next attack, at Sulina on June 12, also encountered obstacles. Three Turkish ironclads, *Idjalieh, Feth-I-Bulend*, and *Mukadim-I-Hair*, and a gunboat lay behind an outer circle of gunboats which were connected to one another by ropes. Lieutenant Makarov arrived in the *Veliky Kniaz Konstantin*, accompanied by the *Vladimir*. After locating the enemy, Makarov decided to attack in two divisions of three boats each. Five of the attacking Russian ships were using spar torpedoes, while the other, the *Chesma*, towed her torpedo. Unfortunately the *Chesma's* towing torpedo was found to be useless and the attacks of the other two boats in the same division also failed. In one case a rope connecting the picket boats exploded the torpedo; in the other, a torpedo net prematurely exploded the torpedo. On June 20 the Turks again employed the boom defense to protect a monitor attacked by some Russian mine laying boats off Ruschuk. Following this experience Lieutenant Makarov turned for a time to commercial targets; in a short cruise off the Turkish coast he sank four merchant vessels.

Then on August 24 Makarov, using a convenient eclipse to cover his approach, sent four boats (*Chesma, Sinop, Torpedoist*, and *Navarin*) against the Turkish ironclad *Assar-I-Chevket*, lying off Sukhumi. The four torpedo boats converged upon the Turkish warship but had difficulty managing their towed torpedoes. The *Sinop* was able to explode her torpedo in a boat anchored alongside the *Chevket*, but the others were unable to claim even near misses. Indeed, the small expedition was fortunate in getting back to Odessa without loss after sighting but not being sighted by a Turkish ironclad en route.

The detailing of the *Veliky Kniaz Konstantin* to army transport duties caused a temporary lull in the attacks. But three months later the Russians struck again. This time a small squadron consisting of a mortar barge, two armed tugs, and seven torpedo boats, all armed with mines and torpedoes, ascended the Kiliya mouth of the Danube. The Turkish fleet then being hunted by the Russians consisted of the ironclads *Medjenieh, Assar-I-Chevket,* and *Muini Zaffir,* and the turret ship *Hafiz-I-ul-Roham.* These ships were discovered anchored between two breakwaters which were connected by a chain, with batteries defending to seaward. Another battery was pointed upstream, as was a fifth ironclad, *Mukadim-I-Hair,* and a gunboat. The Russians had little hope of succeeding in a direct attack on so strong a squadron, but they sent out torpedo boats to sow mines in the river above and below Kiliya. The following day a Russian steamer, sent out as "bait" to reconnoiter, drew attack from the gunboat *Sulina* and a tug. The *Sulina* struck one of the mines laid the previous day and sank. The next day the Russians launched a torpedo attack, but again the affair proved relatively bloodless. The Turks, though adequately protected, were too poor shots to take toll of their attackers.

Following this encounter the Russians discarded the practice of towing torpedoes and armed the *Chesma* and *Sinop* with the Whitehead tubes just then being introduced. These were an improvement on earlier methods, but as measured by later standards they were still very crude and unreliable. On two occasions the Russians were able to test their efficacy. In the first attack, made on a rainy night, the *Sinop*'s torpedo missed its target. That of the *Chesma* was accurately aimed but was prematurely exploded by nets. On January 26, 1878, the two ships scored a success when they penetrated Batum and fired at the steam frigate *Intibakeh,* which sank at once.

It would be easy to underrate the results of torpedo warfare. The forays ordered by Makarov constituted the first flotilla attacks to be carried out by any navy. Because they were undertaken with inadequate weapons they did not claim many direct victims; yet the mere threat of torpedoes forced the Turks to adopt defensive measures which robbed their naval superiority of most of its effectiveness. Ships moored behind chains, booms, and nets may be adequately protected, but they are also of limited tactical value and have virtually abdicated their function of controlling the sea.

When the Russian armies neared the outskirts of Constantinople, the sultan was more than ready to make peace on terms favorable to the Russians. But his British friends once more intervened, sending a squadron under Adm. Sir Geoffrey Hornby to the Sea of Marmora and urging that the Turkish question be referred to a congress to be held in Berlin. The Russians, now having their ancient objective early in view, seriously considered a course urged by Admiral Popov—laying mines to shut the British out of the Black Sea and pushing on with their land campaign. However, the tsar was in favor of peace. And a study by Gen. Count Edward Todtleben showed there was too little time to lay mines before the British fleet could strike, and too much chance of having Russian minelayers sunk by Turkish shore batteries. Reluctantly, the plan was abandoned.

In the last analysis, then, British intervention kept the Russians from reaping the full rewards of their victory. Disraeli brought about the Congress of Berlin in the summer of 1878 in an effort to rescue Turkey, and for his pains England gained the island of Cyprus. Bulgaria was divided and cut off from the Aegean. Austria was permitted to occupy Bosnia and Herzegovina. Russia was awarded Bessarabia, Kars, and Batum, plus a small indemnity. However, tensions before this settlement was finally reached caused the Russians to deploy some 22 cruisers throughout the world in positions where they could raid British commerce: the lessons of the American Civil War had not been lost on them.

THE NEW INTERNATIONAL ALIGNMENT

In the period following the Congress of Berlin (June 13–July 13, 1878), several shifts took place in the alignment of the European powers. Great Britain, choosing to continue for the time being her policies of isolationism and the maintenance of a balance of power, was regarded by the Russians as their principal antagonist. Indeed, the Congress of Berlin was without doubt exceedingly frustrating to the Russians. They had repeatedly vanquished the Turks, but in every instance British sea power and diplomacy had robbed them of the fruits of their victory. Britain, for her part, viewed Russian aspirations for the Turkish Straits as a dire threat to her Mediterranean lifeline. Russian territorial gains at the expense of the tribesmen of Central Asia also filled her with suspicion, since such moves could be regarded as a preliminary to offensive gestures against India.

But if Russia's relations with Britain remained tense, those with France did not. Prior to the Franco-Prussian War, Russia's natural allies among the European powers had appeared to be the absolute monarchies of Austria-Hungary and Prussia. In 1871 Prussia became Germany and soon thereafter attained a level of military strength which made her an uncomfortable neighbor. In addition, Austria's territorial ambitions in the Balkans were in conflict with those of Russia. In 1881 an "Alliance of Three Emperors" was concluded, but it lasted only until 1887. By 1898 most of the ties with Germany and Austria were ended. To France, thirsting to avenge her humiliation at the hands of Germany, Russia now appeared in a benevolent and friendly light. Diplomatic, cultural, and financial ties between the two countries were strengthened. The two navies exchanged visits. A French squadron visited Kronstadt in 1891, and in 1893 a Russian squadron, consisting of *Nikolai I, Pamiat Azova, Rynda, Admiral Nakhimov,* and *Terets,* repaid the gesture with a friendly visit to Toulon. At French invitation Russia maintained a small Mediterranean squadron based on Villafranca-sur-Mer near Nice, a port which France had permitted the Russians to use in the past. In 1893 an alliance was concluded, following which French capital was exported to Russia for the purpose of starting new and important industrial enterprises.

The Franco-Russian naval rapprochement was regarded with doubt and suspicion by Great Britain. Since the Napoleonic wars, the British navy had been supreme, and at times stronger than all other naval forces combined. When during the 1880s and 1890s other nations started building formidable fleets, the British naval policy became more clearly defined into what was known as a "two-power standard." Translated into concrete terms, the British navy was to be stronger than the two next largest. For a time these two were the French and Russian fleets.

The repeated rebuffs to Russia's ambition to control the straits led her to seek expansion in other directions, notably in central Asia and the Far East. Though Russia in 1867 sold Alaska to the United States, this action was a deviation from a policy that was generally imperialistic and expansionist. The territorial ventures of Nicholas I in the Caucasus and central Asia had not encountered serious obstacles. These conquests were continued, first by Alexander II and later by Alexander III. Between 1865 and 1876 Khiva and Bukhara were reduced to vassalage, and the annexation in 1881 of the Transcaspian area completed the seizure of Central Asia. While England resented these activities, there was very little she could do to prevent them.

Russian expansionism in the Far East was resumed during the reign of Alexander III following a long period of relative calm. With the start of the Trans-Siberian Railroad in 1891 the tsar sought to encourage expansion in the Pacific area. The right to build a railroad across Manchuria was acquired in 1896; and in 1898 the Russians occupied Port Arthur, a warm water port close to the rising sea power of Japan.

NAVAL EXPANSION 1878–95

Between 1878 and approximately 1895 the Russian government followed a naval policy that was basically defensive. Influenced by the American Civil War, Russia was still building many coast-defense ironclads as well as large, fast cruisers and torpedo boats. Maneuvers, when conducted, were usually based on the premise that a stronger enemy was blockading the Russian coast and that the major concern would be either to break a blockade or to inflict heavy losses on an opposing force. The Baltic and Black seas were felt to be important areas, but the White Sea was abandoned. Very few warships were maintained on foreign stations. The small internal squadrons on the Aral Sea and the Amu Daria River were also placed out of commission following the conquest of Turkmenistan in 1881.

In 1880 the Council of Empire directed the minister of marine to prepare a twenty-year naval program. Late in 1881 a report was issued recommending an establishment of 19 first-class and four second-class battleships, together with 25 cruisers of assorted sizes and various lesser vessels. All ship hulls were to be built in Russia. The new emperor, Alexander III, approved the program.

Though the legal basis for the recreation of the Black Sea Fleet had been laid in 1871 with the repudiation of the Treaty of Paris, new shipbuilding did not begin until after the Turko-Russian War. The first Black Sea Fleet vessel of any consequence was the 3,050-ton cruiser *Pamiat Merkuriia*, launched at Toulon in 1880. In 1883 three battleships were laid down. They were *Chesma, Sinop*, and *Yekaterina II* of 10,200 tons. The first two were built at Sevastopol, the third at Nikolaev. These ships, of unique appearance, carried three pairs of 12-inch 30-caliber guns in a pear-shaped central citadel. There was a secondary battery of seven 6-inch guns and ten machine guns. An 18-inch armor belt was carried the length of the ship. The designed speed of 15 knots was exceeded in trials by one to three knots. For their day these were unusually formidable vessels, even though the time of building was very slow and the Krupp-made 12-inch guns never proved entirely satisfactory—faults which were to characterize all types of Russian vessels. For some years the *Chesmas* were the best Russian battleships.

Several reasonably efficient armored cruisers were built for the Baltic. The *Dmitry Donskoi* and *Vladimir Monomakh*—each of slightly below 6,000 tons—made only 15-½ to 16 knots but carried four 8-inch and 12 6-inch guns and were regarded by the standards of the middle 1880s as good cruisers. The slightly larger (7,781 tons) *Admiral Nakhimov* and *Aleksandr Nevsky* made 17-½ knots on their trials and were armed with four 9-inch guns in four barbettes, one forward, one aft, and one on each beam. Though constructed of Russian steel their engines were purchased abroad. The armored cruiser *Pamiat Azova* of 6,700 tons, launched in 1888, carried two 8-inch and thirteen 6-inch guns and could steam at better than 18 knots. In 1890 the Russians included in their building program the *Riurik*, a ship that was huge for the day (10,900 tons), fairly fast at 18 knots, and reasonably well armed with four 8-inch, 16 6-inch, and six 4.7-inch guns, besides 22 quick firers. She was, however, highly deficient in armor protection. The British, who believed it necessary to "answer" foreign warships of all types, were sufficiently disturbed by the *Riurik* to build two rivals, the *Powerful* and the *Terrible*, which were even larger and more expensive. Thereupon the Russians laid down two still larger ships, the *Rossiia* of 12,100 tons and the *Gromoboi* of 12,500. These carried much the same armament as the *Riurik* but were faster and better protected by armor. They, as well as similar French and American ships, prompted the British to build a whole series of lightly armed but fast cruisers of large coal capacity. When the *Riurik* was viewed at Kiel she was found to be a full-rigged three-masted ship of a type that had been fashionable much earlier.

The smaller cruisers of the Russian navy were quite unimpressive as a group, being lighter, slower, and weaker than most foreign ships of the same class. One exception was the *Admiral Kornilov*, a commerce destroyer of about 5,000 tons, which had very little military value.

The Black Sea battleships and the Russian cruisers and torpedo craft could be regarded as logical representatives of a naval policy of coast defense and commerce destruction which was, prior to Mahan, commonly accepted as appropriate to the weaker naval powers. The Russian cruisers were viewed with considerable respect by the British, who feared a repetition of the role played by the *Alabama*. In 1880 in the harbor of Nagasaki, Japan, the British battleship *Agamemnon*, whose captain later claimed she had a defective steering gear, headed directly for the *Vladimir Mono-makh*, apparently in an attempt to ram the Russian vessel. This maneuver could have been a deliberate attempt to eliminate a dangerous potential enemy. At any rate, the Russian captain called all hands to action stations and trained the ship's guns on the British vessel, which then changed course.

The Russian battleships of the 1880s and 1890s are much more difficult to classify in terms of naval policy. They were in fact so varied and miscellaneous in type and design as to suggest a somewhat hit-or-miss groping at policy-forming levels. During the 1880s the *Aleksandr II*, *Nikolai I*, *Gangut*, and *Navarin*, ranging from 6,500 tons to 9,500 tons, were completed for the Baltic Fleet, and the *Georgy Pobedonosets* and *Dvenadtsat Apostolov* were built for the Black Sea Fleet. These six vessels represented five different types, most of which were both undergunned and slow. During the 1890s there was a little improvement, though Russian shipbuilders continued to produce some very poor vessels. Three slow coast-defense battleships of 4,200 tons (named for Admirals Ushakov, Seniavin, and Apraksin) which carried either four 9-inch or three 10-inch guns, and the second-class battleship *Sysoi Veliky* were among the less satisfactory ships built for the Baltic during the 1890s. The Black Sea battleships *Tri Sviatitelia*, *Rostislav*, and *Kniaz Potemkin Tavrichesky*, all of about 12,500 tons, were better; unfortunately, however, they represented three separate classes and were not uniform in speed, armor, or guns. The *Rostislav* deserves passing note as one of the first warships to burn oil fuel.

As previously indicated, the lessons of both the American Civil War and the war with Turkey led to heightened interest in torpedo boats. For most of the decade of the 1880s the Russian torpedo-boat flotillas were among the most numerous in the world. Attempts to use towing and spar torpedoes were abandoned, and movable torpedoes fired from tubes were substituted. The first boats built, numbering about 120, were 23-ton torpedo launches each carrying one or two torpedoes and able to steam at 13 knots. Though a big improvement over the improvised boats of Lieutenant Makarov and his colleagues, they were not formidable. They were gradually increased in size to 100 tons, and in speed to about 20 knots. The flotillas were about equally divided between the Baltic and Black seas.

In common with other countries during the period, Russia took intermittent cognizance of submarines and considered but dismissed plans from at least half a dozen inventors. The most promising designs were submitted by a Russian engineer named Drzewiecki, who after 1877 devoted himself to underwater craft. In 1879 interest in one of his experimental craft led the Ministry of Coast Defense to order 50—of which 34 were sent by rail to Sevastopol and 16 delivered to Kronstadt. Each of these craft carried two torpedoes and two periscopes, but the vessels were of very small size. Designed for night attacks, they were expected to be transported to battle areas by fast auxiliaries. Drzewiecki developed various other submarine types, including one that operated on an electric motor and storage batteries. In 1896 his plans for a 190-ton boat capable of making 15 knots on the surface won a prize from the French government, but no Russian orders.

During the 1880s Vickers in England built a submarine of 243 tons from a design by a Swedish inventor. This ship was lost off the coast of Denmark en route to Russia. It had no engine for submerged propulsion but could travel a maximum of 20 miles under water on steam pressure built up on the surface. Two quick-firing guns could be used on the surface.

A 60-ton submarine carrying two 18-inch torpedoes was designed by Lieutenants Kolbasev and Kuteinikov in 1901. This boat could make eight knots on the surface and six submerged. A sister ship, the *Forel*, was finished and sent to Vladivostok. A larger (175-ton) submarine, the *Delfin*, was launched in 1903 after being built from a design prepared by Engineer A. D. Bubnov. This reasonably effective boat carried four 18-inch torpedo tubes and made 11 knots on the surface. The *Delfin* for a time was used for training until, as a result of the blunders of a green crew, it sank with all hands. Between 1902 and 1905 the Russians purchased no less than nine gasoline-engine subs designed by the American inventor Simon Lake.

Though considerable progress was made in naval ordnance, Russia still tended to lag behind other countries. Cast-iron guns were replaced by artillery of iron and later of steel. The 12-inch naval gun became the standard heavy weapon and was increased in length and range from 17 calibers in 1867 to 28 calibers in the 1870s and 35 in the 1880s. Smaller guns were also improved during the same period.

During the 1880s and 1890s there was a sharp rise in the accuracy, range, and explosive power of the Whitehead and Hertz torpedoes then in use. Russian naval engineers also worked on torpedo tubes, and pyrocollodion powder was developed and used more than any other type. Toward the end of the 1890s high-quality steel armor, which was thinner and lighter than earlier armors but had greater powers of resistance, was adopted. Incendiary and armor-piercing fougasse shells were developed. Several types of secondary and rapid-fire guns came into use.

During the 1880s some development of base facilities was undertaken. A canal across the Isthmus of Perekop, connecting the Crimea with the remainder of Russia, shortened substantially the voyages of warships moving along the northern coast of the Black Sea. Forts were reconstructed on either side of the port of Sevastopol, and the entrance was defended by mines and torpedoes. In addition, the Russian government founded the port of Novorossiisk at the end of a deep bay.

The persistent if none too skillful efforts of the tsars to create a strong navy led to an improvement in at least the paper strength of the fleet; by 1893 the imperial Russian navy was ahead of Italy and Germany in size. In terms of first-class battleships, England then held a comfortable lead with 35 ships, while France was in second place with 16 and Russia third with 11. The numbers of armored cruisers were 18, 13, and ten respectively; protected cruisers of the first and second class numbered 67, 27, and three. From these figures it is apparent that England held a commanding overall lead, and that the Franco-Russian alliance could not then hope to threaten her hegemony.

But if the new Russian fleet was not outstanding in efficiency it was worthy of note from an economic standpoint. The efforts expended in its creation had far-reaching effects on the Russian economy; indeed, the requirements of the navy did much to further the Industrial Revolution in Russia. Factories had to be built, workmen trained in new skills, railroads laid, and shipyards and ordnance plants brought into being. Foreign capital, mainly French, assisted in creating many of these enterprises. Even so, because domestic industry could not be expanded rapidly enough to supply all of the new ships, much less their components, a number of Russian warships had to be built in foreign yards.

THE NEW NAVAL POLICY 1895–1904

In about the mid-1890s Russian naval policy began to undergo gradual change. Shipbuilding became devoted to the primary objective of creating a fleet of seagoing battleships. By threatening intervention at the end of Japan's war with China, Russia succeeded in acquiring Port Arthur and in developing a sphere of interest in Manchuria. This foothold was strengthened by the dispatch of first-class battleships to the Far East until the Russian fleet in the Pacific was as strong as that in the Baltic. A small squadron was also set up in the Mediterranean. Though there was no return to the White Sea, Admiral Makarov enjoyed official support in his efforts to explore the Arctic and to develop a northern sea route along the Siberian coast. In short, naval policy became positive in tone and might even be described as offensive and imperialistic in its motivation.

While there is no completely satisfactory explanation of this new attitude, a partial interpretation of the change may be found in the writings of the American Capt. Alfred T. Mahan. During the twenty years which preceded his death in 1915, Mahan's influence was worldwide. In the case of the United States, Great Britain, Germany, and possibly Japan, the effect of his thinking is fairly easy to trace. The effect in Russia was less direct, though Mahan's works were read in translation there and became a naval bible for the younger officers. Among these was Nikolai Klado (1861–1919), a brilliant, persuasive, extremely learned man with a strong literary bent who, though twenty years younger than Mahan, was in fact in some ways his Russian counterpart. In a series of books and articles that attained wide circulation he applied Mahan's theories of sea power to Russia. He was in great demand as a lecturer as well as a writer, and his audience often included members of the royal family. It is not surprising, therefore, that his conclusion that Russia needed a genuine high seas fleet gained a ready response from Tsar Nicholas II, himself a naval enthusiast.

As a member of the faculty of the imperial naval academy, Klado introduced courses in naval history and tactics, writing the necessary textbooks himself since none existed in Russia. A careful study of the Far East, where he served for a time, convinced him that expansion into this area was necessary to the national welfare. Indeed, his first book, published in 1895, was a history of the war between China and Japan. Though Klado was strongly influenced by the traditional concept of naval power as a seaward flank of the army—his interpretations of his own nation's history showed his ability to apply Mahan's theories to Russia's past and present.

The drive in Russia for a genuine seagoing navy was roughly parallel to the building of the "new navy" in the United States. It had much the same motivation, occurred over the same time span, and brought a comparable rise in naval rank. By the end of the century the Russian navy had an apparently firm hold on third-place rank among the world's fleets. In 1898 it comprised 20 battleships, 22 coast-defense ships, 11 armored cruisers, two protected cruisers, 20 cruisers, nine torpedo gunboats, five destroyers, about 75 torpedo

boats of over 100 feet, and various auxiliaries. With respect to the
efficiency of buildup, however, Russia's record was not comparable
to that of the United States. For a long time a heavy dependence
was placed on foreign builders and suppliers. Ship designs failed to
get all the offensive power that could have been expected from a
given tonnage, and as a result most of the ships were undergunned.
Because of the rigorous winters as well as a variety of other factors,
naval construction was slow, costly, and often graft-ridden. A trial
at Sevastopol in 1900 revealed that about 40 officers had accepted
bribes from contractors. During operations, collisions and naval
accidents were frequent, and ships in the Baltic were often
grounded. Shore establishments varied in quality but for the most
part ranked well below those of other countries. In short, the rise in
Russian naval power was more impressive on paper than in reality.
Moreover, the distribution of ships into three widely separated and
mutually independent fleets prevented full concentration in any
one area.

During the mid-1890s naval construction improved and battleships were built in classes rather than as individual ships. The
11,000-ton *Petropavlovsk, Poltava,* and *Sevastopol,* though far from
being top-notch ships, were perhaps equal to most foreign battleships of their date. Designed for 16-½ knots, they carried four
12-inch and 12 6-inch guns. Maximum armor protection ranged
from 10 to 12 inches on the turrets and was 16 inches on the main
belt. The next class, comprising the *Peresvet, Pobeda,* and *Osliabia,*
was larger (12,674 tons), weaker (10-inch rather than 12-inch main
battery guns), somewhat faster (speed up to 19 knots), and less
well protected. Two relatively high quality ships, the *Tsesarevich*
and *Retvizan,* were built in France and the United States respectively. They carried the then normal battery of four 12-inch and 12
6-inch guns, with 48 smaller guns and quick firers, and were
designed to make 18 knots. A still later class, which came into
service about the time of the Russo-Japanese War, consisted of the
Borodino, Orel, Slava, Aleksandr III, and *Kniaz Suvorov.* These
were larger than the *Retvizan* (13,500 tons) but were in other
respects quite similar.

Shortly before the turn of the century the Russians manifested
some interest in protected cruisers and ordered the *Askold, Avrora,*

Bogatyr, Diana, Oleg, Variag, and *Pallada,* as well as the *Kagul* and *Ochakov,* for the Black Sea Fleet. Though not all sister ships, these vessels were similar and were intended as possible commerce destroyers. On a ship with a displacement of about 6,500 tons they carried a battery of eight to 12 6-inch guns and could steam at nearly 23 knots. A smaller cruiser, the 3,000-ton *Novik,* built as an experiment in East Prussia, was lightly armed but even faster, making 25 knots. The *Svetlana* (3,900 tons, six 6-inch guns) was designed to reach 21 knots but proved such a poor steamer and fighter that she became little more than an armed yacht. As a group these cruisers, which were built in Russia, German, and American yards, were of good type and outclassed most foreign contemporaries.

With the increased development of first-class battleships, the earlier Russian interest in torpedo craft lessened. During the 1890s about 20 destroyers were built. Of these the 240-ton *Sokol,* built in England, distinguished herself by making nearly 30 knots during her 1895 trials. Speeds of 17 to 27 knots at that time were far more common.

Of doubtful value to Russian seapower was the Volunteer Fleet, which consisted of merchant ships subject to service as auxiliaries in time of war. The dozen or so small and slow commercial vessels which comprised this fleet were unimpressive in both quality and quantity.

Late in the nineteenth century Russia developed two new types of ships, both designed by the same man. Vice Adm. Stepan O. Makarov (1849–1904) started his naval career with many handicaps, not the least of which was his peasant ancestry, a circumstance that in Russia normally would have barred him from becoming an officer. His abilities and personality, however, were so outstanding that he was permitted to enter the navy as a cadet officer, and he won rapid promotion. His service career was distinguished in many ways. The collision mat, suggested in 1870, was the first of a long series of his inventions. He was a fluent and productive writer of books and magazine articles, some of which were translated into other languages. In the field of science he ranked as Russia's greatest oceanographer, his principal observations having been carried on while commanding the corvette *Vitiaz* during an around-the-world cruise (1886–89). Makarov was also a naval philosopher who coined some much-repeated maxims, one of them stressing the necessity of Russians' becoming "at home at sea."

His contributions to ship design included the world's first ice-breaker, the 8,000-ton *Yermak*. This ship, which was completed in England in 1897, proved a success from the start. Makarov's objective in designing the *Yermak* had been to make possible summer navigation of the seas north of Siberia, thus overcoming in some measure the formidable geographic handicap which had forced Russia to divide her naval forces among the several seas. The final outcome of his invention and vision was, of course, the Northern Sea Route, developed by the Soviets four decades later. The western half of this route was surveyed by Makarov himself, in the *Yermak*. In addition, the *Yermak* and her successors aided winter navigation within ports, permitted additional polar exploration, extended the navigation season in very cold seas by several weeks, and aided in the rescue of marooned fishermen and seamen. Makarov had hoped that the *Yermak* would enable him to be the first to reach the North Pole but in this respect he was disappointed.

Makarov's second major contribution to ship design, made in 1898, was a class of six minelayers named after Russian rivers, the first such ships in any navy. These 2,590-ton ships carried 300 mines each and could steam at 18 knots. Their building climaxed a long period of interest in and development of the naval mine, one weapon in which Russia led the world.[1]

No other man in the Russian navy during this period matched Makarov in versatility and ability. However, Prof. A. A. Popov of the Torpedo School at Kronstadt deserves mention as a pioneer in the development and use of radio. His successes began as early as 1897. In 1899 he transmitted a message a distance of 35 kilometers, and in January 1900 at the island of Lavansaari he used radio to summon the *Yermak* to the rescue of fishermen stranded on the ice in the Gulf of Finland. Unfortunately the follow-up of his achievements was not very aggressive, with the result that radio communications aboard Russian ships were largely inadequate during the Russo-Japanese War.

This slovenliness in the follow-up of an important invention was fairly typical of the Russian shore establishment in the early 1900s.

Most Russian naval bases were of poor quality. Vladivostok was for a time the only base of importance in the Pacific, and its facilities were distinctly second class. After the acquisition of Port Arthur from China, the Russians partially developed both that port and nearby Talienwan (Dalny or Dairen). Even so, Port Arthur, though easy to defend, had several disadvantages: not only was it limited in size, but 1,500 miles of Japanese-held shoreline separated it from Vladivostok.

In the Black Sea the only bases of importance were Nikolaev and Sevastopol. Nikolaev was well guarded and relatively modern, with good dockyards and industrial facilities of various types. Sevastopol was less modern but had docks, two building slips, and reasonably good fortifications.

The largest bases were those in the Baltic, where St. Petersburg was the center of a whole complex of government and private shipyards which included, in addition to smaller establishments, Kronstadt, the Baltic Works, the New Admiralty, Izhora, Obukhov, and Galernyi Island. These yards included industrial facilities of all kinds and employed some well-paid workmen who were as highly skilled as any to be found elsewhere. Yet industrial accidents, whether due to sabotage or carelessness, were of frequent occurrence, and the construction rate on warships was slow. Building slips were roofed over to protect them from icy weather, and during winter most of the ships were frozen in and deserted, the crews confined to shore. With the development of icebreakers, however, this situation was partially remedied.

Aside from the St. Petersburg complex, bases had been developed in the Baltic at Revel, Helsinki, and Libau. Since Libau had the unusual virtue of being ice-free, it served as a base from which vessels could be dispatched to the Pacific or the Mediterranean. Although it had been developed to an elaborate extent, however, this port was exceedingly vulnerable because of its exposed situation only 50 miles from the German frontier. Revel was used mainly as a torpedo boat station.

A major weakness of the Russian navy lay in its personnel. Conscripts did not enter the navy until they had reached the age of twenty-one. While there were a few Balts with some knowledge of the sea, the major proportion of the men came from the interior and had no naval background and little education. The enlisted force normally served for seven years on active duty, plus three years in reserve, and training was in most cases negligible. During the 1890s the yearly intake of recruits ranged from 7,000 to 11,000. Save in wartime there was almost no possibility of becoming an officer and comparatively little chance even to advance in rating. Men in service were forbidden to marry, were poorly paid and often poorly fed. Technicians and experts of all types were very scarce.

Future officers, on the other hand, were almost invariably the sons of officers or nobles. They entered the navy at an early age (twelve to fourteen was common) and received an average of six years' training. Competitive examinations were employed at certain stages to eliminate some of the dullards, but most promotions were by seniority. Because many officers disliked being at sea, extra pay was provided for such duty, and service on foreign stations, since it drew increased salary to defray theoretically higher living costs, tended to find favor among them.

Owing partly to natural handicaps and partly to poor management and refusal to spend money on personnel, the Russian navy during the late nineteenth century never succeeded in regaining the reputation for smartness it had enjoyed after the Napoleonic wars. During the Boxer Rebellion three gunboats, *Bobr, Giulik,* and *Koreets,* gave a good account of themselves in the bombardment of the Taku forts which guarded the approach to Tientsin; but this was an isolated instance and even somewhat misleading, since the opposition was extremely feeble. Sloppy ship handling during the relatively few times ships were at sea only compounded the faulty shipbuilding and the administrative scandals ashore. Blunders and breakdowns of equipment during annual maneuvers were not infrequently attended by ugly hints of sabotage. Overall, then, the power of the Russian navy was more apparent than real: its very considerable nominal strength was greatly reduced both by natural handicaps and by a high incidence of undertrained personnel and poor materiel.

CHAPTER 10

Russo-Japanese War: Life and Death of the Pacific Fleet

BACKGROUND

BASICALLY THE RUSSO-JAPANESE WAR was an outgrowth of the conflicting interests of two expansionist powers, Russia and Japan. Commodore Perry's forceful opening of Japan had unleashed in that island country a feverish struggle to become modern and powerful. At the same time the subjects of the tsar were slowly beginning to settle the northeast coast of Asia. It was during this period that the Russians, making use of a combination of force and diplomacy, were able to gain from China regions north of the Amur and east of the Ussuri. In this new territory, on the western coast of the Sea of Japan, they had founded Vladivostok.

For almost a generation thereafter, Russian ambitions remained quiescent; but in the 1890s, as noted in the preceding chapter, a resurgent interest in the Far East led to a renewed expansionist struggle. Construction of the Trans-Siberian Railroad, begun in 1891, was an attempt to tie Vladivostok more closely to the centers of the tsar's empire. Vladivostok, however, because it was ice-bound for several months each winter, did not fully satisfy Russian desires for a window on the Pacific. A more southerly, ice-free port obviously would be more valuable. Russian hopes for acquisition of such a port suffered a setback when, at the conclusion of the 1894–95 war between Japan and China, the Treaty of Shimonoseki ceded to Japan the Liaotung Peninsula, thus barring to Russia the most likely area of access to the sea. The Russians, backed by France and Germany, brought pressure on Japan to return the peninsula to China. Unprepared to do battle with three major European states, the Japanese assented—but very reluctantly. They spent the next decade in expanding and improving their army and navy, and to protect themselves from having to fight more than one power at a time they also concluded the Anglo-Japanese Alliance in 1902.

Meanwhile the Russians moved steadily forward. By secret treaty they gained the right to construct the Chinese Eastern Railroad through Manchuria. In 1898 they secured the lease of Port Arthur and Dalny, the very ports from which they had earlier forced the Japanese, with the plan that Dalny was to be developed as a commercial port and Port Arthur as a naval base. With most of the construction on the Trans-Siberian and Chinese Eastern railroads completed between 1898 and 1901, they stationed troops in Manchuria to protect their investments (allegedly from the Boxers whom Russia, aided by the other world powers, had earlier successfully suppressed). Their next step was to support a group of adventurers seeking timber concessions on the Yalu River in Korea—a country which Japan regarded as her undeclared protectorate.

During 1903 Japan made several attempts to reach an agreement with Russia regarding their respective interests. None of the negotiations met with notable success, largely because the Russian adventurers in the Far East and Nicholas II alike underestimated the Japanese strength and felt there was no danger of war. Then, on February 5, 1904, the Japanese government severed diplomatic relations with Russia. Three days later hostilities began with a surprise Japanese attack; five days later there were mutual declarations of war.

Although Japan was a sentimental favorite, most European and American military observers felt the war was between unequally matched powers. A comparison of the two countries' resources showed a disparity of ten to one in government revenues, more than three to one in population (140 million as compared to 44 million), and nearly sixty to one in area, all, of course, in Russia's favor. Japanese naval expenditures in 1903 totaled £2.5 million; those of Russia £12.3 million—a ratio of five to one. In total tonnage the Russian navy held almost a three-to-one superiority.

Yet despite these apparent disadvantages the Japanese could claim a number of very important assets. Since battles and wars are usually decided not by superiority in total potential strength but by superiority of forces *in contact with the enemy*, the Japanese had the advantage. Russia was forced to operate far from the centers of her strength; Japan was always close to hers. The Japanese merchant marine was larger, 979,000 tons compared to 679,000. Russia had only two naval bases of importance, inaccessible to each other and both inadequately developed; Japan had four large navy yards and four good private yards. What is more, the Russian people tended to be disaffected and at times rebellious, while the Japanese were intensely dedicated, ably led, unified, and patriotic.

Nowhere was the apparent disparity of strength more misleading than in the case of naval forces (see table 4). As of February 1904 Russian forces in the Far East comprised seven battleships (*Retvizan, Pobeda, Tsesarevich, Sevastopol, Poltava, Petropavlovsk,* and *Peresvet*), four armored cruisers (*Gromoboi, Rossiia, Riurik,* and *Baian*), 25 destroyers and about the same number of torpedo boats, and various gunboats, sloops, minelayers, and auxiliaries. At the outbreak of war a squadron commanded by Rear Admiral Vireniius and comprising the new battleship *Osliabia,* the cruisers *Dmitry Donskoi, Avrora,* and *Almaz,* seven destroyers, and four torpedo boats was also on its way to the Far East, but was forced to turn back in the Red Sea. In December 1903 Russian attempts to purchase two new Chilean battleships, *Constitución* and *Libertad,* were forestalled when the British purchased them instead.

In contrast, Japan's navy was all on the scene. It comprised seven battleships (one a small obsolete ship formerly belonging to China), six armored cruisers, 18 protected cruisers, 10 small cruisers and torpedo gunboats, 19 destroyers, and 85 torpedo boats. Prior to the outbreak of war two additional armored cruisers being built in Italy for Argentina, *Moreno* and *Rivadavia,* were purchased by Japan, delivered, and renamed *Nisshin* and *Kasuga.*

As far as the total of combat-ready ships is concerned, the Japanese were equal to the Russians in numbers of battleships, and far superior in cruisers and torpedo craft. Data in table 4 indicate that Japanese craft also excelled in quality. The Japanese battleships were larger, faster, more heavily armed, and in some cases better

TABLE 4

*Russian and Japanese Naval Forces in the Far East,
February 1904**

DATE OF LAUNCH	NAME	TONNAGE	ARMOR BELT	ARMOR TURRET	MAIN ARMAMENT	SPEED (KNOTS)**

RUSSIAN PACIFIC FLEET
At Port Arthur

BATTLESHIPS:

DATE OF LAUNCH	NAME	TONNAGE	ARMOR BELT	ARMOR TURRET	MAIN ARMAMENT	SPEED (KNOTS)**
1895	Sevastopol	11,000	15c†	10	4 12"; 12 6"	16½
1894	Poltava	11,000	15c	10	4 12"; 12 6"	16½
1894	Petropavlovsk	11,000	15c	10	4 12"; 12 6"	16½
1898	Peresvet	12,674	9	10	4 10"; 12 6"	19
1900	Pobeda	12,674	9	10	4 10"; 12 6"	19
1901	Retvizan	12,500	9	10	4 12"; 12 6"	18
1902	Tsesarevich	12,500	10	10	4 12"; 12 6"	18

ARMORED CRUISERS:

| 1900 | Baian | 7,900 | 8 | 7 | 2 8"; 8 6" | 20 |

PROTECTED CRUISERS: *(DECK)*

DATE OF LAUNCH	NAME	TONNAGE	DECK	MAIN ARMAMENT	SPEED (KNOTS)**
1899	Askold	5,905	3	12 6"	24
1899	Diana	6,630	2½	8 6"	23
1899	Pallada	6,500	2½	8 6"	23
1902	Novik	3,000	2	6 4.7"	25
1902	Boiarin	3,000	2	6 4.7"	24

2 armored gunboats; 4 sloops; 1 gun vessel;
25 destroyers 240-350 tons; 21 torpedo boats

At Chemulpho

PROTECTED CRUISERS:

| | Variag | 6,500 | 3 | 12 6" | 23 |

GUNBOAT:

| | Koreets | 1,500 | ½ | 2 8" | 11 |

At Vladivostok

ARMORED CRUISERS: *(BELT CASEMATE)*

DATE OF LAUNCH	NAME	TONNAGE	BELT	CASEMATE	MAIN ARMAMENT	SPEED (KNOTS)**
	Gromoboi	12,500	6	6	4 8"; 16 6"	20
	Rossiia	12,100	10	2	4 8"; 16 6"	19
	Riurik	10,000	10	—	4 8"; 16 6"	18

TABLE 4

Russian and Japanese Naval Forces in the Far East,
February 1904

DATE OF LAUNCH	NAME	TONNAGE	BELT TURRET		MAIN ARMAMENT	SPEED (KNOTS)

RUSSIAN PACIFIC FLEET

PROTECTED CRUISERS: TURRET

1901	Bogatyr	6,650	3		12 6″	23
	8 destroyers					

JAPANESE NAVY

BATTLESHIPS:

1899	Asahi	15,200	9	10	4 12″; 14 6″	18
1902	Mikasa	15,200	9	10	4 12″; 14 6″	18.6
1899	Hatsuse	15,000	9	10	4 12″; 14 6″	19
1898	Shikishima	14,850	9	10	4 12″; 14 6″	18.5
1896	Fuji	12,500	18	6	4 12″; 10 6″	19.2
1896	Yashima	12,500	18	6	4 12″; 10 6″	19

ARMORED CRUISERS:

1898	Asama	9,750	7	6	4 8″; 14 6″	22.3
1899	Idzumo	9,750	7	6	4 8″; 14 6″	22
1900	Iwate	9,750	7	6	4 8″; 14 6″	21.8
1898	Tokiwa	9,750	7	6	4 8″; 14 6″	23
1899	Yakumo	9,800	7	6	4 8″; 12 6″	20
1899	Azuma	9,436	7	6	4 8″; 12 6″	20
1903	Nisshin	7,700	6	5½	4 8″; 14 6″	20
1903	Kasuga	7,700	6	5½	1 10″; 2 8″; 14 6″	20

PROTECTED CRUISERS:

			DECK			
1892	Akitsushima	3,170	3	—	4 6"; 6 4.7"	19
1891	Hashidate	4,230	1½	4	1 12.5"; 11 4.7"	16
1899	Itsukushima	4,230	1½	4	1 12.5"; 11 4.7"	16
1890	Matsushima	4,230	1½	4	1 12.5"; 11 4.7"	16
1885	Naniwa	3,710	3		2 10.2"; 6 6"	18
1885	Takachiho	3,710	3		2 10.2"; 6 6"	18
1892	Yoshino	4,230	4½		4 6"; 8 4.7"	23
1898	Chitose	4,760	4½		2 8"; 10 4.7"	23
1897	Kasagi	4,760	4½		2 8"; 10 4.7"	23
1897	Takasagi	4,300	4½		2 8"; 10 4.7"	23
1884	Idzumi	2,970	1		2 10"; 6 4.7"	17
1885	Suma	2,700	2		2 6"; 6 4.7"	20
1897	Akashi	2,800	2		2 6"; 6 4.7"	20
1889	Chiyoda	2,440	1		10 4.7"	19
1902	Niitaka	3,400	2½		6 6"	20
1902	Tsushima	3,400	2½		6 6"	20

10 small cruisers, gunboats and torpedo gunboats;
20 destroyers; 85 torpedo boats (47 modern).

---

* SOURCE: Herbert W. Wilson, *Battleships in Action* (Boston, 1926), vol. I, appendix.
** Because of poor engineering practices, service speeds of Russian warships were generally well below the designed figure.
† Letter "c" denotes compound armor. All other armor is steel.

armored. In terms of capital ships *in the area* the Japanese were superior in the ratio of 14 ships with a total broadside of 37,600 pounds, to 11 Russian ships having a broadside of 26,500 pounds. Furthermore, the Japanese ships could be united far more readily than could the Russian vessels. Most of them had been built in British shipyards, while the Russian ships had been built in Russia,

France, Germany, and the United States. The Japanese ships were far more up-to-date and homogeneous in design, equipment, and performance.

As for shore facilities, all the advantages were with the Japanese. Four main bases with large docks were available at Yokosuka, Sasebo, Maizuru, and Kure. Three main supply depots were maintained in southern Japan, the Pescadores, and the Tsushima Island. At least half a dozen harbors with a secure coal supply were available. The Russians had only the two main bases already described. The supplies of coal and munitions were alike limited, and chances of substantial reinforcement from European Russia were dim. On the other hand Port Arthur, with her garrison of 60,000 men and strong artillery and mortar defenses, was militarily formidable. At the beginning of the war Port Arthur had large mortars and batteries totaling 82 cannon directly fronting the coast, and these were to be reinforced during the long siege.

The Japanese navy held a decided advantage in quality of personnel. The 36,000 officers and men were well trained and well disciplined. They were devoted to duty, and they had operated since 1903 under a top-notch commander—Adm. Heihaichiro Togo. Adm. Vicomte Ito headed the admiralty and Admiral Count Yamamoto was minister of marine. The top man in the army was Marshal Baron Oyama.

The Russian high command was of poor quality. The moody, despotic, and arrogant Vice Adm. Yevgeny Alekseev headed the Russian Far Eastern forces. Soon after he was appointed to command the Pacific Squadron in 1897 he had in various ways proved himself incapable, and though he had considerable success in obtaining the allotment of larger naval forces to the Far East, their quality declined steadily under his administration. His requests for increased land forces were refused by Gen. Aleksei N. Kuropatkin, minister of war. Though Alekseev's recommendations were at times excellent, he failed to follow them up. Training, gunnery, tactics— in short, nearly all aspects of preparedness—had been neglected for years during his administration.

Serving under Alekseev at Port Arthur were Vice Admiral Starck, an amiable mediocrity, with Rear Admiral Prince Ukhtomsky second in command, and Rear Adm. V. K. Vitheft as chief of staff. The ships at Vladivostok started the war under Rear Admiral Stakelberg, the first of what was to be a series of commanders. None of these officers had a reputation for outstanding ability. At the start of the war Vice Admiral Makarov, generally regarded as the ablest Russian naval leader of that time, was port admiral at Kronstadt. Soon after the outbreak of hostilities Makarov replaced Vice Admiral Starck, who was relieved of command at Port Arthur after his ineptness caused serious losses.

A Japanese naval officer correctly noted in his diary some wide differences in the two fleets:

> Certainly at sea we shall give the Russians a good account of ourselves, for although they are good fighters they possess little practical experience, and their ships, with a few exceptions, are not worth much. An officer of our General Staff was in Port Arthur a short time ago as a spy—we have been practicing espionage for some time now—and is sure the Russians do not believe in the proximity of war. . . . They do not maneuver, they do not carry out any gunnery exercises, and in a corner of the arsenal there are goodness knows how many torpedoes, quite neglected. For months they have not been inspected by either officers or engineers. What a state they must be in—covered with rust.[1]

In a later diary entry, the same officer noted:

> It must be admitted now that the European newspapers have been very wrong ever since the beginning of the war—in declaring that the Russian squadron in the Far East is as powerful as ours. At first sight it looks as though it might be so, for they have the advantage over us in battleships; but actually we are far stronger, owing to the fact that we possessed six magnificent armored cruisers before the arrival of the *Nisshin* and *Kasuga*. . . . Our battleships are superior to theirs in tonnage, weight of guns, and speed, whilst we possess an enormous advantage over them in torpedo boats and destroyers.[2]

At the beginning of the war the Russian leaders displayed little evidence of talent for strategic planning. Their fleet remained divided, with three armored cruisers, a protected cruiser, and 17 torpedo boats at Vladivostok; the cruiser *Variag* and the gunboat *Koreets* at Chemulpo in Korea; three or four gunboats at Chinese ports; and the remainder of their ships at Port Arthur. They had not considered an attack on the Japanese fleet, and a successful

Japanese offensive was thought impossible. The Port Arthur squadron was expected to command the Yellow Sea, while the Vladivostok squadron was assigned to raiding commerce. Apparently there was no plan for coordination between land and sea forces; nor had the naval and army commanders any idea of what they could expect of one another. Some leaders (Kuropatkin, for one) saw little value in a fleet. Their distrust of sea power almost certainly was based in part on the fact that the Pacific Fleet was tactically unprepared to carry out any role. Thus, apart from a vague plan for a landing in Japan, formulated by Kuropatkin, the Russian navy had virtually no design for the conduct of a war.

Japanese strategy was entirely different. The Japanese were far better students of Mahan, and they appreciated the importance of command of the sea. Though they possessed an offensive spirit, they were not inclined to be rash. By dividing their navy into fleets and squadrons they were able to carry out separate, simultaneous missions; but this splitting of forces was entirely different from that of the Russians, whose forces were separated both in theory and in fact. At all times the Japanese squadrons were in communication with one another and operated on interior lines. At the beginning of the war the main objective of the Japanese navy was to land armies on continental Asia, armies to defeat the Russian land forces. To do this, they had first to isolate and then to capture Port Arthur. They dared not risk heavy naval losses in the process, since their battleships were irreplaceable. There was also the possibility that the Russians, because of their much larger strength in European waters, might conceivably be able to send reinforcements to the Pacific. Hence, when the Japanese sought actively to reduce Port Arthur they correctly assigned a leading role to their army rather than to their navy.

THE INITIAL ATTACK

If the opening moves of the Russo-Japanese War seem to have for the American historian a painful familiarity, it is because they were almost identical with those taken by Japan in World War II. They consisted of (a) crippling the main enemy fleet by surprise attack prior to the declaration of war; and (b) destroying small, isolated enemy forces. Both moves were made possible by excellent intelligence gained through spies in Russia and Korea and by mediocre leadership on the part of the enemy.

As already noted, the beginning of the war found the cruiser *Variag* and the gunboat *Koreets* in Korean waters at the port of Chemulpo. For some time these ships had been watched by the Japanese cruiser *Chiyoda*, which was also in the harbor. When the captain of the Japanese vessel learned that diplomatic relations had been severed, he left port to join Admiral Uriu's Fourth Fleet, which consisted at the time of the cruisers *Asama*, *Chiyoda*, and *Takachiho*, three transports loaded with troops, and four destroyers. At 4:40 P.M. on February 8, 1904, the *Koreets*, bent on leaving Chemulpo harbor, fired at approaching Japanese destroyers. It was the first Russian shot of the war. No engagement followed at that time; but Japanese transports proceeded to the task of landing troops, finishing by 10:00 P.M. At 6:00 A.M. the next day Admiral Uriu warned the senior Russian naval officer that both Russian ships must leave by noon or suffer bombardment inside the harbor. He also urged other foreign vessels to move to safe anchorage. When the two Russian ships got under way to leave the harbor shortly after noon, they were fired on by the Japanese. The *Asama* scored repeated hits on the *Variag*, the *Chiyoda* attacked the *Koreets*, and other Japanese vessels quickly joined the fight. The Russian ships fired rapidly but wildly, and made no hits. Heavily outmatched, they soon sustained serious damages which forced them to reenter the port, where *Koreets* was deliberately blown up and *Variag*, which had 49 men killed and 72 wounded, was scuttled in shallow water. The *Variag* was subsequently salvaged and repaired for further service as the Japanese *Soya*. The Russian crews were evacuated from the port by neutral ships.

At the same time a more important action was brewing before Port Arthur. On February 6 Admiral Togo's combined fleet had emerged from its Sasebo naval base, completely ready for war. The Japanese had decided to strike the initial blow with the torpedo flotillas. The First, Second and Third flotillas were to attack the Russian vessels in the roadstead outside Port Arthur, while the Fourth and Fifth flotillas were to search for targets at the satellite port of Dalny.

The attack on Dalny miscarried. At Port Arthur, however, on the night of February 7–8, several Russian ships were anchored in the roads outside the inner harbor. Though it would seem that the Russians had neglected most safety precautions that night, they had stationed two destroyers on patrol outside the harbor. Most of the crews of the two patrol vessels were ashore celebrating a church holiday. Moreover, the two destroyers had orders merely to report the sight of anything suspicious rather than to fire. The torpedo nets that were supposed to be spread nightly had been forgotten. Because

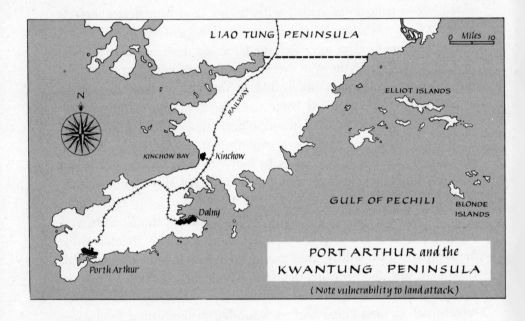

PORT ARTHUR and the
KWANTUNG PENINSULA

(Note vulnerability to land attack)

there was no moon, the approaching Japanese torpedo boats first had great difficulty in identifying targets, and then some were thrown into confusion at the sight of Russian destroyers. Nevertheless, at intervals between 11:00 P.M. and 1:45 A.M. they managed to move in and fire a total of 18 torpedoes, mostly at close range. Though most of the torpedoes missed their targets, so did nearly all the return fire when the Russians became aware of the nature of the explosions. In spite of the failures, the results of the Japanese attack, launched as it was against an unprepared and inefficient foe, were impressive. The *Tsesarevich* had her engine room flooded and developed an 18-degree list to port; both the *Retvizan* and the *Pallada* sustained blows below the waterline: all three ships had to be grounded. The Russians ordered out destroyers to attack the enemy, but they were much too late to be effective. They failed even to contact the retreating Japanese, who escaped with very light damage.

Admiral Togo had planned to follow up the torpedo attack with a major naval onslaught. He therefore headed for Port Arthur at 6:00 P.M. on February 8 with the First, Second, and Third divisions of his fleet, plus a flotilla of destroyers. This force arrived at its destination on the morning of February 9. The Third Division (mostly fast cruisers), under Admiral Dewa, was ordered to begin reconnoitering at 8:00 A.M. and to try to entice the enemy to attack. Dewa found that twelve large Russian vessels, in addition to various gunboats, torpedo boats, and minelayers, were already outside the harbor around the three cripples from the preceding night's attack. Togo approached until at 11:55 A.M., at a distance of about 8,500 meters, the flagship *Mikasa* opened fire. The action soon escalated into a general engagement between the Japanese fleet and the Russian vessels supported by their land batteries. For about half an hour there was a brisk cannonade, with hits being scored on both sides but with no decisive advantage to either. Among the Russian vessels the small cruiser *Novik*, commanded by Capt. N. O. von Essen, distinguished herself. At 12:25 P.M. Togo broke off the action and retired.

The losses in this long-range engagement were fairly even, the Japanese having ten killed and 72 wounded, the Russians 20 killed and 56 wounded. No ship on either side was destroyed. The *Pobeda* was hit 15 times, however, and the *Petropavlovsk, Poltava, Askold, Diana,* and *Novik* each received one or more hits. And though Togo had failed to finish the work started by his torpedo craft, the effect of the action was to keep the Russian fleet immobile until the cripples could be repaired.

Snowstorms and high seas prevented the Japanese from attacking again immediately as Togo desired, but the Russians had a great many other troubles to deal with throughout the remainder of

February. Japanese convoys were steadily putting troops ashore. Two Russian minelayers were lost when they hit their own mines, and two destroyers were damaged when they collided with each other. Finally, just at a time when the dockyards were in need of men to repair the damaged ships, the Chinese workers went on strike, leaving the docks short-handed.

THE WAR OF ATTRITION

For six months following the initial Japanese attacks there were no major battles at sea. The Japanese held the upper hand during this entire period and were able to maintain a reasonably effective blockade of Port Arthur. Such action as occurred at sea can be considered under six headings:

1) Japanese troop landings followed by consistent gains on land —gains designed to isolate and lead to the capture of Port Arthur.
2) Bombardments and torpedo attacks.
3) Attempts to blockade Port Arthur by sinking ships at the entrance to the harbor.
4) A brief period of Russian energy under Admiral Makarov.
5) Relatively effective mine warfare.
6) Raids by Vladivostok cruisers.

By far the most important factor was the first: Japanese gains on land. The Russians, mainly because of lethargy and inadequate intelligence reports but also partly because of lack of force, not only made no serious attempt to interfere with the Japanese troop landings; they consistently failed to support their own ground forces. As a consequence, the Japanese were able to land about half a million troops in Korea and Manchuria without heavy losses. At times the Japanese landings were well guarded, but on several occasions they were made in close vicinity to Port Arthur and with very weak convoy protection. Similarly the Japanese were able to transport munitions and supplies on land with only desultory and almost accidental interference by the Russians.

The land fighting brought an unbroken series of Japanese victories. Troops landed in Korea at Chemulpo on February 8 and marched northward to Yalu, being joined by other contingents en route. By early April, these forces constituted the First Army under General Itei Kuroki. This army crossed the river against fierce Russian resistance and fought its way northward, until by August Liaoyang was menaced from the east. Meanwhile the Second, Fourth, and Third Japanese armies had also landed. The first two directed their push toward Liaoyang, approaching from different directions. The Third Army, under Gen. Count Maresuke Nogi, was given the mission of reducing Port Arthur by land attack. On June 6 General Nogi himself landed at Kinchow, which had earlier been taken by the Second Army, and by early August his force was pressing on the defenses to the north of Port Arthur. Russian communications with that city had already become difficult and uncertain, even though Nogi had not yet come to grips with formidable main Russian defenses.

Although Admiral Togo was dependent on the Japanese Army for the ultimate reduction of Port Arthur, he pursued an aggressive naval strategy of his own. On February 23, two weeks after the initial attack, the Japanese Third, Fifth, and Ninth destroyer flotillas attacked Russian ships outside Port Arthur. This time the Russians were more alert. The torpedo attack resulted in a long-range skirmish between the small but fast Russian cruiser *Novik*, with five accompanying Russian destroyers, and the Japanese Third Flotilla. No damage was done on either side. A second effort, also unsuccessful, was Togo's attempt on February 27 to sink five steamers in the narrow entrance to the harbor with a view to barring the passage to Russian ships. This was the first of several blocking attempts in which Japanese vessels manned by skeleton crews were to be brought in under a hail of projectiles and sunk in a prearranged location. Losses of life among the crewmen, who then tried to escape in small boats, were invariably heavy. On February 23 the Japanese First Division appeared, chased the Russian cruisers inside the harbor, and then, led by the *Mikasa*, fired over the low intervening hills at Russian ships inside the harbor. This indirect bombardment proved quite ineffectual. It is possible that both the indirect fire and the attempted use of blockships had their inspiration in American Rear Adm. William Sampson's blockade of Adm. Pascual Cervera's squadron six years earlier at Santiago de Cuba, where both tactics were used on a smaller scale—also quite unsuccessfully.

On March 10 Togo launched another, virtually identical, attack on the same harbor. This time the Russians lost the destroyer *Steregushchy*, while two Japanese destroyers were damaged in a collision. The blockships were as unsuccessful as they had been in the previous attempt.

Meanwhile a ray of hope had appeared for the Russians: Vice Admiral Starck was relieved of command on February 17 and Vice Admiral Makarov was named his successor. Makarov, however, was unable to report until March 8.

The replacement of the incompetent Starck by the brilliant and versatile Makarov was one of the few truly constructive steps taken by the tsar during the entire war. But the move, made only at the eleventh hour in the hope of redeeming a desperate situation, came five years too late. Makarov was considered Russia's best admiral. During his career as a naval officer, inventor, scientist, and writer, he had repeatedly performed apparent miracles. So great was his reputation and the confidence he inspired that sailors seeing him for the first time often removed their caps and crossed themselves. When, within two days after his arrival, he personally led an attempt to rescue the *Steregushchy* which had been attacked outside Port Arthur by Japanese torpedo boats, he shifted his flag to the tiny cruiser *Novik* in order to join the action as soon as possible. This dramatic assertion of personal leadership won over any doubters and completely restored Russian morale. Makarov and his staff then set to work with frantic zeal and complete unanimity to make a real fleet out of the "floating barracks" at Port Arthur.

The effort to provide in weeks the training that should have been spread over years was inherently hopeless,[3] yet the results achieved were little short of miraculous. Makarov abolished all ceremonies as a waste of time, cut red tape right and left, drilled incessantly, and put tremendous drive into the repair of damaged ships. Meanwhile, unable to seek battle with the vastly superior enemy fleet until repairs were completed on the damaged vessels, he kept his men in training with minor skirmishes and constant exercises. When the Japanese attempted long-range bombardment of Port Arthur the Russians were unable to reply until Makarov had organized a system of fire control from points on the shore. When it appeared that the *Tsesarevich* could not be repaired without a drydock, he invented a new method of doing the work by building a coffer dam.

The time required for the fleet to leave harbor was reduced from 22 to two and one-half hours. Inept handling of ships by untrained personnel inevitably caused some further damages, such as a collision between the *Sevastopol* and the *Peresvet*; the captain of the former vessel was swiftly replaced by Captain von Essen of the *Novik*, an officer in whom Makarov recognized superior talent. Against some opposition from Alekseev and the admiralty, Makarov also pushed the promotion of promising young officers. Mistakes and damages due to ignorance and inexperience were grudgingly accepted as the inevitable cost of training men to the naval trade, but failure to act when action was required was never tolerated. In addition, in going through the arsenal Makarov discovered some overlooked resources, which he promptly utilized. For example, forty new guns found in storage were at once added to the defenses. Ships that had not been examined in years were now inspected at frequent intervals. The commander met the officers, talked directly and personally with the men, gave orders and departed. He remembered everything and forgot nothing; and the common seamen, to whom his every act and word were instantly known, affectionately labeled him "Little Grandfather" and "Old Beardy." Legends and tall tales regarding his prowess spread throughout the fleet.

The Japanese were not long in noting the increased skill and aggressiveness on the part of the Russians. On March 22 they chased the Russian fleet back to port when it emerged for maneuvers. Between March 22 and March 26 they again attempted to block the harbor entrance but again they failed. Turning to indirect bombardment, they did succeed in sinking the Russian destroyer *Silny*, but it became apparent that such tactics were unlikely to bring great results. On April 11 the Russians sent out a task force to bombard the Japanese base in the Elliott Islands. Admiral Togo next ordered an intensification of minelaying, a measure that had been employed by both sides from the earliest days of the war.

Partly because of skill and partly because of good luck, the mine offensive paid off for the Japanese when they won a decisive victory in a prolonged and varied attack in mid-April. On the foggy night of April 12–13, while the destroyer flotillas of both belligerents were at sea, the Japanese minelayer *Koryu Maru* and some torpedo craft laid mines in a new area near the entrance to Port Arthur. Meanwhile, in the darkness out at sea, the *Strashny* unwittingly joined a Japanese formation. In the morning she was recognized, attacked, and sunk. The Russian *Baian* went to her aid, followed by the *Diana*, which picked up survivors and chased off the destroyers. The armored cruisers *Asama* and *Tokiwa* and four protected cruisers then appeared, but the Russians, too, sent in reinforcements, first the *Novik* and *Askold* and at 7:15 the *Petropavlovsk* and *Poltava*. Japanese cruisers reappeared in the mist, and a long-range action ensued from which the Japanese retreated. Other Russian ships arrived, but at the same time the Japanese battleships put in an appearance and it was now the Russians' turn to retreat. A chase developed in which the Japanese gained ground as the 18-knot *Mikasa* slowly overtook the nominally faster (20-knot) *Diana*, rearmost of the Russian ships. By 9:00 A.M. the *Mikasa* had closed the range to 7,500 yards; but instead of firing it abruptly gave up the chase. The reason became apparent as the Russians retreated across the minefield laid only a few hours before. At 9:45 A.M., two miles from Port Arthur, the *Petropavlovsk* hit at least one and possibly two mines. There was a tremendous explosion, and the flagship sank in less than two minutes. So severe was the blast that the turret, funnel, mast, and command post were lofted into the air. Capt. Vladimir Semenov reported hearing three explosions, the last one probably being the bursting of the boiler. Only seven officers and 73 men were saved, while 31 officers—including Admiral Makarov and most of his staff—and 600 sailors lost their lives. Grand Duke Cyril reported seeing Makarov's body lying on the bridge, but a search resulted only in the recovery of his coat.

Rear Admiral Prince Ukhtomsky assumed command to lead the fleet back to Port Arthur. Half an hour later the *Pobeda* hit a mine which blew a hole in her starboard side above the waterline, but she ultimately regained the harbor, listing heavily. The crews of the remaining Russian ships lost their heads, began firing aimlessly and at one another, and the Russian line fell into utter confusion. With no Japanese present, however, the crews gradually recovered and steamed into the harbor.

The next day a very ambitious Japanese attack with 12 blockships failed, while an indirect bombardment between the Japanese *Nisshin* and *Kasuga* and the Russian *Poltava* and *Peresvet* brought the usual disappointing results. However, Russian mines also claimed some victims: the *Kasuga* struck a mine and was damaged and the small cruiser *Miyoko* was sunk.

The events of April 13 were more than a material defeat for the Russians: they were a moral defeat of the first magnitude. The fleet had been deprived of its one first-class admiral, and a sense of intense hopelessness and depression set in. For a time there was a debate as to who should succeed Makarov. The choice of Admiral Skrydlov was finally announced, but this officer was unable to get to Port Arthur. On May 5, as he departed for Mukden, Alekseev assigned the command to Vice Admiral Vitheft and simultaneously decreed a policy of inactivity for the fleet. Vitheft, though honest and hard-working, was neither a forceful leader nor a capable strategist. He accepted without demur the negative policy laid down for him.

For a month following the death of Makarov there were only minor naval actions. A Japanese attack with 12 more blockships was defeated in early May when a storm, three ships hitting mines, and three others sinking in the wrong places disrupted Japanese plans. The Japanese lost 95 men in this attack, but, amazingly, 63 of those aboard the stricken vessels escaped. The Russians attempted nothing on their own. They even failed to make an effort to interfere with a May 5–15 troop landing only 60 miles away. On that occasion the Japanese landed 9,500 men with complete equipment under the protection of two auxiliary cruisers and a few flotilla craft under Admiral Kotaoka. The result of the Russian inactivity was that Dalny fell to General Oku within three days. The laziness and lethargy from which Makarov had aroused the sailors had returned, and it now settled like a blanket over the whole of the hapless fleet.

Then in mid-May came a sudden and unexpected Russian success. How it came about is a subject that requires considerable explanation. The Russians and Japanese were alike in one respect: both had a passion for secrecy. But while the Japanese kept their secrets, the Russians, despite a practice of classifying everything, completely failed to keep theirs. Japanese espionage was generally so efficient that Russian plans were known well in advance. This, of course, enabled the Japanese either to avoid most Russian minefields or to sweep them, and thus to navigate even close to Port Arthur with considerable assurance.

Early in the morning of May 14 Nikolai A. Ivanov, captain of the Russian minelayer *Amur*, left Port Arthur in a heavy fog under escort of six destroyers to unload a cargo of mines. He acted without orders in the sense that he traveled farther than authorized (eleven miles rather than eight) and laid mines in a new area, narrowly escaping detection by Japanese cruisers on his way back. By 6:00 A.M. on May 15 the Russian mining expedition had returned. At about 10:00 A.M. *Hatsuse*, *Yashima*, *Shikishima*, and two small cruisers steamed confidently over the newly laid minefield, secure in the information (from their intelligence reports) that the nearest Russian field was three miles away. The *Hatsuse* struck a mine and limped away, only to strike a second which exploded her boilers and caused a very fast sinking with a loss of 490 men. Shortly thereafter the *Yashima* also struck a mine, but managed to stagger away before she went down so that her loss was concealed until the end of the war. The Japanese suspected activity of submarines and fired wildly, as had the Russians a month earlier.

The almost accidental sinking of two battleships was a major blow to the Japanese, especially since it nearly coincided with the destruction of the cruiser *Yoshino* (rammed by the *Kasuga* in a fog and lost with 318 of her crew), the gunboat *Oshima*, and the destroyer *Okatsuki*. Yet they absorbed the heavy casualties without abandoning their blockade of Port Arthur, and apparently without serious loss of morale.

During the three months following these Japanese losses the naval war was relatively inactive except for a sortie of the Russian fleet on June 23. This was undertaken reluctantly by the Russian naval leaders, who were forced to seek escape to Vladivostok at a time when some of their best specialists were serving as gunners ashore. Abandoning the minecraft and gunboats, Admiral Vitheft's force started leaving the port at 5:40 A.M., but progress was delayed for several hours by necessary minesweeping operations. Scouting Japanese destroyers engaged the Russian minesweepers and their escorting destroyers, and reported the Russian moves. This gave Togo plenty of time to make an appearance. Although the Russians had available six battleships, five cruisers, and 16 destroyers, they were weakened by the absence of twenty-six 6-inch guns, thirty 12-pounders, and many smaller guns which had been landed to aid the defense of Port Arthur. At about 6:30 P.M. the Japanese fleet, consisting of four battleships, four armored cruisers, many smaller cruisers, and about 44 destroyers and torpedo boats, was sighted. When the Russians turned back, Togo ordered in his torpedo craft for a night attack. No hits were scored in this exchange, but the Sevastopol struck a mine and tore a 40 × 7-foot hole in her hull that required six weeks to repair.

Following this abortive sortie attempt the large Russian ships stayed in port, where they were further weakened by the removal of more guns to add to the land defenses while their crews deteriorated from lack of action. The small craft were somewhat more productive. Gunboats at times gave artillery support to nearby land forces; torpedo craft engaged in skirmishes with Japanese picket ships. Minelayers on both sides continued to be very active. The Japanese lost a torpedo boat and a gunboat to mines, and the cruiser *Chiyoda* suffered damage. On the Russian side the *Baian* hit a mine and suffered damage, the destroyer *Lt. Burakov* was sunk, and the *Boevoi* was struck by a torpedo.

While these events were going on before Port Arthur, the Russian Vladivostok squadron, comprising the big armored cruisers *Riurik*, *Rossiia*, and *Gromoboi*, the protected cruiser *Bogatyr*, and a few torpedo craft, had led an entirely independent existence. Since Vladivostok was very difficult to blockade, the Japanese had made no attempt to do so. Vice Admiral Kamimura's Second Squadron, composed at the time of five armored and two protected cruisers, bombarded Vladivostok on March 2 without either causing damage or inducing Vice Adm. Petr A. Bezobrazov to lead his ships out to do battle. A similar attack on March 16 by five armored and five protected cruisers and ten torpedo craft and minelayers also brought small dividends. The only practicable role for the weaker Russian squadron was the *guerre de course* against enemy communications. In this form of warfare the Russians were for a time moderately successful, though their effectiveness against merchant shipping would have been greater had their ships operated as individual vessels rather than as units of a squadron. During April a raid on Gensan, Korea, netted a Japanese transport. In May the Russians received a blow when the *Bogatyr* ran on a rock and was disabled for the rest of the war. Between June 12 and 20 the cruisers were at sea raiding Japanese communications, and three enemy transports loaded with troops were sunk with heavy loss of life. In the Tsugaru

Strait Kamimura tried to intercept the Russians, but they slipped past him during a dense fog. An ineffectual Russian sortie was made at the end of June. This time Kamimura sighted the Russians but lost them on their way to port.

For several weeks the Russian ships stayed in port. Then on July 19 they left Vladivostok, passed through the Tsugaru Strait and into the Pacific, and cruised along the eastern coast of Japan on a voyage that would take them 75 miles south of Yedo Bay. Because most of the Japanese navy lay between Japan and the mainland of Asia, the Russians encountered many merchantmen on the voyage, but no warships. Eight of the former they sank or captured. They returned to port on August 1. Sometimes accompanying the cruisers and at other times acting independently, the torpedo boats also were able to claim several small Japanese vessels in northern waters —at a loss of one torpedo boat, which grounded.

THE BATTLES OF AUGUST 10 AND 14

On August 10, the same day that the Port Arthur Squadron left port, the Vladivostok Squadron again put to sea. Each of these moves brought on a sea battle, but inasmuch as the Port Arthur Squadron was the first to be engaged, the details of this encounter will be given prior consideration.

From late May to August the Russian position at Port Arthur had been steadily deteriorating. By mid-June General Oku's forces had defeated the Russians under General Stackelberg. The First and Second Japanese armies had also won victories over Russian forces and marched northward, further isolating Port Arthur. In late June, despite furious Russian resistance, General Nogi's Third Army started driving in the Russian outposts surrounding Port Arthur. By August Port Arthur was no longer a safe haven for the Russian fleet, and it was ordered to leave. This Vitheft was reluctant to do, but on August 9 when he was ordered in the name of the emperor, he prepared to comply, planning his departure for the early morning of August 10.

With the exception of certain of the ships' quick-firing guns which were ashore together with a portion of their crews, the Russian fleet was now at approximately full strength. It consisted of six battleships and the cruisers *Askold, Pallada, Diana,* and *Novik,* together with ten destroyers. The *Baian,* not yet repaired, was left at Port Arthur under Rear Admiral Loshchinsky, together with various mine craft, gunboats, and torpedo boats. The *Poltava* and *Sevastopol,* though included in the fleet, could make only 12 to 13 knots compared with 16 to 17 for the other battleships. Preceded by mine-clearing launches, the Russian fleet emerged, clearing the harbor by about 8:30 A.M.

Early warning from the Japanese torpedo craft keeping an excellent watch on Port Arthur, plus the five hours required for the Russian ships to get out of the harbor, gave Togo ample time to concentrate his fleet. This comprised eight capital ships—the four battleships *Mikasa, Asahi, Fuji,* and *Shikishima* and the armored cruisers *Nisshin, Kasuga, Yokumo,* and *Asama.* In smaller cruisers and torpedo craft—the latter numbering 60 to 90—the Japanese advantage was overwhelming. Several divisions of small but well-armed Japanese cruisers were on hand to move in and out of the battle, as were the torpedo craft flotillas.

In terms of heavy artillery of the main warships, the two fleets were, on balance, roughly comparable in strength. The eight Japanese vessels carried 16 12-inch, one 10-inch, 14 8-inch, and 53 6-inch guns. The six Russians had 16 12-inch, eight 10-inch, and 36 6-inch guns, the Japanese total being 84 compared to 60 for the Russians. However, even this count is misleading, for the Russian guns were of shorter range, and the 12-inch guns fired a lighter shell than did Japanese guns of the same caliber. Furthermore, the Japanese had an overwhelming advantage in number of guns of lighter caliber. In view of these facts and the great Japanese superiority in cruisers and torpedo craft, the battle of August 10, or the Battle of the China Sea as it has sometimes been called, should have been an easy Japanese victory.

Upon emerging from Port Arthur, the Russian fleet steamed southeast with a view to sailing around Korea and then heading north to Vladivostok. Speed was gradually raised from eight to 13 knots. Togo's fleet was sighted at long range and at about 1:00 P.M., at a distance of about 30 miles from Port Arthur, the battle was joined. For several hours the fight was essentially a spasmodic long-range artillery duel at distances of 8,000 to 11,000 yards, with the flagships *Mikasa* and *Tsesarevich* drawing most of the fire. By virtue of their superior speed the Japanese repeatedly threatened to "cross the T" of the Russians, thus forcing Vitheft to turn in a contracting circle, away from the escape route to Vladivostok.

For several hours the action went on with no great advantage for either side. Because of the long range, the great Japanese superiority in guns of 8-inch caliber and less did not fully register. Indeed, as of 6:30 P.M. the Russians held a slight advantage in that five of the 16 Japanese guns of 12-inch caliber had been knocked out of action as compared to four of 24 10-inch and 12-inch Russian guns. Moreover, despite the Japanese margin in speed they had been unable to "cross the T" of the Russians.

At 6:37 P.M. good luck deserted the Russian side. A Japanese shell burst on the conning tower of the *Tsesarevich*, killing Admiral Vitheft and temporarily jamming the steering gear of the vessel. As the lead Russian vessel sheered to port, the Russian ships following her were thrown into confusion. Some steered to port, some to starboard. Rear Admiral Prince Ukhtomsky, second in command and one of the many high-ranking incompetents in the Russian fleet, was unable to take firm command. With the Russians milling in complete confusion, the Japanese First Division detoured to the north of the enemy; the *Asama* and part of the Fifth Division moved to the northwest; the Third Division headed southeast. By 7:30 P.M. the Russians were virtually surrounded. At this point the Japanese torpedo craft closed in and the larger vessels retired, partly to avoid the chance of accidental attack and partly because they had been somewhat damaged and were short of ammunition. Whether Togo should have retired is debatable. Had the Russians been less disorganized, they might very well have resumed their course toward Vladivostok. Given the tactical and materiel advantages he possessed, it is probably fair to conclude that Admiral Togo ought to have destroyed the entire Russian fleet.

In the night the Japanese torpedo attacks were not very effective: about 40 Japanese torpedo boats, striking at a severely demoralized enemy, succeeded only in damaging the *Poltava*. The bulk of the Russian fleet got back to Port Arthur. Not accounted for were the *Tsesarevich* and the cruisers, whose commander Rear Admiral Reitzenstein, thinking that Ukhtomsky was dead, had ordered a breakout. The *Tsesarevich* stopped for 40 minutes to make repairs but then succeeded in beating off torpedo attacks and limped at four knots into the German-held port of Kiaochow, where she was interned. The *Diana* broke through the Japanese lines and rushed to Saigon, where she was interned by the French. The *Askold* shook off Japanese cruisers and took refuge in Shanghai. The small cruiser *Novik*, commanded successively during the war by two of the ablest officers in the Russian navy, took on coal at Kiaochow and attempted to reach Vladivostok by leaving immediately and sailing around Japan. Unfortunately for that gallant ship, some boiler tubes burst and her speed was cut in half. With enemy cruisers hot on her trail the crew scuttled the *Novik* in the shallow water off Korsakov.

Despite Admiral Togo's failure to destroy a single Russian ship, the battle had decisive results. The five Russian battleships, the two cruisers, and the 12 destroyers left in Port Arthur took almost no part in the remainder of the war, and the Japanese resumed and tightened their blockade. In the battle itself the Japanese had fired some 5,000 projectiles as compared to 3,400 for the Russians, and had secured five to six percent hits as compared to about one percent (32 in all) for the Russians. Broadsides of principal ships had favored the Japanese by about 25,000 pounds to 19,000. Personnel losses were 69 killed and 131 wounded for the Japanese, 74 and 394 respectively for the Russians. The *Tsesarevich* was hit 15 times by 12-inch shells, the *Peresvet* 39 times, and other battleships less often. The Russian protected cruisers had been singularly ineffective all through the battle.

Four days after the Battle of the China Sea the long vigil of Admiral Kamimura was finally rewarded. On August 11 the Russian Vladivostok Squadron left port and headed south. At 4:30 A.M. on August 14 the force was 42 miles from Pusan, Korea, and moving westward when it was sighted by Kamimura. The Japanese admiral had under his command the armored cruisers *Idzumo*, *Tokiwa*, *Azuma*, and *Iwate*, the protected cruisers *Naniwa* and *Takachiho*, and a division of torpedo craft, but these smaller vessels were out of sight to the south when the armored cruiser squadrons came in view of each other. As before, the two fleets did not appear to be greatly unequal. The three Russian armored cruisers were larger but also older than those of the enemy. Their total displacement was 35,389 tons as compared to 38,686 for the four Japanese ships. In armament the Russian ships carried 12 8-inch and 48 6-inch guns; while the Japanese vessels had 16 8-inch and 52 6-inch guns. But the Japanese cruisers held an advantage in fleet speed of about two knots, and furthermore, unlike the Russians, they were supported by smaller craft. Moreover, the 8-inch guns of the Russian ships were not carried in center-line turrets, so that only two could be used on a broadside. Thus the Japanese broadside (not counting Japanese small craft) was superior by a margin of 6,988 pounds to 3,168. Finally, the Japanese vessels were far better protected (particularly around their guns) having been designed for line of battle, while the Russians had been built to raid commerce.

In its essentials the armored cruiser fight was very similar to the Dogger Bank engagement of British and German battle cruisers during World War I. As on that later occasion, the weaker force steamed for home but was hard pressed and lost its weakest ship to the enemy. The fight began at about 5:00 A.M. on August 11 with the two fleets on parallel courses at a range of about 12,000 yards. The Japanese concentrated on the *Riurik*, slowest of the Russian cruisers, and at 8:00 A.M. she sustained decisive damage when one hit disabled her steering gear and another struck below the water-line. Fires broke out but were extinguished by the crew. Leaving the old cruisers *Naniwa* and *Takachiho* to deal with the *Riurik*, Kamimura pressed on after the *Rossiia* and the *Gromoboi*. The two small Japanese cruisers, which should have been out-matched by the *Riurik*, in fact were not. They swept her with fire until her own unprotected guns were put out of action; by noon all fire from the *Riurik* had ceased. She then released a torpedo from her one undamaged tube, but it missed its target. Most of her senior officers had been killed. The acting commander, seeing Japanese reinforcements approaching, ordered his ships blown up. When the attempt failed, he ordered the sea cocks opened. Some time after noon, and after a fight whose heroism and bravery excited even Japanese admiration, the *Riurik* sank. All her life boats had been destroyed; the surviving 21 officers and 583 men, many of them wounded, were picked up by the Japanese. In all, 224 of the *Riurik*'s crew had been killed or wounded.

Meanwhile the main battle had moved northward, until at 10:00 A.M. Kamimura turned back. By that time both of the pursued Russian vessels had been heavily hit. In the *Rossiia* there were 11 holes below the water line, in the *Gromoboi* six. Fires had broken out but were quenched. Decks and upper works appeared to be wrecked. Personnel casualties for the two cruisers totaled 135 killed and 307 wounded; total Russian casualties were put at 332 killed, 558 wounded, 625 taken prisoner. Many of the deaths and injuries were due to unprotected guns. The Japanese lost 46 killed and 81 wounded, mainly on the *Iwate*, which had taken several hits. The Russians apparently scored about 2.5 percent hits, but no Japanese vessel was seriously damaged. The Japanese secured about six percent hits. They had succeeded in wrecking the *Rossiia* and the *Gromoboi*—at least to the extent that their repair required a month's time.

It is difficult to justify Kamimura's decision not to press on and destroy a defeated enemy unless it was because of a shortage of ammunition. Even so, the engagement of August 11 was decisive. The two Russian ships that limped home to Vladivostok were repaired, but they scarcely left port during the remainder of the war. During their wartime careers, the *Rossiia*, the *Gromoboi*, and the *Riurik* had sunk a total of 15 ships and captured three others. Their sinking of the *Hitachi Maru*, with its 18 11-inch howitzers intended for the siege of Port Arthur, had delayed the Japanese victory and exacted heavy enemy casualties. Now the Russian admiralty, striving to continue its *guerre de course*, ordered the auxiliary cruiser *Lena* (11,000 tons, six 4.7-inch guns, 20 knots) from Vladivostok into the Pacific. The crew mutinied and sailed to San Francisco, where the ship was interned on September 12, 1904.

DEATH OF THE PACIFIC FLEET

More than four months were to pass before the Port Arthur ships were finally destroyed, but they were inglorious months from the Russian standpoint. The Japanese continued their blockade, laid mines, pursued their indirect bombardment, and few Russian vessels other than mine and torpedo craft ventured outside the harbor. Meantime, more and more Russian gun crews and guns were landed to aid the land defenses of Port Arthur.

The decisive 1904 battle of the naval war was fought on land, during the latter months of the year. On August 19 General Nogi launched the first of a series of heavy attacks on the defenses of Port Arthur proper. Even by enduring very sizable losses of manpower, he was able to make only slight progress against the Russians, who defended their positions with grim tenacity. The Japanese settled down to siege warfare interspersed with fanatically brave direct charges. The losses on both sides were at times almost unbelievable, but the Japanese could replace theirs while the Russians could not. Gradually, the outmost defenses crumbled.

The main objective of Japanese attack was 203 Meter Hill at the northwestern extremity of the forts surrounding Port Arthur. The highest point of land in the vicinity, the hill commanded a view of the entire harbor and town. Nogi correctly pinpointed it as the key stronghold in the enemy's defenses, and attacks to secure it were launched day and night. The Russians were able to turn back the attacks for several months. Finally, on November 27, the Japanese began a concentrated assault involving nearly all of their artillery and the bravest of their shock troops.[4] On the third day of the attack a detachment of Japanese managed to gain the summit. Nearly a week of the most sanguinary fighting imaginable followed, as the Russians threw in their full forces in a series of counterattacks. It was not until December 5 that the Japanese were able to consolidate their position.

The remainder of the siege of Port Arthur, although it involved much hard fighting, was something of an anticlimax. With the hill in their possession, the Japanese moved up giant mortars that could fire from an elevation, not only on other defenses but also on the remaining ships of the Pacific Squadron. The Russian ships now had no refuge. The idea of a sortie was considered but given up because of the number of guns landed and the shortage of ammunition.

Captain von Essen moved the Sevastopol outside the harbor to escape the fire from the hill. As soon as the Japanese discovered this move they launched repeated torpedo attacks. The Sevastopol finally fell victim, despite torpedo nets and a wide-awake defense. One attacking Japanese torpedo boat was destroyed by the Russian destroyer Stroevoi, protecting the Sevastopol. But Russian ships went down one by one as heavy mortar shells landed on their thinly armored decks, and within ten days the Pacific Fleet had ceased to exist.

Two weeks later, on January 3, 1905, Port Arthur surrendered. Gen. A. M. Stoessel, criticized severely by naval officers for the early surrender, was condemned to death for the action in courtmartial proceedings held in 1908. (The sentence was first commuted to ten years imprisonment, and a year later Stoessel was pardoned.) This decision was probably a just one: rations were short and Russian losses heavy, and the final outcome was already a matter only of time. Nevertheless, Russian troops as well as naval landing parties —whose record ashore had been phenomenally good—could probably have continued resistance for some time longer.

Only six Russian destroyers and some minor vessels succeeded in running the Japanese blockade. They were interned in neutral ports. The conquerors found that the *Poltava* had disappeared, sunk after being literally torn apart by shell explosions. The *Sevastopol*, attacked by torpedo boats which fired the amazing total of 50 torpedoes and scored only two hits, had been scuttled in deep water by her able commander, Captain von Essen. (Two Japanese torpedo boats had been sunk in the attacks on the *Sevastopol*, and 14 damaged.) The *Retvizan* was sunk with eight hits, though her bow remained above water. The *Pobeda*, victim of 15 hits, listed to starboard with huge holes in one side and in the bows. Only the superstructure of the *Peresvet* lay above water as a result of 46 hits. The *Pallada* had received 26 hits before sinking, the *Baian* 41.

The Russians at first had hoped to refloat and restore most of these vessels after the war, but the surrender of Port Arthur changed all that. The Japanese restored the *Poltava* as the *Tango*; the *Retvizan* was renamed *Hizen*; the *Pobeda* became the *Suwo*, the *Peresvet* the *Sagami*, the *Pallada* the *Tsugaru*, and the *Baian* the *Aso*.

At least one more passing mention should be made of the role of Russian naval personnel on land. About 2,000 men served ashore, mainly as gunners. Naval artillery numbering 35 guns in five months fired 46,000 shells. Casualties numbered 56 officers and 289 men. One young naval officer who distinguished himself particularly was A. V. Kolchak, the future admiral.

After the surrender of Port Arthur, the Japanese at once "tidied up" their fleet. First the battleships and armored cruisers, and later all other ships, were overhauled and repaired and their crews rested. Meanwhile Vice Admiral Kataoka, with a squadron of cruisers, auxiliary cruisers, and destroyers, assisted the Japanese army. A long-range blockade was maintained to keep the Vladivostok squadron under cover. Several voyages along the China coast and as far south as Singapore were made by squadrons of cruisers in a show of strength to impress both neutrals and Russians.

It is impossible to conclude this account of the death of the Russian Pacific Fleet without noting that bad luck as well as inept administration and poor leadership played an important part in its demise. Without diminishing in any way the credit due the strategy of the Japanese, who were aggressive and wide-awake throughout, it must be submitted that the Russians were incredibly ill-favored by fortune. In the Battle of the China Sea their fleet, outnumbered and outgunned though it was, had been performing creditably until its admiral was killed. Four months earlier the brave and able Makarov had been eliminated just as he was beginning to get some results from his men and ships. Finally, when given anything resembling able leadership the Russian seamen gave a good account of themselves; it was their tragedy that the tsar's government rarely provided able military leadership.

On the tactical side, the extensive use of mines is worthy of more than cursory notice, since the war presented the first widespread use of open-sea mining. Within a 30-mile radius of Port Arthur possibly as many as 400 small minefields were laid during the period of hostilities. Following the initial Japanese torpedo-boat attacks the Russians mined the entrances to both Port Arthur and Dalny. As for the Japanese, after their first success at mining with the sinking of the *Petropavlovsk* in April, they laid mines continually, usually relying on picket boats and small craft to do the job. The Russians employed several minelayers, but tended to use almost any other class of ship as well.

Ten Japanese ships totaling about 40,000 tons were lost to mines. These included two battleships, four cruisers, a torpedo boat, and a minelayer. The Russians lost a battleship, a cruiser, two destroyers, a torpedo boat, and a gunboat—six vessels in all totaling some 22,000 tons. They also suffered major mine damage to several vessels that were not sunk. In some instances vessels were almost certainly destroyed by their own mines and not those laid by the enemy. Russian mines continued to claim victims even at the very end of the siege; the Japanese cruisers *Takasago* and *Saiyen* were lost and the *Asahi* was damaged as late as December. As of January 1, 1905, the total Japanese losses stood at 16 ships, as compared to a Russian loss of six battleships, two armored cruisers, five protected cruisers, and more than 33 torpedo boats, destroyers, gunboats, and mine craft. In terms of personnel the Russians lost 8,800 men from the Pacific Squadron as well as the 33,500 men of the garrison at the time of surrender. Nearly as many had been killed in battle, where losses were enormous. Those of the Japanese alone may have been as high as 80,000.

One naval resource which the Russians did not use, but which might conceivably have affected the outcome, was the submarine.[5] The Japanese in 1904–1905 had no submarines; the Russians had several underwater craft already built and were building others. When the war began, one small submarine at Port Arthur attracted the attention of one Colonel Meller, an army officer interested in the possible wartime use of underwater craft, but it apparently was promptly forgotten. Though lacking in torpedo armament and periscope, this small boat had a good hull, reliable steering gear, and considerable stability, and could probably have been used. Lt. (later Rear Adm.) B. P Dudarov experimented during the war with a submarine of his own design, but was unable to finish it before the surrender of Port Arthur. The several submarines shipped to Vladivostok via railway cars late in the war (their delivery was in fact delayed by domestic strikes and violence) were never used against Japanese warships; however, their defensive patrols may have discouraged a closer Japanese blockade. Also late in the war the Russians, fearing the Japanese might use submarines to attack, made extensive use of antisubmarine nets at Vladivostok.

It is not difficult to criticize Russian strategy and tactics during the Russo-Japanese war; the errors were glaring and obvious. Basically, they all stemmed from one problem—lack of adequate leadership. No more poignant scene in naval history can be found than that evoked by the lines of a seaman aboard the *Diana*, whose grieving words echo down the years the dense gloom that pervaded the Russian fleet after the loss of Makarov:

> What is a battleship? They are welcome to sink another one and even a couple of cruisers. That's not it; but we have lost our head. Oh, why had it to be just him and not any of the others?[6]

CHAPTER 11

Voyage to Disaster

THE PROJECT

AT THE OPENING of the Russo-Japanese War a more efficient government than that of Nicholas II could probably have decided immediately that reinforcement of the Pacific Squadron was advisable. In St. Petersburg, however, the move was considered and discussed for four months before a course of action was determined. During this period the ministry of marine made no effort to improve the condition of its ships in either the Baltic or the Black Sea. Finally, on June 2 came an announcement that the Russian Baltic Fleet would be sent around Africa to Port Arthur in order to strengthen the outnumbered Russian forces in the Far East. Vice Adm. Zinovy Petrovich Rozhdestvensky was named to command this aggregation of ships, appropriately renamed the Second Pacific Squadron.

Admiral Rozhdestvensky was probably as able as any of the officers available to the Higher Naval Board, although he was an unusual type of man to attain high rank in the Russian service. Following successful service in the war with Turkey he had specialized in gunnery, with results which had impressed the tsar. A large man of great physical strength, he had the reputation of being a severe and ruthless taskmaster—but one who worked himself harder than anyone under his command. Utterly tactless, violent-tempered and abusive, he was completely lacking in those qualities that make

234

a commander loved by his subordinates. But he was honest, and he was possessed of an indomitable will and a great driving force.

The commission given Admiral Rozhdestvensky was virtually unprecedented. He was to select from the hundred-odd vessels comprising the Baltic Fleet a squadron adequate to travel 18,000 miles and join the Port Arthur Squadron—despite Togo's superior fleet standing in the way. The two Russian fleets were then to regain command of the sea, thereby turning the fortunes of the war. Even with first-class ships, experienced and dependable crews, and adequate and accessible bases of supply, such an assignment would have been well-nigh impossible, involving as it did logistic problems of the very first magnitude.

The choice of ships from the Baltic in itself presented a serious problem. At the outbreak of war five 13,500-ton battleships were either newly finished or nearly complete. These were the sister ships *Kniaz Suvorov, Aleksandr III, Borodino, Orel,* and *Slava,* which had been launched in 1901 or 1902 and which, with a normal amount of shipbuilding time, could have been finished and sent to the Far East by the end of 1903. Because of inefficient operations, however, the *Slava* was too far from completion and had to be left behind when the mission got under way. The remaining ships formed the First Division of the Second Pacific Squadron. Each carried four 12-inch and 12 6-inch guns, with 46 smaller pieces in addition. Belt armor measured about 7-¾ inches in maximum thickness, and each ship could steam at 18 knots. Though nominally first-class ships, they had several defects, one of the most serious being that they had been built almost 2,000 tons heavier than the designed 13,500 tons. As a consequence they were topheavy and rode so low in the water that most of the armor belt was submerged. Furthermore, as a class they lacked stability and had a tendency to turn turtle.

The Second Division, commanded by Rear Admiral Fölkersam, comprised four ships of differing types. The *Osliabia,* a sister ship of the *Peresvet,* was fairly speedy but underarmed. The *Navarin* and *Sysoi Veliky* of about 10,000 tons, and the armored cruiser *Dmitry Donskoi,* composed the remainder of the Second Division. The last three were old and very slow ships with short-range guns.

Besides the two divisions of capital ships, the squadron included the old armored cruiser *Admiral Nakhimov*; the protected cruisers *Avrora, Oleg, Izumrud, Zhemchug, Svetlana,* and *Almaz;* nine destroyers; and about 20 auxiliary cruisers and other auxiliaries. The protected cruisers were of two types: the *Avrora* and *Oleg* were of about 6,670 tons and carried 12 6-inch guns; the others were smaller (3,000 to 3,800), and armed with six 4.7-inch or 5.9-inch guns Speeds ranged from 20 to 23 knots.

While the quality of some of the ships was dubious enough, that of the crews was even poorer. For several years most of the better officers and men had been sent to the Far East. About half of the men assigned to Rozhdestvensky's force were unpromising conscripts whom earlier commanders had failed to thrash into shape; others were reservists whose training was not of the most recent. All were relatively green, and most were so ignorant of their duties that they were incapable of carrying out even the simplest orders. Nor was this all. While the Port Arthur and Vladivostok personnel at least had a record of loyalty, the Baltic Fleet was heavily infiltrated with subversive and revolutionary elements who did not wish to see a Russian imperialistic regime victorious lest such a triumph delay the hoped-for revolution. Graft and sabotage were rampant and had to be accepted as a part of class hatred between officers and men, abuse of power by the former, illegal but frequent beatings of sailors, a work day from 5:00 A.M. to 8:00 P.M., poor food and infrequent shore leave, were all grievances which had not been redressed. The *Orel* had mysteriously sunk to the bottom of Kronstadt Harbor while at anchor the year before, and scrap steel was later found inside her low-pressure cylinders—which were closed when the ship went down.

The officers of the Second Pacific Squadron varied in quality, but few were imposing. Rozhdestvensky reportedly once called his second in command, the obese and unimpressive Rear Admiral Fölkersam, a "manure sack," and Rear Admiral Enkvist, commander of the cruisers, was referred to as "the vast space."[1] Three younger officers are worthy of more estimable note, however. Capt. Vladimir Semenov, who had reached Petrograd via the Far East, was treated with respect by Rozhdestvensky, although the squadron commander failed to make use of this aide's extensive knowledge of the faults which the Russian ships had displayed in battle. The chief of staff, Capt. Clapier de Colongue, managed despite a great deal of bullying and abuse from his chief, to be an urbane and charming subordinate. Finally, Comdr. Nikolai Klado, who had first journeyed to Vladivostok as part of Admiral Skrydlov's staff and then, after finding it impossible to reach Port Arthur, had joined the staff of the Second Pacific Squadron, was unique among Russian naval officers. He was a propagandist and publicist of the first rank, as well as a strategist, naval historian, lecturer, and superpatriot. Had he been so disposed and had his superiors been inclined to listen, he could have called attention to such remediable fleet handicaps as poor training, inaccurate long-range gunnery, and the lack of such necessities as range finders, telescopic sights, and wireless. As it was, he spent a great deal of time and energy writing and lecturing— until he was silenced by Admiral Rozhdestvensky—on the more elusive problems of deficient leadership, poorly planned strategy or absence thereof, and defects not only in the construction of Russian ships but also in the entire Russian naval policy.

THE VOYAGE

Departure of the Second Pacific Squadron was originally set for mid-July; but the time required to organize and take on supplies, to repair old ships, and to give some elementary training in navigation and gunnery made long delays necessary. Finally on October 16, following ceremonious farewells, the squadron made a last stop at Libau and headed down the Baltic.

A few days out, the fleet succeeded in making itself thoroughly ridiculous. The long series of Japanese victories had produced in the Russian mind a greatly exaggerated view of Japanese capabilities: among other things the enemy was credited quite falsely, with having secret naval forces in North European waters. The navy ministry allocated 300,000 rubles and 540,000 French francs to intelligence operations to thwart a Japanese surprise attack. One Captain Hartling was sent on counterespionage assignment to Copenhagen, where he and his agents heard rumors of enemy mines, torpedo boats, and submarines, rumors which were daily transmitted (without being checked) to the fleet. Fears thus augmented, combined with the already low morale, produced among the ships' crews some of the strangest hallucinations in military history. There were reports of enemy activity varying from minelaying to balloon scouting at night. Very early in the voyage thoroughly alarmed, trigger-happy Russian gun crews had fired at French, German, Swedish, and Norwegian merchant ships (all of which they missed). Finally, at 8:45 P.M. on October 21, the repair ship *Kamchatka* sent a wireless message that she was being attacked from all sides by enemy torpedo boats. She fired some 296 shots. Though later messages indicated that both enemy ships and torpedoes were illusionary, the first announcement had greatly increased the tension aboard Russian vessels. The fleet passed through the Great Belt and the Skaw and was cruising in a disorderly and strung-out formation in the North Sea when, shortly after midnight on October 22, the First Division ships sighted what they took to be foreign torpedo boats; they were in fact British fishing smacks. Immediately men were called to battle stations, and the Russians began a general bombardment. With hundreds of guns aimed and firing at great speed in their direction, the fishing boats were soon hit and several members of their crews were killed and injured. Four fishing boats, *Crane, Moulimein, Snipe,* and *Mina,* were sunk or damaged. At the same time the First Division also fired on the *Dmitry Donskoi* and *Avrora*—both of which should have been 50 miles away—believing them to be Japanese cruisers. The *Avrora* was hit five times (one man aboard was badly wounded), and the assaulted naval vessels returned the fire with enthusiasm. At last, as the Russian gunners gradually realized that what they had decided were enemy torpedo boats using the fishing smacks as cover were their own ships, the firing ceased. No aid was extended to the fishermen, and the Russians failed to send any ship to port to carry dispatches.

When the news of the Hull Incident—as the attack was to become known—reached England several hours later, there was an outburst of indignation that raised the threat of war. The British press played up the incident which occurred on the 99th anniversary of the Battle of Trafalgar. The Russian government was unable to furnish any information until the First Division stopped to refuel at Vigo on the Atlantic coast of Spain (the Second Division had gone directly to Tangier after coaling off the English coast). There Rozhdestvensky, learning of the diplomatic commotion through the Russian consul general, detached three officers headed by Captain Klado to present explanations at St. Petersburg. Before an International Court of Inquiry consisting of five admirals (three of them neutral) sitting in Paris three Russian officers, Admiral Dubasov, Commander Klado, and Lt. George Taube, presented a case designed to establish the existence of enemy torpedo boats. If they were not there, Klado argued, watch officers on five separate ships must have been simultaneously stricken with identical hallucinations. Ultimately the Russian government paid compensation and the case was settled by a face-saving formula under which no one was blamed. The British remained very antagonistic, however, and thereafter went out of their way to hinder the progress of the Russian fleet. For some days their cruisers or battleships escorted the Russian ships, and the hapless crews were thus able to see how the ships and men of a well-ordered navy behaved. Throughout the remainder of Rozhdestvensky's voyage the British exerted all possible diplomatic pressure on neutrals to prevent them from extending the use of their harbors. Commander Klado did not return to the fleet but remained in St. Petersburg, where he resumed his career of writing and lecturing on naval affairs—activities of great importance, as will be seen presently.

At Tangier the fleet separated. The *Sysoi Veliky, Navarin, Svetlana, Zhemchug, Almaz,* and certain auxiliaries, all commanded by Admiral Fölkersam, were directed to proceed through the Mediterranean and the Suez Canal while Rozhdestvensky was to take the newer and stronger ships around the Cape of Good Hope. The two forces were to meet off the coast of Madagascar, where they would be joined by the *Oleg, Izumrud,* and some destroyers and auxiliary cruisers which were to make the trip by themselves.

The journey to Madagascar, which required about eight weeks, was more easily negotiated by the ships passing through the Mediterranean than by the ones circumnavigating Africa, although those taking the first route did experience a Japanese torpedo boat scare. They also had some difficulty in coaling, an operation which, as a matter of fact, was a serious continuing problem for the entire fleet.

A contract with the German-based Hamburg-America Company

provided for coaling of the squadron during the entire journey, but the voyage had been undertaken with no ports available in which the coaling could be performed. Moreover, stay in any foreign port was limited by international law. Thus coaling had to be done at sea, a practice which some naval officers only a few years before had claimed was impossible. Since Rozhdestvensky never felt sure he would meet colliers when he needed them, he took advantage of all opportunities: not only were the bunkers filled but coal was also carried in sacks on decks, in bathrooms, in engine-room workshops, in officer cabins—in short, in every place conceivable.

By much practice the Russians became so proficient at coaling at sea that the *Kniaz Suvorov* on one occasion set a new world's record by taking on 120 tons in an hour, the previous record of 102 tons having been set by the British. Coal dust in food, clothing, eyes, and mouths constituted a major discomfort as the ships steamed through the heat of tropic seas. All ventilating passages were closed to check circulation of the dust. Cockroaches which throve in the dirt and heat polluted everything. Constant breakdowns which occasioned long and maddening delays only served to add to the misery.

Rozhdestvensky's big ships coaled at Dakar, French Congo, and German Southwest Africa en route to Madagascar, where they arrived on December 29. Fölkersam's smaller ships took on coal at Bizerte, Suda Bay in Crete, Port Said, Djibouti, and Cape Guardafui and reached Nossi-Re, Madagascar, on December 28.

Between breakdowns and coaling, Rozhdestvensky attempted to train his fleet in seamanship. Exercises indicated that months of practice would be required before the ships and men could constitute a formidable fighting fleet. Further, a lack of practice ammunition made it impossible (owing to much of the needed ammunition having been sent to Vladivostok by rail) to give the required training in gunnery and torpedo firing. This limited training and testing also raised grave doubts as to the quality and reliability of the shells and torpedoes carried.

During the journey to Madagascar the Second Pacific Squadron had been out of touch with a world in which momentous changes had been taking place. In the Far East the Japanese had captured 203 Meter Hill and then sunk the First Pacific Squadron. Hence the *raison d'être* of the Second Pacific Squadron had disappeared. If it were to go on, it must defeat the Japanese singlehandedly in order to gain command of the sea, and such command would then have to be exercised from Vladivostok, the only remaining major Russian naval base in the Far East.

Back in St. Petersburg, Captain Klado had been extremely active in the weeks following the Hull Incident. In eloquent speeches and in a series of articles published in *Novoe vremia* under the pseudonym "Priboi," Klado had started a propaganda campaign which had as its objective the dispatch of reinforcements to Rozhdestvensky. In simple, readable language Klado had exposed the faults of the Russian navy with merciless clarity, prophesied the doom of the Port Arthur Squadron, laid out a proposed course of action for winning the war, demanded Admiral Rozhdestvensky's reinforcement, and attempted to explain to a land-minded people the nature and importance of sea power. Virtually overnight he had succeeded not only in creating but giving direction to a powerful public opinion. Once, after he had traced blunders to the ruling system of Russia, he was arrested and imprisoned; but popular opinion forced the government to release him. He then resumed his writing with enhanced prestige and a martyr's halo. He finally won his point when the tsar ordered Adm. A. A. Birilev, minister of marine, to form a Third Pacific Squadron to reinforce Rozhdestvensky.

In the course of his propaganda campaign Klado made numerous enemies as well as friends. Among the former were individuals whose mistakes he had exposed, together with others of whom he had demanded the impossible. His proposed reforms included the creation of a unified command structure in the Far East; the rapid building up of Vladivostok; the disassembling and shipping to that port of torpedo boats and submarines for reassembling; the prompt completion of the *Slava*; and the dispatch, regardless of treaty, of three reasonably modern battleships from the Black Sea Fleet. Klado also urged the immediate dispatch of some older Baltic Fleet vessels which Rozhdestvensky had resisted taking.

Had an imaginative and energetic administration existed in Russia at that time, many of Klado's proposals, advanced as they were, could have been carried out. The disassembling and shipping by rail of torpedo boats and destroyers, for example, had earlier been proposed by Makarov (it was finally accomplished successfully during World War I—when several submarines were actually sent to Vladivostok and there assembled). It occurred to a limited extent from 1900 to 1905, when several destroyers were shipped in sections to Port Arthur while submarines reached Vladivostok in the same manner. But given the laziness and general ineptitude that characterized the tsar's regime, very few of Klado's suggestions were put to use at this time. Indeed, the only one to be adopted without restraint was by far the poorest: old vessels were sent out—under an equally antiquated chief, Adm. Nikolai I. Nebogatov. This force comprised the battleship *Nikolai I*; three small coast defense ironclads, named respectively for Admirals *Apraksin*, *Ushakov*, and *Seniavin*; the old armored cruiser *Vladimir Monomakh*; three destroyers; and half a dozen transports and auxiliaries. These left Russia on February 18 via the Mediterranean route. Coaling arrangements, which proved satisfactory, called for the supply of 30,000 tons of coal by a Kiel firm, Diedrichsen-Jebson and Company. Coaling took place at Cherbourg, Tangier, Suda Bay, and Djibouti.

Rozhdestvensky reached Madagascar on December 29, 1904, intending to depart on January 14. Soon after his arrival, however, he learned that Fölkersam was at Nossi-Be rather than Diege Suarez, by orders of Adm. Fedor K. Avelan, and that he himself was to wait with Fölkersam for Nebogatov's squadron. At the news of the delay Rozhdestvensky had a minor nervous breakdown, and for the next two weeks or so the Russian fleet lay at anchor with no one in effective command. After Rozhdestvensky's return to effective command there were further delays. When his force finally got under way it was mid-March. The departure coincided with the decisive defeat of General Kuropatkin in the Battle of Mukden.

During the nearly three months which the Russian ships spent in the waters off Madagascar, Admiral Togo was able to refit, overhaul, and thoroughly repair his ships, and to rest his crews from war service. The inactivity of the Russian fleet, on the other hand, led generally to the steady deterioration of ships and men. Admiral Fölkersam, whose health was by this time rapidly deteriorating, made no particular effort to control his men. During the first part of the stay officers and men were given a great deal of shore leave, which they spent in saloons, gambling houses, and houses of prostitution that sprang up ashore in a section of the port that came to be known as Hellville. All vessels were soon filled with the stench of animals brought aboard by the men. Barnacles and sea grasses attached themselves to the bottoms of the ships, cutting their speed.

Meanwhile Rozhdestvensky, recovered from his breakdown, requested to be relieved of his command. The request was denied. He thereupon set to work with his usual energy to restore a semblance of order. Inevitably, his success in this endeavor was limited. Gunnery and steaming exercises produced very bad results. Various tropical sicknesses filled the hospital ships and the sick bays. Suicides became common as a result of depression induced by the climate and the uncertainty of the future. Extremely poor officers were largely responsible for two mutinies, one on the *Admiral Nakhimov*, the other on the prison ship *Malaia*.

To make matters worse, for the first time on the voyage the men received letters and newspapers from home, and all the news was bad. In the Far East the Russians had suffered a disastrous series of defeats on land; in Russia peaceable, unarmed workers had been shot down at the Winter Palace; there had been student demonstrations, anti-Semitic pogroms, a mutiny in the Black Sea Fleet. Moreover *Novoe vremia* was publishing the articles of Captain Klado. These provoked suppressed but lively disagreement, for although some of the higher officers regarded him as little better than a traitor, to the sailors and to many of their officers Klado was a hero. In the lower ranks, a young lieutenant aboard the *Suvorov* wrote home:

> More power to Klado's elbow. The Ministry of Marine should have had such a lashing long ago. Besides, he does not disclose the hundredth part of the blunders of this department, which has ruined our ill-fated fleet. If, by God's grace, I ever see you again, I shall have things to tell you past belief or imagining.[2]

Klado's officer-critics could not deny the worsening conditions; nevertheless, they resented his exposure of their own inadequacies. They countered with the contention that his writings were giving valuable information to the Japanese. Even Admiral Fölkersam prepared a reply to Klado, but it wandered from one newspaper office to another without finding a publisher.

The main reason for the long delay at Nossi-Be was logistical. The

Russian government had yielded to the objections of the Hamburg-American Company to supplying coal during an open-sea journey across the Indian Ocean. Rozhdestvensky therefore had to deal directly with his German suppliers. By dint of sheer force of character and by using the name of the Russian government he was able to buy from the Germans 14 colliers loaded with coal to supply his own fuel needs.

But the coal problem was only the greatest of many logistic problems. Supply ships from Russia failed to bring needed ammunition; they brought instead thousands of winter uniforms for use in the tropics! German-made wireless sets, which had never worked well, became utterly useless when the German technicians left. A mysterious power failure (probably caused by sabotage) on a refrigerating ship resulted in the loss of 700 tons of fresh meat. Uniforms ran short on several ships, and though much-needed food could be purchased locally it was available only at extortionate prices and then not in the desired amount or variety.

Probably anticipating that Nebogatov's reinforcements would not be warmly received in Madagascar, the ministry of marine had cautioned that the progress of the Third Pacific Squadron not be communicated to Rozhdestvensky. Nevertheless some news leaked through: it was on March 14, when Nebogatov was at Crete, that Rozhdestvensky left Madagascar.

On the whole, the Third Pacific Squadron had a fortunate journey. Nebogatov was small, mild-mannered, and humane—but he could be firm. With ships that needed overhauling and with crews even poorer than those of his superior, he yet managed to coal easily and to keep his men so busy with gunnery and night torpedo defense exercises that he had little trouble with discipline. When he learned at Suez that Rozhdestvensky had already departed he proceeded across the Indian Ocean, uncertain of the whereabouts of his future commander until this information was supplied him by a Russian sailor named Babushkin who was found cruising in a launch off Singapore. (Babushkin had cruised for three days, part of the time with no food and water, until Nebogatov appeared.)

The Second Pacific Squadron had in the meantime become lost to the world. For three weeks no other ship of any kind was sighted as the fleet steamed along at eight knots, interrupted only by the inevitable stops for coaling and the frequent mechanical break-downs. The main coaling stops were the middle of the Indian Ocean, the Straits of Malacca, Saigon, the Annam Coast, and the Chusan islands. Anxiety over anticipated Japanese attacks continued to haunt the crews, and there were frequent instances of men jumping overboard in an attempt to end their troubles.

On April 5 the fleet sighted the coast of Sumatra. Rozhdestvensky ordered cruisers and scouts ahead, and soon the usual reports of sub-marines, torpedo boats, and shore-based artillery were being sent back, keeping the crews' nerves on edge. Three days later the fleet passed Singapore; and the British, though still hostile, acknowledged that the journey had been impressive. Observers noted that the ships' bottoms were foul with heavy marine growth. At Singapore the Russians received some newspapers as well as dispatches, all of which were immensely disheartening. The newspapers contained reports of the Russian defeat in the Battle of Mukden and made it abundantly clear that only a naval victory could possibly save the Russian cause. Orders from the admiralty directed Rozhdestvensky to proceed to Camranh Bay on the French Indochina coast and there await the arrival of the Third Pacific Squadron. The united fleet was then to push north, defeat Togo, and proceed to Vladivostok where Rozhdestvensky would turn the leadership of the fleet over to Admiral Avelan, at the time already on his way to that port.

For a time Rozhdestvensky considered the idea of pushing on immediately without waiting for Nebogatov's "self sinkers," but an error in computing the coal on board the *Aleksandr III* made this impossible. In despair he ordered the fleet to Camranh Bay and then collapsed in a state of complete melancholy. Once in Camranh he made no effort to have the ships' bottoms cleaned or to instigate repairs. Tropical diseases, food shortages, and inactivity were all taking a heavy toll on the Russians by now, and morale plummeted to even lower depths than had been reached at Nossi-Be. A mutiny that arose when the men were fed a sick cow for Easter dinner forced the captain of the *Orel* to provide better fare. The next day Rozhdestvensky came aboard and gave both crew and officers a fierce tongue-lashing.

The news that the Russian fleet had passed Singapore was highly alarming to the Japanese, who feared that Nebogatov's arrival would

give the Russians an effective superiority in big guns. When the
Mikado's government learned that the Russian ships had anchored
in a French harbor, it protested—at first mildly and then with
increasing vehemence—this violation of international law. On April
22 French Admiral de Jonquieres ordered the Russians to leave.

The Russians obeyed this order in letter but not in spirit. Though
the French admiral reported the next day that the Russian battleships had sailed eastward, Rozhdestvensky actually had merely
moved a few miles up the coast to the uninhabited bay of Van
Phong. Here he might have been safe to await Nebogatov, but by
extreme misfortune a coastal vessel chose that very day to enter the
harbor on its monthly run. As a result the Russians were ordered
out within a few days. Again they complied—only to return and
resume the wait for the Third Pacific Squadron. By now they did not
have long to wait: on May 9 Nebogatov's squadron appeared over
the horizon, and the two Russian fleets united.

Nebogatov boarded the *Suvorov*, but Rozhdestvensky revealed
exactly nothing to him, not his intended route to Vladivostok, not
his battle plans, not even the highly pertinent fact that in the event
of Fölkersam's expected death he (Nebogatov) would automatically
become second in command of the combined fleet.

Though Nebogatov's ships had arrived in relatively good condition, several days were necessary for coaling and repairs. Finally,
on May 14 the combined fleet started north to meet the Japanese.

The foe had meantime been very busy. In mid-February all their
men had been called back from leave. Immediately thereafter the
Japanese fleet engaged in a series of small strategic and tactical
exercises planned especially to enhance the effectiveness of torpedo
craft. Thereafter had come a program of maneuvers and exercises
for the entire fleet. Cruisers were sent out on blockade duty and
captured some additional prizes—60 for the entire war. The Tsugaru
Strait was blocked by mines which were guarded by auxiliary cruisers and torpedo craft. A journey in March which took Admiral
Dewa's forces as far south as Singapore greatly worried the
approaching Russians.

Though the Japanese were aware that there were several ways of
reaching Vladivostok they gambled on the Russians' taking the
shortest route, via the Korea Strait. They developed an early warn-

ing system some 140 miles in depth with auxiliary cruisers and gun-boats positioned to cover all approaches. Torpedo craft and Togo's main fleet were kept close by Tsushima and the Japanese coast.

Before more is said of the further progress of the Russian fleet, it should be observed that in taking a large squadron to the Far East in time of war without effective support from home, without a single friendly naval base, with neither good men nor good ships, Rozh-destvensky unquestionably performed one of the greatest logistic feats in the history of warfare. That the Russians arrived at their objective in poor condition is not surprising. The amazing thing is that they arrived at all.

CHAPTER 12

The Battle of Tsushima

PRELIMINARIES

THE "MOMENT OF TRUTH" was now approaching for the Russian fleet in the Russo-Japanese war. On May 25, 1905, Rozhdestvensky's force took on coal for the last time, enough to carry it to Vladivostok, an excessive load which lowered the ships in the water. During these activities Admiral Völkersam died. Admiral Rozhdestvensky elected to tell no one, not even Admiral Nebogatov, who was supposed to advance to second in command. Admiral Völkersam's flag continued to fly as usual from the *Osliabia*.

The selection of the route to Vladivostok aroused some anxiety. Of the four choices theoretically possible, by far the closest and most direct was the route through the Korea Strait between the coast of Japan and the island of Tsushima. The other routes were more distant and led through narrow seas which could be easily mined. Since Rozhdestvensky had no idea where he would find Togo, he hoped the Japanese admiral had divided his forces in order to cover all the likely approaches. Indeed, with a view to misleading the Japanese he had even told the captain of a merchant vessel that he intended to go through the Korea Strait. He had also despatched the auxiliary cruisers *Kuban* and *Terek* with others to capture merchantmen off the eastern coast of Japan. This diversion probably would not have caused any changes in Japanese plans in any case, but as it happened it had no chance to operate inasmuch as the auxiliary cruisers did not even sight any merchant ships or make their presence felt in any other way.

The problem of auxiliaries vexed Rozhdestvensky. On the one hand, orders from St. Petersburg warned him that he could expect little logistic support at Vladivostok and must not depend on shipment via the Trans-Siberian Railway; on the other hand, he knew that the presence of auxiliaries would constitute a major impediment to fleet action. He concluded that the best solution lay in compromise. Accordingly, two hospital ships, *Kostroma* and *Orel*; two tugs, *Russ* and *Svir*; the repair ship *Kamchatka*; and three auxiliary cruisers, *Irtysh, Anadyr,* and *Koreia,* were chosen to accompany the fleet. Eight other auxiliaries were sent on to Shanghai and six more to Saigon. These were to coal rapidly and, in case the fleet was victorious, to rejoin it at a prearranged rendezvous.

Admiral Rozhdestvensky also issued some rather general battle orders. Cruisers were ordered to protect the supply ships. The other Russian ships were to follow signals from the *Suovorv* or, in case she were disabled, her successor as flagship. The fast cruisers *Zhemchug* and *Izumrud* were to be stationed on the flank. The Third Battleship Division and the Cruiser division were to provide independent support. The destroyers were to be used for transfers of flag officers.

Although a great many of the Russian sailors realized that their fleet would be out-matched, the change from waiting to action, from the tropics to the cooler air of the temperate zone, and from the tedium of a seemingly endless voyage to the promise of an approach to their destination had a stimulating effect. Morale was better than it had been for some time. May 27 was the anniversary of the coronation of Nicholas II, and this fact was regarded as a good omen. In addition, there was considerable confidence that the fleet would get through to Vladivostok—with or without a fight.

Because the Battle of Tsushima was the greatest single naval battle to take place in the period between the Napoleonic Wars and the Battle of Jutland in World War I, it is appropriate to compare the opposing fleets in some detail (see table 5). It will be observed that although each fleet possessed twelve line-of-battle units, the Japanese were easily superior not only in speed and total tonnage but also in the overall newness of their vessels. Their ships carried a total of 127 big guns with a broadside of 28,400 pounds as com-

TABLE 5

*Japanese and Russian Fleets at Tsushima**

JAPANESE—Admiral Togo

NAME	DATE OF LAUNCH	TON-NAGE	ARMOR BELT	TURRET	MAIN ARMAMENT	SPEED (KNOTS)
First Division						
Mikasa *(flag)*	1900	15,200	9	10	4 12″; 14 6″	18.6
Fuji	1896	12,500	18	16	4 12″; 10 6″	19.2
Shikishima	1898	14,854	9	10	4 12″; 14 6″	18.5
Asahi	1899	15,200	9	10	4 12″; 14 6″	18
Kasuga	1902	7,700	6	5½	1 10″; 2 8″; 14 6″	20
Nisshin	1903	7,700	6	z5½	4 8″; 14 6″	20
Second Division—Armored Cruiser Squadron—Vice Admiral Kawamura						
Idzumo *(flag)*	1899	9,750	7	6	4 8″; 14 6″	22.3
Asama	1898	9,750	7	6	4 8″; 14 6″	21½
Tokiwa	1898	9,900	7	6	4 8″; 14 6″	21½
Adzumo	1899	9,500	7	6	4 8″; 14 6″	20
Yakumo	1898	9,800	7	6	4 8″; 12 6″	20½
Iwate	1900	9,750	7	6	4 8″; 14 6″	21
Third Division—Vice Admiral Dewa						
Kasagi *(flag)*	1897	4,760			2 8″; 10 4.7″	23
Chitose	1893	4,760			2 8″ 10 4.7″	23
Niitaka	1902	3,400			6 6″	20
Otava	1903	3,000			2 6″; 6 4.7″	21
Fourth Division—Vice Admiral Uriu		DECK	TURRET			
Naniwa *(flag)*	1885	3,700	3		2 10.2″; 6 6″	18
Takachiho	1885	3,700	3		2 10.2″; 6 6″	18

Akashi	1897	2,700	2		2 6"; 6 4.7"	20
Tsushima	1903	3,400	2½		6.6"	20

Fifth Division—Vice Admiral Kataoka

Itsukushima (flag)	1889	4,230	1½	4	1 12.5"; 4.7"	16.7
Chinyen	1882	7,350		3	4 12"; 4 6"	14.5
Matsushima	1890	4,230	1½	4	1 12.5"; 12 4.7"	16.7
Hashidate	1891	4,230	1½	4	1 12.5"; 11 4.7"	16.7

Sixth Division—Rear Admiral Togo

			DECK TURRET			
Suma (flag)	1895	2,700	2		2 6"; 6 4.7"	20
Chiyoda	1889	2,440	1		10 4.7"	19
Akitsushima	1892	3,170	3		4 6"; 6 4.7"	19
Idzumi	1884	2,970	1		2 10.2"; 6 4.7"	17

21 destroyers, 17 first-class and 40 second-class torpedo boats.

RUSSIAN—Admiral Rozhdestvensky

First Division

Kniaz Suvorov (flag)	1902	13,516 (15,270)	7¾	10	4 12"; 12 6"	18
Aleksandr III	1901	13,516 (15,270)	7¾	10	4 12"; 12 6"	18
Borodino	1901	13,516 (15,270)	7¾	10	4 12"; 12 6"	18
Orel	1902	13,516 (15,270)	7¾	10	4 12"; 12 6"	18

Second Division—Rear Admiral Fölkersam (deceased)

Osliabia (flag)	1898	12,674	9	10	4 10"; 11 6"	19
Sysoi-Veliky	1894	10,400	16	14	4 12"; 4 6"	16
Navarin	1891	10,206	16	12	4 12"; 8 6"	15
Nakhimov	1885	8,542	10	8	8 8"; 10 6"	17

Third Division—Rear Admiral Nebogatov

Nikolai I (flag)	1889	9,672	14c**	18	2 12"; 4 9"; 8 6"	15

TABLE 5

*Japanese and Russian Fleets at Tsushima**

NAME	DATE OF LAUNCH	TON-NAGE	ARMOR BELT	ARMOR TURRET	MAIN ARMAMENT	SPEED (KNOTS)
Ushakov	1893	4,648	10	8	4 10"; 4 4.7"	16
Seniavin	1894	4,126	10	8	4 10"; 4 4.7"	16
Apraksin	1896	4,126	10	8	3 10"; 4 4.7"	16
Cruiser Squadron—Rear Admiral Enkvist						
Oleg (flag)	1903	6,650	3	3	12 6"	23
Avrora	1900	6,630	2½		8 6"	23
Monomakh†	1881	5,593	2		5 6"; 6 4.7"	15½
Dmitry Donskoi†	1885	6,200	2		6 6"; 10 4.7"	16½
Svetlana	1898	3,200	—		6 6"	21
Almaz	1903	3,285	—		12 small guns	20
Zhemchug	1903	3,106	2		6 4.7"	24
Izumrud	1903	3,106	2		6 4.7"	24
8 auxiliaries, 9 destroyers						

† The *Monomakh* carried a 10-inch and the *Dmitry Donskoi* a 7½-inch belt of compound armor. The two were old armored cruisers.

* SOURCE: Herbert W. Wilson, *Battleships in Action* (Boston, 1926), vol. I, appendix.

** c = compound armor.

pared with 92 big guns with a broadside of 32,090 pounds for the Russians. (The apparent Russian advantage in gunpower is misleading, since the Japanese could fire faster and more accurately. Further, their shells carried a much heavier explosive charge that could inflict far greater damage than could the armor-piercing shells used by the Russians.) The tonnage of the entire Japanese fleet was 202,000; that of the Russians, 156,000 excluding auxiliaries. Moreover, outside the battle line the Japanese held overwhelming superiority in cruisers (16 to eight) and torpedo craft (69 to nine). And since they were operating close to their own bases, they had no need to hamper themselves with auxiliaries.

The intangible advantages of the sort which cannot appear in any table were all on the side of the Japanese. The quality of their leadership and personnel was infinitely higher. Their ships were in much better condition, having recently been overhauled and refitted, and were able to make their nominal speeds; the Russian fleet, worn down by the 18,000-mile voyage, was slower than it should have been. For these and other reasons the approaching battle would be far from a contest between equals. In point of fact, the Japanese margin of superiority was nearly as overwhelming as that of the Americans over the Spaniards at Santiago in the Spanish-American War a few years earlier.

A matter of great importance to both sides was the uncertain factor of weather. The Russians hoped for a dense fog to screen their movements; such fogs are fairly frequent in the Korea Strait. Throughout the day of May 25 they steamed through rain, proceeding northward from Formosa. May 26 was bright and clear. The following day brought mist, and with it variable visibility and high seas. The rough waters presented a disadvantage not only to the Japanese torpedo craft but also to gunners of the quick-firing pieces on the *Suvorov* class of battleships, since these overloaded ships were so deep in the water their gunnery was affected.

The conflict between the two fleets lasted for more than a full day and may be logically divided into six periods of time:

1) The Approach: 2:45 A.M. to 1:30 P.M.
2) First Stage: 1:30 to 2:00 P.M.
3) Second and Decisive Stage: 2:00 to 4:00 P.M.
4) Third Stage: Confusion, 4:00 to 7:30 P.M.
5) Fourth Stage: Night Torpedo Attacks, 7:30 P.M. to 5:00 A.M.
6) Fifth Stage: Surrender and Mop-up, May 28–29.

THE APPROACH: 2:45 A.M. TO 1:30 P.M.

The Japanese and Russians in the period immediately before Tsushima were alike in one respect: neither knew exactly where the other was or when contact could be expected. Togo correctly concluded that the Russians would seek the closest route to Vladivostok, the one through Tsushima Strait, between Japan and Korea, rather than any one of the much longer alternate routes. He had stationed his fleet near the southern tip of Korea and had organized his auxiliary cruisers into an elaborate patrol covering all possible approaches to the Korea Strait. However, according to his calculations May 26 was the last date on which the Russians could be expected to arrive if they were indeed taking this route. As time passed and no reports of Russian ships came in, he began to wonder if Rozhdestvensky had in fact chosen a different route.

Meanwhile, the Russian fleet had been moving slowly northward with no attempt to employ its fast cruisers as scouts. At about 5:05 A.M. on May 27 the suspense came to an end when the auxiliary cruiser *Sinano Maru* sighted the well-lighted hospital ship *Orel*, which was traveling in the rear of the Russian formation. The Japanese ship approached to within a mile of the *Orel* and wirelessed the news to Togo. About an hour later the auxiliary ship *Ural* reported she was being shadowed. Her shadow turned out to be the *Idzumi*, which had picked up the *Sinano's* signal and was able not only to report the Russian location at 33°30' north, 128°50' east but also to describe the formation of the Russian fleet—a double column, with the First and Second divisions in one line and Nebogatov's Third Division and Enkvist's cruiser division in the other. Between these lines, and to the rear, were the auxiliaries; the light cruisers and destroyers were ahead on both flanks. For some time the *Idzumi* steamed parallel to the Russian line but beyond effective range. When the *Suvorov* finally turned one of her 12-inch turrets toward her, the *Idzumi* disappeared in the mist. She was very soon replaced by a squadron of light cruisers, which also stayed beyond effective range. The *Ural*, which had requested but been denied permission to attempt the jamming of the Japanese radio communication, also announced a light cruiser squadron shadowing astern.

The silent shadowing was hard on the morale of the Russian gunners: they felt the enemy scouts should be attacked. About 11:15 A.M., acting without directions, Captain Yung of the *Orel* ordered his gunners to fire. Others followed suit, and the Japanese cruisers replied. Because of the long range no hits were made, and at 11:30 Rozhdestvensky ordered his ships to stop wasting ammunition. To put his fleet in better battle formation he now directed the First and Second divisions to raise their speed to 11 knots and go ahead of the other column. Since he did not order a simultaneous slowdown of the other lines, there was for a time a general confusion and jamming together of the two columns. Before this confusion abated and the Russian ships could form a single column, there appeared to the north at a distance of approximately ten miles the gray-green hulls of the First and Second Japanese divisions. Blending perfectly into their ocean background, they furnished a decided contrast to the Russian fleet with its black hulls and yellow funnels.

The time was now 1:30 P.M. Throughout the morning Admiral Togo had been receiving accurate accounts of the Russian fleet as to speed, strength, and course. In order to allow his own forces sufficient room for maneuver, he let the Russians pass through the strait before making an appearance. Then he signaled his fleet: "The fate of the Empire depends upon today's event. Let every man do his utmost."

THE FIRST STAGE: 1:30 TO 2:00 P.M.

At the beginning of the battle Admiral Togo approached from the northeast and crossed in front of the Russian line preparatory to describing a circle. He then planned to move north and east on a course parallel to but ahead of the much slower Russians. The maneuver was unorthodox to the point of rashness, for the Japanese ships, in turning left at the beginning of their circle, would have their sights masked by other Japanese ships while the Russian gunners could concentrate fire on each ship in turn, all within the same range.

Because of the confusion in their own order the Russians were unable to take full advantage of this excellent opportunity to inflict punishment. Rozhdestvensky now ordered the First Division to take its place at the head of the Russian line; but since he ordered neither an increase in the speed of ships of the First Division nor a decrease in that of the remainder of the fleet, the result again was a scramble, with Second and Third Division ships forced to reduce speed, turn in both directions, and even stop their engines. But in spite of the fact that this confusion interfered with their gunnery, the Russian ships nevertheless got in some lusty blows before their foes were in a position to reply effectively. Nebogatov's Third Division, in particular, fired as long as the Japanese ships were within range. The *Mikasa*, the *Shikishima*, and the *Nisshin* all were hit repeatedly. A 12-inch shell from the *Nikolai I* forced the *Asama* out of the battle line to repair a disabled steering gear. Another large Russian shell knocked out the forward turret of the *Yakumo*. Unfortunately for the Russians, these early hits had no effect whatever on the morale of the splendidly trained and well-disciplined Japanese. Repairs were made rapidly, and the killed or wounded were moved speedily out of the way while the firing continued. Shortly after 2:00 P.M. this initial phase of the battle ended.

DECISIVE STAGE: 2:00 TO 4:00 P.M.

Next the Russians resumed their formation and the Japanese passed through their circle. The Japanese cruiser and destroyer squadrons moved to the Russian rear to attack the Russian cruisers and auxiliaries while the main fleets, steaming on parallel courses, began an intense exchange of shelling. The Russians concentrated their fire on the *Mikasa*; the Japanese aimed most of their blows at the *Suvorov* and the *Osliabia*.

In the ensuing contest, with 24 ships exchanging rapid gunfire, superiority in both training and materiel shortly began to pay off for the Japanese. Their greater rapidity and accuracy—once their gunners had found the range—began to make itself felt. Their high explosive shells burst on impact with enormous destructive effect and were far more reliable and effective than the shells of the Russians, which had to pierce armor before exploding and were frequently duds; a Russian observer declared, "A Japanese shell bursting well did as much damage as twelve of ours bursting equally well. And this ours rarely succeeded in doing."[1] As a result of the enormously destructive Japanese fire many Russian ships were almost literally shot to pieces. Although turrets and armor belts provided some security against fatal injury, the smokestacks, masts, and guns were thoroughly and rapidly put out of commission. Hundreds of seamen were killed or wounded.

Taking advantage of their superior speed—15 to 18 knots as compared to nine to 11 for the Russians—the Japanese line pressed steadily ahead, closing the range to less than a mile and forcing the

Russians to turn away from their northward course. Now the fire of many Japanese ships were brought to bear on the Russian van, and the trailing Russian Third Division soon found itself out of range of the main battle.

The first Russian vessels to succumb to the fierce pounding were two flagships—the *Suvorov*, which was initially the target of the *Mikasa* and *Asahi*, and the *Osliabia*, which had taken fire from all the other ships of the Japanese First Division. This pattern of gunnery changed as the Japanese line drew ahead of the Russian line. The *Osliabia* was hit heavily first by *Fuji* and *Shikishima* and later by the Japanese armored cruisers. Her upper works were wrecked and set afire, several shells went through her armor belt and exploded, and dense black smoke poured over her decks. Her own gunfire, wild from the beginning, soon ceased altogether. Then two 12-inch shells struck her forward section on the waterline, peeled off her armor, and opened holes through which the sea rushed in. She swung out of line and settled by the head with a list to port. At 3:30 P.M. she went down. About 330 members of her 900-man crew were rescued from the water by destroyers. Among the free-floating debris of the *Osliabia* was found the sealed coffin of Admiral Fölkersam.

Admiral Rozhdestvensky's flagship, the *Suvorov*, showed far greater powers of resistance under a similar hail of projectiles. The ship had been hit heavily almost from the beginning of the battle, however, and was finally forced out of line at 2:30 P.M. when a shell jammed her rudder. Another hit took out her stern 12-inch turret. Still others blew off her funnels and masts, eventually silenced all of her armament except one 12-pounder gun, and made a shambles of her entire upper works. At 3:00 P.M. Admiral Rozhdestvensky, barely conscious from multiple wounds, had to be removed from the conning tower. The ship was by then a burning ruin, great numbers of officers and men had been wounded and killed, and the hoses were so riddled as to make fire fighting virtually impossible. Four Russian destroyers which had been detailed to the duty of removing flag officers from injured ships failed for some time to appear. Meanwhile the badly damaged and at times almost motionless *Suvorov* lay between the fleets, a target for attack by Japanese battleships, armored cruisers, protected cruisers, and torpedo craft which she tried to repel with ever-waning powers of resistance. Admiral Nebogatov never received Admiral Rozhdestvensky's message to take command, though under the circumstances its delivery or nondelivery made little difference.

With the flagships disabled, the *Aleksandr III* became the leader of the Russian line and the *Sysoi Veliky* led the Second Division. Each of these ships then received concentrated Japanese fire, and though they did not succumb as speedily as had the flagships, both were forced out of the line by damages. The *Aleksandr III* speedily returned, however. The *Sysoi* had the misfortune of losing nearly all of her wounded because the first hits killed her surgeons and wrecked their hospital.

A temporary rescue from destruction developed for the Russians when the growing mist and smoke made it difficult for the Japanese to keep in close touch, and when the very speed of the Japanese line at one time carried it beyond its enemy so that the *Aleksandr III* was able to change its course to the north, pass astern of the Japanese line, and once more head for Vladivostok. This advantage was short-lived, however: Admiral Togo turned back to the fray almost at once. Yet it did gain for the Russians a certain respite for repairs. Meantime, other Russian ships were also suffering injury. The *Borodino* was set afire by repeated hits, and the *Orel* had the muzzle of one of her 12-inch guns shot off and her superstructure severely damaged.

To the south, a quite different and less deadly battle was in progress between the cruiser forces of the two fleets. In this phase of the battle the Japanese out-numbered the Russians 16 ships to eight. On the other hand, most of the Russian ships were larger than the Japanese, and two, the *Admiral Nakhimov* and the *Dmitry Donskoi*, were armored cruisers. In this fight there was occasional intervention by Admiral Nebogatov's Third Division and Admiral Kawamura's Second Division, composed of armored cruisers, but for the most part the light forces were left to their own devices.

The cruiser engagement was slower getting under way than the main battle. At 2:00 P.M. the Japanese Third, Fourth, Fifth, and Sixth Divisions were ordered to the Russian rear to attack the auxiliaries and cruisers. At 2:45 the Third (*Kasagi, Chitose, Otawa,* and *Niitaka,* under Vice Admiral Dewa) and the Fourth (*Naniwa,*

Takachiho, Akashi, and *Tsushima* under Vice Adm. Sokotichi Uriu) found their enemy disoriented and out of formation in the mist, and opened fire on the Russian First Cruiser Division (*Oleg, Avrora, Dmitry Donskoi,* and *Admiral Nakhimov*). The Japanese, on a counter course at the time, passed to the rear of the Russian ships, reversed course, and then ran parallel to Admiral Enkvist's ships. Gunnery was hampered both by the ranges of 5,000 to 7,000 meters and by the heavy seas, and as a result was not particularly effective so far as the combat ships were concerned. Though none of the ships on either side was sunk during this period of the battle, the *Naniwa* and *Takachiho* were forced to repair dangerous hits, at the water line and on the steering gear respectively. At 3:08 P.M. a shell striking *Kasagi* in her coal bunkers started a fast leak, but the vessel managed to reach port under the escort of the *Chitose.* The Russian auxiliaries had fled in every direction while Admiral Enkvist was unable to establish either discipline or protection, so that several of them were set afire and damaged. A Russian destroyer attack made on the Fourth Division at about 3:10 P.M. was beaten off.

The Russian Second Cruiser Division (*Svetlana, Almaz, Zhemchug,* and *Izumrud*) and the Japanese Fifth and Sixth Divisions failed to get into action at this time.

THIRD STAGE: CONFUSION, 4:00 TO 7:00 P.M.

By 4:00 P.M. the Battle of Tsushima had been under way for more than two hours, and already the signs of Russian defeat had become plain. One new Russian battleship had been sunk, one disabled; most of the remaining ships of the Russian battle line were damaged. The pathway to Vladivostok was now effectively barred. The Japanese, though they had been hit repeatedly, were in almost as good condition as at the opening of the battle. And while in the cruiser fight neither side had been greatly damaged, the Russian rear had been separated from the remainder of the fleet and was badly panicked and disorganized.

Then, in the three and a half hours of daylight that remained, the Japanese undertook to turn Russian defeat into overwhelming disaster. The record of events during this period is much less clear, for in the smoke and mist the opposing fleets frequently lost touch with each other. The time of sinking of various ships is only approximate, and the confused courses of both fleets were then, and still are, almost impossible to follow. Identification was difficult, and on occasion both sides mistakenly fired at friendly warships.

Some time soon after 4:00 P.M. Togo's First Division, which had lost contact with the main body of Russian vessels, moved into the group of Russian cruisers and transports and fired at them briefly before leaving for bigger game. Shortly thereafter Admiral Nebogatov's coast-defense ships joined the Russian cruisers, and the main Russian fleet, appearing out of the mist, fired broadsides which scored hits on several Japanese cruisers. At about 4:45 P.M. the Fifth and Sixth Japanese Divisions moved into action, mainly against the light cruisers of the Russian Second Division.

On the whole, the performance of the Russian cruisers was not impressive. The *Zhemchug* collided with the *Ural*; the *Oleg* and *Avrora* were set afire and damaged by numerous hits which did not, however, greatly impair their speed or fighting value. The cruisers of the Second Division were all injured to some extent, the *Svetlana* so seriously that she finally sank. The old and slow *Dmitry Donskoi*, one of the few Russian ships to be well officered, put up a heroic resistance against no less than six Japanese cruisers and succeeded in damaging the *Naniwa* and *Otava*. (On May 29 the *Donskoi* was scuttled near shore by her own crew in order to prevent capture or surrender.)

At about 6:00 P.M. the Japanese cruisers withdrew to the southwest and the Japanese destroyers came up. Instead of attempting to repel attack, the Russian cruisers then scattered. According to Admiral Enkvist's report (which was probably inaccurate), Enkvist's ships at first sought to break through the Japanese lines to the north. It was purportedly only after this attempt failed that they turned south and, with the *Oleg*, *Avrora*, and *Zhemchug*, two destroyers, and three storeships, steamed for the Philippines, where all were disarmed and interned for the remainder of the war.

The Russian auxiliaries, poorly protected by the cruisers, were for the most part either sunk or captured. The two hospital ships, *Orel* and *Kostroma*, were captured by auxiliary cruisers. The tug *Russ* sank, her crew being rescued by the *Svir*. The *Ural* also went down.

At about 7:00 P.M. the *Kamchatka*, which during the entire voyage had been one of the most poorly led ships of the fleet, sank. The *Irtysh* also was lost.

While the Russian cruisers and auxiliaries were scattering like chickens before a hawk, the main battle had been continuing between the battle lines of the two fleets. For about three-quarters of an hour after 4:00 P.M. the opponents faced each other in the mists. At 5:30 P.M. they once more came together and resumed the fight, the Russians clearly badly hurt and firing slowly and inaccurately. During this period the *Aleksandr III* was forced out of line for the second time and her place taken by the *Borodino*, but both ships were already fatally wounded. The *Aleksandr* was listing from a gash in her bows; the *Borodino* had lost most of her officers and was suffering from many hits and uncontrollable fires. Meanwhile, the nearly unrecognizable hulk of the *Suvorov*, unattended by destroyers, continued to draw attacks from all Japanese ships in the area. Eventually the *Buiny* approached the flagship and at great danger to herself succeeded in removing the wounded, including the unconscious Admiral Rozhdestvensky and several members of his staff. Up to this time the fourth member of the First Division, the *Orel*, while it had taken several hundred hits, had not been vitally injured.

The three leading Russian battleships sank within minutes of each other. The *Aleksandr III*, her hull riddled, her superstructure shot away and her interior on fire, fell out, capsized slowly, and sank at about 7:00 P.M. with no survivors. Ten minutes later the *Borodino* was hit in the forward turret by a 12-inch shell from the *Fuji*, sustained two heavy explosions in rapid succession, and sank almost instantaneously, leaving only one survivor. At about 7:20 P.M. the *Kniaz Suvorov* was administered the *coup de grâce* by three or four torpedoes from a Japanese torpedo-boat flotilla.

It was now nearly dark, and Admiral Togo ordered his fleet to sail north to Matsushima. The First Division left the scene of battle at about 7:28 P.M., but the armored cruisers conducted a sweep to the westward before retiring. By 8:00 P.M. all of the Japanese heavy ships retired from the area, leaving night attacks to the destroyers and torpedo boats.

Despite the overwhelming and one-sided nature of the first day's battle, the Japanese had sustained injuries. The *Mikasa* had been hit more than 30 times but had lost only eight killed and 105 wounded, largely because only five of the ten heavy shells hitting the vessel had exploded. The *Shikishima* sustained ten hits with 13 killed and 25 wounded. The *Fuji's* casualties were about the same and those of the *Asahi* lighter. Among the armored cruisers, the *Nisshin* had had three of her main guns destroyed by eight hits and had lost five men killed and 90 wounded. The losses of the other seven armored cruisers were lighter. The *Iwate* was hit 16 times but not in vital places, and had no men killed and 15 wounded. The remaining armored cruisers collectively had been hit no more than 30 times and had lost only a few men. Only the *Adzumo* had been damaged in her armament; several guns were destroyed. The Japanese smaller cruisers had suffered some damage, but all except the *Kasagi* continued to be battleworthy. At the end of the day no major Japanese ship had been sunk, but several had received a sufficient number of blows to cause destruction had the Russian shells been as effective as their own. Total casualties for the Japanese were 144 hits, 72 men killed, and 313 men wounded in the battle fleet. The cruisers had lost 22 men killed and 117 wounded.

Seven of the 12 ships comprising the original Russian line of battle survived, but they were of little value. By about 8:00 P.M. Admiral Nebogatov in the *Nikolai I* led a small line of vessels including the *Orel* (so battered as to be worthless), the *Admiral Seniavin*, the *Sysoi Veliky*, the *Navarin*, and the *Admiral Nakhimov*, with the lone cruiser *Izumrud* on the starboard beam. Several destroyers were wandering about, and one of these, the *Bedovy*, accepted the transfer of Admiral Rozhdestvensky from the crowded *Buiny*, which already held 200 survivors from the luckless *Osliabia*.

FOURTH STAGE: NIGHT TORPEDO ATTACKS,
7:30 P.M. TO 5:00 A.M.

Even before the Japanese battle fleet had retired from the scene the torpedo craft made their appearance. They numbered about 37 torpedo boats and 21 destroyers, some of which had been present during the day but most of which had stayed in port until evening. Very heavy seas impeded operations, but other conditions were now nearly ideal for torpedo attack: several of the Russian ships were damaged and moving slowly; many of their guns were out of action; the surviving crewmen were dog-tired. Moreover several of the Russian ships used searchlights, which made them highly visible targets. The *Orel's* searchlight had been destroyed, however, and Admiral Nebogatov had trained his men in repelling night torpedo attacks without using lights; consequently, while most of the vessels of Admiral Fölkersam's Second Division were destroyed, most of the Third Division ships survived. The *Sysoi Veliky*, already badly damaged, and the *Nakhimov*, largely undamaged, were both torpedoed during the night and sank. At about 2:00 A.M. the *Navarin* was torpedoed twice and sank with her crew of 622 men. The *Monomakh*, not greatly injured in the day's fighting, was hit during the night by a torpedo which blew off her bow. She managed to sink the destroyer that delivered the attack, but because of the severity of her injuries she was scuttled by her crew at 5:00 A.M. Hampered by heavy seas, the Japanese torpedo craft had been able to get only seven hits from 100 torpedoes fired, yet all seven were highly effective. Japanese losses amounted to three torpedo boats sunk and five damaged, and total Japanese personnel casualties numbered 87.

FIFTH STAGE: SURRENDER AND MOP-UP

At 5:00 A.M. on the 28th of May Admiral Nebogatov in the *Nikolai I* had remaining under his command the *Orel*, the *Apraksin*, the *Seniavin*, and the cruiser *Izumrud*. For a time this tiny fleet proceeded slowly through a seemingly deserted sea toward Vladivostok, still 300 miles away. But escape was not in the cards for them. Shortly, smoke was seen over the north horizon, and five enemy cruisers made an appearance. Other ships materialized to the south. By 9:00 A.M. the entire Japanese navy surrounded the remnants of the Russian fleet. Carefully keeping at a safe distance—the maximum range of the Russian guns was 11,000 yards—the Japanese opened fire with their more powerful artillery, scoring first near misses and then hits. After consulting with his officers, Admiral Nebogatov signaled surrender. The Japanese, unable to comprehend at once a decision that was to them a violation of military morality, continued firing for fully ten minutes—until the Russians produced and flew a Japanese flag. At that point the fast cruiser *Izumrud*, declining to surrender, made a sudden dash through the encircling Japanese and escaped. When a Japanese boarding party reached the *Orel*, some sailors who tried to sink her by opening the sea cocks were shot by their captors.

A few of the Russian vessels were still not accounted for. At about 11:00 A.M. the *Svetlana* was sunk after a fight with *Niitaka, Otava,* and *Marakumo*. At 4:00 P.M. Japanese armored cruisers wrecked the *Ushakov*, which was well astern and had put up a very competent fight. The auxiliary *Irtysh* foundered on the Japanese coast; the *Koreia* escaped to Shanghai and the *Anadyr* to Madagascar and eventually to Russia. The *Bedovy* and *Grozny* were overtaken by two Japanese destroyers on their way north. The *Bedovy*, with Admiral Rozhdestvensky aboard, surrendered, but the *Grozny* damaged one Japanese destroyer and steamed on to Askold Island before she ran out of fuel; she was finally rescued by a Russian collier. The *Gromky* engaged in a duel with three Japanese torpedo boats, damaged two, and finally, when she had exhausted her ammunition and two-thirds of her crew were disabled, sank. The *Bravy* reached Vladivostok with her own crew as well as survivors of the *Osliabia*. The *Bodry* headed for Shanghai but ran out of fuel, and finally out of water and rations. With her crew mutinous and considering cannibalism, she was towed to port by a British vessel. The *Buiny* was damaged in action and sunk by the *Donskoi* to prevent her falling into Japanese hands. Two of the remaining destroyers reached Manila while one, the *Bezuprechny*, was sunk by the Japanese.

At Vladivostok Admiral Skrydlov had been operating a fleet of four auxiliary cruisers as commerce destroyers pending the arrival of the second Pacific Squadron. On May 29 the cruiser *Almaz* brought the first news of the debacle. She was followed shortly by two destroyers. The *Izumrud*, bound for Vladivostok by an indirect route, ran out of fuel and was beached on a rock at Vladimir Bay, 150 miles to the north, where she was blown up by her crew. As soon as he had ascertained the magnitude of the Russian defeat, Admiral Skrydlov left for St. Petersburg.

Few naval battles in history have been as decisive as Tsushima.

Thirty-eight of the ships entering the battle were sunk, captured, or interned; and of these all were Russian except three torpedo boats. The Russian loss (counting auxiliaries) exceeded 200,000 tons, greater than the combined losses of both combatants at the Battle of Jutland in World War I. Eight of the twelve Russian capital ships were sunk and four captured. Three of the eight cruisers were sunk or scuttled, one was wrecked, three were interned, and only one reached Vladivostok. Five auxiliaries were sunk and two captured; one escaped. Of the nine destroyers, three were sunk, one captured, three interned, and two reached Vladivostok. As for personnel, the Japanese lost 117 killed and 587 wounded; the Russians had 4,830 killed, an unknown number wounded, 5,917 taken prisoner, and 1,862 interned in foreign ports. The overall Russian loss was the heaviest in the history of naval warfare.

The overwhelming nature of the Japanese victory occasioned a vast amount of post-battle analysis among naval professionals. It was obvious to all that the Japanese had learned from their mistakes, and that they had put on a far better performance from every standpoint than they had the previous year. In August 1904 the possibility of having to fight another Russian fleet had made them excessively cautious. At Tsushima they had "gone for broke," forcing a fight at the close range at which decisive results could be expected.

Equally obvious was the Russian failure to profit from early mistakes. The performance of the Second Pacific Squadron was distinctly inferior to that of the First. The consensus among naval analysts was that while the Russians were fighting against much stronger forces and never had a chance of victory, good leadership would have gone far to make the final contest more nearly even.

Rozhdestvensky undoubtedly faced a hopeless task from the outset. His feat in bringing a very poor fleet around the world against great obstacles excites admiration. But his preparations for and his leadership during the battle do not. He showed little forethought or initiative at any time, and he consistently neglected obvious matters that could have increased the efficiency of his fleet. Admiral Nebogatov, with poorer ships and crews, made a better showing.

The question of Klado's conduct in persuading the tsar to order reinforcements has also been widely discussed, with most modern writers siding with Rozhdestvensky. Without excusing him of insincerity or raising the question as to what he expected of men and ships of whose defects he should have been thoroughly aware, this writer does not feel that Klado's actions unduly handicapped Admiral Rozhdestvensky. The long stay at Nossi-Be arose from coaling troubles rather than from the delayed arrival of the Third Pacific Squadron. Had Admiral Rozhdestvensky arrived in Japanese waters without the Third Pacific Squadron, his fleet would still have been much slower than that of the Japanese, and considerably inferior in force. Nor would he have found the path to Vladivostok any easier. Subsequently, the Russian navy itself rendered a true judgment on the merits of its Russo-Japanese War commanders when it chose to commemorate only one man—Admiral Makarov—by designating a major warship to bear his name.

After Tsushima the Japanese were able to reinforce one phase of their war effort that had until then received very little attention. In the war against enemy commerce, the Japanese had seized 61 merchant vessels as compared to 57 by the Russians. They were now able to blockade the mouth of the Amur and the entire Siberian coast. In July they also sent a task force to invade and occupy Northern Sakhalin; Admiral Kataoka landed 14,000 men who by the end of the month had conquered the island.

CHAPTER 13

Between Wars
(1905-14)

THE LEGACY OF TSUSHIMA

THE BATTLE OF TSUSHIMA was more than a decisive naval defeat; it marked the end of Russian attempts to salvage a lost war. Compared with the military efficiency and selfless patriotism of the Japanese, Russian tsarism had made a very poor showing. Save for their one striking success in mine warfare, the Russians in 17 months of war had managed to lose every engagement both on sea and on land.

Furthermore, Russia herself appeared to be on the verge of disintegration. The outbreak of war had been accompanied by fervent popular expressions of patriotism and loyalty to the tsar. But as defeat was added to defeat support weakened rapidly, and the enemies of tsarism made their presence felt in what Lenin later referred to as a "dress rehearsal" for the 1917 revolution. In July 1904 the unpopular minister of the interior, V. K. Plehve, was assassinated. Workers' strikes, popular demonstrations, and disorders in non-Russian areas such as Poland, the Caucasus, and the Baltic states became the rule. On January 22, 1905, huge crowds of unarmed workers, approaching the Winter Palace to present a petition to the tsar (who was absent), were fired on by troops who killed more than 100 and wounded hundreds more. In the country, peasants seized large estates, burned homes, murdered landlords. In several towns the Bolsheviks set up soviets which attempted to take over the local government. From October 20 to 30, 1905, a general strike supported even by children in primary schools prevailed throughout Russia.

The spreading disaffection even evinced itself in the army and navy, those traditional props to the tsar. Mutiny on the *Pamiat Azova* and four destroyers, plus a mutiny by infantry regiments ashore, occurred at Sevastopol under the direction of Lt. Petr Shmidt. Loyal troops captured the town; the ships surrendered; Shmidt was put to death. But other revolts occurred at Revel, at Kronstadt, and at Sveaborg. Mutineers at Sveaborg managed to seize the fortress before they were bombarded into surrender by the loyal battleship *Slava*. In every case revolutionary organizations were behind the revolts, but the grievances exploited were entirely genuine. The most spectacular revolt began on the new Black Sea Fleet battleship *Kniaz Potemkin Tavrichesky*, when a group of sailors objected to allegedly spoiled and wormy meat used for their borscht. The executive officer ordered that the protestors be seized and shot, whereupon fellow crew members joined in open revolt. They seized the ship after killing or disarming all officers, save those few who had joined them. For eleven days thereafter the *Potemkin* cruised the waters of the Black Sea, firing at shore targets and urging other ships to join her. Finally she sought refuge in a Rumanian port, where she was interned. The ship was subsequently restored to Russia and renamed *Panteleimon*; most of the crew remained abroad.[1]

Faced with so much opposition, Tsar Nicholas II, in order to gain time, agreed to the election of a Duma, or national legislature, based on a wide suffrage but having somewhat limited powers. He also gave his assurance that certain civil liberties would be granted. As soon as pressures subsided his ministers withdrew or whittled down many of the concessions. An armed uprising in December 1905, which Nicholas was strong enough to put down, was taken by the tsar as an excuse for invoking the sternest measures of repression. For a period thereafter, members of the political right joined with police and army to create the infamous "Black Hundreds" who undertook pogroms of Jews, ruthlessly hunted down revolutionaries, and suppressed all liberal and intellectual criticism.

With serious troubles multiplying at home, it was clearly in the tsar's interest to end the war with Japan as quickly and as cheaply as possible. Early in May 1905 President Theodore Roosevelt tendered his good offices as a peacemaker. The tsar at first held back, but once apprised of the destruction of Rozhdestvensky's fleet he was entirely ready to consider a settlement. The Japanese, for their part, were scarcely less willing: though all-victorious, they had exhausted both resources and credit and were in desperate financial straits. England, which had served as Japan's financial angel, was not anxious to see an unlimited extension of Nipponese power. Neither, with the power of Germany growing, could she be entirely happy over a continuing war between her own ally and Russia, an ally of France. Thus after Russia had been humbled England held back the progress of her too-bright pupil by declining to make further loans. By mid-1905 the Japanese had already achieved most of what they could hope for militarily, yet for all its defeats the main Russian army had not been destroyed. Hence after each side had made pro forma protests of reluctance, the plenipotentiaries met at the Portsmouth (N.H.) Navy Yard on August 10, 1905. An agreement was reached in less than three weeks. The Japanese position in Korea was recognized; Russia gave up her claim to Manchuria; southern Sakhalin was ceded to Japan. As a result of her victory, Japan further gained primacy in Chinese affairs. Though they were disappointed in their hope for an indemnity, the Japanese accepted the treaty. It took formal effect on October 16, 1905.

From a naval standpoint the Russian defeat had been catastrophic. The Pacific and Baltic fleets had been wiped out except for a few escapees, a number of ships that were building when the Baltic Fleet departed, and some very old vessels that not even Captain Klado would have wished to send to war. Eleven first-class battleships had been either sunk or captured, as well as seven second-class battleships or coast-defense ships, five armored cruisers, six cruisers, four gunboats, and about 20 destroyers. Almost overnight the Russian navy declined from third to sixth place as a world sea power, being surpassed by the United States, Germany, and Japan.

The Russian navy had remaining only the Black Sea Fleet—weakest of its three main squadrons—and a scattering of ships elsewhere. Either at Vladivostok or in internment were the battleship *Tsesarevich*, the armored cruisers *Rossiia* and *Gromoboi*, and the cruisers

Diana, Askold, Avrora, Oleg, Zhemchug, and *Almaz.* In the Baltic were three unfinished battleships—the *Slava,* already mentioned, and two newer and larger ships, the 16,600-ton *Pavel I* and *Andrei Pervozvanny.* The latter might be termed semi-dreadnoughts, as they carried four 12-inch and 14 8-inch guns and therefore approached the "all big-gun" ship design, though they were slower (18 knots compared to 21) than the contemporary *Dreadnought* in the British Navy. They had been redesigned during construction to incorporate improved armor protection and were consequently slow in building. The *Sv. Yevstafy* and *Ioann Zlatoust* of 12,700 tons were smaller vessels under construction at Nikolaev for the Black Sea Fleet. These were relatively thinly armored ships (9-inch turret and 10-inch belt) carrying four 12-inch, four 8-inch, and twelve 6-inch guns, and were expected to make 18 knots.

An inevitable consequence of thorough defeat is the investigation and apportionment of blame. Captain Klado, first to feel the brunt, was fired from his position and had all of his honors withdrawn shortly after Tsushima. Rozhdestvensky and Nebogatov and their subordinates were not tried for more than a year. A preliminary hearing in the Kriukovsky Barracks in St. Petersburg hinted at the decadent state of the Russian navy, bearing out all of Klado's criticisms and adding many that he had omitted. In November 1906, courtmartial proceedings began. Rozhdestvensky, who manfully claimed and accepted responsibility for everything that happened even while he was unconscious, was acquitted. Nebogatov, who had aired Russian naval deficiencies in articles in the British press following his surrender, was sentenced to death for surrendering, but the sentence was commuted by the tsar to ten years' imprisonment. Enkvist, whose battle record had been far poorer than either of the other two, was not put on trial. Capt. Clapier de Colongue, the captains of the *Nikolai I, Seniavin,* and *Apraksin,* the captain of the *Bedovy,* and a few lesser officers were also sentenced to be executed. As in the case of Nebogatov, these sentences were changed to long prison terms. Some of the seconds in command received shorter sentences. The man who was acting commander of the *Orel* when the battle ended (Captain Yung had been killed in battle) was absolved because of the battered condition of his ship.

To comment on these proceedings and sentences would probably be superfluous: the real culprit, tsarism, was never placed on trial.

Individual naval officers were punished for its faults, which were far more serious than any individual guilt, and the choice of victims made comparatively little sense save in a few instances, justice being a commodity in short supply in tsarist Russia.

Had Russia been a democracy at the time of the investigation of the Tsushima disaster, the public would have learned of many more naval abuses than were ever revealed by Captain Klado. Some of these—such as the failure to issue battle orders, to keep ships in as good condition as possible, to have ships painted to blend with their ocean background, to conduct pre-battle reconnaissance, and to avoid gross overloading at Tsushima—were the fault of Admiral Rozhdestvensky. Far more deficiencies stemmed from the system of naval administration, however, and cannot be ascribed to the fleet commander: failure to put the ships in condition before the voyage; shortage of ammunition; poor quality of shells, powder, and torpedoes; lack of range finders; inoperative wireless sets; neglect of training of the crews and poor quality of both officers and sailors; constant efforts at subversion and sabotage. These problems had their origin in a host of serious defects in the Russian shore establishment.

Some of the survivors of Tsushima who engaged in early operations research concluded that the Russians had fired per minute 134 shots of 20,000 pounds, as compared to the Japanese record of 360 shots of 53,000 pounds. In addition, since Russian shells contained on the average only 15 pounds of pyroxylin compared to 105 pounds of shimose in the Japanese shells, the actual difference in the weight of high explosive was on the order of one to 15, or 500 pounds as compared to 7,500.[2]

THE SEARCH FOR A NAVAL POLICY

For a nation as badly defeated as Russia had been, two steps were urgently needed. First, underlying causes of defeat needed to be determined and removed. Second, active rebuilding of the shattered forces should have begun at once.

These moves were not forthcoming for many reasons. While the tsar and the ministry of marine favored a rebuilding of the fleet, they were greatly opposed to any fundamental changes in either its organization or its methods of operation. In the face of overwhelming evidence they refused to acknowledge any need for administrative reform. On the other hand, the newly created Duma strongly favored change, insisted on debating the navy's (and the army's) shortcomings, and refused to vote money for new ships until such time as a considerable measure of modernization had been effected in naval administration. For two years an impasse existed. Finally, between 1907 and 1912, the tsar, by repeated and widespread disfranchisements and completely illegal alteration of election laws, succeeded in effectively packing the Duma with his own supporters.

The deadlock between the tsar and the Duma, however, was not the only cause of delay in bringing about change. The period between 1905 and 1914 witnessed a great deal of discussion over what should constitute the appropriate naval policy for Russia. The "big navy" school had been temporarily discredited by the outcome of the Russo-Japanese War, but there was no agreement among its foes. One group argued that naval building was useless unless preceded by thoroughgoing reform. Another maintained that a nation of Russia's industrial backwardness lacked the capacity to create a first-class modern navy. To this school, no shipbuilding at all or a building program comprised mainly of submarines, torpedo craft, and mining ships appeared most likely to answer Russian needs. A third and more constructive group consisted largely of younger officers who, though loyal to the tsar, were determined to correct the serious faults revealed by war and to build as large a navy as Russia could afford.

The debate over naval policy continued for several years and on its theoretical side received the attention of at least three prominent writers on strategy: Nikolai Klado, V. Novitsky, and N. Portugalov, the last an officer turned journalist. Of these Klado, who returned to official favor following a brief period of disgrace, was by far the most important. In two books and in a series of articles dealing with strategy, published in *Morskoi sbornik*, Klado examined with clarity and in detail the nature of naval power as it affected Russia. He pointed out that the weapons of naval warfare were more complicated and technical than those used on land, and that defense at sea posed far greater problems than on shore. Because of her geographical position, he contended, Russia's naval strategy was tied up with her land strategy. In the Baltic, in order to protect the

Russian Coast from attack the fleet must defend a line between the Aland Islands and Osel Island (Sarema). It was essential that naval control be maintained to facilitate the movement of Russia land forces in the area. He declared that mines and submarines, when taken alone, were only fragments of the naval organism and were not in themselves sufficient to defend important bases.

Klado saw the Black Sea problem in similar terms. If either Germany or her allies were to control the Black Sea, Russia would lose her main trade route to and contact with Europe. By dominating the Black Sea, Russia would have an easy access to the Danube and the Balkans—an access adequate to assure control and probably also sufficient to ensure military victory.

Klado believed that the territory in the Pacific which was vital to Russia and therefore must be defended was the "green belt," or Primorsk triangle, bounded by lines running from Vladivostok to Nikolaevsk to Khabarovsk and containing most of Russia's Pacific area population. During the war with Japan this area had never actually been threatened. Manchuria, Klado felt, offered the best metallurgical base for future Japanese expansion. He noted in addition the central and dominating position of Korea.[3]

Novitsky and Portugalov had less influence than had Klado. They were alike in pointing out that Russia's conquest of the "Heartland" of Eurasia had failed to give her great military advantages. Portugalov also turned much attention to expansion abroad; he urged the acquisition of overseas naval bases as an indispensable adjunct to the spread of Russian power. Another naval writer was Capt. (later Rear Adm.) A. D. Bubnov, who produced a three-volume *History of Naval Science* and a volume entitled *Naval Strategy*. Gen. N. Golovin, writing slightly later on strategy, foresaw the Japanese push into Manchuria and predicted that in a future Pacific clash the United States would require Russian assistance.

Despite the urgings of all these strategists, however, the tsar's government still was in no hurry to adopt a "big navy" policy even after 1907, when P. A. Stolypin, first as interior minister and then as premier, managed to enlist support from a reasonably tractable Duma. Major plans were brought forward in August 1909 involving a ten-year program to cost 1.125 million gold rubles; but it was not until March 1910 when the sum had been cut to 731 million rubles, that the Council of the Empire issued an approval. Further, only when Vice Adm. I. K. Grigorovich, an unusually able, vigorous, and honest man, became minister of marine in 1912 were any really definitive statements on naval policy forthcoming. At that time it was decided that there would be a concentration of sea power in the Baltic, and that the Pacific and White Sea stations were to be covered mainly by torpedo craft. For the Black Sea, where Turkey was the only likely opponent, a 50 percent margin over the strength of other Black Sea powers was deemed sufficient. Since the Turkish navy was even more drastically obsolescent than the Russian, no great naval increase would be required, but need for better shore establishments and more modern ships was recognized.

For some years there had been discussion of a long-term ship-building program. At length a fifteen-year plan was adopted, to begin in 1913. It stipulated requirements as regards capital ships as follows:

LAID DOWN		JOIN FLEET
1913	4 battle cruisers	1916
1915	4 battleships	1918
1917	4 battleships	1920
1919	4 battle cruisers	1922
1921	4 battleships	1924
1923	4 battleships	1926
1925	4 battle cruisers	1928
1927	4 battleships	1930

A two-a-year building program with a radical reduction in the time of construction was supposed to result in the completion not only of capital ships, but of light cruisers of about 7,600 tons, many large destroyers, and submarines. Most of the new ships were to be stationed in the Baltic. Had the project been completed in its entirety, the eventual makeup of the Russian navy would have been 27 battleships, 12 battle cruisers, 24 light cruisers, 108 destroyers, and 36 submarines. Replacement intervals were set at 22 years for capital ships, 18 for cruisers, 17 for destroyers, and 14 for submarines.

REBUILDING THE FLEET

Although prior to 1913 comparatively little rebuilding took place, some new vessels were completed, the first being ships laid down during or directly after the war. A very large armored cruiser named *Riurik* (15,000 tons) was ordered in England. This ship was armed with four 10-inch, eight 8-inch, and twenty 4.7-inch guns. Instead of a maximum speed, a sustained 21 knots on easy steaming at three-fourths of full engine power was specified. A class of small armored cruisers (*Admiral Makarov, Baian,* and *Pallada*) of 7,900 tons, 21 knots, and two 8-inch and eight 6-inch guns was also laid down. These cruisers were virtual copies of the *Baian* lost at Port Arthur, and were already of obsolete type. The foregoing were about the only major warships projected, and progress in shipbuilding was so often interrupted by strikes and sabotage that the warships ordered abroad were finished years sooner than those built in Russia.

This story of naval change, however, has not taken into consideration one particular phase of shipbuilding. For some time the Russians had shown desultory interest in submarines; and since this form of defense looked to be both promising and cheap, neither the government nor its critics seriously objected to further development in the field. A sizable beginning had been made in the building of a submarine fleet during the Russo-Japanese War. Thirteen boats of 210/235 tons[4] had been ordered in Germany. The 137-ton *Protektor,* designed by Simon Lake, and the *Fulton,* built by the American-owned Holland interests, were both procured in the United States. Orders for five of each of these types had been placed with yards in the Baltic. The Russians had even imported Mr. Lake and a nucleus of American workmen to supervise the building of one submarine of the *Bubnov* type, which was financed by popular subscription, and some others that were financed by the government.

These early submarines had varied fates, but by the time of the Treaty of Portsmouth no less than 14 had been sent in disassembled form to Vladivostok. Although some of these were damaged in transit and required alterations, about half of them could be reassembled, proved operational, and during the last months of the war were used defensively on patrols near their base. No offensive operations were attempted, partly due to the limited range of the submarines themselves but more because of lack of clearly defined organization and leadership. The port authorities also developed net defenses against submarines of the Holland type, which they believed the Japanese to be using.

A later Lake contract called for comparatively large boats of

410/482 tons, with four torpedo tubes and two light cannon and capable of a surface speed of 15 knots and a cruising range of 3,500 miles. When first tested on delivery, these boats stood on end and could not submerge; but after the cause of the difficulty—overloading—was corrected, they were reasonably effective craft.

A training division at Libau in April 1905, designed to prepare personnel for underseas operations, was established under Captain Shchensnovich, formerly of the *Retvizan*; but because of lack of program, equipment, classrooms, and experienced teachers it accomplished little the first two years. In 1907 Commodore P. Levitsky was given command of the department, and by dint of hard work he managed to establish a reasonably efficient training program. Few good officers were available for the submarine service; however, the enlisted force was assured of higher pay and more rapid promotion to petty officer ratings than they could have received in other branches of the navy.

In 1907 submarines maneuvered for the first time with the Baltic Fleet. The next year witnessed the completion at Nikolaev of the *Krab* (512/572 tons), the world's first submarine to be designed as a mine layer. At about the same time three German-built (Krupp) boats were shipped from the Baltic to form the nucleus of the submarine force of the Black Sea Fleet. By the end of 1910 a brigade of submarines, consisting of two divisions of five boats each, was set up in the Baltic under Rear Adm. P. Levitsky. By 1912 the Baltic force consisted of eight submarines and two tenders, and a submarine rescue vessel was under construction. Submarine losses during the eight years since 1904 had numbered four boats, not a heavy rate of casualties considering the newness of the weapon.

Prior to 1912 the Russian submarine program had been mainly experimental and had failed to produce many soundly constructed boats, particularly among those of larger size. During 1912 and 1913, when the Russians started to build ships of 600 to 800 tons, there was a notable increase in numbers authorized and an improvement in types. Unhappily, because Russian industrial facilities were too weak to support so large a project, the much improved models were still not completed by 1914. At the outbreak of war, therefore, the Russians had only eight boats of 1904–1906 vintage in the Baltic, four in the Black Sea, and nine in the Pacific. Nearly all of those suffered from various serious defects which made them either unreliable, unseaworthy, or unlivable for any length of time. Since some of the friends of undersea warfare had talked in terms of a navy composed of 500 submarines and little else, the contrast between dreams and ambitions on the one hand and reality on the other was extremely sharp. Russian administration continued to be weak. Simon Lake complained of officers who were not held accountable for their mistakes, of the always strict and at times inhuman treatment of crewmen, and of the generally poor quality of the Russian service.[5]

Although in 1907 Stolypin was able to secure the election of an unrepresentative and highly conservative Duma, dominated largely by the class of big landowners, support for naval rebuilding was not at once forthcoming. Even the conservative Duma was impressed by the need for reforms in the army and navy, but since it was now weighted by members who were the natural allies of the tsar, Stolypin was able by granting some of their demands to obtain support for a few new ships. Still, progress was slow, and the years from 1907 to 1911—when other powers were building dreadnoughts —were lean years for the Russian navy. Financial difficulties, poor administration of navy yards, and well-grounded suspicions on the part of the Duma all held back the construction of new ships. The government for several years encouraged private citizens to donate funds for the building of small craft. Some fifty new destroyers were built between 1904 and 1909, mainly by popular subscription, the largest being a 625-ton class of ships named after officers active in the previous war.

About 1908–1909 there was a partial easing of the deadlock over ship construction. In 1908, after two committees of the Duma had declared that a reconstruction of the navy without a reorganization of administration was impossible, the minister of marine ordered an inspection of both the fleet and its personnel and an inquiry into dockyard administration. The inquiry confirmed the need for radical reform, whereupon the Duma insisted that the scheme of administration in the navy yards be completely changed. It concluded that the Baltic and Admiralty yards could not build large ships quickly, and that the cost of Russian construction would be at least 40 percent higher than if the same ships were to be built abroad. The admiralty contended that conditions were not that bad, that the country needed to have its naval forces strengthened more than it needed administrative changes. The differences were resolved in a compromise. Some reforms were introduced and several new committees were set up. The naval academy was reorganized with an altered enrollment system. A new rank of senior lieutenant was created. Submarines and radio were placed under control of the inspector of torpedo services.

Finally, four new battleships were laid down, the *Sevastopol* and *Petropavlovsk* at the Baltic yard, and the *Poltava* and *Gangut* at Admiralty. Since these were to be the first dreadnoughts built for the Russian navy, their design was a matter for long debate and much consultation with foreign firms. The plan that was accepted was patterned after the Italian *Dante Alighieri*, and called for 23,000-ton ships of 23 knots speed. They carried the then novel arrangement of 12 12-inch guns in four three-gun turrets, which, combined with a high angle of elevation, resulted in a fire-power superior to that of contemporary dreadnoughts elsewhere. They were built in about four years (most of them came into service in 1914–15), far less time than the seven to eight years required for the *Pavel I* class. Thus, in some respects, the limited reforms which the Duma forced on the admiralty brought a measure of improvement. The anti-destroyer battery of 16 4.7-inch guns, however, was weaker than the 6-inch pieces then common in some foreign navies; and an overall weakness lay in substandard armor protection and crew accommodations. Criticisms of the new ships continued to emanate from both the Duma and the press. Improper expenditure of funds was charged. The side armor was held to be too thin to keep out heavy shells, and the 4.7-inch guns were adjudged to be too close to the big guns to be kept in action. It was further alleged that no steel works in Russia could produce the high-tensile steels needed.

The objections raised concerning the 1910 battleships could not have been applied to the three ships laid down the following year for the Black Sea Fleet. The *Yekaterina II*, *Imperatritsa Mariia*, and *Imperator Aleksandr III* (a fourth vessel, *Navarin*, was planned but not built) were to be 22,500-ton ships with 21 knots' speed, 12 12-inch guns in four turrets, and 20 5.1-inch guns. Armor protection on belts and turrets reached a maximum of 12 inches—then topped only by new German ships. In the design of these dreadnoughts the Russians rectified one major blunder of former years: because the guns were given an especially high angle of elevation and could fire at a distance of about 25 miles, these became the longest-range dreadnoughts afloat. Some bettered their designed speed by as much as four knots. Competently handled, these ships could have given a good account of themselves in combat had they been in the Battle of Jutland.

Four planned battle cruisers, *Izmail*, *Borodino*, *Kinburn*, and *Navarin*, were to be of 32,000 tons and carry nine 14-inch and 24 5.1-inch guns of high velocity. These ships were given the speed of 27 knots, relatively slow for battle cruisers, though this was somewhat compensated for by heavy armor protection. They were laid down as early as 1912, but their construction was interrupted by World War I and the Russian Revolution, and they were never finished.

On the whole, the Russians had greater success in building small vessels than in producing dreadnoughts. Their 7,600-ton light cruisers were excellent ships for their day. The destroyers, which progressed rapidly from about 650 tons to double that size, were superior in design and capabilities to contemporary ships in the German and Turkish navies. In fact, the destroyer *Novik* (1,260 tons) made 37.3 knots on her trials in 1913 and was possibly the best ship of her class in the world. Russian destroyers incorporated four double torpedo tubes, three or four 4-inch guns, and as many machine guns. The vast majority of both Russian destroyers and submarines also had a minelaying capacity.

Because the quality of Russian ship design had often been justly suspect in the past, it is only fair to note that the ships built during this period were in many cases excellent. The battle cruisers were actually high-speed battleships, a type that did not appear in the rest of the world's navies until the 1930s. Both the Black Sea dreadnoughts and the light cruisers were well ahead of their day, as were the Russian destroyers. Subsequently, battleships carrying 12 16-inch guns and destroyers of 2,000 tons, both far in advance of their day, were projected for later years of the program. Certainly in the field of ship design, then, the Russians had learned something from experience.

Just before World War I the Russians started work in naval aviation. As early as 1909 the head of the naval engineer corps, L. M. Maevich, had proposed an aircraft-carrying ship equipped with catapults for launching planes. Another officer named Shishkov had in 1913 recommended a carrier speed of 30 knots. In 1910 a naval flying school was established at Kronstadt and slightly later another at Sevastopol. For several years appropriations were small but 330 planes and eight airships for minelaying were included in the 1913 program. Ninety of these craft were Sikorsky biplanes and mono-planes. Ten were of the giant *Ilia Muromets* type, which could carry 16 passengers or half a ton of bombs, the first models of the eighty that were finally built by the Russo-Baltic Waggon Factory. These were the first four-motored airplanes, and the largest planes of their time. They were built in both a land plane and a seaplane version. Similar in size to the U.S. B-17 Flying Fortresses of the 1930s, these early aerial dreadnoughts had a ceiling of only 10,000 feet and an effective flying radius of about 80 miles. But they had a remarkable war record: only three were lost during the war, and the only one shot down downed three or four of its attackers.

Considerable proficiency was also demonstrated in lighter-than-air aviation, a field in which the Russian navy had been interested since the 1890s. Eight airships of about 290 feet in length were con-structed for purposes of aerial minelaying. As an adjunct to these activities quite a sizable shore establishment was built up, including sheds, airfields, and a flying school at Sevastopol.

Despite the great obstacles interposed by a penny-pinching and critical Duma and a weak ruler, uncertainty over basic policy, inade-quate industrialization, and shortages of non-government funds, the Baltic Fleet improved noticeably in efficiency between 1905 and 1914. Much of this change was due to the efforts of two unusually capable officers who were supported by a group of younger officers determined to remedy some of the more serious faults revealed by the Russo-Japanese war.

Adm. Nikolai Ottovich von Essen, a small, wiry man of unlimited energy and keen intellect whose gifts had been recognized by the great Makarov, was now generally considered the ablest admiral in the navy. As commander of the Baltic Fleet mine-cruiser detachment from 1906 to 1908 he built up a superb offensive mining organiza-tion. Later, as commander of the Baltic Fleet from 1908 to 1915, he emphasized indoctrination, preparedness, and thorough training. He was aware of many abuses in the navy and personally dedicated to reform and improvement. He was handicapped, however, by the massive inadequacies of tsarism and by the incipient revolutionary movement.

What von Essen was to the seagoing fleet, Adm. Ivan Konstantino-vich Grigorovich, navy minister after 1912, was to the shore estab-lishment. A fine and honest administrator with a great deal of driving force and the ability to lead subordinates, Grigorovich attempted not only to build up and modernize the fleet's naval bases but to improve the quality of naval administration through the elimination of graft and the promotion of reforms in organization.

In shipbuilding, as in ship design, the Russians showed an ability to learn from their mistakes. The vessels of the 1912 and later pro-grams were homogeneous in type, and much more capable of match-ing the best foreign warships than were the ships of a decade earlier. Building time had been significantly reduced.

Organizational reforms are much more difficult to evaluate. In 1906 a naval general staff was created. It was modeled after the army general staff though it did not have the distinctive uniform and other special perquisites enjoyed by that body. At about the same time, a council of national defense was created. Changes during 1911–12 placed the chief of staff for the navy directly under the minister of marine rather than the tsar, enhanced the powers of the director of naval construction, and reduced the previously strong technical committees to a purely advisory role—all necessary improvements from the standpoint of concentrating responsibility. Admiral Grigorovich also made progress in modernizing the bases, especially at Revel, where drydocks for battleships and cruisers, a floating dock for torpedo craft, and machine shops and fuel depots were added. Torpedo bases were developed at Ekenäs and Pork-kala, and additional facilities of various kinds were added at Sevastopol, Nikolaev, Sveaborg, Kronstadt, and Vladivostok. Improvements were also made in ordnance, in the quality of metal used, in the rapidity of gunfire (following, it should be noted, similar improvements in other navies), in radio telegraphy, and in the size and range of torpedoes. Other advances brought the begin-nings of promotion by merit, as well as changes in training methods.

Although the movement for reform showed considerable promise, it suffered from three serious limitations. In the first place it either ignored or else dealt inadequately with many fundamental deficien-cies, such as shortages of skilled labor, the general inefficiency of

Russian industry, graft, excessive and unreasonable costs of shipbuilding, the status of seamen, and the navy's significant revolutionary movement. Second, it was very slow getting under way and still had not gathered full momentum at the outbreak of World War I. Finally, the nature of tsarism itself imposed many handicaps to any type of reform, even that of a wholly military character.

All told, both the rebuilding of the fleet and the movement toward its reform were too recent to show decided results by 1914. In terms of *effective* ships, the outbreak of World War I found the Russians with eight battleships (all pre-dreadnoughts), 14 cruisers, 105 destroyers, 25 torpedo boats, and 25 submarines. Building were seven dreadnought battleships, four battle cruisers, eight light cruisers, 36 destroyers, and 18 submarines.

TABLE 6

Russian Naval Expenditures, 1904–13*

	TOTAL EXPENDITURES	NEW CONSTRUCTION	PERSONNEL STRENGTH
1904	£ 11,949,906	4,480,188	69,856
1905	12,392,684	4,576,370	71,529
1906	12,490,444	4,576,583	59,822
1907	8,850,240	2,846,268	55,343
1908	10,222,783	2,703,721	44,949
1909	9,650,167	1,758,487	46,845
1910	9,723,574	1,424,013	46,885
1911	11,693,870	3,216,396	46,655
1912	17,681,207	7,940,094	52,463
1913	24,477,487	10,953,616	—

* SOURCE: *Brassey's Naval Annual*, 1913 (London), pp. 96, 502.

TABLE 7

Russian Naval Ordnance, 1913*

SIZE BASE	WEIGHT OF GUN	CALIBERS	WEIGHT OF SHELL	MUZZLE VELOCITY	WEIGHT OF AMERICAN SHELL
12"	43 tons	40	730 lbs.	2,600	870
10"	22 tons	45	450 lbs.	2,275	500
8"	12 tons	45	192 lbs.	2,950	250
6"	3½ tons	45	91 lbs.	2,600	105
4.7"	2 tons	45	46 lbs.	700	—

* SOURCE: *Brassey's Naval Annual*, 1913 (London), p. 401. The last column was added by the author as an indication of the lightness of Russian naval ordnance compared with that in other navies. During World War I somewhat stronger naval artillery came into use.

CHAPTER 14

World War I:
Baltic, Pacific, and Arctic

STRATEGY OF THE NAVAL WAR

WORLD WAR I brought changes in the systems of alliances that had prevailed in previous wars. Because Austrian ambitions in the Balkans rivaled those of Russia, and because Germany had adopted the formerly British role of protector of Turkey, these two absolute monarchies were ruled out as Russian allies. Indeed, the Austro-Hungarian annexation of Bosnia and Herzegovina in 1908, the German-planned Berlin-to-Baghdad railway, and the 1913 German attempt to reorganize and improve the Turkish army were all developments which the Russians had watched with icy but futile disapproval. The Balkan wars of 1912 and 1913 had interested the Russians as much as they had other powers in Europe. Relations between Austria-Hungary and Russia were near the breaking point well before 1914, while Germany was viewed with a growing hostility tempered by fear and respect.

Meanwhile Franco-Russian relations improved, and a rapprochement occurred between England and Russia. An agreement on respective spheres of influence in Persia eased diplomatic and naval relationships, and in 1907 the Triple Entente of Russia, England, and France came into being, balancing the older Triple Alliance of Germany, Austria-Hungary, and Italy. Later agreements cleared the way for Russian acquisition of the Turkish Straits and Constantinople.

The assassination of the Austrian Archduke Francis Ferdinand by a Serbian terrorist set the mobilization machinery of the European states into motion, and the Austrian declaration of war on Serbia on July 28, 1914, initiated a whole series of counter-declarations. Within a week, Germany and Austria-Hungary on the one hand were facing on hostile terms Serbia, Belgium, Russia, France, and Great Britain. With other nations entering the war later, as their interests became directly involved, "world war" as distinguished from "European war" became a reality.

German military strategists disliked the prospect of a two-front war, but they had long recognized it as a possibility. The "land strategy" for such an emergency was based on the assumption that the Russians would not pose an immediate military threat. The plan, therefore, was to throw everything possible at France in an attempt to score an early knockout, preferably before the British could marshal assistance on land. When France was defeated, the German army could move eastward over an excellent system of state-owned railways to deploy against the slowly gathering Russians.

The early months of the war witnessed the frustration of German land strategy in both West and East. Although the French were indeed forced to retreat, the invasion of Belgium brought Britain into the war with some immediate assistance, ending the German dream of a neutral England, and shortly thereafter, at the Battle of the Marne, the Germans were checked. The Western front stabilized into trench warfare with little possibility of a breakthrough. In the East, the Russians mobilized with unexpected speed and launched initially successful offensives against East Prussia and Galicia, so that the Germans were forced to divert troops they had intended to use against France. Pressure on the Germans was lifted only when their hero of the hour, Gen. Paul von Hindenberg, out-maneuvered and crushed the Russian armies of Gens. Aleksandr V. Samsonov and Pavel K. Rennenkampf at Tannenberg, in the area of the Masurian lakes. Meantime the simultaneous Russian offensive in Galicia brought large territorial gains from the Austrians.

It soon became apparent that a sobering geographical reality stood in the way of success for the Triple Entente powers. Between Russia and her principal Western allies lay the German, Austro-Hungarian, and Turkish empires, which controlled the exits to the Baltic and Black seas. Though Russia's manpower resources were greater than those of Britain and France combined, her lagging industrialization and technical backwardness kept these resources from being fully usable. Hence it was as important for her allies as for Russia herself that large quantities of supplies, munitions, and weapons be imported from the West. The difficult question was the means by which this could be accomplished.

This problem had received some consideration in British and Russian naval circles prior to the war. However, neither at Anglo-Russian naval discussions at Revel in 1908 nor during British Adm. David Beatty's visit to St. Petersburg in the summer of 1914 had there been any substantive agreement on strategy. Sir John A. ("Jackie") Fisher, who was Britain's First Sea Lord from 1904 to 1910 and remained influential in his country's naval councils after that period, favored a bold breakthrough into the Baltic, possibly combined with a minelaying campaign to keep the German High Seas Fleet inactive. These efforts, he maintained, could be coupled with either a British attack on Schleswig-Holstein and the Kiel Canal, or a British-Russian landing in Pomerania that would threaten Berlin directly. Admiral von Essen, on the other hand, favored a naval demonstration by Russian battleships to coerce Sweden into joining the Allies. But these were extremist views and received no more than cursory attention.

The Gallipoli campaign had its origin in a Russian telegram of January 2, 1915, asking for an allied naval demonstration against the Turks to relieve pressure on the Russian armies in the Caucasus. Unfortunately the campaign, a costly one, was badly mismanaged and ended in no relief for the Russians.

For a time the Russians as well as the Germans obtained vast quantities of supplies by shipment through neutral Sweden; but when the British tightened their blockade to eliminate this assistance to the enemy the Russian ally was injured too. There remained only two possible alternate routes of supply for Russia, both of which involved transport over great distance at considerable inconvenience, neither of which afforded unlimited capacity. The first was through the White Sea port of Arkhangelsk which, though free of enemy intervention, was closed by ice from November to May. Even under the most favorable weather conditions, this port had no wide-ranging communication with the rest of Russia. In spite of all its drawbacks, however, this route was the one which came into increasing use as the war progressed; the alternative route lay across Siberia from Vladivostok, a 7,000-mile haul on the Trans-Siberian Railroad.

There was an additional urgent need for a prompt allied breakthrough to Russia—one not recognized by British and French statesmen early in the war. The tsar's regime, for all its defects, was loyal to the allied cause, but the tsar's regime was tottering and a revolutionary government might not be true to the allegiance. The Russo-Japanese war, short-lived as it was, had brought tsardom to the brink of downfall. An upsurge of patriotism at the opening of World War I gave the royal family a temporary popularity, but it was a sentiment that could not last in the face of military defeat and continued incapacity—especially inasmuch as few of the fundamental defects of the tsar's regime had been remedied since 1905. The seeds of new revolution, already sown liberally in Russia, awaited only favorable conditions to spring into active growth.

Regardless of the basic geographic handicap, the Triple Entente allies at the beginning of World War I appeared to be much stronger than the Central Powers. In completed warship tonnage the British navy held better than a two-to-one lead over the German fleet, while the French navy could claim even greater superiority over the Austro-Hungarian fleet in the Mediterranean. With the added sea power of Russia, Japan, Italy, and finally the United States, the allied margin was overwhelming.

Set off against this superiority, however, was the growing effectiveness of enemy mines and submarines. Indeed, so great was the perceived threat from this quarter that the Entente allies felt constrained to exercise their control of the seas only with the greatest caution. On land, too, the manpower edge held by the allies and the greatly superior economic resources they commanded were significantly offset by a number of important advantages favoring the Central Powers. These advantages included a strong geographic position, higher quality materiel, unified direction and control of the entire war effort, generally more able leadership, and (until near the end of the war) better morale.

The outbreak of the war found the Russian navy weak, with a big rebuilding effort just getting under way. Further, even Admiral von Essen's able leadership since 1908 had not sufficed to restore completely the morale and self-confidence lost by the Russians in their defeat by Japan. Sailors of the Baltic Fleet in 1914 could not but compare their four pre-dreadnought battleships with the 17 dreadnoughts and battle cruisers in the German High Seas Fleet, and with this comparison it was perhaps inevitable that they concluded they were hopelessly out-matched, that the Germans could annihilate them at will. Their leaders, also fully cognizant of the disparities, felt forced to a cautious defensive strategy.

In actuality, however, any unit-for-unit comparison between the Russian Baltic Fleet and the German High Seas Fleet was in itself almost completely meaningless. German naval leaders studying the strategy of a two-front naval war had long since concluded that the British must be kept neutral at all costs. Only if this could be done, they decided, would the German navy devote more than light forces to the Baltic or assume the offensive there. The attention of German naval planners was thus concentrated on the superior British Grand Fleet, which they hoped to destroy if it could first be sufficiently reduced by attrition. A diversion of major vessels to strategically unimportant and risky operations against the Russians was, from the German viewpoint, unthinkable. Thus, so far as the Baltic was concerned, the Germans were actually inferior at sea to the Russians in the strength they were willing to divert and, like the Russians, they believed in following a cautious strategy of limited action and limited risk. The German view was set forth by Adm. Reinhardt von Scheer:

If the enemy ever succeeded in securing the command of the Baltic and landing Russian troops on the coast of Pomerania, our Eastern front must have collapsed altogether, and brought to naught our plan of campaign, which consisted of a defensive attitude in the East and the rapid overthrow of the French Army. The command of the Baltic rested on the power of the German Fleet. If we had destroyed the Russian Fleet, our danger from the Baltic would by no means have been eliminated, as a landing could have been carried out just as easily under the protection of English forces if the German fleet no longer existed to hinder it. For such a purpose the English Fleet had no need to venture into the Baltic itself. They had it in their power to compel us to meet them in the North Sea, immediately they made an attack on our coast. In view of such an eventuality we must not weaken ourselves permanently, as we could not help doing if we attempted to eliminate the danger which the Russian Fleet represented for us in the Baltic.

At the outset somewhat weak observation forces had to suffice against the Russians, and these forces had to intimidate the Russians into the same course of action by adopting offensive methods whenever possible. Mines could do us good service in that respect. This method of intimidation, however, could only be effective so long as we could still employ a superior force against the Russians.[1]

The validity of Admiral von Scheer's reasoning may be open to question; but there is no doubt that he correctly stated German naval doctrine of the time. Acting on this policy, the Germans confined their Baltic action mainly to defensive operations which rarely employed the superior sea power they had available.

Russian strategists had paid far more attention to the Baltic than to either the Black Sea or the Pacific. Naval academy war games (1900, 1901, 1903), with Germany as the presumed opponent, had led them to the dismal conclusion that the Germans could be expected to take St. Petersburg, and after the disasters of the Russo-Japanese war this prospect seemed especially likely. Consequently, Russian war plans concentrated on the means of preventing German amphibious landings, with great emphasis on minelaying. While an advanced base for torpedo craft was maintained at Libau (probably an unwise arrangement, as this port was exposed and difficult to defend), the Irben Strait and other passages of the Gulf of Riga were felt to be the most desirable areas for the deployment of advance Russian naval forces. Though a plan for the allocation and operation of ships worked out in 1912 had not been finally approved, Admiral von Essen took it upon himself to follow this plan at the beginning of the war.

In at least one respect the Russians were fortunate: very little of their naval strength was unavailable. The Askold was in the Mediterranean and the Zhemchug and a few torpedo craft were in the Far East. All their other major warships were in the Black Sea or the Baltic.

WARTIME NAVAL DEVELOPMENT

All belligerents in World War I had heavy shipbuilding commitments when hostilities opened, but many of these programs were unable to affect the naval war to any great extent. This was especially true in the case of Russia. Every one of the seven dreadnought battleships under construction at the beginning of the war was eventually completed, but all were behind schedule. Some excellent destroyers of 1,200 to 1,350 tons, carrying long-range 60-caliber 4-inch guns, were delivered in the early days of the war and gave a good account of themselves against both Turks and Germans, and a few new submarines and a number of auxiliaries were also forthcoming. The Russians continued to manufacture excellent and highly lethal mines—by far the best turned out by any of the belligerents (not until 1917 were the British able to produce a mine comparable to those the Russians used as early as 1914). Some progress also was made in naval aviation: by 1917 the Russians had produced 37- and 82-mm. cannon for air use.

But that was about all. Other parts of the naval program were in trouble almost at once, in some instances because of poor performance by the Russian shipbuilding industry, in others because ship completions depended on parts produced in foreign countries. The Russians' great respect for German industry had led them to order the engines and boilers of the *Navarin*, two light cruisers, and four destroyers from German firms, and many Russian destroyers were awaiting turbines on order from German firms in Stettin and Hamburg. The outbreak of war not only terminated the German sources; it also ended all chances of getting these parts elsewhere abroad, so that completion of the affected ships was delayed by as much as two years.

Few of the large ships planned in programs developed in 1912 or later were completed during World War I. The four fine battle cruisers of the 1912 program were never finished, and of those light cruisers that finally were commissioned, some were as much as fourteen years behind the original schedule.

As for destroyers, submarines, and mine craft, the outputs varied. Many destroyers of the 1912 program and some laid down still later were completed during 1915–16. The list of minelayers and minesweepers was lengthened by conversions of merchant ships, many taken from the enemy. Admiral von Essen at the outbreak of war had ordered the speedy seizure of enemy vessels in port or in Russian waters; in this manner the Russians acquired 61 ships, four of which became minelayers and the others minesweepers.

Though no satisfactory submarines were in commission in 1914, some improved types were building, about 20 of which were delivered prior to the Revolution. In late 1914 a naval board decided to order the building of 30 additional submarines, and at about the same time Adm. A. I. Rusin, chief of the naval general staff, proposed a multi-year program calling for 114 new submarines by 1917–18. Orders were placed for several each of a 950-ton Holland type, a 920-ton Fiat model, and a 930-ton Bubnov class. The Holland type was to be capable of 16-knot speed on the surface and nine submerged; of submergence in 20 seconds from an awash condition, and in one minute from a completely surfaced condition; and of immersion to 300 feet. During 1916 two 2,000-ton submarine cruisers were ordered, one each from the Noble-Lessner yards and the Baltic yards, with cruising ranges of 12,000 miles. These boats were to have triple bottoms and subdivided hulls, and to carry the unusually heavy armament of 19 torpedoes, in addition to four 100-mm. and two 57-mm. cannon. Although well ahead of their time, these craft were much smaller than one considered in 1912, a 4,500-ton boat carrying light armor and armed with 60 torpedoes and 120 mines. Plans were also drawn up for a 1,700-ton submarine minelayer.

It is apparent that the vision of the Russian navy vastly transcended its concrete planning as far as submarines were concerned. By World War I Russian naval thinking was clearly looking ahead to the offensive possibilities of undersea craft. The boats were to be of excellent type, far ahead of their time, but the Russian industrial and shipbuilding plants were simply incapable of producing them within any reasonable period of time. Because of this general Russian incapacity, both the United States and Great Britain contributed to the Russian submarine force. In the late fall of 1915 no fewer than 12 disassembled Holland-type boats of 350 tons were shipped from the U.S.A. to Russia by way of Vladivostok. Five of these were sent to the Baltic and seven to the Black Sea, where they were—or should have been—put together. Actually, five of the Black Sea boats were never reassembled. The British contribution, to be considered in more detail later, consisted in the dispatch of royal navy submarines to serve in the Baltic.

During the war, marked progress was made in naval aviation.

At the beginning of hostilities, neither the Black Sea nor the Baltic had a completed hangar for naval planes, and other facilities were lacking as well. One large seaplane ramp existed on Osel Island, later the main naval air base where Sikorsky's *Ilia Muromets*, the world's first four-engine plane, was tested. Although in 1914 the Russian navy was spending more money and showing far greater interest in aviation than was the American navy, the limited number of short-range aircraft it had available were mainly of foreign manufacture, the American-made Curtiss hydroplane being one of the most common types. Originally, side arms carried by crewmen were the only weapons aboard.

During 1915 some flying boats were built and at about the same time the Russians began converting the 5,000-ton passenger liner *Imperatritsa Aleksandra* for use as a seaplane carrier. This ship, renamed the *Orlitsa*, was officially classed as a training ship to hide its true purpose. In its hold it carried eight planes, four of them in reserve status with wings removed. Hangars were placed on deck, and the ship was fitted with winches and booms for handling seaplanes. When the conversion work was completed in the spring of 1915, the *Orlitsa* entered service in the Baltic.

By November 1916 naval aviation had attained sufficient stature to receive tactical recognition, and an order of the supreme naval commander established one aviation division for the Baltic Fleet and one for the Black Sea Fleet. Each division was made up of two air brigades, the brigade being roughly equivalent to the American squadron. The brigade, in turn, included three air "stations," six air "posts," and three air "divisions," each of the divisions comprising three detachments of six aircraft. Thus, provided the organization was complete, there were about 100 planes attached to each major fleet, besides the aircraft carried on the *Orlitsa* in the Baltic and *Aleksandr I* and *Nikolai I* of the Black Sea Fleet.[2] Some of the approximately 15 to 20 dirigibles available were also operated by the navy. Airplanes were used mainly for scouting, although they were occasionally assigned bombing and strafing missions. As a rule little damage was done by such missions, since both bombing and antiaircraft fire were wildly inaccurate.

While there were some able men of advanced ideas in the air force, wartime technical advance was limited in a number of ways.

It was difficult to get planes and engines from abroad, and Russian industry could not supply them in adequate numbers. Thus Russian aviation, qualitatively inferior from the outset, suffered increasingly during 1916–17 from lack of spare parts.

As noted in chapter thirteen, plans drafted before the war called for improvement of base facilities, especially in the Baltic. The plan for establishing the Revel-Porkkala-Kronstadt triangle as the operational base for the Baltic Fleet had not been scheduled for completion until 1917, however, and the outbreak of war found shore facilities incomplete, with Kronstadt alone reasonably well prepared. Plans to strengthen Libau were dropped.

WAR IN THE FAR EAST

While the powerful Japanese and British navies held control of the Pacific for the allies, the small Russian Pacific squadron played an almost wholly inactive role throughout the war. In fact a few Russian ships in the Far East, from both the Pacific Fleet and the Amur River Flotilla, were transferred to other areas after the first year.

There was one exception to this rule of Russian passivity: the Zhemchug, one of the escapees from Tsushima, had the doubtful distinction of being one of the most noted victims of the famous German cruiser Emden. At five o'clock on the morning of October 28, 1914, two days after her arrival, the Zhemchug lay at anchor in the harbor of Penang when what appeared to be a four-funneled cruiser steamed into the harbor. The newcomer was the Emden (3,544-tons, 25 knots, ten 4.1-inch guns), disguised with a dummy funnel to resemble British and Japanese cruisers. At a distance of three-quarters of a mile the cruiser ran up the German flag and discharged a torpedo. The missile struck the Zhemchug aft, flooding the engine room. The Emden then moved in rapidly and opened fire from the point-blank distance of 300 yards. The aroused crew of the Zhemchug rushed to battle stations, but their ship was already sinking. They were able to fire only a few wild shots before the ship went down, within 15 minutes of the opening shots. After firing a second torpedo at the Zhemchug, the Emden moved on to attack harbor shipping and sink a French torpedo boat. She then left the harbor, having closed the most brilliant chapter of a singularly eventful career. The captain and executive officer of the *Zhemchug* were later courtmartialed and dismissed from the service for neglecting precautions. The *Emden* attack had killed 91 Russian crewmen and wounded 108.

THE NAVAL WAR IN THE BALTIC

At the outbreak of war the Russian Baltic Fleet comprised the two semi-dreadnoughts *Pavel I* and *Andrei Pervozvanny*; two older battleships, *Slava* and *Tsesarevich*; ten cruisers of various types (six armored and four protected) ranging in size from the 15,000-ton *Riurik* on down; 36 destroyers; 11 submarines; and six minelayers. At the time of mobilization orders (July 30, 1914) all ships landed inflammables and took on ample supplies of oil, coal, and munitions.

In its initial organization the Baltic Fleet was made up of both active and reserve elements. The active elements included a four-ship battle division; a cruiser division consisting of the *Gromoboi*, *Pallada*, *Baian*, and *Admiral Makarov*; a 21-boat destroyer force; and the new destroyer *Novik*, which served as the fleet flagship. In reserve was a brigade of cruisers (*Rossiia*, *Oleg*, *Diana*, *Bogatyr*, *Avrora*, and *Riurik*); two submarine divisions of four boats each plus three old training submarines; six first-class minelayers and some 31 lesser mine craft; a brigade of torpedo boats; and various lesser vessels. Most of these reserve forces were placed in commission shortly after the outbreak of war. By 1915 the commissioning of new ships had greatly strengthened the fleet.

The German forces facing the Russian ships at the beginning of the war were led by Admiral Prince Henry of Prussia, who operated within a chain of command that made for compromise and accommodation rather than clear authority. His forces included seven old cruisers (*Amazone*, *Augsburg*, *Magdeburg*, *Lübeck*, *Undine*, *Thetis*, and *Gazelle*), plus mining craft, destroyers, and torpedo boats. From time to time the Germans deployed somewhat stronger forces into the Baltic—mainly older battleships—and from 1915 on they also used a few submarines. But during most of the war the German forces in the Baltic were weaker than those of the tsar.

The Russians greatly feared that the Germans, like the Japanese in 1904, would open hostilities in the Baltic with a surprise attack; for this reason they temporarily abandoned the exposed naval station at Libau. Other problems, however, remained unsolved. The coastal forts in the Gulf of Finland had few guns in place and were not ready to protect the minefields. One of the two newest battleships, *Andrei Pervozvanny*, was in drydock after having run aground, while the new dreadnoughts *Gangut* and *Poltava* were still several months from completion. The submarines were not in combat condition and none had a fully competent crew.

In view of Russia's naval weakness it is not surprising that her naval strategy was defensive and tied to the support of land forces. Yet it was highly unfortunate that, with a chief as competent and offensive-minded as von Essen, the Baltic Fleet was subservient not only to the Russian army but to one of its lesser echelons. It received orders from the commander of the Seventh Army who was charged with the defense of Petrograd. Official lack of knowledge concerning the nature and uses of seapower resulted in rigid restraints, such as were imposed by an order that no new battleships be committed to combat without a specific directive from the tsar. Von Essen's early plans to destroy enemy commerce and control the sea east of a line running from Danzig to Karlskrona were vetoed. Under such conditions the navy could wage only a warfare of attrition.

The Russian army's reluctance to employ naval strength, added to German unwillingness to commit strong forces to an area, deemed to be of secondary importance, meant that any naval engagement could come about only accidentally. Meanwhile, each side sought to wear down the other while preserving its own strength. Mine warfare was the order of the day, with some use of sea power as a mobile flank to land armies. Submarines to a considerable extent and seaplanes to a very minor degree were added to the picture as the war progressed.

It is not surprising that the real heroes of the Baltic war were to be the minelayers. In this particular specialty the Russians were well prepared: their mines were effective and the tactics for laying them were well developed. The 1914 Russian minelaying campaign got under way on July 31—two days before the outbreak of war—when Admiral von Essen, unable to secure an answer to his request for permission to lay mines, ordered such action himself. The mine-layers *Ladoga, Narova, Yenisei, Amur,* and *Volga,* under Adm. V. A. Kanin, set out to lay a 2,124-mine Central Position defensive minefield in the Gulf of Finland while most of the other ships of the Baltic Fleet stood by as protection. Within the next few days the Russians had laid three additional mine barrages across the Gulf of Finland and established minefields at both entrances to the Gulf of Riga.

In the meantime the Germans were busying themselves with various minor operations. Early in the war they shelled Libau and destroyed Russian lighthouses at the entrance to the Gulf of Finland. They also mined the entrance to the Great Belt and Little Belt. Because of good Russian intelligence the German minefields were not unduly menacing: at times the Russians even incorporated them into their own defenses.

These early activities led to the first loss of a major naval vessel. On August 28 the German light cruiser *Magdeburg* (4,550 tons, 28 knots, 12 4.1-inch guns) grounded and was wrecked near Oden-sholm lighthouse on the south coast of the Gulf of Finland. The Russian cruisers *Bogatyr* and *Pallada* approached, but before they could take charge German destroyers had evacuated about 200 men from the stricken cruiser. Since the entire operation took place in dense fog, mistaken identity led the Russian ships to fire at each other, fortunately without damaging results.

When the *Magdeburg* was boarded and searched by men from the Russian destroyers *Riany* and *Lt. Burakov,* a Lieutenant Hamilton made a discovery of immense importance—a German signal book lying on a disordered table. A second copy was found by divers on the person of a drowned signalman. A third copy had been obtained in Germany through Russian naval intelligence. From that time on, the Russians (and also the British to whom the Russians passed on their secret) were able to decipher German radio messages, for though the Germans changed their codes several times they never changed their basic system. The Russians exiled the captured German captain to a particularly inaccessible Siberian camp, and the Germans failed to discover that their code had been broken. Since the Germans were often in the dark concerning Russian operations, they were vitally disadvantaged. They were suffi-

RUSSIAN
MINING CAMPAIGN
in Winter 1914-15

GULF OF FINLAND

Stockholm

Baltic
Port

DAGÖ

Norrköping

ÖSEL

SWEDEN

GOTLAND

IRBEN STRAIT

GULF
OF RIGA

Windau

ÖLAND

SWEDISH IRON ORE SUPPLY LINES TO GERMANY

Riga

Karlskrona

Libau

RUSSIA

HANO BAY

Memel

N

BORNHOLM

Königsberg

GULF OF DANZIG

RÜGEN

Danzig

German Shipping Routes
Suspected Minefields
Actual Minefields

Swinemünde

GERMANY

Stettin   0   Miles   100   (Courtesy of Dr. Philip Lundeberg)

ciently impressed by the loss of the *Magdeburg,* however, to conclude that submarines were their best means of attack, and that the employment of cruisers should be more cautious.

The Germans had one clearcut advantage over the Russians: they could reinforce their weak forces in the Baltic at any time while the Russians could not. In the somewhat unrealistic hope of relieving pressure on the Galicia front, where the Russians had as yet received no such check as they had at Tannenberg, the Germans resolved on a naval demonstration which took the form of sending six old battleships into the Baltic in late September to aid in simulating a troop landing near Windau. This shift was not permanent and had no particular effect on the land fighting. Further, it was called off on September 25 upon receipt of a false report that the British were about to attack the German coast.

After the first few weeks of war, when it became apparent to them that the Germans did not intend to risk their main forces in the Baltic, the Russians adopted slightly bolder tactics. Several of their cruisers and nearly all their destroyers were given a minelaying capacity, and operations were expanded to include offensive mine-laying as far west as Danzig. The Russians also conducted cruiser patrols between Gotland and the Gulf of Finland for the purpose of intercepting trade between German and Swedish ports—something they should have done earlier, when commitments of forces else-where would have made it impossible for the Germans to provide effective protection. This was not a well-performed operation. Had it been vigorously undertaken by the larger forces the Russians had available, however, it could have been very damaging to the Germans.

In early September there were a few long-range and indecisive exchanges of fire between Russian and German cruisers. Not only were the Russian cruisers not particularly successful (they captured only four merchantmen during the month), but by cruising at slow speed—and even anchoring—without the protection of destroyers they exposed themselves to U-boats. At that time official Russian instructions concerning antisubmarine tactics were so naive they were regarded as a joke among the junior officers. On October 11 the Russians had the first of several painful lessons thrust upon them when the unescorted armored cruisers *Pallada* and *Admiral Maka-rov* were both attacked by German submarines. The *Pallada* exploded and sank with her entire crew, a victim of the *U-26* under Captain Lieutenant von Berckheim. Three torpedoes passed under the *Makarov*. Russian military authorities then ordered abandon-ment of the patrol.

In November the campaigns of attrition conducted by each side claimed a certain number of new victims. The Russians lost the destroyer *Ispolnitelny* to a submarine during a storm. Her consort, *Letuchy*, capsized when she went to the rescue of the *Ispolnitelny* sailors. On November 17 the Germans made a combined attack by naval gunfire and blockships against Libau but failed to do much damage. The same day the German armored cruiser *Friedrich Karl* was wrecked on mines laid by Russian destroyers off Memel and Danzig. (The crew, who were saved, at first believed their ship had been sunk by a British submarine.) Some German destroyers and 18 commercial craft were also damaged or sunk.

At the end of 1914, neither side had won the war of attrition in the Baltic; it was apparent that the Russians had at least held their own. German losses were in fact greater than those of the Russians, but the cautious strategy forced on von Essen by the Russian army had prevented any serious interference with German trade. During the 1914–15 winter months, Russian minelayers, cruisers, and destroyers laid 14 new minefields. Operating in darkness, often in snowstorms, they planted some 1,600 mines, the main fields being off the coast of Latvia, off German ports such as Memel and Danzig, and east of the island of Bornholm along the route followed by iron ore carriers from Sweden.

1915 IN THE BALTIC

The Germans started their 1915 campaign with half their cruisers either sunk or disabled by mines, and on January 25 the light cruisers *Gazelle* and *Augsburg* were similarly disabled but managed to reach Stettin. Though the Russian campaign had not been carried out in sufficient strength to force the Germans to divert any large force to the Baltic, Prince Henry was sent three more cruisers (the armored cruisers *Prinz Heinrich*, *Roon*, and later the smaller *Bremen*) and a flotilla of torpedo boats.

The Russians entered the year in better shape. Coastal defenses had been strengthened at many points; a number of new submarines of sufficient range for Baltic operations were available, as well as several British undersea boats; and whereas during the preceding year the *Novik* had been the only new destroyer, several additional ones were now in use. Two new dreadnoughts were also scheduled for early commissioning.

Some developments were soon to appear on the debit side, however. The able Admiral von Essen would die in service that spring, and (after a short interlude under Adm. L. B. Kerber) would be replaced by Adm. V. A. Kanin, a far weaker man. Also the *Riurik* would be out of action for several months after February 15 (it grounded during a minelaying expedition and limped into Kronstadt only with the aid of icebreakers).

The decision to send British submarines into the Baltic had been made as early as October 1914, partly in recognition of the low undersea warfare capability of Russian crews. The plan presented navigational problems, since the Germans had minefields in most of the narrow sea lanes in the Belts. However, there was one neutral (Swedish) lane which until October 20, 1914, was not barred to passage by belligerents. When the *E-1* safely passed the Skagerrak and Kattegat to make her presence known by an unsuccessful attack on a German cruiser, the Germans not unnaturally blamed the Swedes. Thereafter they initiated patrols which made entrance to any of the passages leading to the Baltic extremely difficult. Even so, the *E-9, E-11, E-8, E-13, E-18,* and *E-19* also made the attempt, and four of them got through. *E-11* was the only one forced to turn back; *E-13* ran aground and was destroyed, and her crew was interned. In 1916 four small C-class submarines reached the Baltic by way of Arkhangelsk, the Dvina River, and various lakes and canals.[3] Unfortunately this reinforcement was not usable for many months, since the submarines' batteries had been shipped on a merchant vessel that was sunk by a U-boat.

The British submarines in the Baltic were immediately effective, the more so because the first ones arrived at a time when all of the Russian undersea craft were immobilized by engine trouble. During most of the war the British ships were based on Revel, using the old Russian cruiser *Dvina* (earlier *Pamiat Azova*) as a mother ship. Because they were attached to the Baltic Fleet for purposes of accommodation and victualing, Russian naval historians have laid claim to their considerable success. The first operations in which the British submarines in the Baltic participated were routine patrols in company with Russian submarines. In 1915, however, their interference with German attempts to make amphibious landings along the Russian coast and to transport iron ore from Sweden, resulted in the sinking of several enemy transports and destroyers. The armored cruiser *Prinz Adalbert* (9,050 tons, four 8.2-inch and 16 6-inch guns) was badly damaged on July 1, 1915, by the *E-9* and was sunk by her sister boat, *E-8*. The smaller cruiser *Undine* (2,715 tons, ten 4.1-inch guns, 21 knots) was sunk by *E-19* on November 7. The battle cruiser *Moltke* (22,400 tons, ten 11-inch guns, 27 knots) was torpedoed by *E-1* but managed to get back to port. The light cruiser *Bremen* foundered on a mine on December 17. Several German torpedo boats and merchant vessels also were claimed by either mines or submarines. These achievements diminished sharply during 1916, when the timid and vacillating policy of Admiral Kanin kept the boats in port much of the time, but following the Bolshevik revolution the British submarines were almost the only effective Allied naval units in the Baltic.[4]

The principal effort on each side continued to be minelaying. In this endeavor the Russians showed growing tactical proficiency and reaped gratifying success. Most of their minelaying was done in darkness, and when destroyers were employed, mines were dropped with great speed and precision; an entire field could be laid in a few hours. These operations of course were not carried out without losses (the minelayer *Yenisei* was torpedoed on June 4 by the U-26, for instance), nor were they always free of complications. Twice on minelaying expeditions Russian covering forces fell in with weaker German forces, once when four Russian cruisers encountered the *München* (3,250 tons, ten 4.1-inch guns, 23 knots) east of Gotland but allowed her to escape, and again in a foggy encounter on July 2. On the second occasion, the *Augsburg* (4,350 tons, ten 4.1-inch guns, 28 knots), the minelayer *Albatross*, and three destroyers fell in with the *Makarov, Baian, Bogatyr*, and *Oleg* near the coast of Gotland, and the Russian ships forced the *Albatross* to ground. The *Augsburg* put up a strong resistance and succeeded in hitting the *Makarov*. The German ship was soon joined by the armored cruiser *Roon* (9,500 tons, four 8.2-inch and 16 6-inch guns, 20 knots). The Russians received reinforcement from the powerful *Riurik*, which was nearby, and in a long-range, low-visibility duel the *Roon* scored a hit on the *Riurik* but in turn was struck several times by 10-inch shells from the Russian ship.[5] The exchange ended when the *Roon* sought refuge in the fog, and the Germans managed to escape without difficulty from the far more powerful Russians.

In sum, despite the loss of efficiency in the direction of the war following von Essen's death, 1915 must be regarded as a successful year for the Russians in the Baltic. Russian minelaying was markedly more successful than that of the Germans, partly because the Russians managed to keep much better surveillance on the minelaying activities of their foes. At the end of the year the *Augsburg* was the only undamaged German warship larger than a destroyer.

COOPERATION WITH THE ARMY: THE ATTACK ON RIGA

During the early days of the First World War naval forces were rarely called upon to aid the Russian army, despite the fact that there had been some indications of their potential value (for instance, a German attempt to land troops on the coast of Kurland during 1914 had been defeated by Russian destroyers). This under-use of naval strength stemmed partly from the unimaginative, uninformed army command, which was unaware of the services which might be obtained from ships, and partly from the nature of the land war, which until the late spring of 1915 presented few obvious opportunities for joint operations.

As has been noted, the Russians mobilized far more speedily than the Germans expected and during their initial offensive scored large gains in Galicia. This early progress on land was reversed in 1915. Treason, incompetence, and disloyalty among high officials close to the tsar accounted for only a part of the problem. Major transportation difficulties had not been solved; grave shortages of arms and ammunition now crippled the Russian armies. These crises resulted from a too-conservative forecast of war needs, and from the failure of Russia's allies to deliver needed supplies. When a German/Austro-Hungarian offensive was started in the spring of 1915 the Russians began a large-scale retreat. All of Galicia and Poland were abandoned, as were Kurland and areas of White Russia. In some areas the retreat was carried as far as 250 miles.

These losses on land were reflected in reverses at sea. Early in the year the Russians briefly held Memel but then, on March 4, withdrew when German cruisers aided land forces in retaking the city. Two months later the old coast-defense ship *Beowulf*, three armored cruisers, three small cruisers, and some torpedo boats and auxiliaries aided the German Army in taking Libau. Next, Windau had

to be evacuated by the Russians. These were, of course, relatively minor attacks and the Germans themselves were divided as to their value; the loss of advanced bases handicapped but did not halt Russian naval activities.

Eventually, however, advancing German armies came within range of the Gulf of Riga and its bases and defenses. This was a vitally important target; it was, in fact, the northern anchor of a new and fairly straight Russian defense line which extended to Rumania—and it could be attacked by the Germans from both land and sea. When it became apparent that a German attack in the Riga area could be only a question of time the Russians hurriedly mined the Irben Strait, the best and southernmost of several possible entrances to the gulf. The main Russian defenses consisted of

12-inch and smaller guns mounted on Ösel, Dago, and Moon islands, all of which command the narrow passages into the Gulf of Riga, and fixed minefields in these same channels. As long as the minefields could be guarded from German minesweeping by either warships or coastal artillery, the Russian position was reasonably secure from naval attack.

The Germans foolishly gave notice of their intention to attack when in July 1915 they made a preliminary move. Two Russian destroyers, *Dobrovolets* and *Donskoi kazak*, sank on German mines. The Russians were alerted; they brought in the old battleship *Slava*, under escort of the *Gangut* and *Petropavlovsk*, as a reinforcement to the 12 destroyers, four gunboats, and handful of auxiliaries which were already on hand.

On August 8 a major German naval attack began. A German fleet of large size was picked for the attack. It was a force which vastly exceeded the strength of the Russian defenses. It consisted of the Fourth Squadron, comprising the old battleships *Wittelsbach*, *Wettin*, *Mecklenburg*, *Schwaben*, *Zahringen*, *Braunschweig* and *Elsass* newly transferred from the North Sea, besides six cruisers, two destroyers, and 22 torpedo boats and 25 minecraft under Vice Admiral Schmidt. A supporting force under Vice Adm. Franz von Hipper consisted of the dreadnoughts *Östfriesland*, *Thüringen*, *Helgoland*, *Rheinland*, *Posen*, *Nassau*, and *Westfalen*; three battle cruisers, *Seydlitz*, *Moltke*, and *Von der Tann*; five modern light cruisers; 32 torpedo boats; and a mining division.

The German minesweepers at once proceeded to clean up Russian mines. The *Slava* attempted to close with the minesweepers, but was prevented by two *Deutschland*-type battleships (13,200 tons, four 11-inch and 14 6.7-inch guns, 18 knots) which opened fire on the *Slava*, whose guns they could greatly outrange. After being hit several times, the *Slava* withdrew. The Germans then resumed vigorous sweeping operations, but an effort to pass through the channel cost them two destroyers (S-31 and V-109) and two cruisers damaged by mines laid by the *Novik*.

Russian efforts to sow mines in an area the Germans had cleared the preceding day partially miscarried when the armored cruisers *Roon* and *Prinz Heinrich* surprised the Russian destroyers in the act of minelaying, but a quick retreat enabled the Russians to get away with only one destroyer, *Sibirsky Strelok,* being hit. Russian mine-laying continued; on August 16 when the Germans returned, they not only met the fire of coastal batteries but found they had to repeat their earlier sweeping. Once more the *Slava* tried to destroy the minesweepers and once again she was frustrated by the longer-range guns on German battleships. However, two German destroy-ers struck mines, and the *Slava* did sink one minesweeper. On Aug-ust 17 the Germans made their way into the gulf, and Russian defensive forces retreated in good order after losing the gunboats *Sivuch* and *Koreets* and the minelayer *Ladoga.* Two German destroyers penetrated the area seeking the *Slava.* They met the *Novik,* which sank the *V-99* and damaged the *V-100.* The Germans had recently had the *Moltke* torpedoed and damaged in addition to their other losses in attempting to penetrate the gulf.[6] They evidently concluded they were paying too high a price: on August 21, they left. The Russians immediately returned and restored their minefields. Thereafter the *Slava,* the seaplane carrier *Orlitsa,* and several destroyers supported the right flank of the Russian army and fired on German troops ashore.

On October 22 the *Slava* served as cover for the landing of 400 men at Domesnes, and on November 10 she seriously interfered with a German army offensive on shore. Although the German commander termed the attack on the Gulf of Riga a "success," his view was not shared by the High Command, which expressed dis-satisfaction over such meager achievements by such a large force and over the continued effectiveness of the *Slava* and other Russian ships. The German attack with its attendant diversion of German dreadnoughts probably would not have been undertaken in the first place had not the Allied navies at the time been tied up at Gallipoli. As it happened, both campaigns failed for their insti-gators.

During the fighting for the Gulf of Riga and during the remainder of the year considerable activity was carried on by naval air squad-rons, including a torpedo attack by a German seaplane on the *Slava.* On April 27 the *Slava* became the first battleship in combat history to be hit by an aerial bomb, which killed five men and wounded two. The first aerial bombs were thrown by hand and almost invari-ably went wide of the mark; when they did hit the damage was usually very light. The pilots, like those in later wars, invariably exaggerated their successes: one downed German pilot rescued from the sea by a Russian destroyer was convinced his squadron had badly damaged seven Russian destroyers, when in fact not one of the destroyers in question had taken so much as a single hit. Antiaircraft weapons of the time were just as limited, inaccurate, and ineffectual.

During the winter of 1915–16, both Russians and Germans developed heavier bombs, and the Russians strengthened the antiaircraft artillery on their ships. Zeppelin raids in 1915 claimed two enemy airships, *L-5* and *SL-6*, over Riga, but in general this branch of aviation played little part in the naval war apart from reconnaissance and some aerial minelaying. According to German figures, 30 of the 71 German Zeppelins employed on the eastern front were lost, most of them in action against military rather than naval targets.

The larger Russian battleships had stayed in port for the duration of the attack on Riga. Plans for a sortie late in the year were frustrated when mutinies broke out first aboard the *Gangut* and somewhat later on *Pavel I*, and although the *Gangut* and *Petropavlovsk* finally did move as far as the island of Gotland, they returned with no tactical achievements to their credit. In November 1915 Russian minelaying was delayed for about a week by mutinies.

Meanwhile, late in October, the Germans reacted to heavy sinking tolls by transferring two small cruisers and two flotillas of torpedo boats from the High Seas Fleet to the Baltic.

1916 IN THE BALTIC

During the winter of 1916 the Russian fleet was strengthened by the completion of two dreadnoughts, nine fine large destroyers, five new Russian submarines, and five small American submarines. None of the new cruisers was completed, but the navy yards managed to rearm most of the older cruisers and destroyers. The *Makarov* and *Baian* were provided with additional 8-inch and 6-inch guns to bring armament complement on each vessel to three 8-inch and 14 6-inch guns. The *Oleg*, *Diana*, and *Bogatyr* had their 6-inch guns replaced by heavy machine guns and antiaircraft guns, thus becoming in effect the first antiaircraft cruisers. *Rossiia* and *Gromoboi* each carried six 8-inch and 22 6-inch guns in addition to their new antiaircraft pieces. The destroyers were given longer-range guns of the same 4-inch caliber they had carried earlier.

At this time two important command changes occurred. The first advanced Capt. A. V. Kolchak to the rank of rear admiral and then, after only two months of service in that grade, to the position of vice admiral and commander of the Black Sea Fleet. This unprecedentedly rapid advancement, even for a well-liked and energetic officer,[7] was highly questionable in view of the fact that it displaced a competent admiral who was in excellent health. Then, in October, Adm. A. I. Nepenin replaced Admiral Kanin as commander of the Baltic Fleet—an improvement, for Nepenin, though far less able than von Essen, was a sound organizer and logistician.

The war of attrition continued in fairly low gear. The German cruisers *Danzig* and *Lübeck* were damaged on mines early in the year, but until November, when the Germans again attacked the Gulf of Riga, neither side had lost many ships. The heavier antiaircraft armament carried by the Russians paid off in an occasional downed German aircraft. In June, three Russian cruisers fell in with a German convoy but sank only one merchant ship before the enemy force entered Swedish territorial waters. Other losses—mainly of destroyers, minesweepers, and minelayers—were shared about equally by the two sides. The old Russian submarine *Som* and the British *E-18* were additional casualties, the latter being lost the day after she torpedoed the German destroyer *V-100*.

The Germans had not forgotten the performance staged by the *Slava* in the Gulf of Riga; in early September they put on a demonstration in the Irben Strait to lure the Russian ship into a position in which submarines and seaplanes could attack her with torpedoes. The attempt failed.

Then on November 10, the German Tenth Torpedo Flotilla forced its way into the Gulf of Finland, hoping to catch the Russians by surprise—and promptly encountered a Russian minefield. Only four of the eleven boats making the trip to bombard Balticport returned; the remainder all hit mines and sank. Amazingly, the personnel loss was only 16 men killed. Although from a Russian standpoint this was the greatest naval victory of the entire war, the success was due chiefly to a most uncharacteristic display of German stupidity.

Two weeks later the Russians came close to losing the *Riurik* when she struck a submerged rock and her forepart was flooded. No one was killed, however, and the armored cruiser managed to crawl back to port and drydock at speeds of two to eight knots.

THE WAR IN THE ARCTIC

Long before the outbreak of World War I the Russians had deemphasized the White Sea as a possible combat theater. In this area they started the war with only a few small patrol vessels and auxiliaries, plus a small complement of naval personnel which was third-rate even by Russian standards. The only port available in the area was Arkhangelsk, on the Dvina River about 30 miles from the open sea. Arkhangelsk was in no sense a naval base. In 1914 it received something like a regular organization only during the summer months, when the tender *Bakan* made the trip from the Baltic to assist Russian fishermen and traders.

By the end of 1914, however, it became clear that Arkhangelsk, as the most direct port of entry for munitions supplied by the British and French, had acquired an unexpected importance. In view of Arkhangelsk's very limited ice-free navigation season (only five months), the Russians decided to develop an additional port at Murmansk on the Kola Inlet, much farther north but usable during most of the year because of its proximity to the Gulf Stream. They began construction of a railroad connecting Murmansk with the center of European Russia, and new defenses and naval installations were constructed at both Arctic ports. A few fishery protection vessels, trawlers, and merchant cruisers were also put into service.

Because of its distance from German bases, the Arctic did not at once attract the attention of German submarines. By the spring of 1915, however, the Germans had sent in the minelayer *Meteor* and occasional submarines to mine the entrance to the White Sea. The Russian force in the area at the time (a dispatch boat, an armed yacht, three armed merchant cruisers, and eight small craft) was far too small to furnish efficient patrol and antisubmarine service

even had the ships been well manned, which they were not. Adm.
James Glennon, USN, drily observed:

> Russian patrol vessels spend practically all their time in port—when it
> is tried to send them to sea, they develop repairs absolutely necessary
> to be made.[8]

The inability or unwillingness of the Russians to handle their
own defenses in the White Sea of course presented a problem to
allied suppliers. In February 1915 the British sent the battleship
Jupiter to the Arctic to substitute for a Russian icebreaker which
had broken down, and in June they sent in half a dozen trawlers
armed with 12-pounder guns and minesweeping gear. The Russians
themselves had very few ships available to reinforce the White Sea,
but they recalled two damaged destroyers from the Pacific, repairing them in England en route. They also purchased from the Japanese, for ten million yen, two ex-Russian battleships, the former
Peresvet (*Sagami*) and *Poltava* (*Tango*), and the cruiser *Variag*
(*Soya*). The *Peresvet* was sunk in the Mediterranean, however, and
the other ships did not reach the White Sea until 1917.

At the end of August 1915 Vice Adm. A. P. Ugriumov was placed
in command of the new northern fleet. Operating under him were
Russian and British minesweepers commanded by Capt. Thomas W.
Kemp of the Royal Navy. At the end of the 1915 shipping season
Russian and British naval units had escorted 198 merchant vessels
in the area and destroyed most of the mines laid by the Germans.

In 1916 both the Allies and the Germans put forth greatly
increased efforts along the northern supply route. More than 600
steamers put in at Arkhangelsk during the months that the port
was open; and the coal and military cargo delivered amounted to
two and a half million tons, five times the deliveries in 1915. Unfortunately, Russian facilities were unable to handle such quantities.
Mountains of supplies accumulated, awaiting shipment on Russian
rail lines. Work was pushed on the railroad to Murmansk. When
objections were raised to the Russian use of prisoners of war to
build the road, Chinese laborers were imported. Even these docile
laborers became irritated by broken promises, but bad conditions
were skillfully concealed from inspectors and the work went on. For
all the sustained drive, the railroad was not completed until the end
of the year.

Belatedly realizing the size of the Allied supply effort, the Germans sent in at least five submarines. One, the *U-56*, was attacked on November 2, 1916, by four Russian patrol vessels and later sank as a result of damage sustained—but in view of the fact that *U-56* had sunk 24 Allied ships en route, the exchange rate was certainly acceptable from the German standpoint. In all, 36 Allied merchant ships were sunk by submarines in 1916, four others were run ashore, and three were damaged by mines. Though the Russians obtained patrol vessels from the United States and torpedo boats by rail from their Pacific Squadron, the bulk of the minesweeping and patrol work in the Arctic continued to fall on the British.

In December 1916 the Russian forces in the Arctic were placed under Adm. L. B. Kerber, the same officer who had filled in briefly as top admiral in the Baltic after the death of von Essen. Kerber had the status of fleet commander, was subordinate only to chief of naval staff Admiral Rusin, and held control over both military and naval units, and over ports, inland waterways, access roads, and garrisons. In late 1916 and the first half of 1917 the Russian Arctic Squadron gradually began to take shape. It finally consisted of the old 11,000-ton battleship *Chesma* (ex-*Poltava*), the 6,000-ton cruisers *Variag* and *Askold*, two small and two very small submarines (the latter were harbor-defense types of less than 50 tons), four small tenders, six destroyers of the 350-ton type, and 43 minesweepers. The chief of staff was Rear Adm. A. I. Posokhov and the squadron commander Rear Adm. Vasily N. Bestuzhev. Because the Russians were short of naval personnel, some of these vessels were actually operated by American or British personnel then stationed in northern Russia.

Whereas the end of 1916 marked the conclusion of effective prerevolutionary Russian naval activity in the Baltic, the Arctic, because of its remote location, was little affected by the tsar's abdication. The Allied supply operation, which was to bring in two million tons of cargo during 1917, continued with the help of the Russian navy. The Germans suffered a small setback when their *U-76*, sent to mine the Kola Gulf near the newly opened port of Murmansk, was damaged by ramming a surface ship and subsequently lost in a storm off the North Cape. In February 1917, however, when the Germans started unrestricted submarine warfare, Allied shipping losses rose sharply. Two German submarines in particular (*U-45* and *U-75*) sank a number of merchant ships near Murmansk despite concentrated minesweeping and convoy duty there by British and Russian vessels. In all, the Allies managed to deliver five million tons of war supplies by the Arctic route during World War I, compared to about four million in World War II. The British navy did by far the greatest share of the work.[9]

Russian naval strategy in World War I deserves brief summarization and analysis. Admiral von Essen had favored waging an active naval war outside purely German coastal waters. Military dominance of strategy blocked this course, and neither of von Essen's successors questioned the purely defensive role assigned by the generals to the navy. The very weak state of the navy prior to reinforcement by ships of the 1912 and later programs would seem to lend some justification to the military decision; but on balance, in view of the very weak forces which the Germans used in the Baltic, the Russian strategy must be judged unduly inactive and timid. Too many powerful Russian ships were either unemployed much of the time or used only as protection for minelayers. Russian commanders repeatedly failed to take advantage of their greater strength in more or less accidental contacts with German forces. On the other hand, the Russians waged their mine warfare campaign with a skill in both defensive and offensive operations that may fairly be said to have surpassed that of the Germans. The Russian record in the Arctic was not good, but here their forces were so small, so miscellaneous, and so limited by time and conditions of operation that there is perhaps little basis for evaluation.

CHAPTER 15

World War I: Black Sea

FORCES AND STRATEGY

IN THE BLACK SEA the Russians started World War I with a clear-cut superiority of force. The Turkish navy, nearly always highly defective, was in especially poor condition during the early years of the twentieth century. When the war approached, its best vessels were three old battleships—the ex-German *Torghout Reis* and the *Haireddin Barbarossa* (10,000 tons, six 11-inch guns, 17 knots) which dated from 1894 and 1891 respectively, and the forty-year-old *Messoudieh* (10,000 tons, two 9.2-inch and 12 6-inch guns, 14 knots). Two first-class dreadnoughts which were being completed in England, the *Sultan Osman I* (27,500 tons, 14 12-inch guns, 22 knots) and *Reshadieh* (23,000 tons, ten 13.5-inch guns, 21 knots) were taken over by the British on the outbreak of war. However, fortune brought the Turks an unexpected reinforcement to partially offset the loss. The German battle cruiser *Göben* (22,400 tons, ten 11-inch and 12 6-inch guns, 27 knots) and the light cruiser *Breslau* (4,550 tons, 12 4-inch guns, 28 knots) were caught in the Mediterranean when hostilities began. Hunted by far superior British forces, they entered the Bosphorus and were bought by the Turks and renamed *Yavuz Sultan Selim* and *Midili*. The crews remained with the vessels, and the French-born German Rear Admiral Souchon became chief of the Turkish navy. By assigning his own officers and noncommissioned officers to various strategic positions, Souchon was able in a few months to improve greatly both training and war readiness. Besides the three old battleships already noted, his command included two light cruisers, *Hamidieh* (3,800 tons, two 6-inch and eight 4.7-inch guns, 22 knots) and *Mejidieh* (3,800 tons, two 6-inch and eight 4.7-inch guns, 22 knots); eight destroyers; nine torpedo boats; and a variety of lesser craft, mostly small, old, and obsolete.

The Russians' Black Sea Fleet started the war without a single dreadnought, although they had three 22,500-ton dreadnoughts under construction (see chapter 13, p. 278). The fleet's five battleships, Sv. *Yevstafy, Ioann Zlatoust, Panteleimon, Tri Sviatitelia,* and *Rostislav* (with the ancient *Georgy Pobedonosets* in reserve), were about equal in fighting value to the German battle cruiser and the old Turkish battleships. The *Rostislav* was of 8,800 tons, four 10-inch and eight 6-inch guns, and 16 knots. The other four were of similar design. Each displaced about 12,500 tons and was designed for 17 to 18 knots, but the armament differed. The *Yevstafy* and *Ioann Zlatoust,* the newest, each carried four 12-inch, four 8-inch, and 12 6-inch guns. The *Panteleimon* had four 12-inch and 16 6-inch guns, and the *Tri Sviatitelia* had four 12-inch and 14 6-inch guns. Besides these five battleships, all relatively old, there were two fairly effective cruisers (*Pamiat Merkuriia* and *Kagul*: 6,500 tons, 12 6-inch guns, 23 knots), nine new destroyers, 17 torpedo boats, six submarines, and a scattering of gunboats, minelayers, and lesser craft. Most of these ships were not in prime working shape, and several were in use as floating barracks. Two additional cruisers and four submarines, ordered in 1914, were expected by 1917–18. Until mid-1916 this fleet was commanded by Vice Adm. A. A. Eberhardt, a Russian of Swedish descent. Eberhardt was replaced by Vice Adm. A. V. Kolchak.

In training, discipline, gunnery, and morale the Black Sea Fleet was superior to the Baltic Fleet. It also contained a much smaller revolutionary element. The gunnery, regarded as good, was directed aboard the battleships by a very short-wave radio system superior to anything then in use in the British navy.

A comparison of the more modern ships of the two fleets reveals that while the Russians were collectively superior in gunpower, the Turko-Germans had an edge of several knots in speed and therefore could escape any engagement if they chose.

So far as basic strategy was concerned, the Russians desired what they had actively pursued for more than two hundred years—control of the Turkish Straits and access to the warm waters of the Mediterranean. These rewards the French and British conceded in a secret treaty (the Sazonov Agreement) of March 4, 1915. It is ironic that the Russians were to fail militarily in a war in which they had at last gained diplomatic concurrence with their desires.

At the beginning of the war the naval general staff had three plans for Black Sea operations. Though for various reasons none of these was carried out, in day-to-day operations the Russians aimed at two objectives. The first was to support their armies on the Caucasus front, mainly by interfering with Turkish water communications so as to leave the sultan's armies dependent on an inadequate network of roads. The second was to aid the French and British in forcing their way through the Dardanelles. In addition, some Russian naval actions were taken which, though not closely related to either objective, did have certain values in a war of attrition.

OPERATIONS DURING 1914 AND 1915

The war in the Black Sea did not get under way until late October 1914. At that time, though Turkey and Russia were still at peace, Admiral Souchon decided without notifying Turkish minister of marine, Jemal Pasha, to attack the Russians without warning. In pursuance of this plan the *Göben* with a minelayer and two destroyers was dispatched to bombard Sevastopol. En route she met the Russian minelayer *Prut*, which refused a demand to surrender, opened fire with her puny 47-mm. guns, and was speedily sunk.[1] The *Göben* was undamaged in the encounter, but was later hit three times by shore batteries at Sevastopol. In other phases of the surprise attack two Turkish destroyers and a minelayer attacked Odessa and sank the torpedo gunboat *Donets* and damaged her sister ship *Kubanets*; and the *Hamidieh*, the *Breslau*, and the minelayer *Berk* attacked the port of Feodosiia on the Kerch Strait.

From a tactical standpoint the surprise attack was militarily unsuccessful in that the Russians did not sustain important damage. But it signaled a major strategic setback, for Turkey's entrance into the war closed an Allied supply line into the Black Sea.

When the British demanded on behalf of Russia that Turkey disassociate herself from Souchon's activities, the demand was refused. Only then did Russia and Britain declare war on Turkey.

The long period between the opening of hostilities and the specific declaration of war against Turkey gave the Russians time to prepare for the type of warfare they best understood—a campaign of attrition. In late October they were able to start minelaying, using a number of converted merchant ships manned by mixed naval and civilian crews. On November 4 four Russian destroyers laid a minefield north of the Bosphorus while covering forces fired into the coal port of Zonguldak and sank four transports.

These early actions set the pattern of the Turko-Russian naval war. On the Caucasus front the Turks were heavily dependent on coastal transportation. Because no railroads were available in the area and other roadways were of small capacity and wretched quality, they usually moved supplies and munitions from Constantinople along the south coast of the Black Sea to Trebizond and other coastal ports. In turn an important west-going trade in coal moved out of the port of Zonguldak. The Turks now attempted to continue their coastal trade by the use of escorted convoys, while the Russians undertook to disrupt it completely by such tactics as bombardments of the ports at each end of the Black Sea, minelaying about the Bosphorus, and submarine and destroyer attacks on merchant ships. Though Russian tactics caused heavy Turkish losses, they did not stop the trade altogether.

Probably the greatest Turkish success came late in 1914 when the *Göben* and the *Breslau* intercepted and sank some Russian vessels preparing to make a fireship attack on shipping in Zonguldak Harbor. The success was dearly bought, for on December 26 the *Göben* hit two mines in the area, and though she was able to limp home for repairs she suffered some loss of speed and was out of action for several months. Even less fortunate was the *Mejidieh*; which subsequently hit a minefield off Odessa and sank in shallow water. The Russians raised and repaired her and added her to their own fleet under the name of *Prut*, honoring the destroyed minelayer.

Occasional unplanned brushes also occurred between Turkish and Russian warships in spite of the fact that as in the Baltic, neither belligerent actively sought battle. On November 18, 1914, for

A Soviet *F* class large attack type fleet submarine.

A Soviet *D* class guided missile submarine.

This 5,000-ton *Echo II* class nuclear-powered submarine was photographed during Soviet fleet exercises in the North Pacific. The submarine carries eight cruise missiles and a crew of about 100.

A Soviet Y class nuclear-powered ballistic missile submarine.

A Soviet merchant tanker refuels a Soviet *Mirka* class escort ship while they are at anchor off the coast of Kithira, Greece.

U.S.S.R. bomber *Bounder* with *Fishbed C* escort.

A Soviet MIG-21 *Fishbed* short-range delta-wing fighter aircraft in flight.

A Soviet 201-M *Bison* bomber aircraft in flight with a U.S. F-4 *Phantom II* fighter aircraft in flight in the background.

A Soviet *Kamov* KA-20 antisubmarine helicopter, with tracking gear extended in flight near the British antiaircraft frigate HMS *Lynx*, pennant number F-27.

A Soviet-built TU-16 *Badger* aircraft with Egyptian markings in flight to watch over the North Atlantic Treaty Organization exercise Dawn Patrol. A U.S. Navy F-8 *Crusader* fighter aircraft of Fighter Squadron 13 (VF-13), assigned aboard the antisubmarine warfare support aircraft carrier USS *Shangri-La* (CVS-38), flies alongside.

A Soviet TU-20 *Bear* bomber aircraft in flight during the Soviet worldwide naval exercise Okean.

Soviet warships on maneuvers in the Mediterranean Sea.

A Soviet navy task group lies at anchor about 25 miles south of Honolulu. In the foreground is one of the two *F* type conventional submarines in the force. In background a *Kotlin* class destroyer takes on fuel from the Soviet merchant tanker *Zhitomir*. Slightly ahead is a destroyer of the modern *Krupny* class.

n left, models of a Soviet *Sawfly* stage solid-propellent subma- launched ballistic missile, a Navy ZUGM-73-A *Poseidon* d-propellent submarine- hed missile, a Soviet SS-N-6 le, and a U.S. Navy UGM-27C is A3 submarine - launched propellent missile.

From left, models of a Soviet SS-9 *Scarp* liquid-propellent intercontinental ballistic missile, a U.S. Air Force LGM-306 *Minuteman* solid- propellent intercontinental ballistic missile, a Soviet ABM-1 *Galosh* antimissile missile, and a U.S. Army *Spartan* antimissile missile.

A model of a Soviet *Goa* two-stage surface-to-air missile.

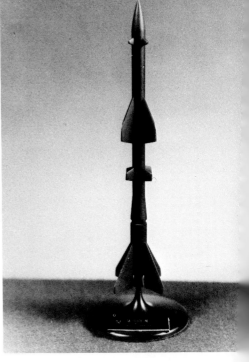

A model of a Soviet SA-2 *Guideline* two-stage surface-to-air missile.

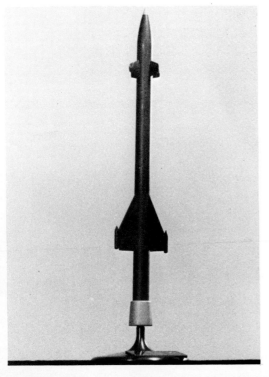

A model of a Soviet *Guild* surface-to-air missile.

instance, when the Russian fleet was returning to port in foggy weather following a bombardment of Trebizond, the *Göben* and *Breslau* were sighted by Russian ships at a distance of about four miles. A brief action followed in which the *Ioann Zlatoust* and *Sv. Yevstafy* were hit four times, had 55 men killed, but managed to deliver an accurate fire. The *Göben* was hit by the *Yevstafy's* first salvo; one shell bursting on the center of her freeboard started a fire. After about 15 minutes of combat the Turks used their greater speed to move away into the fog. No ships had been sunk; the Russians reported 334 killed and wounded, the Turks about 100. On December 7–10 the *Göben* and the *Hamidieh* escorted a convoy along the south coast of the Black Sea and ended by bombarding Batum. The disabling of the *Göben* shortly thereafter placed the Turks' main naval weapon out of action.

For the next several months the Russians clearly held the upperhand. On January 6, 1915, they engaged and severely damaged the *Breslau* and the *Hamidieh*. During the next two days they conducted a sweep of the south coast during which they bombarded Khopi and destroyed more than 50 ships at Trebizond, Sinope, Pletona, and Surmene. Later that month they sank 11 small schooners and 15 feluccas between Batum and Trebizond. On January 27 Russian cruisers of superior size pursued but did not overtake the newly repaired *Breslau* and *Hamidieh*. The completion in July 1915 of the *Imperatritsa Mariia*, first of the new Black Sea dreadnoughts, assured the Russians of continued superiority even after the *Göben* returned to service and enabled them to hold an edge even after the entrance of some German submarines into the Black Sea and a declaration of war by Bulgaria. In October, when the *Yekaterina II* joined the fleet, Russian strength became overwhelmingly superior.

The second Russian objective, support of the Allied Dardanelles campaign, was pursued with less success. The November 3, 1914, long-range British bombardment of the forts at the entrance of the Turkish Straits succeeded only in alerting the Turks. This poorly handled campaign began on February 19, 1915, and lasted until early January 1916, involving about 120,000 men in army units plus reinforcements and large naval forces. It had as its objective the control of the straits, the capture of Constantinople, and the establishment of a supply line to relieve the 1915 Russian shortage of guns and ammunition. While in April 1915 the campaign came very close to success, the Allies, owing to poor intelligence, failed to attack heavily at a time when such an attack would have meant victory. They finally withdrew after incurring heavy losses on both land and sea. The Turks suffered less, but the *Messoudieh* and *Haireddin Barbarossa*, two of their three old battleships, were lost to British submarines which penetrated into the Sea of Marmora.

The Russians, of course vitally concerned with the success of this campaign, had at first considered providing an army corps to attack the Bosphorus from the Black Sea side. Unfortunately the corps was sent instead to Galicia, where its losses were heavy because of munitions shortages. For some time the *Askold* was attached to the Allied forces as a liaison ship, but it proved extremely difficult to maintain the communications and coordination so necessary to forces separated by the enemy. When the threat of a possible landing of a 20,000-man Russian force stationed at Odessa obliged the Turks to disperse their troops, the Russians did not make the contemplated move for two reasons: the *Imperatritsa Mariia* was not ready for sea in March 1915, and they were uncertain about the condition of the *Göben*.

The battleships of the Black Sea Fleet, firing from ranges of about eight miles (i.e., beyond the range of most Turkish shore batteries) conducted bombardments of the forts on both European and Asiatic shores from March 29 to May 2, 1915, in support of the troops landed under Sir Ian Hamilton. These bombardments were necessarily sporadic because returns to port had to be made for coaling. At times the Russians were fired upon by the battleship *Torghout Reis* and by torpedo craft, as well as by guns from local forts. A 30-minute engagement on May 4 between the *Göben* and the two best of the older Russian battleships, *Ioann Zlatoust* and *Yevstafy*, was won by the Russians when the *Göben* retreated after receiving four hits. But although the Turkish land defenses received a thorough going-over, there is no indication of any results greater than those attained by the somewhat futile Allied bombardments at the other end of the Dardanelles. An imaginative plan of Vice Admiral Kolchak—pouring oil on the sea at the Bosphorus and setting it afire to cover the landing of Russian troops in Thrace—was never tried.

Meanwhile, the *guerre de course* took another turn with Russian attempts to stop Turkish trade by employing torpedo craft against enemy merchant vessels and the two cruisers still available to the Turks. It was a turn which brought the Russians moderate successes and many skirmishes with Turkish escorts. On the night of June 10–11 two Russian destroyers, *Gnevny* and *Derzky*, fell in with the *Breslau*. Spotlighted by the *Breslau*'s searchlight, the *Gnevny* was fired upon and badly damaged before the *Derzky*, under Comdr. A. O. Gadd, succeeded in moving to the stern of the *Breslau*, opening fire at close range, and holding her position until the enemy ship retreated. The *Imperatritsa Mariia* had two brushes, one with the *Göben* and the other with the *Breslau*, in which it demonstrated good marksmanship and remarkable speed, forcing retreat on both occasions. In September 1915 the Russian destroyers *Bystry* and *Pronzitelny* and the submarine *Nerpa* attacked the *Hamidieh* and a Turkish destroyer which were escorting four supply ships. On that occasion the two clearly superior Turkish ships made off, leaving the supply ships to their fate. On September 22 three Russian destroyers (*Shchastlivy*, *Bespokoiny*, and *Pronzitelny*) under Rear Admiral Sablin met but escaped from the *Göben*.

At the beginning of the war the Turks had had no submarines, but by mid-1915 German U-boats were finding their way into the Black Sea. The main port used by German submarines was Varna, which became available on October 14, 1915, when Bulgaria entered the war on the side of the Central Powers.

Similarly, there was virtually no Russian submarine activity during 1914, as the six obsolete submarines of 100-200 tons—the only ones available—could not be used in operations beyond the Russian coasts. But the Russians had a number of better, 500-ton undersea boats building at Nikolaev, and smaller Holland-type submarines had arrived at Black Sea ports in sections. Before the end of the war six of these two types (*Nerpa, Tiulin, Morzh, Narval, Kit,* and *Kashalot*) had become operational and the older submarines were being used only for training. The completion of even these six was something of an achievement, considering that their diesel engines, on order in Germany, were never delivered, and the two small 250-horsepower engines used in each submarine had to be taken from river gunboats of the Amur Flotilla. These weak engines limited the surface speed of the submarines to no more than seven knots. While the boats were at sea the crews normally consisted of four officers and 33 men. Russian undersea forces also included the submarine minelayer *Krab*, mentioned in chapter 13.

In the later months of 1915 Russian submarines operated along the sea lanes from Constantinople to Zonguldak, 150 miles to the east. Their conquests consisted mainly of sailing ships carrying supplies to Constantinople and a few larger cargo vessels. The *Krab* added to this toll when the *Breslau* went to drydock for seven months after hitting one of her mines. Opponents were Turkish small craft and occasional airplanes which bombed and strafed with sufficient effectiveness to keep the Russians under the surface during most of the daylight hours.

Though the strategic role of naval aviation during World War I was not large, it is worthy of note that the Russians in the Black Sea theater were among its foremost practitioners. At the beginning of the war two nearly new cargo ships of 9,000 tons each were converted to carriers of seven or eight seaplanes. Each ship carried six 120-mm. and four 75-mm. guns and was officially classed as a hydrocruiser. The *Nikolai I* and *Aleksandr I* were used not only in attacks on the Bosphorus but for raids of Turkish commerce and shore targets. As early as 1916 they were paired with *Tri Sviatitelia, Rostislav*, and *Panteleimon* in forming a primitive battleship-carrier task force. The planes were handled with skill and an American observer reported launching of seven in 14 minutes—compared to British launching of one plane in 20 minutes. Though the bombs carried were not particularly lethal they sank a 7,000-ton collier off Zonguldak in February 1916 and may have sunk the German submarine *UB-7* later in the year.[2]

OPERATIONS: 1916 TO THE REVOLUTION

Operations throughout 1916 and the first months of 1917 followed much the same pattern as during the earlier part of the war. In January, off Eregli, the *Yekaterina II* showed her excellent qualities when with the two destroyers, she met the *Göben* in a duel. The *Yekaterina II* pursued at almost 24 knots and fired at a range of 24,000 meters in what was probably the longest-range gunfire performance of the entire naval war. The Russians continued to hold the upper hand until the revolution destroyed the efficiency of their navy. In July Vice Adm. A. V. Kolchak came from the Baltic to replace Vice Admiral Eberhardt. The relatively young and vigorous Kolchak was able even after the revolution to deal successfully with sailors' committees until support from the Baltic Fleet arrived.

By far the greatest threat to Russian control of the Black Sea during 1916 was the handful of U-boats whose operations forced the Russians to use destroyers to guard their merchant shipping. Despite this protection the submarines still torpedoed a great many cargo ships. German submarine minelayers proved a particular hazard. In April 1916 the destroyer *Zhivuchy* foundered on a mine laid by U-27. This loss followed by a month that of the destroyer *Lt. Pustoshkin.* The Russian submarine offensive during 1916 was relatively less effective than that of the Germans, though it did claim a few large cargo ships and some smaller craft. The Turkish cruisers were only moderately active, but early in the year the *Imperatritsa Mariia* forced the *Göben* to retreat from a long-range duel.

The Russians continued their support of the Caucasus Army, both by repeated blows at Turkish supply lines and by direct artillery support. During April 1916 a task force consisting of the *Imperatritsa Mariia*, the *Kagul*, and a destroyer squadron covered an amphibious landing of some 30,000 troops near Trebizond and thereafter bombarded the city until it surrendered to Russian land forces. Varna and several Turkish ports were repeatedly shelled. On several occasions seaplanes from the two somewhat primitive Russian seaplane carriers (*Aleksandr I* and *Nikolai I*) were also employed in bombardment missions, though the light bombs they carried were relatively ineffective. Naval aviation at that time was used most efficiently either in reconnaissance missions or against U-boats. On August 25, 1916, in a combined operation of naval and air forces oddly prophetic of World War II, Admiral Kolchak with the *Imperatritsa Mariia*, a cruiser, eight destroyers, and two seaplane carriers with 19 seaplanes aboard attempted to bomb the German U-boat base at Varna. They were foiled by an alert German defense; German seaplanes attacked the squadron, preventing the Russian seaplanes from taking off.

By far the hardest blow suffered by the Russians was the loss, on

October 22, 1916, of the *Imperatritsa Mariia.* The battleship sank in
the port of Sevastopol, a victim of fires and explosions apparently
of accidental origin but possibly caused by sabotage (no official
report was issued). Nevertheless, the loss in strength was only
temporary, as the *Yekaterina II* was already available and the
Aleksandr III was nearly ready for commissioning.

The arrival in the Black Sea theater of Vice Admiral Kolchak, an
expert in mine warfare, was followed by an important development
in the system of light-vessel minelaying, a procedure designed
mainly to bottle up U-boats which had by now become such a menace. Kolchak's teams consisted of two to four destroyers, one or
more submarines and, occasionally, seaplanes operating from parent
ships. Submarines, which were the first to arrive on the scene,
planted buoys in predetermined positions; then following destroyers
rapidly laid mines. At times during such an operation seaplanes
attacked the enemy in order to divert attention from the minelaying.
Existing minefields were replenished by shallow draft motor boats
transported to their destination aboard the *Pamiat Merkuriia*, which
had been converted to a mother ship. A 500-ton shallow draft ship
with 220 mines was used for laying inshore mines. Minelaying
sorties were the most common offensive Russian naval activity
from mid-1916 to mid-1917, with the Bosphorus, Varna, and Constantsa the most favored areas in the order named. The last such
operation, on June 25–26, 1917, involved a battleship, nine destroyers, and nine special vessels which laid 880 mines. From July 1916
to July 1917 the Russians planted 4,000 mines in and around the
Bosphorus, and in one sortie, on July 31, 1916, the submarine minelayer *Krab* alone planted 60 mines. The losses thus forced on the
enemy (including the German *UB-45* blown up outside of Varna)
made it very difficult for the Turks to keep the coastal trade lanes
clear; they probably also accounted for a period of relative inactivity on the part of the *Göben.*

In a war so general as World War I the Black Sea contest between
Russian and Turko-German forces can be counted as no more than
a minor engagement. Yet in its limited sphere the Russian performance in the Black Sea was truly commendable. Here the Russians held the upper hand for most of the war and proved more
effective in the war of attrition than did their foes. Here enemy

losses totaled one cruiser, four destroyers, five submarines, five gunboats, and some small craft. Here successful Russian minelaying
greatly complicated Turkish military supply problems, and in fact
did much to worsen a 1916 shortage of coal which greatly hurt
both Turkish shipping and industries even in Constantinople. And
finally, unlike in the Baltic, here the Russians were comparatively
aggressive in their contacts with enemy ships.

In the Baltic and Black seas combined the Russians claimed one
battleship, the *Rheinland* (not sunk but badly damaged on a reef
and towed back to Germany), two armored cruisers, seven light
cruisers, a monitor, 23 destroyers and torpedo boats, nine submarines, a Turkish minelayer, six German dirigibles, and many small
craft and auxiliaries. Though a few of these claims are open to question, the overall achievement was a creditable one for a comparatively weak fleet.[3]

CHAPTER 16

Revolution, Intervention, and Civil War

GENERAL HISTORY OF RUSSIA 1917–22

BY EARLY 1917 Russia was ripe for revolution, and her naval history for the next five years can be understood only in relation to the larger picture of a highly confused and bloody period.

World War I had gone badly for the Russians. After two and a half years of fighting, troops at the front were completely demoralized by incompetent leadership and repeated defeats. Patriotic efforts to bring about reform had gotten nowhere. The tsarina, and to a lesser extent the tsar, had fallen under the influence of the dissolute monk Rasputin, whose hypnotic powers appeared beneficial to Nicholas' only son, the sickly Alexis. Ministers had been disgraced and speculators enriched at Rasputin's whim until at length even aristocrats and nobles were fully as prepared to welcome a palace revolution as the radical parties were to achieve their revolution from below. On February 27, in the midst of food riots, strikes, and pitched fighting which involved police, both loyal and mutinous troops, and workers, the Duma met in defiance of an order of dissolution from the tsar. With the support of the Petrograd soldiers they formed the provisional government and induced Nicholas II to abdicate. When Grand Duke Michael declined to succeed his brother, the way was paved for the creation of the Russian republic —first under Prince Georgy Evgenevich Lvov and later under Aleksandr Kerensky—which the principal Allied powers immediately recognized.

The establishment of the provisional government marked only the first stage of the Russian revolution, however. The new Russian leaders proved unable to maintain or extend their power, to prosecute the war successfully, or to grapple with a host of other important problems that clamored for attention. In point of fact, their efforts were being steadily sabotaged by the Bolsheviks who, though at first a very small minority, had on their side strong leadership, great powers of organization, and a clear-cut and appealing program: "Peace, Land, and Bread." They had organized "soviets" which in turn arrogated to themselves the right to act as governing bodies. Instead of trying to enforce its authority, the provisional government repeatedly made concessions to this militant group and at the same time apparently failed to discern the enormity of the threat they posed. Even an unsuccessful attempt at a new Bolshevik revolution in July 1917 did not alert the government. After July the soviets abandoned all pretense of cooperation and set about openly to undermine not only the authority of the provisional government but the discipline of the army and navy. As Kerensky's power declined, the power of the Bolsheviks grew. In early November they seized control, and two months later they dispersed with bayonets a newly elected constituent assembly which they found they could not direct.

A principal issue between the provisional government and the Bolsheviks was the question of continuation of the war. For the first seven months of 1917 Russia remained in the war despite a steadily dwindling military effectiveness. *Order No. 1* issued by the Petrograd Soviet—and weakly accepted by the provisional government—provided that soldiers' committees were to take charge of all weapons, while the orders of officers were to be obeyed only when they were not in conflict with the decisions of the soviet. Needless to say, this directive effectively destroyed the Russian army. Discipline was hopelessly undermined; thousands of men deserted. A July 1917 offensive against the Austrians (which proved to be the last gasp of the Russian war effort) soon dissolved in complete military disintegration. The Germans helped things along with propaganda of their own to promote the independence of outlying areas of Russia, especially the Ukraine.

Unfortunately for the Bolsheviks, this destruction of the armed forces was to prove a handicap once they had consolidated their power and were ready to end the war: the Germans insisted on a Carthaginian peace. By terms of the Treaty of Brest-Litovsk (signed March 3, 1918), outlying areas including Finland, the Baltic States, Poland, and the Ukraine were detached under German protection for purposes of economic exploitation. Russia lost, in fact, more than a quarter of her population and arable land and a third of her industry, and in addition agreed to pay a huge war indemnity. The Bolsheviks accepted these stiff terms partly because they had little choice, partly because they anticipated a world revolution which would restore their losses.

The new Soviet state faced formidable foreign opposition from the first. The separate peace treaty, which freed 40 German divisions for action on the Western front, prejudiced the Allies to regard Lenin and his followers as traitors; and later Bolshevik policies of persecuting religion, attacking private property, repudiating the foreign debt, and waging propagandist warfare against the capitalist states antagonized virtually every other government as well. The Western powers, anxious to gain a new Eastern ally in the fight against Germany, expressed their position by blockading Russia and declaring support for any forces fighting the Bolsheviks. In April 1920 the new government of Poland, hoping for territorial aggrandizement, ordered its armies into a sudden attack on Russia. The Poles were victorious at first, then beaten back almost to Warsaw by forces under twenty-seven-year-old Gen. M. N. Tukhachevsky. Finally, with French help, they defeated the Russians and gained a relatively favorable boundary.

The fact that the Bolsheviks were able to conduct military offensives deserves some explanation. Shortly after November 1917 the Red army was created under the leadership of Leon Trotsky. Loyalty was re-inculcated, this time on the basis of service to the Revolution, and communist cells charged with restoring discipline replaced the soldiers' committees. The Red army was not large, but enjoying as it did the best rations and equipment available, it proved able to fight and win the three-year Civil War.

The Civil War was an involved affair complicated by Allied intervention and by the resistance of separatist movements which derived from various ethnic minorities. The main White Russian forces were (1) a group led by Gens. L. G. Kornilov and A. I. Denikin, which had the support of the Kuban Cossacks; (2) a People's Army in Siberia; (3) Adm. A. V. Kolchak's conservative forces, which at one time controlled nearly all of Siberia as well as much of southeast Russia and in league with the forces of Denikin were able to pose the greatest threat to the new regime; and (4) forces based in Estonia under Gen. M. N. Yudenich. The Bolsheviks were able to force Kolchak out of European Russia and Denikin into the Crimea. There Denikin gave way to Baron Petr N. Wrangel, who held out until the end of the Polish war freed the main forces of the Red army, whereupon he escaped with 145,000 followers to Constantinople. In October 1919 General Yudenich, with British backing, scored early gains in a surprise attack on Petrograd but later was forced to retire before a counter-attack. In addition to these main White Russian forces there were many lesser groups whose members ranged from disinterested patriots to bloodthirsty brigands.

There were several reasons for Allied intervention—aside from mere dislike and distrust of communism. Huge supplies of munitions had been shipped to the Russian ports of Murmansk, Arkhangelsk, and Vladivostok. The Allies had no desire to see these fall into either German or Bolshevik hands. Moreover, Allied leaders persistently pursued the will-o'-the-wisp idea of a reestablished second front in the east. One possible Allied hope of giving substance to this dream lay in a considerable force of Czechoslovak prisoners of war who had enlisted in the tsar's armies to fight against the Austrians for the liberation of their native land. Unable to get out of Russia to the west, this force seized control of the Trans-Siberian Railroad and made its way across northern Asia toward Vladivostok, fighting as it went all Bolsheviks who attempted to impede its progress.

In all, about six major interventions occurred, involving a total of fourteen countries but in no case a large commitment of either manpower or economic resources. Most of the interventions were weak and halfhearted; nevertheless, they posed certain problems for the Bolsheviks. The main interventions—and those which brought the greatest problems—took place (1) in the White Sea area, where an Allied force, mainly British in composition, established itself at the ports of Murmansk and Arkhangelsk and interfered with local government affairs; (2) at Vladivostok, where some 72,000 Japanese, 9,000 Americans, and smaller forces of other allies landed on the eastern coast of Siberia in 1918 (in the case of the Japanese the venture was purely imperialistic, and the Mikado's officers at one time held a tenuous control over Siberia east of Lake Baikal; the Americans had been ordered to assist the Czechs but to remain neutral in the Civil War, and as far as possible the American Gen. William S. Graves complied and also acted to check the Japanese); (3) in the Ukraine, where German forces occupied territory as far east as Rostov and the Austrians held Odessa (the Germans assisted the Don Cossacks against the Bolsheviks and also secured an economic treaty from the short-lived Ukrainian Government, but the German collapse enabled the Bolsheviks to regain much of the territory they had lost); (4) again in the Ukraine, when in March 1919 a French expedition invaded on the heels of the Germans and actively fought the Bolsheviks (this venture failed because of the susceptibility of war-weary French troops to Bolshevik propaganda); (5) in the Transcaucasia area, where the British seized Batum and Baku and actively aided a volunteer army then fighting the Bolsheviks; and finally (6) in the Baltic, where the British supported a wide circle of allies which included Finland, the new Baltic republics, certain Germans, and the White Russian forces of General Yudenich.

REVOLUTION AND WAR IN THE BALTIC 1917–18

Conditions favorable to revolution were perhaps as fully present in the Baltic Fleet in 1917 as they were anywhere in Russia. Most of the long-standing abuses which had prevented Admiral Rozhdestvensky's force from becoming a real fleet had not been corrected. Officers and men were from different social classes and were too often divided by a curtain of hatred; discipline was inexact, at times brutal, and dependent largely on the whim of the commanding officer; police regulations in ports discriminated against seamen. To be sure, certain improvements had come about prior to 1914 as a result of the reform efforts of younger officers under the able and forceful direction of Admiral von Essen. However, old regulations remained in force and the improvements effected had not proved sufficiently well grounded or numerous to withstand the effects of war. Morale had suffered sorely with the unrelievedly bad news from the front and the boredom of staying in port with too little to do.

Similar conditions throughout the nineteenth century had led to mutinies in both the army and the navy. What is more, the events of the Russo-Japanese War had revealed that social Revolutionaries even then had a strong foothold in the Baltic Fleet. Though the navy was outwardly loyal at the outbreak of World War I, revolutionary organization had spread widely and become especially strong in Kronstadt. Minor revolts on the *Rossiia* and the *Gangut* had been put down early in the war, but Bolshevik agitators continued to operate with increasing boldness and success.

The year 1917 opened inauspiciously in the Baltic. The work of repairing and refitting ships was slow and insufficient, and new construction was almost at a standstill. Accidents were more common than usual. Even the diversion of going to sea was unavailable to the men; it was not possible during the Russian winter.

Meanwhile, Bolshevik agents kept busy channeling dissatisfaction into revolutionary acts and breaking down loyalty and discipline, with the result that the February 1917 revolution at Helsinki and Kronstadt was in all essentials a Communist revolution. The Russian sailors there were merely a bit ahead of the rest of the country. When Admiral Nepenin, after a severe inner struggle, pledged support to the provisional government, he was promptly murdered by a petty officer. His successor to the command of the Baltic Fleet was Vice Adm. A. S. Maksimov, former commander of the Baltic Fleet mine defense. Maksimov, a turncoat who covered himself with red ribbons and declared himself the "People's Admiral," was acceptable for the time being to the Bolshevik leaders.

Capt. M. J. Nikolsky of the *Avrora* became the navy's first victim of the revolution when he was killed at Kronstadt attempting to prevent agitators from boarding his ship. On the *Pavel I* and the *Andrei Pervozvanny*—both in Helsinki Harbor—there was a wholesale slaughter of officers, warrant officers, and petty officers which took the lives of some 88 men. The provisional government, weak and beset with other problems, made no effort to apprehend those responsible or to restore discipline. Agitators continued to make speeches from morning until night and to organize ships' committees of various types.

At Kronstadt some 3,000 young men had been attending various naval schools, all under the command of Rear Adm. A. D. Sapsay. The few instructors were petty officers for whom the men had little respect, and Admiral Sapsay himself was regarded as incompetent and lazy. In contrast to these men, the decisive and ruthless local Bolshevik leadership had greater appeal to the students. As a result, what took place in February at Kronstadt was a well-organized and well-directed *Communist* uprising. The Kronstadt sailors, in fact, were among the most vigorous and militant elements in the entire Russian revolution.

The outbreak itself was led by the naval base forces, but they were joined in March by the ships' crews in manifestation of the growing spirit of mutiny. Three admirals, N. G. Rein, R. N. Viren, and A. G. Butakov, were killed (Viren in particular, though generally regarded as personally brave and honest, had been a whip-wielding martinet). At least 78 officers of lower rank were also murdered, some by torture and mutilation. For several days permission could not be obtained for their burial, and when it was finally granted, mobs interrupted some of the funerals by throwing the corpses out of their coffins. Those officers left alive were arrested, questioned, and occasionally charged with fanciful offenses. Some remained in prison under extremely punishing conditions; others were freed, a few at a time.

The leadership vacuum created by the murder or disgrace of the officers was not entirely filled for the remainder of the year. Of the new officers either elected or appointed to take the place of those killed, a few learned to change color with the times. Many more became completely discouraged, and the ablest of them left at the first pretext. Each vessel had its elected "ship's committee" to serve as mediator between officers and men.

Though initially intended to concern themselves only with the personal provisions and duties of the sailors (work, food, shore leave, etc.) the committees soon interfered with all directions aboard ship. They generally followed the suggestions of the local soviets, secret Bolshevik agents, or the Central Committee of the Baltic

(TSENTROBALT). The Central Committee consisted of 68 representatives (one per 1,000 men) from the various units of the fleet and bases. Though it had no legal standing whatever, it moved rapidly into complete de facto control. While only 13 of its members were Bolsheviks or their sympathizers, TSENTROBALT was dominated from the beginning by this forceful and radical minority, which was so strong that orders from the commander in chief were often refused. Its own program was aimed at dissipating bonds between officers and men, and to this end rumors of corruption and distrust were instigated. Shoulder straps were prohibited, the warrant officer rank was abolished, and the privileges of long-service men were withdrawn—thus depriving the navy of its few specialists. Ships were even renamed. An order of May 24 by the Central Soviet of Petrograd placed all matters of discipline in the hands of the ships' committees.

At Revel the Bolsheviks had to work harder to achieve success. The vessels there had been more active in fighting the war than those at the other two bases; leadership was reasonably acceptable; discipline was strict, with the men being kept busy. For a time the ships' crews were isolated from the mobs on shore, but news of important events reached them through daily orders. When the tsar abdicated, those officers unable to shift their allegiance were allowed to resign. Hence, in February Revel witnessed much the same type of partial revolution as the rest of Russia. This resistance to change only caused the Bolsheviks to redouble their efforts, and before long the Revel sailors too had become suspicious of their officers, ceased saluting, started taking orders from the local soviet, and joined red flag demonstrations on shore.

Was nothing done to halt this trend? The answer is, nothing effective. Officers formed a union of their own, but they proved inept in politics and were regarded with suspicion by other groups. Though most of the Russian officers were by no means unthinking reactionaries, as a group they were fatally lacking in flexibility and unequipped, either by native endowment or by education, to talk personally and persuasively with their men. Most of them were deliberately nonpolitical. No help or guidance of any kind came from the provisional government, and officers who went to see Kerensky found him uninterested in naval problems. In such circumstances the legal provisional government became an ever more shadowy abstraction which was increasingly disregarded and defied by those looking to the soviets for their direction.

In July the Bolsheviks failed in an attempted revolution against the provisional government. During the revolt the provisional government requested that destroyers be sent to its aid, but when TSENTROBALT protested, Admiral Verderevsky (who had just replaced Maksimov), instead of obeying orders, merely went to Petrograd to report. He was badly received, accused of treason, and arrested. Eventually he was freed as a concession to the Bolsheviks and made minister of marine. He was replaced as commander of the Baltic Fleet by Adm. A. V. Rozvozov, former commander of destroyers.

Rozvozov's appointment, an excellent one, came far too late, for the days of the navy were numbered. The July revolt had brought some setbacks to the Bolsheviks—such as the order for the dissolution of TSENTROBALT, the arrest of some of its members, and the closing of party newspapers (promptly reopened under new names) —but none of them proved a serious hindrance.

As a result of a series of misunderstandings Kerensky quarreled with the strongest army commander of loyal troops, General Kornilov, whom he had ordered to Petrograd to dissolve both the Petrograd Soviet and the Kronstadt base. Later, fearful that Kornilov might be preparing to seize power himself, Kerensky removed him and appealed to the Kronstadt garrison for support! This move was fatal.

On November 7 the Bolshevik Revolution began. TSENTROBALT now requested (successfully) that destroyers as well as the cruiser Avrora be sent to Petrograd to support the soviets. The Avrora fired a few rounds of blank ammunition on the Winter Palace; Kerensky fled; the council of ministers was arrested.[1] The ministry of marine was at first replaced by a "naval college" of fleet representatives, but in December the office of Baltic Fleet commander in chief was abolished and its powers conferred on TSENTROBALT. The popular Rozvozov left and was replaced by an ex-bluejacket named Izmailov who was "assisted" by Admiral Ruzhek. The destruction of the Russian imperial navy was now complete. Sailors deserted at will, and even the most subservient officers began leaving the ranks.

In January 1918 the Kronstadt sailors rendered one more service to the revolution when they dispersed the newly elected constituent assembly. Then, early in February 1918, the Soviet of People's Commissars announced the demobilization of the navy.

To note that a war was taking place in the Baltic during 1917 seems almost an anticlimax. Yet such was the case, though only one important naval action occurred during a year that saw unusually heavy Russian losses brought about by incompetence. There were no Russian initiatives of any importance, but in October 1917 the Germans revived, this time with success, their favored objective of capturing the Gulf of Riga. At this time the Russian forces were under the command of Vice Adm. M. K. Bakhirev, one of the last of the truly capable Russian officers. Because they were closer to the war, the Gulf of Riga naval forces were in a better state of discipline than those farther north. But their efficiency had been greatly undermined by events elsewhere. The first indications of unusual German activities came in late September, when the destroyer *Okhotnik* struck a mine in the Irben Strait area and quickly sank. At about the same time German minesweepers started working to clear Russian mine fields from coastal areas. On October 12 the Germans moved into the Bay of Riga under cover of a very strong escort which included dreadnoughts of the High Seas Fleet. These forces, under the command of Vice Adm. Eberhardt Schmidt, included ten dreadnoughts, eight light cruisers, six submarines, 56 destroyers and torpedo boats, six airships, 94 planes, about 80 mine-searching and sweeping vessels, and about 70 submarine search ships. By far the strongest fleet the Germans were to place in the Baltic during the entire war, this aggregation vastly outclassed the Russian defenders. German army forces numbering about 25,000 under General von Kathen were landed on Ösel Island, the largest of the several islands dominating the entrance to the Gulf of Riga. Because of the poor marksmanship of the Russians, the Germans lost only one destroyer, though they shelled Russian positions so heavily as to force their abandonment. Later Admiral Bakhirev sent in *Iziaslav, Grom, Zabiiaka, Samson,* and *Novik* against German destroyers which had entered the Kassarsky Basin. An engagement of the two forces proved indecisive, and the next morning the Russian destroyers *Novik, Grom, Konstantin, Pobeditel,* and

Zabiiaka, entering the basin to scout, chased away some enemy steamers but were in turn driven off by a German cruiser of the Graudenz class. At this point the crew of the minelayer Pripet decided that minelaying was too dangerous, and that the orders of Admiral Bakhirev were "inopportune."[2] The same indifference and disloyalty prompted the surrender of the Zerel Island battery of four 12-inch guns which outranged any German artillery on the dreadnoughts.

Among the remaining islands, the Russians elected to defend only Moon Island. On October 14 their naval forces in the Kassarsky Basin came under the fire of far stronger German units. The Russians retired with the loss of the Grom. The old armored gunboat Khrabry, however, sank a German destroyer, thereby making the honors about even. The next day the Russian Third Destroyer Flotilla (Iziaslav, Avtrail, and Gavriil) was sent in, only to meet seven German destroyers. The Flotilla sustained some damage before being reinforced, first by two gunboats and later by the armored cruiser Admiral Makarov, which forced the Germans to leave.

On October 17 the Germans directed a serious attack into the Moon Sound entrance to the Gulf. The Russians held back the heavier German forces as best they could, meantime sweeping mines to permit their own withdrawal and laying new ones to delay the Germans. Enemy ships were attacked by seaplanes, by the Sixth and Ninth Destroyer Flotillas, and by the Baian, Tsesarevich, and Slava. Baian and Tsesarevich were damaged but made good their escape. The Slava, which had as opponents the German dreadnoughts Kaiser and Kronprinz, received several hits which made her draft too great to permit escape. She was sunk by her own men in the entrance of the channel, though not in a position to block it. Her crew was taken off by destroyers. By October 20 all Russian naval forces were out of the gulf. In the last phase of the operation the Germans lost only the destroyer S-64, although the Bayern, the Grosser Kurfurst, and the Markgraf struck mines and suffered some damage and Russian mines sank several small craft and damaged a great many others. Some Soviet naval historians, however, have claimed huge and wholly imaginary German losses of five battleships, a cruiser, and 23 destroyers and minesweepers sunk or damaged for the whole operation.

The success of the Germans' 1917 Baltic campaign was only partly due to their larger forces. The Russian defenders actually had greater strength at their disposal than had been the case when they defeated the Germans in 1915. However, the effects of the revolution sent Russian efficiency into such a decline that by the end of the year the Russian navy was almost completely worthless. The Germans could and did undertake naval enterprises with complete assurance and no risks other than those presented by old minefields. In March 1918 a division of German cruisers captured Revel, and a German invasion of Finland in April encountered absolutely no resistance from the Russians. For the invasion the Germans used the older dreadnoughts *Posen, Rheinland,* and *Westfalen* under Vice Adm. Alexander von Meurer as the backbone of their task force. Army troops under Gen. Count Rudiger von der Goltz freed all of southern Finland from the Bolsheviks in a few days.

Decreasing efficiency also accounted for an unusually long list of losses which included five submarines—*Gepard* (on her first cruise), *Bars, Lvitsa, AG-14,* and *AG-15* (later raised)—and the destroyers *Bditelny, Lt. Burakov,* and *Stroiny.* After their success in the Gulf of Riga the Germans and Austrians, aware that internal decay was doing their work for them, avoided disturbing the Russians unnecessarily, having no wish to revive wartime patriotism in Russia.

The dismal 1917–18 record of the Russian navy was relieved by one exceptional performance, which deserves some emphasis. Under the terms of the Treaty of Brest-Litovsk, Finland and the three Baltic states were to be freed by Russia and to be placed under German protection. In addition, Russian ships in Finnish or Baltic state ports such as Revel were to be either moved out of port or disarmed. What this meant was that unless the Russian ships at Revel, Helsinki, and other bases could be transferred in midwinter to Kronstadt they would be lost to the Soviet state.

The task of moving several hundred ships of all sizes through frozen seas at a time when both officers and men were demoralized and the ships were in a state of very bad repair was not an easy one. In fact, it would have proved impossible but for one man, a quiet, retiring, nonpolitical officer named Rear Adm. A. M. Shchastny, who during the war years had spent most of his time on radio communications. He yielded to the plea of the Bolsheviks to save the fleet in exchange for their assurance that his orders would not be countermanded. The first movement from Revel had to be made in February prior to the Treaty of Brest-Litovsk, since the Germans, tired of Russian delays in accepting the inevitable, had announced on February 16, 1918, the resumption of an offensive on land. On February 17 Shchastny began a transfer of the Russian ships to Helsinki. The first group, led by the icebreaker *Yermak*, reached Helsinki on February 27, after a journey slowed by heavy ice. Another group, leaving on February 24, was the target of an air attack and cleared harbor only a few hours in advance of German land forces. In this way some 56 ships of all sizes were taken out of Revel before the arrival of the Germans.

The transfer to Helsinki assured no more than temporary security, since the Treaty of Brest-Litovsk in effect required that the ships be moved out of Finnish waters as well. This operation, an equally difficult and complicated one, was in no way eased by the seizure by White Finns of the icebreakers *Tarmo* on March 21 and *Volynets* on March 29; both ships were taken to Revel. The *Volynets*, together with the *Yermak*, had already been used by the Russians to escort four dreadnoughts and three large cruisers which sortied on March 12 and reached Kronstadt through the ice five days later. Even so, three later detachments were successfully moved out of Helsinki and to Kronstadt, the last detachment reaching safety on April 22, 1918.

The importance of this evacuation, proclaimed by Soviet historians as "the first strategic move" of the Red navy, has been largely overlooked outside the Soviet Union. It enabled the Bolsheviks to transfer to relative safety six battleships, five cruisers, five mine-layers, seven icebreakers, 54 destroyers and torpedo boats, 12 submarines, 25 patrol boats, 28 tugs, and 69 auxiliaries.[3] It is true that the Red navy continued to decline for many years thereafter, but at least in the Baltic some of the remnants of Russian seapower had been preserved. Moreover during the Civil War some of the small craft were shifted, mainly by internal waterways, to active fronts where they constituted the nuclei of river flotillas used against the White Russians. Given existing conditions, the movement of ships to Petrograd and Kronstadt was an outstanding achievement.[4] And considering later uses made of the ships, it was also a significant one.

Fears that the Germans would shortly assault Petrograd, the treaty notwithstanding, led to a further Russian attempt (undertaken despite the unreliable character of many of the ships and crews) to lay a series of minefields west of Kronstadt in mid-August 1918. When a British squadron entered the Baltic after the defeat of the Germans, these mine defenses were renewed and extended.

A good many of the Russian ships lost during the German occupation were destroyed by their crews in the smaller ports to prevent their capture. For instance, at Hangö the Russians sank the submarines *AG-12, AG-15, AG-16,* a supply ship, and a patrol boat shortly before the German arrival on March 21. The British submarines *E-1, E-8, E-9, E-19, C-26, C-27,* and *C-35* also were sunk by their crews. Some vessels were lost at other ports as well, but considering the narrow coastline left to Russia it is surprising that the naval losses in the Baltic were not greater.

The fact that the Russians carried out even such operations as minelaying and the moving of ships is some indication of change in policy soon after the revolution. After the Bolsheviks were in power their purpose was no longer served by a weakened and disunited navy. On February 12, 1918, a decree by Lenin created the new Red Fleet under the People's Commissariat of Naval Affairs headed by P. E. Dybenko. The administration of the Baltic Fleet was vested in a Soviet of Baltic Fleet Commissars and the operational aspects placed under TSENTROBALT. The energetic new regime also attempted to restore a certain degree of order and efficiency, but they soon found naval organization to be rather more complicated than the creation of a Red army. When commissars continued to side with crews rather than with the officers without whom ships could not be operated, the officer class was deeply disaffected. The result was that the indiscipline of the revolutionary days continued to plague the new rulers of Russia.

THE BALTIC: INTERVENTION AND CIVIL WAR 1918–20

Immediately after the November 11, 1918 armistice, the British sent into the Baltic Adm. Sir Edwyn Alexander-Sinclair with a small naval force comprised mainly of light cruisers and destroyers. The situation there was incredibly complicated and chaotic, with the Germans in actual occupation of most of the area of the Baltic states though their de facto control was disputed by Red and White Russians alike and by the native Lithuanians, Latvians, and Estonians. Under the terms of the armistice, the Germans were to return to their native land; but the British, though they wanted to see Finland and the Baltic States remain independent, were not eager to have the German overlords replaced by the Bolsheviks. For the time being, then, they insisted that the status quo be maintained.

The Germans were ready to oblige. Gen. Count Rudiger von der Goltz, commander of the German Iron Division, arrived on the scene in February 1919, apparently hoping to remain as a permanent overlord with the assistance of the numerous Balts of German derivation, and possibly with a White Russian serving as figurehead. The ideal man for the latter role seemed to be the self-styled prince Avelov-Bermondt, who proclaimed allegiance to Admiral Kolchak. He gathered an army of about 15,000, principally Germans, and proclaimed a "West Russian Government." In the latter half of 1919 General Yudenich, under British protection, was also recruiting a large force at Narva in Estonia in preparation for a march on Petrograd. Because Yudenich opposed the separation of the Baltic states from Russia, he was not fully trusted by either the British or the Estonians. Finally, intermittent fighting had broken out between Red and White Finns; under Gen. Carl von Mannerheim, the White Finns proved the stronger—with some help from the Germans.

The directive under which Admiral Alexander-Sinclair and his successor (after January 19, 1918) Rear Adm. Sir Walter Cowan, operated, was apparently none too clear. However, both commanders interpreted their mission as being mainly to protect the Baltic States and see to the evacuation of the Germans, although they also undertook to rescue Allied prisoners of war and disarm German forces. Their tasks entailed a great deal of compromise as well as considerable fighting on both sea and land.

British arrival in Russian waters was delayed by the necessity of sweeping a pathway through old German and Russian minefields, an operation accomplished with minimal risk thanks to German, Russian, and Swedish mine charts, but which even so resulted in the loss of the light cruiser *Cassandra*. Once in the eastern Baltic, the British ships dispersed to Revel (named Tallinn by the Estonian government), Libau, Danzig, and Helsinki. On paper the Russian force in Kronstadt appeared far stronger than that of the British, but its general demoralization made figures meaningless. All the Russian ships were in an extreme state of disrepair and grossly undermanned. With shortages of ammunition and fuel as well as scanty and undisciplined crews available, it was only with great difficulty that the Bolsheviks managed by November 15, 1918, to activate the battleships *Andrei Pervozvanny* and *Petropavlovsk*, the cruiser *Oleg*, four destroyers, seven submarines, and some auxiliaries. Nevertheless the Reds showed a certain enterprise, both on land and at sea. The minelayer *Narova* laid a minefield around Kronstadt, and destroyers supported the Soviet land forces.

In the spring two Russian destroyers bombarded Revel, but they were pursued and captured by a British light cruiser and a destroyer.[5] These captured vessels were given to the Estonians as a nucleus for a navy composed mainly of miscellaneous German and Russian ships which proved valuable in landing marines behind Red lines. In April 1919 Rear Admiral Cowan's ships shelled Red land troops advancing out of Windau. General von der Goltz assumed command of local German forces, and was able to defeat the Bolshevik armies so promptly that General Mannerheim called him to Finland to help suppress a Red revolt in Helsinki. Admiral Cowan lent assistance to the Helsinki project, too, and in the process nearly lost the light cruiser *Curaçao*, which hit a mine and was barely able to limp back to Revel. From the grateful Finns Cowan received permission to establish a fleet base at Bjorko, only about forty miles from Kronstadt. Here the British improvised a small airfield, blockaded Kronstadt, and were reinforced by the monitor *Erebus* (with two 15-inch guns), a small converted aircraft carrier, additional cruisers and destroyers, and some fast "hush-hush" coastal motor boats armed with two torpedoes—clear predecessors of the motor torpedo boats of World War II but at that time almost unknown to the Russians in the Baltic. According to Soviet accounts, the British employed in the Baltic a total of twelve cruisers, a monitor, an aircraft carrier, 20 destroyers, eight coastal motor boats, and various other craft, not all of which were present at any given time. During the summer a French destroyer flotilla joined the British. Two American ships cruising in the Baltic did not take part in hostilities.

The very weak Baltic naval forces with which the Reds began 1919 were gradually increased to three battleships, the cruiser *Oleg*, six destroyers, four mine boats, six guard ships, seven submarines, four torpedo boats, and some auxiliaries. Both Russians and Estonians had small flotillas on Lake Peipus, that of the Russians consisting of two torpedo boats, five guard ships, four transports, and two minor craft. The small Finnish and Estonian navies were allied with the British forces, and from May to August there were constant brushes between Red ships and the British blockaders with the fighting closely related to land warfare between the Estonians and Whites on the one hand and the Reds on the other. A vital bone of contention was Fort Krasnaia Gorka, which covered the sea approaches to Petrograd and was first held by the Reds, then by the Whites, and finally lost to Red landing forces under Joseph Stalin.[6]

During May several indecisive skirmishes occurred in which Red warships advanced to the edge of their mine defenses and attempted to entice the British blockaders into the range of shore batteries. These efforts resulted in no sinkings, though on occasion vessels on either side were damaged. On July 4, 1919, in a battle between small destroyer and submarine forces, the Soviet destroyer *Azard* sank the British submarine *L-55*, and shortly thereafter the British lost two large minesweepers to Soviet mines. On the night of June 17, 1919, two coastal motor boats under Lt. Augustus Agar successfully torpedoed the *Oleg* which, however, went down in shallow water with the loss of but 40 of her men. Possibly because coastal motor boats were unknown to the Russians, the British were able to conceal information about their weapons and Soviet guesses regarding the fate of the *Oleg* ranged from destruction by internal sabotage to loss from a submarine torpedo. The British lost one destroyer to a Soviet submarine in November 1919, but the Russian penchant for staying within the protection of their own minefields largely deprived British submarines of reciprocal targets. On Lake Peipus two Red ships surrendered to the Estonians on May 20, 1919, and were incorporated into their flotilla. British bombing attacks on the ships at Kronstadt were generally unsuccessful.

After May 30 shortages of fuel resulting from a prostrate economy forced the Reds to turn their battleships into fortresses. Wisely or unwisely, Admiral Cowan decided to use the opportunity to make a general attack, using all the weapons at his disposal. The night of August 18 was chosen for this purpose. Eight recently arrived coastal motor boats with the shallow draft needed to clear the boom defenses of Kronstadt were selected as the decisive weapons. Russian attention was to be distracted by an aircraft bombing attack while the fast boats entered the harbor. Cruisers and destroyers were to play supporting roles. The plan was skillfully carried out and brought complete success. The *Marat* (ex-*Petropavlovsk*), the *Andrei Pervozvanny*, and the submarine depot ship *Dvina* were torpedoed; they sank in the shallow basin of Kronstadt, thus making salvage entirely feasible though the British attempted to discourage it by air attacks.

The defeat effectively discouraged Soviet naval activity involving ships larger than torpedo and mine craft, but even so, Russian mines and submarines continued to claim occasional victims. The British destroyer *Verulam* was lost to a mine on September 4, five days after the submarine *Pantera* sank the *Vittoria*. On the other hand, the Soviet destroyers *Gavriil* and *Konstantin* were lost to British mines while en route to surrender to the British, their tsarist commanders being out of sympathy with the Bolsheviks. This development came some six weeks after an announcement by Stalin that a conspiracy had been discovered among naval officers and battery commanders to fire at the rear of Red army forces. That announcement had been followed by the execution of some 66 Russian naval officers.

Fortunately for the Soviets, their warfare on land was relatively successful. During the summer months of 1919 they were heavily attacked by forces under General Denikin and Admiral Kolchak, who advanced to within 200 miles of Moscow. Had General Yudenich been ready to attack at the same time the Reds would have been in great peril, but by the time he mounted an offensive—in October —other White forces were in retreat. For several days after he began his attack, Yudenich appeared to be successful as he advanced to within eight miles of Petrograd. However, his failure to take forts on his left flank (an omission causing heavy losses to his Estonian allies), in addition to a sharp Red Army counter-attack, turned victory into defeat and then defeat into rout. Yudenich retreated into Estonia, where his forces were eventually interned. During his brief offensive the British ships supplied artillery support, while on the Soviet side the *Sevastopol* and about a dozen destroyers fired from positions in the Neva River. The Reds also employed from 6,000 to 10,000 naval personnel ashore, partly in the trenches and partly as crews for batteries and armored trains.

Meanwhile the German forces of General von der Goltz had clearly outlived their usefulness and were becoming a problem to the British. Since Mannerheim had forced the German troops to leave Finland following the suppression of the Red movement in that country, von der Goltz moved into Latvia and tried to set up a regime with Avelov-Bermondt as the nominal head. Cowan ordered the Germans out of the area and supplied naval assistance under Admiral Brisson, the French naval leader in the Baltic, to aid Latvian forces in dislodging them. In addition, the British blockaded German ports to force a government recall of von der Goltz. Under this pressure the German leader retreated to Libau, where an attempted German rally was ended by the gunfire of the monitor *Erebus* and British light cruisers.

On December 28, 1919, Admiral Cowan left the Baltic, barely making his way through encroaching ice. For all practical purposes his departure ended the Baltic war. Finland and the Baltic States were reasonably secure from conquest by the Bolsheviks; the Germans had been eliminated from the region; the White armies were no longer threatening; the Reds were exhausted and had at least temporarily abandoned hopes of reconquest. Convinced that keeping the Baltic states at war with the Soviets no longer served any sound purpose, the British decided to conclude a peace on the basis of the status quo. This was done in the later months of 1920. During the period of undeclared war the Bolsheviks had had two battleships disabled, a cruiser sunk, five destroyers sunk or captured, and two submarines sunk. The British had lost one cruiser and had a second badly damaged, lost two destroyers, one submarine, and some lesser craft.

One last chapter remains to be told in the story of the Baltic. The Soviets discovered to their sorrow that the lawless habits they had encouraged among Baltic Fleet personnel before the revolution tended to persist during their own regime. Crews containing many Bolsheviks and some anarchists could not always be depended upon to follow orders. At Kronstadt on February 28, 1921, the crew of the *Marat* (salvaged and renamed since her 1919 sinking as the *Petropavlovsk*) issued a resolution attacking the regime. Angry at the recent suppression of a Petrograd strike, the sailors demanded a secret ballot, free speech and press, free elections to the soviets from *all* left-wing parties, the release of certain Socialist political prisoners, and the abolition of special privileges. Entirely loyal to the revolution, the sailors yet viewed themselves as a pressure group and called for support in their demands. At a mass meeting on March 1 they drew up an entire program of reforms, and two Soviet officials who were charged with divers misdeeds were arrested. To meet this emergency the Soviets placed M. N. Tukhachevsky, their best field commander, in charge of a group of elite Red officer cadets to suppress the mutiny. On March 7 the Soviets began an attack on Kronstadt, but artillery and machine-gun fire broke up the first and second assaults. A third assault on March 17, following an artillery barrage, fared better. The attackers freed 300 loyalists in prison and prevented the firing of demolition charges. On March 18, after heavy loss of life, the Cheka and Red army forces took Kronstadt. Some rebel sailors walked across the ice to Finland and escaped, but large numbers of those surrendering reportedly were executed. Soviet figures put losses of the rebels at 700 killed and 2,500 wounded, and their own at 600 killed and 1,000 wounded. Had the revolt not occurred when the ships were frozen in the sea, the Bolshevik's problem would have been far greater.

From a political standpoint it should be noted that the Kronstadt revolt was most significant. It served very clear notice that the system of war communism under which Russia had been operating was basically defective. Gifted with a far greater ability to learn from mistakes than Nicholas II had possessed, the Soviet leaders retreated from the previous party line and adopted the New Economic Policy to allow Russia to recover from her wartime and revolutionary devastations and losses.[7]

THE BLACK SEA THEATER

The effect of the revolution of the Black Sea Fleet took a somewhat different course than it had in the Baltic. Here there was no entrenched Bolshevik minority, and the distance from the center of events was far greater. Revolutionists from the Baltic reached the Black Sea Fleet by railway and were accompanied by letters from the provisional government to Admiral Kolchak directing that they be provided free access to all ships and base installations. Kolchak, far more aware of their disruptive intentions than was the provisional government, permitted them the access ordered, but also presented to his crews a different version of events. For this he was accused of counter-revolutionary activity and became a special object for execration. On June 19, 1917, after several weeks of agitation, the Bolshevik agents succeeded in persuading the Council of Soldiers, Sailors, and Workers to pass resolutions refusing allegiance to the provisional government, stripping all authority and arms from the officers, and removing Admiral Kolchak.

At this point the Communist program received a bizarre and wholly unexpected interruption. Shortly after the United States declared war on the Central Powers she had decided to send a mission to Russia to make arrangements for cooperation in fighting the common foe. Rear Adm. James Glennon, who headed the naval section of the mission, was a volatile Irishman of considerable personal charm. He visited Russian naval and industrial installations, conferred with whatever Russian officers were temporarily in control, and finally recommended that some $49 million of a proposed $250 million loan to Russia be devoted to such needs as port facilities and small craft. Since friendship for the United States was traditional in Russia, the Americans had been received everywhere with a warm welcome.

Admiral Glennon's party arrived at Sevastopol on June 29, the day after the Bolshevik coup. Invited to address the Executive Committee of Soldiers, Sailors, and Workers, he made some impromptu remarks that were well received; and he was invited later the same day to address the whole council of about 1,200 members. The startling results were later reported by Admiral Glennon:

At a meeting of the Council of 1,200 in Sevastopol, June 20, 1917, speeches were made, that of the Admiral being received with manifest attention and enthusiastic approval. The final vote that night decided by 60 committees for, 3 against, to reverse in large part the vote of the preceding day and to support the Provisional Government; to restore arms and authority to the officers of the fleet and to arrest the agitators who were responsible for the propaganda against constituted authority. Vice Admiral Kolchak was not returned to office.[8]

For one moment an American admiral had succeeded in reversing the course of history and within one day, by personal force and eloquence, had suppressed a mutiny in the navy of a foreign power. One is left to wonder whether there is in all military history a single counterpart of this feat.

On June 24 the Glennon party went north on the same train as Admiral Kolchak, and for a time there was talk of a Russian naval mission to the United States under Kolchak's leadership. This project came to naught, but not before it had given rise to many rumors, the most extreme of which was a report that Admiral Kolchak was to command the United States navy. After receiving a stream of applications from Russian officers eager to transfer and serve under Kolchak, the U. S. Embassy was forced to issue a denial of the report. However, Admiral Kolchak was sent to the United States, where he remained for a short while before returning to Russia by way of Vladivostok. In Asia he worked at one time for the British, though it is not clear to this day in what capacity. At any rate, he finally was selected by dissident Russians to head the White forces in Siberia.

For practiced Communist agitators the defeat by Admiral Glennon was no more than a minor setback. They returned to the attack and by the time of the November Revolution had thoroughly undermined all authority, murdering more than 35 officers in the process. But in their efforts to convert the Sevastopol sailors into a hardened corps of loyal shock troops equal to those of the Kronstadt garrisons, they were relatively unsuccessful. A Sevastopol naval force pitted against the Don Cossacks not only deserted and plundered en route to battle, but was defeated on reaching the front.

Although neither the Germans nor the Turks offered a serious threat at sea, their land advances in early 1918 were causing the Bolsheviks considerable uneasiness. Orders were issued for the port of Novorossiisk to be prepared to receive the fleet, but at the same time, since no attack on the Crimea was expected, instructions were given not to interfere with the German operations. The Russian Danube Flotilla was withdrawn and the shores of the Danube evacuated because of the presence of Rumanian monitors. Instead of preparing to defend Sevastopol the local leaders merely led pogroms against officers (about 40 more were murdered) and the more prosperous townspeople. This situation continued until March 1918 when the workingmen of Sevastopol, organized to fight the lawlessness of the sailors, succeeded in putting a stop to night thefts and murders.

German and Ukrainian troops met no resistance when they entered the Crimea in April 1918. In a state of chaos and panic, Red groups had by then fled to Sevastopol, whence they left the country on supply ships. Admiral Sablin was called out of retirement and given dictatorial powers. On April 12 he stated that the Black Sea Fleet had become Ukrainian. This prospect was so unsatisfactory to most of the crews that 14 destroyers and four supply ships left: they entered Novorossiisk on May 14. Learning that the German advance was continuing, Admiral Sablin ordered all ships able to do so to put to sea and detailed Rear Admiral Ostrogradsky to take an explosives party of 100-120 men and blow up the remainder. The plan miscarried when the Germans, supported by the *Goeben* and *Breslau*, arrived earlier than expected and the men who were to have opened the boom defense to allow the Russian ships to leave, ran away instead. When the booms were finally opened only the *Volia* (ex-*Aleksandr III*) had time to get away to Novorossiisk. German artillery opened fire on the other ships at pointblank range. The *Svobodnaia Rossiia* (ex-*Yekaterina II*) was hit several times but only one Russian gunner disobeyed orders by returning the German fire. *Gnevny* ran aground and was then blown up. It was the only destroyer to be thus lost, the explosives party supposed to destroy the ships having fled. The new Ukrainian flag was then raised over all remaining ships, and Rear Admiral Ostrogradsky was rewarded for his treachery by being given command under German protection. After the armistice, when the Germans retreated before a British landing, the British exploded the machinery and boilers of the old battleships and sank 12 submarines to prevent their seizure by the Bolsheviks.

The ships that had escaped to Novorossiisk found themselves under the nominal suzerainty of the Kuban-Black Sea Soviet Republic. While a group of southern Bolshevik leaders were concentrated in the area, their authority was far from complete, and they requested naval help in suppressing irregular and rebellious Red forces. The fleet personnel persuaded Admiral Sablin to take charge, and on May 17, 1918, he ran up the St. Andrew flag, a clear challenge to the local Bolsheviks who had the desire but lacked the strength to get rid of him. In the two companies of sailors organized to keep order and restore discipline there were many who favored a campaign of killing Bolsheviks. A heavy exodus of local Communists resulted from the airing of this suggestion. The ships' boilers were then cleaned, engines tested, and destroyers repaired—such maintenance being long overdue but almost unknown among Russian ships in 1918. Before the Soviets turned off the supply Sablin also obtained some badly needed oil.

A week after his arrival Admiral Sablin received a letter from German Field Marshal Eichorn demanding that the ships be returned to Sevastopol on pain of a continued German push along the coast. This threat had serious implications, since Novorossiisk was the last available Black Sea port, Tuapse being too shallow for the big ships. Admiral Sablin replied, denying there had been any breach of the Treaty of Brest-Litovsk but offering to send representatives to talk the matter over with the Germans. Eichorn made no reply but kept watch on the Russian ships by seaplane and submarine. Meanwhile the Germans continued their advance as far as the Isthmus of Kerch and at the same time brought heavy pressure on Moscow to compel the surrender of the ships. The Reds, who much preferred that their ships be sunk rather than fall into German hands, hoped to throw the responsibility for the decision on the sailors. When the officers made this proposal, the indignant crews chased away the Red commissars. By secret ballot on June 28 the men voted to return to Sevastopol. The local populace demonstrated against the decision, and hundreds of sailors left their ships. Finally two lines of action were taken. The *Volia*, six destroyers, and the converted cruiser *Troian* left for Sevastopol; the *Svobodnaia*

Rossiia, nine destroyers, a supply ship, and eight subchasers remained. The battleship was then torpedoed repeatedly by the destroyer *Kerch*. The sea cocks were opened on all other ships, and they sank in deep water.

The armistice found the Germans spread out along the Black Sea almost as widely as they had been in the Baltic. However, that was the end of any similarity between the two areas. The French were the first of the Allies to arrive in the Black Sea, and they established a zone around Odessa and later occupied Sevastopol. Their naval forces in the Black Sea were never involved in the same kind of minor naval war as were the British in the Baltic. Moreover, some of their crews were decidedly receptive to Red propaganda and refused to fight the Soviets. When the Germans were forced to evacuate the area, they gave up their gains not to the Bolsheviks but rather to the White Russian forces of General Denikin and his successor, Baron Wrangel.

In the Black Sea proper, the Whites, aided to some extent by the Allies, controlled the remnants of the fleet and held clear-cut naval superiority over the Reds. The principal naval forces consisted of the dreadnought *General Alekseev* (ex-*Volta*), the old battleship *Georgy Pobedonosets*, the cruiser *Kornilov* (ex-*Ochakov*, ex-*Kagul*), five new and five old destroyers, three torpedo boats, a gunboat, and four submarines, together with the naval bases at Sevastopol and Nikolaev. The Whites also organized river flotillas for service on the Don, Bug, Dnieper, and Dniester rivers. Had this strength been properly used, it could have made the task of the Bolsheviks much harder. As it was, the ships were asked to get along almost without repairs, ammunition, and coal. They managed nevertheless to give some support to White land forces by gunfire, transport, and support of the seaward flanks.

Following their defeat on land, the White Russians fell back into the Crimea only to be forced later to move out in large numbers. With the assistance of Allied warships and commercial vessels, the remnants of the Black Sea Fleet, carrying some 146,200 refugees and commanded by Rear Admiral Kedrov, departed for Constantinople between October 29 and November 10, 1920. Between November 14 and 23 all the approximately 120 ships reached their destination. The refugees were permitted to intern in French North

Africa. This second leg of their voyage was made in echelons which reached Bizerte between December 22, 1920, and February 17, 1921. At Bizerte the force came under the command of Rear Adm. M. Behrens. Here the ships, which had no legal owners, presented a problem. A few were put to use as floating hotels or schools; four were taken over by the French navy as mine vessels or oilers; most gradually rotted. From 1921 to 1924 (when France recognized the U.S.S.R.) White Russians daily raised and lowered the St. Andrew flag over their ships and even conducted a naval school and government of Russia in exile. Finally, in 1936, after most of the vessels had decayed, the French ordered the remainder broken up and the proceeds of their sale distributed to Russian émigrés.[9]

THE WHITE SEA

In the Arctic as in the Baltic, the Russian revolution brought about an extremely complicated situation. Russian naval forces there were limited; indeed, the British, the French, and later the Americans actually operated more ships from the ports of Murmansk and Arkhangelsk than did the Russians themselves. Here ships' crews were as demoralized by the revolution as those in the Baltic, though they were not so quickly affected. Early in 1918, when the Soviet government disbanded the Russian navy, many sailors left; and for a time thereafter the cruiser *Askold* and four Russian destroyers were operated by Allied crews. With the interruption of normal railroad traffic, immense ammunition dumps began to accumulate which the Allies were reluctant to surrender to the Soviets in view of Lenin's determination to end Russian participation in the war. Further, there was a distinct danger of the supplies being captured by the Germans after their invasion of Finland in April 1918.

These considerations, together with Allied eagerness to aid Russian factions interested in continuing the war, accounted for a minor but vigorous intervention involving British, French, and American forces under the command of the British General Poole. The first occupation, at Arkhangelsk in August 1918, caused the Red regime to flee. But the Allied forces were at first more strongly anti-German than anti-Bolshevik (on at least one occasion they cooperated with the Bolsheviks to protect Russian territory from seizure by the White Finns, who were at the time being aided by the Germans), and to this end they were consistently interested in protecting the northern supply line regardless of what ally was on the opposite end. At one time they sought to assist in the evacuation of pro-Allied Czechoslovak troops anxious to fight the Germans. But Allied intervention in the White Sea also involved, among other things, support of a counter-revolution in Arkhangelsk, begun for the purpose of restoring the conservatives to power; training and arming Russian peasants to fight the Bolsheviks; protection of the north Russian railways; an amphibious expedition down the Northern Dvina River; and the advance of a small international army to within 300 miles of Petrograd.

A substantial number of naval engagements took place in the White Sea area and on the Northern Dvina. Here the Reds had about fifteen steamers of 40 to 300 tons, with patrol boats, minelayers, and gunboats available at their main northern naval base at Petrozavodsk on Lake Ladoga. The Red flotillas were commanded by former naval officers operating under the supervision of commissars. British and White naval forces in the area varied in size but generally consisted mainly of small steamers and coastal motor boats with a few seaplanes in support. The White flotilla was manned by regular naval personnel, whereas some of the British crews were soldiers serving under naval officers. On August 9, 1918, in a river engagement on the Dvina, the Reds captured the British steamer *Zaria*. Five days later the Reds lost the steamer *Moguchy*. The next day a British motor boat was blown up on a mine. The small British monitor *M-252* sank a Red steamer. After these skirmishes the British withdrew for the winter, and for the next seven months very little happened.

Then, in early May 1919, a Red advance up the Dvina with army forces and a river flotilla was repulsed. During the summer months the British lost two trawlers and a motor boat to mines. And farther south, British and White Russian forces entered Lake Onega from the north to make what was initially a very good showing: on August 13 the White Russian flotilla—a yacht and three patrol boats under Captain Kara-dindzhan—encountered and defeated a much more heavily armed Red flotilla. Two of the four Red ships were forced ashore and one was captured. On the same day two British motor launches captured a Red tug. Unfortunately, such successes proved illusory. The Reds strengthened their flotilla from the Baltic and regained command of the lake, and on land the Whites were forced to retreat.

The Allied intervention in the north had involved only about 15,000 soldiers, very small naval assistance, and comparatively limited White forces. By September 1919 the British realized they would have to make a far greater effort if the Bolsheviks were to be dislodged. Since they were unwilling to risk the large commitment that would have been necessary, they destroyed the supply dumps and withdrew their land and river forces to Arkhangelsk. A few White Russians managed to escape by sea, but more were executed by the Reds. In March 1920 the Bolshevik occupation of Murmansk marked the end both of the Civil War and of Allied intervention in the Arctic.[10]

THE FAR EAST

The Russian revolution was several months late in reaching the Far East. When it finally arrived, it encountered a great deal of opposition from White Russian forces. The issue in eastern Siberia was by no means a simple one of Red versus White Russians, however. Here the principal Allies had united to send into Siberia joint landing forces—some 10,000 for each ally, though the French and British soon withdrew. In June 1918 small Bolshevik groups holding Vladivostok were driven out by an international army which arrived in foreign ships. In September 1918 an American force of some 9,000 men under Gen. William S. Graves debarked; the Japanese landed 72,000 men at about the same time. The motives behind these landings were never completely clear, although there were claims that the troops were there to expedite the evacuation of Czechoslovak troops through Siberia. The Japanese occupied territory as far west as Lake Baikal and indicated that they hoped to exploit the country on a permanent basis. They remained in the area until 1922. The Americans withdrew in April 1920.

Naval warfare of small dimensions took place from 1918 to the end of 1922. The Amur Flotilla, composed mainly of river monitors, river gunboats, and motor boats based on Khabarovsk, was operated at various times by the Whites, Reds, and Japanese, and suffered heavy damage each time it changed hands. For example, in September 1921, when pressure from the Reds forced them to evacuate Khabarovsk, the Japanese sank the river gunboat *Korel*, destroyed the guns of several other ships, and took with them, first to Niko-laevsk and finally to Sakhalin, seven of the better boats as well as machine parts from the others. The stolen ships were returned much later, in 1925, when the Japanese surrendered northern Sa-khalin to the Soviet Union.

On the seacoast, where most of the ships were in the hands of the Whites, there was also minor naval activity. After the territory about Vladivostok had changed hands several times it came to form part of the Far Eastern Republic, which was nominally independent but actually a Bolshevik satellite state. On May 26, 1921, with consider-able assistance from the Japanese, the Whites in Vladivostok revolted and announced the formation of a Primorsk-Amur provi-sional government. The naval forces of this new state, first under Captain 2nd Rank Solovev and later under Rear Adm. Y. C. Stark, consisted of a gunboat, six transports, 14 torpedo boats, and about 26 other craft, all with small crews. However, on September 23 a steamer carrying 80 officers and 200 seamen from the Caspian Flotilla entered Vladivostok. The newcomers became the nucleus of a navy of about 1,300 officers and men. The ships, which were then in wretched shape, were cleaned and repaired to the extent that local facilities allowed. Despite its obvious weakness, this force was a great deal stronger than the two five-ship Bolshevik squadrons that were based on the Bay of St. Olga and the Tatar Strait.

The varied activities of the Siberian Flotilla included gunfire and transportation support of the White Army forces, blockade duty off Red-held ports, and on occasion supply of naval infantry and land-ing parties. In the only direct conflict that occurred between White and Red naval forces the *Patrokl* took the Red cutter *Pavel*. In November 1921 a small task force under Captain 1st Rank Ilin was detached to give close support to White army units who suc-ceeded in recapturing the city of Khabarovsk; but when the Whites attempted to move farther west, the tide turned. When the last reserves from Vladivostok were committed to action (their places in guarding the city being taken by naval personnel), the effort proved insufficient: the Whites lost Khabarovsk and went into retreat. They held ground to the south and east for a time, despite a withdrawal of Japanese support, but in a battle on October 13–14, 1922, they were beaten decisively. The ships of the flotilla were evacuated—first to Gensan, Korea, and ultimately in most instances to Shanghai.

THE INTERNAL WATERWAYS

The period from 1918 to 1922 witnessed a great deal of naval activity along Russia's major rivers and lakes. Unfortunately, the story of that activity is one that probably will never be told in its entirety. Documentation from both Red and White sources is incomplete, often violently prejudiced, and so lacking in detail that even Soviet historians avidly searching for favorable material on this phase of Russia's naval history have been forced to deal in generalities. However, it is possible to note the nature and scope of the fighting and, in some instances, to supply a few particulars.

During the civil war the Bolsheviks held one great naval advantage over the Whites. Because nearly all of the Baltic Fleet remained in Soviet possession, it was possible for the Reds to transfer the fleet's smaller craft, usually via inland waterways, to other parts of Russia. Thus though they were unable to accomplish much in the Baltic against the British, they moved destroyers, torpedo boats, submarines, gunboats, and patrol boats—in fact nearly every kind of small vessel—to inland trouble spots. They also transferred their best naval personnel. Meanwhile the Whites were compelled to rely largely on haphazardly recruited personnel with little naval experience, and on whatever merchant vessels, barges, or river steamers might be at hand.

In the course of the intervention and the civil war, flotillas serving primarily to assist the Red army were created on the Northern Dvina to fight the English; on the Dnieper and Bug in 1920 to fight the Poles; on Lakes Ladoga, Piepus, Onega, and Baikal, the Caspian and Azov seas, and the Amur, Kama, and Volga rivers to fight the

Whites. These flotillas transported troops, defended the river and lake flanks of land forces, gave artillery support to troops, laid and swept mines, brought in supplies, and in a few instances engaged in pitched naval battles with White flotillas.

The nature of the problem presented to the Whites can be illustrated by the experiences of Admiral Kolchak's forces. In late 1918, when Admiral Kolchak was made supreme commander by the White Russian council of ministers, he announced the formation of a naval ministry. At that time he had no ships, no guns, and very few sailors. But in mid-December, when Perm (modern Saratov) was taken by the Whites, they seized craft left by the Bolsheviks. After several months spent in getting equipment and armament, they put together a river flotilla consisting of *Strashny* (four 3-inch guns), *Silny* (four 3-inch guns), *Gordy* (three 75-mm. guns), *Grozny* (three 4.7-inch guns), *Kent* (four 12-pounder guns), *Suffolk* (one 6-inch gun, as the vessel was a barge), and *Bystry* (four 3-inch guns). This makeshift flotilla was used mainly for artillery support of the army. Nevertheless, it fought in one full-sized engagement at the junction of the Kama and Viatka rivers with a somewhat larger Red flotilla. One White vessel was put out of action in the encounter, and the Whites retreated. Three later river battles were fought, but the flotilla was never able to do more than delay the Bolshevik forces, which finally pushed on to Perm and forced the Whites to evacuate. The Whites then retreated into Siberia and their river flotillas disbanded, but the crews continued to fight on land.[11] Some of the men later joined a temporary Ob-Irtysh flotilla in Siberia.

THE CASPIAN

In the Caspian area the civil war and the intervention period involved not only the expected conflict between Reds and Whites but local independence movements, small-scale British intervention, military conquest by the Turks, and a substantial amount of naval action as well. As early as January 1918 the British had considered sending a small force under General Dunsterville from Baghdad to Engeli, Persia, on the south coast of the Caspian. The objective was to assist General Bicharakov's Cossack force in resisting both the Turks, who were threatening the Caucasus, and the Bolsheviks. In May 1918 Georgia, Armenia, and Azerbaidzhan all declared their independence and attempted to negotiate recognition from the Turks and the Germans. Their attempts failed, and in the summer of 1918 the Turks struck through Armenia at Baku on the Caspian. At the moment, Baku was held by a weak Red force which had just defeated a small army of Tatars. The Caspian Fleet, though loyal to this Red regime, was in a state of demoralization.

In June the British moved the Dunsterville Force to Engeli and in August to Baku, ousting the Reds and installing a White regime. Most of the crews of warships and merchant vessels in the Caspian were persuaded without undue difficulty to support the White regime, and by organizing the ships into a flotilla under Capt. David T. Norris, the British were able to hold complete dominance of the big lake. The small British land forces had less success. In September 1918 they were forced out of Baku by a Turkish army which immediately instituted a slaughter of Armenians. With the collapse of the Central Powers the British once more moved into Baku, where they held fairly effective control until they left in the summer of 1919.

Well before the British departure, the White Russian forces of General Bicharakov had taken independent steps to establish a naval force of their own. After some delays a detachment of officers and men from the Black Sea Fleet arrived on March 22, 1919, at Petrovsk in the northern Caspian. The British were at that time unwilling to transfer any of their own ships, so the White Russians put together a detachment of castoffs—cutters, motor boats, fishing smacks, and small merchant steamers which were armed with mines and small guns. Meantime the Bolsheviks had organized a squadron consisting of three steamers and five old destroyers from the Baltic. In May the British Caspian Flotilla soundly defeated this Red force, sinking several ships and demoralizing the remaining crews.

The next month the British started to withdraw. They now transferred most of their flotilla, which included several large steamers and eight coastal motor boats, to White Russian forces which had already been strengthened by additional experienced personnel from the Black Sea, and for the time being the Whites held naval superiority. A number of Red naval officers from Astrakhan also attempted to join them, but most of these men were captured and executed by the Bolsheviks. The principal duties of the White Caspian Flotilla were to support land forces along the shores of the northwest Caspian, to escort convoys, to conduct reconnaissance missions, and to evacuate the wounded. In carrying out these activities the White flotilla lost two vessels to mines and joined in battle with Red naval forces repeatedly—more often than not successfully. Red forces continued to increase: in late 1919 they included 11 torpedo boats and destroyers, four small submarines, four schooners, 17 coast-defense vessels, and eight cutters. However, it was not the rising strength of the Red naval forces but rather the defeats on land, first of Denikin and then of Wrangel, that eventually made the Caspian Flotilla insecure. After Wrangel's defeat and the loss of its bases at Baku and Petrovsk, the squadron moved to Engeli, where the ships were returned to the British. About 80 officers and 200 men reached Basra and were transported aboard the *Franz Ferdinand* to Vladivostok, where they joined the Siberian Flotilla.[12]

CHAPTER 17

Rise of the Red Navy

(1922-40)

T HE END OF THE CIVIL WAR marked the nadir of Russian naval power. The country over which the Bolsheviks were finally able to maintain control showed marked devastation from border to border. Internationally, the new regime was a pariah which no established government was willing to recognize. Territorially, the Soviet Union was weakened by the *cordon sanitaire* of new states created out of territory previously Russian and allied to France. Finland, Estonia, Latvia, Lithuania, and Poland had all achieved independence at Rusian expense, while Rumania had extended her borders by the annexation of Bessarabia. The Russian window to the west on the Baltic, smaller than at any time since the reign of Peter the Great, included only Leningrad and a small strip of the Gulf of Finland. Petrograd was within artillery range of Finland. The Baltic peoples, who had been the only "natural sailors" in Tsarist Russia, were now independent of Soviet rule. Finally, the Soviets were for the time being confined within limited borders even in the Far East, for Japanese troops had not yet evacuated eastern Siberia.

In a naval sense the 1917–22 period was significant for two further reasons. First, events of the war had emphasized the importance of sea power. Second, the imperial Russian navy had been reduced to junk. The first theme requires some elaboration.

During the period of intervention and civil war the Allied blockade of Russian ports had prevented needed goods from reaching the country, with the result that there had been extensive suffering and the Bolsheviks had been forced to rely on their own resources. But this was only one side of the picture. The various White Russian forces had at the same time enjoyed secure lines of communication over the ocean lanes and had been fed supplies which the Reds, lacking sea power, were unable to disrupt. This lesson was not lost on the followers of Lenin, but it was to be some time before the new regime would or could apply it. After all, the creation of a new fleet was not one of the top-priority tasks facing the Bolsheviks; there were even more important problems to be solved. For about a decade after the close of the civil war Soviet policy was mainly isolationist, and very little news of any kind was circulated regarding the navy. Such efforts at rehabilitation as were made lacked the necessary support to be successful. The ill-fated revolt of the Kronstadt sailors had tended to make the Bolshevik leaders somewhat wary of a strengthened navy. Indeed, Lenin might have scuttled the remnants of the Baltic Fleet had he not been persuaded against this course by the militarily more astute Trotsky.

Under any circumstances the rehabilitation of Soviet sea power would have been a most formidable task—far harder than the rehabilitation of the army. At the end of the civil war the Black Sea Fleet had almost ceased to exist, most of the ships having either sunk, escaped to Bizerte, or been damaged to the point of ineffectiveness. Only a handful of mine craft, destroyers, and submarines were left in working condition. In the Baltic the four *Borodinos*, launched but not finished, were scrapped—two being towed to Germany for demolition. The three remaining older battleships (now named *Andrei Pervozvanny, Grazhdanin*, and *Respublika*) and the prewar cruisers were also broken up after cannibalization for guns to be used ashore and spare parts. Each of the new Baltic states fell heir to a few small warships. The four dreadnoughts were maintained, together with eight destroyers and a few submarines, but usually no more than one dreadnought was in active service at a time. Such efforts as were made to keep ships in good condition were expended on the destroyers, submarines, and mine craft. Most of the prewar ships in these categories had disappeared—some going to the Baltic states, others lost to poor handling or incompetent maintenance. By 1921 there were only five submarines and about fifteen destroyers left of the wartime fleet. Some unfinished light cruisers and destroyers and a few submarines from early programs were left on the stocks. Also a few small craft were at Vladivostok and in the Arctic and some gunboats and small craft were stationed on the Caspian, Volga, Amur, and Dnieper. For years training and upkeep had been so neglected that nearly all the ablest officers who had not been killed had escaped from Russia. Shore establishments were in chaotic condition, and navy-supported industries were prostrate.

Considering its condition at the close of the war, it is amazing that the Red navy could revive at all. Yet it not only revived in less than a generation; it actually lost less ground in world naval competition than might have been expected.

The last statement becomes credible when it is recalled that the decade from 1922 to 1932 was a comparatively peaceful and stable period in which naval limitation treaties retarded maritime progress. The Soviet Union was not a participant in the 1922 Washington Treaty on Naval Limitation or in the related Nine Power and Four Power treaties affecting the Far East; yet she received substantial benefits from these agreements. The ten-year moratorium on the building of battleships, the scrapping of many vessels in other navies, and the qualitative limitations placed on future battleships, airplane carriers, and cruisers, as well as the maximum tonnage permitted each naval power, were all of definite if indirect value to the Red navy in that they greatly slowed the pace of naval development elsewhere during a period when Russia was in no condition to compete. Moreover, Japanese withdrawals from China and Siberia gave the Soviets a new measure of security from territorial aggression.

For six years following the Washington conference the Red navy made virtually no progress. For a time it was even necessary to employ German mechanics to do essential upkeep work on the few remaining ships. Former tsarist officers who had changed color with the times formed the nucleus of the greatly reduced officer corps available to train crews, but training was an uphill effort even though the Bolsheviks had hastened to reestablish naval discipline. Gunnery, torpedo, and mine schools, together with two cadet ships,

a small air station, and a ship for mechanics, were maintained at
Kronstadt. Maneuvers were conducted in the Baltic in 1922, 1925,
and 1926; each time they were marred by a multitude of accidents,
blunders, and breakdowns. In 1926, for example, an exercise of two
battleships, ten destroyers, and several cruisers and submarines in
the Gulf of Finland resulted in one lost torpedo boat (it struck a
mine), two collisions of destroyers, a turret explosion on the battleship *Marat*, and a submarine lost after it struck bottom. While such
accidents were caused mainly by unskilled handling, they also
reflected to some extent the worn-out state of the Red navy's materiel. The Communist leaders were well aware of these deficiencies
but made only occasional and halfhearted efforts to correct them.
Leon Trotsky, commissar of defense and head of both army and
navy, was too busy with other concerns to give much attention to
his expressed interest in naval aviation programs, and although
shipbuilding programs were announced from time to time they produced scant results aside from a few new icebreakers and mining
vessels and the completion of submarines and destroyers that had
been on the stocks for years. There was also a certain amount of
repair to dockyards and industrial plants serving the navy. Apart
from these efforts the material condition of the naval establishment
deteriorated steadily.

In connection with this picture, one should keep clearly in mind
the limitations of the Soviet system at the time. Given the degree of
devastation in Russia and the undeveloped condition of industries
on which a navy necessarily depends, it is doubtful if the Soviet
leaders could have accomplished much more than they did before
1928. Until old industries were rehabilitated and new ones established and until technical personnel were trained and available,
there could be no real revival of sea power.

Given these considerations, the period from 1922 to 1928 was not
wholly unproductive. In 1922 Germany and the Soviet Union, both
international outcasts, signed the Treaty of Rapallo, by which the
Soviet regime received its first diplomatic recognition. This agreement was advantageous to the Soviets in at least two ways. In the
first place, it paved the way for a series of pacts providing for both
nonaggression and political recognition—pacts which were to result
in complete international acceptance of the Soviet regime about a

decade later. It also bore benefits from a naval standpoint. One of
the Soviets' greatest needs was for the technical information and
human skills necessary to rehabilitate their navy; these the Germans
were well equipped to supply. A compensating factor to Germany
was the possibility that the manufacture of weapons in the Soviet
Union might offer a means by which she could get around the provisions of the Versailles Treaty. Hence, from 1922 to 1930 a series of
naval exchanges took place, involving visits, sales of plans, and
transfer of intelligence between the two countries.

The first German naval mission arrived in the U.S.S.R. in 1922. At
that time the Soviets acquired plans for wartime submarine types;
received advice in addition to orders and manuals on training, shipbuilding, airplane catapults, and engines; and benefited by information on wartime experience.

From the 1926 German naval mission headed by Adm. Arno
Spindler, historian of the U-boat war, the Russians got plans for
the B-III type of U-boat which later became the basis of the Soviet
S class. During this exchange, however, whereas the Russians were
generally eager and willing to accept any help, the Germans tended
to become increasingly cautious and uncommunicative. Talks concerning a possible wartime cooperation against Poland or against
France and Poland did not result in an agreement, and it was clear
the Russians were gaining far more in the exchange than the Germans. In any case, the Germans had already discovered other ways
of evading the Versailles Treaty. After 1930 they adopted a naval
policy which, by emphasizing the maintenance of good relations
with Great Britain, the United States, and the Baltic states, virtually
precluded a close relationship with the Soviets.

Unable to build new ships, the Russians attempted to acquire
additional vessels by salvaging a number of their own and foreign
ships sunk in home waters. The *Novik* was raised in 1934, sank
again, and was salvaged a second time. The British submarine *L-55*
was also raised (as a gesture of good will the Soviet Union shipped
the remains of the crew members home to Great Britain) and was
finally used in the design of a new class of Soviet submarines. At
the same time, the Soviets attempted to discourage navigation of the
Black Sea and the Baltic by nonriparian states. And though they
shied away from the French quid pro quo, the assumption of tsarist

debts, they repeatedly demanded the return of the vessels at Bizerte.

Probably because of the Kronstadt mutiny, the political reconstruction of the navy outweighed its material reconstruction in the
minds of Bolshevik leaders. The officer corps was suspect because of
its aristocratic background, but at the same time the navy could not
be operated without officers. Faced with this dilemma, the Soviet
leaders hedged: in 1924 they purged about 750 officers. Since a
large proportion of those left had non-working-class backgrounds,
the Soviets fed into the navy hundreds of Komsomols (young communists). Whatever their technical limitations, they proved to be
politically reliable and filled with revolutionary ardor. In 1922,
3,000 were taken in after brief naval schooling and from 1923 to
1927 at least 10,000 more were trained.

Though the Soviet leaders were believers in education, they did
not at once make revolutionary changes in this field. Rear Admiral
Klado, who had made the transition to the new regime without too
much difficulty, was director of the naval academy immediately
after the revolution. For the time being old naval doctrines continued to be taught, partly due to the tolerance of Trotsky (who did
not believe that Marxism could be applied to war), and partly
because the Soviet leaders, then far more concerned with the army,
did not take the time to reevaluate policies or to formulate any naval
philosophy. It is significant, however, that a congress of Communist
marines and soldiers in April 1922 passed resolutions favoring close
naval cooperation with the army and rejecting both the battleship
and submarine theories of sea power.

About the only test of Soviet sea power in the decade following
the Civil War occurred in 1929 in Manchuria, against the Chinese
warlord Chang Hsueh-liang. The Chinese leader, irritated by Soviet
political propaganda, closed the Soviet consulate in Mukden,
arrested a consul, and moved against the Chinese Eastern Railroad
(originally built by the Russians in the days of the tsars with
capital obtained in France). The Soviet government demanded a
withdrawal of anti-Soviet measures; and when the Chinese refused
to yield, there was a brief period of warfare. The Amur River
Flotilla, which had been considerably strengthened since 1922,
proved far superior to Chinese river forces on the Amur and the
Sungari. Here the flotilla covered the retreat of an outnumbered

Soviet force, bombarded villages, captured nine Chinese river boats, and interfered constantly with Chinese troop movements.

During the 1920s the Soviet state participated in the first of a series of disarmament efforts while simultaneously seeking to protect its sea approaches through peace settlements and nonaggression pacts. But in 1922 it proposed closure of the Baltic to ships of nonriparian states and refused to include the Red navy in disarmament talks. Two years later, at the Rome Naval Disarmament Conference, it opposed the Lausanne Treaty demilitarizing the Dardanelles and refused to discuss limitations of capital ships. And when, at the invitation of the Council of the League of Nations, representatives of major and minor naval powers met at Geneva in 1925 to discuss the best methods of limiting naval armaments of the smaller states, the attitude of the Soviet Union prevented any progress. Specifically, Soviet representative M. Berens stated that though his country wished to maintain its 1921 tonnage of 540,000, it would accept 280,000 tons—provided the Council of the League was replaced by another organization, the Bosphorus and Dardanelles were closed, ships of nonriparian states were not allowed in the Baltic, the Korea Straits were disarmed, and the interned ships at Bizerte were returned to Russia. Since the experts were not even authorized to discuss such terms, much less accept them, an impasse followed. This offer is of considerable interest, since it exemplifies a tactic that in later years became all too common: an apparently generous offer was tendered, with impossible and nonnegotiable conditions attached. When the inevitable rejections followed, the assertion could be made that Soviet attempts at disarmament were frustrated by the capitalist countries.

In 1927 the Soviet Union proposed "complete, immediate, universal, and simultaneous disarmament" without going into any details as to how such a step was to be achieved. Again the outcome was rejection, and again the proposal and its defeat were exploited in Soviet propaganda.

Soviet progress in shipbuilding prior to the first five-year plan (1929) was limited to the completion of vessels already on the building ways. Three of the prewar light cruisers were finished: *Profintern* (ex-*Svetlana*)[1] of 6,800 tons, and *Krasny Kavkaz* (ex-*Lazarev*) and *Chervonaia Ukraina* (ex-*Admiral Nakhimov*),

7,600 tons. Speed was 30 knots. Each ship was equipped to carry 100 mines and to operate two seaplanes. The main battery comprised 15 5.1-inch guns in the case of the *Profintern* and *Chervonaia Ukraina*, and four 7.1-inch and 12 3.9-inch antiaircraft guns for the *Kavkaz*. Seventeen fairly modern destroyers of 1,260–1,610 tons, 35 knots, and nine to 12 torpedo tubes were also maintained, though most of these were completed before the war. Submarines were of small size, ranging from 355 to 650 tons. Naval policy, so far as any may be said to have prevailed, emphasized isolation and extreme secrecy; some interest was shown in naval aviation, in minelaying, and in flotilla craft; there was apparently no interest in capital ships and cruisers. Rarely was there more than one battleship in operating condition, and neither airplane carriers nor heavy cruisers were built. Defenses in both the Black Sea and the Baltic consisted of minefields and submarines; there were a few gunboats in the Caspian.

THE FIVE-YEAR PLANS: LAYING AN INDUSTRIAL BASE

No genuinely important steps to rehabilitate the Red navy were taken until the inauguration of the first five-year plan in 1929, when a series of vitally important developments occurred. The five-year plans were conceived out of a Soviet determination to escape the backwardness that was the heritage of tsarism and to build a modern economy. They involved planning, heavy economic sacrifices, concentration on building capital goods, and the transformation of millions of ignorant peasants into trained industrial workers—all within a brief period of time. These developments formed the basis on which sea power might rest as certainly as had the activities of Peter the Great more than two centuries earlier. It is obvious that such projects as the improvement of port facilities, construction of a merchant marine, establishment of airplane factories, increase in steel production—to name only a few—were of great and tangible assistance to the navy. It would be too great an undertaking to cite all the other perhaps less obvious aspects of the five-year plans that were useful to the navy, but no history would be complete without mention of some of the more important ones.

Without question the greatest of these contributions lay in the fields of heavy industry and education. Undeveloped industries and uneducated seamen had plagued Russian sea power for three-quarters of a century, placing it at a critical disadvantage in contests with more advanced states. In attempting to cast off their nation's economic and educational backwardness the Soviet leaders were also laying the groundwork for great national power.

The new regime took up the improvement of internal waterways and navigation facilities. The completion in 1933 of the White Sea canal opened a link from the Baltic to the White Sea via several rivers and Lake Ladoga. The complex of installations for this canal included 19 locks, 15 dams, 12 sluice-gates, 49 dikes, and 33 secondary canals, and made it possible for ships as large as destroyers to be shifted with some dispatch between the Arctic and the Baltic.

The Volga-Don canal, first proposed by Peter the Great, was also undertaken, at last, though it was not completed until 1952. A third system of canals, the Volga-Moscow, permitted the use of naval facilities at the nation's capital and made possible a connection between the Baltic and the Caspian. In the Arctic, shipbuilding facilities were created at Arkhangelsk, Murmansk was developed, and a new base was established in the Kola Inlet at Polarnye. Completion of the Dnieper dam at Dnepropetrovsk linked the Ukraine with the Baltic and provided a water route around the Zaporozhe Rapids. Harbor facilities were modernized at Kherson, Batum, Baku, Mariupol, Vladivostok, and Murmansk. At Vladivostok construction capacity was increased; in 1937 a floating drydock was added, and an additional 6,000-ton drydock was towed from the Black Sea for use at Petropavlovsk. In addition, shipbuilding facilities were established at Komsomolsk on the Amur River.

Probably the most glamorous of the many improvements to navigation was the development of the northern sea route, another idea that had been under consideration for a long time. For more than three centuries intermittent attempts had been made to find a northeast passage, and in 1878–79 Nils Nordenskjöld in the *Vega* had traveled the entire length of the northern Siberia coast, a feat unequaled until 1914. The Russo-Japanese war focused attention on a possible Siberian route to the Far East, and before World War I there were some mild attempts to explore a possible northern route and to erect wireless and weather stations. The project held a commercial as well as a military attraction since, with the exception of the Amur, all the big Siberian rivers—the Ob, Yenisei, Lena, and Kolyma—flowed into the Arctic and offered a potentially cheap if hazardous export system.

Indeed, as early as 1912 this route had been advocated as an inexpensive outlet for wheat exports from the Yenisei area, and a commercial company had gone so far as to collect a small fleet of steamers for the purpose. These had been confiscated during the revolution. Immediately after the revolution Bolsheviks were too busy to pursue the northern route project. But in 1919 a preliminary move was made in the form of an expedition to the Kara Sea, a part of the Arctic Ocean lying between 70° north and the ice pack and so difficult of navigation that as late as 1924 only three ships had crossed it. Thereafter the gradual development of aerial reconnaissance of sea ice and the establishment of meteorological stations, plus the services of a handful of old icebreakers, made the navigation of first the Kara Sea, and later the entire northern sea route, more practicable. Because of lack of trade along the Kolyma and the Lena, development along the eastern end of the route was slower than in the western area. The 1920s witnessed many scientific expeditions to the Arctic in which personnel of the Red navy at times played a prominent part. In the summer of 1932 the *Sibiriakov*, a small (1,384-ton) icebreaker, journeyed from the Atlantic to the Pacific via northern Siberia.

After 1933 there was a decided increase in the use of Arctic waters as the government embarked on a sustained program of Arctic development. All shipping was in charge of the chief of administration of the northern sea route. Two of the men who held this position, O. Y. Shmidt (head until 1939) and Adm. Ivan Papanin (1939–46) were easily the foremost leaders in Russian Arctic development. In 1934 the icebreaker *Litke* made the first east-west traverse in a single season. The following year four freighters made the traverse, two from Pacific to Atlantic and two in the reverse direction. Though handicapped by antique icebreakers and severe ice conditions, the Soviets made the route north of Siberia increasingly usable for commercial and naval vessels during the short summer season of two to three months. In 1937, in an unusually bitter winter, no fewer than 26 vessels, including seven of the eight icebreakers, were caught in the ice and had to spend the winter at sea. The one remaining icebreaker, *Yermak*, rescued all but one of the ships during the following year. In 1938 the first new and improved 11,000-ton icebreakers, *Stalin* and *Kaganovich*, also came into service. Ten ships made the traverse that summer, and the *Stalin* became the first ship to make the round trip in one season. By the eve of World War II a limited but important navigation north of Siberia had passed the experimental stage and was in successful operation. In the development of this capacity to operate in far northern waters, the Russians were nearly two decades ahead of their American and Canadian neighbors.

To some degree Soviet interest in the Arctic affected foreign relations. In 1924 the Soviet Union sent a note to all foreign states claiming all territories claimed by the tsar in 1916. This note was probably a reaction to what the Soviets considered a case of trespassing. Canadians in 1921 had landed on Wrangel Island, one of the Arctic islands claimed by the tsars, and in 1923 that landing party had been reinforced by a new group. In 1926 the Soviets took forcible action: the *Krasny Oktiabr* reached the island, raised the Soviet flag, and arrested the Canadians. In 1929 the Soviets annexed the archipelago of Franz Josef Land and prior to World War II refused recognition to the Arctic claims of other countries, whose capitalistic natures, they contended, made impossible any efficient development of the Arctic.

REBUILDING THE FLEET

The five-year plans not only laid the basis for future naval strength, they also envisioned a new navy, to be created as rapidly as the expanding industrial base would permit. The first meaningful naval construction program was announced in 1928 as part of the first five-year plan. In its naval aspects this plan aimed at the creation of a modern shipbuilding industry and the completion of transports, merchant vessels, more than 400 towed and self-propelled barges, some submarines and small naval craft, and naval planes. But despite this marked progress the Soviets still lacked the capability to produce battleships, airplane carriers, large naval guns, turrets, armor plate, and main battery fire control machinery. Most of these lacks were remedied by the second five-year plan, which also called for the laying down of additional submarines, destroyers, and torpedo boats, and the modernization of old battleships. Under the third five-year plan consideration was given to three battleships, some cruisers and destroyers, a great many more submarines, and hosts of motor torpedo boats. Every plan called for steady expansion of facilities of all kinds.

Soviet shipbuilding under the five-year plans was at first unimpressive, handicapped as it was by poor workmanship and technical backwardness. However, after a period of trial and error (mainly the latter) the Soviets altered their policy of naval isolation and availed themselves of French and Italian and, to a lesser extent, American and German plans. In some instances foreign firms even built and delivered the ships, as in the days of the tsars. This method of enhancing sea power had some obvious limitations, for the ships so acquired rarely represented the best designs attainable, and they differed so greatly in structure and design as hardly to constitute a fleet.

Generally, the Soviet Union at this stage showed little interest in large ships. The four dreadnoughts were retained and from time to time refitted and overhauled. In 1931 the *Parizhskaia Kommuna* (ex-*Sevastopol*) and the cruiser *Profintern* were sent into the Black Sea, where they remained to strengthen the Black Sea Fleet to a point of near equality with the Turkish navy. Turkish sensibilities were partly soothed by an agreement whereby each power undertook to provide the other six months' notice of any increase in Black Sea forces.

In the years immediately preceding World War II, negotiations were opened with American firms looking to build 35,000-ton, 16-inch-gun battleships in American yards, but these efforts fell through as did Soviet attempts to obtain armor plate, large naval guns, and blueprints. A naval mission headed by Adm. I. S. Isakov, then vice commissar of naval affairs, failed because the U.S. Navy refused to discuss such classified matters as ship armament and design or to talk about very large battleships of, say, 62,000 tons. Efforts of the Soviets to obtain plans and specifications for the latest carriers also failed. After two and a half years the Russians had only empty hands to show for their exertions.

Following these disappointments the Soviets decided to build their own battleships, using some materials acquired abroad. Thereafter there were persistent but unconfirmed reports of large battleships being built in Russia. According to German sources one such ship, the *Krasnaia Ukraina,* was captured on the building ways at Nikolaev in 1941, and a similar vessel had been destroyed by the Russians before their retreat (the machinery intended for *Krasnaia Ukraina* was in Switzerland and was bought by the British to prevent its falling into German hands). The French *Les Flottes de Combat* for 1950 stated that two 45,000-ton ships with speeds of about 30 knots and armaments of nine 16-inch guns had been laid down in 1938, the *Sovetsky Soiuz* at Leningrad and the *Krasnaia Bessarabiia* at Nikolaev. The report of a third ship of the same type building at Leningrad or near Arkhangelsk turned out to be false. Projected building of aircraft carriers was left for the last year of the third five-year plan and then further postponed.

The uncertainty of reports regarding new battleships was typical during the period prior to World War II, for in those years little reliable information was available concerning the Red navy. Though the Soviet government from time to time made boastful announcements of progress, these announcements usually referred to a gross number of new ships without revealing whether the newcomers were tiny minesweepers or huge battleships. Sometimes progress would be represented in terms of a percentage increase over completions of the previous year, the latter always an unknown number. If the purpose of these indefinite and at times contradictory announcements was to mystify outsiders, it succeeded. Even such standard reference books as *Brassey's Naval Annual* and *Jane's Fighting Ships* for several years published the names of ships later found to be nonexistent.

The Red navy showed even less interest in aircraft carriers than in battleships and, except for one or two small vessels converted from ships of other types, paid no attention to tenders. Yet, paradoxically, Russian naval aviation was to become relatively strong after a laborious buildup from modest beginnings.

At first the Russians made use of seaplanes for a great many purposes not common elsewhere. Under the second five-year plan their program included 12 torpedo seaplanes, 63 bomber seaplanes, 242 fighter seaplanes, 86 reconnaissance seaplanes, 18 school seaplanes, six escort airships, and 16 observation balloons. *Savoia* flying boats were also purchased from Italy. These planes required mother ships; and for that purpose the Red navy operated a number of small seaplane tenders. About 35 Russian warships, including some of the larger destroyers as well as gunboats, icebreakers, and training ships, could carry planes. This dependence on seaplanes was mainly due to an early lack of technical knowledge on the part of Soviet airplane builders. During the 1930s, after the Soviet government concluded contracts with several German firms, land-based naval aircraft came into service in greater numbers. At the beginning of World War II about 700 aircraft of all types were in Soviet service.

In cruisers the Red navy scarcely kept pace with obsolescence. The *Kirov* class (8,800 tons, nine 7.1-inch guns, 34 knots) was based on plans drawn up by the Ansaldo firm in Italy. These ships were somewhat larger than those of the Italian *Condottieri* class, which they otherwise resembled. They were designed for great speed but had very little armor protection. Authorized in 1935, they were the first warships of any size built by the Soviets. Four of them, *Kirov*, *Maksim Gorky*, *Voroshilov*, and *Molotov*, were finished before World War II, and others of the same class were completed later. Far larger cruisers were considered, including a 22,000-ton class of battle cruisers carrying four 14-inch guns.

The French *Fantasque*, a very large destroyer, served as the model for about fifteen 2,900-ton *Leningrad* class flotilla leaders, only a few of which were finished prior to World War II. These were designed for a speed of 36 knots and carried five 5.1-inch and four 37-mm. antiaircraft guns, in addition to six torpedo tubes. They were unusually fast ships, but were regarded by foreign critics as highly deficient in antiaircraft protection. Many smaller destroyers and torpedo boats were also completed during the 1930s. The *Stremitelny* class destroyers of 1,800 tons, four 5.1-inch guns, and 37 knots were built from 1936 on. Torpedo boats of 500-700 tons, equipped to act as fast minelayers, were also built in considerable numbers. Finally, some of the older World War I destroyers—relatively good ships for their day—were reconstructed.

By far the greatest attention was given to submarines. As late as 1933 League of Nations sources credited the Red navy with no more than 16 submarines. This number may have been too small. It is certain that thereafter the undersea fleet increased in numbers very rapidly, to the point where the Red navy with an estimated 175 submarines in 1940 was regarded as numerically the strongest in the world.

As to quality of construction, the Soviet Union could make no such impressive claim to progress. The first new submarines were coastal-defense craft of about 215 tons, with very limited cruising radius and offensive capability. Further, they failed to give good service within these limitations. The next group of boats, built from 1934 to 1940 and intended for somewhat wider activities, were of the *Shch* class—about 500 tons with six 21-inch torpedo tubes and 13 knots surface speed. There was also a larger (800 to 1000-ton) class which resembled British submarines of the same size, in addition to the World War I vintage boats ranging from 350 to 650 tons and a few of miscellaneous types. The latter included a small number of 1,200-ton boats of the *Pravda* class, and some of the 650-ton *Nelim* class, laid down in 1937.

Since records were kept secret, the degree to which the Red navy was actually increased by rebuilding under the first three five-year plans is still impossible to determine. The 1930 edition of *Brassey's Naval Annual* gave the strength of the Red fleet as four battleships; six light cruisers; 17 fairly modern destroyers of 1,260-1,610 tons, 33-35 knots, four 4-inch guns, and 9-12 torpedo tubes; 35 destroyers of older vintage; and 21 submarines. This listing excluded the ships at Bizerte which the Russians claimed but could not recover and which the French finally broke up in 1936. Ten years later the same publication credited the Soviets with having four battleships (all modernized between 1931 and 1937), nine cruisers built or nearly finished, 36 destroyers and flotilla leaders, about 20 torpedo boats, and 150-175 submarines. There were also about 200 motor torpedo boats as well as 20 gunboats, nine minelayers, 14 minesweepers, one tanker, 14 icebreakers, four training ships, two guard ships, and six depot ships.

In the 1940 listing the number of minelayers and minesweepers is far too small; other sources indicate that many more ships of these two classes existed at the time. Mining operations received a very heavy emphasis in the Red fleet, and nearly all combat vessels possessed a minelaying capacity. Also, while the increase in total vessels between 1930 and 1940 was fairly modest in every class except submarines, the increase in fighting value was considerable. The 1930 list included virtually no ships laid down after 1916, while nearly all the torpedo craft listed in 1940 were new ships.

Naval shore facilities of all kinds were markedly improved during the early five-year plans. New naval bases were developed in the Arctic. The site at Polarnye (adjoining Murmansk and personally selected by Stalin), was blasted out of solid granite. Molotov (Perm) was a dockyard and warship building center close to Arkhangelsk. Outside the Arctic, the improvement of bases took the form of new dockyards and maritime industries at ports already in use as naval bases.

SOVIET NAVAL POLICY 1928–41

During the years of greatest naval weakness Soviet theoreticians paid comparatively little attention to the navy and the classical views of such naval academy men as Klado and M. G. Petrov were not brought into serious question. Diplomacy rather than naval strength was relied on for protection. Such naval doctrine as could be said to exist was of a purely defensive nature and emphasized cooperation with the army.

Russian naval thinking came to life about 1930 when A. P. Aleksandrov wrote a penetrating monograph criticizing the concept of command of the sea. His paper argued that modern warfare had demonstrated the impossibility of a close blockade, and that submarines, torpedo boats, and torpedo launches (i.e., defensive weapons) could be produced during a war. The rapid development of weapons, Aleksandrov contended, had changed the forms and methods of warfare to a point where production during war, rather than strength at the beginning of war, was the principal arbiter of victory. The essay argued that naval doctrine should be based not on history but on a defensive interpretation of the current five-year plan, that independent naval operations should be rejected and the doctrine of close coordination with the army proclaimed.

Aleksandrov's concept won the acceptance of Adm. R. A. Mukle-vich, then the navy's highest officer, who announced it in a 1931 speech to the sixteenth congress of the Communist Party. Muklevich went on to emphasize the notion of conducting a small war by submarines, mines, and naval aircraft. The January 1932 issue of *Morskoi sbornik* carried an article by M. Krupsky entitled "Toward Purging Marxist-Leninist Theory on Naval Questions," and during the early months of the year Adm. V. M. Orlov, then commander in chief of the navy, mercilessly attacked the classicists who believed in high-seas fleets built around battleships. Thereafter, Professors Petrov and B. Gervais of the Voroshilov naval war college, both classicist naval thinkers, were denounced and fined.

The new doctrine, though it routed the classicists in Russia who believed in command of the sea, was actually no more than a rationalization of the defensive naval policy which industrial and naval weakness had thrust on the Russians. The goal of command of the seas would present the navy with strategic problems not neces-sarily related to those of the army. In tactics, the new school approved of "combined attack" by surface, air, and submarine forces. Great battles of the past were not considered of interest, but guidance was to be found in the experiences of the Russian civil war with its emphasis on guerrilla activities. Training was to be based on conditions in the theater and on the weapons available. Torpedoes, aerial torpedoes, bombs, and mines would be used on a huge scale in war. In battle the problem would be one of close cooperation between all kinds of ships and coastal defenses. Persistence and aggressiveness would be in great demand. Air attacks would be especially important.

Though the concepts of the "new school" were accepted for sev-eral years with little dissent, they were not in harmony with the changing facts of either international relations or Soviet industriali-zation and were therefore not likely to prove lasting. In Manchuria the displacement of a weak and divided China by a militant Japan was an unpleasant development for the Russians. The 1933 acces-sion in Germany of Adolf Hitler, with his claim to being a savior of the people from Bolshevism, was even less propitious. Then in 1934 Japan denounced the Washington and London naval treaties which, as noted earlier, had been of considerable indirect value to the Soviets; in 1935 Germany abrogated the Versailles Treaty; and in 1936 came the announcement that Italy, Japan, and Germany had signed the Anti-Komintern Pact.

Each new development made rapprochement with the West seem increasingly desirable to the Soviets. However, years of accumulated mutual fear and suspicion, plus the British and French hope of channeling fascist aggression toward the Soviet Union, continued to prevent anything resembling an alliance. Soviet efforts to order battleships built by American firms fell through, and even the conclusion of a somewhat meaningless naval limitation agreement in 1937, when naval limitation itself was for practical purposes a dead issue, required long and time-consuming diplomacy.

Meanwhile, the buildup of Soviet industry had proceeded to a stage where genuine naval reconstruction was becoming possible. The assumption of Soviet industrial ineffectiveness which was clearly inherent in the views of the "new school" was, at least by implication, a criticism of Stalin himself. Never wholly a convert to the narrow seas concept, Stalin had taken steps to reestablish Soviet sea power in its four traditional areas and to secure battleships even before naval expansion on a large scale was practicable. The Black Sea Fleet, virtually destroyed during the civil war, was reestablished in 1930 following the transfer of the *Parizhskaia Kommuna* and *Profintern*. Two years later the Pacific Fleet was established, and in 1933 the Northern Fleet. For some time all three of these fleets were quite weak; at no time prior to World War II did any one of them contain many large ships. The 1935 maneuvers in the Pacific, for example, involved five destroyers, 15 submarines, and some planes, but nothing larger. German press reports in 1937 credited the Red Baltic Fleet with possessing two battleships, one cruiser, eight destroyers, three torpedo boats, 60 motor boats, 40 submarines, two minelayers, and 16 minesweepers. The Black Sea Fleet comprised at the same time a battleship, four cruisers, five destroyers, two torpedo boats, 20 submarines, 20 motor torpedo boats, and mine vessels. Six destroyers, five torpedo boats, and six submarines were believed to be in the White Sea, and 30 submarines, 30 motor torpedo boats (no destroyers?), six gunboats, and mine vessels on the Pacific station. Finally, there was an Amur River Flotilla of 75 armed motor boats and 32 river gunboats and a small force, mainly for training purposes, in the Caspian. To a limited degree these fleets were capable of reinforcing each other.

The Red navy, like the Red army, was organized on the basis of a dual command system, in which political commissars were present on all levels to keep an eye on the activities of their naval opposite numbers in order to report suspicious deviations. This system developed naturally enough during the revolution when both army and navy required the services of certain "technicians" (officers), but it subsequently was extended to such a degree that the loyalty of officers was more or less automatically questioned. Understandably unpopular as it was among officers, it continued to be regarded as necessary to protect the revolution.

In September 1933, the old titles of military rank were restored. Thereafter the presence of political commissars was regarded as particularly onerous, and there was considerable agitation to abolish these posts altogether or to reduce sharply the authority of those holding them. Instead, Stalin (presumably to strengthen his hand for the approaching purges) ordered the universal reintroduction of the system of commissars. This order affected the army, in which the system had somewhat lapsed, more than it did the navy. On June 12, 1937, the execution of Marshal M. N. Tukhachevsky, chief of staff of the Red army, and eight other high-ranking officers, signaled the beginning of the singularly bloody purges which were to eliminate a large proportion of the country's senior officers.

The Red navy probably lost even more top officers than the army during this period. R. A. Muklevich was shot. In addition to Admiral Orlov, commander-in-chief of the navy, the fleet admirals commanding in the Black Sea (Koshchenov), White Sea (Dushkanov), and Baltic (Zivkov) all were liquidated, as were three leaders of the naval academy (Stashkevich, Petrovich, and Aleksandrov), the commander of the Amur River forces (Kadotsky), and Adm. Ivan S. Ludri, former chief of the naval staff. At a slightly lower level three high political commissars, many captains of ships and shore bases, and hundreds (or possibly thousands) of officers of lower rank simply disappeared, fate unknown. As these large numbers of leaders were swept away, often very young and inexperienced men were elevated to fill the vacancies.

The purges in the Red navy had strong policy overtones. The only fleet commander to escape liquidation was Admiral Viktorov, who commanded the Pacific Fleet. He was known to be sympathetic to Stalin's concept of an ocean-going fleet as contrasted with the

essentially defensive new-school thinking of many others in the
navy. He and several of his younger officers had in 1934 been sum-
moned to a Moscow conference to discuss the new strategy and the
merits of the new ships. They had given Stalin exactly the type of
advice he wanted to hear.

Shortly after the disappearance of Orlov, a new and independent
commissariat of the navy was set up. The top post in this commissariat went to Adm. N. G. Kuznetsov, a relatively young man.
During 1938 and 1939, as large numbers of new warships were commissioned, every effort was made to arouse popular enthusiasm for
the expanding fleet. In 1939 a Soviet Navy Day was proclaimed
and since has been celebrated annually. Simultaneously came
wholesale promotions of high officers. The ranks of admiral and vice
admiral which had been abolished in 1918 were restored in May
1938, L. M. Geller, I. S. Isakov, and Kuznetsov attained the higher
rank while V. F. Tributs (Baltic Fleet) and I. S. Yumashev (Pacific)
became vice admirals.

The new naval policy which emerged from the purges had as its
goal the "most powerful navy in the world." Despite the geographical and industrial limitations of his country, Stalin demanded, and
speedily, an offensive navy of powerful surface warships, though the
did not in any way repudiate the submarine which he felt could be
used as an offensive weapon. Navy commissar P. I. Smirnov was
quoted in the February 3, 1938, issue of *Pravda* as stating:

> We need a still more powerful navy, a more modern sea and ocean
> navy. So decided the Party. So decided the government. The whole
> Soviet people so decided.

As it applied to naval building programs, the new line meant that
the 1938 and 1939 programs were to be much larger than those of
previous years. The plans for these two years included two 35,000-
ton battleships, an aircraft carrier, eight or nine cruisers, about 30
destroyers, and at least 65 submarines.

In adopting this policy and demanding a huge increase in naval
strength Stalin was not necessarily demonstrating a superior understanding of sea power. The argument that Russia was not equipped
to create such a fleet was a reflection on the success of the five-year
plans and therefore, by implication, on Stalin himself. Battleships,

in Stalin's view, were prestige symbols, indispensable to the power-ful industrialized state which he believed Russia had become. But the Soviet leader expressed no clear philosophy of how the naval power he intended building was to be employed. Nor had he or his associates any formula for achieving great naval strength overnight. In accord with the new line as expressed by Molotov, Stalin, Admi-ral Kuznetsov, and *Morskoi sbornik*, the enhanced status of the navy was recognized by the creation of separate commissariats for navy and shipbuilding, by the appointment of Andrei Zhdanov, a Polit-buro member, to the Supreme Naval Council, by extension of the active service term from four to five years, and by a lively pro-navy propaganda. Yet at the outbreak of World War II the Red navy was still tied to the old naval doctrine and any immediate attempts to equal or surpass the British were clearly unrealistic.

The foregoing pages have given some of the details of the early buildup of a Red navy insofar as these can be gathered from the sparse, often misleading, and at times contradictory statements which have emerged from behind the screen of official secrecy.

With regard to the accomplishment of Soviet aims, two sets of evaluations must be considered. The Russians have *claimed* that during the first two five-year plans—1929 to 1937—a total of 480 warships of 850,000 tons were built, and that the number of ships was four times as great and the tonnage three times that of the decade preceding World War I.

On the other hand, few foreign naval critics believe these figures are accurate. Some critics have pointed out that before World War I a great many of the reports which came out of Russia concerning the secret expansion of the imperial navy were later revealed as wholly false and intended merely to mask glaring weaknesses. This low estimation of the Red navy has necessarily been based on very fragmentary data: the obvious imbalance in types of ships; an exceedingly poor performance by the *Profintern*, which twice put into port for repairs during her 1930 voyage to the Black Sea; the slowness in commissioning ships started during World War I; the dual system of command; the general inefficiency of the tsarist navy from which the Red navy was an outgrowth; the period of naval isolationism followed by a patchwork use of ship plans developed in other services; the infrequency of fleet exercises and overseas voyages; and the purges of the high-ranking naval officers. Moreover, most foreign observers have failed to take into consideration Stalin's ambition and that of others about him to create an ocean-going navy, or the fact that the education level of the crews was rising steadily and the efficiency of the Soviet industrial plant was increasing rapidly.

While the Soviet leaders were indeed correct in believing they had made great progress compared to previous years, they were entirely wrong in the representation that their navy was on a par with those of other major powers. Even in the Baltic the Red navy before World War II was probably weaker in actual fighting value than either the German or the Swedish fleet.

CHAPTER 18

World War II: Black Sea and Baltic Operations

STRATEGY ON THE EASTERN FRONT

DURING THE EARLY DAYS of World War II a prominent American political scientist was asked by a newsman to say who he expected to win the war. Instead of replying directly he told the reporter to list in a vertical column the names of the four principal leaders in the following order: Mussolini, Hitler, Chamberlain, and Daladier. He then told his interviewer to add to that list the two words "which" and "wins." This done, he directed the reporter to spell down the column the third letter in each word. The result: "Stalin."

Without question the role of war profiteer was the one most agreeable to the Soviet leader in World War II. When he failed in his efforts to join with France and Britain in a common front against the spread of fascism, Stalin entered on the eve of war into his own private agreement with the Germans. This gave him almost two years to play the role of profiteer. During this period Hitler conquered Poland, Denmark, Norway, the Low Countries, and France, and by a combination of threats and military force took over the Balkans and parts of northern Africa as well. By June 1941, though he had been unsuccessful in the aerial assault against Britain that was intended to be the forerunner of invasion, Hitler had established over continental Europe a degree of domination unequaled in history.

During the same period Stalin had also made territorial gains, though on a smaller scale. Soviet troops occupied eastern Poland following the German attack and seizure of western Poland. Rumania was forced to give up Bessarabia and part of the province of Bukovina. And the Baltic states were occupied and annexed after first being forced to grant the use of their territory for military bases.

Finland was another story. This small country possessed a power out of all proportion to its size. Under the leadership of Field Marshal Carl Gustav Mannerheim, who served as chairman of the national defense council from 1931 to 1939, the Finnish nation had developed a small but superbly trained army and had erected along its southeastern border a defense system known as the Mannerheim Line. In mid-October 1939 the Russians bluntly demanded the rental of the Hangö Peninsula on Finland's southern coast, the cession of several islands in the Gulf of Finland, and the surrender of the small area of the Rybachi Peninsula which formed Finland's only access to the Arctic. They also wanted part of the Karelian Isthmus and the ultimate dismantling of Finland's border fortifications. The Finns reacted with counter-proposals which the Soviets promptly refused. On November 30 the Russians, without first declaring war, bombed Helsinki.

In the beginning the war on land brought several sharp Russian defeats, partly as a result of the hardened quality of the Finnish troops and partly because the overly confident Russians did not bring in their best troops and equipment for what they expected to be a minor operation. By the end of December only one of six major Soviet attacks had made any significant gains. When the Soviet government became aware of the difficulty it faced, additional troops and equipment were rushed in and more experienced leadership provided. Early February saw the Soviets once again prepared for a general offensive. This time, in spite of major losses from their nearly continuous attacks on the Mannerheim Line, the Red army gradually wore down the defenders and prevailed. Vyborg, which the Russians wanted as a naval base, was won in an across-the-ice attack at the cost of very heavy casualties.

At sea, handicapped by the advance of the season and by increasingly icy water, the Russians proclaimed a blockade of the Finnish coast, effective December 8, and tried to sever Finnish sea communications with Sweden. Within the next few days they destroyed two merchant vessels, one Swedish and one Finnish, but also lost at least one of their own. The Baltic Fleet also repeatedly bombarded Finnish coastal points, and a foray by the cruiser *Kirov* and some destroyers against a coastal fort near Hangö resulted in the sinking of the destroyer *Stremitelny* and minor damage to the cruiser. On December 18 the *Oktiabrskaia Revoliutsiia* and four destroyers followed up an air raid with an attack on Koivisto. The *Marat* fired some 160 rounds at the port before it was hit and forced to withdraw. Minelaying proved relatively ineffective because the Russian mines were promptly and easily swept up by Finnish minesweepers. During the entire Winter War, as it is called, the Russians sank four Finnish vessels and one Swedish vessel by bombing, and damaged an icebreaker and six merchant vessels.[1]

On March 13, 1940 the war ended with a treaty granting Russia more than she had initially demanded, including territory holding some ten percent of the Finnish population. Both the war and the treaty were strategically important. Though the vast majority of the Finns were democratic, some small independent groups of pro-Soviet and pro-German sympathizers existed among them. The latter were especially strong in the Finnish army, and indeed their presence may account in part for the original Soviet demands, since the Russians would have considered pro-German groups in a neighboring country a serious threat in the event of a war with Germany. During the Winter War the Finns had received considerable moral support and sympathy but very little material aid from France, Britain, and the United States. It is not strange, therefore, that after the war they moved into alliance with Germany. By May 1940 the Luftwaffe was already setting up bases on Finnish soil and the Finns had changed the organization of their army and were keeping 100,000 men under arms.

During the period of Russo-German collaboration Stalin did a great many things to keep the Germans happy. The Soviet Union provided a means by which rubber and other scarce supplies could reach Germany. The northern sea route was made available for the German auxiliary cruiser, *Komet*, as was Soviet help for most of the distance of the passage. The Soviets in return attempted to obtain various German plans and blueprints for submarines, firing directors, and gun turrets. Especially coveted were the designs of the *Bismarck* and *Tirpitz*, Hitler's two super-dreadnoughts. The Germans sold to the Russians the partly built 10,000-ton heavy cruiser *Lützow* (minus the 8-inch guns, which were taken by the German army) and added some technical assistance, but far less than the Russians wanted. Additional efforts by Molotov to obtain agreement to Soviet control of the Danish Straits, the Dardanelles, and several Aegean islands are said to have shocked Hitler.

Amazingly, Stalin appears to have been completely taken in by the agreement with Hitler. In the Baltic, building of new forts was suspended; at Vyborg, the new naval base was not properly equipped. Neither warnings from foreign intelligence services nor definitely suspicious German actions were enough to stir Stalin to any precaution against attack. Even the late-May withdrawal of the German naval mission, a June 16 order prohibiting Russian ships from leaving German ports, and the June 14 sailing of thinly disguised German minelayers and their escorts for the Gulf of Finland, were insufficient to arouse apprehension.

Early on the morning of June 22, 1941, war began between the world's two strongest land powers. The Wehrmacht attacked the Soviet Union in full force, spearheaded by large fleets of planes and powerful armored forces along a wide front stretching from the Black Sea to the Arctic. Though the German plan had been in preparation since August 1940 their attack achieved full surprise against an unprepared foe. For a time the tremendous impetus of the attack carried all before it. In a series of large-scale battles along the entire front, the Russians fell back with heavy losses. After a few months the Red forces, at first numerically superior in armor, planes, and personnel, had lost 5,000 planes and had two million men taken prisoner. In the south, it was questionable whether reserves could be brought up in time to make any effective resistance to an enemy that had dealt stunning defeat to Marshal S. M. Budenny's forces. Approximately one-third of European Russia was occupied in three months and about one-half in five months—an area including the Baltic states, most of the Ukraine and the Black Sea coast, and large sections of central Russia. In October, as the German Central army began drawing a noose about Moscow, Stalin moved the government to Kuibyshev. Russia faced one of the gravest perils in her history.

Yet the end of the 1941 campaign found the Germans short of their objectives. The southern armies had failed to reach the Caucasus; in the north Marshal Wilhelm Ritter von Leeb's besieging forces had not taken Leningrad; forces based in Finland had been unable to cut the Murmansk supply line by which Russia was receiving a growing volume of munitions from Britain. On October 23, with the first snows falling a month earlier than expected, the forces of Col. Gen. Fedor von Bock were extended in a semicircle about Moscow.

The reasons for the failure of the Wehrmacht to attain complete success, despite its surprise attack, are varied. Russian roads were relatively poor. Guerrillas made supply lines still less reliable, though they did not play as large a role in 1941 as they would later. German intelligence had not provided an accurate estimate of the great number of Russian forces which enabled the Soviets to absorb huge losses and yet continue to throw in reserves. All Russian troops, regular or irregular, had the full support of a Russian population welded by German savagery into loyalty to the Stalin regime and willing to carry out a "scorched-earth" policy that spelled self-sacrifice. The vastness of the Russian territory permitted a resiliency that other Hitler victims could not achieve. Lend-lease and British aid were both important contributors to Russian strength. And finally, considerable credit is due the weather that winter of 1941–42. The harshest winter in half a century arrived earlier than expected; and the Germans, trying desperately to land a knockout blow before extreme cold could cut down their mobility, greatly overextended their forces. The Russians, better acclimated to the increasing severity, first contained enemy attacks and then gradually forced their opponents back, regaining some of the approximately 500,000 square miles they had lost until by April 1942 their offensive had spent its force.

Springtime found the German forces at least 25 percent weaker than the year before. Realizing they lacked the resources for an advance along a 2,000-mile front, they now undertook a more limited offensive in the center and south which enabled them to capture Sevastopol and much of the Black Sea coast, to reach the Caucasus, and to besiege Stalingrad on the Volga. But by November the tide had turned again: the Germans once more had attempted too many objectives without fully achieving any. Their efforts to continue a drive in the Caucasus incurred heavy losses, and Hitler's unwillingness to accept expert advice turned a defeat at Stalingrad into a disaster that marked the turning point of the war. The Soviet second winter offensive, lasting roughly from November 1942 through March 1943, regained much of the ground lost earlier in the year.

From July 1943 on, there was little doubt of the outcome of the war on the eastern front. The Russians proved themselves better able to replace heavy losses than the Germans, and the Wehrmacht gradually lost what margin of superiority in planes and armor it had possessed earlier and had to content itself more and more with stubborn defensive fighting and small-scale counterattacks. Axis satellite forces also were reduced in numbers and quality. By November 1943 more than half of the territory lost to Germany had been regained, and during 1944 and 1945 the Soviet armies outnumbered the Germans by two and three to one. Large shipments of weapons and equipment from Britain and the United States enabled the Red forces to move forward with increasing speed and into areas far west of the Soviet Union's prewar frontiers. The Germans were pushed out of the Baltic states, the Ukraine, eastern Poland, and part of the Balkans. By May 1945, when the final German collapse occurred, Russian troops occupied most of the Balkans, Poland, Hungary, eastern Germany, northern Norway, most of Czechoslovakia, and the Danish island of Bornholm.

The story of the land fighting along the eastern front has been briefly outlined because it determined the nature of the naval war. On the Baltic, German conquests soon limited the Russians to a seacoast comprised of Leningrad and very little else. In the Black Sea, where the Russians held a clear-cut naval superiority, the Germans followed much the same strategy of seizing the fleet's land bases and attacking it from the air.

The Germans' attempt to blockade Russia and isolate her from her allies was highly successful in the Baltic and Black Seas, where the Soviets did not control the outlets, but far less so in the Arctic. There, although they were able to exact a heavy toll of Allied shipping by operating from bases in Norway and Finland, vast quantities of aid still came into Russia via Murmansk and Arkhangelsk. And in the Pacific and the Persian Gulf where lines of transportation were both long and indirect, German efforts had very little effect on Allied shipments. There were no large landing operations by the Germans, no fleet battles, and only occasional brushes between light craft. Yet the war at sea was continuous. Torpedoes and mines were the typical weapons rather than guns, for the main Russian effort was directed toward protecting the flanks of the Red army against enemy landings. Typical Red fleet activities included the defense of naval bases, small landing operations, the escort of convoys, minelaying and minesweeping, the bombardment of enemy bases, and some attacks on enemy shipping by submarines and torpedo bombers. A great deal of the active fighting by personnel of the Red navy was done ashore.

At the beginning of the war there was a certain resemblance between the Russian and German fleets. Each was a subordinate service of a power primarily interested in land warfare. Each had been developed within the previous decade, though the German buildup had been the more effective. Each was primarily concerned with undersea warfare and possessed a navy in which submarines formed the striking edge.

The naval war as it involved the Soviet Union was fought in no less than five theaters. Two, the Black Sea and the Baltic, were traditional areas of conflict for Russian sea power. They will be treated in the present chapter. Three other theaters, to be discussed in the following chapter, were the Arctic, the inland waters, and the Pacific. The Arctic and inland theaters remained important throughout the war, while the Pacific saw only a brief period of action near the end of hostilities.

NAVAL PREPARATIONS FOR WAR

Several writers have failed to correctly interpret naval events in Russia from 1939 to 1941. The publication of the six-volume *History of the Great Patriotic War of the Soviet Union*[2] and the controversies over its subsequent revision have yielded considerable information which was previously unavailable.

From this information it is clear that before the war, so far as naval doctrine was concerned, the top Russian leadership had departed from the new-school philosophy with its defensive war concepts based on mines, submarines, airplanes, and torpedo boats, and was thinking in terms of a "high-seas fleet." Between 1939 and 1941, 108,718 tons of surface warships were delivered for the Red navy, and 50,385 tons of submarines. The same period saw a 43-percent increase in coast artillery and a 90-percent increase in antiaircraft batteries. At the end of 1940 no fewer than 269 warships were under construction. The Danube and Pinsk flotillas were formed. Early work was completed on several new naval bases which were to be active between 1943 and 1945. The fleet air force emphasized fighter planes; 45.3 percent of its planes were of this type, as compared to 14 percent bombers, 9.7 percent torpedo planes, 25 percent reconnaissance, and 6 percent special types. This division of force indicates little or no interest in long-range strategic missions but some appreciation of the tactical possibilities of aircraft.

With the benefit of hindsight the Soviets have concluded that their navy was deficient in several important respects when the war began. They have cited a lag in mine warfare, great early deficiencies in technical equipment and armament, outdated airplane designs, a major shortage of antiaircraft artillery, and despite considerable prewar attention to such operations, a decided lack of modern craft for carrying on amphibious warfare. Except in the last-named instance, they also claim that there was constant improvement in these respects during the period of the war.

Plan Barbarossa, Hitler's master blueprint for the conquest of the Soviet Union, envisioned a largely defensive role for the German navy. The Red Banner Baltic Fleet was to be weakened by surprise minelaying and by air attacks at the very beginning of war, but there was to be no large-scale transfer of German naval forces to face the Russians. It was assumed that the progress of the German army would incapacitate Russian sea forces by depriving them of their bases. While these moves were in progress, the German navy would protect the German coastline and prevent any Soviet breakout from the Baltic. German sea supply was to be suspended with the outbreak of the war, but was to be resumed after the capture of Leningrad.

Aside from the dynamic nature of the German ground attack, the situation in the Baltic at the beginning of World War II was not wholly dissimilar to that of World War I. At that time the entire strength of the German navy had been far superior to that of the Russian Baltic Fleet, but because the Germans were primarily interested in the fight against England they had allotted very weak forces to the Baltic. In June 1941 German forces in the area consisted of five submarines, 28 motor torpedo boats, ten minelayers, three flotillas of M-boats (100-ton motor minesweepers), three magnetic minesweepers, and two mine clearance vessels carrying motor boats. The Finnish navy had, in addition, two coast-defense monitors, four gunboats, five submarines, six motor torpedo boats, and a handful of auxiliaries, minesweepers, and patrol vessels. In September 1941 Hitler formed a German Baltic Fleet, consisting of the superdreadnought *Tirpitz*, the pocket battleship *Admiral Scheer*, two light cruisers, three destroyers, and lesser vessels, for the purpose of preventing the escape of Russian ships to Swedish ports when Leningrad was taken. As events transpired, this fleet was very short-lived since its ships were soon called to duty elsewhere.

From an organizational standpoint the German navy in the Baltic was weak in several respects. There was poor liaison with the Finns, who operated independently. The command structure was complicated and unwieldy, with several shore-based admirals commanding different sectors of the Baltic. The German navy, unlike the Soviet, did not control its own aviation but depended upon the reluctant and erratic cooperation of a separate military organization under Hermann Goering.

On paper the Russians held a decisive superiority in the Baltic. They had the two old battleships *Oktiabrskaia Revoliutsiia* and *Marat*, two cruisers, 47 destroyers and large torpedo boats, at least 75 submarines, 110 motor torpedo boats, large forces of gunboats, minesweepers, and patrol vessels, and a shore-based naval air force. In the builders' yards were three or four cruisers, a dozen destroyers, and about 50 submarines.[3]

Where the Germans were strong in experience and technical skills, the Red navy was weak. Commanding in the Baltic was Adm. V. F. Tributs. The member of the war council was Rear Adm. N. K. Smirnov and the chief of staff was Rear Adm. J. A. Pantelev. Adm. I. S. Isakov, the ex-tsarist officer who had become the principal theoretician of the navy, commanded the battleships and cruisers,

Vice Adm. V. P. Drozd the destroyers, and Rear Adm. G. Levchenko the submarines. None of these leaders had performed distinguished service and none would establish much of a war record. Drozd, probably the ablest, died in an auto accident in 1942. Immediately below these men were equally unheralded subordinates.

The theoretical Soviet superiority did not alarm the Germans. Vice Adm. Friedrich Ruge, writing after the war, observed:

> No German officer who fought the Russians in 1914–1917 had any real respect for their fleet. It is true that the ships' crews knew well enough how to fire their guns and in a tight corner they would fight bravely to the end. But what the Russians had always lacked in the Russo-Japanese War, as well as in 1914–1917, was the ability to make quick decisions and to exploit the ever-changing tactical and operational opportunities inherent to a war at sea. In the First World War the Germans, using only their oldest and most poorly armed second-rate warships, had done as they pleased with the Russian Baltic Fleet. Thus there was no reason whatever to fear the opponent, for now the Germans possessed well-tried flotillas of efficient ships. In the Second World War the sea and air operations in the Mediterranean and the unproductive Italian submarine campaign had already demonstrated the relative insignificance of numbers and the supreme importance of ability and self-confidence.[4]

THE INITIAL GERMAN ATTACK IN THE BALTIC

The opening German naval offensive, which included minelaying just before the outbreak of war and air attacks on Russian ports coincident with the start of hostilities, was extremely successful, though the Russians at sea appeared to be somewhat less bewildered by the attack than their comrades on land. Prior to the invasion the Germans had moved 48 small warships to Finnish waters and put 32,000 troops on land, in addition to establishing a naval base at Helsinki. Making use of Finnish facilities as well as their own, they laid minefields from the Åland Islands to the Latvian coast. Other fields were laid along the Baltic Coast in front of ports at Libau, Windau and Memel, and in the Irben Strait. To the north, the German fields were placed so they would join others laid by the Swedes to protect their own territorial waters. These fields caused very heavy initial losses of Soviet destroyers and submarines, and German motor torpedo boats and submarines added to the casualties. During the first three weeks of the war losses were running at a higher rate than in any previous Russian war. On June 23 the cruiser *Maksim Gorky* hit a mine off Ösel but managed to reach Revel and later Kronstadt. The same day the *M-78* was torpedoed by the German submarine *U-144* off Windau. *S-3* and *S-10* were sunk in the Baltic by motor boats. *M-80*, *M-79*, and *M-101* were lost to German mines on June 28. *M-94* was sunk by *U-14* near Dagö Island. During most of July the toll continued. On July 1, *M-81* hit a mine in Moon Sound. On July 12 the destroyers *Smely* and *Surovy* were lost to mines. On July 26 the German destroyer *T-3* sank the Russian destroyer *Tsiklon*. Submarines and other small craft were lost in great numbers. Meantime the Germans were not suffering in anything like the same degree. Aside from a few remarkably minor sinkings, such as occurred in the Irben Strait on the night of June 26–27 when the Germans sank the Russian destroyers *Gnevny*, *Tuchka*, and *Taifun* at the cost of two motor torpedo boats of their own, German losses were inconsequential. Indeed, the most serious was due to a German blunder: on July 9 three German minelayers, *Tannenberg*, *Preussen*, and *Danzig*, blew up in a Swedish minefield whose existence German headquarters had simply neglected to report to the operating personnel.

An even greater threat to the Baltic Fleet was the advance of the Wehrmacht, which seized one by one the Baltic coast ports and bases. Nearly all of the 20 airfields used by the fleet fell into German hands. On June 28 Libau fell, and with it went the old destroyers *Desna* and *Karl Marx* and five submarines which were blown up. On July 1 Windau was taken; on July 4 Riga; on July 8 Pernov. Each involved small naval losses.

Vigorous Red army resistance at this point slowed down the speed of the Wehrmacht's advance and forced it inland. As a consequence, when the attack came on Revel, the principal Russian advanced base, it came from the east where defenses were weak rather than the south as the Soviets had expected. Three divisions plus the cruiser *Kirov* and some lesser craft put up a fairly strong resistance, however, and it was not until August 28 that the German Twentieth Army attained the outskirts of the city.

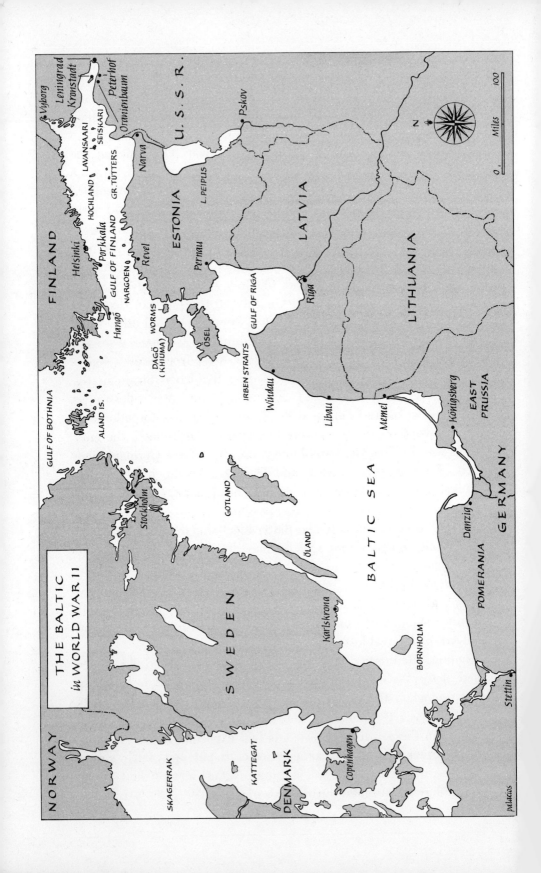

THE BALTIC
in WORLD WAR II

NORWAY

SWEDEN

FINLAND

Vyborg
Leningrad
Kronstadt
Peterhof
Oranienbaum

Helsinki
Porkkala
Hangö
Hochland
LAVANSAARI
SEISKARI
GR. TUTTERS
NARGOEN
GULF OF FINLAND
Revel
Narva
Pskov

U. S. S. R.

L. PEIPUS

ESTONIA

WORMS
DAGÖ
(KHIUMA)
ÖSEL
Pernau
GULF OF RIGA
Riga

LATVIA

LITHUANIA

IRBEN STRAITS
Windau
Libau
Memel
Königsberg

EAST
PRUSSIA

GERMANY

Danzig

POMERANIA

Stettin

GULF OF BOTHNIA

ALAND IS.

Stockholm

GOTLAND

ÖLAND

BALTIC SEA

Karlskrona

BORNHOLM

SKAGERRAK

KATTEGAT

DENMARK

Copenhagen

N

0   100
Miles

palacios

Because a very large share of all Baltic shipping, both naval and merchant, was at Revel at that time, as well as thousands of refugees and troops, the Red navy now undertook one of the fastest high-pressure evacuations of the entire war. Aided by a huge smoke screen laid by destroyers and a great deal of antiaircraft fire, no less than 170 naval and merchant vessels loaded and prepared for sea under the direction of Vice Admiral Drozd. In the city, street fighting was still taking place. At three in the afternoon the first convoy left the harbor. It was led by the *Kirov* and included 15 destroyers, four torpedo boats, six submarines, 28 minesweepers, and 26 merchantmen. It was followed by a second convoy consisting of six minesweepers, 12 guardships, ten subchasers, and 62 merchant vessels.

The *Kirov* silenced a German battery and antiaircraft fire discouraged somewhat weak air attacks, but a way had to be cleared through the closely set Juminda minefield. Although the sweepers went to work immediately, some ships got into the field and blew up. Both convoys then anchored for the night only to have additional ships hit mines in the darkness. The next day it was possible to continue the voyage. In all, the Soviets lost five destroyers (including the former *Novik* and *Azart*), a submarine, six minesweepers, and 42 merchantmen. Six additional damaged ships were seized the next day by the Germans, who also found sunk the old Makarov-designed minelayer *Amur* and two cargo steamers. This "mine battle off Revel" (to quote the German title) was by far the greatest German naval success of 1941. Yet the energy and bravery displayed by Vice Admiral Drozd and his men in saving nearly two-thirds of their ships certainly was one of the more noteworthy aspects of the battle. The fall of Revel meant the loss of the Baltic, for this had been the major port used by Soviet destroyers and submarines laying mines and by minesweepers trying to keep open the sea lanes.

The Germans had found themselves hampered in their northern march by coastal and island batteries; therefore the elimination of these and the seizure of the Russian-occupied islands was the next order of business. Almost simultaneously they took steps to insure against any escape of Soviet naval forces.

The steps to prevent escape were twofold. The first step, the creation of a short-lived German Baltic Fleet, has already been mentioned; with the exception of the light cruisers those vessels left the Baltic on September 27. In the second step, Germans and Finns laid 19 new minefields containing over 4,300 mines of several types between August 9 and August 23. Amazingly, the Soviets made no efforts to interfere with the planting operation.

The Axis offensive against the Baltic islands actually started the first day of the war, June 22, 1941 (four days before Finland's declaration of war), when the Finns landed 5,000 men in the Åland Islands. The forces were escorted by Finland's two 4,000-ton coast-defense monitors, *Ilmairinen* and *Vainamoinen*, plus some smaller ships. Though two Soviet dreadnoughts and six destroyers were nearby they made no attempt to interfere. Instead they steamed to Kronstadt, where the dreadnoughts stayed for the remainder of the war.

The Germans were somewhat slower to occupy the area, but before mid-September they were gathering special troops and landing craft for an assault on the main islands in the Gulf of Riga. A Finnish task force sent to support these operations lost the *Ilmairinen* on the evening of September 13, probably to a mine or torpedo. The loss occurred at Khiuma, where the Axis forces were making a demonstration to conceal their attack. Moon Island, invaded the next day, was subdued in only three days. The island's Red army defenders retreated by causeway to Ösel with the Germans in pursuit. Here, mop-up operations took longer, especially after the defenders reached the Sworbe Peninsula. The Germans were greatly assisted by gunfire from the light cruisers *Leipzig* and *Emden*, which Soviet planes and motor torpedo boats attacked fruitlessly. Khiuma, invaded on October 12, held out until October 21 against the invaders, who were aided by gunfire from the light cruiser *Köln*. In the three islands the Germans lost less than 3,000 men while capturing more than 15,000 prisoners.

On September 22 the Germans scored a major success when the *Marat* (ex-*Petropavlovsk*) was sunk during an air raid over Kronstadt. The *Marat* went down on an even keel in very shallow water so that many of her guns remained operable, however; when the ship was scrapped after the war the stern turret was left standing out of the water as a memorial to the defenders of Kronstadt.

In the fiercely contested struggle for the main islands in the Gulf of Finland, which started still later, many islands changed hands several times. In early December the Russians evacuated several garrisons which they could no longer hold in the western portion of the gulf. Eventually they held only four main islands in the eastern end of the gulf, the main one being Lavansaari, 60 miles west of Kronstadt, a base for small naval craft and planes.

In view of the long recitation of German-Finnish successes it is startling to consider that the Allies started the war with a decided superiority at sea. Why was it never used?

Actually, the Soviets did make a few feeble attempts at offensive action. The *History of the Great Patriotic War* mentions early air attacks on Finnish airdromes, the use of naval aviation against enemy land forces, aerial minelaying in enemy waters, and Soviet mine barrages in the Gulfs of Finland and Riga and Irben Strait. The account claims numerous German casualties from these and later actions. Soviet claims for the sinking of enemy ships are subject to very heavy discount, however, and the Soviets have never published figures of their own naval losses. On the basis of generally reliable German sources it can be stated that losses for the Axis during 1941 totaled 25 naval vessels lost (including four minelayers and a U-boat) and 24 damaged, besides 18 merchant vessels sunk and seven damaged. The first Soviet submarine success that year, and nearly the only one, was the sinking of the steamer *Baltenland* on October 23. The general failure by submarines was occasioned partly by the disorganization and very heavy damage accompanying the initial attack, and partly by the difficulties of operating in shallow Baltic waters against sophisticated German antisubmarine devices and tactics. For the most part, however, it resulted from poor administration and lack of technical skill. Baltic submarines were, in fact, so ineffective that four were transferred by internal waterways to the Caspian and 15 to the White Sea. It should be added that the ten or so German and Finnish submarines in the Baltic also failed to do much, and even lacking radar and sonar the Soviets had developed reasonably effective antisubmarine tactics.

The air force of the Red navy achieved some damage in the area but was almost completely destroyed in the early days of the war. Mines, the most effective Soviet weapons, claimed the minelayer

Königin Luise and some 17 other German warships, as well as about ten merchant vessels.

The culmination of the German campaign in the Baltic was supposed to be the siege and capture of Leningrad, where for the first time the larger ships of the Soviet Baltic Fleet served a conspicuously useful purpose. At Kronstadt and Leningrad its ships gave artillery support afloat while many members of the crews—a total of 80,000 men, eventually—manned shore batteries or otherwise aided in the defense of the port. Lack of sufficient food and fuel were to cause great privation among the civilian population, inasmuch as neither the Red army nor the Soviet government had been farseeing in stocking food and preparing the means of defense. Moreover, the garrison was weak and recent reinforcements were of low morale and dubious discipline. Certainly in late autumn 1941 German expectations of conquering the city did not appear unreasonable.

By mid-December the Germans' initial offensive had ended. Their losses at sea had been low, those of Russia very heavy; the Baltic Fleet had not seriously interfered with their progress up the Baltic and the Gulf of Finland; only a very short stretch of coastline about Leningrad and Kronstadt remained in Russian hands; and most of the strategically located islands in the Gulf of Finland had been taken by the Germans and Finns, though to be sure the Russians were making good use of the four they still held. Almost no Soviet naval air arm remained. Satisfied that the Russian naval power once considered so superior was not in fact unduly menacing, the Germans in December resumed supply of the Wehrmacht by sea convoy routes. Nothing resembling a naval battle had yet occurred, although there had been a few brushes, mostly favorable to the Germans, between R- and M-boats (small and large minesweepers), ferries, motor torpedo boats, and occasionally destroyers. There had been no action involving battleships either, though the possibility of such action may have deterred the Germans from attacking the gulf islands still in Soviet hands. Each foe limited its use of cruisers mainly to shore bombardment operations, and even Russian mine operations were relatively ineffective when compared to previous wars. Yet despite their great gains the Germans were unable to take Leningrad, then closely besieged, or to end the sea war by depriving the Baltic Fleet of its bases.

DEADLOCK IN THE BALTIC 1942 AND 1943

During 1942, 1943, and the beginning of 1944 there was little change in the Baltic. The Germans enjoyed a magnificent strategic position but lacked sufficient strength to capture Leningrad. The Russians' position could hardly have been worse, but still they retained forces sufficient to stave off disaster. For two years positional warfare prevailed, with considerable fighting but no significant victories. The relative strength of the combatants did alter to some degree during this period, however. The Russians were far weaker in submarines than during 1941, but they became steadily stronger in the air (280 naval planes in early 1942, 600 by year's end) and on land as the Germans weakened in both areas. Finnish naval strength increased somewhat, especially in submarines and motor torpedo boats. German strength varied, depending on the demands of other theaters as compared with the Baltic.

In 1943 the Germans moved to improve their position by strengthening their minefields and taking more islands in the Gulf of Finland. The Russians made no attempt to maneuver their surface warships through the minefields; rather they swept up German mines, laid mines of their own, and employed their submarines to brave the fields and harass enemy commerce.

German occupation of the coastal islands was delayed and to some extent limited by either the unwillingness or the inability of the Wehrmacht and Luftwaffe to furnish the necessary troops and planes. Nevertheless, progress was made. On March 28 a Finnish force took the island of Hochland. Next, the Russians evacuated Teutters Island, which was in turn occupied by the Finns, retaken by the Soviets April 8 in a successful counter-attack, and soon lost again to a German attack. On the other hand, the Germans finally abandoned all plans to seize the strongly held islands of Lavansaari and Seiskari, owing to continuous harassment by Soviet minesweepers, aircraft, and submarines based there.

The battle of the minefields still slightly favored the Germans, and in May 1942 they set out to lay several new fields to compensate for those feared destroyed by the winter ice. The attempt, on the whole, proved unsuccessful. As early as mid-1942 the Russians held quantitative superiority in the air (though both the planes and pilots of the Luftwaffe were superior in quality), so that German minelayers were subject to constant air attack which also drove away subchasers attempting to protect fields from Russian minesweepers.

Apparently their extremely heavy submarine losses taught the Russians certain lessons, for in the winter of 1941–42 they conducted crew training in the limited area of sea available, and demagnetized their ships by adding a heavy layer of paint and various antimine devices. During daylight hours the submarines attempted to pass the minefields submerged, but at night they surfaced to recharge their batteries.

By May 10, with the ice in the Gulf of Finland broken up sufficiently to permit navigation, the Russian submarine offensive got under way. The Germans, heartened by their successes of the preceding year, had altered neither their defensive weapons nor their tactics despite Finnish urgings that they lay nets to keep in the Soviet submarines. Hence mine barrages protected by subchasers were their principal means of defense. The mine barrages had been renewed to the extent that more than 12,000 German mines had been laid in three main areas.

Soviet submarines, aided by diversionary attacks from naval planes and occasionally by minesweepers, attempted to run the mine barrier in some eleven waves over a period of six months, usually by running either very close to the bottom of the sea or very close to the shore. The first wave of seven boats left on June 13–14. Three got through; three were damaged and returned to the port; one was sunk. Two of the next three departing on June 23–24 got through. The blockade-running continued until mid-December when gathering ice put an end to such activities. Meanwhile the Finns, unable to use their submarines for conventional purposes, employed them for antisubmarine attack and thus accounted for at least three or four of the approximately ten submarines lost by the Russians.

The 1942 Soviet campaign must be regarded as mildly successful. It showed that Red navy submarine personnel had learned, but still had a great deal left to learn. In all, the successful blockade runners sank 27 German, Finnish, and neutral merchant ships—20 by torpedo, three by gunfire, and four by mines—and damaged probably seven or eight others more or less seriously. Five Russian submarines accounted for four ships each. While this represents a vast improvement over the 1941 Soviet record, it suffers by comparison with the achievements of German, British, or American submarines during the same period. Further, the cargo loss to the Germans, only one percent, was one which could be accepted with equanimity.

While submarine warfare was Russia's main naval response to the Germans in 1942, it was not the sole activity. On July 8 a Russian amphibious force attacked Someri Island, 23 miles east of Hochland and one of the most advanced Finnish bases near Leningrad; but the attack, conducted by forces much too small, failed. In the meantime most of the surface vessels damaged in the initial German air attacks were repaired, and considerable activity was shown by very light Russian naval units. The most important fighting, however, took place on Lake Ladoga and is discussed in chapter 19.

The modest successes achieved by Russian submarines in 1942 prompted the Germans to further defensive measures in 1943. Accepting the earlier suggestion of the Finns, they manufactured over 60 miles of heavy steel netting which when fitted together could be lowered to a depth of almost 200 feet. In April 1943, under cover of severe weather, they laid a new barrage across the Gulf of Finland between Porkkala and an island west of Revel. The completed barrage consisted of two rows of netting with more than 11,000 blownup fuses and 8,454 mines between the nets. The task required the coordinated effort of 141 ships; aerial attack could have made the operation impossible. Yet, either through lethargy or failure to understand the significance of the move, the Russians made no attempt to interfere—a fact which the Germans regarded as incomprehensible: the use of nets as antisubmarine defenses dates back to the days of Commo. John Rodgers and Robert Fulton and was common enough in both world wars. Probably no net system of defense was ever more successful than this one. During the entire year of 1943 not a single Russian submarine reached the Baltic, and at least three submarines are known to have been destroyed in the net barrage. Several submarines made repeated attempts before returning damaged. German losses were nonexistent. The only effective use of Russian submarines during 1943 was in landing saboteurs and special agents.

Aside from the submarine war, 1943 followed much the same pat-

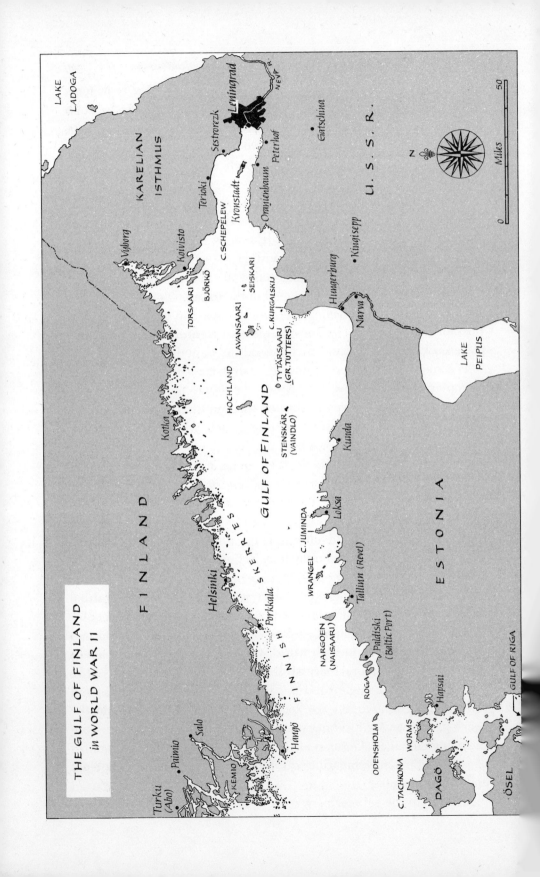

THE GULF OF FINLAND
in WORLD WAR II

LAKE LADOGA

KARELIAN ISTHMUS

Leningrad

NEVA R.

Sestrorezk

Trioki

C. SCHEPELEW

Kronstadt

Oranienbaum

Peterhof

Gatschina

U. S. S. R.

Kingisepp

Narva

Hungerburg

C. KURGALSKIJ

LAVANSAARI

SEISKARI

TYTÄRSAARI
(GR. TUTTERS)

LAKE PEIPUS

Vyborg

Koivisto

TORSAARI

BJÖRKÖ

HOCHLAND

STENSKÄR
(VAINDLO)

Kunda

FINLAND

Kotka

GULF OF FINLAND

Loksa

C. JUMINDA

WRANGEL

ESTONIA

Helsinki

SKERRIES

Porkkala

FINNISH

NARGOEN
(NAISSAARI)

Tallinn (Revel)

Paldiski
(Baltic Port)

ROGA

Hapsai

Turku
(Åbo)

Paimio

Salo

KEMIO

Hangö

ODENSHOLM

WORMS

GULF OF RIGA

C. TACHKONA

DAGÖ

ÖSEL

N

Miles

50

0

tern as 1942. The Germans attempted unsuccessfully to increase restrictions on Russian maritime traffic in the Leningrad-Kronstadt area by aerial minelaying and the use of coastal batteries. During August 1943 three German minelayers were sunk at the cost of one Russian patrol boat—one of the few times that the exchange rate at sea favored the Russians. Russian minesweepers also held their own in a contest with enemy minelayers while the Russians increased minelaying activity near Hochland and Someri. Soviet motor torpedo boats laid mines in the Finnish skerries and from time to time landed saboteurs and spies. The Red air force, steadily growing in strength with the addition of American planes, was employed against German patrol vessels guarding the nets and minefields, as well as against merchant shipping. German accounts report that Soviet planes sank five German vessels in the Baltic in 1943; Russian accounts claim fifty.

RUSSIAN BREAKTHROUGH AND VICTORY

The end of the siege of Leningrad came in January 1944 when the German general staff was forced by the gradual wearing dôwn of the Wehrmacht to withdraw troops from that front. On January 8, 1944, with artillery assistance from the *Oktiabrskaia Revoliutsiia* and the cruisers, the Soviet army near Leningrad broke through the weakened German Sixteenth Army. Another Russian breakthrough from Oranienbaum, supported by naval gunfire, hit the flank and rear of the retreating Germans. The enemy forces, bereft of all heavy artillery and many critical supplies, retreated to a new Narva front between the Gulf of Finland and Lake Peipus. Here they were able to hold—at least temporarily. But time was now on the side of the Russians. During June 1944 Russian drives along the south coast of the Gulf of Finland cut off German Army Group North. The following month a massive Russian attack produced a collapse on the Narva front. A Soviet drive toward Riga and Libau forced German evacuation of Riga on August 23.

Meanwhile the Finns were being gradually pushed westward along the Karelian Isthmus. Their leaders, not anxious to have their bleeding country involved in the final German collapse, started peace negotiations. The terms reached on September 4 provided, among other difficult conditions, for the complete evacuation of Finland by German forces no later than September 15. The Finns were not expected to declare war on Germany, but they were obliged to sweep mines out of their territorial waters and to make commercial vessels, ports, and islands available to the Soviets.

Even with complete cooperation and good faith on the part of the 200,000 Germans then within Finland, these conditions would have been difficult to carry out. As it was, bloody fighting broke out, and the Germans left a path of devastation in the wake of their gradual retreat into Norway. Hitler's original plan for holding Finnish vessels then in German ports and seizing the Åland Islands was abandoned when his foreign affairs minister, Joachim von Ribbentrop, persuaded him the action would incur an unfavorable Swedish reaction. In the Gulf of Finland, however, the Germans were deterred by no such scruples. Misled by intelligence reports which pictured the Finnish garrison of Hochland as eager to continue the wartime partnership, the Germans staged an amphibious landing of 2,500 men from 35 ships on September 15. Finnish motor torpedo boats destroyed seven of the landing craft, and German troops ashore, lacking artillery support, were soundly beaten by the Finnish garrison and forced to surrender. In the days that followed, German submarines sank two Finnish vessels and each country seized the other's shipping. By early November the German Twentieth Army had reached Norway. The bulk of the German-Finnish fighting was over, though the last of the German troops did not leave Finland until April 1945.

Until the surrender of Finland, Russian territorial gains had been more evident in the interior than along the Baltic coast, where the Germans continued to hold many pockets of land. Though their position had been fatally undermined, the Germans sought to delay translating their losses on land into losses at sea; with courage and skill they turned to the defense of their mine and net installations in the Gulf of Finland. By March 1944, when enough ice had melted to permit some naval activity, they were attempting not only to hold their existing minefields but to build new ones farther west, including a double net from Nargoen to Porkkala. Meanwhile the Russians, under cover of their aircraft, began a massive campaign of mine clearance. Soviet air superiority made the task of the German defenders virtually impossible. The German craft protecting the minefields—minesweepers, trawlers, drifters, and barges—could venture out of base only at night, even when reinforced with destroyers and torpedo boats. German losses were high (one of the heaviest being the minelayer *Roland*) and undoubtedly would have been much greater had the Russians used their heavy surface vessels. After three years of war the Soviets still had available a battleship, two cruisers, eleven destroyers, six torpedo boats, 22 submarines, 50 motor torpedo boats, 19 minesweepers, and many auxiliaries and small craft. The corresponding German strength was four destroyers, two torpedo boats, 17 minesweepers, six R-boats, 15 fishing steamers and whalers, 85 patrol boats, 46 naval ferry barges, nine artillery ferries, three floating heavy artillery carriers, and three minelayers. But the Soviets opted to use only their small and very small craft, while the Germans employed all they had. In July the Germans added to their forces the Sixth Destroyer Flotilla, the Fifth Motor Torpedo Boat Flotilla, and a dozen submarines. The antiaircraft cruiser *Niobe* (formerly the Dutch cruiser *Gelderland*) was also brought in, only to be sunk with 400 of her crew during an attack by more than 100 Soviet planes. By June 26 the Russians had recaptured Plissari, Tiuinsaari, and Koivusaari in amphibious landings. During July 5–6 they retook Teikaari, Melansaari, and Lammasaari islands and were able to command the entrance to Vyborg. In the same month they broke through the main Seeigel minefield, bringing heavy if unskilled MTB and submarine attacks against the German defenders. The hazards of night navigation also took their toll: in one disastrous foray (August 18) three (*I-22, I-30* and *I-32*) out of four new German destroyers on a minelaying mission were lost in their own minefield.

In their all-out effort to retain sea defenses the Germans even made minefield protection a main mission of U-boats which had been engaged in attacks on Soviet shipping between Kronstadt and Vyborg in the eastern end of the Gulf of Finland. Meanwhile they capitalized on the opportunity afforded by Russian preoccupation with the crumbling mine defenses to move troops from both shores of the Gulf of Finland. In this hurried and almost impromptu evacuation, carried out mainly by ferry barges, artillery transports, fishing cutters, and other small craft, German losses were light; Soviet naval air strikes proved ineffective and there were no attacks by heavy ships. German naval forces were able to transfer 91,000 soldiers, 85,000 refugees and prisoners of war, and 82,000 tons of war materials at a loss of only one convoyed steamer—though several others were damaged.

For the Allies, the evacuation automatically reduced the danger posed by German mine defenses in the Gulf of Finland by opening up bypasses at each end. The Russian occupation of several islands formerly held by Axis forces further improved the situation, and by the close of September 1944 Soviet submarines and MTB boats were able to skirt the minefields and reach the Baltic by remaining close to either the Estonian or the Finnish coast. During their last operation in the Gulf of Finland, in mid-December, the Germans once again blundered into one of their own minefields and lost two new destroyers and 600 men. On December 12 *U-497* also was lost on a mine. Shortly thereafter *U-779, U-776,* and *U-745* were lost.

Although the way was now open for a larger Russian naval participation in the war, the Red navy still made little use of its surface vessels. Soviet naval airplanes, however, had become increasingly active, and their ever-expanding numbers were making the sea extremely risky for the Germans. They claimed 17 steamers besides some small warships during the last three months of 1944. On October 10 the Germans sighted a Russian submarine in the Baltic, the first in nearly two years. Though Red submarine forces were not large and were out of practice, they managed to sink 14 ships during the next three months.

Between October 1944 and the final German surrender in May 1945 the main focus of the naval war was the German evacuation of land bases in the Baltic. Continued victories brought the Red army into East Prussia, and in mid-January 1945 the German eastern front collapsed. On January 25, 1945, the Russians crossed the Oder and occupied Elbing. From that time on, remnants of the German army reached ports along the Baltic and managed to hold onto them while awaiting evacuation by sea. In February the German Fourth Destroyer Flotilla was recalled from Norway to assist in evacuation. Other ships of all types were pressed into service, and with great daring and efficiency (and with no little aid from the

Soviets, who repeatedly failed to take advantage of obvious opportunities) the German navy managed to take troops and refugees out of situations that should have been wholly disastrous.

The first Russian landings in the Baltic were made on September 24, 1944, at Worms (Vormsi), on October 1 at Khiuma, and on October 5 at Ösel. The Germans retreated in good order in the face of superior forces but held on to the Sworbe Peninsula on Ösel for seven weeks before evacuating, again in an orderly manner, on the night of November 23–24. On several occasions during the autumn of 1944 the Russians made amphibious landings behind German lines, none particularly successful; and although they had no less than 236 single-engine planes on the nearby Pernau airfield they did not use them to interfere with German evacuation. Also during the same period, Germans ashore enjoyed the support of a battle group built around the *Prinz Eugen* and the *Lützow*—which, again, the Russians chose not to attack. Soviet inaction in this case gave the Germans a particularly important advantage, since none of the Soviet surface ships was providing comparable gunnery support to the Red army. Much of the German evacuation traffic was routed to and out of Memel, where the Russians were able on October 6 to sink the transport *Nordstern*. The Red army reached the outskirts of Memel on October 10, but artillery support from warships offshore enabled the Germans to hold the city until January 1945.

Logistic support for the isolated German garrisons awaiting evacuation along the Baltic coast presented a difficult problem that was never fully resolved. The German Ninth Defense Division, using 350 very small craft (the largest were fishing cutters), was able to furnish support for the Baltic beachheads at an acceptable rate of loss, however, and these garrisons were moved out during 1945. On March 14 two German torpedo boats were lost to Russian mines. Sinkings by Red navy submarines during this period were not heavy (five steamers of 10,000 tons in the Kurland supply operation). On April 1 Russian MTB boats, assuming an offensive role for the first time, attacked a German convoy but were turned back. In the air, British and American strikes in Pomerania achieved greater results than any the Russians were able to produce.

Aircraft from the Baltic Fleet aided other Soviet forces in taking Königsberg which was surrendered on April 5, 1945. This ended the

German mission of supplying East Prussia (for a time thereafter the fire of the *Prinz Eugen*, the old battleship *Schlesien*, and the *Leipzig* helped to delay the fall of Danzig), but it did not end German naval activity: the fleet remained to remove troops which were on the verge of capture by the Red army. From May 6 to 10, seven destroyers and five torpedo boats entered the Hela anchorage, took survivors from ferry barges (at least 2,000 per ship), and provided escort for several crowded steamers. Some 60,000 soldiers had to be left behind, not because of Russian opposition (there was none) but simply because of inadequate resources. On May 8 five convoys with 25,000 men were moved out of Libau and 13,000 men were evacuated from Windau. One of these groups was subjected to constant strafing; it suffered little damage and reached Kiel on May 11.

At the end of the war, by making the best possible use of scanty shipping and with little help from the Luftwaffe, the Germans had accomplished the remarkable military and logistic feat of moving some 700,000 able soldiers, 300,000 wounded, and a million and a half refugees. Tonnage lost to submarines during the last eight months of the war was only 33 ships (112,000 tons). Naval planes during the same period claimed 34 warships and 57 merchant vessels totaling 163,000 tons. About 15,000 lives were lost, nearly all on three crowded refugee ships, the *Wilhelm Gustloff*, the *General von Steuben*, and the *Goya*.[5]

The Soviet Union to this day has not published any listing of its naval losses during World War II. According to a compilation of war losses in the Baltic by a former officer in the Russian imperial navy, the Soviet Union lost one battleship, 15 destroyers, three torpedo boats, 39 submarines, three minelayers, about 40 minesweepers, 60 merchant ships, and an undetermined but sizable number of motor torpedo boats, subchasers, and patrol vessels. German and Finnish official figures list, for the Finnish navy, a coast-defense monitor, two minelayers, six minesweepers, seven patrol boats, two motor torpedo boats, one mine transport, and 39 merchant ships, some of which were very small. German loss figures include one old battleship (the 13,000-ton *Schlesien*, sunk by a mine on May 4, 1945), two large and 10 small destroyers, seven submarines, five auxiliary minelayers, six auxiliary gunboats, 67 minesweepers, 27 patrol boats, 21 subchasers, three training ships, 56 landing ships, 11 miscellaneous types, and 160 merchant ships, many quite small.[6] No reliable figures for total naval plane losses have so far appeared.

According to figures published by the Germans, Soviet planes were their most formidable adversaries in the Baltic and accounted for more than half of the losses. Submarines sank only about 107,000 tons of German shipping, mines claimed 89,000 tons, and other causes combined to take an additional 19,000 tons. These are raw figures; they are in disagreement with other Western (not to mention Russian) figures; and they are probably too low. However, they are almost certainly correct in placing naval planes first as a cause of losses. While the Germans believed they discerned Anglo-American influence in the Russian air tactics at times, they were also probably correct in attributing the limited Russian successes mainly to the weakness of the Luftwaffe.

Neither the Germans who fought the Russians in the Baltic nor the few British and Americans who were cognizant of the Soviet record there have shown great admiration for the wartime performance of the Red Banner Baltic Fleet. The extremely cautious record of the Russians has been variously ascribed to early damages sustained by Soviet ships in the surprise German attack; to icy conditions and the limited sea area which restricted preparations and training; and to the combined effects of a reactionary continental concept of sea power, an absence of a naval tradition, a lack of combat experience on the high seas, and the destruction of the tsarist officer corps during the revolution and civil war. Any of the above could be a true explanation of Soviet actions, but until official documentary evidence is available the assessment of Soviet motives must remain largely guesswork. Regardless of interpretation, there is little doubt that Russian leadership was poor, unimaginative, and slow-moving, and that it failed time after time to take advantage of obvious opportunities. The Germans employed full combat strength continually while the Russians used a very small proportion of their potential. In the occasional skirmishes between German and Russian craft the latter were almost always in superior force, yet they displayed little combat aggressiveness. The Germans were able to erect new defenses and to evacuate their forces from strategically hopeless positions with little or none of the Russian opposition which almost certainly could have hastened victory at little additional cost. In the Baltic, the Russian navy did not produce a single major war hero comparable in stature to any of at least a dozen Red army generals and marshals. German Adm. Theodor Burchardi summed up the situation with the comment: "The Soviet naval warfare was as though paralyzed in the early war years, and in the following period only minimally active."[7]

THE GERMAN OFFENSIVE IN THE BLACK SEA
MAY 1941–NOVEMBER 1942

The chronology of Black Sea operations differs considerably from that in the Baltic since in the Black Sea theater there was no period of deadlock. Here the initial German attack was even more vigorous than that farther north, and here it brought a series of prompt and disastrous Russian defeats. The territory which the Soviets had taken from Rumania, and nearly all of the Ukraine (including the cities of Nikolaev, Kherson, Rostov, Zaporozhe, Dnepropetrovsk, Kharkov, and Taganrog), was occupied by the enemy within a few months. Yet in the south as in the north the Wehrmacht proved unable to land a knockout punch during 1941.

In the Black Sea as in the Baltic, the Germans hoped to eliminate Russian sea power by occupying its bases. However, they had not included in Plan Barbarossa a naval attack scheme for the area as they had for the Baltic. Hence German Navy Group Command South, headquartered in Sofia, was as much surprised as the Russians by the German attack, and was forced to do some very rapid improvising.

The lack in German planning could have been due either to a deliberate decision to place complete reliance on land strategy or to a high-level conviction that since German forces in the Black Sea would be hopelessly outmatched prior planning would be all but useless. If the latter was indeed the case, the German high command was correct in its premise but wholly wrong in its conclusion. For despite a much greater disparity of force at sea than was the case in the Baltic, and in the face of extreme strategic difficulties affecting the transfer of reinforcements, the German navy was to give an excellent account of itself. The Russian Black Sea Fleet, on the other hand, avoided some of its past mistakes but never lived up to its potential.

At the outbreak of war the Black Sea Fleet consisted of an old battleship (*Parizhskaia Kommuna*), two new cruisers (*Voroshilov* and *Molotov*, 8,800 tons and 33 knots speed), four old cruisers (*Krasny Kavkaz, Chervonaia Ukraina, Krasny Krym* [ex-*Profintern*, ex-*Svetlana*], and *Komintern*, 6,500 to 7,400 tons, 29 knots), 27 new and ten old destroyers and torpedo boats, about 50 submarines, and various small flotilla craft. On the building ways, mainly at Nikolaev, were a 35,000-ton battleship, several cruisers, some destroyers and submarines, and lesser craft. As was the case with the Baltic Fleet, this organization was not fully modern either tactically or technically. The high command in the Black Sea consisted first of Vice Adm. F. S. Oktiabrsky and later (after May 1943) Vice Admiral Vladimirsky, Rear Admiral Kulakov as member of the war council, and Rear Adm. I. D. Yeliseev as chief of staff. Four flotillas in the general area were commanded respectively by Rear Adm. Ya. A. Panteleev (Volga), F. S. Sadelnikov (Caspian), N. O. Abramov (Danube), and S. G. Gorshkov (Azov and later Danube). Probably the ablest man in this generally mediocre group was Gorshkov, who subsequently became commander in chief of the Soviet navy.

The only nearby naval force approaching the Black Sea Fleet in size was the Turkish navy, which throughout World War II remained neutral. Germany began the war with no ships in the Black Sea. The two Axis satellites had very small naval forces: Bulgaria's navy included some obsolete torpedo boats, a few S-boats (the German type of motor torpedo boat), and some patrol types; the Rumanian fleet included four destroyers, three torpedo boats, three gunboats, eight S-boats, two submarines (both unready for action), three minelayers, and a few tugs and auxiliaries. Three Germans directed the naval forces in the Black Sea—Admiral Fleischer from 1941 to 1942, followed by Adm. Hans H. Wurmbach in 1942 and Vice Admiral Kaiseritsky in 1943.

The Germans were able to reinforce the modest Axis naval strength to some degree by arranging to move the Danube Flotilla (consisting of 12 small river minesweepers, a tender, a repair ship, and a few river tugs) to Galatz. Other reinforcements included Siebel

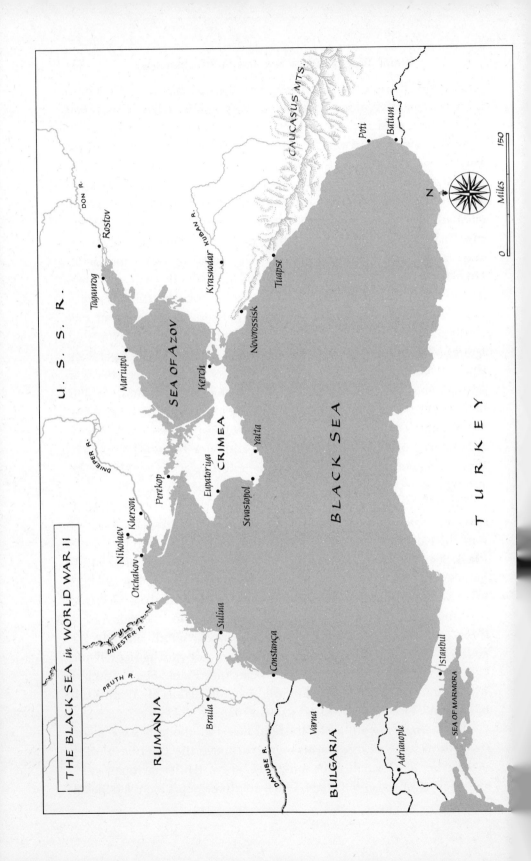

THE BLACK SEA in WORLD WAR II

U. S. S. R.

DON R.
Rostov
Taganrog
Mariupol
SEA OF AZOV
Kerch
CRIMEA
Perekop
Eupatoriya
Sevastopol
Yalta
Nikolaev
Otchakov
Kherson
DNIEPER R.
DNIESTER R.
Sulina
PRUTH R.
RUMANIA
Braila
DANUBE R.
Constança
Varna
BULGARIA
Adrianople
Istanbul
SEA OF MARMORA
TURKEY
BLACK SEA
Novorossisk
Tuapse
Krasnodar
KUBAN R.
CAUCASUS MTS.
Poti
Batum

N

0   150
Miles

ferries (large, slow craft designed for the invasion of England), S-boats, minesweepers, a squadron of Italian MAS boats, six 250-ton U-boats and an equal number of Italian midget submarines, and a few other types. Since most reinforcements had to come either by way of the Danube or by rail and had afterwards to be reassembled at Constantsa, the main Rumanian base, no very large ships were to be expected. The Germans did an outstanding job of shipping small craft; in the course of the war they moved 500 boats. To some extent they also built their own reinforcements, using captured Russian shipyards. They sought to improve the performance of the Rumanians by giving them training courses.

The first naval objective of the Germans was the establishment of a sea transport route between Constantsa and Ochakov on the Dnieper, a distance of only 120 miles. This route was designed to furnish a supply line into the Ukraine that would be unaffected by such normal hazards of overland transport as muddy roads and guerrilla warfare, would not require rolling stock or motor vehicles, and would be of unlimited capacity. To maintain it the Germans would need to control the coastline as far as the Perekop Isthmus. It was felt that protection must be assured primarily against submarines, mines, and torpedo boats, since the threat of the Luftwaffe would discourage interference by sizable Russian ships.

A particularly thorny problem concerned the city of Odessa which, for political reasons, the Germans had decided should fall to the Rumanians. But after the Rumanian attack on the city proved relatively ineffective, Russian defenders under Rear Admiral Gorshkov made excellent use of their naval superiority to defend the city and minimize losses. Most of the warships under construction were towed to safety. To move in men and supplies, the Soviets set up a convoy system involving 27 ships under protection of the cruisers *Krasny Krym* and *Krasny Kavkaz* and four destroyers. They disconcerted the besiegers by staging a small-scale airdrop combined with an amphibious landing in the Rumanian rear, and when pressure on the city at last became too severe in mid-October, they ended a 73-day siege by a skillful evacuation, leaving behind them a thoroughly sabotaged, scorched, and booby-trapped port which the Germans were unable to restore to service for several months.[8]

Shortly after the fall of Odessa the Germans opened their new sea line of transportation and by the end of the year had sent through three convoys. For protection they relied on flank minefields, shore-based aircraft, and occasional shore batteries, in addition to the motor torpedo boats and other small craft used for escort purposes. As the Germans had expected, the Russians were unwilling to risk heavy vessels to interrupt this sea transport. However, they did employ offensive minelaying, torpedo attacks by submarines, and occasional attacks by MTB's, and these were enough to cause sizable losses to the early convoys. On October 25 the Germans lost four tugs to mines in the Ilichevka minefield. Their second convoy lost its flagship and suffered damage to an S-boat and a rescue boat, both of which later sank. The river minesweepers proved too frail for their task, especially in cold weather when crews were unprotected and the ships became sheathed in ice. After the Christmas of 1941 operating conditions became impossible, and the German ships returned to the Danube for the winter.

Despite their superiority at sea, the Soviets followed an almost completely defensive strategy. The one exception occurred shortly after the outbreak of war when a Soviet task force of cruisers and destroyers joined forces with air attackers to bombard Constantsa. This combined force accomplished little, however, and in course of the action, on June 26, 1941, the flotilla leader *Moskva* was first hit by shore gunfire and then blown up when she entered a minefield.

One of the prime objectives of the German land attack was the vital Soviet naval base of Sevastopol, That port was still in Soviet hands when the 1941 offensive finally ground to a halt in November after passing far to the east and penetrating the Crimea. Though always cautious in employing its forces, the Black Sea Fleet was thoroughly aware of the importance of its main base; it had kept the port reasonably well supplied by sea—at the cost of the cruiser *Chervonaia Ukraina* (sunk on August 16 by the Luftwaffe) and some lesser vessels. *Parizhskaia Kommuna*, *Krasny Krym*, and the large destroyer *Kharkov* particularly distinguished themselves during these supply operations, which involved 31 ships in all and at times even entailed the evacuation of wounded men by night on submarines. Despite their commitment to Sevastopol, however, the Russians did not repeat their error of the Crimean War and the Russo-Japanese War: they did not risk allowing their ships to be trapped in one main port.

Between December 26 and 29, 1941, the Russians conducted their largest amphibious operation of the entire war in an attempt to relieve the pressure on Sevastopol. Following bombardment of shore targets by a task force which included *Comintern, Krasny Krym, Krasny Kavkaz,* destroyers, and MTB boats, the Russians took advantage of darkness and a calm sea to essay landings at no less than ten points about the Kerch Isthmus. This operation was poorly carried out and the Russians were able to make good their foothold at only four of the locations. One tangible result was the speedy capture of the city and port of Feodosiia. An early expansion of the Russian bridgeheads was soon brought under control by the Germans, and in January the *Krasny Kavkaz* was damaged when the Luftwaffe, which had been grounded by snow, became active again. While these Russian landings could not be developed successfully, the time required to wipe them out delayed by many months the German assault on Sevastopol. However, the Russians bought the delay at the cost of 170,000 prisoners.

The city finally fell on July 1, 1942, after a bitter 250-day siege in which the Red fleet played a major defensive role. Submarines played a role in getting in supplies after the use of surface warships became too risky. About 20,000 of the initial garrison force consisted of sailors and marines. In what was probably the best known of many acts of heroism performed by Red navy men at Sevastopol, five marines, out of ammunition, threw themselves with their last hand grenades under advancing tanks to forestall the German breakthrough. A key element in the city's defenses was the use of main battery turrets and guns salvaged from the scrapped battleships of the tsarist era. These guns were silenced only by direct hits from monster German siege mortars. Unlike the case at Odessa, effective Soviet evacuation by sea proved all but impossible; the Germans claimed 95,000 prisoners.

Russian naval losses in the last weeks of the siege included three submarines, two subchasers, and several patrol boats. Ironically, the destroyer *Tashkent,* which had up to that time been attacked 96 times by air in the course of more than 40 supply trips from Novorossiisk to Sevastopol, survived the siege only to be sunk the day after the surrender by a German bomber off Novorossiisk. Russian manpower losses during the siege of Sevastopol were reported to be 97,000, not counting prisoners.

With the fall of Sevastopol the German supply routes in the western Black Sea became relatively secure. During 1942 the Germans were gradually able to bring in somewhat better craft and simultaneously to deprive the Russians of other bases. As a result, despite the paper superiority of the Russians, the Germans were able to extend, protect, and operate their inshore supply line at a cost of losses from submarines and mines which they regarded as acceptable. The Russians sent small task forces, including destroyers, into the western Black Sea on three occasions, but these raids accomplished little. On most raids only very small naval vessels or submarines were employed, especially following losses of six destroyers in 1941 and seven in 1942.

On May 8, nearly two months before the capture of Sevastopol, the Germans had retaken the city of Kerch and had liquidated the large Russian beachhead in that area. During July the Wehrmacht pushed east and north of the Sea of Azov, regaining ground it had lost the previous winter. Kherson and Voronezh fell in early July, and Rostov on July 24. With this the German encirclement of the Sea of Azov was complete. By July 27 the last of the Russian small craft in the area had been bombed to bits by the Luftwaffe and the Black Sea Fleet found itself deprived of all of its prewar bases. Only the stretch of coast from Tuapse to Batum remained in Soviet hands and the ships were forced to base at Poti and Batum, both secondary ports with grossly inadequate facilities.

The German gains on land continued for about two months more. On August 2 they successfully crossed the Kerch Isthmus and shortly thereafter took Maikop and Krasnodar. Soviet naval forces, dispirited as they were after the fall of Sevastopol, nevertheless succeeded in impeding German progress to some extent by night bombardments of enemy bases, a great deal of aerial minelaying in the Sea of Azov (especially in the Kerch Strait), relatively small amphibious landings behind German lines, and extensive but comparatively unskilled air and submarine attacks on German transportation. On one occasion Russian naval planes acting on highly accurate intelligence from partisans attacked the Italian MAS (motor torpedo boat) base at Yalta one day after its antiaircraft guns had been removed. They scored a complete triumph, destroying two boats and badly damaging three others. Despite all the naval activity, however, the Germans continued their ground gains in a drive aimed at the Caucasus and the oilfields near Baku on the Caspian Sea. The Taman Peninsula opposite Kerch was fully in the hands of the Germans on September 6 following a successful amphibious landing on September 2. On September 7 they seized Novorossiisk. They had moved deep into the Caucasus—but failed to reach a source of oil (which the German war machine desperately needed)—when bad weather, mountainous terrain, stiffening Soviet resistance, and perilously long supply lines combined to stop them in October.

Accompanying the land campaign was an active war of attrition at sea. In this contest Black Sea Fleet submarines accomplished a bit more than their counterparts in the Baltic. They were able to sink occasional enemy vessels but were not sufficiently well handled to be a major threat to the Germans whose antisubmarine defenses were relatively sophisticated. Moreover, 24 Russian submarines had been lost by the end of 1942. Russian naval air strength, almost decimated in the original German attack, was gradually built up with American and British as well as new Soviet planes to the point where it was quantitatively superior to the Luftwaffe. But here again the Russians failed to get the most out of what they had owing to crude tactics and inaccurate bombing. Aerial minelaying, while unsophisticated, did tie up a great deal of German effort, and the Russians also used several types of small surface craft to some advantage. The small-turreted motor gunboat, able to travel at 24 knots, was introduced in the autumn of 1942 with considerable success. PAT's, as the Russian motor torpedo boats were termed, were extensively employed. They were faster—52 knots—than either their German or Italian counterparts, but their gasoline engines made them far more vulnerable. In their occasional brushes with German S-boats they almost invariably retreated under cover of smoke screens, and they scored few successes against convoys. The Germans' loss rate from the combined efforts of Soviet naval air, undersea, and light surface forces was appreciable but bearable: in September 1942, a fairly typical month, they lost two MAS boats, two ferry barges, a tug, three lighters, and a supply craft.

The Germans' superior skill and experience were not enough to compensate for their relative weakness in force, however, so that in the war of attrition they never came close to achieving victory in the Black Sea theater. Axis submarines in the area were used mainly against Russian coastal traffic and claimed few victims. The Luftwaffe was extremely effective at the beginning of the war but thereafter gradually weakened in numbers if not in quality; on bombing raids over Poti and Batum its achievements were not impressive. German S-boats, though not numerous, were widely respected and invariably gave a good account of themselves.

Neither side, then, can be said to have won the war of attrition. The Russians, who according to German estimates had 400,000 tons of shipping at the beginning of the war and about 100,000 tons after the defeats of 1942 (the true 1942 figure was probably larger), continued to supply the immediate necessities of amphibious movements and sea transport. The Germans, by using every conceivable type of ship, were also able to care for their own minimum needs.

THE TURN TOWARD VICTORY
NOVEMBER 1942–MAY 1944

From the time the German reverses at Stalingrad began, the tide of victory flowed ever more strongly in favor of the Russians. During this latter phase of the war the Russians continued to enjoy a decided superiority of force on sea as on land, although an exceedingly unfavorable strategic position and lack of adequate bases made the superiority at sea very hard to exploit. At the end of 1942 the Russians had available in the Black Sea a battleship, four cruisers, eight destroyers, 67 motor torpedo boats, and 29 submarines, besides minesweeping craft, landing ships, and patrol vessels. The Germans had seven destroyers and torpedo boats, an auxiliary cruiser, ten gunboats, 18 motor torpedo boats, 12 submarines, more than a hundred minesweepers, landing craft and ferries, and about 360 planes. The Red navy's air arm, of comparable size, was thenceforth to grow steadily while that of the Germans steadily declined. The Germans held an enormous advantage in strategic position and in bases, while inadequate base facilities kept a sizable proportion of the Russian forces inactive. During most of 1944, in fact, only about 16 Soviet submarines and the same number of motor torpedo boats were in commission.

These considerations were secondary, however, in a naval war whose nature was determined by the war on land. The Red army drive in the winter of 1942–43 recovered most of the territory the Germans had taken the preceding summer and fall. The recapture of Rostov in February 1943 threatened the Germans' deep penetration farther east and caused them to withdraw to a new defense line east of Taganrog. To add to German woes, the Soviets landed at Novorossiisk, also in February, and captured Cape Myskhako, which commands the port. The naval part of this operation, commanded by Vice Admiral Kholastiakov, chief of the Novorossiisk base, involved some 150 patrol and motor boats—no larger vessels. This involvement pointed up a Soviet weakness in landing craft (ironic in that the first modern landing craft were evolved by the Russians in the Black Sea area in 1916), and was attended by large losses. The beachhead, which was eventually liquidated, was able to do no more than interfere with German operations.

In late winter the German Caucasus Army retreated to the Kerch Strait but continued to hold the Kuban bridgehead and hence to control the exit to the Sea of Azov. Since no very large forces were required for what had become essentially a holding operation, the Germans late in March began a massive evacuation—of some 105,-000 troops, 45,000 horses, 7,000 vehicles, and 12,000 horse-drawn vehicles—across the Kerch Strait to the Crimea. The Russians made some not very successful attempts to interfere, partly by persistent large-scale aerial minelaying in the Kerch Strait and partly by two amphibious landings of their own. The Luftwaffe, by now numerically weaker than the Soviet air force, was able to concentrate its forces sufficiently to give local support, and under the additional protection of defensive minefields and escorts of lighters, S-boats, and minesweepers, German troops were removed by ferry barges without unduly heavy losses. The Germans were able to contain the Russian amphibious landing northwest of Novorossiisk and at the same time to interfere with Russian seaborne supply to the extent that during April their R- and S-boats were claimed to have sunk 23 barges, lighters, and small supply ships. The Soviet failure to use heavier ships obviously worked to the Germans' great advantage. With far weaker forces the Germans yet managed to play the role of the stronger naval power, and even Russian land forces were bombarded from the sea by artillery lighters.

Following the German evacuation came a lull of several months in the land fighting near the Black Sea while the Russian offensive moved to the central front. Then in August 1943 the Russian army under General Fedor Tolbukhin launched a powerful attack on German lines north of the Sea of Azov. The Germans retreated to a line stretching from Zaporozhe to the Sea of Azov and still covering the Perekop Isthmus leading into the Crimea. But this position proved impossible to hold and the Russians were shortly threatening the Crimea from both north and east. On the night of September 9–10, after months of skirmishing, Russian navy MTB's made an amphibious attack on the Novorossiisk harbor. They were followed by landing craft which disembarked 2,000 troops. This time the Russians were able to support their landing, and on September 16 the Germans withdrew. On September 21 the Russian 318th Division took Anapa. Four days later Russian troops landed on the Taman Peninsula (not in great enough force to bring immediate results), and by October the Russians had reached the Dnieper, sealed off the Crimea from the north by taking Genichesk, and finally forced the Germans to abandon the Kuban beachhead. The Germans then destroyed their Azov Flotilla.

On September 7 the Germans began a new evacuation to the Crimea. In the 34 days which followed, using about 240 craft for transport and every conceivable plane, S-boat, minesweeper, U-boat, tug, and lighter for protection, they moved 202,500 men, 55,000 horses, 15,237 motor vehicles, 20,000 horse-drawn vehicles, 95,000 tons of army equipment, and 1,200 guns across the Kerch Strait, mainly to Sevastopol. Once more the Russians limited their opposition to an amphibious landing (at Eltigen), and to vigorous but unskilled air attacks which sank two ferry barges and damaged several other vessels. Once more they failed to apply their superior naval strength where it was needed and thus allowed the Germans to succeed in an inherently difficult operation. The Soviet fight to supply the Eltigen beachhead was finally lost to the Germans, but not before it proved expensive for both sides. The Germans admitted losses of eight ferry barges sunk and three minesweepers and 14 ferry barges damaged, and their leader, Vice Admiral Kaiseritsky, was killed. They claimed to have sunk at least six times as much Russian tonnage. Russian losses appear to have been about 60 supply craft of very small size.

The largest naval setback of the year for the Russians occurred on the night of October 5–6, 1943. The destroyers *Kharkov, Boiky,* and *Sovbrazitelny* had completed a bombardment of German positions at Yalta and were delayed by a motor torpedo boat attack during their retirement. Dawn found them still within range of land-based planes; all three vessels were sunk in three attacks by the Luftwaffe. This disaster, instead of inspiring the Soviets to perfect their aerial cover operations, merely made them even less willing to risk their ships. Thereafter, most of the larger ships were kept in harbor and their crews were dispatched to join in the land fighting—a fate which had already befallen the crew of the *Parizhskaia Kommuna* after that ship was damaged by air attack in Poti harbor during September.

The year 1943 brought scant reward to the Russians waging the naval war of attrition. The Germans had been able to maintain their communications all the way from the Bosphorus by using convoys under the escort of Rumanian destroyers, minesweepers, subchasers, ferry barges, Danube Flotilla boats, torpedo boats, and gunboats. These convoys were seldom attacked, even by Soviet minelayers, as long as they stayed in the western portion of the Black Sea. In the eastern Black Sea, where only about six of the approximately 30 Russian submarines were usually active at any given time, the situation was different. Here submarine attacks on convoys during the year cost the Germans four ferry barges, five steamers of 20,000 tons, and a lighter. For these gains the Russians paid the price of six submarines. The naval air force was more successful: in 1,270 attacks on ships and ports Soviet fliers destroyed a total of 13 barges, two R-boats, an S-boat, eight harbor defense boats, a tug, three steamers, and eight lighters—14,500 tons in all—at a cost of 91 planes downed by naval forces and shore batteries.

For 1943 the Germans claimed their S-boats destroyed a torpedo boat, an MTB, three motor gunboats, a tanker, three freighters, 19 coastal freighters, and 15 lighters—29,000 tons in all. U-boat claims included 12 vessels totaling 29,300 tons and four smaller craft, in addition to two steamers sunk by mines. R-boats accounted for six motor gunboats and five patrol craft. These claims are probably reasonably accurate. In addition, the Russians lost to shore batteries and to the Luftwaffe three destroyers and various other vessels. German sources place the total Russian Black Sea loss during the

year at 103 small warships, 191 planes, and 86 merchantmen totaling 58,200 tons. They admit a German loss of 43 warships and 27
merchantmen of 40,850 tons.

At the beginning of 1944 the German position in the Crimea was
critical. In December 1943 Hitler had refused permission to evacuate, although the Germans did continue to move out prisoners,
wounded, and noncombatants. They were cut off by land, and while
their supply lines by sea were still open, Russian submarine attacks
and extremely bad weather made convoy sailings so irregular that
serious shortages developed. Even mines ran short. The Russians
moved their submarines west of the Crimea to prey on this supply
traffic, and succeeded at the cost of two of their own submarines in
sinking more than a dozen ferry barges. Also lost were the German
transport *Lorissa*, the 4,000-ton steamer *Peter*, and the minelayer
Charlotta. From a German standpoint the only bright spots were
the liquidation, in mid-December, of the Eltigen beachhead, the
defeat of several new Russian landing attempts, and the continued
failure of the Soviets to use their Black Sea Fleet. A severe blow was
the successful amphibious landing on January 10, 1944, of Russian
forces at Cape Tarkhan, north of Kerch.

With the strategic situation in the Crimea clearly overwhelmingly
in their favor, the Soviets now withheld attack for several weeks,
meantime forcing the Wehrmacht to retreat farther north. Then, on
March 23, the Third Ukrainian Army launched a drive to the west
and south. On March 26 Nikolaev and Ochakov were taken, and
on April 10 the Germans' most direct line of evacuation was severed
when Odessa was recaptured. On April 7 the Russians attacked the
German positions in the Crimea from both north and east. The
German lines gave way quickly; Feodosiia was taken on April 11
and Balaklava a week later. Hitler still resisted evacuation (for a
time further evacuation probably could not have been carried out
in any case, since the German ships available were loaded with
nearly 90,000 evacuees from Odessa), and ordered that Sevastopol
be held at all costs.

But order and execution were two different things, as the luckless
German soldiers soon were to learn. The larger and better-equipped
Russian forces were everywhere victorious. By May 8 the Russians
were within the city and the port could no longer be used. Only at

this time, when the German positions were irretrievably lost and the remaining troops faced imminent annihilation, did Hitler's head-quarters authorize evacuation. By employing the Kherson beach-head, using naval units on land (at costs of up to 80 percent casualties), and loading and moving troops under constant enemy air attack, the Germans succeeded in transferring about two-thirds of the Crimea survivors to Constantsa. The official Soviet claim is that 37,000 German and 5,000 Rumanian troops were lost.

Two motor torpedo boat brigades under Captains 2nd Rank Dish-chenko and V. T. Prozenko received special mention by the Soviets for aid in cutting off the German evacuation. The German transport *Janina* was sunk at Sevastopol. The *Teya* and *Totilla*, carrying a total of 8,500 troops, were sunk at sea on May 10. The tanker *Tirus* was hit by three torpedoes and sunk. The minelayer *Ruminia* went down under air attack. The *Dorostor* was blown up by submarine A-5. Another Russian submarine sank the *Geyzerich*. At least 6,000 German naval personnel lost their lives. Of some 130 ships taking part in the evacuation, 40 percent by numbers and even more by tonnage were lost. About 25,000 prisoners were taken and other thousands were killed during the siege. Nevertheless, the Germans claim some 87,000 of their men and 40,000 Rumanians were moved out by sea, and reached Rumanian ports safely despite attacks by submarines, airplanes, and MTB boats. It is only fair to note that these figures are disputed by the Russians, some of whom claim that no more than 30,000 escaped. And as usual, German shipping losses reported by the Russians differed greatly from those admitted by the Germans, as the following tabulation indicates.[9]

While the evacuation of Sevastopol was defeat enough for the

TABLE 8

Two Claims of German Naval Losses

CLASS OF SHIP	RUSSIAN CLAIM	GERMAN CLAIM
Transports	69	8
Landing craft	56	20
Subchasers	2	5
Gunboats	2	0
Fishing steamers	3	0
Patrol boats	27	7
Other craft	32	10
Total	191	50

Germans, it might with better employment of Russian naval forces have turned into a disaster of the proportions of Stalingrad. This point was brought out by German Capt. H. D. von Conrady in a postwar report on Black Sea operations:

> No German soldiers would have reached the Rumanian coast from the Crimea and not one of them would have seen his homeland again if the Russian Black Sea Fleet had not remained inactive, thus making possible the removal of the bulk of the German troops in the Crimea by the Navy, despite very heavy losses.[10]

With the conclusion of the Crimean campaign, the Black Sea phase of World War II was nearly but not entirely, at an end. Naval activity went into low gear for a time. German ships from the Crimea were transferred to the command of German Sea Defense Rumania. Italian and German submarines were able thereafter to sink a Soviet torpedo boat, a tanker, a freighter, a patrol boat and a tug (their score for the entire year of 1944 was only ten small ships). The Germans also laid defensive minefields off Sulina. A noticeable drop in Russian air and submarine attacks was partially offset by the greater activity of MTB boats. Russian cruisers and destroyers reportedly were at sea, but they did not play an active role.

The lull ended in August 1944 when the armies of Gen. R. Ya. Malinovsky and Fedor Tolbukhin launched a heavy attack in the area between the Carpathians and the Black Sea. On August 22 Russian naval forces comprising 600 small craft made an amphibious landing back of the German lines. Two days later there was a similar landing at the mouth of the Danube. Things then happened fast: Jassy was taken; a coup in Rumania brought to power a government which promptly declared war on Germany; following a heavy raid by 191 planes, Bucharest and Constantsa were occupied by land forces; and, finally, Bulgaria resolved a one-day formal state of war with the Soviet Union by declaring war on Germany.

Though two German destroyers and 13 MTB's had raided Odessa as late as the first week of August, German naval efforts were now at an end. Ships short of ammunition and manned by discouraged crews failed to put up an effective resistance. Some were destroyed by the Russians. More were scuttled by their own crews at Constantsa and Varna, and about 200 small craft retreated up the

Danube seeking safety in flight (see chapter 19). On September 10 the last three German U-boats, no longer having a base, were destroyed by their own crews in Turkish waters.

A war of attrition deserves a final word. According to German figures, a total of 27 merchantmen of 63,236 tons were lost to Russian submarines in the Black Sea. Ten German ships (10,290 tons) were sunk by mines, 22 (35,806 tons) fell victim to planes, and 16 (11,029 tons) were accounted for by shore artillery or miscellaneous causes. The grand total, about 120,000 tons, is far from impressive. No reliable figures exist on Russian plane losses, but sinkings of Red submarines numbered more than 20.

One remarkable feature of the Black Sea fighting was that it involved almost no ship-vs.-ship or fleet-vs.-fleet battles. In the few such actions that occurred the Axis forces almost invariably won or at least held their own despite unfavorable odds. For example, on December 14, 1942, two Russian destroyers encountered a convoy of three Rumanian steamers escorted by a torpedo boat and four launches. A one-hour fight at a range of 3,000 yards concluded indecisively when the Rumanian steamers escaped and the Russians retired.

In the overall Russian conduct of naval war in the Black Sea, several points stand out clearly. First, all naval activities were closely related to the war on land. Second, although the Black Sea Fleet did not always take the actions that might have been of greatest benefit to the Red Army, its tactics and know-how showed a degree of improvement over a period of time, it avoided some of its mistakes of past wars, and its general performance was definitely better than that of the Baltic Fleet. Third, the Russians were consistently weak in operational planning and initiative, displayed virtually no understanding of the meaning or potential of modern seapower, and in these and other ways wasted an overwhelming margin of naval superiority. Direction by the Red army was doubtless of no help in overcoming these deficiencies. The added factors of untrained personnel (admitted even by Soviet authors) and the lack of satisfactory port facilities may have influenced this record, but clearly they did not determine it wholly. The Black Sea Fleet was unquestionably hurt late in the war by the distance of its bases from the scene of operations, and its effective force was certainly lessened by the difficulties and delays incident to making repairs at bases lacking in proper facilities. Yet the fact remains that the force available was not used effectively: the larger Russian vessels, for example, rarely left port for any purpose other than aimless cruising —well out of harm's way. Had the British, Germans, Americans, or Japanese been operating the Baltic and Black Sea fleets it is quite possible the conclusion of the European phase of World War II would have been advanced by several months. Or to put it a bit differently, had the Soviets shown a propensity to use their sea superiority as well as they did their land superiority, the Germans perhaps would have abandoned all hope of escaping defeat during 1944.

CHAPTER 19

World War II: Arctic, Pacific, and Inland Waters

THE ARCTIC THEATER

THE ARCTIC prior to World War II had never been a main theater of interest to the Russians. Both the tsars and the Soviets included the area in strategic planning, but it remained of secondary importance because of its sparse population and undeveloped resources. Accordingly, far smaller military and naval forces were allotted there than to installations farther south. The Soviets, to be sure, were somewhat more aware than their predecessors of the latent possibilities in the Far North and had done more to promote transportation and economic development in the area. To the already existing important Siberian ship traffic in coal and timber, valuable fisheries, and northern coastal air terminals, they added a small Northern Fleet which in 1936 comprised three destroyers and three submarines, plus tankers, icebreakers, and a small naval air force. It is probable, however, that before hostilities erupted between them in 1941 neither the Russians nor the Germans had any real appreciation of the strategic potential of the Arctic theater.

The Germans in successfully attacking Norway in 1940 had at least two objectives clearly in view. Most immediate was the acquisition of U-boat bases fronting on the open sea, removed from the mine barrages in the North Sea and English Channel that had hindered their operations in World War I. But a Norwegian conquest would also serve another end: it would cut off the Soviet Union from easy communication with and aid from the Western allies—if and when German actions brought the Soviet Union into the Allied camp. In World War I, even without the loss of Norway to the Germans, the isolation of Russia from Western supply lines had contributed to her defeat. The German expectation that the same thing could happen again, especially if the situation were worsened for the enemy, was not unreasonable.

Germany's opponents possessed their own share of strategic sense; and once the Soviet Union became allied with Britain and the United States, first Churchill and then Roosevelt recognized the importance of supplying the Soviets with the sinews of war. Both reluctantly assumed the difficulties and costs of doing so. Three routes were available for the movement of supplies. The first, the North Pacific, was used by Russian ships to transport half of all the supplies the Soviets received. The Japanese were tacitly willing to ignore this trade so long as they were not directly fighting the Soviet Union. The Persian Gulf route was also used extensively and with comparatively few losses, although some violence was done to international law in the Allied occupation of Iran. But it was the northern supply line, around Norway, that was much the shortest and fastest of all the possible routes. Thus, despite risks and losses that were at times exceedingly great, both the British and the Americans continued throughout the war to deliver munitions by this route, and by their determined efforts this vitally important joint enterprise grew up and succeeded.

Initial German strategy sought both to capture the principal land terminal of the northern supply line by an attack on Murmansk and to cut the rail line by which supplies were carried. The offensive against Murmansk was opened by two specially trained German divisions. Petsamo was occupied on June 22, 1941, but the attempt to take Murmansk encountered much more difficulty. First an amphibious landing with gunfire support by Soviet destroyers forced the Germans on the defensive and then, farther south, the lack of roads and a stiffening of Russian resistance stalled the attack in mid-July. In September, when the Germans renewed their efforts, they were forced by heavy losses to settle into prepared fortifications. Thus three months after the outbreak of war the land front was stabilized. The Russians held strong defenses; their batteries on the Fischer Peninsula covered the entrance to both Pet-

samo Bay and the Kola Fjord leading to Murmansk. German efforts
to cut the railroad behind the Russian line had failed.

In June 1941 neither the Russians nor the Germans were particularly well prepared for a naval war in the Arctic. The Soviet naval
forces were based on Murmansk and Polarnye in the Kola Inlet.
Both bases were poorly equipped, but waters warmed by the Gulf
Stream allowed them to remain open the year around. Three sum-
mer-only bases, all in the White Sea area, were Molotovsk, Arkhangelsk and Belomorsk, the last located on the southwest coast of
the White Sea at the entrance of the Joseph Stalin canal. The
Russian fleet based on the Arctic consisted of eight destroyers (one
of which was lost to a divebomber in the initial German attack),
three torpedo boats, eight minesweepers, 20 motor torpedo boats,
20 subchasers, 15 icebreakers and about 27 submarines. The fleet
was under the command of Rear Adm. Arseni G. Golovko, possibly
the ablest of the Soviet fleet commanders at the beginning of the
war.[1] The war council member was Rear Adm. A. A. Nikolaev, and
the chief of staff Rear Adm. M. I. Fedorov, who was to be replaced
in 1944 by Rear Admiral Platonov.

Although no Western historian has taken note of the fact, the
Northern Fleet was not the only Russian naval combat organization
in the area. The White Sea Flotilla under Rear Adm. G. A. Stepanov
contained more than 100 small craft (patrol vessels, minesweepers,
cutters, motor launches, etc.) and was reponsible for guarding the
northern sea route and protecting ships in coastal waters. A main
early activity of this organization was the clearing of mines from
the West Siberian Sea in the summer of 1942.

In spite of its small size the Northern Fleet had a very long list of
functions which included U-boat hunting, assistance to Soviet
ground forces, protection of Allied convoys as they neared Soviet
ports, harassment of German shipping, and protection of air bases.
These duties involved far more responsibility than Russian Arctic
forces had carried in any previous war and, as it happened, greater
activity than fell to the lot of either the Baltic Fleet or the Black Sea
Fleet. Because the level of training and the technical competence
of personnel was comparatively low, the Northern Fleet was never
during World War II more than moderately successful in fulfilling
its many missions.

The secrecy connected with Plan Barbarossa in some ways handi-

THE ARCTIC THEATER, WORLD WAR II

ARCTIC OCEAN

ICELAND

GREENLAND

JAN MAYEN I.

SPITZBERGEN IS.

FRANZ JOSEPH LAND

NORWEGIAN SEA

BARENTS SEA

TAIMYR PENINSULA

YENISEY R.

Port Dickson

KARA SEA

NOVAYA ZEMLYA

OB R.

PECHORA R.

Tromso

Narvik

Petsamo

Polyarnoye

Murmansk

Archangelsk

Molotovsk

WHITE SEA

L. ONEGA

UNITED SOVIET SOCIALIST REPUBLIC

NORWAY

SWEDEN

FINLAND

GULF OF BOTHNIA

Stockholm

Helsinki

Leningrad

L. LADOGA

BALTIC SEA

N

0   Miles   500

capped the Germans at sea almost as much as it did the Russians. German pre-attack preparations had included the improvement of airfields in northern Norway and the completion of Route 50, a main roadway paralleling the Norwegian coast. But German naval forces in the area on July 10, 1941, numbered only five destroyers, two submarines, a few flying boats and torpedo planes and some sub-chasers and escorts. The experience and general quality of the personnel, however, far surpassed that of the Russians. Admiral Ciliax commanded in Norway from 1943 to 1945 when he was replaced by Admiral Krancke.

Each belligerent was reinforced in the course of the war. During the summer of 1941 the Soviets moved 15 unfinished submarines from the Baltic to the White Sea via the Joseph Stalin Canal. Five other submarines from the Pacific, under the command of Capt. 1st Rank A. V. Tripolsky, reached the Arctic via the Panama Canal after a long and adventurous voyage in which a companion boat was lost in the North Pacific, possibly torpedoed in error by a Japanese submarine.[2] A squadron of destroyers from the Pacific also reached the Arctic by way of the northern sea route. Various other small craft were moved from the Baltic during the war, and in 1944 the fleet was strengthened by the transfer of several British and American vessels.

For the Germans, reinforcement by sea was much easier. Additional ships and planes were shifted to Norwegian waters from time to time; the first real increase early in 1942 was a substantial addition to escort and antisubmarine forces.

Beyond any doubt the most important single phase of the naval war in the Arctic was the one involving the Anglo-American convoys. Hitler considered this traffic of sufficient importance to devote most of the German surface navy, strong Luftwaffe squadrons, and a great many U-boats to its extermination. His success was limited, as indicated by the figures in table 9. Of 3,964,231 long tons of Allied cargo sent by this route some 3,700,000 tons reached destination; of 811 merchant ships used in 40 northbound convoys and 715 ships in 37 southbound convoys, only 98 were lost, though individual convoy losses were sometimes extremely heavy. Table 10 gives a breakdown of British and U.S. supplies shipped to the Soviet Union, mostly through Arctic waters, between March 1941 and

April 1946. Both British and Germans—and to a much lesser extent the Soviets—experienced fairly heavy warship losses in battles to push through the convoys. Although many of the warships and merchant vessels were American, the overall command of this operation rested with the Royal Navy. Russia's contribution to the Allied enterprise consisted in aiding in the escort of convoys as they neared their destination; supplying destroyers as escort for incoming convoys, mainly in purely Russian waters as between the Kola Inlet and Arkhangelsk; furnishing aerial cover; and at times conducting preventive aerial attacks on German-held airfields.

The level of losses experienced by British and Americans depended partly on the efficiency of Russian participation. In the first two years of the war results were seldom satisfactory, possibly owing in degree to the slenderness of Russian naval resources. Of 203 ships used to escort convoys during this period, only five were Soviet. But British officers complained that Soviet escorts often

TABLE 9

*Analysis of Russian Convoys, World War II**

	1941	1942	1943	1944	1945	TOTAL
Number of convoys to north Russia	8	13	6	9	4	40
Number of ships in convoy to north Russia	64	256	112	284	95	811
Number of convoys from north Russia	4	13	6	9	5	37
Number of ships in convoy from north Russia	49	188	93	249	136	715
Ships obliged to turn back due to ice or weather damage	45	21	8	6	1	81
Ships sunk by U-boats	1	24	4	7	5	41
Ships sunk by aircraft	—	36	—	—	1	37
Ships sunk by surface vessels	—	3	—	—	—	3

Ships sunk by aircraft or mines after arrival at Kola Inlet	5
Foundered in a gale	1
Sunk in a British minefield	5
Sunk sailing independently	6
TOTAL number of ships sunk	98

In addition to the above a fleet tanker and a rescue ship were sunk by U-boat and aircraft respectively, making 100 ships in all with a gross registered tonnage of 60,837.

* SOURCE: Brian B. Schofield, *The Russian Convoys* (London, 1964), Appendix I, p. 212. Reprinted by permission.

TABLE 10

British and American War Equipment Shipped to the Soviet Union**

1. BY BRITAIN†
    Between October 1, 1941 and March 31, 1946
    5,218 tanks (of which 1,388 from Canada)
    7,411 aircraft (of which 3,129 from U.S.A.)
    4,932 antitank guns
    4,005 rifles and machine guns
    1,803 sets of radar equipment
    4,338 sets of radio equipment
    2,000 telephone sets
    473,000,000 projectiles

    9 MTBs
    4 submarines
    14 minesweepers

    Total value £308,000,000

    Raw materials, foodstuffs, machinery, industrial plant, medical supplies and hospital equipment to the value of
    £120,000,000

2. BY UNITED STATES‡
    Between March 11, 1941 and October 1, 1945
    14,795 aircraft (67 percent fighters, 26 percent bombers, 7 percent miscellaneous)
    7,537 tanks (including 5,797 medium)
    51,503 jeeps
    35,170 motorcycles
    8,701 tractors
    375,883 trucks
    8,218 antiaircraft guns
    131,633 submachine guns
    345,735 tons of explosives
    1,981 locomotives
    11,155 flatcars and wagons
    540,000 tons of rails
    Over 1,050,000 miles of field telephone cable
    Food shipments to the value of $1,312,000,000
    2,670,000 tons of gasoline
    842,000 tons of chemicals
    3,786,000 tires
    49,000 tons of leather
    15,000,000 pairs of boots

    Total value $11,260,343,603

** SOURCE: Brian B. Schofield, *The Russian Convoys* (London, 1964), Appendix 2, pp. 213–14. Reprinted by permission.
† Statement by Prime Minister in House of Commons, April 16, 1946, and 3rd report on Mutual Aid, 1946.
‡ From information contained in lease-lend reports 19, 20, 21 and 22 to U.S. Congress.

failed to appear and were forever developing defects or fuel shortages which led to a speedy return to port followed by a party in
celebration. At sea, the technical backwardness of Russian crews
and their tendency to unorthodox behavior caused the British to
station Soviet ships well astern of the convoy, where they would be
unlikely to cause confusion, and where they might rescue survivors
of submarine attacks. All in all, the deficiencies of Russian cooperation were sufficiently marked to cause the British to ask for additional help in 1942. In reply, Stalin promised more aid east of 28°
east longitude. Shortly thereafter, on July 15, 1942, a British convoy
was forced to disperse under heavy attack. Two-thirds of the ships
were lost, but two Russian destroyers and an icebreaker transported
the survivors to Arkhangelsk. During this fight the Russian submarine *K-21* got inside the screen of a German task force which
included the superbattleship *Tirpitz* and the heavy cruiser *Scheer*.
The commander later claimed a hit on the *Tirpitz* and the sinking
of a destroyer, but German records do not even indicate an attack.
Apparently the submarine failed to fire a torpedo.

During 1943 there was some easing of problems in convoy operations, though taxing demands on the British Home Fleet continued
because of the presence of heavy German ships in Norwegian
waters. Growing Soviet air strength allowed increased bombing of
German air bases and helped to bring about an improvement. Soviet
bombers were materially aided by the presence on Russian bases of
part of the Royal Air Force, an arrangement to which the Soviets
had assented only with reluctance. Allied convoy losses continued
to decrease throughout 1944, despite a heavy diversion of strength
which was required until the destruction of the *Tirpitz* in late
October. Thereafter, the Germans could present only U-boat and
aerial threats, with the result that subsequent convoy escorts
included only antisubmarine and escort types. In the summer of
1944, the Soviets added to their fleet the battleship *Arkhangelsk*,
(ex-*Royal Sovereign*), the light cruiser *Murmansk* (ex-*Milwaukee*),
an ex-Polish flotilla leader, nine ex-American World War I destroyers, and four ex-British submarines (one of the submarines was
accidentally destroyed en route by a bomber). They received these
vessels in lieu of a share in the surrendered Italian navy which
would have been difficult to move to Soviet waters. The added ships

were occasionally and temporarily used on convoy duty. However, on January 11, 1945, a submarine torpedo was fired at the *Arkhangelsk* and the destroyer *Deiatelny* was lost; after that the Russians ordered the dreadnought to Vaenga Bay, where it remained for the rest of the war.

About March 1945 the first German snorkel submarines appeared in the Arctic, too late to affect the outcome of the war but in time to cause a sharp increase in Allied shipping losses. Russian aid to convoys in the last months of conflict included unskilled but massive air attacks which did some damage to German bases, the employment of Catalinas (U.S. patrol planes granted under lend-lease) to hunt submarines, and the operation off Kola Inlet of a subchaser unit (partly British) to keep U-boats out of the way of approaching convoys.

During the summers of 1942, 1943, and 1944 the Germans staged raids into the Kara and West Siberian seas, probably with a view to intercepting the summer convoys along the northern sea route. The 1942 raid, Operation *Wunderland*, involved the pocket battleship *Admiral Scheer*, the heavy cruiser *Admiral Hipper* and the minelayer *Ulm*, three destroyers, half a dozen submarines, and a few naval reconnaissance planes. The raid started on August 16 when the *Scheer* and two U-boats sortied. Four days later the *Scheer*'s planes reported an eight-ship convoy near Kravkova Island and on August 23 an even larger convoy in Vilkitsky Strait. In neither case were the Germans able to mount a successful attack, since fog in the first instance and pack ice in the second prevented any close approach. They achieved their first success on August 25 against the icebreaker *Sibiriakov,* Sr. Lieutenant Kacharov commanding. The Soviet ship put up a courageous and skillful defense which ended with the crew opening the sea cocks in order to sink with flag flying rather than surrender. Early on August 27 the Germans sailed into Port Dickson off the northwest coast of Siberia, where they destroyed the radio station and shelled the icebreaker *Taimyr* and the tanker *Kuibyshev* (Russian accounts claim injury to the *Scheer* by gunfire at Port Dickson). On August 30 the *Scheer* returned to Narvik. Meantime the U-boats had sunk a 6,000-ton steamer and five tugs and lighters, and had destroyed radio stations. With the aid of the *Hipper*, four submarines and a minelayer had laid a great many small minefields, one of which was at the northern end of Novaia Zemlia and probably the most northerly minefield ever laid. Soviet losses from mines are unknown, but the Germans admitted the sinking of their minelayer *Ulm* and their submarine *U-589*, in both instances by British forces and on the return from Operation Wünderland. The German exploits forced the Russians to divert forces from the Murmansk area to protect the summer traffic, and to set up patrols between Novaia Zemlia and the Kola Peninsula.

During 1943 and 1944 the Germans attempted to repeat their tactics of 1942, but they had lost the element of surprise which so aided their past success. The 1943 raid, which involved the *Lützow* (ex-*Deutschland*, a pocket battleship and sister ship of the *Admiral Scheer*), began in mid-July with minelaying in the Pechora Sea and continued with attacks on merchant shipping and radio stations that netted the destruction of six steamers and two stations. In the exchange two German submarines were lost, the *U-255* to Soviet survey ship *Akademik Shokalsky* and the *U-639* from an unknown cause. Russian countermeasures included the transfer of three destroyers from the Pacific by way of the Siberian Seaway, increase in the armament of icebreakers, and the preparation of subchasers and patrol boats to operate in the Kara Sea.

The 1944 raid, involving six U-boats but no surface forces, was less successful. It cost the Germans one submarine lost in the process of sinking two small steamers.

From the beginning of the war to the end, the largest share of Soviet efforts went into attacks on the German supply lines. In this endeavor the Russians made use of submarines, airplanes, light surface craft, mines, and shore batteries. There was never any lack of targets, since the Germans used vessels both to supply Gen. Eduard Dietl's army in Norway and to transport ore cargoes out of Narvik and Petsamo. This shipping invariably hugged the coast, but in doing so it had to pass several promontories where it was exposed to attack. Though the operations of attacking submarines were not limited by shallow water, as in the Baltic, they were handicapped by fog and inadequate weather reports as well as by the difficulty of distinguishing camouflaged ships against a mountainous coastal background. A more important drawback for the Allies was the

Soviet lack of technical sophistication, instances of which have been noted earlier. The loss of the World War I officer corps, the lateness of attempted rebuilding, and above all twenty years of naval isolationism had left the Red navy far behind those of other powers. The Russians had poor hydrophone detecting gear, no magnetic mines, no degaussing equipment, no radar, and no knowledge of how to sweep magnetic and acoustic mines. Many officers were aware of these weaknesses and avidly sought British and to a lesser degree American blueprints and equipment. However, their mistrust of outsiders, sedulously cultivated by the commissars, made them somewhat skeptical of advice and instruction concerning the newer tools of sea power, so that they learned less than might have been possible.

In view of this background it is not surprising that the Soviet naval response to a *guerre de course* was neither prompt, skillful, nor effective. In fact, the approximately 10 to 12 submarines which the Soviets were able to put to sea in the first few months of the war accomplished almost nothing while two British submarines, *Tigris* and *Trident*, based in Russian waters beginning in August 1941, sank nine ships. Soviet submarines in the same waters sank three. The Russians undoubtedly learned something from the British example, for in November they began submarine minelaying along the Norwegian shipping lanes and within Norwegian harbors, and from December 1941 on these efforts began to pay off in occasional German sinkings. The Soviets claim such sinkings were frequent and that they sank 95,000 tons in 1941 but Jürgen Rohwer, the German naval historian, reports only 28,000 tons in all and only 6,000 tons of this to submarines. Notwithstanding the Soviet official World War II history gives great credit to certain submarines commanders in the area at that time; but captured German records do not sustain these claims.

By early 1942 the Germans were compelled to bring in reinforcements to protect their convoys. For ships following the coast they laid defensive minefields flanking their shipping lanes. The business of sweeping up the uncomplicated Russian mines posed no undue technical difficulties, but it did force the Germans to divert men and ships from other tasks and thus had a certain negative value.

The Russians made considerable use of other weapons. Their batteries on the Fischer Peninsula, well concealed among granite cliffs, were never in the course of the war silenced by the Germans, despite repeated bombing attacks. However, because the guns had to be sighted visually and thus scored very few hits on German ships entering Petsamo, their prime practical value was that they proved a continuing nuisance. Destroyers were not generally employed against German shipping; PT boats were used successfully at times. Naval planes, not present at the beginning of the war, entered the area in increasing numbers in 1942, became much stronger than the German capability in 1943, and throughout 1944 and 1945 held overwhelming superiority over the Luftwaffe. Russian airmen proved adept at improvising operations when faced with formidable obstacles of terrain and climate, but they proved less successful in attacks on convoys. On only a few occasions were there any sinkings to show for several all-out attempts, and Soviet air losses in such attacks were likely to be heavy. Late in the war the Russians attempted with some success to coordinate their various weapons in joint aircraft-submarine-PT boat attacks.

While the Soviet Union's war of attrition in the Arctic also claimed a certain number of victims, it never represented an important threat to the Germans, who calculated their losses of tonnage convoyed at .82 percent for 1942, .63 percent for 1943, and .45 percent for 1944. The small figure for 1944 is especially impressive since it includes losses incurred during the evacuation of Finnish and Norwegian territory and at a time when the Northern Fleet had expanded to a force which included about 80 submarines as well as strong naval aviation and PT boat flotillas. Unless German records are greatly in error, Soviet submarines from November 1944 to the end of the war failed to record a single major sinking. In all, the Soviets lost some twenty submarines and sank about thirty cargo ships and some armed trawlers—certainly not for them a favorable exchange rate.

The Northern Fleet was also responsible for the protection of purely Russian convoys, especially in Soviet coastal waters. Except in the case of the already noted German raid into the Kara Sea, this work was usually somewhat prosaic in character. Since the Germans considered the great Allied convoys more important, it was seldom that any action was demanded beyond escort and patrol duty near the coast. One exception was the Kola Gulf where some 20 percent of the British and American sinkings occurred and where their allies tended to be critical of Soviet naval operations. These tasks were the main concern of the smaller patrol craft, subchasers, and occasionally destroyers, and were usually performed by the White Sea Flotilla.

Because of the relatively inactive land front, there was no strong demand for naval assistance to the Red army in the Arctic until 1944. During the three-year hiatus in land fighting Soviet destroyers and minesweepers occasionally bombarded German coastal positions. Efforts were uncoordinated and did little damage to an enemy who was deeply entrenched. Then the surrender of Finland on September 3, 1944, forced a German retreat through areas occupied by hostile Finns. Although a Russian amphibious landing near Petsamo in October 1944 slightly increased the hazard of the retreat from northern Finland, however, the German operation had been skillfully completed by mid-November. The Germans also abandoned several ports in northern Norway, beginning October 11, 1944. Soviet attempts to disrupt the evacuation took the form of very heavy air attacks combined with submarine and PT boat offensives, but entirely failed to make use of larger surface ships. In three weeks the Germans lost four medium-size transports and cargo ships as well as a minesweeper, a subchaser, and four very small vessels. In the same period the Russians, besides having many planes shot down, lost three PT's.

Because the Arctic was the one theater in which Soviet naval officers and men came into extensive contact with their British and American opposite numbers, the subject of inter-Allied relations in the area is of considerable interest. Few of the sailors who were stationed in Murmansk or Arkhangelsk for any length of time were pleased by their experiences. Bad weather, inadequate food and fuel, and extreme boredom were the most frequent complaints. British observers reported a tremendous confusion and gross inefficiency at the wharves, where most of the cargo handling was stupidly and carelessly done by convict gangs. Occasionally conditions grew so bad that an important official had to be dispatched from Moscow to clean things up. Long delays and constantly encountered obstructionism apparently had their origins in the intense suspicion of foreigners which was cultivated by the Soviet government. These conditions were further aggravated by the built-in red tape of the Communist system under which local commanders had to request instructions from Moscow on virtually every matter, as well as by the common practice of deliberate needling by petty officials. While local Soviet commanders almost never refused requests outright, they frequently failed to notify their allies of difficulties or delays. Some directives, such as a refusal (later reversed) to permit a British hospital unit to operate at Arkhangelsk or an unexplained slowness in permitting a Royal Air Force base to be established near Murmansk, obviously injured their own interests. Yet the Russians as individuals were friendly, grateful, and willing to share with their allies the little they possessed.

So far as Russian naval efficiency was concerned, foreign observers with few exceptions tended to be critical. British Vice Adm. Sir Ian Campbell acknowledged that antiaircraft gunners of four Russian destroyers attached to one convoy had "put up a splendid performance when put to it."[3] He nevertheless complained that Britishers in Soviet posts were subjected to petty restrictions and inconveniences and received neither help nor appreciation. He further criticized the Russians' misuse of American subchasers and their refusal to patrol for U-boats for fear of mistaking their own fishing boats, and concluded:

> It was an inescapable fact that the Russians lacked all flair for naval warfare at that time, whatever they may have developed since. The success of the Arctic convoys owed almost nothing to the efforts of those for whose benefits they were run. The Soviets, for their part, were not unduly complimentary to their allies. The captain of one of the submarines the British transferred in 1944 complained in a book that British ships were disorderly and unkempt and that the British were claiming credit for the defeat of the U-boat which was obviously due to the defeat of the Germans at Stalingrad![4]

INLAND WATERS

The Soviet Union is like the United States in its geographical endowment of lakes and rivers large enough to set the scene for historically important naval action. In fact, as noted in chapter 1, the earliest Russian naval power was employed on the great rivers. During the Russian civil war the Caspian, the Volga, the Don, and the Siberian rivers held much the same importance as did the inland waterways of the United States during the American civil war. In World War II they were at least equally vital.

During the rapid German advance of 1941, the Pioneers (Army) of the Third Reich set up on their own internal waterways local flotillas of assault boats and such other craft as they could find. In the early stages of the war these German flotillas dominated the rivers. Opposing Russian boat patrols were either destroyed by the Wehrmacht (as on the Prut, Dniester, and Don) or else were scuttled by their own crews. But on some rivers it proved possible for small Russian flotillas either to retreat out of harm's way or to transfer to other waters. The Germans, as noted in chapter 18, brought in ships from the Danube for the Black Sea battles. Similarly, the Russians in 1944 used parts of the Lake Ladoga Flotilla in the Sea of Azov and later in the Danube. The Soviet use of naval power on the rivers was slightly more advanced and of less improvised character than that of the Germans, however; the Soviets assigned naval personnel to serve on the inland waterways while the Germans not only used inexperienced army personnel but frequently satellite crews as well.

There were other factors, too, which made the Soviets better prepared to wage war on the internal waterways. River flotillas had played important roles in the civil war, the brief war with Poland, and the occupation of Belorussia in 1939. While the craft that fought in those wars were mainly converted merchant ships, barges, and other small non-combat vessels, the Soviets between 1933 and 1941 had designed monitors, motor gunboats, gunboat minesweepers, and rocket-launching craft for use specifically on rivers. Though these new types were not sufficiently numerous to alter entirely the ad hoc character of some of the flotillas, their development indicates a high degree of continuing Soviet interest. Ships of this kind were typically small and fast, usually carried guns, howitzers, and machine guns, and occasionally were equipped with mines. The missions of lake and river flotillas, basically the same in all theaters, included gunfire support for ground forces and for river crossings, landings on enemy flanks and in the rear of their defenses, antimine operations, escort of shipping, and transport of troops and supplies, as well as opposition to enemy landing efforts.

The greatest strategic contribution of any of these flotillas was unquestionably made by the Lake Ladoga Flotilla during the siege of Leningrad. Within less than three months of the initial German attack in June 1941 the Wehrmacht had established a blockade around Leningrad and cut the last railroad communications. Hitler had announced that he would completely destroy the city and accept no surrender. Food stocks for three million people were low, and for more than a month there was confusion and disorganization in the defense effort. Then Gen. Georgy K. Zhukov was sent to the city and virtually overnight produced order, purpose, and an adequate plan for defense. Yet for all Zhukov's moves and despite all the efforts of the defenders, Leningrad would have died of starvation had it not been for the Soviet success in opening and protecting a new supply line across Lake Ladoga. During the winter the thick ice supported a roadway; during the warmer weather a fleet of old steamers, barges, lighters, launches, and miscellaneous floating craft transported troops and supplies, not in sufficient quantity to prevent inconceivable suffering but in quantity great enough to sustain resistance for nearly two and a half years. Thus the control of the lake was strategically vital to both sides—and it was the Lake Ladoga Flotilla which supplied protection for the entire Soviet operation.

Following the Winter War of 1939–40 the shores of Lake Ladoga lay entirely within the Soviet Union. But the progress of German and Finnish forces was such that as early as August 6, 1941, the Finns were reestablishing a lake flotilla comprised of two tugs, four barges, and some 150 motor boats which carried small cannons, machine guns, and, in a few instances, mines. While this force was too small to counter the Russian flotilla—which at that time consisted of three gunboats, the old destroyer *Konstruktor* (ex-*Sibirsky Strelok*), about 20 patrol boats, and numerous lesser craft under Rear Adm. V. S. Cherokov—it cooperated with the Finnish army in the encirclement of a Russian division. In the largest of a number of small actions on the lake the Russians landed on two islands held by weak Finnish forces, then failed to use their naval superiority to block Finnish reinforcements.

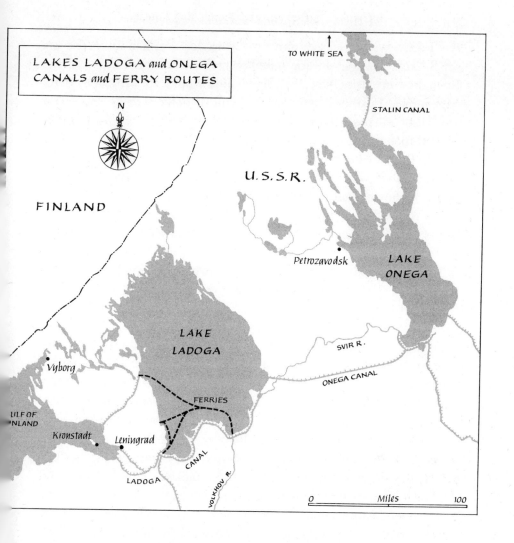

LAKES LADOGA and ONEGA
CANALS and FERRY ROUTES

Meanwhile the land war was going badly for the Russians, who were forced to evacuate two infantry divisions pressed against the coast as well as to give up the western shore of the lake and a number of islands. When the land fighting subsided into positional warfare, naval activity on the lake died down. Despite their acquisition of a Latvian steamer, whose crew they murdered, the Finns were too weak to attack the Russians. The Russians for their part made no attempt to interfere with the Finnish supply traffic in the northern end of the lake.

An early German effort to cut the naval supply line across the south end of the lake received comparatively little assistance from the Finns, who released only one ship for German use. The six small craft brought in for minelaying accomplished little, as the Russians were using wooden ships which would not ordinarily detonate mines. Further, they were too full of defects to be usable for any other purpose. Three small minelayers brought in by rail also proved ineffective. Four Italian MAS boats, however, destroyed one of the Russian gunboats and a 1,300-ton lighter. These boats also demonstrated versatility in guarding German shipping, hunting a mythical Soviet submarine, and landing saboteurs and spies. But the northern lights disturbed the Italian crews and the boats themselves were unable to operate in the very shallow waters used by the Soviet supply craft.

The real backbone of the German naval forces on Lake Ladoga were to be the Siebel ferries, which could be broken down and shipped by rail. When put into operation, however, they proved very slow, and so noisy as to undo any plan of surprise. Also, their completely inexperienced crews were not ready for action until late August 1942. When on August 25–26, 1942, a fleet of the ferries finally ventured into central Lake Ladoga with two MAS boats in support, they failed to contact any Soviet ships and suffered some damage from air attack. They made two attacks on the Russian base at Sukho, on the second occasion landing a demolition party which silenced the Sukho battery and did considerable damage ashore. But the small German squadron was in turn attacked by both planes and warships of a better-trained force of Russians. In this, the only Soviet fleet engagement of the entire war, the Germans were soundly beaten with the loss of at least five ferries (the Soviets claimed 19 of 38 German ferries and 15 planes destroyed). During 1943 the Russians were able to regain enough territory to establish a land supply line; hence the German opportunity to take Leningrad was definitely lost.

After the fleet action in 1942 Lake Ladoga was to see little activity until the beginning of the big Allied offensive of 1944, when the Soviets made good use of their naval forces there to land troops. In June of that year the flotilla was used to counter Finnish batteries and to support landings during the Russian offensive between Lakes Ladoga and Onega. And as the extent of the Axis defeat on land became apparent, the Finns withdrew all possible naval forces from the lake.

It is obvious that the Russian performance on Lake Ladoga was a success. It undoubtedly saved Leningrad, though at a cost of about 124 ships and boats of some 50,000 tons, and contributed materially to other Soviet concerns as well. As for the Finns, they made good use of what they had, but their forces were too small and too widely dispersed for any outstanding accomplishment.

Lake Peipus, located along the pre-1940 boundary between Estonia and Russia, was not a bone of contention for the entire war nor did it possess great strategic importance. Yet it was the scene of some action. It fell into German hands in 1941, and the Germans, to aid their own communications, set up a small squadron of police and motor boats. In 1943 during forced German retreat on land the squadron was strengthened to include 24 MAL's (naval artillery lighters of about 280 tons), 30 launches, 27 heavy assault boats, four minelayers, and some command boats, Siebel ferries, barges, etc., in an attempt to hold back the Red army. When the Soviets gained a foothold on the lake they established a similar but much smaller fleet comprising chiefly shallow draft gunboats armed with searchlights and small cannon. For a time thereafter, the Germans' naval superiority allowed them to retain considerable freedom in carrying on transportation plus some protection from surprise Russian landings. However, in several skirmishes that took place on the lake and despite a limited amount of minelaying, the Germans were unable to dislodge the Soviet squadron or to silence its covering coastal batteries. Meantime the strength of the Red air force was steadily increasing, and the German vessels were subjected to very heavy and almost continuous air attacks which did considerable damage. In August 1944 the Germans reluctantly recognized the inevitability of defeat. Wherever possible they removed their vessels by rail; those remaining were scuttled.

Lake Ilmen, south and slightly east of Leningrad, is one of the larger Russian lakes, but strategically not one of the most important. In 1941 the Germans seized its western shore together with some fifty of the eighty sailing fishing boats that normally operated on the lake. Only the swampy east shore of the lake and the thirty remaining fishing boats remained in Russian hands. A Russian attempt to repossess the lake during the winter of 1941–42 was repulsed, but the Germans, convinced that their security was endan-

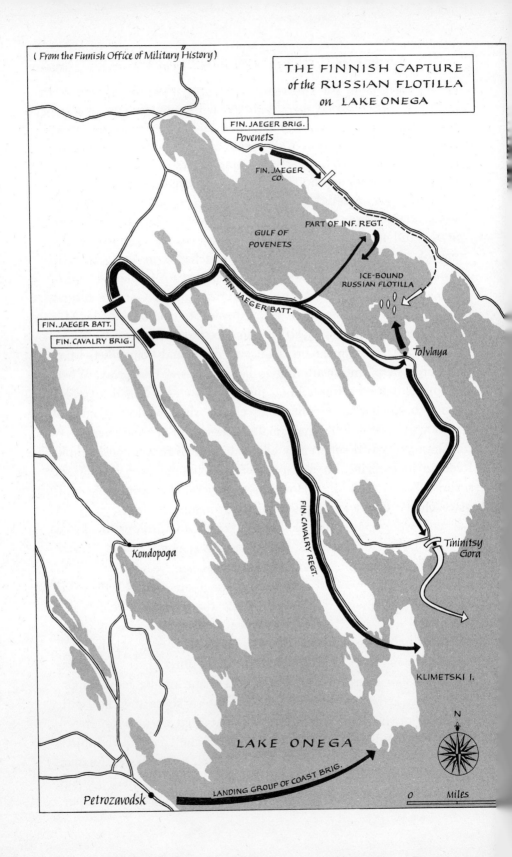

(From the Finnish Office of Military History)

THE FINNISH CAPTURE
of the RUSSIAN FLOTILLA
on LAKE ONEGA

FIN. JAEGER BRIG.

Povenets

FIN. JAEGER
CO.

PART OF INF. REGT.

GULF OF
POVENETS

ICE-BOUND
RUSSIAN FLOTILLA

FIN. JAEGER BATT.

FIN. JAEGER BATT.

FIN. CAVALRY BRIG.

Tolvlaya

FIN. CAVALRY REGT.

Kondopoga

Tininitsy
Gora

KLIMETSKI I.

N

LAKE ONEGA

LANDING GROUP OF COAST BRIG.

Petrozavodsk

0   Miles

gered, brought in Siebel ferries, converted their fishing boats to naval use, and manned them with 300 army personnel. Such a large squadron was entirely unrelated to the needs of the area and in fact had been opposed by the German navy. The Russians made no effort to organize a fleet on Lake Ilmen but continued to land agents either by boat at night or by air. These constant threats by an estimated 500 Russians tied up at least 5,000 German troops.

Lake Onega, directly east of Lake Ladoga and connected with it by the Svir River, witnessed some extremely brilliant and daring Finnish naval operations. During the high-water mark of Axis attack the Finns reached and damaged the Joseph Stalin canal, obtaining a foothold on the coastline of Lake Onega before the Russian defense stiffened. Because their control was incomplete, the Finns had to make the most of the limited resources available. They raised and reconditioned 14 small ships and commissioned six tugs seized in a shipyard, brought in 17 motor boats of their own and a naval supply battalion, and set up a base on the lake. On November 11, 1941, their scouts sighted an ice-bound Russian convoy. On the orders of Lt. Col. Wahlbeck, the Finnish battalion commander, the vessels were attacked at midnight November 12–13 by a party under one Lt. Lehtonen. By 4:00 A.M. the Russians had surrendered and the Finns were in possession of 41 small vessels including tugs, barges, and motor and sailing boats loaded with food, clothing, fuel, and machinery. In addition there were 1,000 prisoners of war. Acting with great speed the Finns next brought in the necessary personnel and fuel, repelled ineffective attacks by Soviet bombers and a demolition party, and evacuated their new fleet through a narrow channel which the Russians had blasted through the ice. The entire operation was completed in about one week. The Finns also took over some trawlers, and a lighter which was building in a Soviet shipyard. The captured fleet was organized into patrol and transport divisions and quickly armed. Though the Soviet fleet continued to remain inactive, it had learned a lesson in alertness: a later Finnish effort to seize Russian ships by a 100-man attack across the ice failed, and Finnish air strikes which destroyed one lighter were otherwise ineffective.

After this violent beginning, naval activity on Lake Onega died down appreciably. In the meantime both sides reinforced their flotillas so that ultimately the Soviet force (originally 15 tugs and 25–30 lighters stationed at the mouth of the Vodla River) included about 23 gunboats of several types, approximately 25 tugs, and numerous motor boats and lighters. The Finnish force comprised three gunboats, an armed motor boat, a picket boat, a transport, nine trawlers, three passenger steamers, 18 tugs, two lighters, eight 900-ton barges, two tank lighters, 173 small motor boats, and a few other lighters and barges, mostly captured from the Russians. The two flotillas never met in battle. The Finns were able to transport men and supplies very much at will, though at a cost of several vessels lost. The principal Soviet activities were minelaying, occasional shore bombardments, and the landing of agents. Despite the tremendous performance put on by the Finns, the contest for Lake Onega was decided by the course of the war on land, where the Finns were finally forced to yield to the greatly superior man power and resources of their opponents. In late June 1944 the Finns evacuated what ships and war materiel they could and destroyed the rest.

The Caspian Sea, by far the largest inland body of water in the world and the site of a great deal of fighting throughout the civil war, remained comparatively quiet during World War II. In the summer of 1941 Russians from the north and British in the south seized Iran and deposed the shah. The British in the Persian Gulf sank about eight minor Iranian warships, the Soviets seized all Iranian shipping in the Caspian (returned after the war), and Iran for the next four years served as a main link in the transport line between the Soviets and their Western allies.

In a naval sense the Caspian remained almost completely inactive, and was in fact used as a training area by the Soviet navy. At the height of the German offensive during 1942 the Luftwaffe mounted air and mine attacks on targets at the mouth of the Volga. On October 27, 1942, the Germans claimed to have set fire to two Russian patrol boats in the Caspian and on November 1 to have sunk four tankers and five transports. There is a possibility that there were also some losses from German mines. But these claims, even if true, are not indicative of extensive damage. German plans called for the establishment (in 1942) of a Caspian flotilla comprising wooden minelayers and S-boats, but the Wehrmacht was stopped before it seized the necessary area to carry out this project.

In any case it is doubtful whether the operation, as conceived, could have been effective: the German plans contemplated using only very small forces, and the Soviets, to whom Caspian oil transported by both Volga tankers and rail lines was absolutely essential, would certainly have put forth a great defensive effort.

The Volga Flotilla, created in 1941 from ships based on the Caspian, from private boats and new construction, performed a strategic mission on inland waters second only to that of the Soviet flotilla on Lake Ladoga. Its small wartime missions included protection of the vital barge traffic from the Caspian, and the service provided consisted of sweeping up magnetic mines and supplying antiaircraft protection. During the siege of Stalingrad the flotilla, reinforced ashore by several battalions from the Pacific Fleet, sent in its best vessels to furnish antiaircraft fire and artillery support, to transport and land troops, and to protect river shipping. Several individual vessels distinguished themselves, among them the *Usyskin* and the *Chapaev*. The Volga Flotilla also was charged with preventing possible German attempts to cross the river. Though the Soviet vessels were mainly out of effective range of the Luftwaffe, the Germans claimed they sank a few gunboats and two monitors by artillery gunfire, bombing, and mines.

Probably the most active of the Soviet Union's regularly constituted river flotillas was the one on the Dnieper. In June 1940 that force was divided into the newly created Danube Flotilla and the Pinsk Flotilla. The latter operated in the same area as the Dnieper Flotilla and at the outbreak of war was commanded by Rear Adm. D. D. Rogachev. In June 1941 it consisted of nine monitors, eight gunboats, nine patrol boats, 16 motor gunboats, 14 gunboat-minesweepers, and various older small craft, in addition to base facilities ashore, especially at Pinsk and Kiev. In mid-July the flotilla was divided into three detachments (Pripet, Berezina, and Dnieper), each subordinate to the army command in its particular area.[5]

The river detachments performed under extremely trying conditions, under constant exposure to enemy air, tank, and artillery attack. In some cases they also had to operate in areas where one or both river banks were held by the Germans. Further, the armies they were supporting were reeling back in defeat. They remained in action in 1941 for periods of up to three months before being destroyed by either the Luftwaffe or the Wehrmacht, and during this time their support for river crossings, together with determined opposition to similar enemy attempts and to artillery harassment, probably helped prevent a decisive defeat from becoming a complete rout. As in the case of the fleets, there were inadequacies in both organization and training. The crews, after the destruction of their ships, joined either the partisans or the Red army forces.

When after more than two years of fighting the Red army was able to return to the scenes of its 1941 defeat, the Soviet leaders decided one of their first steps would be to recreate river flotillas. On September 14, 1943, the Dnieper River Flotilla was formed once more. The winter was spent in organization and training, but from April 1944 on the ships were used to provide support for a wide variety of land operations along the central and southern fronts. The flotilla's principal activities were landing troops, furnishing gunfire support to the army ashore, and moving men and equipment in swampy and hard-to-reach regions bordering rivers. On occasion the small ships penetrated far behind the loosely held front to disembark the army units which seized strong points in the German rear. Units of the Dnieper Flotilla were transferred by rail where water movement was impossible, and in 1945 they supported the Red army on the Vistula, the Oder, and even the Spree.

The Soviet Danube Flotilla was created in the Sea of Azov on April 20, 1944, for the purpose of giving naval support to the Red armies in their planned penetration of the Balkans. It originally consisted mainly of PT boats and armored landing craft and was definitely inferior to the opposing German naval forces. However, it had the support of greatly superior Red army and Red air force units, so that its relative weakness did not prove decisive.

Approximately four months after its creation the Danube Flotilla was used in combat. Brought to Zaporozhe by railroad, the ships descended the Dnieper to the Black Sea. Their August 24, 1944, landing at the mouth of the Danube brought about the destruction of three Rumanian river monitors and the surrender of most other Rumanian warships. As the Red army moved inland along the Danube, the small naval vessels accompanied it. The German vessels on the river seldom resisted although they were usually superior in numbers, but they did seek to evacuate persons from the Balkans.

The progress up the Danube of the two flotillas, German and

Russian, furnished one of the more colorful adventure stories of World War II. A German river fleet of 200 assorted vessels gathered at Brăila under Rear Admiral Zieb on August 25, 1944, to begin what the refugees hoped would be a successful voyage into Germany. By dint of a great deal of improvising and bluffing, plus occasional fighting, the German force was able to pass through hostile Rumania with the loss of only 20 small craft. For more than a week all went well. By the time the flotilla entered Yugoslavia, however, the Red army had already seized the Iron Gate on the Danube below Belgrade. A projected Axis counter-attack to regain the position long enough to enable the flotilla to pass failed to materialize. The force then disbanded and Zieb scuttled nearly all of his ships; only about a dozen fell into Russian hands.[6]

The Russian Danube Flotilla, delayed somewhat by the necessity of sweeping new German and old Allied mines, moved more slowly and in a less improvised manner. It aided the Red army in crossings of the Danube, mopped up the resistance of a few Rumanian diehards still loyal to the Germans, and landed Red army forces to liquidate the retreating Germans. When it started up the Danube about three days later than the Germans it was in considerably less force. Two Rumanian river monitors were sunk en route, as well as a German vessel which had failed to join Zieb's force. Further delays were incurred while the Red army troops eliminated German-manned batteries at Galatz. On August 27 the flotilla accepted the capitulation of five monitors and other vessels of the Rumanian river flotilla.

For eight more months a steadily increasing Soviet Danube Flotilla participated in the war, its forces swelled by captured Rumanian and German craft as it moved upriver. A few Soviet boats were damaged by shore fire or mines, but on the whole losses were low. The flotilla supplied river transportation for more than 100,000 troops, carried on troop landings, and furnished mobile artillery support for the advance of the Red army. It played an active part in the battles of Prakhov, Belgrade, and Budapest, and on April 11, 1945, it had a distinguished role in the capture of Vienna when naval infantry moving in armored motorboats seized intact the one surviving bridge across the Danube and removed Axis demolition charges.

Other small craft fought on Lake Balaton in the interior of Hungary. At the time of the final German surrender the foremost detachment of the Danube Flotilla and the 83rd Brigade of naval infantry were operating at Linz, Austria.

THE PACIFIC

Stalin could scarcely have found a role more to his liking than the one he played with regard to Japan in World War II. By withholding Soviet involvement in the Pacific phase of the war, he had both enhanced the value of Soviet neutrality in the eyes of the Japanese and stimulated American desire to secure his aid. As a consequence, when a promise of future Soviet belligerency was secured at Yalta, the Russians obtained extremely generous territorial concessions which allowed them to occupy northern Korea and Manchuria, and to annex outright Sakhalin and the Kurile Island chain. By August 1945, when Japan was hopelessly defeated and actually looking for a way to surrender, Stalin appeared likely to reap a sizable profit for minimal participation. He had tentatively committed the Soviet Union to entering the Pacific war three months after the downfall of Hitler, and the dropping of the atomic bomb may or may not have hastened his decision to act. Certainly it did nothing to retard it: the bomb opened up the possibility of Japanese surrender prior to a Soviet declaration of war, and that might have deprived the Russians of a share of the spoils.

By August 9, 1945, when the Soviet Union declared war on Japan, Russian preparations were complete and the Red army and Pacific Fleet were ready to launch simultaneous attacks in many directions. Army, navy, and air force were under the supreme command of Marshal A. V. Vasilevsky. On the land side the leaders were Marshal K. A. Meretskov, Gen. M. A. Purkeyev, and Marshal R. Ya. Malinovsky; they commanded respectively the First Far Eastern, Second Far Eastern, and Zabaikal fronts. Fleet Adm. N. G. Kuznetsov was in charge of coordinating naval forces, which included the command of the Soviet Pacific Fleet under Adm. I. S. Yumashev and those of two subordinate organizations—the North Pacific Flotilla under Rear Adm. V. A. Andreev and the Red Banner Amur Flotilla under Rear Adm. N. V. Antonov. According to Soviet figures, the

Pacific Fleet then consisted of two cruisers (*Kalinin* and *Kaganovich*) of the 8,800-ton *Kirov* type, a flotilla leader, ten destroyers, 78 submarines, 204 motor torpedo boats, 19 destroyer escorts and frigates, 49 subchasers, and 34 minesweepers—the minesweepers and frigates being lend-lease ships from the United States. Naval planes numbered 1,549. The fleet was based mainly on Vladivostok, with the Northern Pacific Flotilla principally at Sovetskaia Gavan and in lesser strength at Petropavlovsk. The Amur Flotilla contained about 200 small warships of the river monitor, gunboat, motor gunboat, patrol boat, minesweeper, and similar types. The Japanese, decimated by four years of war, were far weaker in the air, on the sea, and on land.

Soviet participation in the Pacific phase of World War II started on August 9 and ended formally with the surrender of the Kuriles on August 23. Informally, it lasted into mid-September due to the presence of Japanese units that continued to resist after surrender. From a naval standpoint it may be divided into four phases: (1) the occupation of North Korea, (2) the conquest of Sakhalin, (3) the fight for the Kuriles, and (4) activities of the Amur River Flotilla.[7]

The Soviet landings in Korea followed in general outline the amphibious methods developed by the United States in the Pacific, though they were far more hurried and impromptu, on a much smaller scale, and carried out with less impressive weapons and simpler techniques than those used by the forces of Admiral Nimitz. Preliminary reconnaissance was not always employed by the Russians due to the pressure of time affecting their operations, but where used it was performed by submarine or airplane. Landings were almost always preceded by aerial bombing and in some instances also by naval gunfire. This preliminary softening up seldom required more than two days and in a few cases was omitted altogether.

Four main Soviet landings were made in Korea. The Yuki assault landing on August 11 was made from a task force of two frigates, two escorts, a trawler, and eight motor torpedo boats under Rear Adm. N. S. Ivanovsky. Because most of the Japanese had left the area, the landing was virtually unopposed.

The Rashin landing of August 12, under Capt. 1st Rank E. E. Poltavsky, may be regarded as complementary to the Yuki landing,

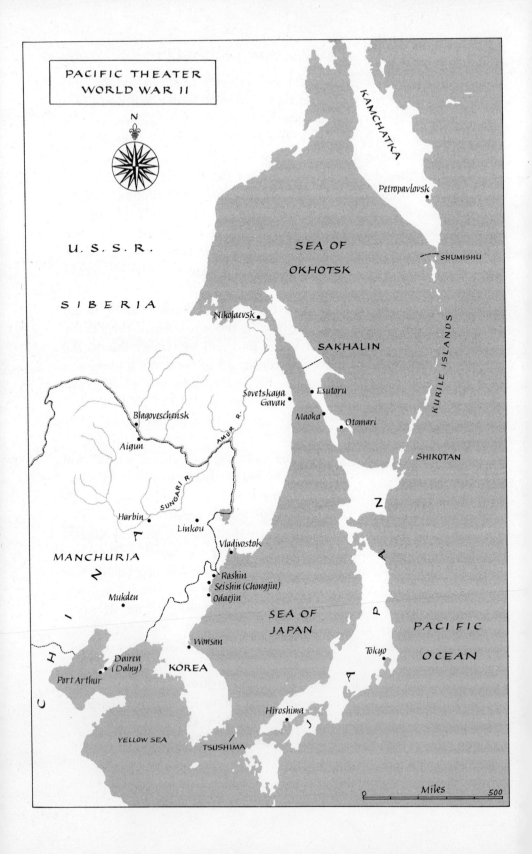

PACIFIC THEATER
WORLD WAR II

N

U.S.S.R.

SIBERIA

KAMCHATKA

Petropavlovsk

SEA OF
OKHOTSK

SHUMISHU

Nikolaevsk

SAKHALIN

Sovetskaya
Gavan

Esutoru

Blagoveschensk

Maoka

Otomari

AMUR R.

Aigun

SHIKOTAN

SUNGARI R.

Harbin

Linkou

Vladivostok

MANCHURIA

Rashin
Seishin (Chongjin)
Odaejin

Mukden

SEA OF
JAPAN

J
A
P
A
N

PACIFIC

OCEAN

Tokyo

Wonsan

Dairen
(Dalny)

KOREA

C
H
I
N
A

Port Arthur

Hiroshima

YELLOW SEA

TSUSHIMA

KURILE ISLANDS

Miles

0   500

since some of the Yuki troops helped capture Rashin. Rashin was cleared on August 18 at a cost of seven Russians killed and 37 wounded, compared to Japanese losses of 277 killed and 292 captured. Three Soviet landing ships and later six other craft struck mines, probably laid earlier by American planes.

The Seishin (Chongjin) landing on August 13, made under the direction of Admiral Yumashev, met fairly strong opposition and the initial troops of the 390th Infantry Battalion encountered hard going and very heavy losses. Much stronger forces embarked at Vladivostok landed August 15 under command of Lt. Gen. of the Shore Service I. S. Kabanov. The ships for this landing force consisted of six escorts, ten landing ships, four transports, and three trawlers, all commanded by Capt. 1st Rank A. F. Studenichnikov. They gave fire support, but the victory was won on land after a vigorous but brief fight for which Soviet casualties have not been published. Those of the Japanese amounted to more than 3,000 killed or taken prisoner.

The Wonsan-Odaejin landing on August 21 was made to prevent evacuation or reinforcement of the Japanese in Korea. The original landing forces were heavily outnumbered; but reinforcements, plus news of the main Japanese surrender, prevented the Soviet position from becoming critical. By the end of August all Japanese forces north of the 38th parallel had surrendered.

Unlike those in Korea, the Sakhalin landings were spur-of-the-moment affairs, decided on only when the resistance of the Kwantung army in Manchuria proved weaker than originally expected. They involved a southward march of Soviet troops already stationed in northern Sakhalin, plus three landings by men and ships of the North Pacific Flotilla. Since the Soviets held a decisive superiority on land and sea and in the air, there was little doubt of the outcome of the campaign, though air support was at times ruled out by heavy fogs and storms. The initial landing at Esutoru on August 16 was virtually unopposed, and the landing force captured Toro the next day.

The main objective of the Sakhalin campaign was Maoka, where a preliminary reconnaissance by submarine indicated that opposition might be expected. For that move the Soviet landing force consisted of 3,500 troops, plus an escort vessel, a minelayer, two large subchasers, five patrol craft, four minesweepers, six transports, and four motor torpedo boats. These were organized into a detachment of support ships and three detachments of landing craft. On the evening of August 19 the landing party sortied from Sovetskaia Gavan, and the next morning landed at Maoka, in a fog and against light Japanese opposition. Soviet troops were put ashore in waves and by nightfall had secured the town. Later part of the Maoka task force was shipped to Otomari, where it landed on August 25. On the same day other Russian forces who had broken through the Japanese Koton defense line in the north also reached Otomari. The 3,400-man Japanese garrison surrendered, ending a campaign which netted over 18,000 Japanese prisoners.

The Kurile Islands, northernmost of Japan's main outposts, were reported to be well fortified and garrisoned by a force which Soviet estimates put at 80,000 men, with space for 600 aircraft on nine separate air fields (actual strength turned out to be only seven planes and 65,000 troops). Shumishu, a small island with a garrison of about 8,500 men only six and a half miles from Kamchatka, was believed to be the most heavily fortified of all. It thus appeared that although Japan had officially surrendered on August 14, the Japanese had the means to make any enemy landing in the Kurile chain expensive if they chose not to lay down their arms.

Soviet plans called for occupation of the northern islands of the chain, including Shumishu, prior to an assault on Paramushiru farther south. The initial landing on Shumishu was made early on August 18 with the aid of about 30 transports and landing craft which had been dispatched from Petropavlovsk under escort of two destroyers and a submarine. There was a preliminary softening by planes and ships. In the process, enemy gunfire claimed one Soviet patrol craft and four landing boats and damaged others. Once the troops reached the beachhead and were able to move forward, they had considerable difficulty in unloading heavy equipment under enemy fire. Japanese aircraft also put in an appearance and made attacks on the ships.

After this unpromising beginning the situation improved rapidly. The local Japanese had acted before receiving any news of the surrender, and by August 19 the Japanese commanding general in the Kuriles was offering to discuss surrender terms at Kataoka. However, when Soviet ships approaching for the scheduled meeting were

fired on by shore batteries the Russians withdrew to make preparations for an all-out assault. Meantime spreading news of the surrender enabled the Japanese general at Kataoka to gain command
of his bitter-enders. On August 13 the island surrendered.

The Shumishu surrender proved definitive: in no other instance
did the Soviets encounter resistance. The remaining islands of the
group were occupied one by one, the final surrender being on Shikotan September 5. The conquest of the Kuriles netted nearly 64,000
prisoners.

The major Soviet military operation against Japan was the occupation of Manchuria against the opposition of the famous Kwantung
army. As a major military test, it was a fiasco. All through World
War II the once mighty Kwantung army had been weakened by
the dispatch of its best units to shore up Japan's crumbling defenses
in her island empire; Americans had, in fact, fought ex-Kwantung
army troops all over the Pacific. At the time of the Soviet attack this
highly regarded Japanese force was only a shell of its former
strength, outnumbered in manpower by the Russians and even more
greatly outmatched in all kinds of weapons and equipment. Despite
heavy Japanese counterattacks the Soviet troops experienced no
difficulty penetrating into Manchuria. The Soviets made free use of
air-dropped troops, partly to confuse the defenders and especially
to occupy Port Arthur and Dairen, where they feared possible American landings. After heavy fighting and one day after the occupation
of Harbin, Stalin announced the surrender of the Japanese, although
some Japanese units fought on after that date.

The Amur River Flotilla played a classical and highly important
role during the conquest of Manchuria with gunfire support, organization of river crossings, and transport of troops. Expected opposition from the Japanese Sungari River Flotilla, which consisted of
about 30 monitors and river gunboats, did not develop; indeed,
Japanese river ports were seized with almost no opposition from any
quarters. In the north the flotilla assisted General Purkeyev by
moving his troops along the rivers. When heavy fighting developed
on August 15–16 at Linkou, the flotilla moved in troops which reinforced the 34th Division and defeated the Japanese. In the Blago-
veshchensk-Aigun area the vessels provided both transportation and
fire support for three major river crossings, and in the battle for
Aigun they rendered similar valuable assistance. Finally, on August

21–22, the flotilla landed Soviet forces at Harbin to accept the Japanese surrender.

The Pacific fighting, though it was waged very briefly and against an already beaten enemy, showed the Red navy in a somewhat better light than did the fighting in the Black Sea and the Baltic. In the Pacific the Soviets used rather than hoarded their ships, with performance results that ranged from adequate to good. Major weaknesses, mainly due to lack of experience, were evident in command, coordination, and communications, and are in fact recognized by Soviet writers. The official Soviet claim for damage to the Japanese by the Pacific Fleet totals two destroyers, 28 transports, three tankers, five cutters, and 12 barges. It is not possible to check these claims against Japanese official loss figures, but they are probably excessive. Admiral Yumashev's far more modest claim of a Japanese destroyer and eight transports sunk by the Soviets seems more realistic and may well be accurate.

No Japanese statistics on the short war with Russia have so far been made available. Soviet figures released in September 1945 claim Japanese losses at 80,000 killed, 594,000 prisoners (later accounts revise this number upward to total losses of a million men), and 925 planes. Russian casualties were stated to be 8,000 dead and 22,000 wounded. Even allowing for the weakened condition of Japanese forces the Soviets are substantially correct in claiming a major victory. But their official propaganda line—that destruction of the Kwantung army ended a war that otherwise might have lasted for years and led directly to Japan's surrender—cannot be taken seriously outside the Communist world.

The end of the Pacific war left a bad taste in the mouths of Russians and Americans alike. The Russians were alarmed at American atomic achievements, and the Americans felt the Russians had reaped major gains for very small effort. In line with his decision that Japan would not be divided into occupation zones, President Truman rejected a Soviet proposal that the Japanese in northern Hokkaido surrender to Soviet troops. A proposal by Truman that the Russians permit the United States to maintain an air base on one of the Kuriles was in turn declined by Stalin. Bit by bit, American hopes for a harmonious Big Three peace and a more liberal regime within the Soviet Union gave way to harsher realities.

CHAPTER 20

World War II: An Evaluation

GENERAL STRATEGY

THE SOVIET UNION has not within recent years produced a naval historian of the first rank, nor has she seen fit to make more official records available to scholars of other nations. These two circumstances make any definitive estimate of the strategic thinking of Soviet leaders difficult. Consequently, the World War II strategy of the Red navy must be inferred from its performance record, with some assistance from voluminous postwar naval writings by the Soviets themselves and some excellent foreign accounts, mainly from German sources.

On the basis of the available evidence it is clear that Soviet planning insofar as it proceeded from any system of military philosophy was exclusively defensive and at the same time rigid to the point of being static. In postwar propaganda publications issued for the purpose of glorifying the wartime record of the navy, two main themes stand out: the navy is seen as a brave defender of the Russian coastline, and it is the close ally of the Red army. There is very little evidence to suggest a concept of an offensive role of any kind, aside from submarine activity aimed at strangling an enemy by blockade. In general the purpose of the navy is to preserve Soviet use of the sea—though not primarily to deny such privileges to an enemy. There is no apparent understanding of the term "sea power" as expounded by Mahan and his disciples and as understood in the British, American, Japanese, and German navies.

This apparent lack of a basic conception of sea warfare and its possibilities is borne out in the Soviet naval record throughout World War II. At no time did the Russians make full use of the tools of sea power in their possession; theirs was a strategy of minimum risks and minimum gains. In both the Baltic and the Black Sea a resolute use of surface warships might well have shortened the war. Yet such use was never made, though the reason for the caution is sometimes somewhat obscure. Did the Soviets hope to preserve their ships so as to improve their postwar bargaining position, or did they simply fail to recognize the opportunities before them? Were they shackled, as was the German navy on several occasions, by unrealistic orders from high command or Red army levels? There is no certain answer to these questions.

The most probable explanation of their cautious action lies in the general qualitative inferiority of personnel and materiel. Postwar Soviet publications have acknowledged deficiencies in training, organization, and doctrine, and indeed the wartime record of almost any branch of the Red navy reveals a far lower level of efficiency than that prevailing in other navies. The Red navy was suffering from the recency with which its ships had been placed in service, from twenty years of isolationism, and from an incompetent intelligence system. The Soviet navy no longer had to contend with the subversive elements that had wrecked the tsarist navy, and wartime morale was generally high; yet a German naval historian observed with considerable accuracy that the Soviets fell into nearly every trap the Germans laid. And where the Soviets could have learned from their allies—as in the Arctic—they were handicapped by the suspicions of their leaders.

Soviet materiel, while serviceable, was too often outdated. In spite of the fact that Red navy ships were ruggedly built and their fighting planes were roughly equivalent in quality to those obtained through lend-lease from the United States, handicaps still existed in that newer and better types were in use in other navies. Even though German observers expressed considerable respect for Russian coastal and ship artillery, as well as for the accomplishments of their PT boats, bombs, and rockets, the Soviets lacked whole series of inventions in communications, electronics, submarines, amphibious equipment, and (surprisingly) mines.

In short, the poor performance of the Soviet navy in World War II was due to (1) a failure to understand sea power and its capabilities; (2) insufficient training in the proper use of naval equipment and weapons; (3) lack of up-to-date materiel; (4) unwillingness to learn from allies.

SURFACE WARSHIPS

The goal of control of the surface of the sea, from time immemorial the *raison d'être* of navies, has during the twentieth century yielded some of its former priority to the struggle for airpower and underwater domination. Nevertheless, its continuing importance should not be underrated.

In control of the surface of the sea the Soviets in World War II were unnecessarily weak. Their three battleships were scarcely used at all (although the *Marat*, even after it had been sunk with main turrets above water, still provided artillery support for the defenders of Leningrad). The performance of the *Arkhangelsk* after its delivery to the Russians in 1944 was certainly not outstanding. Cruisers were almost equally neglected. The *Murmansk* remained in port in the Arctic most of the time. In the Baltic, the *Kirov*, whose guns had aided the land fighting on several occasions in 1941 and assisted in the evacuation of Revel, remained in port for the rest of the war. While the Black Sea cruisers played roles in the defense, supply, and evacuation of Odessa and Sevastopol, they were rarely employed after mid-1942.

Nor were Soviet destroyers and torpedo boats much more active. They were put to their greatest use in the Arctic, where they carried out escort and shore bombardment duties. Destroyers fared poorly during the first months of the war in several brushes with German surface vessels in the Baltic. On July 6, 1941, two of them retreated before German minesweepers in the Irben Strait, and in another conflict involving German minesweepers and Soviet destroyers and PT boats, the Russians retreated after losing a PT. Indeed, during most of the war Baltic Fleet destroyers stayed in harbor, only occasionally employing gunfire against the German positions about Kronstadt. The somewhat more active Black Sea Fleet destroyers were used for the support of Odessa and Sevastopol, for shore bombardments, and occasionally for minelaying. Yet in this theater, too, they remained inactive for the greatest part of the war.

So generally limited was the movement of battleships, cruisers, and destroyers that during the entire war Soviet surface vessels failed to sink a single major warship or merchant ship of the Axis powers. On the other hand, one Soviet battleship, two cruisers, and about fifty destroyers were lost.

The most important surface warship as far as the Soviets were concerned—the real naval workhorse—was the motor torpedo boat or PT. It was used to attack convoys, provide escorts, move troops ashore, bombard coastal fortifications, and attack enemy submarines. Made of aluminum, the Soviet PT boats were about 53 feet long, and carried two stern torpedoes, two machine guns and antiaircraft guns, and crews of 20 men. Extra torpedoes or three or four mines were optional additions. The boats were hard to replace because the Ukrainian source of aluminum at Zaporozhe fell into German hands early in the war; and the fact that their gasoline engines made them susceptible to explosion and their hulls tended to corrode did not lessen the problems. Despite such shortcomings, however, the PT's were seaworthy and rugged, and with their 1,500-horsepower engines which provided a regular speed of 32 knots and a maximum of 52 knots, they were faster than their Axis equivalents, the Italian MAS boats and the German S-boats. A preparatory course of five months in navigation and one month of theory was required of Soviet PT commanders, as well as special training in the use of torpedoes, mines, and net barrages. With a range in operations of 200 miles they were more than a purely local weapon. The losses they inflicted were small, partly because handling tended to be less than optimal and partly because they were seldom effectively coordinated with airplanes, the second main weapon employed by the Red navy. Yet the Soviet PT's were responsible for most of the sinkings of German surface craft, and several German observers rated them equal to the best British motor torpedo boats in the English Channel.

A detailed account of the scores of encounters between PT's and enemy vessels would require a very long treatment. In general the PT's sought to achieve surprise; when this failed they retired at high speed—invariably under cover of smoke—and often without blood-shed. In most instances when they fought small German craft they were worsted. To take a few examples at random:

1) In the Baltic on August 1, 1941, six PT's attacked the German Third M-boat Flotilla. The Russians retreated after losing one boat.

2) On June 2, 1944, fifteen PT's attacked several German torpedo boats in the Gulf of Finland and sank *T-31*, but with the loss of three of their own boats.

3) On August 1, 1942 two PT's entered the Bay of Ivan Baba in the Black Sea and blew off the stern of a ferry barge. They were mistakenly identified as German by personnel at the harbor batteries and got away undamaged.

4) In February 1944 six German S-boats fell in with and sur-prised two Russian gunboats and four PT's southeast of Novorossiisk. In a fifteen-minute engagement the gunboats were destroyed, and three of the PT-boats were burned following a confused and ineffec-tive resistance. There were no German casualties, though two of the German S-boats sustained light hits.

5) On April 8, 1944, in a fight between German subchasers and four PT's in the Arctic, one of the latter was sunk and the other three were hit.

6) On August 19, 1944, PT boats broke through a smoke screen to attack a German Arctic convoy. A steamer and a patrol boat were sunk by torpedoes, at the cost of two PT's hit and burned.

These incidents are reasonably typical of an enormous number of small-boat naval actions. The Baltic in 1941 and 1944–45, the Black Sea throughout the war, and the Arctic in the last two years of the war (where PT's were present but inactive earlier) all witnessed a great deal of motor torpedo boat activity. At times during these periods PT operations were handicapped, especially when the Ger-mans held nearly the entire coast of the Black Sea and PT's were forced to base on the old cruiser *Komintern* which was anchored in a river. Though the number of losses directly attributable to PT's was not especially large, their presence in an area often had suffi-cient influence on enemy tactics to tie up large defensive units. To that degree these small surface warships may be judged to have been successful.

UNDERSEA WARFARE

At the beginning of World War II by far the largest submarine fleet in the world belonged to the Soviet Union; and of about 250-260 Red navy submarines only 15 were of old types. Further, the men in the Red submarine force constituted an elite who were loyal, hard-working, and self-sacrificing. Yet Soviet submarines had probably the least impressive record of any submarines that participated in World War II. During the entire war period they sank about 100 cargo ships and 30 small craft, totaling less than 300,000 tons—roughly one-tenth the tonnage of Soviet propaganda claims. Soviet submarine losses were approximately 40 for the Baltic and about 20 each for the Black Sea and the Arctic—a total of 80. The exchange rate, therefore, was only a little better than one-for-one, anything but satisfactory from a Soviet standpoint.[1]

The story of the Russian submarine campaign has been told in great detail by Jürgen Rohwer, a capable German scholar,[2] and has received some attention from other authors. A detailed account here would only distort the scope of this book without adding much to the known data. What should be of interest, however, is an analysis of the reasons for the Soviets' unimpressive performance.

To some degree the lack of success of the Soviet submarine campaign stemmed from material disadvantages. These included lack of access to the open sea, ice conditions which in the Baltic and the Black Sea restricted the scope of both operations and training, the loss of the best operational bases in the Black Sea, and the isolation and lateness of the Soviet naval buildup.

To these factors should be added certain organizational considerations. The submarines of each fleet comprised what was known as the "submarine unit" under the fleet commander. In the Black Sea and the Baltic this unit consisted of three brigades, each of which in turn comprised three to five divisions, the division consisting of three to five submarines of the same type. Training and reserve boats were organized as a fourth brigade in the case of the Baltic, and in other areas as independent divisions. The Arctic had only one brigade in its submarine unit when the war opened. In general, submarines were employed singly in sharply defined grid squares to wait for the enemy. Soviet and foreign naval writers alike agree that this system, conceived in the absence of prewar plans for group action, was not the best possible. Superficially it resembled that of Japan, whose highly touted submarine arm also failed to live up to prewar notices.

Besides these disadvantages there were two others of vital importance. The first was lack of a clear and mature concept of how to employ undersea boats: submarine warfare requires quick adaptation to changing conditions, a quality absent in the inflexible, static, and completely unimaginative Soviet naval leadership. The hackneyed description used for Union soldiers in certain battles of the American civil war, "lions led by jackasses," is not wholly inappropriate in this context.

Equally cogent is the effect of the closed mind upon the operations of submarine warfare, and indeed upon naval warfare in general. In a highly technical field, undeviating loyalty to Marxist doctrine is of no assistance in discovering solutions to difficult and demanding problems. It can lead only to tactical backwardness. In underseas warfare, where the more complicated maneuvers, inventions, and doctrines were foreign to the Soviets, the rigidities of their system handicapped them in learning. Small wonder that their submarine service, despite its large size, compiled so poor a wartime record.

NAVAL AVIATION

Despite the virtual annihilation of the Russian naval air force by the Luftwaffe and Wehrmacht during the early days of the war, it continued to be the most successful branch of the Red navy. With lend-lease shipments and the output of their own factories, the Soviets were able to reconstitute their naval air force so effectively that in 1944–45 it was overwhelmingly stronger than the Luftwaffe.

Throughout World War II this branch of the service operated as an integral part of the navy, even though it was almost entirely land based. In both organization and titles of rank it much resembled the Red army, operating from four types of bases, as follows:

Class A: 750-800 men with extensive equipment supporting an entire brigade or combat group

Class B: smaller than Class A but servicing a brigade or group

Class C: 70 officers and 640 men servicing two or three airfields
Class D: auxiliary base with 500 men supporting one airfield

Each fleet and flotilla had its complement of air stations. As of September 1, 1942, for example, the Black Sea Fleet Air Arm operated from nine bases. Support personnel included many women and some civilians.

The uses of Soviet naval planes were exceedingly varied, perhaps the most important being in attacks on convoys. They were also employed against enemy bases and installations, in the dropping of agents and propaganda leaflets, for reconnaissance purposes, in aerial minelaying (very extensively), and in occasional torpedo attacks. Late in the war naval bombers went farther afield, to attack the Ploesti oil fields, the Danube bridge at Chernovoda, and Finnish and East Prussian ports.

In raids on convoys and individual ships the Soviet planes became increasingly effective as the war went on. In the Baltic Sea, for example, where they claimed only two launches in 1941 and one launch in 1942, the 1943 bag included five merchant ships, three launches, and three minor warships. The next year sinkings again rose sharply: 25 minor warships, a torpedo boat, an antiaircraft ship, and 25 merchant vessels. Finally, in 1945, the Soviet planes sank at least 30 minor warships and 40 merchant vessels.[3]

Though the Germans repeatedly expressed the opinion that the Russian performance was improving as a result of Anglo-American instruction, this increased toll of shipping was not entirely due to better methods. The change resulted principally from the six- or seven-to-one superiority which by 1944 the Russians held over the Luftwaffe and their strategy of throwing in planes in continuous mass attacks, however unskillful. This inference is further indicated by Black Sea statistics which show that during 1943 the Soviets made 311 air attacks on ships at sea and 959 on ships in port, involving an average of 10-15 aircraft per attack. In such attempts they lost 91 of their own planes but destroyed 22 minor warships and ten merchant vessels. In short, one attack out of 40 achieved some measure of success.

As in the case of submarine warfare, the lack of greater success did not stem from the quality of personnel (in the U.S.S.R. as else-

TABLE 11
*Types of Planes Used by Soviet Union in World War II**

TYPE	NO. OF EN- GINES	CREW	ARMA- MENT	MAXI- MUM SPEED (KM/HR)	RANGE (KM)	SERVICE

I. Attack Planes (bombers, ground attack, torpedo, and minelayers):

Russian:

TYPE	NO. OF EN- GINES	CREW	ARMA- MENT	SPEED	RANGE	SERVICE
SB-2	2	3	4 flex. MG**	450	2600	lt bomber, 1000 kg load
DB-32	2	3	3 flex. MG	495	3000	1000/3000 kg bomb, also tor- pedoes
IL-2	1	1-2	2 cannons; 2 fixed MG; 8 rockets	360	750	heavily armored
IL-4 DB-3F }	2	3	3 flex. MG	445	3000	standard bomber after 1943
TB-2 TB-3 TB-4 }	4	7-10	4 flex. MG	280	2000	obsolete bomber w/2000/4000 kg load; mine carrier in Sea of Azov
PE-2	2	3	2 fixed MG; 2 flex. MG	540	1500	divebomber and reconnaissance
MBR-2	1	3-4	2 flex. MG	250	1500	flying boat and night bomber

Foreign:

TYPE	ENGINES	CREW	ARMAMENT	SPEED	RANGE	SERVICE
Douglas A-20 Boston III	2	3-4	2 fixed MG; 2-3 flex. MG	490	1800	reconnaissance, torpedo, and bomber
Handley Paige Hampden	2	42	1 fixed MG; 6 flex. MG	400	3500	torpedo plane
B-25 Mitchell	2	5	1 fixed MG; 5 flex. MG	495	4500	torpedo and long-range reconnaissance bomber

II. Fighter Planes:

Russian:

TYPE	ENGINES	CREW	ARMAMENT	SPEED	RANGE	SERVICE
YAK-1 YAK-4 }	1	1	2 fixed MG; 1 cannon	585	700	fighter w/6 rockets; also used as fighter bomber
YAK-7b YAK-9 }	1	1	2 fixed MG 1 cannon (37 mm)	580	700	larger machine guns; YAK-9 all metal

TABLE 11—Continued

TYPE	NO. OF EN- GINES	CREW	ARMA- MENT	MAXI- MUM SPEED (KM/HR)	RANGE (KM)	SERVICE
MIG-3	1	1	3 fixed MG; 6 rockets	620	820	obsolete after 1941
LAGG-3	1	1	1 fixed MG; 1 cannon (12.7 mm)	600	750	explosive shells and fighter cover for IL-2
Foreign:						
Spitfire	1	1	4 fixed MG; 2 cannons	600	800	few in use, mainly in Black Sea area
Aircobra (Bell)	1	2	6 fixed MG	570	1000	Soviets armed w/1 20 mm cannon, 2 x 12.7 MG, 4 x 7.6 MG
III. Reconnaissance Planes:						
Russian:						
MBR-2	1	3-4	2 flex. MG	250	1500	flying boat, night bomber
RE-3	2	2	2 fixed MG; 2 flex. MG	500	2000	long-range reconnaissance
GST-	2	5-7	4 flex. MG	300	6000	med. bomber, 1 rocket torpedo, flying boat and transport
IV. Transport Planes:						
DB-3F	2	3	3 flex. MG	445	3000	transport for 7 men or towing plane
TB-3	4	7-10	4 flex. MG	280	1200	34 paratroops or 40 men

* SOURCE: Vice Adm. Friedrich Ruge, "The Soviet Russians as Opponents at Sea: Analysis of German and Russian Naval Operations in the Second World War" (unclassified ms., U.S. Office of Naval Intelligence, Washington, D.C., 1955), Vol. II, pp. 126–29.
** MG = machine guns.

where an elite group) or the materiel involved. While Soviet bombers proved inferior to the American and British models, Russian fighter planes were excellent. The true weakness lay in poor training and inadequate leadership, as well as in poor flight discipline and navigation which led to too widely dispersed attacks. Accuracy in bombing and gunnery was very poor, and lack of coordination with other arms was the rule rather than the exception. In 1945, for example, large German warships operated in the Baltic within a few miles of Soviet airfields whose planes made no effort to attack them. The Germans were unable to observe any system at all in Soviet aerial minelaying. Only one well-known type of mine was used, and it was laid by primitive means which made sweeping simple and relatively safe, though also laborious. So far as naval war was concerned, the Soviets at no time showed an understanding of what airpower might accomplish, nor did they carry out systematic operations within the framework of an overall strategic concept. Aid from the Western Allies did not alter this condition, but it did place in Soviet hands weapons so strong that even when clumsily employed they could do a great deal of damage.

MINE WARFARE

The Russians entered World War II with a tradition of effective mine warfare stretching from the Crimean War through the Intervention and Civil War. They had failed to make much progress since World War I, however, and as a result their campaign in World War II was far less successful than in previous wars. Offensive minefields were laid by ships of destroyer size or less; and there was no single instance, as there had been in World War I, of the employment of sizable surface vessels to lay minefields behind enemy lines. PT boats for the most part, and submarines to a lesser degree, were employed to fill the gaps or to lay attrition minefields of their own. Minesweepers, mainly of the *Fugas* class, and of 100-150 tons or less, were also used for other purposes than the removal of mines, so that they became naval jacks-of-all-trades. The Soviet minesweeping chore in both the Baltic and the Black Sea did not involve any large area, but the narrow sea lanes about Kronstadt and along the Caucasus required constant sweeping in order to permit the uninterrupted transfer of supplies and the departure of submarines.

Both Germans and Russians made extensive use of mines, the German devices being far the more sophisticated. Yet aside from the German minelaying prior to the declaration of war neither side was especially successful save insofar as its minelaying forced the other to divert considerable manpower and equipment. One exception was the highly effective German net barrage, bolstered by mines, which was laid across the Gulf of Finland. The Russian efforts brought one reasonably fruitful venture—an early minefield near Odessa in which the Germans lost several ships—in addition to a measure of success in the Sea of Azov and Kerch Strait where uncomplicated Soviet aerial mines forced the Germans to do a great deal of sweeping. Minelaying by Soviet submarines was unimpressive.

But if their minelaying campaign was less effective than in previous wars, the Soviets did develop some innovations which indicated future progress. These included the development of very small mines for use in rivers and lakes, mines for use in extremely shallow waters, and aerial mines able to penetrate ice by chemical action.

INSHORE AND INLAND WATERS

Because of Russia's geographic characteristics and traditions, a much larger percentage of her naval force has always served close to the coastline or even inland than has been the case with other navies. In modern times these inland and inshore naval forces have included coastal artillery, naval infantry, gunboats, minesweepers, motor gunboats, patrol boats, and converted merchant vessels. Motor torpedo boats, naval planes, and minelayers, which could also be included in this general grouping, have been considered elsewhere in this book.

The Russians have frequently been quite astute in the employment of light coastal and inland forces. During World War II the narrow stretch of Baltic coast about Leningrad, Kronstadt, and the island of Lavansaari was held successfully by such forces, which were enhanced during the war by the addition of the flat-bottomed motor gunboat which carried a gun in a tank's turret and could steam at high speed. Dredges armed with 5.1-inch guns and used as gunboats were among types that found successful employment in both inshore and inland waters. Some other small vessels were used successfully in the Arctic and Pacific. At both Stalingrad and Leningrad these same small types made major strategic contributions, as noted in chapter 19.

AMPHIBIOUS WARFARE

Probably few American military men are aware that the Soviets were among the foremost practitioners of amphibious warfare during World War II. In both the Black Sea and the Baltic at least twenty Soviet amphibious assaults were made. There were also several in the Arctic and nearly a dozen during the brief period of Soviet belligerency against Japan. If small landings are included the number is far greater. In fact one Soviet writer, Kh. Kh. Kamalov, has listed 159 landings in which Soviet marines participated.[4]

In general, the Soviet amphibious assault varied markedly from the American or Japanese. Soviet landings were often impromptu affairs which involved short-distance movements of troops, improvised landing craft, minimal naval support following the landing, and very low logistic requirements for the troops landed. A large proportion of these attempts were outright failures, while some that succeeded in their strategic objectives also lost virtually all troops landed. On several occasions personnel involved were largely untrained, and at times they were also poorly led. In every instance the amphibious attack was closely connected with land warfare and had no independent or far-reaching objectives of its own. Once on shore, the men could be depended upon to take difficult conditions in stride and to fight to the last. The larger American amphibious operations would have been completely beyond either the logistic or naval capacity of the Russians. But inasmuch as the Soviet strategic situation did not necessitate far-flung operations, their landings, crude as they were, adequately answered strategic needs.

Soviet amphibious operations can be roughly classified on the basis of size. The smallest were those attempted from a single submarine or motor torpedo boat and were of the commando type. A team of spies and/or saboteurs was put ashore with a small amount of equipment and with a definite but limited objective which might involve no more than the destruction of a bridge or ammunition dump or the transmission of orders to guerrillas. On occasion a single agent might be landed. As a rule ships did not wait to pick up the men, though most saboteurs are reported to have escaped. Probably hundreds of these small landings were carried out in the

Crimea, Bulgaria, Rumania, the islands of the Gulf of Finland, and Norway.

Larger landings involving forces from company to regimental size were also numerous, including some unsuccessful assaults against Finnish-held islands early in the war. The September 1941 disembarkation of infantry behind the Rumanian lines before Odessa was another such operation, and a number of others were made in the brief period of Russian belligerency with Japan. Of the medium-sized assaults carried out in the Baltic, a high proportion were failures for reasons ranging from inadequate training and poor leadership to lack of air-sea or sea-land cooperation. One of the larger attempts of this type was made by a force of 5,000 men near Narva on February 1, 1944. During the early stages of these landings the movement of men ashore was usually rapid, but if a plan miscarried or unexpected resistance occurred the Soviet troops tended to become confused and uncertain and could be readily placed on the defensive.

The third type was the full-scale invasion, which might involve a division or more. The largest single example of this type is furnished by the landings at Kerch Isthmus toward the end of 1941. In this operation the strategic purpose, reduction of pressure at Sevastopol, was accomplished at an ultimate cost of the loss of all twenty-two divisions employed. (It should be added that these divisions were under strength and smaller than U.S. army divisions.) A majority of the large-scale assaults were carried out in the Black Sea, but during 1944 several occurred in the Baltic as well. Between June 30 and July 5 of that year invasions of the islands of Teikaari and Melansaari were supported by more than 100 Soviet ships; the defending Finns fought bravely but were finally hopelessly outnumbered and forced to evacuate. In September 1944, when four or five divisions of the Eighth Estonian Army were landed on the islands of Worms, Khiuma, and Ösel, Soviet leadership proved excellent and German coastal forces were soon driven back. Two Soviet marine brigades, escorted by more than 100 small vessels, supported a June 23, 1944, landing near Tuulos on Lake Ladoga. Soviet landings on the Kuriles, Sakhalin, and Korea toward the end of the war are also classifiable as either large or medium-sized. As compared

The destroyer *Novik*, one of the best Russian warships of World War I.

Russian submarines in Revel Harbor, 1915.

The *Orlitsa*, Russian seaplane carrier in the Baltic during World War I.

Sinking of British destroyer *Vittoria* by the Soviet submarine *Pantera* in 1919.

British bombardment of Kronstadt, 1919.

Adm. A. V. Kolchak, leader of the White Russian forces during the civil war.

Battle on the Kama River during the civil war.

Battle of Irben Strait, 1941.

Minesweeping in the Gulf of Narvik after German evacuation.

Landing on Baltic island in 1944.

A Soviet *Petia I* class escort patrol vessel.

A Soviet *Krivak* class guided missile frigate (DDGM) at anchor.

The Soviet *Riga* class destroyer escort, pennant number 618, underway.

A Cuban *Komar* class guided missile patrol boat.

A Soviet *Kresta* class guided missile armed destroyer leader.

A Soviet *Kotlin* SAM class guided missile armed destroyer.

he Soviet *Kashin* class guided missile armed destroyers, pennant num-
rs 523 and 871, at anchor.

From front to back: A Soviet *Krupny* class guided missile armed destroyer, a Soviet *Kotlin* SAM class guided missile armed destroyer, and the U.S. Navy escort ship USS *Sample* (DE-1048) in the waters off the coast of Hawaii. The Soviet ships were units of a Soviet task group that cruised through the Hawaiian waters from September 13 to 15, 1971.

The Soviet *Sverdlov* class cruiser *Aleksandr Suvorov* (CL-834) during the world-wide Soviet naval exercise Okean.

A Soviet *Moskva* class helicopter ship.

The Soviet helicopter carrier *Moskva*, pennant number 857, underway with a U.S. Navy SP-2H *Neptune* patrol aircraft of Patrol Squadron Seven (VP-7) overhead.

U.S.S.R. research vessel *Vityaaz* photographed from Honolulu.

Soviet AGR class, pennant number 621—this is a former fleet mine-sweeper of the T-43 class, converted into a radar picket.

The Soviet intelligence trawler *Gidrofon* underway with the attack aircraft carrier USS *Coral Sea* (CVA-43) and her escort ships in the background.

The Soviet *Don* class ocean-going submarine support ship, pennant number 963, underway during the Soviet world-wide naval exercise Okean.

The Soviet missile detection ship *Kosmonaut Vladimir Komarov*.

A Soviet *Ugra* class nuclear support ship.

A Soviet *Alligator* type landing ship (number 411) underway.

The Soviet oceanographic research ship *Gavril Saritshev* underway.

A Russian fish-factory trawler, capable of staying at sea for eighty days, was photographed in international waters off Cape Cod by a USN patrol aircraft.

The Soviet direction trawler *Gidrofon* (foreground) cruises in the vicinity of the attack aircraft carrier USS *Coral Sea* (CVA-43).

to earlier such attempts, they were relatively luxurious operations, for by then American-built lend-lease landing craft were available in considerable numbers.

ESCORTS AND ANTISUBMARINE WARFARE

The fight against the U-boat never constituted as important an aspect of naval activity for the Russians as it did for the Americans and British, so that Soviet progress in this area during the war was only modest. The Black Sea and Baltic were distinctly secondary theaters for the German U-boats, and their Arctic activities were directed primarily against the Western Allies rather than the Russians.

Both antisubmarine and escort weapons of the Soviets were primitive and relatively ineffective at the beginning of the war. In the Baltic only the *U-250* was lost to antisubmarine forces, the other four submarines lost by the Germans being claimed by mines which may or may not have been placed by the Soviets. In the Black Sea, where German defenses were somewhat better, not a single U-boat was lost to Soviet action. The Soviets employed PT-boats as submarine chasers and escorts with some success. No long-range Soviet convoys were used during the war, but the Red navy gained considerable experience in protecting small coastal convoys within purely Russian waters.

Partly due to their own increased experience and partly because of gifts from their allies, however, the Russians made some progress during the war. Lend-lease shipments from the United States included about 200 modern antisubmarine craft of various types, and the Russians on their own were able to increase the number of vessels equipped for submarine chasing and the ships carrying sonar. They employed such devices as net barrages, mines, camouflage paint, searchlights, direction finders, a monitoring service, and smoke screens. Even by the end of the war, however, they had not developed radar location of submarines by airplane. U-boat commanders correctly concluded that the Soviets were far behind their allies; even when they had the best American and British equipment, they tended to be rigid and unimaginative in using it.

CONCLUSIONS

Probably the most illuminating explanation of the Soviet naval record in World War II is to be found in the writings of Russian naval philosopher and strategist Adm. Nikolai Klado. In his studies of strategy published before World War I, he noted that for Russia, primarily a land power, the building of a good army was a far less demanding task than was the creation of a modern navy, whose sophisticated tools would require so much greater industrial advancement.

After the Bolshevik seizure of power, one of the first steps taken was the creation of an effective army. This army in World War II was tested to the utmost, and despite some discernible weaknesses it was able to recover from surprise attack to wage a war of attrition that would "tear the guts out of the German army" (to quote Churchill). But the Red navy was an afterthought. It had been built up too incompletely and too recently for the best possible results— and in a state whose industry and technology in 1941 was not sufficiently advanced to supply the newer tools of sea power.

This is not, of course, the full story. In 1940 the Soviet leaders did not have a mature or usable naval philosophy, nor did they have an understanding of what services they should expect from their navy. As noted in chapter 17, Stalin had proclaimed a new naval doctrine shortly before the war, but there had not been time for the change to become effective. Ships had been produced very rapidly, but the *trained* personnel to put them to good use did not exist. And finally, for all the raw materials of sea power that were present, yet, all through World War II a finished product was never achieved. As a result Russia's World War II naval record was poorer than in any of her previous conflicts.

However, the record still is not as bad as some critics have depicted it. The Soviet failure to use large ships in the Baltic and Black Sea toward the end of World War II seems inevitable when it is remembered that their crews were then busy fighting on land. If well led, they doubtless could have contributed more to the war effort acting as sailors; yet as soldiers they made an important and undeniable tactical contribution.

CHAPTER 21

The Fight for Sea Power

THE RED NAVY'S POSTWAR POSITION

At the end of World War II the Soviet navy was in a paradoxical position. Not only had the cost of war been heavy in terms of both manpower and industry; it included in addition ship losses (made even more onerous by the enforced cessation of building), and wrecked internal waterways, ports, and other industrial facilities on which seapower depends. Added to these debits was a poor war record as far as "sea activity" was concerned.

Yet in Soviet eyes this was not the dominant side of the picture. So far from excoriating the naval war record, the Soviet leaders took pains to extol the deeds of naval personnel at Leningrad, at Sevastopol, in the Caucasus, at Berlin and Warsaw. In this they were merely being consistent with a long-held philosophy: the Red navy, whatever its failings as an independent force, was expected to aid the army; in this respect it had served loyally. Exaggerated claims of wartime successes were made and maintained to raise service morale, particularly with regard to the submarine fleet, whose captains were extravagantly praised even though their boats had done no damage to the enemy; apparently it was considered feat enough that an officer had completed numerous voyages. Official propaganda was contrived to convince the Russians that they were a naturally maritime people with lofty naval traditions.[1] As soon as possible, the country resumed the policy of naval modernization and expansion which the war had interrupted and which was intended to support the Soviet Union's expansionist aims abroad.

Before considering in detail the enormous postwar expansion of the Red navy, it is worthwhile to turn briefly—though only briefly—to naval doctrine. As was pointed out in chapter 17, the defensive concept of sea power was liquidated by Stalin in the late 1930s, together with most of its advocates. In 1940 *Morskoi sbornik* published a new statement of naval doctrine derived from an amalgam of concepts of Marx, Engels, Stalin, Frunze, and Voroshilov. Before the new doctrine was generally accepted or plans based on it could be carried to fruition, World War II erupted. As we have seen, the Red navy fought the entire war—and fought it quite poorly—under the older defensive doctrine.

On July 22, 1945, in a Navy Day address, Stalin reaffirmed the new doctrine which, in essence, called for grafting Communist ideology and purposes onto the naval theories of Adm. Raoul Castex, the eminent French naval writer. Under the new policy the Red navy was to bring aid to Soviet-sponsored revolutions in various parts of the world. Fast cruisers and submarines were to be the principal agents of a new imperialism. The Red fleet was to move onto the world's oceans and seek Russia's release from enclosed seas and other geographic limitations. On the other hand, the new naval enthusiasts looked back on World War II as a glorious triumph of Soviet arms in which the Red navy had performed brilliantly, and for which Comrade Stalin had been the principal architect of victory. Adm. I. S. Yumashev, in the 1947 celebration of Navy Day, proclaimed Stalin "the initiator and inspirer of a great fleet; of the naval forces of the Soviet Union; . . . [of] all our successes and victories." *Pravda* on July 27, 1947, declared:

> As the great patriotic war showed, Soviet warships followed their own technical-tactical talents, and not only refused to yield to the Germans but surpassed them. During the course of the war the fleet was the faithful assistant of the Red army.

The idea that a strong economy would strengthen the Soviet Union as a great naval power was also repeatedly stressed.[2]

A close observer will note at once some inherent contradictions in the new doctrine. It clearly approves the wartime role of the navy as a subsidiary to the army while at the same time envisioning a Soviet role in revolutionary disturbances thousands of miles from the Soviet Union. The latter projection is one which calls for independent naval action. In 1951 Admiral Golovin once again stressed the role of the navy in liberating colonial areas, and in the light of recent history there is every reason to expect this policy will continue. Again, the partial acceptance of the doctrines of such Western writers as Mahan and Castex, to which are then added the purposes of leading Communists, would seem likely to produce a kind of strategic indigestion. Because under Khrushchev none of these inherent contradictions was resolved, the Soviets since World War II have at times stressed an overseas naval strategy and at other times equally emphasized cooperation with the Soviet army.

BASES OF EXPANSION

Though the new policy and doctrine announced by Stalin would in itself have served as a springboard for naval expansion during the decade following World War II, it was powerfully aided by four other factors. These, in approximately reverse order of importance, are (1) wartime aid from allies; (2) geographical expansion; (3) ships and information gained from former enemies; (4) an enormous expansion in the Soviet industrial, technical, and scientific base.

Aid from allies was probably the least important factor on a long-term basis. During the war the British and American navies, having every reason to wish success to their Eastern allies, sought to enhance both the technical competence and the material strength of the Soviets. Under various protocols the United States sent vast quantities of munitions to Russia. While most of these were intended mainly for land warfare, the naval items included the light cruiser *Milwaukee* (7,500 tons, twelve 6-inch guns, 33 knots), eight destroyers, four submarines, and large numbers of subchasers, tankers, frigates, and landing craft, as well as minesweepers and escort vessels. The cruiser, which the Russians renamed *Murmansk*, was for five weeks a veritable tactical school as the officers and men who were to take her over learned from their American opposite numbers exactly how the ship operated. A subchaser school was conducted in Miami for Soviet officers who were to operate the 49 subchasers given under lend-lease. Similar arrangements were made elsewhere. For their part the British, whose main contributions were the battleship *Royal Sovereign*, nine destroyers, and four submarines, provided all the new devices, technical aid, and practical instruction the Russians would accept. The Russians were happy enough to get blueprints, ships, and munitions; but the degree to which they actually benefited from the new weapons would be difficult to determine. British liaison officers reported a Soviet tendency to ignore instructions and to rely on blueprints. When the equipment was incorrectly installed and failed to work, the Russians then blamed the British for defective materials.

It must not be forgotten that ships were not the sole items covered by lend-lease. Also included was a vast volume of naval weapons and equipment, such as antiaircraft and antisubmarine weapons, steering gear, anchors, clothing, medicines, leather, and other supplies.

From a geographical standpoint, the aids to Russian sea power gained by the victory were immense, especially in the Baltic and the Far East. At the end of the war Russia occupied the former Baltic States as well as most of East Prussia. Satellite regimes were set up in Poland and in the Russian zone of Germany, and Finnish independence was precarious. To a greater degree than ever before, the Baltic had become a Russian lake, with the Soviet coastline now lengthened from 75 miles to nearly 1,000. The acquired coastline included numerous ports and bases, a few of them ice-free, all of them available for potential development.

Geographical gains in the Arctic were slight and in the Black Sea they were inconclusive, consisting mainly of the use of facilities and ports of satellite Rumania and Bulgaria. But on the Pacific, Soviet territory was markedly expanded. For her approximately two weeks of participation in the war against Japan, the Soviet Union had gained the Kurile Islands, southern Sakhalin, and the northern half of Korea. The cession of the Kuriles and northern Sakhalin was of particular strategic importance since it made of the Sea of Okhotsk virtually a *mare clausum*.

At the same time it would be easy to overestimate the importance of these gains. Because of ice, Soviet bases in the northern part of the Sea of Okhotsk were of only seasonal value. The outlets to the Sea of Japan—the Tsugaru, Tsushima, and Soya straits—were still mainly controlled by the Japanese. Ports south of Vladivostok could be denied to the Russians by the Chinese and were subject to some further discount because of American bases running from Japan through Okinawa and Formosa to the Philippines. In European Russia, the outlets to the Black Sea and the Baltic were still under the control of other powers, and Soviet attempts to pressure the Turks into sharing control of the Dardanelles and to set up a communist regime in Greece led ultimately to the Truman Doctrine.

Ships, facilities, components, and expertise acquired from the Axis navies were also used to reinforce Soviet sea power and to make up for the wartime hiatus in normal shipbuilding. The 1945 Berlin Conference awarded the Russians ten German destroyers, ten U-boats, the light cruiser *Nürnberg* (6,000 tons, nine 5.9-inch guns, 31.5 knots), the badly damaged and incomplete 20,000-ton aircraft carrier *Graf Zeppelin*, the very old battleship *Schleswig-Holstein* (13,000 tons, four 11-inch guns), and the incomplete heavy cruiser *Lützow* (10,000 tons, eight 8-inch guns) which was renamed *Petropavlovsk*. From the surrendered Italian fleet came the old battleship *Giulio Cesare* (23,662 tons, ten 12.6-inch guns, 27 knots), the light cruiser *Emanuele Filiberto Duca d'Aosta*, four destroyers, 14 torpedo boats, two submarines, and a variety of small craft. The Soviet Union returned to Great Britain and the United States the *Royal Sovereign* and *Milwaukee* as well as some lesser vessels which had been loaned earlier. Eventually the Russians also obtained six surrendered Japanese destroyers and many smaller vessels.

These acquisitions more than compensated for wartime losses, for the vessels were all comparatively modern if (in some cases) worn out with hectic wartime service. Russian crews, however, found it hard to master the complex machinery of the German ships. As a result the *Graf Zeppelin* and a U-boat were lost and several boilers of the *Admiral Makarov* (ex-*Nürnberg*) were burned out. Moreover, Soviet yards lacked the necessary experience and equipment to overhaul torpedo craft with high-pressure steam installations, and for some time maintenance of these ships was carried out at Rostock and other East German ports.

Naval assistance of a more fundamental sort was obtained from the Soviet zone of Germany. In East Germany the Red army found guns, unfinished ships, U-boats, sections of U-boats, machinery, factories, and scientific and technical data, as well as expert personnel and specialists in every field. Recognizing the value of these resources, the Russians hastily set up an administration in Berlin to deal with scientific and technical matters and placed the German elite in research centers and offices. They also sent to Moscow for evaluation everything of interest. The new German U-boats (types XXI, XXIII, and XXVI) and hydrogen peroxide propulsion were of especially great naval interest. So were the Japanese submarines of the I-200 class, completed too late to participate in the war but in their hull design and high underwater speed prophetic of future models.

The absorption and evaluation of German technical and scientific development did not take place overnight, but it was rapid, and German inventors who had not escaped to the West were moved to the Soviet Union to pursue their specialties on a "contract" basis. The resultant new technical knowledge was pumped into current Soviet weapons programs.

Without question, then, Soviet naval technology greatly benefited from the Axis defeat. Yet it would again be easy to overestimate this contribution; it was valuable mainly because the Russians were themselves ready to make rapid advances in industry, science, and technology.

It had been the objective of the prewar five-year plans to bring the Russian economy abreast of the more advanced Western industrial states. While this purpose was not fully carried out prior to 1941, the degree of success was far greater than most foreigners realized, as evidenced by the success of the Soviets in finally defeating the German army. Despite losses of population variously estimated at 16, 20, and even 30 million (the Soviets put this figure at 22 million), and in spite of the destruction of nearly half of her industry, the Soviet Union finished the war as a major power. Under the leadership of Joseph Stalin the Soviets immediately set about restoring their industrial losses (a process which would require about six years), and at the same time building up the scientific and technical know-how which they hoped would enable them to surpass the

United States. Though neither their resources nor their scientific personnel were sufficient to permit an all-out attack on American leadership in every field, the Russians selected certain branches of knowledge which they regarded as of such importance as to receive most of their money and skilled personnel. Meantime, by greatly encouraging education in selected scientific and engineering fields, they sought to ensure the future supremacy of their industry, armed forces, technology, and ideology by out-producing the United States in trained personnel.

Partly because of the long record of Russian technical mediocrity and partly out of ignorance of the process that was going on, key Western generals, newspapermen, educators, scientists, and politicians persisted for years in underrating the Russians. Thus atomic and thermonuclear weapons, modern airplanes, sophisticated submarines, "Sputniks," rockets, and satellites were all developed by the Soviets years earlier than most of the world expected. With almost unlimited funds available for research and development, and with great prestige and monetary rewards attached to their work, the Russian scientists displayed such great ability that by the late 1950s few Western leaders were unwilling to accord to the Soviet Union the status of a great technical power. A worldwide espionage system was of assistance in that transformation, to be sure, but neither the handful of Western traitors and turncoats nor the information gained by Soviet spies was sufficient to generate this scientific revolution. At most they slightly speeded it.

Without a recognition of this overall developmental trend it is impossible to understand Soviet naval progress—for the establishment of a strong navy was one of the most cherished goals of the Soviet leaders. Since the end of World War II the Soviet Union has built more warships than all the other nations of the world combined. Moreover, it has simultaneously sought to produce a navy of optimal quality and technical sophistication.

Because the Soviets are extremely close-mouthed on certain subjects, their motivation in seeking a strong navy is not completely clear. There is considerable evidence that a greater fleet was and is viewed as a requisite accompaniment of great-power status, and there is some indication that even those men in the Kremlin who do not understand sea power—as many certainly did not in World War

II—are impressed by both the deeds of German submarines and the victory of the United States in the Pacific, as well as by American strategic airpower. During Stalin's last years Soviet naval policy remained unresolved at many points. Cmdr. Robert Herrick, in his excellent work entitled Soviet Naval Strategy, notes:

> Stalin chose an unorthodox strategic mixture of naval forces that combined with the forces suitable for a young school naval strategy, major elements of the other two strategies of "Fortress fleet" and "fleet in being."[3]

By 1950 Stalin had approved a large surface fleet which apparently was to include four large carriers. The carrier phase of the project was never carried through and appeared to have died with Stalin. The dictator was more successful with his program for building heavy cruisers, which is described elsewhere in this chapter.

Stalin also sought to popularize and glamorize the navy by a heavily supported propaganda campaign. This effort, pushed vigorously during the early 1950s, appears to have been aimed at glamorizing the sea and overcoming the repugnance which many Russians displayed toward life afloat. In this campaign the naval section of DOSAAF, a society established to foster civilian cooperation with the armed forces, played the roles elsewhere familiar to a navy league, naval militia, and naval reserve. Tsarist champions of naval strength, such as Peter the Great, Makarov, Ushakov, and Nakhimov, became national heroes, and such incidents as the Crimean War defense of Sevastopol, the fight of the Variag, the revolt on the battleship Potemkin, and the story of the Kronstadt sailors provided the themes for heroic propaganda films. The old cruiser Avrora, whose shots at the Winter Palace marked the beginning of the Bolshevik revolution, became a national museum. In short, the Soviets discovered naval traditions and used them to arouse enthusiastic support for the new fleet.

The eventual replacement of Stalin by Nikita Khrushchev brought several changes. Khrushchev himself never even remotely understood sea power. By 1955 Soviet naval thinking had largely reverted to a defensive strategy based on submarines. The Soviets failed to demand base rights in several overseas areas where they had given economic and military aid, and in 1956 they even gave up such rights at Porkkala in Finland and Port Arthur in Manchuria.

These retrogressive steps were possibly balanced by the appointment of Adm. Sergei Gorshkov, to replace Fleet Admiral Kuznetsov. Gorshkov is the ablest naval officer the Soviet Union has thus far produced. Though he was unable or unwilling to oppose Khrushchev directly and was forced to operate within the system of Communist speech and thought, he was able to influence Khrushchev's thinking in some respects and to drag his feet on such matters as the scrapping of new cruisers.

In about 1955–56 an important and continuing change occurred in Soviet military policy. Khrushchev apparently concluded not only that military expenditures were too high but that some forms of military expenditures were altogether unjustified. With the support of Marshal Zhukov he therefore launched a campaign to cut costs, preferably while reducing as little military muscle as possible.

One result of the change was a great reduction in the manpower allocated to all of the armed services. Three successive cuts, averaging 1,200,000 each, were announced between 1955 and 1960, though the Berlin crisis of 1960–61 prevented the final one from being carried out fully. In round figures this series of cuts ran to almost 50 percent, or from a total force approaching six million men at its largest to one slightly in excess of three million. In 1957 the navy was decreased from about 600,000 men to less than 500,000, and 375 warships were mothballed—a then fairly uncommon practice in the Soviet navy, where formerly almost everything available had been kept in commission. The full extent of this cut was not realized outside Russia for some time, and American military analysts who had long credited the Soviet army with 175 divisions continued to do so when 75 was closer to the correct number.

In the case of the navy the cut was accompanied by much deliberation concerning value of a conventional surface navy; threats to scrap all cruisers, the cancellation of some, and the scrapping of several uncompleted hulks (four at Leningrad alone); a reduction in the plane and personnel strength of the naval air arm—possibly by as much as two-thirds; a great decrease in the number of submarines being built (followed shortly by a marked improvement in submarine sophistication and general quality); a press campaign devoted to the changes which nuclear weapons dictated in the country's fleet; and the replacement of Fleet Admiral Kuznetsov by Admiral Gorshkov as commander of the navy. Probably unconnected with these changes was the abolition of the Soviet marine corps in the early 1950s (it was reestablished a decade later).

Changes as important as these could not normally occur without extensive debate, but if such a debate occurred within the Soviet Union it was well concealed; details have not leaked out. It may be presumed that some of the military professionals were less than anxious to give up their more familiar weapons and types of organization, but the Soviet system did not encourage either the development or propagation of dissenting views. Also, despite the size of the cuts involved it would be rash to conclude that they resulted in weakened forces; the accompanying development of missiles and nuclear submarines clearly made the Soviet Union more and not less formidable.

In striving to create a powerful navy virtually overnight the Soviet leaders showed an awareness that naval strength is dependent on far more than ships. Simultaneously they expanded inland waterways, fisheries, merchant shipping, shipbuilding, and the training of personnel, thus creating not only a formidable fleet but also the industrial, economic, and propaganda base to sustain it.

ORGANIZATION

The Soviet Navy is currently under the Ministry of Defense, which is headed by Marshal Andrei Grechko. Grechko fills the position created by the death of Marshal Rodion Malinovsky, one of the leading Red Army generals of World War II. He differs from his predecessors in not having been particularly prominent in World War II and may therefore be the first of a new generation of leading military men. Subordinate to Grechko are the Commanders in Chief of the Strategic Rocket, Land, Air, Sea, and Air Defense forces, who however are not necessarily and automatically of equal rank (the land commander is customarily at least a grade higher than the sea commander). Directly below the Commander in the Chief of the Navy, currently Adm. of the Fleet Sergei G. Gorshkov, are the Naval War Council, the Chief of Naval Staff Adm. of the Fleet V. A. Kasatonov, and the Director of Naval-Political Administration, Adm. V. H. Grishanov. The last named official reports not only to the Commander in Chief but also ultimately to the Central Committee of the Communist Party of the Soviet Union. The main naval services under the Commander in Chief are administered under Fleets and Flotillas, Central Administration, Training School, Naval Air Arm, and Logistics.

The Soviet Navy is divided into four fleets and four flotillas (Danube, Caspian, Dnieper, and Amur).[4] The fleet commanders are currently (1970) Adm. V. V. Mikhailin of the Baltic Fleet, Adm. Semen M. Lobov of the (Sysoev) Northern Fleet, Adm. V. S. Sysoev of the Black Fleet, and Adm. Nikolai N. Amelko of the Pacific Fleet. Each commands a force of 700 to 800 ships. The forces are generally similar in their composition, but submarine forces are stronger in the Pacific and Northern fleets. The Baltic and Pacific fleets are both divided into Northern and Southern groups, respectively based on Tallinn (Revel) and Baltiisk (Pillau) in the case of the Baltic, and Petropavlovsk and Vladivostok in the case of the Pacific. Each commander in chief of a fleet commands both surface and subsurface craft, a naval air arm, naval bases and ports, a hydrographic department, and coast-defense forces consisting mainly of artillery and naval infantry. The doctrine of sea power as an extension of land power is still strong in Russia, and the mine fleets, motor torpedo boats, coastal submarines, and land-based air fleets are actually as much coast-defense forces as are the artillery and infantry. The flotillas depend directly on the land forces commanders in their respective areas, in spite of the fact that they are organized as miniature fleets. A recent change is the creation in the Pacific and Arctic of long-range strategic submarine forces.

Naval bases are classed as main, secondary, and operational. The main bases include Vladivostok in the Pacific; Polarnye, Murmansk, and Severomorsk for the Northern Fleet; Sevastopol in the Black Sea; and Tallinn (Revel), Kronstadt, Riga, Kaliningrad, and Baltiisk in the Baltic. Secondary and operational bases are listed elsewhere in this chapter.

Though the administration of the Northern Sea Route has been under the Minister of Mercantile Marine since 1952, it has a very close connection with the navy, which makes use of its ports and assists it in various ways.

The organization of naval forces on the fleet level is indicated in the table on page 480.

THE NAVY ASHORE

Almost the first problem faced by the Soviet Union in expanding its fleet after World War II was that of inadequate facilities. Most of the shipbuilding yards in the Baltic and the Black Sea had been ruined, as had many of the river yards, and the naval bases were in no better state. Furthermore, with the longer seacoasts gained from the war and with naval expansion in prospect, the available bases even as they existed before the war were no longer adequate. This lack of base facilities was especially pressing since the prewar navy had possessed few and relatively inefficient auxiliaries.

The policy that was followed in satisfying these logistic needs is

TABLE 12

*Organization of a Fleet**

```
┌─────────────────────┐
│ Commander in Chief  │
│    of the fleet     │
└─────────────────────┘
           │
┌─────────────────────┐          ┌ ─ ─ ─ ─ ─ ─ ─ ─ ─ ─ ─ ┐
│  Military Council   │            Political Directorate
│    of the fleet     │          └ ─ ─ ─ ─ ─ ─ ─ ─ ─ ─ ─ ┘
└─────────────────────┘
           │
┌─────────────────────┐
│     Fleet Staff     │
└─────────────────────┘

┌─────────────────────┐          ┌─────────────────────┐
│   Surface Forces    │          │      Logistics      │
└─────────────────────┘          └─────────────────────┘

┌─────────────────────┐          ┌─────────────────────┐
│   Fleet Air Force   │          │      Services       │
└─────────────────────┘          └─────────────────────┘

┌─────────────────────┐
│   Coastal Defense   │
└─────────────────────┘

┌─────────────────────┐
│   Submarine Force   │
└─────────────────────┘

        ┌─────────────────────┐
        │  Naval Air Forces   │
        └─────────────────────┘
```

* Source: *Revue Maritime* (December 1964), p. 1285.

of considerable interest. Many new bases were established, especially in the Baltic and on the Pacific. The Soviets, however, avoided the mistake of crowding facilities together. Especially in their Arctic bases, shore installations were widely dispersed and in some cases buried beneath heavy granite cliffs to provide protection against nuclear attack. In recognition of American logistic achievements in the Pacific during World War II, as well as the probable vulnerability of bases in a nuclear war, the Soviets also gave some attention to developing new types of auxiliaries which would permit their fleets to operate at a greater distance from home bases.

Developments in the Arctic are believed to have been extensive, but they have been shrouded in almost complete secrecy (especially those along the northern sea route). Known new bases along the northern coast of European Russia include Severomorsk on the Kola Inlet, Polarnye, Petsamo, Severodvinsk (Molotovsk) near Arkhangelsk, and Belushia on the island of Novaia Zemlia. New ports have also been established along the northern coast of Siberia, most notably at Andermo, Narian Mar at the mouth of the Pechora, Salekhard on the Ob, Dikson on the Yenisei, Nordvik near the mouth of the Khatanga River, Tiksi on the Lena, Ambarchik on the Kolyma, and Ueleu on Bering Strait.

From available evidence it is possible to conclude that the northern sea route is economically rather less important today than it was expected to be during the 1930s. While 200,000 miles of navigable rivers are available in Siberia, most of them run through barren and almost uninhabited territory. Between 1960 and 1967 annual total transport rose 70 percent. However, the double-tracking of the Trans-Siberian railroad and the development of local industries in southern Siberia have reduced the dependence of northern Siberia on consumer goods shipped by sea from European Russia. Most goods move on the Siberian rivers from south to north. The products of northern Siberia include coal, timber, a small surplus of meat from reindeer herds and fishing, and the products of a few mines. The shipment of grain by the northern sea route has proved too costly, and furs can be moved more rapidly and safely by air. As a consequence this route has lost much of its interest to the Russians, though the navy retains a fleet of 28 icebreakers of the Northern Fleet devoted to keeping the channels open.

TABLE 13

Organization of the Soviet Navy

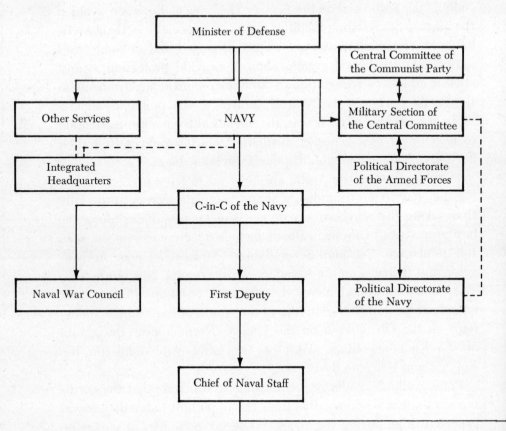

Command of the Soviet Navy as of 1 January 1969

Commander: Admiral of the Fleet of the USSR S. C. Gorshkov
Political Direction: Admiral V. M. Grishanov
Chief, War Soviet* of the Navy: Admiral of the Fleet V. A. Kasatonov

Northern Fleet

Commander: Admiral of the Fleet S. M. Lobov
Chief of Staff: Rear Admiral N. M. Baranov
Political Director: Vice Admiral F. Ia. Sisov

Baltic Fleet

Commander: Vice Admiral V. V. Mikhailin
Chief of Staff: Vice Admiral F. I. Savelev
Political Director: Vice Admiral Ia. G. Pochupailo

* This organization was established in 1932.

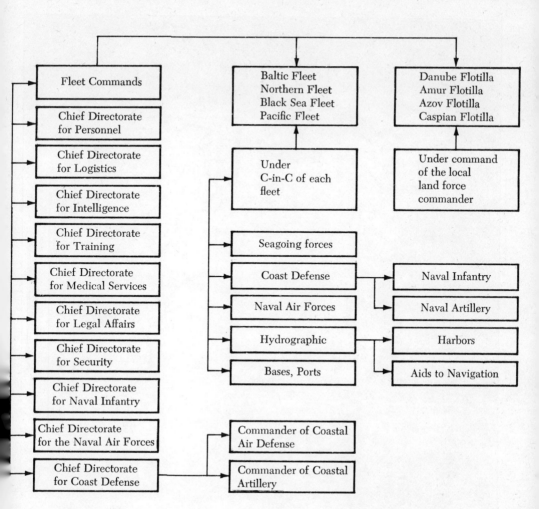

Fleet Commands	Baltic Fleet Northern Fleet Black Sea Fleet Pacific Fleet	Danube Flotilla Amur Flotilla Azov Flotilla Caspian Flotilla
Chief Directorate for Personnel	Under C-in-C of each fleet	Under command of the local land force commander
Chief Directorate for Logistics		
Chief Directorate for Intelligence		
Chief Directorate for Training	Seagoing forces	
Chief Directorate for Medical Services	Coast Defense	Naval Infantry
Chief Directorate for Legal Affairs	Naval Air Forces	Naval Artillery
Chief Directorate for Security	Hydrographic	Harbors
Chief Directorate for Naval Infantry	Bases, Ports	Aids to Navigation
Chief Directorate for the Naval Air Forces	Commander of Coastal Air Defense	
Chief Directorate for Coast Defense	Commander of Coastal Artillery	

Black Sea Fleet

Commander: Vice Admiral V. S. Sysoev
Chief of Staff: Vice Admiral L. V. Mizin
Political Director: Rear Admiral I. S. Rudnev

Pacific Fleet

Commander: Admiral N. N. Amelko
Chief of Staff: Vice Admiral G. M. Egorov
Political Director: Admiral M. N. Zakharov

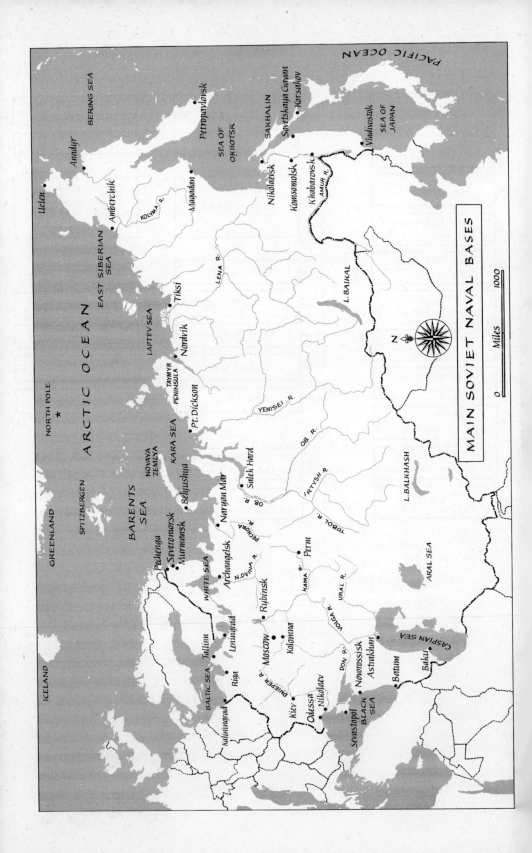

MAIN SOVIET NAVAL BASES

With the development of widely dispersed base facilities in the Baltic, Leningrad no longer enjoys its former predominant position. Ice-free bases are maintained at Libau, Kaliningrad (Königsberg), and Baltiisk, the last serving as the main base for approximately half of the Baltic Fleet. The northern half of the fleet operates out of Tallinn (Revel), though Leningrad, Kronstadt, and Balticport are also used to varying degrees. Other base facilities are maintained at Windau (Ventspils, Latvia) and Oranienbaum (Lomonosov).

Developments in the Pacific have been extensive and are much better known than those in the Baltic. Here the Russians have worked long and hard to improve a climatically handicapped and naturally barren terrain, with the result that eastern Siberia is much further advanced than is Alaska, an area similar in geographic characteristics.[5] Yet neither strenuous work nor gains from World War II have entirely freed the Russians from handicaps in the Pacific. Japan controls the exits to the Gulf of Tatary, which in any case are shallow and frequently iced. Although the exits to the Sea of Okhotsk are in the Kurile Islands, now held by the Soviet Union, they do not provide favorable access to the sea. Petropavlovsk on Kamchatka is the only port which opens directly on the Pacific. Russian naval and air installations are well dispersed from Vladivostok to Bering Strait, the principal activities being centered in Vladivostok to the south and Petropavlovsk and Sovetskaia Gavan (on the Tatar Strait opposite Sakhalin) to the north. Petropavlovsk has no railway connections and is extremely isolated, but it is well located as a submarine base. Vladivostok supports a wide range of military and naval activities; so to a somewhat lesser degree does Sovetskaia Gavan.

Other facilities are scattered. Nakhodka, east of Vladivostok and like Vladivostok fronting on Peter the Great Bay, is a submarine base. Korsakov, Nevelsk, and Kholmek are minor bases on the island of Sakhalin. Nikolaevsk on the Amur is an industrial city and oil storage center. Khabarovsk, headquarters of the Amur River Flotilla, operates small shipyards, as does Komsomolsk. Magadan and its twin city Nagaeva form the only important naval base on the Sea of Okhotsk. Korsakov on the southern coast of Sakhalin is a naval supply and destroyer base. Profideniia on the Bering Strait is a deep-water port and a stop on the northern sea route. Anadyr provides a coal depot for Arctic shipping as well as an airfield and a base for light naval forces. Paramushiro, largest island in the northern Kuriles, is also reported to have sizable naval facilities, and several other small ports have minor facilities.

The Black Sea has seen comparatively little change. Sevastopol continues to be the main headquarters of the Black Sea Fleet, with Odessa and Nikolaev playing less important roles. Poti, Tuapse, Novorossiisk, and Batum are secondary stations. Rostov, Kherson, and Zhdanov Mariupol are ports which could be used in case of necessity. Some use has also been made of Rumanian and Bulgarian ports.

There have been intermittent efforts by the Soviets to gain a foothold in the Mediterranean. In 1946 Stalin tried to secure a United Nations trusteeship over Eritrea and Libya. Failing that, the Soviet Union established a submarine base at Valona in Albania and maintained it from the early 1950s to 1961, when Albania's support of Communist China cooled relations between the two East European countries. Subsequent naval developments in the Mediterranean are reported in chapter 22.

While the Caspian fronts only on Iran, it is nevertheless of considerable naval importance to the U.S.S.R. Most of the Russian domestic oil transport is carried on in the Caspian and on the Volga. The Caspian is also used extensively for naval training, and ships are built at its main port, Baku. Ships can, of course, reach the sea via the Volga-Don Canal, Don River, and Black Sea.

Shipbuilding in Russia, never as important a part of the general economy or as efficient an industry as in such European countries as Germany and Great Britain, virtually ceased during the revolution and civil war and was not revived until 1928. Between that date and the beginning of World War II there was a steady expansion, with most of the early activity centering in Leningrad, Odessa, Nikolaev, Sevastopol, and ports on the Volga. The second five-year plan, which carried shipbuilding to Komsomolsk on the Amur, also expanded some of the Volga yards. At the time of the German invasion there were approximately 500 building and repair yards of all sizes in Russia, including the river yards capable of constructing only small craft. During the war 98 yards were destroyed, many were damaged, and most of the work was halted at all of those not occupied by the Germans.

The extremely rapid Soviet rebuilding and recovery involved the

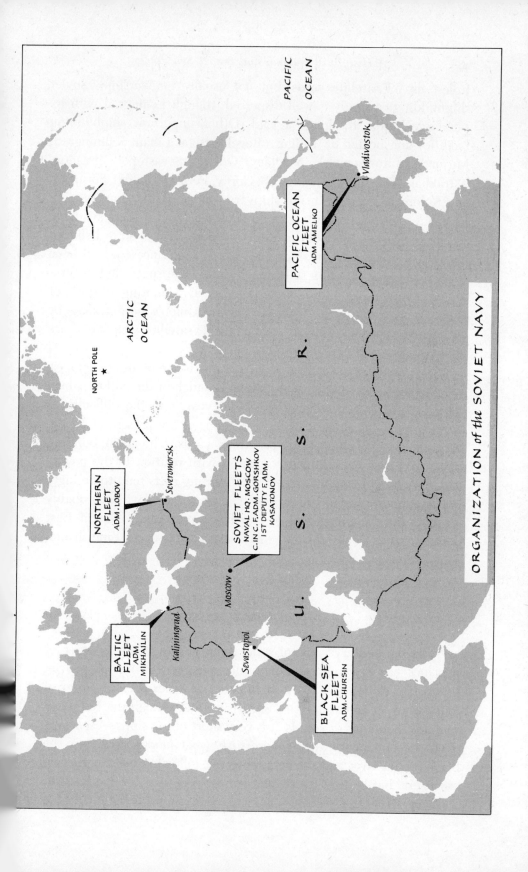

PACIFIC
OCEAN

• Vladivostok

PACIFIC OCEAN
FLEET
ADM. AMELKO

U.   S.   S.   R.

ARCTIC
OCEAN

NORTH POLE
★

• Severomorsk

NORTHERN
FLEET
ADM. LOBOV

SOVIET FLEETS
NAVAL HQ. MOSCOW
C. IN C. F. ADM. GORSHKOV
1ST DEPUTY F. ADM.
KASATONOV

• Moscow

BALTIC
FLEET
ADM.
MIKHAILIN

Kaliningrad •

• Sevastopol

BLACK SEA
FLEET
ADM. CHURSIN

ORGANIZATION of the SOVIET NAVY

fullest use of satellite yards, but not usually for warships. Soviet shipbuilding currently is well dispersed, though Leningrad with its ten large yards still holds a lead. Other important shipbuilding facilities are located at Tallinn (Revel), Riga, Libau, Kaliningrad, Murmansk, Komsomolsk, Nikolaev, Odessa, Sevastopol, Zhdanov, Astrakhan, Volgagrad (Stalingrad), Gorky, Perm (Molotov), Sormovo, and Kolomna. Fourteen major shipyards on the Baltic alone employ a total of some 86,000 workers. Approximately 600 yards are available within the Soviet bloc, but of these no more than 100 are believed capable of taking care of ships over 1,000 tons. Since 1947 all have been working at virtually full capacity and have succeeded in turning out about 150,000 tons of warships yearly. Counting all types of commercial shipping as well the Soviet Union's output may be closer to 1,000,000 tons a year and, if satellite shipyards are included, as much as 1,500,00 tons.

Soviet shipbuilding suffers from certain inherent disadvantages. They include the severity of climate over much of the nation, which restricts activity several months of the year, and the difficulty of operating in such shallow-water conditions as are present at Leningrad, on the Volga, and in the Amur yards. The main building centers are also inconveniently located with relation to the power, coal, iron, and oil supply, so that shipbuilding costs tend to be high. Quality of work has at times been suspect, a factor which probably accounts for the great deal of warship repair carried on in East German yards. Many Soviet vessels are also built in Finnish and West European yards.

THE SURFACE FLEET

While the military value of submarines and to a lesser degree of airplanes has been almost universally accepted within the Soviet Union, the value of surface warships has at times been a matter of controversy. It is therefore not surprising that though the Red navy contains thousands of vessels, it is very short of big ships—especially since the sinking of the *Novorossiisk* (ex-*Giulio Cesare*) in the Black Sea in 1955 and the scrapping the following year of the old tsarist-era battleships. Persistent rumors circulated directly after

World War II regarding possible Soviet construction of both battleships and airplane carriers, but no actual building occurred in
either category; a 9,000-ton aircraft carrier, *Stalin*, was found to
exist only in naval annuals.

Except for the new helicopter carriers (see chapter 23), the
largest warships in the Soviet navy are cruisers. All of these, save
some very old ships and surrendered Axis vessels, are of three main
types. The oldest are the five *Kirovs* (*Kirov*, *Slava* [ex-*Molotov*],
Kalinin, *Maksim Gorky*, and *Voroshilov*), designed before World
War II but nearly all finished after the war. Two complete or nearly
complete sister ships were lost early in the war, one in the Black
Sea and one in the Baltic. On an 8,800-ton hull, the *Kirov* types
were originally armed with nine 7.1-inch guns, and about 30 antiaircraft guns ranging from 13-mm. to 4-inch size. They carried a
side armor belt 3 inches thick, and while turret armor up to 4 inches
was used, deck armor measured only 2 inches in thickness. Designed
for 35 knots, they usually fell short of this speed in practice. Like
most Russian warships they were equipped with both torpedoes and
mines.

The *Chapaev* class consisted of four ships (*Chapaev*, *Komsomol-
ets* [ex-*Chkalov*], *Kuibyshev*, *Zhelezniakov*) of 11,500 tons, which
were laid down at the beginning of World War II but not completed
until 1948–50. Larger and probably better built than the *Kirovs*
which they resembled, the ships of this class were also somewhat
better armed, carrying 12 6-inch guns in four triple turrets and
eight 4-inch and 28 37-mm. antiaircraft guns.

The latest Soviet cruisers, designed during the early 1950s, are
the ships of the *Sverdlov* class. Several of these ships have been
observed in foreign ports, and they have favorably impressed
observers even so critical and knowledgeable as the British. No less
than 24 were at one time named in *Jane's Fighting Ships*, but not
all of them were completed. The fourteen now in the Soviet navy
are named *Sverdlov*, *Admiral Lazarev*, *Admiral Nakhimov*, *Admiral
Ushakov*, *Aleksandr Nevsky*, *Aleksandr Suvorov*, *Admiral Seniavin*,
Dmitry Donskoi, *Dmitry Pozharsky*, *Dzerzhinsky*, *Kozma Minin*,
Mikhail Kutuzov, *Oktiabrskaia Revoliutsiia*, and *Murmansk*. The
names are of considerable interest as indicative of the extent to
which the Soviet leaders are willing to accept the events and lead-

ers of the tsarist navy to promote a naval tradition.[6] The designed
tonnage of this class is 15,450, with full-load tonnage 19,200. The
main battery consists of 12 6-inch guns with 44 pieces (12 3.9-inch
and 32 37-mm.) for antiaircraft use. Ten quintuple-mounted 21-inch
torpedo tubes and 140 to 240 mines are carried on each vessel.
Turrets and conning tower have 5–6-inch armor; the side armor belt
is 4-inches thick. Normal personnel complement is 1,050 men. Speed
is the same as that of the earlier cruisers, but fuel capacity is considerably greater; at 20 knots the ships have a cruising range of
about 5,000 miles. Some of these cruisers have undergone modification to change their armament from guns to guided missiles. The
relatively light armament of these ships, especially against submarines and aircraft, had aroused some foreign criticism.

A new and highly formidable class is that of the missile-armed
frigates, at least some of which carry nuclear-armed sea-to-surface
missiles. In size these resemble small cruisers, ranging from 3,000 to
6,000 tons. They date from 1958, and are of several types which
vary in size and armament. The *Kynda, Kashin, Krupny,* and *Kotlin*
types have all been noted by observers. With relatively long-range
missiles of great destructive power these ships pose a serious threat
to both sea and land targets. Due to their varied weapon systems
which also include rockets and torpedoes they could operate inde-
pently over a wide area.

Since World War II there has been a gradual merging of several
types of ships, such as frigates and destroyers on the one hand and
various types of smaller escorts and destroyers on the other. Of the
destroyer class proper, the Soviets apparently have 100–110 units of
post-World War II construction and may still have a few earlier
models. The *Skory* class, probably numbering about 55, are the most
numerous. These are of 2,600 tons, 38 knots speed, and have a personnel complement of about 250. Armament consists of four 4.8-inch
guns and 17 antiaircraft guns, ten 21-inch torpedo tubes, and 80
mines. The 30 or so *Kotlins* are 250 tons larger, have the same speed
and mining and torpedo equipment, but a slightly different gun
armament. All 16 antiaircraft guns are of 57-mm. caliber (vs. 37-mm.
for the *Skory*) but the main battery guns are of only 3.9-inch
caliber. The new *Tallin* class (of which a prototype is known to be
completed) is much larger, displacing 3,500 tons; but aside from an

increased mine capacity of 100 and the addition of an on-board helicopter, it is no better armed and actually carries weaker antiaircraft defenses (12 37-mm. AA guns) than the *Kotlins*. Recently built Soviet destroyers are believed to be armed with guided missiles. The Soviet destroyers are equipped mostly for minelaying but are regarded as weak in antiaircraft protection, and a number have been modernized in recent years.

In the category of small surface vessels for inshore naval work, the Soviet navy is extremely strong. In addition to an estimated 400 escort ships of many types, gunboats, minesweepers, motor gunboats, patrol boats, and motor torpedo boats all run into the hundreds.[7] Soviet policy favors keeping many of these inshore naval vessels available at all times. For some years antisubmarine warfare was neglected by the Soviets, but the very large force of escorts points to a growing interest in this field.

So far as auxiliaries are concerned, the Soviet navy is in a much better position than formerly; and because of the needs of its strategic submarines and some other long-range types, is apt to be increasingly well supplied. Many highly specialized types have been developed. There is an icebreaker fleet of 30 to 40 vessels, which includes the 16,000-ton nuclear icebreaker *Lenin*. There are also depot ships, tenders, fishery protection vessels, an estimated 350 mine tenders, minelayers, minesweepers, aircraft tenders, survey ships, salvage vessels, boom defense vessels, about 100 landing craft, and an expanding fleet of tankers. These would be inadequate to support any large-scale operations away from Soviet waters, but they are sufficient to care for the needs of a large and growing fleet. Continued stress is laid on mine warfare and most surface fighting ships of any size have a minelaying capacity. For an overall comparison of the Soviet and American navies, see table 14.

THE UNDERSEA FLEET

At the end of World War II the Soviet Union still had some 150 of the approximately 250 submarines with which she had entered the war. For a time the poor condition of the shipyards prevented anything more than the completion of numerous hulls already on

TABLE 14

*Composition of American, Soviet, and British Navies**

	USA	USSR	UK
Large aircraft carriers	33	0	2
Light aircraft carriers	0	0	2
Escort, helicopter and commando carriers	7	2	2
Command ships	9	0	0
Nuclear powered submarines	93	75	8
Conventional powered submarines	64	320	33
Cruisers	32	25	3
Large destroyers and frigates	33	0	8
Destroyers	295	100	11
Destroyer escorts and frigate escorts	229	100	68
Patrol vessels and submarine chasers	0	275	0
Motor torpedo boats, missile boats, fast patrol	37	425	4
Fleet fast minelayers, mine support ships	13	1	1
Coastal minelayers	0	0	5
Ocean and fleet minesweepers	91	170	0
Coastal minesweepers and mine hunters	20	130	66
Inshore sweepers	43	0	22
River gunboats, motor launches and motor patrol	400	120	4
Landing ships	115	100	2
Landing Craft	100	130	26
Net layers and boom defense vessels	4	18	20
Depot and repair ships	70	50	8
Transports	40	25	0
Supply ships	120	125	11
Oilers	75	50	38
Training ships	2	20	4
Tugs	250	140	20
Survey Ships	26	55	1
Miscellaneous	440	450	185

* SOURCE: *Jane's Fighting Ships*, 1970–71 (London).

hand, but between 1948 and 1950 the Soviets were able to start work on massive programs of new construction. Though they had captured some extremely sophisticated German types, such as the Type XXI U-boat, their first new submarines were quite conventional. Sacrificing quality for quantity, the Soviets attained an output of 50 to 60 boats a year aimed at a total estimated force of some 500 by 1959.

Before they had reached this point, however, Soviet naval leaders became concerned over the development of the far less numerous but more complicated and sophisticated American undersea craft. Technological advances following World War II had produced a capability for diving deeper, moving faster, staying submerged almost indefinitely, and discharging infinitely more destructive weapons. It now became clear to the Soviets that since their earlier postwar submarines did not embody these characteristics, they could present little threat to sophisticated antisubmarine forces apart from that inherent in their great numbers.

As a consequence, since 1959 a completely new submarine building policy has been adopted: the navy's leaders have concentrated on reducing the long qualitative lead possessed by the United States. In course of this program they have been forced to grapple with some very difficult technical problems which have greatly slowed their progress, so that in both submarine output and in total vessel output the Soviet submarine force has decreased, the former figure to an estimated twelve boats a year, the latter to 370 boats or less. In the meantime, many of the older types have been either sold or given to satellites or neutrals. Red China probably has 33 of the older submarines, the United Arab Republic 16, Indonesia 12, Poland six, and Bulgaria two.[8]

If this change in policy has meant a smaller submarine fleet, it emphatically has not resulted in a weaker one. The coast-defense and medium-range types have been replaced by larger and far more powerful undersea boats. While the process is far from complete and the force is apt to continue to shrink below the estimated number of 350-370, there can be no doubt that the new types represent a much greater threat. The larger boats now range widely in every ocean.

The most numerous class of Soviet submarines is the 1,050-ton W (or *Whisky*) class of seagoing, snorkel-equipped submarines. These are of low speed and short range but carry both mines and torpedoes. No less than 220 were built during the middle 1950s, but large numbers have been given away or scrapped and only about 170 are reported to remain. Some have been adapted to carry two to four short-range missiles. Some 15 short-range coastal types of 350 tons are still reported in service, as are about 25 of the O class medium-range (7,000 miles) 650-ton submarines which carry torpedoes but no mines. Some 20 R class boats of 1,100 tons, armed with torpedoes but capable of speeds of 15 to 18 knots, are also reported.

None of the above types is especially formidable. Nor are the one-man midget submarines in which the Russians have shown some interest. About 85 Z class large oceangoing attack submarines, with diesel engines and able to carry either 40 mines or torpedoes, were built from 1954 on. Of these, about ten have been converted to missile submarines carrying two 500-mile ballistic missiles as well as torpedoes. Where conversion has not occurred the Z-boat is a 1,900-ton ship of 16 knots surface speed, with eight loaded torpedo tubes and 24 torpedoes in reserve. It has a great enough cruising radius to remain at sea for four months, and some of the boats in this class may be much faster than indicated. The 40 F class submarines in the Red navy incorporate a number of improvements on the Z design and are slightly larger, faster, and better armed. They can probably cruise up to 30,000 miles, and some are probably equipped with nuclear propulsion. There are also two J class 1,600-ton missile submarines carrying four missile launchers, and some 30 G class submarines which are reported to be of 2,350 tons and to carry three tubes for missiles. The G class boats may represent several variations on a basic type, with some designed for nuclear attack and others as high-speed minelayers, nuclear radar pickets, and nuclear antisubmarine types. Though neither as quiet nor as fast as their American counterparts, they are less complicated and considerably less costly. Those carrying missiles have armaments only a fraction as powerful or as long-range as the American Polaris type vessels. However, since most large American cities lie within a 500-mile radius of the sea, the nuclear missiles they carry would probably suffice for a "city busting" assault on the United States. If the Russian submarines can fire their missiles while submerged, as they are credited, this capability would add to their threat.

Other than the above, the most recent Soviet boats are of the E, H, and N classes. The 15 E class boats of 5,600 tons carry six tubes for missiles and crews of 92 men, but make the relatively low speed of 22 knots. They are the largest of Russian submarine types. The H class (13 vessels), of 3,500 tons, is a nuclear-powered ballistic missile type, carrying three launching tubes for missiles as well as torpedoes. It can make 25 knots on the surface and 30 or more under water. The 12 boats of the N class are of 3,200 tons. They are nuclear-powered, high-speed antisubmarine submarines. The Leninsky Komsomol, first of the class, required an abnormally long construction time.

The search for quality in the submarine force has recently attained a high degree of success. Improvements have been made in torpedoes, in the streamlining of conning towers, and in the development of sonar. A variety of missiles have been developed, ranging from simple tactical types capable of making strikes at distances of six to forty miles, to strategic weapons able to reach at least 350 to 500 miles. Recent reports tell of much longer-range missiles capable of 2,000 to 3,000 miles. Russian mines, though simple, are reliable and powerful. Huge stockpiles of mines of all types, including some very sophisticated models, are on hand. Mobile transport forces which have been built up include tenders, drydocks, repair ships, and supply ships. An extensive program of oceanic research by fishing and hydrographic vessels also functions mainly to support submarine operations.

The submarine force is organized into divisions of six boats each, with brigades made up of four to six divisions. Each Russian fleet contains one or more brigades of cruiser, attack, and coastal submarines.

About 5,000 officers (one-fourth of the entire naval officer corps) and 45,000 men are in the submarine fleet. Although in theory an elite corps, the submarine service has in the past waged not-always-successful battles with the surface fleet for the best jobs and the greatest prestige. However, the introduction of missiles aboard ships within the past several years has certainly given the undersea forces an advantage in this struggle. Also helpful has been the rapid expansion of the undersea force, which has tended to speed promotions.

The training of officers and men for Soviet submarine service has improved greatly since World War II, but is probably still less thorough than in the United States navy. About half of the officers come from the ranks, and the remainder from universities and naval schools conducted at Arkhangelsk, Leningrad, Kaliningrad, Sevastopol, and Vladivostok. Political reliability is an important factor in determining their advancement. The training of enlisted men, which also stresses the dogmatic, is at times impractical. Foreign observers have reported a general lack of initiative and of interest in sea service, and brief and somewhat lackadaisical instruction ashore. The severe climate in itself serves to curtail the length of training. Doctrine still tends to stress the combined-arms approach rather than the possibility of independent action by naval forces alone;

however, the development of the long-range force of strategic submarines seems likely to produce a change in this respect.[9]

While a more detailed assessment of the military capabilities of the Soviet submarine force is contained in chapter 23, it should be mentioned here that the Soviets appear to have made up most of the technical and tactical lag which they displayed in World War II. This does not mean that their undersea boats are on a par with British or American submarines. In World War II the Russian submarine effort was weakened by crews that were undertrained as well as by the tactical doctrine governing submarine employment. Unless both of these conditions have been altered substantially, Russian submarines still are not likely to attain maximum effectiveness. In point of fact, Soviet submarines at sea have repeatedly shown a somewhat high susceptibility to breakdowns and engine trouble. Nevertheless, the sheer bulk of this improving fleet is enough to command respect: it is nearly twenty times as great as that with which Germany started World War II, and it now includes boats having nuclear propulsion and equipped with missiles with nuclear warheads. According to the best unclassified sources the present Soviet submarine fleet consists of some 370-385 boats in all. Of these about 65 are nuclear submarines of various types and 320 are conventional diesel boats; probably 30 nuclear boats of five classes are building. In armament some of these newer types will equal (or have already equaled) the *Polaris* with its 16 missiles, and the missiles carried may be of comparable range and destructive power. Ballistic missile types, cruiser missile types, missile submarines, fleet submarines, and antisubmarine boats are the modern types now in service. The Soviet medium-range missiles planted in Cuba in 1962 represented far less a threat to the United States than do the Soviet nuclear submarines operating today off the American coast.

NAVAL AVIATION

The Soviet naval air force is commonly credited with having approximately 750 to 850 planes of all types, as compared to some 10,500 for the Soviet army. Most of the naval planes are attached to the four main fleets; but the organization of the naval air force strongly resembles that of the army force. Each fleet operates an air corps consisting of several divisions. An air division in turn includes two or three regiments, each composed of several squadrons. As a rule, a squadron is trained and equipped to perform just one particular job, though dual-purpose squadrons do exist. Titles of rank are the same as in the army. Until 1950 the naval air force reported to the ministry of defense and operated in the shadow of army aviation, but when at that time three separate ministries were established, naval aviation was placed under the naval staff.

The main missions of the naval air arm include oceanic reconnaissance, minelaying, attacks on enemy ports and bases, antisubmarine warfare, and attacks on enemy surface forces. Available for these missions are probably 300 TU-16s (*Badgers*) with a range of 2,000 miles, a few new TU-22s (*Blinders*), and perhaps 50 TU-95 turbo-props (*Bears*) with a range of 7,800 miles. Fifty or more *Beriev* patrol planes are available for antisubmarine warfare, as are helicopters, aerial transports, fighters, and interceptors.

The tasks and procedures of the air arm of the Soviet navy differ in so many respects from those of the equivalent force in the United States that comparisons are difficult. Russian planes, for the most part, are excellent products of a number of able aircraft designers and manufacturers. Qualitatively, they rank at least equally with the American carrier-based planes, and this standard is likely to be maintained. Practically all Soviet planes are land based, since the Soviet Union operates no carriers. But since countless satellite bases supplement those available in the Soviet Union and the plane crews are skilled in speedy transfer, the naval air force nevertheless unquestionably has wide mobility and range.

Aviation schools are maintained in each fleet command area, as well as at Nikolaev, Perm, and Novaia Ladoga. Airmen, like submarine crews, are a naval elite, eager and of high morale. During World War II the Germans gave Russian airmen credit for their ability to perform well with primitive facilities and under very trying conditions. This quality has not been lost. Russian personnel have a great deal of experience in operating at night, under polar conditions, and in "blind" flying by radar under severe weather handicaps. They are proficient at improvising landing fields in snow and in very rough country. Tactical skill is less certain, though in one field, aerial minelaying, there was a vast improvement between World War II and the Korean war. Russian fighters have had training in port defense, in the support of ground troops, as convoy escorts, in combat air patrol over surface forces, and often in conducting ice patrols over the Arctic. But there has been no experience in the coordination of long-range reconnaissance with submarine attack, and until recently there was also very little use of any type of plane in long-range flights over the sea. By early 1963, however, certain types of Soviet planes were flying over American naval forces in both the Atlantic and the Pacific in sufficient numbers to prove a growing capability to detect and reach fleets at sea.

In general, the conclusion appears warranted that the naval air force of the Soviet Union is as yet basically defensive in character and has relatively little long-range power. Without long-range air assistance, the nation's mighty submarine force could be crippled in its operations. Nevertheless, the Soviet naval air force appears to be adequate to accomplish most of its defensive objectives, and the recent development of distance flying indicates a likelihood of future effective support for the submarine force.

THE MERCHANT MARINE AND THE FISHING FLEETS

Since merchant and fishing fleets and internal waterways are all connected with sea power, the part they play in Soviet naval operations should not be overlooked. For many decades the Russians appeared to have no idea whatever that there might be a connection between naval power and merchant shipping. At the beginning of World War I the merchant marine totaled only about 1.3 million tons. The cessation of normal building together with losses during the revolutionary and civil war periods brought this figure down to 200,000 tons in 1925, of which more than a third operated in the Caspian. This total represented the nadir; succeeding years have brought a steady increase. In 1932 the figure advanced to 500,000 tons, and in the next five years merchant tonnage doubled. By the beginning of World War II the merchant fleet had returned to its 1914 level. War losses, commonly estimated at about 500,000 tons, were more than replaced by Liberty ships from the United States and by about 750,000 tons of vessels seized from the Axis. Hence, despite a wartime absence of shipbuilding, the merchant fleet gained in size. It continued to grow: by 1955 it totaled 3 million tons and by 1966 more than 8 million tons deadweight. A further increase of 50 percent to 12 million tons (15 million if fishing vessels were included) took place by 1970, as well as an increase of 80 percent in cargo capacity. In 1968 tonnage was going up at a rate of a million tons yearly, and 80 percent of the vessels were less than ten years old.

This steady increase has been sufficient to make Soviet Bloc shipping a major factor in world trade, though not as yet a dominant one. The Soviet Union still controls only about five percent of the world's merchant tonnage instead of the ten percent it hopes to control at the conclusion of present building plans. About half of the Soviet Union's foreign trade and all of its coastal commerce is moved in Soviet ships. The main commodities transported are oil, timber, and grain. Transport is not always rapid or efficient, owing to cumbersome and bureaucratic administration, shallow harbors, inadequate harbor installations, and poor use of facilities available; on the other hand, because Soviet shipping is never impeded by strikes and is not required to show a profit, it has a competitive edge over the West's private shipping lines.

The merchant marine presents a somewhat unbalanced appearance in its role as a part of sea power. It has very few passenger ships or large liners, and transports carry the bulk of the load into and out of Pacific coast ports. Oil tankers have been increasing but are still deficient in numbers. Special shallow-draft tankers have been developed for service in shallow stretches of the Caspian and the Volga.

As of January 1968 the Soviet merchant marine comprised 1,449 vessels of 10,958,000 deadweight tons and 283 tankers of 4,148,000 deadweight tons. Surpassed in size at that date by the merchant fleets of the United States, Great Britain, Japan, Norway, and Liberia, its rating was no better than sixth, or fifth if the Liberian flag of convenience is omitted. However, the Soviets' standing was advancing and they hoped to attain first place in oceangoing vessels by 1980. On March 13, 1966, merchant marine minister Viktor G.

Bakaev announced that the Soviet Union then ranked sixth in merchant marine tonnage (having just surpassed Greece). With the exception of East Germany, China, and Poland, no other Communist states had merchant fleets of much importance.

The Soviet merchant fleet has a number of important advantages which enhance its growth aspirations. At the outset, it has behind it a good educational plant, with large merchant marine academies at Leningrad, Odessa, Arkhangelsk, and Vladivostok as well as some ten lesser schools. It is also supported by large government expenditures for research and development, and by a ship procurement program which is implemented by all Soviet shipyards and by many overseas as well. Since it is unhampered by special-interest groups, the Soviet government is free to improve productivity by the prompt adoption of new inventions; as a result, some excellent cargo ships and tankers have recently come from Soviet yards. Weaknesses exist in passenger service, in the handling of cargo in ports, and in coordination of water and rail transport. Existing plans call for new and improved piers and jetties, expanded space in pier sheds, and a high degree of mechanization in cargo loading. Other plans provide for the completion of modern passenger terminals in Odessa and Sevastopol and the building of sea stations at other ports. Accounting, planning, and evaluation data concerned with the fleet will in future be processed by electronic computers. Finally, because the merchant marine is now completely integrated with the regular navy in both operations and planning, the coordination gap between seagoing services which exists in other countries is not present in the Soviet forces.

The U.S.S.R. is a nation rich in fishery resources, but it has only recently made a vigorous effort to exploit this wealth. Prior to the revolution, fishing was largely limited to lakes, rivers, and coastal waters; the annual catch was small. Since World War II, however, spurred by the inadequate meat production of Soviet livestock husbandry, the Russians have turned increasingly to fish as a source of protein. While some progress had already been made in the number of trawlers built in Russian yards before World War II, and although German and Finnish vessels received as reparations helped to replace wartime losses, there was a great dearth of fishing tonnage during the late 1940s and 1950s. The Soviet government therefore placed very large orders with foreign shipyards. Denmark built sealers; Great Britain, Belgium, Japan, and Sweden delivered hundreds of trawlers; West Germany supplied fish transports and factory ships; and Polish, East German, and Bulgarian yards were called upon to contribute in accord with their capacity. By 1955 Russia had become the world's third largest fishing nation. Baltic fisheries were expanded, and in the Pacific the Soviets ousted the Japanese from the Sea of Okhotsk and the herring fisheries off southern Sakhalin. Inland waters, especially the Caspian, the Volga, and Lakes Peipus and Ilmen, began producing approximately 20 percent of the total catch. During the 1960s large whalers and other fishing vessels were venturing into most parts of the Atlantic, Pacific, Arctic, and Antarctic, and had penetrated Alaskan, northeast coastal, and west coast American waters where they were competing successfully with the declining and technically obsolescent American fishing fleet.

The rapid Soviet expansion of fishing has reaped a sizable harvest of international ill will. Soviet ships have been accused of trespassing in the territorial waters of the United States, Norway, Iceland, Japan, and Iran; of using fishing methods generally condemned by other nations; and occasionally of capturing foreign fishing vessels in disputed waters. They are also alleged to have served as vehicles for espionage, and for the training of naval personnel in waters where Soviet warships would be suspect. Certainly the large reserve of small ships and trained personnel of the fishing fleet is a naval asset of considerable potential value. The major gains of the Soviet fishing industry, however, must be attributed primarily to the use of more modern methods and equipment than are employed by other nations (see chapter 22).

Mention should also be made of the marked Soviet interest in oceanography. Since World War II the Russians have led the world in most fields of oceanic research, and currently about 100 Soviet agencies and bureaus are involved in some aspect of ocean exploration. Though much of this is pure research (which has engendered a vast number of technical publications), a good deal of effort has been directed toward improving the northern sea route and aiding the ministry of maritime fleets, the fisheries, and the navy. It is quite possible that other nations have conducted similar research that is as valuable, but none has participated on such a large scale. One authority estimates there are at least 1,500 senior Soviet oceanographers and places total oceanographic personnel at 8,000 to 9,000. Comparable figures for the United States are 1,000 and 3,000 respectively. There have been no fewer than 14 Soviet expeditions located on drifting ice in the Arctic since 1950. In the same period the U.S. has activated five such expeditions. Water movements, currents, ocean circulation, wind, tides, and drift all have been under study. The Soviet oceanographic program probably lags behind the U.S. program in certain areas, notably in computer processing of data, instrument design, offshore oil drilling, deep submergence equipment, and underwater use of nuclear power. But in addition to the greater size of their total effort, the Soviets appear to hold a lead in overall planning and direction, in all phases of fishing, in fish farming, in general studies of the ocean, and in control of ocean pollution (in the Soviet Union a criminal offense).

Partly because of the deficiencies of Soviet railways, the inland waterways of Russia have retained their historic position of importance well into the twentieth century. The 80,000 miles of navigable waterways still offer what is ordinarily the most economical means of transportation, despite heavy freezing from two to seven months of the year. Most river ships and waterway facilities were destroyed during World War I and the civil war and were not brought back to prewar standards until 1937. Then World War II took a toll of 4,280 river steamers and motor ships and 4,029 other craft—roughly two-thirds of the total. Post-World War II rebuilding, however, was exceedingly rapid and continued to show improvement. It has been aided by the output of Balkan and Finnish yards, and has included high-speed freighters especially developed for the Siberian rivers, motor tankers which move Caucasian oil as far as Moscow, and recently some very fast catamarans. In 1961 river fleets of about ten million tons total capacity transported more than 200 million tons of cargo. River ports have been developed, the largest being Kiev, Shcherbakov (Rybinsk), Volgograd, and Moscow; narrow rivers and canals have been widened; and facilities have been greatly improved. The principal cargoes carried have been timber, building materials, oil, grain, and coal. Outside the Soviet Union the most important inland waterway under Russian control is the Danube and its tributaries. The main Polish rivers, the Bug and the Vistula, carry comparatively little traffic.

Since World War II the glamor formerly attached to the northern sea route has diminished, largely because electrification and other improvements of the Trans-Siberian railroad have reduced the need for a second system of transportation. Nevertheless, development has continued. In 1956 a naval task force of destroyers, submarines, and two cruisers moved to the Pacific by this route. The administration of the northern sea route employs some 40,000 persons and in order to facilitate its tasks has divided the navigable waters along the route into three sections. Since 1960 the activity of more and better icebreakers has lengthened the navigation season from 90 to 100 days to 140 to 150 days.

Russian security measures along the Siberian route were for a time extremely far-reaching; until recently the Soviet Union claimed a monopoly on use of the sea north of Siberia. (In 1965 the U.S. Coast Guard icebreaker *North Wind* abandoned an attempt to use this route when challenged by Soviet warships and planes.) In March 1967, however, Soviet authorities announced they were preparing to relax their claims.

Polar exploration programs of the Soviet Union continue to absorb naval and scientific manpower. The Soviets maintain several scientific research stations in the Arctic, as well as about 20 ice-based radio reporting stations. Aerial ice reconnaissance is carried on as an aid to navigation. In the Antarctic the Soviets maintain one large base, with a crew of more than 100 men, and several smaller bases. The scientific effort here is largely devoted to land exploration and aerial reconnaissance, though many technical disciplines are represented in the staffs present. Cooperation and good relations are normally maintained with other nations in the Antarctic region. The Soviet Union has signed and reportedly abides by the international convention prohibiting military forces in the Antarctic or use of the area for military purposes.

PERSONNEL AND TRAINING

In recent years total Soviet naval personnel has ranged from 450,000 to 750,000 men—approximately the same as that of the United States. Two-thirds of the men in the ranks are undergoing a three-year period of compulsory service; the rest are long-term volunteers. DOSAAF, the important Soviet civilian organization for cooperation with the military, trains certain groups prior to their entering service and calls them back for periods of refresher training after service, the navy assisting the process by the loan of small vessels. Komsomol also provides some pre-induction training. Men normally enter the navy at the age of eighteen and do not leave the reserves until the age of fifty. During the first two years no leave is normally given and pay is low. Food is nourishing but monotonous. Most petty officers are long-term enlistees. Progress from the ranks to a commission is theoretically possible (as it was under the tsars) but from a practical standpoint very difficult and rare. A vast gap in pay, status, and privileges exists between officers and men and between senior officers, junior officers, and flag officers. Contractual services and services performed by women cover sizable areas of the activity at bases. While there has been some disenchantment among navy personnel, strict discipline, educational opportunities, and the employment of sailors during their complete leisure time have kept overt disaffection at a low level.

In theory commissions are open to all citizens, but in actuality most of them go to graduates of certain schools which accept many sons of officers and party officials. Before 1946 preparatory schools at Saratov, Leningrad, and Vladivostok offered three-year naval courses to students who had finished the seven primary grades. The curricula included naval subjects as well as non-maritime training and were taught by both civilians and naval specialists, and graduates were admitted to the higher naval schools without medical or entrance examinations. Because they were not a success, these three schools were discontinued. Today the major proportion of commission aspirants attend one of four Nakhimov schools at which the education covers six years, from the fifth through the tenth grade. The curriculum is based on tsarist concepts altered to conform to Communist Party doctrine. It includes instruction in mines, torpedoes, and artillery as well as the normal academic subjects. Summers may be spent in practice cruises or in special camps. The Nakhimov schools (which have been criticized as divorced from real life and lax in discipline) are supplemented by three-year schools designed to prepare officer cadres for the technical branches. These schools accept boys who have finished the standard seven-year primary school. They include the Kronstadt Mine and Torpedo School, the Kiev Naval Medical School, and the Odessa Naval Medical School.

On a higher level there is no one large school in the Soviet Union that corresponds precisely to the United States Naval Academy at Annapolis. There are, in fact, about a score of schools that turn out naval officers. Probably the best known is the Frunze Academy, named after one of the founders of the Red army, which graduates 180 to 200 officers a year and refuses nearly 90 percent of its applicants. The academy course lasts four years and features Marxism-Leninism, mathematics, and science besides naval studies. Similar schools have operated for some time at Baku and Vladivostok. Since World War II, these have been supplemented by two schools on the Baltic, one on the Black Sea, and one on the White Sea. These seven colleges combined graduate some 1,400 officers yearly. Because the training these schools offer is quite general, a need has developed for further specialized training, and a great many additional institutions have been established to meet this requirement. A well-known example is the Voroshilov School, successor to the tsarist school which included Admirals Klado and Belli on its faculty. It provides a two-year graduate level course which may be said to correspond very roughly to the United States Naval War College. The Krylov School for Engineers is on a similar level. The Dzerzhinsky School in Leningrad (with two branches elsewhere) offers a five-year eight-month course for naval engineers. The six-year Naval Medical School is also at Leningrad, as is the Engels Higher Naval Political School. There is a higher naval radio school at Pushkin and a higher naval radar school at Petrodvorets (Leninsk). The Naval Quartermaster School and the Naval Infantry School are at Vyborg, and the Coast Defense Artillery School is at Riga. Technicians' schools for men promoted from the ranks are located at Sevastopol, Riga, and Vladivostok. Air officers may attend the Pilot's School at Nikolaev, the Mechanics School at Perm, or the Signal School at Novaia Ladoga. An institute at Arkhangelsk bearing the name of Admiral Makarov specializes in Arctic studies. There are also schools for musicians, language specialists, hydrographers, and a few other specialities. Aboard most ships "Lenin centers" combine the functions of a study, an institute, and a recreational hall. In addition, each fleet operates several schools on a lower level.

The Soviets have made every effort by both education and preferential treatment on matters of pay, housing, clothing, and food to produce a contented elite corps of officers. Naval officer pay, while slightly lower than that of the Soviet air force, is better than that of the army and ranges from two to four times as much as civilian professions requiring a similar level of education. Pay consists of basic salary plus allowances determined by a complicated system that considers rank, length of service, food, knowledge of foreign languages, unpleasant climatic conditions, service aboard ship rather than shore (especially in the case of submarines, motor torpedo boats, and mine vessels), transfers, and accommodations. By Soviet standards, then, naval officer pay is excellent. The same cannot be said of housing. Married officers receive one to two rooms for themselves and family, while as many as four unmarried officers may live in one small room. Ships' rations range from tolerable to poor depending on whether the vessel is a warship or an auxiliary. The state provides clothing for officers but not for their families. Small pensions are paid retirees, the amount depending on record and length of service.

Generally speaking, army and navy officers exhibit a strong sense of social solidarity, rank consciousness, and military in-breeding. They are a favored group but have to inure themselves to such perils as investigations by police, political officers, and counterintelligence men.

It would be difficult to say how able Soviet personnel actually is. During World War II the Soviet navy failed to produce a single admiral of notable achievement comparable to those of Makarov, or even of von Essen and Eberhardt in World War I. The wartime service of a few of the present officers, including Fleet Admiral Gorshkov, was creditable, but the names of Oktiabrsky and Tributs, commanders in chief in the Black Sea and Baltic at the beginning of World War II, are scarcely known even in Russia—and with good reason. Today the Soviet admirals and captains tend to be relatively young. Almost without exception they are Communist Party members; yet the Soviet command system has tended to perpetuate the subordination of the navy to the army and to discourage initiative on the part of commanders. On the other hand, the general personnel condition of the Soviet navy is in many ways improved. Though the education of naval officers in a great many institutions would seem to deprive them of a common background, there is no indication that the education itself is not sound and thorough. It emphasizes political regularity and technical expertise, two weak points in tsarist navy days which have certainly been rectified.

The Soviet leaders themselves appear to be aware of many deficiencies: in *Morskoi sbornik* there are periodic attacks on "formalism," which according to one critic leads to "complacency, indifference, red tape-ism, window dressing and windbag-ism." Training aboard ship often leaves a great deal to be desired. Higher officers at times neglect drills, and poor leadership of enlisted men, negligence, and falsification of records are commonly reported. Inadequate recreation for both officers and men, excessive drinking, and the persistence of religious beliefs are felt to be other defects.[10] Some Soviet leaders, after the manner of Admiral Makarov, have sought to produce in the navy an oceanic mentality. Soviet warships on recent foreign cruises have looked far better than those of a generation ago. The French Adm. M. A. Peltier, an acute and not unfriendly observer, has indicated, however, that this smart appearance has been largely achieved by paint over dirt, and that most of the time Soviet warships are ill-kept and slovenly. Soviet seamen generally are politically loyal, reasonably well educated, hardy, and adaptable.

Two big questions that remain regarding Soviet personnel are: (1) Do the navy's leaders understand sea power and how to employ it? (2) Has the navy fully erased its heritage of tactical ignorance and technical backwardness? There are indications of great improvement in both areas. Far more overseas cruises are being undertaken than prior to World War II and much of the naval isolationism of that period has broken down, even though Soviet warships other than submarines still do not venture outside Soviet waters in large numbers. Presumably the widespread espionage carried on by trawlers, intelligence ships, planes, and submarines has provided better naval intelligence than was available to the Russians in World War II when they repeatedly fell into traps set by the Germans. Ship and group exercises are frequent, even under conditions of severe winter ice. Large fleet exercises occur at least once a year, and combined exercises involving troop landings and coast defense in coordination with air elements are common. Furthermore, because the Soviets keep most of their navy in commission, unlike the United States and Great Britain, the navy is always close to a war footing. On the other hand, a survey of Soviet naval publications still fails to reveal any clear, consistent concept of sea power. The Red navy is still hailed as a protector of the seacoast. Submarines are regarded as offensive weapons, but the conditions needed for their successful operation apparently are not always understood. There is also a notable dearth of publications dealing knowledgeably with defense against submarines and aircraft.

OTHER COMMUNIST NAVIES

The navies of other Communist states are mainly Russian-equipped but of small size; taken all together they do not exceed ten percent of Soviet strength. Yet because of their likely assistance to the U.S.S.R. in the event of war they are worthy of brief notice. Communist China possesses the second strongest fleet among the Communist states. Poland stands third. The East German and North Korean navies are of very small size. The Bulgarian, Rumanian, and Hungarian navies are limited in tonnage and in manpower by treaty, (but such disarmament treaties have in the past been more honored in the breach than in the observance). Certain satellite craft, such as motor torpedo boats, submarines, destroyers, patrol boats, and minesweepers, would in time of war have some defensive value as escort, coast defense, and antisubmarine forces, but are of limited strategic significance. In the Baltic, where the strongest showing could be made, the East German and Polish navies have 100 missile-carrying vessels of patrol and gunboat types, 95 minesweepers, 30 subchasers, seven frigates, and ten or more submarines. In the Black Sea the Rumanian and Bulgarian navies might be able to add 140 small vessels to Soviet strength.

The one non-Russian Communist naval force which does have some strategic importance is the Chinese navy. When the Communists gained control of the mainland they inherited from Chiang Kai-shek only a few ships which had either deserted or been left behind owing to defective machinery. Those so obtained were the *Chungking* (ex-British *Aurora*, six 6-inch guns), which the National-ist air force soon sank, and a motley array of ex-U.S., ex-Japanese, and ex-British patrol and amphibious types and minesweepers, all in disrepair. Save for defectors, there was no nucleus of trained personnel. Politically reliable army officers were detailed to the navy to fill the large gap, and a People's Naval Academy was established with strong Russian staffing. Two naval air schools were set up later. Between 1954 and 1960 the Soviet Union gave a large measure of naval assistance. Several destroyers, more than a dozen submarines and many subchasers, and some auxiliaries and old motor torpedo boats (mostly of pre-World War II vintage) were transferred, along with some 1,500 to 2,000 Soviet "advisers" to provide instruction. A naval headquarters was opened at Peking, and three fleet commands were set up—the Northern at Tsingtao, the Eastern at Shanghai, and the Southern at Canton. The Soviet Union also assisted in the establishment of a small shipbuilding industry that was able to turn out *Riga* class destroyer escorts, W type submarines, subchasers, minesweepers, and motor torpedo boats. Battle experience, some of it successful, was gained in skirmishes with Nationalist naval forces. In one of these a Nationalist Chinese destroyer escort was sunk in a night torpedo attack by Communist forces, while in another a gunboat was lost. The withdrawal of Soviet aid about 1960 caused retrenchment in all naval plans.

The present navy of the People's Republic of China apparently consists of four destroyers, four destroyer escorts, about 50 amphibi-ous craft, 25 to 30 submarines, 140 motor torpedo boats and fast motor gunboats, 24 subchasers, 20 or more minesweepers, 300 service craft, and a small land-based naval air force manned by about 50,000 men. Leadership quality is at best dubious and the ships, which operate very close to the coastline, have shown navigational weaknesses.

Nevertheless, this all-small-craft fleet is probably the strongest naval force in Asia and has considerable defensive potential.[11] What is more, despite recent political upheavals in China there are signs of future growth. Under Communist China's first and second five-year plans coastal shipping capacity was expanded by modernization, new construction, and waterway improvements. Orders for modern cargo ships have been placed in British, Dutch, and French yards, and the nation's own shipbuilding industry has been built up to a point where it can supply both naval and merchant vessels. The fuel oil industry is now reaching a level of self-sufficiency after a hard struggle. Modern metallurgical, electronics, and machine tool industries have been established, and China has entered the restricted circle of thermonuclear powers.

Some of the Soviet-equipped navies are relatively efficient and are closely geared to cooperation with the Soviet Navy; others are not. The fleet of the United Arab Republic, for example, has made an extremely poor showing against Israel. In the case of China, even during the 1950s there was no evidence of coordinated training exercises or maneuvers with the navy of the U.S.S.R., and Soviet support of China during the Korean war was very limited. Though the Soviets gave considerable assistance to the development of military industries in China during the mid-1950s, any offer of closer cooperation was refused by the Chinese. They were unwilling to accept a joint naval command in the Pacific under Soviet leadership and later failed to carry through an important secret agreement on the "new technology for national defense" which would have established Soviet control of joint enterprises. The degree of scientific maturity achieved by the Chinese was revealed by their development of nuclear and thermonuclear weapons after the Soviets had refused to supply such weapons. With or without Soviet assistance, Communist China is a formidable contender in the world power arena and as such poses problems which are certain to grow more serious.

THE DOCTRINAL DEBATE

Since 1955 the Soviet Union has operated under what is to all intents and purposes a new naval policy. During Stalin's lifetime there was still an incomplete realization on the part of Soviet strategists that short-range weapons, such as coastal submarines and the Red army, were incapable of seriously threatening any such foe as the United States. American air and sea strength, operating from either carrier task forces or bases close to the Soviet Union, then could have greatly damaged Russian targets in the event of war.

Without question one of Khrushchev's main objectives was to supply the Soviet armed forces with a longer-range punch while simultaneously seeking to weaken the ability of the United States to strike from nearby bases. The policy formulated during his regime has dictated the rapid buildup of long-range rockets and missiles, a radical improvement in the quality of submarines, and a variety of efforts to interfere with American overseas bases, often through the encouragement of nationalist movements in host countries.

There has been a significant change in overseas employment of Soviet seapower. Surface warships, submarines, naval planes, and electronically equipped trawlers are now ranging widely over the oceans of the world. The Soviet Union has taken a decided interest in Antarctica, to which it may lay some claim on the basis of the long-ago voyages of Bellingshausen and Lazarev. Probably more significant is the attempt to extend Soviet influence over such trade bottlenecks as Skagerrak, the Dardanelles, the Panama Canal, the Straits of Malacca, the Suez Canal, and the Straits of Gibraltar. Brig. Gen. James D. Hittle, Jr., USMC (retired), writing in *Life* magazine, has pointed to Soviet threats to communications at these bottlenecks. Morocco, opposite the British position at Gibraltar, for example, has recently profited from Soviet deliveries of planes, arms, and ammunition. Khrushchev's courtship of Egypt and Yemen offers another case in point, as did the Soviet presence in Cuba. Indonesia while under Sukarno received substantial military gifts from the Soviet Union, including a large cruiser, four destroyers, eight patrol boats, several submarines, and numerous motor torpedo boats. Her aggressions had tacit Soviet and overt Chinese approval. None of these actions, however, has involved moves likely to cause war. The recipients of gifts cannot be counted on to welcome Soviet control, as Nasser in Egypt and the new regime in Indonesia have demonstrated, but they do serve to extend Soviet influence abroad and to facilitate a highly modern and sophisticated employment of seapower.

The Khrushchev years were accompanied by a great deal of military writing as Soviet theoreticians sought to think through the changes implied by modern weapons and to arrive at a national strategy. In 1962 a weighty study on military strategy written by a team of Red army Officers under the direction of Marshal V. D. Sokolovsky, made an appearance. American publishers who had overlooked most previous Soviet military writing at once translated the work into English and put out two different translations.[12] Within the Soviet Union the work engendered heavy and continued criticism, which led to a revised edition in 1963. Future naval operations, as viewed by these land warfare officers, will have a far greater scope than at any time in Russia's past, but they are not expected to be decisive. For naval warfare, large surface ships and most naval task forces are regarded as an expensive luxury, highly vulnerable to nuclear attack. Landing operations in a future war will have to feature small units and great dispersion. Seaborne supply will be far more difficult than in the past, particularly for the United States. The introduction of nuclear rocket-firing submarines favors the Soviet Union, which has relatively few worthwhile coastal targets and moreover can now carry war into enemy waters to a degree that would have been impossible with the short-range sea power of the past.

The Sokolovsky team concludes that the primary missions of the Soviet navy, in approximate order of importance, are (1) destruction of enemy striking forces based on carriers; (2) defeat of American submarines, especially those of the *Polaris* type; (3) disruption of the support of enemy ground troops by defeating enemy landings and (4) aiding Soviet land forces; (5) mine warfare to defend Soviet coasts, blockade enemy ports, bases, and straits, and generally disrupt enemy communications. The use of submarines in a strategic sense against enemy population centers is not listed among the navy's missions and may have been beyond the capability of Soviet forces available in 1962.

Submarines and naval planes are seen as the principal naval weapons to carry out these tasks, though Soviet naval thought also supports the existence of numerous small surface ships for amphibious operations, commerce protection, and coast-defense responsibilities. A significant qualitative development, now under way, is the substitution of rockets and missiles for conventional artillery, even in ships of less than 100 tons.

Continued criticism of the Sokolovsky work by Soviet naval officers has taken the form of a prolonged debate. The second edition
of the work, presumably intended to answer both naval and other
criticisms, has succeeded mainly in demonstrating that army officers are not competent to develop naval doctrine. Indeed, both
editions tend to gloss over the genuinely difficult naval problems,
such as defense against carrier task forces or *Polaris* submarines.
On the other hand, published comments by naval officers in *Izvestiia, Krasnaia zvezda* (Red Star), *Morskoi sbornik*, and elsewhere
have not only pointed out the new freedom of Soviet submarines to
play an important strategic bombardment role; they have also
emphasized the need for *real* answers to the principal American
naval threats and have directed new attention to such largely overlooked areas of defense as antisubmarine warfare.[13]

Soviet views of strategy have of course been expounded in many
forums other than the Sokolovsky volume, and they have changed
in several respects since the end of World War II. Had war with
the United States erupted before the Soviet Union gained nuclear
weapons, the Russian leaders would have depended on the Red
army to expel U.S. forces from Western Europe and then waged a
submarine war on communications to prevent an American buildup
and re-invasion. This short-range strategy, even if successful, would
have left the United States entirely intact. It would also have left
the territory of the Soviet Union open to long-range sea and air
attack to which the Soviets would have had little means of reply.

In the Soviet view the availability of nuclear weapons to both
sides strengthens Soviet security by undermining American naval
strength. It makes capital ship and/or carrier task force survival
much more difficult: ships are obliged to sail in such widespread
formations (up to 300 miles diameter for a task force) that they
must operate virtually as separate units; and the requirements for
accuracy on the part of an attacker are greatly reduced by the
wider area of destruction of nuclear weapons. The United States
fleet is therefore to a large degree obsolescent. Soviet submarines
might in a future war exceed the success of German submarines in
World War II. Landing operations would be far more difficult than
in the past, and would have to be made by relatively small, dispersed units. For while nuclear air bursts to clear an area might be

useful to an attacker, the threat of defensive nuclear weapons would rule out the large convoys, artificial harbors, and massed landings of World War II. Prior to gaining nuclear weapons themselves, the Soviets endorsed the belief that the United States would have to win a war *in Europe* and that ground forces and submarines would prevent this. They later favored the belief that defensive nuclear weapons would prevent the United States from crossing the sea in force. Both views were based on an assumption not necessarily shared by American military thinkers: that physical occupation of enemy territory is essential to victory.

From the above it is apparent there has been a sizable gulf between American and Soviet concepts regarding the nature and conduct of war. By American standards Soviet thinking has been highly land-oriented and essentially short range. Only quite recently have the Soviets begun to free themselves from short-range strategic thinking and to realize the possibilities that modern weapons offer, both to themselves and to their opponents.

It is surprising that in a period of intellectual ferment neither the Soviet dual-command system of control by both naval and political officers nor the distribution of ships among the fleets has given rise to much open controversy, though both have undergone change in the very recent past. The dual-command system has been a source of friction and delay in conducting operations for nearly half a century. At present, military officers hold an additional political command: as political officers they receive all directives and make all reports through Communist Party channels. Though this procedure appears to make for fewer conflicts than occurred in previous systems, it cannot necessarily be expected to be a permanent change.

For a decade following World War II the four Soviet fleets were approximately equal in strength; but this policy was altered under Khrushchev. The historically older fleets in the Baltic and the Black Sea were given ample strength to dominate local waters, especially since continued improvement in waterways between the Dnieper and the Niemen made transfer easier. But the Arctic and Pacific fleets were supplied with both more and better ships and personnel. While the exact distribution of forces is not openly proclaimed by the Soviets, each of the main fleets is said to have from 700 to 800 vessels of all types. The Black Sea force (including the Mediterranean) was credited in the late 1960s with seven cruisers as compared to three or four in the Baltic and White Sea and four to six on the Pacific station. The Black Sea also had the two helicopter carriers, and about 50 destroyers types as contrasted to 25–35 in the other fleets. On the other hand, the nuclear submarines were probably all in the Arctic or Pacific fleets. Over two-thirds of the conventional submarines were also with these two fleets, and the December 1964 issue of *Revue Maritime* credited them with substantially stronger naval air forces as well.

TABLE 15

Fleet Distribution of Soviet Sea Power

	NORTHERN	BALTIC	BLACK SEA	PACIFIC
Nuclear Submarines	45	0	0	25
Conventional Submarines	105	75	40	80
Helicopter Carriers	0	0	2	0
Cruisers	5	6	7	7
Missile Destroyers	5	6	13	6
Conventional Destroyers	15	12	20	23
Missile Patrol Boats	20	40	20	50
Naval Aircraft	250	250	250	250

The above table, taken from Fairhall's *Russia Looks to the Sea*, is probably roughly accurate as regards fleet distribution. The number of nuclear submarines is probably greater than listed above. Not included are coastal escorts, minesweepers, missile patrol boats, torpedo boats, amphibious ships and auxiliaries, each of which would be numbered in the hundreds. The number of naval aircraft listed above may also be slightly excessive.

CHAPTER 22

The Achievement of Sea Power
(1962-72)

DECISION IN THE DOCTRINAL DEBATE

FOREIGN NAVAL ATTACHÉS in the Soviet Union look forward each year to July 30, Navy Day. On that day they may not only see new machinery and weapons but learn the views of the Soviet leaders regarding naval questions.

For the years 1966, 1967, and 1968 these opinions have been especially important. In 1966 Adm. Sergei Gorshkov proclaimed "an end . . . to the complete domination of the sea by the traditional naval powers." In contrast to the defensive themes he had expressed in earlier years, he also announced a "new way of building up an ocean-going submarine and rocket missile fleet, capable of solving strategic tasks of an offensive nature." A year later the lengthy inspection of the Arctic Fleet by General Secretary of the Communist Party Leonid Brezhnev, Premier Aleksei Kosygin, and other top officials preceded Navy Day, and on the customary day of celebration rocket-launching nuclear submarines were on display at Leningrad. Admiral Gorshkov was only one of many high defense officials to make a speech befitting that occasion, but what he had to say strongly reaffirmed his position of the preceding year. Speaking aboard the rocket cruiser *Kirov*, the Soviet Union's highest admiral criticized the presence of the United States Sixth Fleet in the Mediterranean and the close aerial inspection of Russian ships supplying North Vietnam. He declared the Soviet navy's "firm determination to defend the state interests of the Soviet Union against the imperialists" anywhere in the world, and directed a warning to Americans: "Sooner or later they will have to understand that they have no mastery whatsoever of the seas. The flag of the Soviet navy today flies proudly over the oceans." During the same celebration *Pravda* carried a report by Viktor Bakaev, minister of the merchant fleet, that Soviet shipping was then visiting 800 ports in 90 countries; and Adm. Vasily M. Grishanov, writing in *Izvestiia*, stressed the Soviet mission of guarding the interests of Warsaw Pact allies.

For Navy Day 1968, Fleet Admiral Gorshkov and his deputy, Adm. Vladimir A. Kasatanov, gave a report on "Operation North," the July 1968 combined exercise of the Soviet Baltic and Northern Fleets and the Polish and East German navies. The exercise had been conducted over an immense area in the Baltic, the North Atlantic, and the Arctic, and from the standpoint of size it was without precedent in Russian naval history. Included in the variety of operations carried out were difficult joint landing operations. Concerning this Warsaw Pact exercise (which followed by one month a NATO operation, "Polar Express," involving the navies of the United States, Great Britain, West Germany, Holland, Belgium, Norway, and Canada), Admiral Gorshkov commented:

> We now have forces capable not only of checking imperialist aggression, but also, if needed, of delivering a blow from which the aggressor could not recover.
> Our fleet cannot only break up the attack of an aggressor, but also inflict annihilating blows in distant oceans and deep in enemy territory.[1]

On July 21 Gorshkov set forth as the navy's long-range aims the continued development of nuclear submarines, naval and military aviation, and the marine corps with its landing ships.

From the tactical standpoint, Navy Day 1968 occasioned a claim by Radio Moscow that Soviet nuclear submarines could strike at distances of several thousand miles. Also, the aerodynamic surface-to-surface rockets carried by 6,000-ton small cruisers of the *Kresta* and *Kynda* classes were reported to have wings, and an initial high-altitude trajectory but a very low-level approach to target, making detection difficult.

Many of the claims made by Soviet leaders in celebrating Navy Day have perhaps been excessive, but those which announced a point of maturation in the naval building following World War II were essentially correct. Soviet merchant vessels, surface craft, and submarines were indeed spread widely over the seven seas. Their crews were steadily gaining in technical skill and knowledge, learning, as Makarov had counseled, to be "at home at sea." There could be no question that Russia for almost the first time in her history was actually moving abreast of the times in employing sea power and understanding its uses. Though well behind the United States in some aspects of naval power, the Soviet navy had gained sufficiently in others to cause genuine, even acute, alarm in American naval circles. After a long and discouraging period of tutelage and inferiority, the Soviet navy had come into its own.

The Soviet navy would probably have reached a high level of development earlier had not the opinionated and often incorrect views of Nikita Khrushchev held back its progress. Though he had selected an excellent chief in Admiral Gorshkov, and though he was friendly to submarines, Khrushchev regarded large surface vessels as obsolete and money spent on them as wasted investment. He scrapped several huge cruisers still on the building ways (he regarded them as useless save for state visits); other building programs he halted or curtailed. Informally, he ridiculed naval power and threatened to disband the navy and scrap its surface vessels. Morale suffered.

So did Admiral Gorshkov. This man, who joined the navy at the age of 17, was (and is) the ablest naval leader the Soviet regime has produced. An admiral at the age of 31, thanks partly to wholesale purges of officers higher in rank, he was one of the few top Soviet officers to establish a creditable record during World War II, first at Odessa and later as commander of the Danube Flotilla. His wartime experience in cooperating with the army impressed Khrushchev and Brezhnev, both of whom held important army commands in the south. Unable to oppose Khrushchev directly after the war, Gorshkov could and did drag his feet so far as the dismantling and reduction of the navy was concerned.

The 1962 Cuban crisis apparently taught Khrushchev and his successors some lessons concerning the value of surface vessels as a means of exercising sea power. For several years preceding that crisis the Soviet leader had relied largely on boasting and bluffing as means to win victories in the cold war. He was greatly interested in destroying the Western presence in Berlin, but he was also acutely aware that since the United States then held vast superiority in both numbers of nuclear warheads and means of delivering them, the Soviets could hardly win a showdown. They might win by bluffing. Their edge in medium-range missiles and rockets was then a threat to the European allies of the United States but not a direct menace to the United States.

The scheme of planting medium-range nuclear missiles on Cuban soil to menace the United States directly was conceived in the hope of forcing an American retreat from her stand on Berlin; it was, in a strategic sense, harebrained. American command of the sea could stop the Soviets at any time: the plan could have succeeded only against an opponent too weak, too fearful, or too irresolute to use force.

The American discovery of Soviet activities in Cuba, the mobilization of American land, air, and sea forces, the use of the U.S. navy to enforce a blockade, and the ultimatum to Khrushchev form collectively one of the classic diplomatic and naval case histories. What the Russians were given was a choice between hostilities and major diplomatic defeat. Except for an American assurance that Cuba would not be invaded if the Soviets agreed to dismantle their bases, there was no sugarcoating for the defeat. So severe was this setback that it ultimately contributed greatly to Khrushchev's forced retirement. It was immediately obvious that the Russians, operating in an unfamiliar area, suffered from a great shortage of usable forces. They could not support their position in Cuba by air, nor would their surface navy have had a chance against the much greater strength of the United States. Five or six Soviet submarines sent to Cuban waters were easily tracked by American antisubmarine craft and could have been destroyed with little difficulty; one of them developed serious engine trouble. Escalation of the crisis to the point of a nuclear exchange might have meant grave injury to the United States, but it would also have meant a catastrophic Russian defeat.

SOVIET MILITARY POLICY AFTER CUBA

The outcome of the Cuban missile crisis had a profound effect not only on the tactics of the cold war but on Soviet military and naval policy as well. Relations with the United States after 1962 improved noticeably in many respects. Threats and bluffing—"missile rattling"—were virtually abandoned as cold war tactics of the Russians, in part because the improved reconnaissance techniques of the 1960s greatly reduced any chance of success. Limited accommodations between the two superpowers gradually became more numerous.

Russian military policy was also greatly altered. As compared to the United States, the Soviet Union during the Cuban crisis lacked (a) nuclear parity, (b) the possibility of employing a graduated response, and (c) naval power. The last deficiency was in fact twofold: not only were surface vessels missing; the few submarines the Soviet navy sent across the Atlantic were qualitatively unimpressive. In the ensuing years the Soviets have repaired the major military weaknesses revealed in 1962. They have also followed a very cautious policy vis-à-vis the United States. Since the United States has exercised similar prudence as regards the Soviet Union, there have been no major confrontations.

U.S. military policy under Secretary of Defense Robert S. McNamara had a profound influence on Russian military planning. McNamara attempted to build a strategic nuclear force of missiles, bombers, and submarines sufficient to discourage attack, and in case of surprise attack to guarantee survival of planes and missiles by dispersal and a hardening of land bases. To insure its 41 strategic nuclear submarines against successful tracking and attack by an enemy, the United States provided in their design for speed and offensive power. Attainment of the greatest possible strength was not considered a major objective. The United States pursued an orderly buildup to a predetermined strength level without the extreme pressure of constant escalation. In other words, the McNamara policy was one which permitted the Soviet Union to catch up without undue effort.

Most military analysts agree that by 1968 the Soviet Union had fully made up arrears and was ready to move ahead in strategic strength. The number of Soviet intercontinental ballistic missiles, estimated at 340 in 1966, was put at 720 in October 1967 and 934 in early 1968. The comparable American figure for 1968 was 1,054. During 1969 the Soviet figure probably surpassed that of the United States, and military men began worrying about the possibility of the Soviets' attaining a first-strike capability. By 1972 the Soviet figure exceeded 1500. Further, the American posture was static while the Soviet Union was adding missiles at a rapid rate. The earlier Soviet missiles were much larger and had far greater payload than their American counterparts, so that the total megatonnage of explosive power of the Soviet weapons was considerably greater than the American. On the other hand missile accuracy was believed to be well below that of the United States. Also, the development of multiple warheads promised to give the United States a major advantage. So far as hardening and dispersion of missiles was concerned, both powers had taken similar steps.

In other forms of nuclear power the patterns of armament were quite dissimilar. After the Cuban crisis the Russians disposed of a force of intermediate range missiles estimated at 725 units by the British Office for Strategic Studies. This force would have been valuable against Old World targets but hardly capable of reaching the United States; it was not matched by anything in American possession. The Soviets in 1968 possessed about 1,000 medium-range bombers whose principal value would be in attacking targets in Europe and Asia. On the other hand, the United States in 1968 held a margin of about four to one in heavy long-range bombers (680 to 155) and about as great an advantage in numbers of submarine missiles. Moreover, the American carrier task forces, though ordinarily classed as tactical weapons, were quite capable of strategic bombardment use.

The United States is far more vulnerable than the Soviet Union in the concentration of its population and industry, and this vulnerability was heightened in the 1960s by the neglect of civil defense programs. The Russians had a disciplined population trained in civil defense; they had also made considerable progress on an antiballistic missile defense covering not only the areas around Moscow and Leningrad but much of European Russia; and their force of fighter-interceptor planes was growing far faster than that of the United States. The whole question of defense against ballistic missiles was regarded with skepticism in the United States. The Defense Department, feeling that an assured second-strike capability was the best deterrent to enemy attack, had concentrated on giving U.S. missiles electronic aids to permit penetration of enemy defenses. Hence in 1968 the United States was only starting to consider a "thin" defense allegedly aimed at blunting a possible Chinese attack in the 1970s. It should be added, however, that many officials within the American military hierarchy viewed the anti-Chinese ballistic missile defense system as one which would later be strengthened to counter possible Soviet attack.

The immense change in relative Soviet-United States strength positions between 1962 and 1968 is explainable in some degree by the fact that many Soviet gains were made with the entire agreement of the United States. But two other factors contributed to the speed of the Russian advance. The first was the war in South Vietnam; the second was the comparative activity of the two powers in the areas of research and development.

The war in South Vietnam was always an expensive involvement, particularly after 1965 when it came to cost the United States between two and three billion dollars a month. This cost was sufficient to cause major delays not only in vital civilian programs but in important military programs as well. Thus, even though a certain strengthening of American forces resulted from combat experience, progress slowed down elsewhere.

The matter of research and development is more complicated. Many American policy makers during the 1960s tended to look at military research as having reached a plateau and were therefore conservative about launching new projects. This attitude, coupled with the hardboiled cost-effectiveness approach of the McNamara scientists and administrators, no doubt frequently prevented money from being wasted on weapon systems that would have proved unproductive. Yet the whole tempo of technical advance was slowed, and it was with justification that generals and admirals complained of lack of plans for more sophisticated and powerful submarines and airplanes, and of the lack of action on such plans.

The American delays occurred at a time when the Soviets, who

did not share the belief concerning a plateau in weapons development, were making a supreme effort to catch up with and pass the
United States. Lt. Col. V. Bondarenko, writing in the September
1966 issue of the magazine *Kommunist vooruzhennykh sil* (Communist of the Armed Forces), was probably expressing the official
viewpoint when he argued in favor of a massive and imaginative
research and development effort to assure military-technological
superiority. So zealously did the Soviets pursue this effort that by
1968 most of their relative deficiency in military technology had
disappeared.

SOVIET NAVAL PROGRESS 1966–68

By 1968 Soviet policies had resulted in a naval force which was
clearly more potent than American naval analysts had realized or
predicted. Since World War II the two navies had played deadly
serious games aimed at testing and evaluating each other's forces on
the high seas. These contacts usually went unreported until the
appearance of the motion picture *The Bedford Incident*,[2] in which
an American patrol vessel "hunted" a Soviet submarine. Previously,
the United States navy had made no open acknowledgment of this
type of war game. In early 1968 a Soviet submarine was detected
"tracking" an American carrier crossing the Pacific. The carrier captain deliberately increased his vessel's speed, whereupon the submarine did likewise until it had achieved a greater speed than any
Soviet submarine was supposed to possess. In a later incident a
Soviet attack submarine following an American nuclear submarine
showed the same unexpected speed. The United States navy had
already reported Soviet development of three classes of teardrop-
shaped high-speed attack submarines; the 1968 Navy Day review at
the port of Baltiisk showed what may have been one of the new class
of ships—a very large vessel whose superstructure towered above the
conventional submarines anchored nearby. Television photos indicated a steel bulge around the conning tower. Other reports indicated high speed and a capability for launching as many as eight
missiles.

Actually it is hard to conceive a sound reason for the official secrecy which the Department of Defense imposed regarding the operational characteristics of the newest Soviet submarines, unless it is that the department hopes to avoid acknowledging its blunder in failing to counter the newest Soviet submarines years earlier, as Adm. Hyman Rickover and others had repeatedly urged it to do. After all, the Russian leaders know the characteristics of their own submarines; presumably so do the United States Office of Naval Intelligence and members of certain congressional committees. During 1967–68 at least four or five completely new types of Soviet submarines were detected and their operational characteristics determined. Soviet underwater speeds have certainly equaled and probably surpassed the 35 knots ascribed to the fastest United States submarines. Diving depths of 2,000 feet or more, significantly superior to the best American performance which is believed to be 1,000 feet, have been reported in unclassified publications.

The *Christian Science Monitor* of July 18, 1968, reported:

New Soviet submarines are of three types. Ballistic missile submarines capable of launching attacks against the United States and its allies. Earlier submarines of this type were diesel-powered, with only three crude, short-range missiles in the sail, or super-structure, of the submarine. Later models have more missiles of longer range positioned in the hull capable of being fired from below the surface, as are United States Polaris missiles. Some sources believe the Soviets may now have a submarine with sixteen advanced missiles similar in many ways to the United States Polaris submarine. Last year, the Soviets exhibited a submarine-launched missile with a claimed range of between 2,300 and 3,000 nautical miles and a 1,500-pound payload.

Cruise missile submarines capable of attacking allied shipping and naval forces as well as striking coastal installations. Strategists were taken aback by the sinking of an Israeli destroyer with such a weapon, and the Navy is busily trying to devise more effective countermeasures. The United States has no such missiles, either on ships or submarines, preferring to rely upon guns and airpower to accomplish the same thing. New heavily armed, and very fast attack submarines pose an increasingly serious threat to surface ships and United States attack submarines, as well as to the United States Polaris fleet.

There have been unconfirmed reports of a Soviet submarine capable of operating at a depth of 2,000 feet. If such a submarine were built in quantity, the Soviets would have an extremely useful advantage, for

United States submarines are now believed capable of operating only at around one-half that depth or a little more.

Other Soviet submarines have been found operating extremely quietly, and some have demonstrated great speed, it is believed.

To counter the developing undersea threats, the United States is planning to develop a new and very fast submarine with advanced detection equipment and weaponry.

Such reports are extremely revealing to any careful naval observer. Both carrier task forces and nuclear submarines depend partly on speed for their success. If Soviet attack submarines could successfully track and overtake them, and report their position, the Soviets in 1968 were well on the way to the development of a sophisticated defense against these twin naval threats, and only the very rapid production of faster American attack submarines or a new generation of higher performance missile-carrying nuclear submarines would restore the balance. Subsequent intelligence reports supplied further details but did not completely clarify the picture. Four classes were being built in numbers of seven to 12 a year. The *Y* class, first to be identified, was deployed in small numbers in the North Atlantic late in 1969. These boats carried 16 missiles of more than 1,000 miles range. They were very fast but, like some earlier types, were also reported to be noisy by American standards and therefore detectable at considerable distances.

Nor are speed and diving depth the only facets of Soviet development that have aroused American apprehension. The sinking of the Israeli destroyer *Elath* by a Soviet *Styx* missile fired by an Egyptian naval officer revealed what close observers had already concluded: though the Soviet Union lacked aircraft carriers and therefore ship-based planes, it had developed a missile system which at medium ranges was far superior to conventional naval artillery. In addition to the *Styx* with its effective operational range of about 20 miles, the larger SS-N-1, capable of destroying targets at a distance of 100 miles, was known to be a potent weapon. Both of these weapons are carried on vessels as small as the 200-ton patrol boats of the *Osa* and *Komar* classes. Soviet torpedo boats also ordinarily carry the *Styx*, while destroyers of the *Krupny* and *Kildin* classes carry both surface-to-surface and surface-to-air missiles. The five *Kresta* class small cruisers carry surface-to-surface missiles with a range of about 450 miles. These missiles fly at about 700 miles per hour and steer by either radar or infrared systems. Longer-range cruise missiles are expected in the immediate future, if they are not already in operation. Indeed the United States, which at an earlier date had decided against developing this particular weapons system, has found itself in the embarrassing position of having to find defenses against it and simultaneously to start work on similar missiles.

Another development of importance in 1968 was the completion of the 25,000-ton carriers *Moskva* and *Leningrad* in the Black Sea and the information that a sister ship would shortly be finished. The first conclusion of some naval analysts, that the Soviet Union had at last built conventional airplane carriers, was proved incorrect when more details became available. The new Soviet carriers were not for conventional airplanes but rather for helicopters and vertical-takeoff airplanes, and they had landing areas only in the rear—behind the superstructure—with antiaircraft guns and missiles installed forward. Estimates of carrying capacity ran from 30 to 40 helicopters and possibly a battalion of naval infantry. These ships appear to be intended—along with the 10,000-man black-bereted naval infantry which was reorganized in 1964—to bolster the amphibious capacity of the Soviet navy. It is significant that during the *Moskva*'s stay in the Mediterranean in 1968 she reportedly was engaged almost continuously in antisubmarine exercises—a threat and a warning to the American *Polaris* force.

Various types of landing craft and amphibious tanks are currently used by the naval infantry. Admiral Gorshkov in a recent interview boasted that 500,000 naval men saw service in land battles during World War II; the comparatively small size of the present force indicates it is intended for selective landings far afield rather than service as a main ally of the Red army.

The Soviets have recently made at least equal progress in the three interrelated fields of oceanography, fishing, and commerce. Their fleet of 200 oceanographic vessels is by far the largest in the world and the 8,000 to 9,000 full-time person in the field compare favorably with the 3,000 Americans similarly employed. The 45,000 ton *Yury Gagarin*, largest scientific vessel in the world, is a Soviet ship. Considering that this force is combined with the largest submarine fleet in the world and the most modern fishing fleet—a fleet devoted to intelligence-gathering as well as fishing—it is apparent that the Soviet knowledge of currents, depths, ocean bottoms, and other marine phenomena must be at least equal to that of any other power. In all probability it is superior. Recent developments include operation of tidal power stations, dredging manganese from the bottom of the Pacific, and extracting chemicals from the ocean.

The recent progress of the Soviet fishing industry affords an excellent illustration of the multi-dimensional nature of the new Soviet challenge at sea. Whereas 90 percent of the 12,000 boats of over five tons in the American fishing fleet are obsolete, practically all of the 18,000 Soviet vessels are new and are, moreover, being augmented at the rate of 1,500 units a year. The Soviet Union doubled its catch to a total of five million tons between 1955 and 1965—years in which the United States catch remained static at about three million tons. During 1967 the Soviet catch totaled 5.8 million tons, that of the United States 2.4 million. In 1970 the catch was up to 7.8 million tons—or to 8.7 if whales and other marine mammals were included. Russian fishing fleets acted in concert, with free and constant exchange of information, whereas American captains, competitive to the core, kept information to themselves. Trips to port after five or six days were a necessity to the Americans—but not to the Russians, whose floating factories could salt, can, cook, dehydrate, or produce fish meal with equal ease and speed. Even directly off the American coasts the U.S. fishing fleets were being thoroughly outfished. Apparently determined to improve its somewhat sullied reputation for disregard of sea resources, the Soviet Union in 1967 joined with the United States in two fish conservation agreements, one covering waters off Alaska and the Aleutians and the other the North Atlantic fisheries south of Cape Cod. On January 31, 1969, a similar agreement was ratified reducing the Russian king crab catch in the eastern Bering Sea from 100,000 cases a year to 52,000. One negative development during the period was reduction of the catch in inland waters from 40 percent of the total to ten percent, this being caused by steadily increased pollution which has endangered sturgeon and the caviar industry especially.

The Soviet merchant marine in August 1968 consisted of about 1,320 ships of over 1,000 tons. It claimed about seven percent of the world's merchant-ship tonnage and stood in fifth place among the world's merchant fleets. These facts are not, on the surface, overly impressive. But the fleet they describe is far more potent than the figures indicate. Eighty percent of its ships are less than ten years old. Since 1950, world merchant tonnage has gone up 93 percent while Soviet merchant tonnage has advanced 435 percent. The rate of increase from 1966 to 1970 was projected at 50 percent as compared with 25 percent for the world average. Nearly one-quarter of all ships being built in 1968 were for the Soviet Union, and at that time the 1980 fleet was planned to total over 27 million tons. It is apparent that such a rate of increase will make the Soviet fleet steadily more important.

Late in the 1960s Soviet ships were operating over the entire globe, making stops at some 800 ports. Shore liberty for their crews, as for those in the Soviet navy, does not mean an alcoholic celebration and the reckless expenditure of money. By comparison with sailors of other nations, the men of the Red fleets are extremely well behaved and restrained in their conduct. (Whether the regimentation and indoctrination which produce this high standard of behavior also impose the inability to mix freely with the natives of host countries may well be a question.) Because the Soviet merchant ships carry far more exports than imports, they often operate on home-bound voyages as tramp steamers, carrying foreign cargoes from one intermediate port to another. For example, Soviet freighters after delivery of war materials to North Vietnam have frequently stopped at Australian ports to carry cargoes to Europe—at as much as 20 percent below standard rates. The purpose of the merchant marine is primarily political and only secondarily economic, so that a large share of Soviet carrying capacity is expended on such states as North Vietnam, Cuba, and Algeria. Like the Soviet navy, the merchant marine operates in four main fleets. About one-third of the ships operate out of the Black Sea, one-third out of the Pacific, about one-fifth from the Baltic, and one-eighth from the Arctic.

Soviet trade patterns in 1968 revealed a total foreign trade valued at 18 billion rubles. Of this about two-thirds was with other socialist countries. Outside of Eastern Europe the principal trading partners were Cuba, the United Kingdom, Japan, Italy, West Germany, France, Egypt, and India. Trade with the United States was quite small and with Communist China negligible.

In the past, because Soviet shipyards were frequently inadequate to produce both naval and merchant vessels, warships were built in Russian yards and merchant ships were ordered abroad. Indeed the East Germans have complained of the small capacity left for their own construction activities with so many of their yards preempted for Soviet ships. While this dependence on foreign yards still obtains to some extent, about half of the new merchant ships—probably 500,000 tons a year—are now turned out in Soviet yards. Further, Russian yards have recently begun building ships on foreign orders. Provisions of a long-term barter deal concluded in December 1965 between a Greek businessman and the Soviet government included $105 million worth of agricultural products in exchange for 400,000 tons of Soviet-built ships. This deal failed to attract much attention, but it was followed by a series of freighter sales to West Germany. The Soviet ships concerned—12,000-ton freighters which sold for less than 3.2 million dollars each—were clearly both better and cheaper than those being offered by competitors. The unit price was about a million dollars below the average market price elsewhere for similar vessels, and the ships were so fully automated as to require only one man in the engine room instead of the usual three or four. Moreover, the ships were able to load and unload faster than Swedish and German-built vessels operated by the German-owned Afrika Line, and the sellers not only provided ship-to-ship radio but offered the services of three engineers to make repairs for the first year of a ship's operation. Improvements, mainly to provide better living quarters, cost the buyers about $125,000 per ship.

Plans of the main Soviet yards in 1968 included a sharp 33 percent increase over 1967 in new ships built. As of October 1969 the Russians had 250 vessels of 1,414,000 tons on order, more than any other country. Further, the Soviets were developing a number of new types, including a 36,000-ton ore carrier with unusual stability, the 49,000-ton *Safie* class tanker, some 16,000-ton freighters, the *Amguema* class of ice breaking freighters, a few 19,000-ton passenger liners, small 1,200- to 2,000-ton ships for the Siberian timber trade, shallow-draft *Izmail* type ships for use at river ports previously considered inaccessible to oceangoing vessels, and the first 100,000-ton tankers to be built by the Soviets (the Russians previously had concentrated on small or medium tankers). The Russians had also shown marked interest in hydrofoils.

But the Soviet Union's estimable secondary forms of sea power, such as the merchant marine and the fishing fleet, and the sharp improvement in its new types of warships, are in the last analysis merely secondary manifestations of a far more important change. Soviet ships in 1968 were manned by a far better trained, educated, and experienced group of men than had manned Russia's vessels in all her history. Soviet naval personnel may or may not be fully equal to their American counterparts today. Certainly they are not equal in terms of naval tradition or in successful combat experience. But they are now directed by an offensive-minded admiral, a man determined to produce a force equal to any task at sea. Behind Admiral Gorshkov lies the determination of the leading members of government and party. As U.S. Secretary of Navy Paul Ignatius recently put it, the Soviets

> have developed the techniques, the base of experience, and the capabilities to operate, both in peacetime and in periods of high tension, on the high seas.[3]

The process by which Soviet seamen have gained in experience and know-how is not easy to describe in its entirety. To some extent the gain is a product of a changing philosophy. The once clearly predominant position of the Soviet army in the military pecking order has been somewhat altered, and, too, force reductions under Khrushchev hit the army harder than other branches of the armed services.

In 1963 a reorganization divided the forces into five major organizations. To the three traditional services (army, navy, air force) were added—as equals—the strategic rocket troops and air defense organization. The former did not include the navy's nuclear submarines forces. The latter was assigned antiaircraft defense covering what in the United States would be termed civil defense, antimissile defense, and cosmic defense—the last being mainly research and development aimed at reconnaissance satellite and orbiting weapons. The air defense organization was divided into national, troop, and fleet commands, with the fleet command given the mission of destroying enemy missile submarines.

This reorganization indicates an entirely new set of priorities. Marshal Malinovsky, in an article written shortly before his death and published in *Kommunist* (January 1967), stated that first priority was being given to strategic missile forces and to atomic missile-launching submarines. Within months thereafter, Admiral Gorshkov received a fifth star making him a fleet admiral and equal in rank to the army's chief of staff. A difference from American military philosophy is observable in the high status accorded the various forces engaged in defense against air, missile, and cosmic attack.

A great improvement in personnel performance has been noted recently. During the entire Soviet regime the personnel has been potentially first-class, but it long lacked training and skills. In the present fleet, 90 percent of the officers have the equivalent of a college education while 70 percent of the enlisted men have achieved specialist ratings. The attainment of a much higher level of competence than was present during World War II has resulted from frequent cruises (even in winter), rigorous discipline, and constant training, plus a great deal of learning from foreigners. Soviet submarines have traveled under the ice to the North Pole and have circumnavigated the globe in groups without surfacing, thus equaling achievements of their American counterparts. In such areas as mine warfare, electronics, and new forms of propulsion, Soviet progress has been most marked. Planning of operations, a weak point in World War II, has vastly improved.

The process of learning from others has necessarily involved some abandonment of the naval isolationism of the past. For example, Russian translations of American books dealing with naval power have appeared in far greater number than Russian-to-English translations of equivalent publications. But most of the transferred learning has taken place on the high seas and has involved watching, tracking, harassing, and at times "playing chicken" with Western vessels, mainly American. Soviet warships and electronic intelligence trawlers stalk American and British warships nearly everywhere. Spy ships often follow the fleets and task groups, and maintain a watch outside Cape Kennedy, Holy Loch in Scotland, Rota in Spain, Puget Sound, Norfolk, Pearl Harbor, and other important bases. During the Allied naval exercise "Silver Tower" in the eastern Atlantic during September 1968 the Russians employed nearly a dozen ships plus long-range planes for spying purposes. In

April 1969 "Dawn Patrol" was monitored by 69 ships and a second exercise in October by 63. The 1972 Allied exercise "Strong Express" drew about 50 Soviet ships as observers, including 12 submarines. Destroyers and trawlers frequently steam into the midst of U.S. formations or cut across the bows of American ships, and at times they even steer a collision course with American ships. The United States destroyer *Walker* was scraped twice by a Soviet destroyer in the Sea of Japan in 1966 during antisubmarine warfare maneuvers of Japanese and American units. Soviet bombers flying far from their land bases regularly approach carrier task forces in the hope of getting within the 100-mile range at which they could, in time of war, launch air-to-surface missiles. American radars are usually able to report the snoopers at a greater distance, however, and the three or four fighters of CAP (Combat Air Patrol) are then sent to meet the Soviet planes, hopefully at a distance of 200 miles or more, and to escort them in their flight over the task force.

Aerial and naval surveillance is not entirely one-sided, of course. Soviet warships and merchant vessels have long been of great interest to the United States and are subjected to a close western aerial surveillance at all times when outside purely Russian waters. United States Pacific Fleet Headquarters in Hawaii plots the course and location of every Soviet ship detected in the Pacific. In sensitive areas, near Vietnam and off the American coasts, for example, Russian snoopers may be buzzed by U.S. planes several times a day.

The most dangerous and sophisticated of naval war games is the one played beneath the surface of the sea between submarines and antisubmarine forces. The latter may include attack submarines and various types of surface vessels, such as antisubmarine carriers, destroyers, and frigates. In the past this game generally involved Western antisubmarine forces as the hunters and Soviet submarines as the hunted. However, the recent appearance of high-performance Soviet attack submarines could bring alterations in the game as the Soviets attempt to track American *Polaris* or *Poseidon* type nuclear submarines.

For Soviet submarines, the undersea game has involved evasion of opposing antisubmarine forces bent on detecting and tracking down undersea intruders. Heat- and sound-detecting devices in U.S. satellites and planes have given generally good results against the conventional types of Soviet submarines, which make enough noise to leave "scars" (traces of their passage through the water) and "electronic signatures" (the total of all the ship's sounds) that are easily detectable by sonar technicians aboard submarines, planes, and surface warships. Sonar cable networks in the ocean depths are also used for detection purposes. Once the sound of an unknown submarine has been received it can be flashed to an American base, where a computer can analyze it and flash back the name and description of the submarine. From time to time an American destroyer is able to "lock on" a Soviet submarine, track its every move, and eventually force it to surface.[4]

Probably the roughest future undersea games will be played between American *Polaris* (or *Poseidon*) armed nuclear submarines and Soviet attack submarines. The Soviet navy contains about 250 attack submarines; the United States has 41 nuclear submarines fitted for bombardment purposes. The U.S. vessels operate in the Pacific out of Guam; in the Arctic and North Atlantic out of Holy Loch, Scotland; and in the Mediterranean out of Rota, Spain. Because submarines operating out of these bases can fire from unknown stations which unlike land installations cannot be targeted, it is potentially a matter of national survival for the Soviets to know the coordinates of each firing station.

From these three bases *Polaris* submarines move out to sea for 60-day patrols, during which they make no signal that would provide a clue to their position. However, Soviet attack submarines outside the bases can and do attempt to follow the *Polaris* submarines, and when this happens American attack submarines slash in to run interference and provide a decoy. The attack submarines are fast. By following a scissors maneuver, moving in and out of the wake of the *Polaris* submarines, they can distort and confuse the sound tracks of the American submarines. At times the game can be extremely dangerous: one American attack submarine is reported to have been so severely damaged in an underwater collision it required two months at Rota for repair.

In the past American ships have had an advantage in submarine games because they were quieter and faster. That advantage was apparently enormously reduced, if not wiped out, during a five-year period in the mid-1960s when the United States navy laid down no new nuclear submarines and the Soviets continued developing submarines with greater speed and deeper diving qualities.

Of course this summation greatly oversimplifies the causes and the dynamics of Soviet gains. Since World War II a major part of Russian naval research and development effort has gone into anti-submarine warfare, with its many pitfalls and uncertainties. The search for effective growth has represented a long, highly technical priority struggle between offensive and defensive weapons. It has also had to confront the problems inherent in all submarine opera-tions. The success of detection always depends to a large degree on the skill of equipment operators in distinguishing ship sounds from scores of other underwater sounds, and present efforts on all sides to disperse heat and produce silent operations are certain to make detection more difficult in the future. Moreover, just as a submarine in wartime often spends weeks or months patrolling empty ocean, so antisubmarine forces are likely to put forth great exertion and effort for a very limited number of kills.

One of the handicaps of the Russians in the past has been a psychological one. Against the Germans in World Wars I and II the Russian navy was greatly handicapped by unimaginative direc-tion from the army. But even discounting this factor, its men were inclined to be overawed by the Germans and to show against them far less initiative and innovation than against other foes. Whether because of official propaganda or other reasons, the Soviet navy today shows little of this inferiority complex; indeed at times the behavior of men and ships can only be described as "cocky."

An examination of Soviet maneuvers over the past decade reveals how completely the naval isolationism of the past has been aban-doned. In 1961 (the last year before the Cuban crisis) Soviet war-ships exercised in the Norwegian Sea. In 1962 Black Sea warships got into the Atlantic to join the Northern Fleet in the Arctic; 1963 saw exercises in the Northeast Atlantic. In the following year Cuba and the Mediterranean were visited and in 1965 this was intensified. In 1966 exercises were in the Faroes-Iceland area. In 1967 the Mediterranean Fleet was made permanent while research vessels entered the Indian Ocean. This was followed in 1968 by a small squadron. In 1969 the Soviet Mediterranean Fleet was strengthened to the point of being larger than the South Fleet. The 1970 Exercise

Okean in celebration of the centenary of Lenin's birth was worldwide and is described in the Foreword to this volume.

Much of the insecurity and fear which in the past led the Russians to demand that only ships of riparian states be permitted in the Baltic and the Black Sea has passed away. The northern sea route, once viewed by the Soviet Union as a veritable *mare clausum*, was declared open to non-Soviet vessels in 1966 and was even promoted among foreign shippers following the closing of the Suez Canal in 1967. The northern sea route is now open 100 days or more a year with the aid of icebreakers, and the Soviets are attempting to extend the season. By use of five icebreakers, including the *Lenin*, they succeeded in January 1973 in running a four-ship convoy from the metallurgical center of Norilsk on the Yenesei River to Murmansk. It affords Western shippers a 29-day voyage to the Far East —about ten days shorter than even the Suez route, and far shorter than the route around Africa. Whether it will "catch on" is a moot question; however, Polish ships carried coal to Japan over it during the summer of 1968.

The foregoing discussion is not intended to imply that all Soviet sailors had suddenly grown to be nine feet tall or that the Soviet Navy in 1968 was in no way deficient. Its lack of combat experience and a naval tradition has been noted. Geographic handicaps remained. The absence of aircraft carriers and fleet-based air power on the basis of American, British, and Japanese experience was a vital lack, and despite the formidable threat of ship-based missiles the Soviet navy was hardly ready for a battle test. Yet the rapidity of force development since 1962, the navy's avid support by the government, and the great research and development effort behind it, all argued that the Soviets had come closer to being "at home at sea" than ever before. In at least a few respects the Soviet navy had probably already surpassed the achievements of its American exemplar. By 1970 its fighting ships outnumbered those of the United States by a margin of 1,575 to 894,[5] and whereas the average U.S. warship was built 17½ years before, a slim one percent of the Soviet vessels were as much as 20 years old. Finally, the fact that 456 new warships were building in Soviet yards in midsummer of 1968 as compared to only 51 in the United States indicated no letup in future pressure.

SOVIET SEA POWER IN THE MEDITERRANEAN

There is no justification whatever for the constant presence of the U.S. Fleet in waters washing the shores of Southern Europe. One would like to ask: what are the grounds, twenty years after the end of World War II, for the U.S. Sixth Fleet to cruise the Mediterranean and to use military bases, ports and supply bases in a number of Mediterranean countries? This poses a serious threat to the independence of all coastal countries. The time has come to demand the complete withdrawal of the U.S. Sixth Fleet from the Mediterranean.[6]

So spoke CPSU Secretary-General Leonid Brezhnev on April 24, 1967, at the Conference of Communist and Workers Parties of Europe at Karlovy Vary, Czechoslovakia. His words may be regarded as representative of the Russian thinking which attends the end of one historic era and the beginning of another. Eleven centuries after the Varangian Russians made their first offensive gestures toward Byzantium and two hundred years after Catherine the Great's fleets circumnavigated Europe to defeat the Turks at Chesma, the Russians had succeeded in bypassing old obstacles and establishing their sea power in the Mediterranean.

The long and largely fruitless Russian quest for warm water has been told in detail in previous chapters of this volume. So far as a legal basis for the presence of Soviet warships from the Black Sea in the Mediterranean is concerned, it is necessary only to point to the Montreux Convention of 1936, which ran for twenty years and was then automatically renewed in the absence of objections. The convention provided that Black Sea powers could send warships through the Dardanelles without limit as to number or tonnage, stipulating only that Turkey be notified eight days in advance of the intended passage. During the calendar year 1967 this privilege was exercised freely: 167 Soviet warships entered the Mediterranean from the Black Sea that year, and only 62 made the return trip. Among those which made the outbound journey were three cruisers, 11 destroyers, nine minesweepers, two submarines, 51 minelayers, 21 motor torpedo boats, and various auxiliary and supply vessels. Of the warships which did not return via the Dardanelles in 1967, by no means all remained in the Mediterranean. Some went elsewhere to return later or by different routes, others were gifts to satellite navies. But the Soviet naval presence in the Mediterranean that year often included between 40 and 50 vessels and at times was even larger.

Paradoxically, the Soviet presence in the Mediterranean and the budding effort to oust the far stronger United States Sixth Fleet were by-products of two stunning defeats. The first was the six-day war in June 1967, in which Arab client states of the Soviet Union were speedily and crushingly defeated by Israel. The second was the defeat of the Soviet-Arab attempt, in the United Nations during July 1967, to turn military defeat into political and diplomatic victory.

Following World War II the Mediterranean became the southern flank of NATO and was dominated by the United States Sixth Fleet plus the navies of countries allied to the United States—Great Britain, France, Italy, Greece, and Turkey. Postwar Soviet demands for two Turkish provinces and a share in the control of the straits were successfully denied by Turkey. The guerrilla war in Greece was won by the government, Yugoslavia later became largely independent of Moscow, and with each of these developments Russian influence in the Mediterranean faded. Even the submarine base provided by tiny Albania was unavailable after 1961 when Albania finally drifted decisively into the Chinese Communist camp.

The beginnings of effective Soviet penetration in the area date to the middle 1950s and the successful exploitation of the quarrel between the Arab states and Israel. Though the Soviet Union had been as prompt to recognize Israel as had the United States, the Soviets concluded there was more to be gained by a posture friendly to Arab nationalism than from support of Israel. During the Franco-British seizure of the Suez Canal and Israel's invasion of Egypt the Soviets joined the United States in opposition, to what the Soviets alleged to be the "imperialist" forces. Soviet financing of the Aswan High Dam followed. During the 1950s and early 1960s the Soviets may have hoped to sell Communist ideology to the Arabs. They customarily distinguished between "progressive" or "socialist" Arab states, such as Egypt, Algeria, Syria, and Iraq, and the "reactionary" regimes allied with the "imperialists." However, in nearly every Arab country local Communists went on being jailed and the efforts

of the Russians to sell their ideology failed. Opposition to Israel
was the one issue uniting Arab states which varied greatly in the
degree of their political and economic development, and this theme,
combined with denunciations of the United States and Great Britain, was constantly stressed. Meanwhile it proved that the anti-
imperialist line appealed to countries emerging from colonialism.

During these years small fleets of Soviet vessels in the Mediterranean numbered from three to as many as a dozen vessels. In 1964
the Soviets created a special Mediterranean unit as part of their
Black Sea Fleet.

From 1964 to mid-1967 world events seemed to play into Russian
hands. The overcommitment of the United States in southeast Asia
after 1965 appeared to rule out the possibility of a vigorous U.S.
response to any challenge in the Middle East. The withdrawal of
France from NATO not only weakened Allied naval forces in the
Mediterranean but brought France, an able and unscrupulous competitor, into the scramble for oil concessions. Though they had
earlier supplied much of Israel's air force, the French now adopted
an anti-Israel posture. At the eastern end of the Mediterranean, the
Cyprus issue pitted Greece against Turkey and thus promoted
NATO disunity. Great Britain's announced intention to withdraw
from "East of Suez" raised the threat of a power vacuum between
Aden and Hongkong. At the other end of the Mediterranean, the
revival of Spain's claim to Gibraltar—a claim which the U.S.S.R.
promptly supported in the United Nations—brought in a new element of uncertainty. Turkey and Iran, long the major obstacles to
Soviet southward pressures, were responding favorably to Russian
diplomacy.

In view of all these developments, even leaders as cautious as
Kosygin and Brezhnev could reasonably deem conditions propitious
for an Arab political victory over Israel and a Soviet political victory
over the United States; it was also reasonable for them to assume
that the chances of disastrous defeat were not too great. Yet it is
debatable whether it was deliberation and calculation or widespread bungling which brought on the six-day war. The Arab terrorist organization known as Al Fatah had in late 1966 and early
1967 increased both the frequency and severity of its raids into
Israel. Some of these raids were made through Jordan, but most

originated in Syria, where a radical and irresponsible young men's government had recently come to power.

Israel on November 13, 1966, retaliated massively for past provocations—but against Jordan rather than the principal culprit Syria, in an action which fully merited the censure she received from the United Nations. In Arab eyes the attack may also have justified protests on the part of Jordan that Egypt and Syria had failed to shoulder their burden in the struggle against the common foe. During early 1967 there was a great increase in disorders along the border between Syria and Israel, and on April 7, 1967, the Syrians suffered a severe repulse in which they lost six planes. A wave of minor aggressions from Syrian territory followed, and by mid-May the Israeli government announced it was prepared to take further punitive action. At the same time President Nasser, apparently stung by earlier criticisms of his inactive role, entered the fray. Between the middle of May and early June there was a rapid procession of events which included the movement of Egyptian forces into the Sinai Peninsula and close to the Israeli frontier, the withdrawal of U.N. peacekeeping forces at Nasser's request, the proclamation of a blockade of the Gulf of Aqaba on May 22 (in flagrant violation of international law), the failure of the United States to oppose this blockade or to persuade a group of naval powers to do so, promises of support for Nasser from all countries of the Arab world, and the conclusion of a mutual defense pact between Egypt, Jordan, and Iraq. These steps were accompanied by enthusiastic paeans and exuberance throughout the Arab world, and by promises of support from the Soviet Union.

By June 1 Nasser appeared to have won a war without fighting, and his Soviet backers must have felt extremely hopeful. Israel was surrounded by a ring of foes greatly superior (on paper) in every aspect of military manpower and equipment. Most of the equipment was of first-class Soviet manufacture, and most of it had been contributed since the January 1964 Cairo summit conference which drew up plans to destroy Israel. According to a June 19, 1967, statement by Israeli Foreign Minister Abba Eban, Soviet military contributions to the Arabs since 1955 had included some 2,000 tanks, 700 modern fighters and bombers, ground-to-ground missiles, 540 field guns, 130 medium guns, 200 120-mm. mortars, 695 antiaircraft guns, 175 rocket launchers, 650 antitank guns, *Luna M* and *Sappa* missiles, seven destroyers, 14 submarines, and 46 torpedo boats. Most of this equipment had been awarded to Egypt, whose army had been trained by Soviet experts.

Although not all of this equipment was available to them at the outbreak of the June war, the three Arab states immediately involved outmatched Israel in weapons and manpower by about a three-to-one margin. But modern weapons require modern men to operate them successfully, and in this respect the Arabs were hopelessly inept with their poor leadership, untrained men, and low morale. Further, some of the best Egyptian troops were tied up with hostilities in Yemen. On June 1, Gen. Moshe Dayan, a hero of the 1958 war, was made minister of defense in Israel. With his appointment an Israeli military response became a certainty.

On June 5 the six-day war started with a highly successful air attack against Egyptian bases, as Israeli planes moved in from the west at low altitudes to escape radar detection. This strike caught nearly all the Egyptian planes on the ground, and destroyed most of them. It also gave rise to a charge by Nasser that British and American planes were helping Israel, a convenient face-saver for the Arabs and one which was widely believed.[7] Following the destruction of enemy air strength, Israel's air force went to the aid of its army in Sinai, where the larger forces of Egyptians were easily defeated and bypassed and soon became an unorganized mob without water and with little chance to escape destruction in the desert. Vast quantities of virtually unused Arab equipment were captured. On June 7 the Gulf of Aqaba was taken by the Israelis without loss. Meantime Israeli action had started against the Jordanian and Syrian forces, which were speedily vanquished.

The naval forces of the Soviet Union and of NATO were both within the general area of conflict. The Arabs may have expected Soviet intervention in time to ward off defeat, but the Russians acted with extreme caution. There was never any great prospect of an armed conflict between their forces and those of either the United States or Great Britain. Diplomatically, the Soviets who had opposed any United Nations action in the early stage of the conflict were finally willing to accept an unconditional cease-fire. So was Israel, whose forces had reached the Suez Canal, occupied Jerusalem and the west bank of the Jordan River, and routed the Syrians from the Golan Heights. So, after slight hesitation, were the Arab states.

That the six-day war was not to be followed by peace speedily became apparent. Defeated militarily, the Arab states with their communist and neutralist sympathizers now took their case to the United Nations and once more failed to score a victory. Nasser announced the indefinite closing of the Suez Canal. Several Arab states broke off diplomatic relations with the United States and Great Britain, and some announced—but did not effectively carry out—a selective oil embargo. The Arabs demanded that Israel abandon all conquests prior to peace negotiations. Israel demanded face-to-face bilateral negotiations—and recognition of Israel—as a preliminary to any settlement. With Egypt and Jordan facing economic ruin, the three "reactionary" Arab states, Saudi Arabia, Kuwait, and Libya, decided at a Khartoum foreign minister's conference held August 1–5, 1967, to provide financial aid amounting to nearly 300 million dollars.

The outcome of the June war may have hurt the Arabs more than the Israelis, and the Soviet Union more than the United States. But it also brought triumphs—though expensive ones—to the Soviet Union. Capitalizing on the Arab states' grief and humiliation, their need of a strong friend, and their widespread resentment of the United States for her pro-Israel role, the Russians moved rapidly. They concealed whatever disgust they may have felt at the miserable military record of their protégés and re-equipped the Syrian and Egyptian forces in a gigantic 800-plane-flight air lift. The value of this second arms gift was estimated by Israeli sources at three billion dollars.

There are indications that the Russians did not completely replace all weapons, and that they asked for—and received—certain new concessions. For one thing, they may have demanded some control over the promotion of officers, since they were known to be critical not only of the class structure of the Egyptian army but of its entire attitude which, in the Russian view, put pleasure and personal profit before responsibility and hard work. An estimated 4,000 Russian technicians were believed to be active in Arab countries in 1968 training Arab troops in the handling of sophisticated new weapons, and Arab pilots were being taught in the Soviet Union to fly Mig-21's. While the bulk of Soviet equipment has gone to Egypt, gifts have also reached some unlikely recipients, including Sudan and even Morocco, one of America's closest African allies, which received Czechoslovak tanks and field artillery.

Economic penetration has accompanied military instruction. During the year following the Arab defeat at least 1,000 Soviet civilian technicians were reportedly in the Arab world advising on all types of economic activities. Many barter deals were concluded involving the exchange of the Arab states' primary products for Soviet equipment and weapons. Cultural ties were emphasized, and an increased number of Soviet scholarships were made available for Arab students. Agreements concluded since June 1967 have included contributions to dams and irrigation facilities, an airline, and even Soviet acceptance of surplus citrus fruit. Allied intelligence services report substantial Soviet sums being channeled to key military and political personnel, editors, and teachers.

In return for these very large outright gifts, the Soviet Union has gained the use of certain ports as naval bases. Latakia in Syria, Alexandria and Port Said in Egypt, and more recently Mers-el-Kebir in Algeria (newly evacuated by the French) have become available as rest and repair stops. The Soviets apparently have permanent shore parties and repair facilities at these ports and there have been recent reports of Soviet planes being stationed there. It should be noted, however, that the bases are probably not absolutely necessary to the support of the Soviet navy since it has adopted a fleet train system for supply of ships at sea, much like the one developed by the United States during World War II.

Another Soviet gain has been a considerable degree of control over the foreign policy of the Arab states. The Soviet Union is at present the buyer of 70 percent of the Egyptian cotton crop and supplies 80 percent of the U.A.R. food imports. According to one source, a Nasser move to renew diplomatic relations with the United States was defeated by Soviet opposition.

The Soviets have also lost ground in certain important respects.

The closing of the Suez Canal has hurt some nations but has not seriously disturbed others. It has directly and deeply injured Egypt, for example, but has been of little significance to most of the other Arab states. The United States' supply of oil has been little affected by it, but for most of the nations of Western Europe as well as for Japan it has come to mean an estimated billion dollars a year in increased costs to transport oil around Africa. The building of extremely large tankers whose draft is too great for the Suez Canal has been greatly speeded up. The Israeli 42″ pipeline running from Elath to Ashkelon pumped its first oil in February 1970 and in full operation could carry 60 million tons a year—more than a third of the tonnage previously moved through the Suez Canal.

But other than Egypt, probably no country has been more unfavorably affected by the canal closing than the Soviet Union itself. The Red Sea, Persian Gulf, and Indian Ocean have all been made more distant and difficult to penetrate. The shipment of Russian military supplies to North Vietnam, already difficult in view of the distance involved and the uncooperative attitude of the Chinese Communists, has been made doubly hard. Neither land shipment through Chinese territory nor shipment of supplies to Vladivostok (either by the Trans-Siberian railroad or by the northern sea route) for trans-shipment to Haiphong has proved a satisfactory alternative to the long route from Black Sea ports around Africa.

The sizable naval presence of the Soviet Union in the Mediterranean at present has greater psychological than military significance. In any conflict with a major power the Soviet forces in the Mediterranean, lacking air cover, would doubtless be defeated. Though the size and composition of this force has altered, in the summer of 1968 it included one 20,000-ton cruiser (either *Sverdlov* or *Dzerzhinsky*), one *Kynda* and one *Krupny* class destroyer armed with long-range surface-to-surface missiles, and five *Kotlin* class destroyers, five escorts of the *Riga*, *Petia* or *Meska* classes, three landing ships, 12 nuclear submarines (some carrying as many as eight missiles), and support and landing craft. Later that year the new carrier *Moskva* also made an appearance in the Mediterranean, where it remained for about six weeks, engaged mainly in antisubmarine exercises.

Compared to this small force the NATO alliance has usually had in the Mediterranean some 300 ships which were entirely separate from the vessels of the U.S. Sixth Fleet. Either British or Italian forces in the area would be more than a match for the Russians. The Sixth Fleet, which is organized in three forces (strike, antisubmarine warfare, supply), has comprised some 60 vessels. These have included two large carriers with a complement of about 100 planes each, many capable of carrying nuclear weapons to a range of 1,000 miles; one antisubmarine carrier; a cruiser; 16 destroyers; 12 to 14 submarines, half of them of the *Polaris* type; a marine landing force of 2,000 men; the usual complement of landing and supply ships; and a land-based (Sicily) air force. Effective November 21, 1968, a new NATO command, Maritime Air Forces Mediterranean, was formed for the purpose of coordinating aerial surveillance of the Soviet fleet. Further, French cooperation with British, Italian, and American forces reportedly has been arranged.

Without doubt the Russian move into the Mediterranean also represents the assumption of sizable risks. With client states as volatile as are the Arab countries, there are good chances the Soviets may find themselves enmeshed in many commitments and responsibilities which afford no ideological payoff and very little influence over the governments involved. Soviet technicians "advising" native Arabs are almost certain to create tensions and dislikes. Finally, while legitimate Soviet interests exist in the Mediterranean they are not preponderant there. Of the approximately 2,600 ships cruising the Mediterranean on any typical day at least 80 percent belong to NATO nations. The fifteen nations which border the Mediterranean are diverse in many respects, but the great majority are basically anticommunist. The Russians control none of the three exits to the Mediterranean (though their commercial and fishing vessels have recently made great use of Gibraltar). Under these conditions it is hard to imagine how the Soviets could sever Western supply lines. There remain at least three other possibilities.

First, they might try to interfere with the oil supply of Western Europe. The Soviet Union herself probably is in little need of Middle East oil since she already has numerous domestic sources, including some fields in Siberia that may prove exceedingly productive. Nations such as Italy, West Germany, Japan, and Great Britain are less independent and thus more vulnerable to oil blackmail, which could prove disruptive to the NATO alliance. Second, the possibility of demanding Sixth Fleet withdrawal from the Mediterranean was openly acknowledged by Brezhnev in his Karlovy Vary speech of April 1967. This theme has subsequently been sounded by the Soviet press and echoed, though faintly, by the Communist parties of

Western Europe. A third and grimmer prospect, full Soviet backing or participation in another Arab war against Israel, could give the United States some highly unpalatable options.

SOVIET SEA POWER EAST OF SUEZ

As anyone familiar with these pages will know, the Russians have long been interested in the land and sea routes to southern Asia and especially to India. It is Great Britain's present intention to move out of all areas between Suez and Hongkong. Such a withdrawal will be likely to create a power vacuum which the United States, overcommitted in other areas, probably will not attempt to fill. Therefore a major shift of Soviet attention to the Indian Ocean must be viewed as a definite possibility.

Prior to the six-day war Soviet actions in the vast Indian Ocean area had been mainly by proxy. Foreign aid programs have usually been related to strategic needs, and Indonesia—with its control over the straits linking the Pacific and Indian Ocean—was the recipient of very large Soviet gifts when it was still under the rule of Sukarno. This experiment in foreign aid proved to be a failure. Sukarno drew progressively closer to the Peking camp and steadily away from the Moscow version of the Gospel of Marx. Further, when an attempted Indonesian Communist coup against the army miscarried, no efforts by Sukarno were able to avert the pogrom which virtually destroyed the party.

At the other end of the Indian Ocean, Soviet activities have been somewhat more effective. In Yemen the Soviet Union has provided air support for the republic of Yemen against royalist forces backed by Saudi Arabia. Soviet engineers have constructed a harbor at Hodeida, a city on the Red Sea which enjoys a direct air-line link with Moscow. And when Great Britain moved out of the Red Sea area in November 1967, Aden swiftly became the South Yemen People's Republic. In June 1968 the Soviet cruiser *Dmitry Pozharsky*, a missile destroyer, a nuclear submarine, and an oiler, anchored in the harbor at Aden to pay a courtesy visit to the new country. These ships, in course of a four-month cruise, had previously paid visits to Iraq, Somalia, India, Iran, and Ceylon. In the autumn of 1968 two other small Soviet squadrons, one from the Black Sea and the other from the Pacific, made courtesy visits to the Indian Ocean countries, where American and British forces are very weak. Other probings to establish good relations with the small and weak states of the area are now under way. Somalia is benefiting from this trend by securing Soviet aid in constructing the new port of Berbera.

The Soviet Union has established friendly relations with India, and to a lesser degree with the Pakistanis (since successful Soviet mediation of their 1965 war). American withdrawal of military aid to these two countries merely opened up another competitive arena, one in which the Communist giants compete against each other: Communist China has since tendered military aid to Pakistan while the Soviet Union has supplied India. In February 1968 a visit of Admiral Gorshkov to India was commonly believed to be for the purpose of securing Indian ports for refuelling and repairing Soviet warships. Whatever the outcome of these preliminary feelers, the Indian navy has received Soviet submarines and patrol and landing craft, and in late 1968 it was slated to receive five destroyer escorts.

Ever since the beginning of the war in Vietnam the Soviet Union has supplied sinews of war to Hanoi. The main line of supply at first ran from Odessa through the Dardanelles and from the Suez Canal to Haiphong, a distance of well over 7,000 miles. That trip ordinarily took somewhat over a month using the Soviet Union's largest and fastest cargo ships (*Belitsk* class, 14,000 tons and 18-½ knots). An average of 47 cargo ships a month reached Haiphong. (Most of them were closely inspected en route by "hazing" American ships and planes, and perhaps for this reason a detachment of the Soviet Far Eastern naval forces, including cruisers, was reported operating near Vietnam in spring of 1968.[8])

The closing of the Suez Canal lengthened the supply route around Africa to more than 14,000 miles. Even at top speed the round trip now required nearly five months, and the number of ships arriving at Haiphong fell to an average of 22 to 25 per month. To maintain the former level of aid the Soviets would have had to employ nearly all the large cargo ships turned out in their shipyards during a two-year period—probably 300 ships as compared to the 150 or so employed previously.[9]

The fourth role played by Soviet sea power east of the Suez Canal has been that of active supporter or defender of Soviet-aligned powers or nations. For example, Soviet *elint* (electronic intelligence) ships almost daily harassed U.S. forces in the Gulf of Tonkin—this not only to gain information for the U.S.S.R. and her allies but also to deter American actions and ensure that the Russian presence was felt. When the *Enterprise* task force entered the Sea of Japan after the *Pueblo* capture in January 1968, the Soviets immediately reinforced North Korea with a 16-ship task force of cruisers, missile frigates, and destroyers. Similarly, the presence of the U.S. carrier *Hancock* (following the Blue House raid and a large-scale infiltration attempt against the South Korean coast) was matched by a countering Soviet naval force. After the shootdown of the U.S. EC-121 reconnaissance aircraft over the Sea of Japan, the U.S. task force in the area was assisted—and monitored—by a sizable Russian force. While the Soviet intent in the above instances cannot be ascertained, it can be assumed with confidence that in all cases the Soviet presence caused concern among American forces, and that the United States very well understood that the Soviets were more than casually interested in ascertaining U.S. objectives.

One thing more should be clear: in a cold war situation the mere presence of an opposing force, even a much weaker force, has an inhibiting effect on naval action.[10] In the case of the six-day war, Soviet threats to help the Arabs diminished with the approach of the U.S. Sixth Fleet. Rightly or wrongly, the United States (until late in the war) refrained from mining Haiphong harbor or bombing its piers, because of unwillingness to sink Soviet merchant ships. And consonantly, in their grim undersea encounters neither the Soviet navy nor the United States navy issues statements regarding possible damage or losses on either side. In the sense that the presence of ships of one party inhibit open action by the other and tends to neutralize its force, then, Admiral Gorshkov is justified in claiming that United States mastery of the sea is at an end.

SOVIET NAVAL DEVELOPMENT 1968–72

In the foregoing discussion 1968 had been employed as a cutoff date. The military buildup of nuclear and naval forces which followed the Cuban missile crisis had by 1968 provided a substantial military equality with the United States, so far as numbers of missiles was concerned. In 1962 the United States with 200 ICBMs, 100 submarine based missiles, and 1700 bombers had vastly outclassed the Soviet Union's 50 ICBMs and 200 bombers. By 1967, however, the American missile buildup was complete with 1,710 missiles, both land- and sea-based, and about 600 bombers. Though the United States then held about a two-to-one margin Soviet progress thereafter was extremely rapid. By 1968 Soviet megatonnage probably exceeded that of the United States. However, because of better technology the Soviet Union was believed to be behind in actual strength.

Since the Soviet buildup continued while the United States stood still, by 1972 the Soviet Union possessed a theoretical superiority in most areas. The development of this theoretical superiority will be considered first. Secondly, attention will be given to the far-reaching accords signed in Moscow in May 1972.

By far the greatest interest attached to the development of Soviet submarines. As the details gradually leaked out it became apparent that the Soviets in their *Yankee* class nuclear submarines had made a quantum jump over the early H class submarines carrying three missiles of 650 miles range. The *Yankees* carried 16 missiles, each having a range of some 1,750 miles. They were thus roughly equal to the American A-2 *Polaris* submarines but less formidable than the A-3s carrying *Polaris* type missiles with their range of nearly 3,000 miles. By doubling the size of the principal yard producing these submarines, at Severodvinsk in the Arctic, the Soviets further developed the ability to finish at least eight or nine submarines per year, a rate vastly greater than the capacity of the United States yards. From a technical standpoint the *Yankee* submarines had several faults, the worst one being that they were inordinately noisy and therefore easy to detect. During May 1972 the Soviets laid down their forty-second *Yankee* class ship, thereby outnumbering the *Polaris* type of the United States. Twenty-six *Yankee* submarines were then complete, with 16 others building and probably at least 20 others projected.

Aware that the *Yankee* type was not equal to the best *Polaris* submarines, the Soviets decided on a program of modification to enable their submarines to carry the SS-N-8 Sawfly missile with its

3,500-mile range instead of the SS-N-6. This was certain to present problems due to the much greater length of the Sawfly.

Meantime the United States had not been inactive even though it had deliberately permitted the Soviet Union to catch up in numbers. American progress in multiple warheads (sometimes referred to as MIRV) was believed to be much more advanced than that of the Soviets, possibly by as much as five years. Accordingly, a program of modifying both land- and sea-based missiles was showing results. In the summer of 1971 the air force announced that a Minuteman 3 had been altered to carry three warheads instead of one. This was the first step in a conversion program ultimately involving 550 such missiles.

The Navy's MIRV program involved converting 31 of the country's *Polaris* type submarines. The first submarine so converted, *James Madison*, put to sea on April 1, 1972. The conversion to ten-warhead *Poseidon* missiles would increase the total warheads from 656 to 5,120. The individual warheads were of low yield as nuclear yields went, from 17 kilotons in the case of some *Poseidon* warheads to 1.2 megatons in the case of the Minuteman. Compared to the 25-megaton warheads of some of the Soviet land-based missiles the American warheads were positively puny. However, the initial atomic bomb which destroyed Hiroshima and killed more than 78,000 people was of only 20 kilotons.

The real question was one of accuracy. Rightly or wrongly American military men believed that their own missiles were far more accurate than those of the Russians. Submarine-based Soviet missiles were believed to be no particular threat to the *Minutemen* and *Titans* in their concrete silos. However, airfields were much larger targets and the Strategic Air Command in early 1972 announced a program of dispersing to 47 airfields the B-52 bombers and of taking additional measures to assure quick takeoffs. The huge land-based missiles of the Russians were believed to be so inaccurate as to make it likely that 80 percent of America's land-based missiles could survive a surprise attack. So far as American submarine-based missiles were concerned it was assumed that 50 percent would land within a few hundred feet of their target. Thus the United States hoped to achieve by extreme accuracy what the Russians sought to achieve by brute force.

So far as future programs were concerned, the U.S. navy appeared to be in a vastly better position than the air force. Air force missiles were in known locations which could be targeted and attacked while the navy's submarines were moving about constantly. In the event of hostilities air force missiles would have to be fired or face the risk of destruction. *Polaris* and *Poseidon* missiles did not face this threat and could always be used as part of a second strike. For these reasons the only nuclear missile program which in 1972 appeared to have a good chance of enactment by Congress was a navy project. ULMS (for undersea long-range missile system) was certain to be costly—opponents claimed the cost would hit $30 billion—though the navy used a much lower figure. What the program envisaged was the construction of an entirely new fleet of nuclear submarines, each carrying 20-24 missiles of such long range that they could attack Soviet targets from virtually any point of the earth's surface. About double the size of the most modern *Poseidon* submarine and with better passive and active defenses built in, such ships would be subject to very few area limitations. Conceivably even a submarine in dry dock could fire missiles at Old World targets. Estimates of cost of construction were $500 million for the first ship and $350-400 million for each later submarine.

While nuclear submarines occupied the forefront of interest they were not the only area of Soviet progress. The new Backfire bomber was regarded by some American military analysts as superior to anything the United States had at a similar stage of development. Another Soviet project involved improvement in one of the Soviet navy's most successful ship types, the small guided missile cruiser. Three cruisers of some 12,000 to 15,000 tons were reported to be building while a similar number of *Sverdlov* class cruisers were having their guns removed and being converted to guided missile ships. Another question to concern naval experts was attack submarines. Here the Soviet superiority over the United States in numbers was 236 to 100. Yet the Americans were known to be ahead in the techniques of antisubmarine warfare. Did this technical lead compensate for more than a two-to-one Soviet superiority in numbers?

Undoubtedly the most intriguing question concerning the Soviet navy involved aircraft carriers. By previous experience of other navies lack of carriers would be a fatal weakness in a showdown.

But did previous experience govern the present and the future? Some American naval critics boldly stated that the Soviets were right and that the capital ship of the present was the submarine and not the carrier. Yet the practical disadvantages attached to a navy lacking carriers were very great. The guided missile cruisers and destroyers, for example, would be formidable only within a short range unless their missiles received guidance in reaching targets from some outside source such as a plane or satellite. Again, lacking air protection, Soviet surface vessels would find it difficult to operate for any length of time in case of hostilities. For these and other reasons reports and rumors of the building of carriers continued to circulate. Soviet progress with VTOL planes was followed with special interest, since these could be accommodated by the two helicopter carriers already in the navy. Should the Soviet Union enter the field of carrier aviation a time period of seven to eight years was thought by the U.S. navy to be necessary to develop not only forces but competence in using them.

By the fall of 1972, it had become apparent that the Soviets had at least partly realized the advantages of carrier aviation. A carrier of about 45,000 tons and some 900 feet long, named *Kiev*, was launched in the Black Sea at Nikolayev, and a similar ship immediately was laid down. The new carrier, which was expected to be completed in 1974, was apparently a compromise type. The flight deck of 600 feet in length, twice that of the *Moskva*, was still very short by American standards. As there was no evidence of launchings by steam catapults, as in the United States Navy, the indicated conclusion was that these ships were to operate vertical or short takeoff (VTOL or STOL) planes rather than more conventional types. Such planes are limited in range because of the very high fuel requirements for takeoff. The plane expected to operate on these carriers was reported to be a short, sturdy jet of about 600 knots' speed with a range of only 350 miles.

Some naval observers saw these ships as improvements on the earlier helicopter carriers whose limitations had apparently disappointed the Russians. The ideological basis was apparently set forth by Admiral Gorshkov in a series of articles in *Morskoi sbornik*. He pointed out that, though carriers might be vulnerable in a nuclear war (as the Russians had long insisted), the extension of influence in underdeveloped areas required a naval air capability which in remote areas could hardly be shore-based. That this change in traditional Soviet doctrine was both important and likely to prove permanent was indicated by promotion of the head of naval aviation, Colonel General Ivan I. Berzov, to the rank of Marshal of Aviation.

THE SALT AGREEMENTS

The entire process of allowing the Soviet Union to catch up with the United States, adopted as a deliberate policy during the regime of Secretary of Defense Robert McNamara, was conceived to be in the world interest. As long as the United States held superiority the Soviet Union was not likely to negotiate arms limitation agreements which would spell out Russian inferiority. Therefore at least a rough parity was regarded as being in the interests of both countries and a necessary prelude to limiting the costly arms competition.

As early as 1969 meaningful disarmament talks occurred between Soviet and American representatives. These were continued at several locations and at several different times. By the late spring of 1972 these long-continued private negotiations came to the surface in what was known as the Moscow summit. President Nixon and his advisers journeyed to Moscow and in about a fortnight reached final accords with the Soviet Union in more than half a dozen different fields. These included space exploration, science, technology, medical research, public health, the environment, encounters at sea and in the air, anti-ballistic missile sites, and arms control. Some were executive agreements and some were treaties. Collectively they formed possibly the most promising single breakthrough since World War II. Neither side pretended that the agreements constitute a diplomatic love affair. What was significant was the fact that neither Russians nor Americans let basic differences concerning Vietnam and the Middle East stand in the way of a marriage of convenience that could serve the interests of both parties. Only in the area of trade, in which negotiations were to be continued, was it not possible to reach an agreement. No end to competitive coexistence was in sight. Yet the Moscow accords signified many areas of common interest. Also embodied in the agreements was American recognition of the complete equality of the Soviet Union, a valuable psychological tool.

Although several of the agreements are irrelevant from the standpoint of this *History*, two concerning arms control and avoidance of incidents at sea (nicknamed by some the "anti-playing-chicken" agreement) are definitely pertinent, while the ABM Treaty is worth at least a glance.

The arms control agreement covered a period of five years but was revokable by either party on six months notice. Put very briefly, it froze the status quo so far as land-based missiles, submarine missiles, and bombers were concerned, though it did permit replacements, presumably by later models and more formidable weapons. In numerical terms the agreement appeared to favor the Soviet Union if simply because the Russians had more missiles (though fewer bombers) in existence. This point was seized on by certain opponents such as Senator Henry Jackson of Washington. Thus the total missiles (both land- and sea-based) was 2,300 for the Soviet Union and 1,710 for the United States. Deliverable warheads favored the United States by a margin of 5,700 to 2,500. In terms of total megatonnage or explosive power the Soviet Union held a great margin. The respective bomber fleets numbered 190 for the Soviet Union to 530 for the United States. Because the areas of greatest American technical superiority such as the MIRV system, better guidance systems, and much greater accuracy were not subject to limitation it is doubtful if the agreement favored the Soviet Union.

Also involved in the general field of arms limitation was a formal treaty limiting each country to two ABM sites. This was generally interpreted to mean Moscow and Washington, plus one weapons site for each country. Moscow already had such a system involving 64 missile launchers. Washington did not, and whether such a site could be protected in the future was a matter of guesswork, as considerable opposition existed. The American weapons site defense would probably be erected in Montana or North Dakota.

The accord for the prevention of incidents at sea was an executive agreement which went into effect on May 25, 1972, upon its signature by Adm. of the Fleet Sergei Gorshkov for the Soviet Union and John Warner, Secretary of Navy, for the United States. The agreement had been worked out first by Mr. Warner, who had then

aken the trouble to go to the Soviet Union to become acquainted
with leading Soviet naval figures months before the Moscow summit.[11] It consisted of nine articles. Effective for three years and
renewable for the same length of time it provided for annual meet-
ings to arrange for the implementation of the terms of the agreement. A joint committee was created to set up distances to be
observed in encounters involving ships and aircraft. Under Article
II the parties recognized as a basis of operations the 1958 Geneva
Convention on the High Seas. Article III set forth rules to be
observed and practices to be avoided in navigation. Steaming into
a formation of the other country's ships, for example, was forbidden.
Surveillance ships were to stay at a distance sufficient to avoid risk
of collision and avoid endangering ships under surveillance. Simula-
tions of attack such as aiming guns or torpedo tubes and illuminating navigation bridges by excessively powerful searchlights were
forbidden. Article IV applied these same principles to aircraft. Other
provisions prescribed adherence to rules of the road and the
increased use of signals.

Whether this agreement would put an end to the numerous cases
of "playing chicken" on the high seas that had occurred since the
end of World War II remained for the future to determine. The
document itself set forth general principles and left the details to be
filled in by a joint commission. With Soviet sea power fully mature
and the Soviet Union recognized as fully equal to the United States
there seemed, however, to be no lasting reason not to expect Russian
seamen and airmen to act with the maturity and responsibility to be
expected of representatives of a great power.

CHAPTER 23

Strategic Capabilities of Soviet Sea Power

POSTWAR GAINS AND DEFEATS

IMMEDIATELY FOLLOWING World War II the Soviet Union, despite the devastation and loss which she had suffered, embarked on an expansionist course. Through a combination of internal subversion, threats, and direct force, she secured effective control over the bordering state of Czechoslovakia and all nations overrun by the Red army during the war. Rumania, Hungary, Poland, Czechoslovakia, Bulgaria, Albania, and East Germany all became Soviet satellites, and all rebellions which have since taken place in the Communist states of Eastern Europe have been crushed by local militias and the Soviet army. Soviet attempts at further gains in Europe have, however, been successfully repelled.

In the Far East the addition of China to the Communist camp, while certainly not an unmixed blessing for the Soviet Union, has been an incalculable loss to the West. It has signified a Communist increase in manpower of possibly 700 millions and the acquisition of bases from which Communist attacks can be launched all over Southeast Asia and along India's northern borders. It has also presented to the Soviets a rival for leadership of the Communist world, with the result that the unity and power of international Communism have been greatly weakened.

In the Middle East, after the failure of encroachment attempts in Iran and Greece and of threats against Turkey, the Russians substituted a new policy of economic and military aid and ideological penetration for their former heavy-handed aggression in neighboring countries. While this policy of indirect conquest bypassed Greece and Turkey and fomented trouble for the West in Egypt, Syria, Iraq, Lebanon, Yemen, and other Arab states, it has not gained many converts to the Communist camp. The government of Egypt, for example, has accepted Soviet aid even while severely suppressing local Communists. However, the independence of the former colonies of France, Great Britain, Belgium, and Holland has created a host of new small and weak states—anticolonial, nationalistic, suspicious of their former masters, and naive in their understanding of the Soviet Union. In these troubled areas the Soviets, posing as enemies of colonialism yet themselves practicing it elsewhere, have gained converts. In pro-Soviet states not contiguous with the U.S.S.R., however, the Red army troops have not been able to extend control to adjacent areas—the standard method of expanding Red imperialism under Stalin. The overall result, therefore, has been that overseas gains are less than expected, insecure, and dependent on ideology rather than force.

Progress made by the international Communist movement has also brought with it certain penalties. Perhaps the greatest potential threat to the movement itself is the inability of any one power to maintain complete control. The Communist bloc today is no longer a monolith. Dissent has appeared, and the Yugoslav and Chinese interpretations of the Gospels of Marx and Lenin differ from that of the Soviets. Rumania, in the economic field at least, has partly escaped from Soviet domination. The suppression by military force of political liberalism in Czechoslovakia, while temporarily successful, has added greatly to the internal strains in the Communist camp.

Meanwhile, Soviet success in domestic economic development has changed the U.S.S.R. from a "have-not" to a "have-got" power with a great deal more to lose by war than have, for instance, the peasants of China. Soviet leaders are realistically aware of the threat posed by thermonuclear warfare and cannot welcome its possibilities for destruction. Consideration of the great risk and expense of such a war may lead the Soviets to continue their present strategy of cold war, or at most to risk a limited or conventional war. Nevertheless thermonuclear war could occur, either by accident or as an outgrowth of a conviction that a surprise attack on the United

States, accompanied by energetic Soviet civil defense measures, would achieve victory at an acceptable cost. In fact, as Raymond Garthoff has shown, Soviet military doctrine has stressed this very possibility.[1]

Before considering the role of Soviet sea power in each of these three possible types of conflict—cold war, conventional war, or thermonuclear war—it would be well to review the Soviet Union's natural limitations and advantages. Lastly, the present role of the Soviet navy will be considered on a geographic basis in the present setting of competitive coexistence.

In the first place, Russia is almost impregnable so far as land attack is concerned. Its only truly successful land enemies were the Mongols. In more recent times Charles XII, Napoleon, and Hitler have all met defeat before the Russian strategy of retreating and trading space for time until ever-lengthening lines of communication and supply weaken the enemy to such an extent that he becomes vulnerable to counter-attack.

Protection also exists against direct sea attack. The vast area of the world's heartland makes the Soviet Union largely immune from blockade, while much of its coastline is protected by ice. Nevertheless, in some past wars that were less all-out than a future conflict might be, such as the Crimean and Russo-Japanese Wars, enemy sea power concentrated on limited areas has been sufficient to defeat the Russians. Moreover, the Russians are sadly equipped geographically to exploit sea power themselves, outside purely local waters. Four fleets must be maintained with only limited possibilities of shifting ships from one fleet to another. The Danish and Turkish straits keep the Baltic and Black Sea Fleets fairly effectively bottled up. The Pacific and Northern Fleets, though not completely contained by foreign outlets to Russian seas, are hampered by ice blockade during the winter months.

SOVIET CAPABILITIES

The Surface Fleet

In terms of surface vessels, Soviet capabilities are decidedly limited against a major opponent such as the United States. Khrushchev's cutback in the building program of large surface warships, plus Soviet weakness in long-range aviation, has left the surface forces unequipped for distant operations. Apart from some missile-carrying frigates and large destroyers, Soviet warships are not especially dangerous. Further, in recent history Russian surface forces have consistently avoided coming to grips with more powerful opponents on the high seas (Admiral Rozhdestvensky's voyage during the Russo-Japanese War is a possible exception). Hence, it is unlikely that Soviet surface forces will in the future seek to do more than inhibit by their presence naval moves on the part of other major powers; they probably do not constitute a direct threat to the United States navy.

Within local waters, where they can operate under the protection of land-based air power, the Soviet surface fleets might be far more effective. The Black Sea Fleet is overwhelmingly superior to the Turkish navy. In the Arctic, 15 submarines, 26 motor torpedo boats, escort, and mine craft of the Norwegian navy would have little chance against the Soviet Northern Fleet. The Swedish navy is extremely efficient with its one cruiser, 15 destroyers and frigates, 24 submarines, 42 motor torpedo boats, 35 minesweepers, and other craft; backed up by the 600 planes of the Swedish air force and possibly by the small Danish navy, this force would doubtless give a good account of itself; but it too would be heavily outmatched. In the Far East, the reborn Japanese navy is still far too weak to put up anything beyond a token defense. None of these defensive forces would be able to hold its own very long against Soviet forces without powerful assistance from the U.S. Sixth and Seventh Fleets and the Royal Navy. Thus the Soviet Union's surface navy must be regarded as a definite threat by its immediate neighbors. Within a distance of 150-250 miles from its own bases it probably could dominate the sea, but its lack of longer-range weapons such as naval planes and carriers would severely limit its effectiveness in mid-ocean.

Joint Army-Navy Operations

During the entire Soviet period and for at least two centuries earlier, as our survey of Russian history has shown, a principal use of sea forces has been to assist land forces. This role is still emphasized in Soviet naval propaganda. The Soviets have constructed literally thousands of small craft for local use, and thus have a much greater capacity for army-navy cooperation than existed in World War II. This is an essentially short-range capability, and would be of limited value in a war with a power far from Russia's borders. As noted in chapter 22, however, the beginnings of a much longer-range capability are now present.

Amphibious Operations

So far as amphibious operations are concerned, the Soviets have advanced far beyond their very creditable World War II record. Greatly improved landing craft obtained first from the United States under lend-lease and later from the Germans after their surrender, have spurred a substantial development of theory and techniques for carrying on amphibious operations. An amphibious training center in the U.S.S.R. has turned out many thousands of graduates. A growing inventory of specialized landing ships includes the 4,000-ton *Alligator* tank lighters capable of moving 30-40 tanks and 2,400 tons of cargo. Exercises in airlifting troops and in gunnery and air support have been frequent. For the short-range lifts characteristically carried out by the Russians, amphibious capacity has been conservatively estimated as sufficient for one division in the Arctic and two divisions in the three other fleet areas. Soviet capability for long-range operations is well below that of the United States; the Soviet marine landing force is smaller, and effective aerial coverage is seriously deficient.

Protection of Commerce

Historically the Russian navy has had relatively little experience protecting its nation's commerce in time of war. The merchant marine has usually been small and has operated within coastal waters and under protection of shore batteries. During both world wars most of the protection of Russian oceanic commerce was provided by the British navy and the Soviets had no need to demonstrate capability in such matters as convoy defense and antisubmarine warfare. Concurrent with the vast expansion of Soviet commerce since World War II, the Red navy has added hundreds of escort vessels of various types. Until recently, little material on this phase of sea power (other than translations from foreign sources) appeared in Soviet naval publications; but it is now clear that the Soviets have become fully conscious of the possible threat of submarine warfare and have made a belated start on commerce protection as a naval mission. Late in 1966 Vice Adm. Charles B. Martell stated that in antisubmarine warfare technology the Soviet Union was still about 20 years behind the United States. The Soviets probably could guard their commerce in areas near their own bases, but hardly on a worldwide basis.

Defeat of Enemy Amphibious Operations

Although a favorite propaganda line continues to glorify the Red navy as defender of the Soviet shores, it is questionable whether the greatest land power on earth truly perceives the possibility of a seaborne enemy invasion as unduly menacing. At any rate, the Soviets have ample forces available in the form of strong armies, shore-based aviation, short-range submarines, coastal-defense forces, and large numbers of torpedo and mine craft to meet any such threat.

In the unlikely event of a war involving a land invasion of the Soviet Union, an enemy might consider revising the strategy of the Crimean and Russo-Japanese wars. In both of those wars Russia's enemies did not attempt a genuine full-scale land war; instead they secured beachheads and then concentrated all forces on a small area which could be supplied and reinforced more easily by the invader than by the Russians. Soviet nuclear weapons, however, tend to make this an unattractive proposition.

Mine Warfare

Minelaying represents one tactical naval field in which, with the exception of World War II, the Russians have historically excelled. Almost all Soviet ships are built to carry mines as either primary or secondary armament; so are many aircraft. During the Korean war, North Korean forces using Soviet mines and tactics taught the United States navy the perils of mine warfare. They demonstrated in the process a far greater spirit of innovation and far more sophisticated weapons than were displayed against the Germans in World War II.[2]

Soviet defensive minelaying capability is even greater, with submarines, airplanes, and hundred of surface ships available for the purpose. Unquestionably the Russians could easily close their contiguous waters with mines, and it could be done quickly.

Offensive minelaying is quite a different story. Here the Russians also possess a sizable capability, though the tactics would have to be quite different from those used in defensive mining. The force of surface minelayers, for example, probably could operate only prior to the outbreak of war—and then clandestinely, after the fashion of the Germans in the Baltic at the beginning of World War II. Long-range planes and submarines would have to be the wartime offensive weapons; the Red navy has strong, though far from overwhelming, forces in each category.

These air and undersea minelayers would have a wide choice of possible targets, though areas such as the Pacific Coast of the United States would probably be ruled out because mining is most effective in shallow waters. The areas which most effectively combine shallow water with target density are (1) the Atlantic Coast of the United States, with its heavy traffic of ships, its long coastline, and its numerous ports; (2) the coastal waters of continental Europe, outside the principal ports; and (3) natural oceanic bottlenecks through which traffic is funneled, such as the Suez Canal, the Panama Canal, the Straits of Malacca, the Dardanelles, the Straits of Gibraltar, and the Danish Straits. It is significant that Soviet postwar policy has shown great sensitivity to each of these bottlenecks, as witness friendly overtures and support offered the United Arab Republic, Yemen, and Morocco, and the encouragement and support of Castro Cuba and Indonesia. Whether outstanding I.O.U.'s could be translated into effective assistance to Soviet sea forces in the event of a major war in which the Soviet Union did not control the seas, is another question.

The Guerre de Course

By far the greatest naval threat which the Soviet Union could offer in a major, wide-ranging war lies in its immense fleet of submarines. Most of these could be used in the traditional role of commerce destroyers, and a growing number of them possess important strategic capabilities. Because these threats are basically different, they will be considered separately.

The Russian threat to commerce would seem to be less than might appear on the surface. It has been noted that the World War II record of the undersea branch of the Red navy was mediocre, reflecting a combination of technical backwardness, defective direction and doctrine, and undertrained crews. While there can be no doubt that much of the technical naivete has disappeared, the Soviets apparently have not yet equaled most of the achievements of recent U.S. navy submarines. To produce such achievements, U.S. submarine crews were put through a long process of highly technical indoctrination and operation involving many types of naval vessels and aircraft using a wide variety of weapons. There is little evidence to suggest the Soviets have provided such exhaustive training for the crews of their approximately 370 submarines, though indications point to material progress beyond the World War II level and some very recent major achievements. Nor does it appear that the Soviet navy has developed a modern doctrine for undersea operations. All told, there is little reason to believe that the Soviet undersea boats would be comparable in effectiveness to the same number of British, German, or American vessels.

Even if the Soviet submarines were in all ways equal to the best afloat, they would still face handicaps. About a third of them are bottled up in the enclosed waters of the Black Sea and the Baltic, and not even a successful rapid transit of the Danish and Turkish straits would fully free them to operate in wide waters. Russian submarines based in the Arctic and Pacific are far distant from the main shipping lanes and would have to expend a disproportionate share of their cruising radius in transit. A still greater problem would probably be lack of aerial direction, without which submarines would waste a great deal of time patrolling empty ocean. Effective land-based aircraft would need very long-range capabilities as well as special training for their crews; there are some indications of recent development of this capacity. A final drawback, lack of experience in ocean cruising, is currently being overcome, as Soviet submarines are now venturing far from their bases.

So far as the direct threat of submarines against commerce is concerned, it is necessary to keep in mind certain logistical considerations. During World War II the Germans were able to maintain only about a third of their U-boats on station at any one time, and in the Black Sea the Russians usually kept only one-fifth active, the remainder being en route or in port. In view of the fact that in our postulated future war the Russian submarines would be much farther from their targets, it would hardly be reasonable to expect them to better this record. Also, unless they are aided by very efficient intelligence, submarines in war will spend most of their time in fruitless hunting, as convoys and individual ships will diverge from their peacetime routes and be difficult to locate.

With these considerations in mind, the Soviets might attempt to get all their long-range submarines on station along the busiest shipping lines prior to the outbreak of war. At a prearranged date the submarines could then swing into action, torpedoing all the unprepared shipping possible during an early period of surprise attack. Later there would be a time when almost no submarines could be on station, but the size of the initial bag might more than compensate for this difficult situation.

The practical disadvantage of the strategy of maximum early attack against an unprepared foe—or a second Pearl Harbor—is the difficulty of carrying it out. While the means of detecting underwater submarines are less effective than might be desired, they do exist and are comparatively effective in narrow waters. A Soviet attempt to filter hundreds of submarines through the Dardanelles, the Great and Little Belts, the Barents Sea, and the line of American Western Pacific bases, without detection, would be so formidable an undertaking as to have virtually no chance of success. In the Danish Straits, for example, surface passage of submarines is recognized and legal but submerged passage is not. Also, all these waters are shallow and difficult to navigate and are under continual scrutiny by antisubmarine craft. The discovery of an attempt at very large-scale infiltration would almost certainly bring about counter preparations. In short, Soviet preparations for a massed submarine offensive could initiate a general war. A large-scale concealed exodus of Black Sea and Baltic submarines would probably be impossible in any case. A gradual buildup of at-sea forces over a considerable period, however, might attract little notice.

A move almost certain to be taken in either a thermonuclear or a conventional war would be a Russian attempt to seize the exits to both the Baltic and the Black Sea. This attempt would require combined naval, air, and land attack on a large scale, for both outlets are readily defensible by mines, coastal artillery, and naval craft. However, neither the Danes and West Germans in the case of the Baltic, nor the Turks in the Black Sea, could hold these exits against full-scale Soviet attack for any length of time. In World War II Hitler captured the Danish Strait in a matter of hours. It is possible the Russians could do as well. The Danish and West German navies, though they demonstrate considerable ability, comprise small craft between the size of destroyers and motor torpedo boats. Whether American and British aid could be rushed in in sufficient time and force to hold these exits might well be a top priority question.

In a *guerre de course* neither surface nor air naval forces are apt to present as great a threat as undersea craft. Nevertheless, and despite a likely unfamiliarity with naval conditions on the part of the crews of land-based planes, Soviet bombers would doubtless sink some ships in European waters. The number of very long-range planes available for missions outside European or East Asian waters is believed to be limited, and the main mission of those planes available would probably be to hunt targets for submarines rather than to initiate direct attack. The latter cannot, of course, be entirely ruled out: late in World War II B-29 bombers attained great success in sinking Japanese merchant vessels, though it was at a time and under conditions in which Japanese defenses were not particularly efficient. Surface warships would probably not be very effective outside Soviet waters even if their capabilities have improved. Defenses against them have also improved.

NEW ROLES

Thus far only roles historically familiar to the Russian navy have been discussed, but at least four new duties have been thrust on the Soviet navy by recent changes in technology. In approximate order of importance these are (1) strategic bombardment; (2) defense against *Polaris* submarines; (3) defense against carrier task forces; (4) promotion of Communist revolutions and overseas expansion of the Communist empire.

The Strategic Role

The first of these activities, strategic bombardment by nuclear submarines, has had an effect on Soviet naval thought that can only be described as exhilarating. Accustomed to the largely defensive psychology of the past, Soviet naval thinkers have not only found the offensive and defensive implications of the nuclear submarine difficult to grasp but have been a little intoxicated by the prospects of carrying on distinctly offensive operations thousands of miles from the Soviet Union. It was not until 1962 that Soviet writers began to show an awareness of the possibilities involved. The subsequent development of techniques was not immediate, but in April 1966 Marshal Rodion Ya. Malinovsky announced that several Soviet submarines had succeeded in circumnavigating the globe submerged. Analysis of current Soviet naval publications reveals that considerable thought is being devoted to these future vistas.

As noted earlier, the Soviets in building their underseas fleet were bemused by quantity for many years and were tardy in appreciating quality of weapons. The best evidence available suggests that most of the missiles carried by Soviet submarines are not at present as long-range as those carried on the *Polaris*. On the other hand, they need not be tactically equal to the American *Polaris* submarines to constitute a major threat. Even a 500-mile missile fired from coastal waters not only could reach such coastal cities as Seattle, Portland, San Francisco, Oakland, Los Angeles, Long Beach, San Diego, Houston, New Orleans, Miami, Norfolk, Washington, Baltimore, Philadelphia, New York, and Boston; it could also reach Pittsburgh, Cleveland, Buffalo, San Antonio, Dallas, Atlanta, and many other of the principal cities farther inland. Roughly 70 to 75 percent of American population and industry would be vulnerable; the entire northeastern Boston-through-Washington target system is within close range of the sea. Further, the Soviets have under development missile submarine systems at least as good as those of the United States. Barring tremendously improved means of detecting and destroying, therefore, Russian missile submarines in a bombardment role appear to present a major threat. The development of a satisfactory answer to this threat has undoubtedly been given high priority by United States defense planners. For now, the American reply will be the same as in the case of a missile attack from land bases, namely the threat of overwhelming nuclear retaliation from both land and sea.

Defense Against the Polaris

Soviet strategists were slow to perceive the threat of the *Polaris*, and despite a great deal of recent discussion published in military and naval journals, no one has yet come up with a convincing answer. Writings on the subject reveal a good deal of surface optimism based largely on misinformation, plus some sober warnings that the task of defeating *Polaris* submarines is by no means simple. The Sokolovsky volume's second edition, for example, still professes a belief that homing missiles from submarines and surface craft can destroy the *Polaris*, but it contains no analysis of weapon effectiveness and deals in sweeping generalizations. Adm. V. A. Alafuzov, in an article in the January 1963 issue of *Morskoi sbornik*, questioned the treatment of this subject as well as scores of other weaknesses in the book and concluded that the tasks being glossed over were "not so easy." On the other hand, Capt. 1st Rank V. P. Rogov argued in the same magazine four months later that the *Polaris* was vulnerable in its base, that it had a low percentage of successful test launches, that it was inaccurate in aim due to navigational errors in positioning, and that it faced difficulties in communications and control. Adm. A. Chabanenko in the December 1, 1963, *Izvestiia* cited noise made by the *Polaris* submarines and claimed they could be detected by special atomic submarines. A news release by TASS in February 1965 echoed Soviet navy claims of being able to detect, monitor, and destroy American missile submarines, but a report by Capt. 1st Rank K. Penzin in the November 7, 1966, issue of *Morskoi sbornik* made no such claim.

In the view of most American and other observers, Soviet claims to possession of an answer to missile submarines have been too general to be convincing, and indicative of a tendency on the part of army and navy officers to make assertions for purposes of propaganda regarding matters which they have hardly yet recognized as major and unsolved problems. Though the Soviet Union is less vulnerable than the United States to sea-fired missile attacks, the

2,500-mile range of the A-2 version of the *Polaris* and the 2,900-mile range of the A-3 (not to mention the projected *Poseidon*) could mean attacks launched from the Irish Sea, Bay of Biscay, Arabian Sea, waters about Iceland, northern Pacific, and north African waters. To defeat the *Polaris* threat the Soviets would have not only to develop a tactical reply but to patrol 2,500 miles from their own coasts.

A possible related application of sea power for the future might involve using ship-based missiles to shoot down incoming missiles, instead of relying wholly on land-based antimissile defenses. This type of system, which has been suggested as a future development of American sea power, might also be used by the Russians—though perhaps less advantageously since more of their frontiers are on land. Conceivably it could involve the positioning of task forces as close to American (or Soviet) launching sites as possible with a view to intercepting missiles in mid-course rather than near their targets. Those not intercepted at sea would then be countered by land-based defenses.

Defeating the Carrier Task Force

Soviet naval officers have devoted far more thought and action to carrier task forces than they have to missile submarines. At least insofar as their long-range plans have demonstrated an ability to detect and overfly such forces, some of their actions have been pertinent to the threat. Yet here again much of the *Polaris*-type thinking is to be found in naval publications. The official Khrushchev line, not yet abandoned, was that large surface vessels were obsolete. The Sokolovsky volume supports the contention that CTF's are highly vulnerable and can be destroyed by a few missiles launched by submarines and aircraft outside CTF defenses.

Earlier Soviet writers were less sanguine. In 1957 D. I. Solovev pointed out that owing to the mobile nature of a task force, attacks could come from an unknown distance and direction; it was his hope that shore-based air forces and fast nuclear-powered submarines would offer a sufficient means of defense, either operating separately or with the aircraft performing reconnaissance for the submarines. I. A. Bykhovsky, writing during the same year, developed the thesis

that Russia's submarines with fast underwater speeds could seek
out enemy task forces, attack them at long range, and follow them
for lengthy periods, and could easily break contact with enemy anti-
submarines forces.[3] Other Soviet naval writers have put their faith
in homing torpedoes with nuclear warheads, fired from either missile cruisers and destroyers, aircraft, or submarines.

The problem of how to neutralize the threat of the carrier task
force presents two aspects: detection and destruction. On the first,
at least, the Soviets have made important gains with their development of very fast nuclear submarines and long-range *Bear* and
Blinder planes and reconnaissance satellites. These craft, which in
combination are able to detect and track American task forces from
above and beneath the ocean's surface, seem likely to rob the carrier
of much of its elusiveness. Earth satellite detection systems presumably have added to Soviet spotting capabilities. There remain
the problems of penetrating task force defenses and delivering a
fatal blow, of course, but on the basis of visible progress it is reasonable to suppose that carriers will become increasingly vulnerable in the foreseeable future.

Promotion of Communism Overseas

The final new mission for the Red navy calls for its assistance in
the spread of communist doctrine and/or Soviet power overseas.
This essentially cold war mission involves both warships and merchant vessels. Warships can be used as a threat, as a medium of
propaganda, or as a link to overseas allies. Since the Soviets employ
trade for political as well as economic purposes, their growing merchant marine is also a primary political and military tool. The commitment of the few Soviet tankers available to the task of supplying
Cuba and other friendly powers overseas with essential oil is an
excellent example of the uses to which the Soviets have put their
growing maritime strength. Indeed the entire Cuban-Soviet trade
relationship, with its barter deals, purchases of Cuban sugar at low
prices, and supply of industrial machinery and parts, appears economically senseless unless viewed in the light of political and
ideological considerations. It is significant that the change in Soviet
cold war tactics and the projection of the Soviet offensive into non-
contiguous and distant areas did not occur until the Soviet naval-

merchant ship buildup had begun to show results. This mounting strength on the seas is an indispensable element of Soviet expansionism.

The general success attending this particular use of sea power has doubtless been highly disappointing to communist theoreticians. Cuba, the lone clear-cut victory for communism in the Western Hemisphere, was something in the nature of an unearned dividend and has proved to be far from subservient. In other areas, nations which have accepted Soviet aid have remained steadily unyielding to communist doctrines and interests. Finally, the Soviet navy cannot act at a great distance to serve its nation's interests in the same way that the Red army could perform in contiguous areas during the Stalin era.

It should be noted that the Soviets have also sought to influence overseas countries in other and complementary ways. Between 1955 and 1968 their military assistance to areas outside the Soviet bloc amounted to $5,510 million, with the United Arab Republic, Indonesia, India, Iraq, Syria, Algeria, Congo (Kinshasa), and Afghanistan the main beneficiaries. At the end of 1967, 14,425 students from developing countries were in attendance at universities in the U.S.S.R. (mainly at Lumumba University in Moscow), East Germany, and Czechoslovakia. The average length of attendance was five years per student. The fact that this number is lower than in previous years may indicate, however, that the educational program has not proved entirely effective as a means of ideological penetration.[4]

WAR CAPABILITIES: SUMMARY

What the Soviet navy capabilities enumerated signify would depend on the type of conflict situation which might arise. It is doubtful that a major war with the Soviet Union and the United States in opposite camps could, under present conditions, be confined to a limited or conventional type. Yet most of the Red navy is better designed for such a war than for a thermonuclear holocaust, and, in fact, all of Russia's four fleets are suited to limited operations rather than to all-out attack or defense.

For operations in the context of a conventional war, the Red navy has important capabilities. In mine warfare its defensive potential is immense, its offensive capacity much smaller. Its minesweeping vessels are probably sufficiently numerous to keep Soviet coastal areas reasonably clear. The lift and support are available for relatively short-range amphibious operations, and the Russians have had considerable experience in carrying out such activities. Naval aviation strength is unknown, but the navy's land-based planes are undoubtedly able to dominate coastal waters. Russian coastal areas almost certainly could be protected from conventional attack by planes and short-range submarines. The surface fleets are everywhere superior to those of adjoining states and, as some Soviet naval writers have suggested, might well provide effective "operational control" in local waters; only with American air and sea power present could the comparison swing heavily against the Russians. In a conventional war the huge submarine fleet would present a major threat to any adversary, though the handicaps facing Soviet undersea craft would be formidable. While an extensive withdrawal of submarines from the Black Sea and Baltic prior to the outbreak of war appears unlikely, the presence in most areas of some Red navy submarines would be too common a phenomenon to serve as a warning of attack; it could be assumed that some submarines— possibly 30 to 60—would be scattered widely along major oceanic trade routes.

Another area of Soviet strength in conventional war is land power, which could be exerted with decisive effect against contiguous countries allied to the West. South Korea in the Far East, Iran in the Middle East, and to a lesser extent the states of Western Europe are all countries whose military weakness vis-à-vis the Soviet Union dictates ultimate dependence on alliance with the United States.

In case of a general war fought with thermonuclear weapons, the picture of Soviet capabilities changes. Defensively the Soviet navy is weak against the two most obvious American threats, the carrier task force and the *Polaris* submarine. A strong defensive asset, however, is the dispersion and protection of its base facilities, especially in the Arctic and Pacific. The greatest counter weapon against the CTF would probably be massed air assault from large numbers of planes attacking at different courses, speeds, and altitudes and employing diverse tactics and weapons in order to complicate the problems of interception and defense. The possibilities of such varied air attacks were demonstrated effectively by the Japanese Kamikazes in the latter months of World War II, especially in the Okinawa campaign (the Japanese, to be sure, knew where American forces were located, an advantage which conceivably might not rest with the Russians). However, the intricate planning involved, as well as the large force requirements, make it exceedingly difficult to mount massed air attacks successfully, particularly if loose and widely spaced cruising formations are adopted by CTF's. All in all, carrier task forces are rather less vulnerable than has often been assumed and could probably survive the more conventional types of submarine and air attack.

So far as the *Polaris* threat is concerned, Soviet leaders have from time to time claimed to have an answer, though they have been far from specific concerning its form and capability, and comments of Soviet navy officers have often evidenced no understanding of the basic problems involved.

If the defensive powers of the Soviet navy in a nuclear war are weak, the same cannot be said of its offensive potential. The threat of nuclear submarines strategically employed against coastal targets is an extremely serious one, whose answer, aside from the counter threat of nuclear retaliation, may not yet have been found. If used to lay nuclear mines, the Soviet submarines might well be able to tie up Atlantic coastal shipping from both the European and American shores of the Atlantic for months.

In evaluating possible Soviet wartime capabilities it is wise to consider not only all available data on current strength but also the fact that the continuing Soviet drive for power on the seas has behind it a great deal of determination and force, has clearly not reached its peak, and is realizing steady qualitative improvement. It is also important to remember the persistence with which the Russians, despite geographic handicaps, have sought the sea. Historically, industrial backwardness and frequent misdirection of naval affairs by army officers have held back the pace of naval development; during periods when these handicaps were inoperative, as was the case during most of Russian history before the Crimean War, the Russian naval record was excellent.

Before closing the subject of strategic capabilities it is appropriate to note the publication in 1968 of Cmdr. Robert W. Herrick's book entitled *Soviet Naval Strategy: Fifty Years of Theory and Practice.* Based on a thorough study of Soviet publications, this volume is one of the few authoritative works available on recent phases of Soviet sea power.

The author concludes that current Soviet naval strategy is deterrent and defensive in concept, and that its every aspect is determined by Communist Party leaders and the army—even to the selection of number and type of weapons. Moreover, it is very difficult to change party directives during the process of administration. Offensive missions appear to be limited to missile strikes against land targets and submarine warfare against shipping. Unable to obtain airplane carriers themselves, Soviet naval leaders attack them as "obsolete" and contend that submarines have wholly replaced them. This is seen as part of a rationalization process in which qualitative inferiority is obscured by sweeping assertions of overall world naval superiority. Commander Herrick predicts that Soviet strategy will remain defensive for the foreseeable future, and will continue to be dominated by army and party men whose views are dictated by budgetary considerations, men who not only do not understand sea power but who furthermore do not believe their navy will be obliged to fight a war. These are men who first select weapons and then determine strategy. In time of war the Soviet navy could scarcely control the seas but might be able to interfere with their use by NATO forces.

This writer does not agree with Commander Herrick's evaluation at all points. It has often been a Soviet tactic to keep the West off balance and reacting to Soviet moves. But many a move which may be defensively conceived from a Soviet viewpoint certainly runs the risk of being considered offensive in nature by the West. Furthermore, some of the more recent Soviet naval moves (see chapter 22) appear to reflect a growing awareness of the meaning of sea power and a willingness to pay the costs involved in attaining it. The major contradiction to this statement is, of course, the persistent fact that the Soviet navy has not acquired as yet the airplane carrier, which the U.S. navy regards as the very bedrock of command of the sea. It is indeed quite possible that the Soviet leaders do not anticipate fighting a naval war; this is a reasonable expectation, since in the interests of avoiding a general war the United States would probably avoid, if at all possible, any showdown with Soviet naval forces.

COMPETITIVE CAPABILITIES
IN A NON-WAR SITUATION

The naval capabilities of the Soviet Union have thus far been evaluated as they might be in a war situation with the United States. Yet such a condition does not look probable in the immediate future. It is therefore also necessary to survey the uses of Soviet sea power from a different standpoint, namely that of a competitor but not an active enemy. The entire course of world history since the 1962 Cuban missile crisis indicates that competitive coexistence between the Soviet Union and the United States is a more likely state of affairs for the 1970s and probably the 1980s than is either a conventional or nuclear war.

For this type of analysis a geographical as well as a functional approach is required. Soviet sea power in 1972 is, in its several forms, at least as widespread as is that of the United States. In one area, the Mediterranean, it operates within a tension situation. In other theaters no immediate threats to peace are visible. Indeed the strategic parameters vary from one area to the next and concern not only military force but alliances, cultural factors, geographic advantages, trade relations, investments, and other factors.

THE INDIAN OCEAN

In no other theater has a recent Soviet naval presence attracted so much attention as in the case of the world's third largest ocean. When Great Britain in January 1968 announced withdrawals of forces "east of Suez" the Soviets apparently believed that a naval vacuum was created in the Indian Ocean and within one month sent a small naval task force into the sea south of Asia. A reader of this history will, of course, realize that this interest was not a matter of the moment. Peter the Great's interests in Madagascar and the Molotov-Ribbentrop conversations of 1940, with the expression by the former of Soviet desires to gain a sphere of influence, will come into mind.

From a historic standpoint the Indian Ocean had never been dominated by a single power until the arrival of the Europeans, led by Vasco da Gama of Portugal. A struggle for hegemony during the sixteenth, seventeenth, and eighteenth centuries among the Portuguese, Dutch, French, and British was finally won by the latter. Thus from the time of the French and Indian War until World War II the Indian Ocean had been virtually a British lake. The withdrawal of British power, largely completed by 1972, left no nation predominant in the area.

Most of the states on the Indian Ocean littoral were weak, underdeveloped, and lacking in internal stability. Australia and South Africa were developed countries with small but efficient naval forces. There was also an Indonesian navy, hopelessly moribund. Indian and Pakistani naval forces existed, as well as an Iranian navy possibly strong enough to keep order within the Persian Gulf. Communist China showed some interest in the Indian Ocean area, especially in Tanzania, but hardly enough naval and economic power to dominate. Economically rich but militarily weak Japan has aided in certain ways, especially in dredging operations in the Malacca Straits. Inasmuch as the United States, the world's strongest sea power, evinced no great or immediate interest, the Indian Ocean must have appeared to the Soviets as a power vacuum into which they could well expand. One of the two principal entrances into the Indian Ocean, the Suez-Red Sea route, was largely dominated by the United Arab Republic, a near satellite. The Straits of Malacca, the best though not the only passage leading from the Indian Ocean into the Pacific, had at one time been controlled by a friendly Indonesian regime. Further, even the Western-oriented Suharto regime which had succeeded Sukarno had claimed the right to control the passage of shipping through the straits.

Because the United States felt itself to be overextended and moreover relied on British domination of the sea lanes south of Asia it had not, prior to 1968, exhibited much military concern with this area. The vast oil interests of American and European companies in an area containing more than half of the world's known oil reserves, and the fact that the Indian Ocean carried more commerce than the North Atlantic, were only dimly recognized. Still the ANZUS, CENTO and SEATO pacts extended some American protection to the region. A tiny American naval contingent of a seaplane tender and two destroyers was stationed in the Persian Gulf at Bahrain. Though the United States never officially admitted their presence *Polaris* submarines cruised in the Indian Ocean carrying missiles that could reach the nuclear installations in Western China as well as cities as distant as Moscow. Satellite communications facilities were maintained in Asmara, Ethiopia, and Northwest Cape in Australia. In case of need Australian and British facilities were open to American use.

Soviet moves in the direction of the Indian Ocean were underway well before the six-day war. Apparently Admiral Kasatanov had them in mind when on Navy Day 1971 he proclaimed, "The flag of Soviet naval forces is today flying in all latitudes even on waters traditionally considered as preserves of the British and American navies."

Despite the handicap of a closed Suez Canal small Soviet naval task forces had reached the Indian Ocean from both the Pacific and Black Sea Fleets. Between 1968 and 1972 Soviet ship days in the Indian Ocean tripled. Ships sent included submarines, escort and destroyer types, auxiliaries and occasionally a cruiser—not antisubmarine types that might logically have been dispatched to watch Polaris submarines. Though replenished by the Soviet system of at-sea supply they received certain port services at friendly harbors within the area. Friendly visits of a showing-the-flag type were made to more than 50 ports in Iraq, India, Somalia, Yemen, Tanzania, and other countries. The Soviet airline Aeroflot also served several routes within the area and transported certain war materials to India during the latter's 1971 war with Pakistan.

Despite the fact that both the United States and the Soviet Union have exhibited a "low profile" in the Indian Ocean, something which looked like a power confrontation developed late in 1971. During the Bangladesh war for independence the Nixon administration chose to support Pakistan while the Soviet Union aided India. The quick Indian victory combined with the well advertised atrocities of Pakistani troops put the United States in an embarrassing position. In December a strong task force headed by the carrier *Enterprise* was sent into the Bay of Bengal with a secondary mission of evacuating Americans from Dacca should this move prove necessary. Within days of the dispatch of this American force two guided missile destroyers, two submarines, and certain other vessels were sent south from Vladivostok. As it happened this transfer of American forces coincided also with the routine arrival of a Soviet relief task force in the Indian Ocean for the purpose of replacing ships ready to leave. The appearance given was therefore that of a strengthening of Soviet naval forces followed by a retirement of the much more powerful American fleet from the scene. Hence, the United States suffered and the Soviet Union greatly gained from the incident.

The episode may have aided the Nixon administration in formulating a new policy. The United States and Great Britain went ahead with the development of small naval facilities at Diego Garcia in the Chagros Archipelago. On December 23, 1971, in an unpublicized executive agreement, the United States took over a small portion of the British base on Bahrain in the Persian Gulf. In other actions the Persian Gulf area was put under the European Command while the jurisdiction of the Seventh Fleet was extended to most of the Indian Ocean. The administration also signified that with the winding down of the Vietnam war task forces would be sent into the Indian Ocean from time to time.

In all probability the present accommodation in the Indian Ocean area is a compromise which will be temporary. It has been estimated that should the United States attempt to maintain a task force in the Indian Ocean a total of 30 ships would have to be programmed in order to maintain ten on station. Given the low-key Soviet presence, plus pressures to cut the Navy's budget and the general feeling that the United States has been overcommitted abroad, such a change does not look likely. Yet the West's interests in the Indian Ocean are very great. Further, the present low-tension situation could change in any of several ways. New radical regimes in such countries as Saudi Arabia, Iran, or Ethiopia, possibly ushered in by a Libyan-type coup, could greatly upset the present balance of power and put American interests in jeopardy. On the reopening of the Suez Canal which would change the distance of the Black Sea from the Indian Ocean from the present 9,000 miles around Africa to 3,000 miles could greatly strengthen Soviet sea power. In any case, the desire of the strongest littoral state, India, to see the Indian Ocean empty of the warships of nations outside the area seems unlikely to be realized.

THE MEDITERRANEAN

The Soviet leaders must view the eastern Mediterranean with a mixture of triumph and frustration. Their naval force in the Mediterranean has been gradually increasing in size and they have established a firmer warm water foothold than was ever true under the tsars. At the same time the costs of their backing of the Arab states are authoritatively estimated at more than eight billion dollars. Efforts either by threat or diplomacy to force the Israelis out of the gains achieved during the six-day war have all failed. Nor has the United States failed to act decisively when such action was necessary to preserve its major interests. Palestine guerillas, though able to gain world headlines by occasional highjacking of planes, have been soundly beaten and lost strength and prestige. At best Soviet actions and reinforcements have saved Egypt from a humiliating defeat and preserved a status quo which has in fact meant the hegemony of Israel. Further, the hoped-for acceptance of communist ideology or of revolutions on the Soviet model have been conspicuous by their absence, and the Suez Canal, gateway to the Indian Ocean, is still closed. As if to add insult to injury a vicious anti-Zionist press campaign within the Soviet Union has boomeranged to the extent that the Soviet Union has found it expedient to permit increased immigration to Israel of its own Jews. Thus Jewish immigration, which in 1970 was about 1,200, jumped to approximately 14,000 for 1971 and 15,650 for the first six months of 1972.

Following the six-day war peace-making efforts by the United Nations were pursued but proved unavailing largely due to Arab refusals to negotiate unless Israel would first evacuate all territories seized by force. When Israel, comfortably in control of boundaries which gave her more military security than ever before, refused this demand, the United Arab Republic, which had in the meantime never demobilized from a war footing and which had profited from a massive influence of Soviet military aid, denounced the United Nations cease-fire and proclaimed a war of attrition.

In taking this step President Nasser probably had in mind ground force and artillery action along the Suez Canal, a form of warfare in which casualties might be fairly even or even favor the Egyptians. But he reckoned without the Israeli air force, which in a series of damaging raids won victories deep within Egypt and thoroughly and rapidly humiliated the Egyptians, demonstrating that the air defenses of the country were all but worthless. To save Egypt from the consequences of its own military folly the Soviets simply took over the air defense of the country. Numerous SAM batteries were constructed and manned by Soviet technicians. Squadrons of Soviet interceptor planes of the latest models were flown in and based on Egyptian soil. Easy and cheap Israeli victories in the air war then ceased to be the order of the day. However, an estimated 20,000 Soviet advisers penetrated many levels of native life and, despite their services, were not liked by the natives. Indeed, in July 1972 the Egyptian government ordered the military advisers to leave.

A peace initiative based on the so-called Rogers Plan was tried in the summer of 1970 and was accepted by the Soviet Union and Egypt. The first step, a cease-fire along the Suez front, was accepted by Israel only on condition that the military status quo be preserved. This was promised by the United States, but violated on a large scale and at once by Russians and Egyptians, a fact reported immediately by Israel but accepted only tardily and reluctantly by an embarrassed State Department. Though there was no immediate resumption of large-scale fighting the United States resumed shipment of certain weapons to Israel. By September 1970 the Suez front could correctly be termed a stalemate. The Soviet Union had been generous with equipment though it had given the Egyptians few weapons for carrying on an offensive.

Following the dying down of conventional warfare the Palestinian guerillas took the center of the Middle East stage. Though they had been relatively ineffective against Israel they tended to receive special consideration in such countries as Jordan, Lebanon, and Syria. Supported by donations, and claiming to be the heroes of the Arab struggle against Israel, they were difficult to deal with by any country harboring them. In the case of Jordan a decisive struggle took place between the guerillas and the regular government of the country. A major crisis developed when the Syrian government (presumably on Soviet advice) sent in a force of tanks to support the guerillas against the Jordanian army. Because this Syrian tank detachment was soundly defeated by a smaller Jordanian force and then retreated into Syria, hostilities did not spread. However, Israeli armor was moved to the border and a reinforced United States Sixth Fleet containing five airplane carriers was dispatched to the eastern Mediterranean, while two American divisions were alerted.

Behind the moves of Arab and Israeli governments lies the power struggle of the world's two strongest nations. Soviet naval forces in the Mediterranean have frequently been more numerous than those of the United States and its allies and at times have included more than 20 submarines. Yet while the Sixth Fleet is stronger in terms of fire-power it is operating under risks of possible threats from numerous Soviet submarines as well as from planes operating from the numerous airfields on the North African coast.

Further, the Middle East situation possesses certain long-range strategic threats. These were succinctly set forth in a bulletin of the Foreign Policy Research Institute authored by Col. William R. Kintner and Robert L. Pfalzgraff.

> Two dangers seem paramount in the current Middle East crisis. First, resumption of war between Israel and Egypt could lead to further Soviet intervention, eventually compelling an American response and the danger of confrontation. Second, the unsettled Arab world will probably continue its drift towards policies more favorable to the Soviet Union if only by virtue of their extreme antagonism to the West.[5]

The authors raise a sobering question. In view of the present large-scale Soviet involvement (150 Mig 21 J planes in Egypt alone, plus personnel) would the Soviet Union tolerate a fourth defeat of the Arab forces?

An extremely bizarre development worked for the interest of Israel when President Anwar Sadat on July 18, 1972, in a dramatic and unexpected gesture, ordered Soviet advisers and military personnel out of the country. To the surprise of many Westerners, the Soviet Union complied, in some instances removing also sophisticated weapons systems. A month after Sadat's request, only a few hundred technical advisers remained in the country, while only two Soviet warships were found in Egyptian ports.

The motives of Sadat in taking this step were not fully spelled out. Yet they are not altogether obscure. On trips to Moscow in February and April 1972, the Egyptian leader had attempted to get offensive weapons necessary for a renewal of war, such as amphibious craft and long-range bombers, to assist in crossing the Suez Canal. The Soviets, however, showed themselves far more interested in continuing a crisis than in openly moving into a war situation which could involve either a direct confrontation with the United States or, more likely, a fourth defeat for their Arab protégés. At any rate, they failed to meet Arab desires. Other factors, such as mutual dislike between Soviet advisers and Egyptian officers, the restlessness of the Moslem religious community, and the psychological need to assert independence, may also have influenced Sadat's decision. He may also have hoped to secure military gifts from other sources and thereby lessen dependence on the Soviet Union.

Regardless of motives, there is little doubt that both the Egyptian and Soviet military postures were significantly weakened. The Soviets courted other Arab states than Egypt but tried to keep relations with Egypt open. They were, however, hurt in the Eastern Mediterranean by the loss of logistic and air support from Egyptian shore facilities. Meantime the Egyptians failed to find a generous protector among other powers. Further, the loss of know-how caused by the departure of Soviet personnel was perhaps as weakening as was the withdrawal of mobile surface-to-air missile batteries and squadrons of Soviet fighting planes.

Not surprisingly, Sadat weakened in his desire to exclude Soviet personnel. Hence, after a few months, at least a portion of the banished personnel returned with the tacit concurrence of Egypt. It is doubtful, however, if there has been any return to June 1972 strength levels. Most marked and earliest in order of return were Soviet naval units to such harbors as Alexandria, Port Said, and Mersa Matruh. By October 1972 shore facilities were reported to be operating at about normal strength.

SOUTHEASTERN ASIA

So far as sea power is concerned, southeastern Asia could hardly be more completely in the hands of the United States. The Soviet supply effort to North Vietnam, partly described in the last chapter, has been carried on with the tacit consent of the United States. Further, when in May 1972 President Nixon decided on a blockade of North Korean ports enforced by minelaying, the Soviet Union did no more than object for the record. No steps were taken to withdraw an invitation to Moscow for a summit meeting a few weeks later.

This tacit acquiescence in an American military action which had been considered for years and deemed too risky by President Johnson's advisers is an indication that American tactics in Vietnam were unnecessarily timid. Neither the Soviet Union nor any other power was in a position to challenge American naval actions in southeastern Asia. Had the mine blockade of 1972 been instituted in 1965 as part of a strategy aimed at victory the saving of American and other lives could well have been large and the country spared the strain of an interminable badly supported war.

Should American power be withdrawn completely from this area, there will very possibly be a power struggle between China and the Soviet Union. The latter may present itself as a successor to the British. On the other hand, the Chinese enjoy the advantage of propinquity. Should American withdrawal appear to be either certain or probable there will inevitably be a shift in position of our present allies as they seek to reach an accommodation with either the Soviets or Chinese. If the impression grows that American withdrawal is the result of a military disaster, then this process of rapprochement will doubtless be expedited.

EUROPE

The present balance in Europe, as between the NATO powers led by the United States and the Soviet Bloc, could well be described as a state of "dynamic equilibrium." Neither group is on top and each faces major problems which in the long run may prove insoluble. Yet the Continent is not standing still and changes are under-way. Finally, the outlines of a possible long-range accommodation may well be present. The recent agreements involving West Germany and countries of the Soviet Bloc could be the beginnings of such a settlement.

To some degree the Soviet Union is on the defensive. The dominance over Rumania, Bulgaria, Czechoslovakia, Hungary, Poland, and East Germany has been difficult to maintain and over a period of time is likely to prove impossible. Nationalism is a powerful force and is essentially denied by the Brezhnev Doctrine. The author has traveled widely in all of the satellite countries but one, and only in Bulgaria did he find a people that genuinely liked the Russians. In this connection, however, it should be obvious that the limiting or discontinuance of news broadcasts from the West gives to the Soviets a wholly unnecessary victory, which makes the maintenance of their system with its illiberal features considerably easier than would otherwise be the case.

The Soviets are also on the defensive as regards Yugoslavia. Not only does the Yugoslav version of communism differ greatly from any other but it possesses many semiliberal features such as freedom of movement, openness to foreign newspapers, partial freedom of the press, support by the West, and a mixed economy. These characteristics make Yugoslavia a relatively attractive example even though the country has sought to protect itself by maintaining technically pro-Soviet foreign relations and a low profile. The death and/or retirement of President Tito could well mean the covert Soviet use of disruptive tactics designed to destroy the precarious unity among the varied groups which comprise this country.

The West's problems in Europe are perhaps more clearly defined than those of the Soviet Union. The German problem which for long was regarded as predominant now appears to be less of an issue since the construction of the Berlin Wall and the economic boom in East Germany. The coexistence of two Germanys, each operating under a different system, has been a fact for nearly three decades. While not ideal, there are few groups passionately dedicated to changing this division, while many neighbors of Germany favor its continuation.

A far more threatening problem is the continued weakening of

NATO. While the French pullout and the construction of an independent *force de frappe* did not end all forms of cooperation, it certainly weakened the system. Again, the democracies of Western Europe have not in the view of many Americans made the military contribution commensurate with their resources and generally strong economies. This situation has therefore tended to place a major emphasis upon the American land forces. It is not that the size of these land forces—generally about five divisions—is decisive in itself. The Warsaw-Pact powers could probably outmatch them. It is the fact that American ground forces are a kind of security guarantee of the nuclear forces being used in case of necessity and despite the certainty of Soviet nuclear retaliation.

Actually the entire strategy of flexible response and a graduated deterrent is in some trouble. John Erickson of Cambridge University, one of the best students of Soviet military publications and author of *The Soviet High Command*, states that the Soviets never believed in a flexible step-by-step response. Instead their military writings emphasize a mass nuclear strike in great depth followed by land action. The Air Transport Command with its 1,700 short-range and medium-range transports, with about 1,500 helicopters on call, and probably 300 Aeroflot planes in reserve, seems very well designed for carrying on such a campaign in Europe.

Even were there a certainty that the Soviets would play the flexible response game other problems would be involved. The fighter bombers of the NATO alliance are at least matched by medium-range Soviet missiles. The use of tactical nuclear weapons in defense would undoubtedly result in widespread devastation, especially in Germany, the most likely battleground. The fact that the Soviet Union now outmatches the United States in nuclear strength raises some doubts as to the reliability of the American deterrent. Yet withdrawal of American land forces would tend to confirm such doubts.

Soviet strategy in Europe, short of war, would seem to have two options. One of these would seek to further disrupt NATO, detach the United States from Europe and emphasize European unity. The end result might well be the Finlandization of Western Europe. A less risky course of action might be the acceptance of the status quo on both sides.

THE PACIFIC

In the general area of the Pacific, as distinguished from south-eastern Asia, the situation from an American viewpoint is relatively good. An approach has been made toward ending the quarter century of mutually bad relations with Communist China. Soviet policy has been less aggressive than in some other areas. To some extent, China and Russia check each other. Our principal allies among the countries of Asia, Japan, Formosa, and South Korea, have been experiencing an economic boom. Australia and New Zealand are both prosperous and loyal. Both South Korea and Formosa presently possess high-grade armed forces. Though Japan has been unwilling to assume the role of policeman, she possesses great and growing economic strength.

While the above are all factors of American strength they are not the only ones. While the Soviet Pacific Fleet is large it is quite hard to deploy effectively. Not all of the Pacific naval bases (Petropav-lovsk for example) have secure rail connections. Moreover these bases are too far north to be close to the centers of Pacific commerce. Further, the vast reaches of the Pacific, far from land-based air power, are not naturally fitted to a navy lacking aircraft carriers. The Pacific would be the theater in which this Soviet weakness would be most grave. Hence, Soviet sea power in the Pacific (aside from submarines) tends to be local sea power. It can be used effectively close to shore but has no special advantages farther at sea.

There are, notwithstanding, several weaknesses in the American strategic position. President Nixon's summit visit to Peking and the surtax on foreign imports decided on in August 1971 have had their costs. The Formosa regime has been alarmed. Japan, formerly the most obedient of American satellites, has been shocked at brusque treatment from Washington and may very possibly decide on new policies of her own devising. The unwillingness or inability of the United States to meet the problem of brushfire wars in Southeast Asia may mean that this tactic will be repeated elsewhere as in Thailand or the Philippines. Finally, not all American allies are thriving. The Philippines, for example, are at the present moment a poor advertisement for the United States, with corruption and misgovernment at a high level. Indonesia, the perennial dropout among developing nations, though free from Sukarno, is struggling with a host of problems.

SEA POWER IN THE WESTERN HEMISPHERE

Essentially there are two phases to sea power in the Western Hemisphere. One is the effort to detect in peace and defeat in war the missile-carrying submarines of the Soviet Union seeking to maintain patrols off the American coast. This is a grim constant fight involving a great use of very advanced weapons and technology. The other phase is the use of sea power in Latin America. In the case of Cuba, the two phases converge and constitute a different strategic problem so far unsolved by the United States.

Though it is quite possible for Soviet submarines to enter the Atlantic from either the North Sea or the Mediterranean, the bulk of long-range Soviet submarines come from the complex of bases in the Arctic around Murmansk. To enter the North Atlantic by this route they are forced to pass through fairly narrow straits in two locations. The sea area between northern Norway and the Arctic ice pack is the first area in which submarines might be observed and, in case of war, attacked, probably by American killer submarines. The second such bottleneck is the sea between Scotland and Iceland, or less likely, between Iceland and Greenland. Here aerial observation planes are apt to detect their passage.

As the submarines turn south other detection devices come into use. Along the Atlantic coast the United States maintains what is known as the Sousos system. The individual mechanisms are underwater mikes or listening devices lying on the bottom of the ocean. Under most conditions detection is successful. Sousos has, for example, informed the navy that most Soviet nuclear submarines avoid provocation by operating outside the normal firing range of possible targets. Other devices either in use or in process of development include CAPTOR, LAMPS, and DIFAR. CAPTOR is a Mark 46 torpedo anchored to the ocean bottom but equipped with mechanical ears and an electronic brain which tells it when to shoot its warhead of TNT. This weapon is within the letter of a treaty though its use might still be regarded as questionable in view of the February 1971 Seabed Treaty in which the United States, the Soviet Union, and Great Britain pledged themselves against using nuclear weapons on the seabed. LAMPS (Low Altitude Multi-Purpose System), a system regarding which the U.S. navy is very hopeful, is a hunting helicopter equipped with sonar and able to destroy enemy submarines at ranges of 25 to 50 miles. DIFAR, a sonobuoy with an electronic brain capable of transmitting information, has been in production since 1969 but is now in trouble as few items produced have met requirements and been acceptable to the U.S. Navy.

Methods of detection along the Atlantic coast of the United States are considered relatively efficient. However, detection means have their limitations and the 52 million square miles over which the Atlantic Fleet's Anti Submarine Warfare Command holds jurisdiction is far too large for complete aerial, or any other type of surveillance with existing weapons. The Soviet submarine threat is regarded with complete soberness and is certain to increase within the foreseeable future. Y class submarines which are the backbone of this threat though not the only types used carry 16 SS-N-6 missiles of one or two megatons explosive power. They are thus about equal to the *Polaris* A-2 type of the United States.

Intelligence reports as to the number of Soviet submarines on station off the coasts of the United States have varied, the highest estimate being eight to 12, a majority being off the Atlantic rather than the Pacific coast. The low estimate is three off the Atlantic coast and one off the Pacific. The threat is steadily growing as the Soviet missile submarine force is expanding rapidly while the last American *Polaris* submarine was completed in 1967. However, due to geographical handicaps mentioned, it is doubtful if the Soviet threat per missile submarine is as great as the American. Like their American counterparts the Soviet missile submarines have replacement crews and appear to be at sea about 60 days. In February 1972 an *H* class submarine (only three 650-mile missiles) became disabled off the coast of Newfoundland and was escorted home by a Soviet task force with the British frigate *Puma* trailing as an observer.

Though the United States has not built *Polaris* submarines for several years it has, as pointed out in the last chapter, taken certain steps to retain its lead. All but ten of the 41 *Polaris* submarines are being refitted to carry the *Poseidon* missile. Thus a typical submarine would still carry only 16 missiles but each missile would contain 10 separate warheads quite capable of reaching as many destinations and overwhelming defensive systems with the multiplicity of missiles. In the projected stage but quite likely to be accepted by even a critical Congress is a new and larger type of submarine, ULMS, about twice the size of the *Polaris* and able to fire missiles from a far greater range.

So far as Latin America is concerned Soviet strategy is basically long range and, with the exception of Cuba, is not primarily keyed to any nuclear threats.[6] It is designed to take advantage of mistakes of omission and commission of the United States in its relations with the republics to the south. These mistakes include at least a decade of deliberate neglect. The Alliance for Progress raised hopes that proved unfulfillable, largely due to the population explosion and to the unwillingness of autocratic regimes to accept reforms. The result has been gradually worsening relations punctuated by occasional explosions of nationalism and anti-Americanism. The seizure without compensation of American-owned companies in Peru and Chile, the voting into power of a Marxist president in Chile, black power movements in the Caribbean states, oftentimes justified complaints over trading and commercial relations, the seizure of American fishing vessels, a right-wing dictatorship in Brazil are all expressions of a basic malaise. All is not well south of the Rio Grande, but this fact is receiving very little recognition in Washington.

The above ills do not, of course, mean that Latin America is ready for a communist takeover. Marxism has, in fact, experienced hard sledding in most of the area. The popular mood is rarely pro-Russian; but it is often anti-American.

Immediately following the 1962 Cuban missile crisis the Soviet Union was extremely cautious. However, it is now pursuing a fairly active policy on a wide front. The policy is normally peaceful though it may involve backing armed struggle. The object is to weaken and neutralize the influence of the United States, to defend Cuba, to establish cordial relations where possible, and in short to use commercial and diplomatic contacts to present the Soviet Union in a favorable light. Although virtually unrecognized a decade ago, at present 13 countries now have diplomatic relations with the U.S.S.R. This has permitted the introduction of many Soviet agents who at times have interfered in the internal affairs of the host countries. Soviet sea power in its many forms is one method for asserting the Soviet presence in areas felt to be important strategically. Though hopeful for an ultimate Soviet-style revolution, the Soviets are sufficiently realistic to know that such a takeover is not immediately in sight.

If there is such a thing in the Western Hemisphere as a flash point that conceivably could trigger a general war, then Cuba is that flash point. Between 1969 and 1971 visits of Soviet ships increased and a submarine tender was frequently found in Cienfuegos Harbor on Cuba's south coast. President Nixon became sufficiently concerned that a Soviet strategic submarine base was in the making, to state that such an effort would be "viewed with the utmost seriousness." He noted that this would be a violation of the 1962 understanding in which the United States undertook not to invade Cuba in return for a Soviet pledge to keep out strategic missiles. The general picture is far from clear as to either the nature of Soviet naval activities or the objectives back of such activities. The Soviet Union might well be quietly presenting a series of quiet fait accomplis to which response could be very difficult. Quiet and unspectacular Soviet-Cuban actions have brought about a situation which could hold greater possible menace for the United States than the land-based missiles which Khrushchev was forced to withdraw in 1962. The developing situation has in the view of a number of military analysts given the coup de grâce to the Monroe Doctrine, effectively ending a 150-year protectorate of the United States over the Western Hemisphere.

To appreciate the potential importance of the Soviet foothold at Cienfuegos on the southern coast of Cuba it is necessary first to note some of the peculiarities of the theater. Geographically Cuba lies in reasonably close proximity to (1) the Panama Canal, (2) Norfolk, Virginia, the main operational carrier base on the Atlantic Coast, (3) Charleston, South Carolina, the main East Coast base for *Polaris* submarines, and (4) Key West, Florida, a major antisubmarine warfare development and training area. For geographical reasons alone it forms an ideal base for submarine surveillance.

Yet it has another and greater value. The sea area between the U.S. Gulf Coast and northern South America is dotted with islands of which Cuba is the most important. Following three centuries of European tutelage these lands successfully revolted against their colonial masters and set up governments in nations that were typically weak, poor and lacking in stability. About the beginning of the twentieth century the United States gained hegemony in the area and became its policeman. However, because no strong enemy was present these forces were of the gunboat variety. The United States was, and is, comparatively open to attack from the south. The submarine detection systems quite capable of monitoring Soviet submarines from Murmansk to Florida have never been set up in the Caribbean and Gulf of Mexico. Furthermore, the island of Cuba itself offers a land barrier against detection by Sousos systems off the East Coast. Hence, submarines would either launch missiles from directly south of Cuba or move into the Gulf of Mexico and—still undetected—lob from close range missiles capable of destroying any city in the United States.

To quote from a study done by the author for the Center for Strategic and International Studies and subsequently published by Praeger:

> The role of Cienfuegos should not be overlooked. The proportion of submarines that can be kept on station under wartime conditions is never very large. Germany, with a thoroughly efficient submarine organization during World War II, was able to keep only about one-third of all submarines on station. The Soviet Union, with a much less efficient submarine service in the Black Sea, kept only one in five on station in a relatively small theater involving short distances. Considering the length of a submarine cruise from, say, Murmansk to the Gulf of Mexico and the possibilities of detection and destruction en route, one submarine in five would probably be a generous estimate. However, should a well-equipped base be available in Cuban waters, this time on station—and hence the effectiveness of the entire submarine effort—could be raised, possibly by a factor of two or more. It is not surprising that the late Congressman Mendell Rivers suggested a forcible American reaction, while a White House statement, after referring indirectly to the 1962 agreement concerning the withdrawal of Soviet missiles from Cuba and the prohibition of strategic weapons system in the hemisphere, warned that the United States would consider a Soviet strategic base in Cuba with "utmost seriousness." Modern Soviet submarines, operating un-

detected in Cuban waters, would offer far more of a threat to the
United States than all the medium-range missiles in Cuba with which
Khrushchev sought to improve Russia's strategic posture.

It is thus apparent that the threat of nuclear submarines in a strategic
bombardment role in the waters south of the United States is a very
real one and is far greater than in those areas from which monitoring is
readily possible. Nonnuclear submarines, operating from Cuban bases,
would also possess a greater potential for destruction of commerce than
would the same number of undersea craft operating in an area in which
monitoring is readily possible. On precisely the same basis, the absence
of passive listening devices in the Gulf of Mexico would permit submarine minelayers to plant clandestine minefields in the shallow Gulf
waters which, like those of the U.S. East Coast but not its West Coast,
are ideal for offensive minelaying. Although the Germans in World War
II did not employ this particular tactic, preferring to torpedo merchant
vessels, the use of a few mines off such cities as Houston, Mobile,
Tampa, and New Orleans and the sowing of mines in passages along
the coast could probably tie up both ship and barge traffic for several
months.

Whether the Soviets envisage all of the above possibilities or are
merely acting out of opportunism is another matter. The speeches of
Admiral Gorshkov quoted in chapter 22 provide one set of clues as
to Soviet intentions. In his 1970 Navy Day speech he declared:

> Soviet Navy ships are constantly on the ocean, including the stomping
> grounds of the NATO strike fleets. The presence of our ships in these
> regions ties the imperialists' hands and deprives them of the oppor-
> tunity freely to interfere in the people's internal affairs.

At least two conclusions emerge from these and other quotations. One
is the possibility of a Soviet bargaining stance. Soviet sea power out of
the Western Hemisphere in exchange for U.S. Sixth Fleet withdrawal
from the Mediterranean would certainly be in the interest of the Soviet
Union but hardly that of the United States. The Western Hemisphere is
for the Soviets an area of opportunity where real Russian interests are
negligible while both countries have major interests in the Middle East.
Khrushchev's suggested tradeoff of American missiles in Turkey for
Soviet missiles in Cuba during the 1962 crisis might form an earlier
parallel.

The last words of Admiral Gorshkov are even more significant. They
indicate a concept of seapower which, while differing obviously from

Admiral Mahan's doctrine of command of the sea, has a great deal of relevance to a cold war situation which neither side cares to see move into a hot war. The Soviet Navy, while clearly inferior at the moment to that of the United States, is quite strong enough to have a cautionary effect on American actions. It serves as a trip wire and inhibitor of offensive action in the same sense that NATO land forces in western Europe play this role on land. Almost any military analyst would agree that the Soviet Army could defeat the NATO forces. Yet such action is more unlikely because of the probable triggering of a nuclear response. In the same way, a sizable Soviet naval presence is felt, probably correctly, to prevent possible American action. Using the Mediterranean as an example, it is at least questionable whether the American landing of troops in Lebanon would have occurred in the face of a Soviet naval task force. One military historian of the six-day war observed that the closer the Sixth Fleet moved to the eastern Mediterranean, the more reasonable and less interventionist the Soviets became. More recently, the Soviets may well believe that the position of their naval forces during the Libyan revolution staved off a possible American intervention favoring King Idris. Still more recently, the 1970 visit of President Nixon to the Sixth Fleet and its movement to the eastern Mediterranean at the time of the Jordanian conflict probably contributed to the strength of Israel, the failure of Syria to carry through a land intervention, and the apparent unwillingness of the Soviets actively to back an Egyptian military solution.

As applied to Cuba, the introduction of a Soviet naval presence, with the probability that increased trade and fishing activity will follow, is, at least on the surface, well within the bounds of military effort and costs for a theater formerly taken for granted by the United States. It also tends to neutralize the American capability for nuclear retaliation. Although it is not in itself a sign of loss of American naval superiority, it certainly indicates a relative decline in strategic position. The rapid aging of American naval forces in contrast with the very rapid construction of a new navy by the Soviets indicates that American naval supremacy can no longer be taken for granted.[7]

The foregoing does not, to be sure, entirely exhaust a strategic survey of the Western Hemisphere. Worthy of at least passing note is Soviet use of patrols by naval surface task forces off the coast of Guinea, apparently to protect against possible Portuguese intervention. Canadian exasperation with the United States over draft dodgers, the Vietnam war, and American investments is also worthy of note. A well advertised trend is the gain in the Soviet nuclear and naval balance, as compared to the United States, and its increase in funds devoted to research and development, a development likely to permit the Soviets to gain technical superiority. Again, the demands to decrease the military budget, the attacks on foreign and military policy, and the tolerance of draft evasion and desertion so common in the United States have no parallel in the Soviet Union. In short, present trends indicate very real doubt as to whether the future will not belong to the Soviet Union rather than to the United States.

Notes to Text

CHAPTER 2

1. Navy Records Society, *The Russian Fleet Under Peter the Great* (probably written by John Deane) (London, n.d.), p. 162.
2. One American attained flag rank under Peter: George Paddon of New York, who previously had served in the British navy. So far as the writer has been able to determine, he was the first person born in what is now the United States to become an admiral in any navy.
3. Figures from different sources are not agreed on the subject of losses. Those cited here are from Serge Terestchenko and Victor Llona, *Pierre le Grand* (Paris, 1931), 2 vols. F. F. Veselago gives the Russian loss as 300 killed and 1,200 wounded, compared to a Swedish loss of 700 of the 900 men engaged. Obviously the Swedes gave a good account of themselves. It is of interest to note that Peter accorded the captured Swedish leader every courtesy and later sent him back to Sweden with a warm letter of appreciation for his ability and courage.
4. The snow was a small square-rigged sailing vessel similar to the brig.
5. England had a naval interest in the Baltic, where she obtained most of her masts and some other maritime products. She intervened from time to time to prevent any one power from acquiring a position that could mean interference with this trade.
6. G. M. Trusov, *Podvodnye lodki v russkom i sovetskom flota* (Submarines in the Russian and Soviet Fleets) (Leningrad, 1963), p. 12.
7. Walter C. Hucul, in his "The Evolution of Russian and Soviet Sea Power, 1853–1953," a Ph.D. dissertation for the University of California (Berkeley, 1954), discusses Peter's interests in the Far East and central Asia and his unrealized plans for Russian expansion in these areas. See also R. J. Kerner, "The Russian Eastward Movement," in *The Urge to the Sea: The Course of Russian History* (Berkeley, Calif., 1926).

CHAPTER 3

1. Nikolai A. Nazikov, *Russian Voyages Around the World* (London, 1945), p. xx.
2. The best and very nearly the only reference on the subject of administration during the period is L. G. Beskrovny, *Russkaia armiia i flot v XVIII veke* (The Russian Army and Navy in the Eighteenth Cenutry) (Moscow, 1958).
3. The term "pram" or "praam" has no exact English equivalent but denotes a flat-bottomed ship with two masts and a pointed stem.

CHAPTER 4

1. Count Grigory Orlov was at this time Catherine's lover as well as her adviser.
2. Soviet writers fail to give the British any credit whatever for the victory at Chesma or even to mention the names of British officers who served there. Both tsarist and Soviet historians tend to regard Chesma as the greatest Russian naval victory of all time.
3. No love was lost between the Russian and foreign flag officers. Elphinstone

in September 1770 had grounded the *Sviatoslav* on a reef near Lemnos during a voyage not ordered by Orlov, and the ship eventually was lost. Orlov later ordered Elphinstone to Kronstadt, where he was courtmartialed for the loss of the ship. Though not convicted he was retired, and shortly thereafter he left Russia. Following a quarrel with Admiral Ylmanov, Admiral Arf also was sent back by Orlov, who then requested that no more foreign officers be sent to the area.

4. Anonymous, "John Blackett and the Russian Navy in 1774," *Mariner's Mirror* (London), July 1955.

5. Jones' service in the Russian navy was controversial from first to last. A remonstrance had been drawn up by British officers in the Russian service when Jones' commission was announced, but it was not handed to Catherine as originally intended; the protesters were partly mollified when Jones was sent to the Black Sea. Jones' position in the Black Sea hierarchy was undermined by the intrigues of others plus his own negative qualities. Finally his enemies used a scandal concerning his deflowering a young Russian girl to get rid of him. Whether he was guilty or framed remains a moot question.

CHAPTER 5

1. A number of terms for ships have been used in this chapter which are not in common usage even in maritime publications. Galleys were low vessels, usually of one deck and propelled by oars, though sailing galleys were not unknown. They carried sizable crews. Because the gunpower of early galleys generally was considered weak, naval architects developed a number of types of coastal vessels which were variants on the original galley. The turumas and hemmemas, small but heavily armed shallow-draft frigates, were the most formidable of these; some of the larger ones were as much as 140 feet in length. The pojama type was somewhat smaller and usually carried two rather than three masts. Udemas were 80 to 90 feet in length and commonly carried guns on deck along the center line of the vessel; thus placed, they could be trained in more than one direction. Gun sloops and gun yawls were about 60 feet long, had crews of 37–55 men, and each carried one gun, usually a 12- or 18-pounder. Still smaller was the gun dinghy, which carried a crew of 24 men and an 18- or 24-pounder built into the hull at the stern. Most of the types mentioned originally were named after Finnish counties. On the whole these types were of limited value, since their shallow draft discouraged carrying much sail and they were too heavy to be rowed in a light breeze. After 1757 the Swedish galley fleet, unlike that of the Russians, was operated by the army rather than the navy. See Gustav Halldin, "Frederik Henrik af Chapman," *American Neptune* (July 1946); and Rear Admiral J. Hagg [Swedish Navy], "Some Peculiar Swedish Coast Defense Ships of the Period 1782–1808," *Mariner's Mirror* (February 1913).

2. Frederick T. Jane, in *The Imperial Russian Navy* (London, 1904), gives the strength of the respective fleets as follows: Swedes—195 ships with 1,124 guns and 14,000 men; Russians—141 ships with 1,412 guns and 18,500 men.

CHAPTER 6

1. This was not as great a compliment as it might appear to be; for a time before their defeat in a series of ship duels with the Americans, the British were notoriously sloppy in their ship construction. The French at that time

customarily built better ships, and the Russian battleships in the North Sea, even though lacking copper bottoms, frequently were speedier than their British counterparts.

2. Yevgeny Viktorovich Tarle, *Tri ekspeditsii russkogo flota* (Three Expeditions of the Russian Fleet) (Moscow, 1956), p. 391.

CHAPTER 7

1. Alexander I had a scholarly side to his character. This probably accounts for his creation, in 1808, of the post of naval historian which was held by several able men during the nineteenth century, perhaps the most outstanding being N. A. Bestuzhev and F. F. Veselago. Several earlier historians had almost been prevented from operating by the unwillingness of bureaucrats to open their archives for any purpose.

2. Quoted in Nikolai A. Bestuzhev, *Opyt istorii rossiiskogo flota* (A Study of the History of the Russian Fleet) (Leningrad, 1961), p. 9.

3. Mikhail Alekseevich Sergeev, *Oborona Petropavlovska na Kamchatke* (Defense of Petropavlovsk-on-the-Kamchatka) (Moscow, 1954).

4. Figures are taken mainly from Nestor Monasterev, *Histoire de la Marine Russe* (Paris, 1932), p. 158.

5. This incident so displeased the tsar that he issued orders that the *Rafail* was to be burned if captured; he declared the vessel unfit to associate with other Russian ships and not worthy to fly the Russian flag. The Russian commander of the *Rafail*, when freed by the Turks, was ordered never to marry lest his breed be perpetuated.

CHAPTER 8

1. The ruler of Prussia in 1853 was the son-in-law of Nicholas, who in 1849 had done Franz Joseph of Austria a favor by suppressing the Hungarian rebellion which threatened to end the Austrian monarchy.

2. Tarle, probably the most reliable of the Soviet historians, sets the British naval strength at 70 battleships, 63 frigates, and 108 steamers; the French at 25 battleships, 48 frigates, and 108[?] steamers; and the Russian at 43 battleships, 48 frigates, and 24 steamers. Yevgeny Viktorovich Tarle, *Krymskaia voina* (The Crimean War) (2nd ed., Moscow, 1950), vol. I, p. 48.

3. Nobel was a man of little education but vast mechanical ability. He arrived in Russia in 1837 and busied himself with steamboats, mines, and other coast-defense developments under contracts with the Russian government. After the war, orders lagged. Nobel's operations eventually went bankrupt and he returned to Sweden.

4. A. M. Zaionchkovsky, *Sbornik oborona Sevastopolia* (Record of the Siege of Sevastopol) (St. Petersburg, 1904), p. 113.

5. During his visit to the Soviet Union in the summer of 1969, the author learned that this shrine was obliterated by German bombardment during the World War II siege of Sevastopol.

6. Sir William L. Clowes, *et al.*, *The Royal Navy: A History* (Boston, 1897–1902), vol. VI, p. 469. The official Russian statement of losses lists 12 sailing battleships, 2 sailing frigates, 5 corvettes and brigs, and 5 steam vessels, and thus is in reasonably close agreement.

7. E. H. Nolan, *History of the War Against Russia* (London, 1857), vol. VI, p. 321.

8. British and Russian accounts of the Battle of Petropavlovsk differ in several

respects. According to Tarle and other Russian authorities, the allies got ashore and seized positions on a hill, whence they were routed by a Russian attack which first employed sharpshooters and then a bayonet charge.

9. This visit in some respects must have been more surprising to the Americans than to the Russians. The Russians had been highly secretive about their shipbuilding, and the American task force, under Adm. David Farragut, was the first to be welcomed at Kronstadt. And a warm welcome it was—ten Russian monitors in line abreast were deployed to meet the visitors. Lavish entertainment and mutual ship inspections followed.

CHAPTER 9

1. Admiral Makarov is the subject of numerous biographies in Russian. Probably the best English language account of his career is Donald W. Mitchell, "Admiral Makarov: Attack! Attack! Attack!" *United States Naval Institute Proceedings*, July 1965.

CHAPTER 10

1. Capt. R. Grant, tr., *Before Port Arthur in a Destroyer: The Personal Diary of a Japanese Naval Officer* (London, 1907), p. 2.
2. *Ibid.*, p. 144.
3. Makarov must have regarded his assignment with inward despair. He wrote, "Oh, to know what to do! Truly our men are in need of everything. They do not know how to walk in the night. Mismanaged and confused, they continue to elbow each other near Port Arthur. Incapable of identifying themselves, they hesitate to return [to port] for fear of being mistaken for Japanese!" B. G. Ostrovsky, *Stephen Osipovich Makarov 1848–1904* (Leningrad, 1951), p. 379.
4. Among the shock troops were General Nogi's two sons. Both were killed in course of the assault.
5. It is one of the ironies of Russian naval history that Makarov, one of the greatest innovators in the history of naval warfare, overlooked a decommissioned submarine which had been shipped to Port Arthur by rail and then forgotten. Had this weapon been used in 1904 Russia conceivably might have had a chance of victory, or at least of achieving a more nearly acceptable outcome. Also ironic is the fact that Makarov, who had conceived the technique of using towed mines in flotilla attacks and designed the world's first regular minelayers, lost his life to a mine.
6. Cmdr. Vladimir Semenoff, *Rasplata* (The Reckoning) (London, 1909), p. 115.

CHAPTER 11

1. A. S. Novikov-Priboi, *The Battle of Tsushima* (London, 1936), p. 85. It should be noted that this particular account was written by a Russian sailor who was a revolutionary, and that when his manuscript was discovered and published long after the Revolution of 1917 it won the Stalin Prize. A number of White Russian naval officers, therefore, have questioned its authenticity.
2. *Ibid.*, p. 85.

CHAPTER 12

1. Capt. Vladimir Semenoff, *The Battle of Tsu-Shima* (London, 1907), p. 77.

CHAPTER 13

1. There are countless printed Soviet accounts of the *Potemkin* episode. The best in English is Richard Hough, *The Potemkin Mutiny* (London, 1960).
2. A. S. Novikov-Priboi, *The Battle of Tsushima* (London, 1936), p. 386.
3. It is perhaps appropriate to remark that Japan's occupation of eastern Siberia after World War I, her exploitation of Manchuria prior to World War II, and the struggle between the United States and the U.S.S.R. over Korea, all serve to bear out Klado's geopolitical views.
4. In the stated displacement figures, the first figure refers to surface tonnage, the second to submerged tonnage.
5. Most of the foregoing discussion is based on an article by Lt. Cmdr. Bernard M. Kassell entitled "Russia's Submarine Development 1850–1918," in *Journal of the American Society of Naval Engineers* (Washington, D.C.), vol. 63, 1951. Kassell's study in turn is based on archives maintained in New York by the Society of Former Officers of the Russian Imperial Navy. These Russian accounts give far less credit to Simon Lake than is claimed by his biography. See Herbert Corey, *Submarine: the Autobiography of Simon Lake* (New York, 1938).

CHAPTER 14

1. Adm. Reinhardt von Scheer, *Germany's High Seas Fleet in the World War* (New York, 1934), p. 20.
2. The foregoing account is based mainly on Rear Adm. B. P. Dudarov, "Aviation in the Baltic Sea, 1912–1917," *Morskiia zapiski* (New York), vol. VI, nos. 1 and 2 (April and July 1948).
3. A study by P. A. Warneck, "The Baltic Straits in the First World War" (*Morskiia zapiski*, vol. X, no. 3, September 1952), indicates that about ten ships purchased for the Baltic Fleet and some 90 allied warships, plus numerous Swedish merchant ships carrying contraband for both sides, passed through the Baltic Straits during three years of war. Obviously, though the straits were dangerous they were not impassable.
4. See Capt. David MacIntyre, "A Forgotten Campaign," *Journal of the Royal United Service Institution* (London), vol. 106, 1961.
5. Official German accounts deny that the *Roon* sustained damage in this encounter.
6. All told, two German torpedo craft had been sunk, and the *Moltke, Thetis,* and two other torpedo boats had been damaged.
7. Kolchak was an 1894 graduate of the naval academy who had spent his earlier years of service in the Far East and in Arctic exploration. At Port Arthur he had commanded first a destroyer and later a battery ashore. After the war he was a leader in the movement for naval reform, especially in the creation of a naval general staff. He also was interested in the possibility of finding a sea route north of Siberia and was instrumental in promoting many exploratory expeditions in the Arctic. Before leaving the Baltic he had organized the defenses of the Gulf of Riga and had made himself an expert in mine warfare. Small, highly ethical, astute, dictatorial, and energetic, Kolchak was a man who aroused fear and respect but hardly love among his subordinates. Later, as supreme commander of the White forces in Siberia during the Civil War, his good qualities as a naval officer were in eclipse and he was a total failure.
8. "Report of Admiral Glennon" in *Annual Report of the Secretary of Navy 1916* (United States Naval Archives, Washington, D.C.), p. 32.

9. The best Russian source on the naval war in the Arctic, and the one mainly used here, is P. A. Warneck, "The Russian North During the First World War," *Morskiia zapiski*, vol. VI, nos. 2–4 (July-December 1948); vol. VII, nos. 1–4 (March-November 1949); vol. VIII, nos. 1–4 (March-December 1950).

CHAPTER 15

1. In an incident similar to that of the American "Four Chaplains" in World War II, an aged priest called Father Antoine blessed the crew of the *Prut* and then went down with the ship rather than enter one of the few lifeboats available.
2. An interesting account of pioneer Russian aviation is by R. D. Layman and Boris V. Drashpil, "Early Russian Shipboard Aviation" in *U.S.N.I.P.*, April 1971.
3. These figures are from Louis Guichard and Dmitri Novik [pseud.], *Sous la Croix de Saint André* (Paris, 1929), p. 253. This book is one of a number written in French by émigré Russian naval officers. Most of the émigré officers in the United States have chosen to write in Russian.

CHAPTER 16

1. The old protected cruiser *Avrora*, a survivor by flight from Tsushima, is now glorified as a floating museum at Leningrad. She can be regarded as the Soviet opposite to the U.S.S. *Constitution* and H.M.S. *Victory*—even though her battle honors are limited to the defeat of the Winter Palace.
2. Nestor Monastérev, *Histoire de la Marine Russe* (Paris, 1932), p. 323.
3. Figures are from V. I. Sapozhnikov, *Podvig baltiitsev v 1918 godu* (The Baltic Fleet Sailors' Heroic Deed in 1918) (Moscow, 1954). The author has not been able to compare them with other sources; they may be excessive.
4. Admiral Shchastny, who played the main role in evacuating the ships, was later executed as a counterrevolutionary. He was summoned to Moscow, ostensibly to be decorated for his achievement, and charged with planning to use his popularity to "embarrass" the Bolsheviks.
5. Named *Avtrail* and *Spartak* while in Red service, the captured vessels became the Estonian *Lennuk* and *Vambola*. After sale in 1933, they became the Peruvian *Almirante Geise* and *Almirante Villar*, respectively.
6. St. Petersburg was renamed Petrograd in 1914 and Leningrad in 1924.
7. An extremely well-researched account of the Kronstadt Mutiny is to be found in Avrich's *Kronstadt 1921*. Estimates of Bolshevik casualties run as high as 10,000 men. One estimate of the defender's losses puts death at 600, wounded at 1,000 and prisoners at 2,500. Several hundred prisoners were shot at once while others were sent to concentration camps (as were some of their families). About 8,000 persons are known to have escaped over the ice to Finland. A few of these became homesick and returned to the Soviet Union where they were liquidated.
8. *Annual Report of the Secretary of Navy, 1916* (United States Naval Archives, Washington, D.C.), pp. 9–10.
9. Rear Admiral R. Lepatier, "La Flotte Wrangel," *Revue Maritime* (Paris), March 1966, affords a detailed account of the experiences of this refugee fleet.
10. Reliable and complete accounts of the action in the White Sea and northern Russia during the Civil War are nonexistent. This section is derived mainly

from partial and scattered British sources and from two White Russian accounts. One of the Russian sources is Nestor Monasterev, *Sur Trois Mers* (Tunis, 1932); the other is an unpublished English translation by George Taube of New York City (formerly Lt. Cmdr. Baron Taube of the imperial Russian navy) of an eye-witness report from a Russian officer active in the northern theater during the civil war.

11. This account of the flotilla action is based mainly on Lt. Cmdr. V. S. Makarov, "Material for a History of the Navy during the Civil War, 1917–1920, Siberia," *Morskiia zapiski* (New York), vol. I, nos. 4 and 5 (September and November 1943). A Soviet account of the same warfare contained in D. I. Kornienko, *Flot nashei rodiny* (Our Homeland's Fleet) (Moscow, 1957), notes that the Volga Flotilla fought 30 battles in 1918 in support of ground forces, and in 1919 aided the Red army by landings, gunfire support, and aircraft-bombing of White ships and bases. After the Volga Flotilla had cleared the Kama River of White ships, it moved to the Volga to assist in the defeat of Denikin. Still later, together with the Caspian Flotilla, it waged a defensive fight against English and White forces at Astrakhan.

12. The foregoing is based largely on archival material generously made available to the author by the Association of Russian Imperial Naval Officers in America.

CHAPTER 17

1. The *Profintern* well may be the most renamed warship in modern naval history. At various times she also bore the names *Klara Zetkin*, *Sovnarkom*, and *Krasny Krym*.

CHAPTER 18

1. For a careful account of naval operations in the Finnish-Soviet Winter War, see the Ph. D. dissertation by Allen F. Chew entitled "The Russo-Finnish War, 1939–1940: The Facts and the Communists' Versions of Soviet Military Operations in Finland" (Georgetown University, Washington, D.C., 1960).

2. *Istoriia Velikoi Otechestvennoi voiny Sovetskogo Soiuza* (Moscow, 1965).

3. Finnish sources credit the Russian Baltic Fleet at the outbreak of the war with 35 destroyers and torpedo boats, 94 submarines (44 more building), and 124 motor torpedo boats and patrol vessels.

4. Vice Adm. Friedrich Ruge, *Der Seekrieg: The German Navy's Story, 1939–1945* (Annapolis, 1957), p. 81.

5. It should be noted that these figures have not been confirmed officially and are at wide variance with Soviet claims.

6. Sr. Lt. Karl von Notbeck, "The Soviet-German Naval War in the Baltic Sea," *Morskiia zapiski*, vols. XVII and XVIII, nos. 49, 50, and 51 (1959 and 1960). This account, unfortunately available only in Russian, is probably the most complete concise source available for the naval war in the Baltic.

7. Vice Adm. Friedrich Ruge, *et al.*, "The Soviet Russians as Opponents at Sea: Analysis of German and Russian Naval Operations in the Second World War," U.S. Office of Naval Intelligence, tr., United States National Archives, Navy Department Section, Washington, D.C. (unpublished manuscript compiled under the direction of Vice Admiral Ruge), vol. I, study 2, p. 88.

8. The soundest Soviet source concerning the siege of Odessa is K. V. Penzin, *Chernomorsky flot v oborone Odessy: 1941 god* (The Black Sea Fleet in the Defense of Odessa: 1941) (Moscow, 1956). This interesting and relatively objective account differs from German accounts mainly in the very large number of people (195,000 troops and 300,000 civilians) it claims were evacuated.

9. Ruge, *op. cit.* n. 7, vol. I, study 2, p. 277.

10. *Ibid.*, p. 230.

CHAPTER 19

1. Adm. A. G. Golovko, in 1960, wrote *Vmeste s flotom* (translation by Peter Broomfield published under the title *With the Red Fleet*, London, 1965), a story of his wartime experiences which faithfully parrots the Party line that the Soviet Union owed victory entirely to its own resources and was not assisted by Great Britain and the United States.

2. See *United States Naval Institute Proceedings* (Annapolis), January 1962, pp. 115–16 fn. This incident occurred on October 11, 1942. The lost Soviet ship was the *L-16*. The Japanese *I-25* reported sinking an American submarine, but no American boat was reported lost at the time, nor could one be located in the area of the sinking.

3. Vice Adm. Sir Ian Campbell and Capt. Donald Macintyre, *The Kola Run: A Record of Arctic Convoys, 1941–45* (London, 1958), p. 127.

4. *Ibid.*, p. 222.

5. The combat operations of this flotilla are recounted in detail in I. I. Loktionov, *Pinskaia i Dneprovskaia flotilii v Velikoi Otechestvennoi voine* (The Pinsk and Dnieper Flotillas in the Great Patriotic War) (Moscow, 1958).

6. For an interesting account of this operation see David Woodward, *The Russians at Sea: A History of the Russian Navy* (New York, 1966), pp. 219–21.

7. Aside from a recent article by Dr. Raymond Garthoff in *United States Naval Institute Proceedings* (May 1966), little has appeared in English regarding Russia's brief participation in the war against Japan. Japanese accounts appear to be all but nonexistent. Besides the official Soviet World War II history (*Istoriia Velikoi Otechestvennoi* . . . , 6 vols. [Moscow, 1965]), the author has made extensive use of a Soviet monograph by Captain Grigory Mikhailovich Gelfond, *Sovetsky flot v voine s Yaponiei* (The Soviet Fleet in the War with Japan) (Moscow, 1958). A popular account appears in Nikolai Alekseevich Pitersky, ed., *Boevoi put Sovetskogo Voenno-morskogo Flota* (Battle Path of the Soviet Navy) (Moscow, 1964).

CHAPTER 20

1. Siegfried Breyer in his excellent *Guide to the Soviet Navy* (p. 145) concludes that in the Baltic the Russians sank 51 enemy vessels but lost 51 submarines. In the Arctic the exchange was 45 sinkings for 25 submarines lost and in the Black Sea 32 sinkings for 34 submarines. Total: 110 submarines sunk and 128 enemy vessels lost.

2. Jürgen Rohwer, *Die Sowjetische U-Boatwaffe in der Ostsee: 1939–1945* (Frankfurt, 1956).

3. These figures are taken from an article on the Soviet Air Force by Jürgen Meister, which appear in the December 1957 issue of *Navy* (London). They are not totally in agreement with those derived from the studies by

Vice Adm. Friedrich Ruge which largely have been used in compiling this section. See Ruge *et al.*, "The Soviet Russians as Opponents at Sea . . ." (unpublished ms., U.S. Office of Naval Intelligence, Washington, D.C., 1955), 4 vols.

4. See Kh. Kh. Kamalov, *Morskaia pekhota v boiakh La Rodinu* (The Naval Infantry in Battles for the Fatherland) (Moscow, 1966).

CHAPTER 21

1. During the 1950s there was an immense output of popular books, pamphlets, and films dealing with the navy. Though most of these were pure propaganda, a few good studies emerged. Several good biographies of major leaders, such as Ushakov, Lazarev, and Nakhimov, appeared; there were also some fairly reliable subject studies.

2. A number of discussions in professional magazines provided valuable data for this discussion of Soviet naval doctrine in the early postwar period. In addition, the author has drawn upon Walter C. Hucul's unpublished Ph.D. dissertation, "The Evolution of Russian and Soviet Sea Power, 1855–1955" (University of California, Berkeley, 1954), and Lt. Cmdr. Sumner Shapiro's paper entitled "The Kremlin Views the Sea" (U.S. Army Institute of Advanced Russian Studies, March 1, 1961).

3. Cmdr. Robert W. Herrick, *Soviet Naval Strategy: Fifty Years of Theory and Practice* (Annapolis, 1968), p. 61.

4. Siegfried Breyer in *Die Seerüstung der Sowjet Union* (Munich, 1964), easily the best and one of the most recent treatments of the present Soviet navy, claims additional flotillas have been established on the Sea of Azov, the Volga, and Lakes Ladoga and Onega.

5. For a fine review of developments in the North Pacific area, see Lt. Cmdr. S. A. Swartztrauber, "Alaska and Siberia: A Strategic Analysis," *Naval Review* (Annapolis), 1965.

6. Building of cruisers of the *Sverdlov* class was discontinued when Khrushchev lost interest in them. One completed vessel, the *Ordzhonikidze*, was sold to Indonesia in September 1963 and renamed *Irian*.

7. Ships of similar types were built for the United States navy after World War II began, but they were disposed of at the end of the war.

8. *Jane's Fighting Ships*, 1970–71.

9. Three excellent discussions of the Soviet submarine force are Cmdr. Claude Huan, "The Soviet Submarine Force," *Naval Review*, 1964; Hanson Baldwin, "The Soviet Submarine Threat," *The Reporter*, September 24, 1964; and J. Labyle-Couhat, "La Marine Soviètique en 1964," *Revue Maritime* (Paris), December 1964.

10. See Cmdr. Sumner Shapiro, "The Soviet Naval Officer," *Naval War College Review* (Newport, R.I.), vol. 18, 1966.

11. See Lt. Col. Frank B. Case, "Red China's Seapower," *Military Review* (Ft. Leavenworth, Kan.), December 1965; and Capt. E. J. Cummings, Jr., "The Chinese Communist Navy," *United States Naval Institute Proceedings*, September 1964.

12. This work is available in official English translation under the title *Military Strategy: Soviet Doctrine and Concepts* (introduction by Raymond L. Garthoff; Air Force Systems Command, tr. [New York, 1963]).

13. For a digest of Soviet views on and criticisms of the Sokolovsky volume, see Georgetown University, Center for Strategic Studies, *Soviet Materials on Military Strategy: Inventory and Analysis for 1963*, Włodzimierz Onacewicz and Robert Dickson Crane, eds. (Washington, D.C., 1964).

CHAPTER 22

1. *Christian Science Monitor*, August 12, 1968.
2. Columbia Pictures Corp., 1966.
3. Paul Ignatius, "The Soviet Navy: We Are Still Ahead," *Vital Speeches of the Day* (New York), June 1, 1968.
4. Much of the material for this account of naval war games is taken from *Time*, February 23, 1968.
5. See *Jane's Fighting Ships*, 1970 (London), p. 74.
6. Leonid Brezhnev, as quoted in *The Reporter*, December 1967.
7. Nasser may have been somewhat misled by the speed with which Israeli pilots completed one mission and returned for another—at a rate at least three times as fast as was deemed practicable for Arab pilots.
8. *Pravda*, April 11, 1968.
9. For an excellent discussion of the logistics involved in the transport of supplies to Vietnam, see Rear Adm. John D. Hays, "Russian Seapower in the Mediterranean," *America* (New York), January 27, 1968.
10. That the same principle applies on land is evident in the effects of the similarly conceived "trip-wire" strategy employed by NATO land forces in western Europe vis-à-vis the Soviet Army.
11. Interview, Dr. Donald W. Mitchell with Secretary of Navy John L. Warner, June 23, 1972.

CHAPTER 23

1. See Raymond L. Garthoff, *Soviet Strategy in the Nuclear Age* (New York, 1958).
2. For recent discussions of minelaying, see Cmdr. C. W. Saar, "Offensive Mining as a Soviet Strategy," *United States Naval Institute Proceedings* (August 1964); and Donald W. Mitchell, "Russian Mine Warfare: The Historical Record," *Journal of the Royal United Service Institution* (London), February 1964.
3. See Izrail Adolfovich Bykhovsky, *Atomnye podvodnye lodki* (Atomic Submarines) (Leningrad, 1957).
4. See Philip L. Gamble, "Soviet Aid and Trade and Its Threat to the Free World," *Naval War College Review* (Newport, R. I.), vol. 21, 1969.
5. William R. Kintner and Robert L. Pfalzgraff, Jr., *Soviet Military Trends: Implications for U.S. Security* (Philadelphia, 1971), p. 14.
6. For a very recent study of the strategic position of Latin America in general, and Cuba in particular, see James D. Theberge (ed.), *Soviet Seapower in the Caribbean: Political and Strategic Implications* (New York, 1972). For Cuba, note particularly the chapters by Carl Gasteyger, Michael MccGwire, and Donald W. Mitchell.
7. Theberge, pp. 34–37.

Bibliographical Notes

See Bibliography for full citations of works mentioned in this section.

CHAPTER 1. Beginnings

Sources which treat Russian naval history before Peter the Great are scanty and no single satisfactory English source is available. Nestor Monasterev's *Histoire de la Marine Russe* contains a rewarding chapter dealing with this period. Edward Gibbon's classic, *The History of the Decline and Fall of the Roman Empire*, offers an account of the attacks on Byzantium, as does Frederick T. Jane's *The Imperial Russian Navy*. Robert J. Kerner's *The Urge to the Sea: The Course of Russian History* is particularly good on the role played by the rivers and by early explorations. Several standard histories of Russia—among others, those by Sir Bernard Pares, Jesse Dunsmore Clarkson, and George Vernadsky—contributed an overall framework for the chapter. Mairin Mitchell's *Maritime History of Russia* was valuable at certain points; so was S. M. Solovev's 29-volume Russian language *History of Russia from the Earliest Times*.

CHAPTER 2. Peter the Great: Father of the
Russian Navy (1689–1725)

This period of Russian naval history is thoroughly documented, though unfortunately the sources are not always in agreement. Among the better Russian-language sources is the 17-volume *Materialy po istorii russkogo flota* (Materials for a History of the Russian Fleet) (Glavnoe arkhivnoe upravlenic), which is a mine of information on the eighteenth century. Other good references are: M. M. Bogoslovsky, *Petr I: Materialy dlia biografii* (Peter the First: Materials for a Biography), 5 vols.; I. I. Golikov, *Dieianiia Petra Velikago* (The Deeds of Peter the Great), 12 vols.; E. V. Tarle, *Russky flot i vneshniaia politika Petra I* (The Russian Navy and the Foreign Policy of Peter I); N. G. Ustrialov, *Istoriia tsarstvovaniia Petra Velikago* (History of the Reign of Peter the Great), 8 vols.; K. G. Zhitkov, *History of the Russian Navy; Petrine Period, 1672–1725*; and L. G. Beskrovny, *Russkaia armiia i flot v XVIII veke* (The Russian Army and Navy in the Eighteenth Century). Beskrovny is far the best writer on naval administration among the Russian writers. An account little known in the United States but first-class in every respect is provided in Volume II of Alfred Stenzel's magnificent five-volume study, *Seekriegsgeschichte in Ihren Wichtigsten Abschnitten mit Berücksichtigung der Seetaktik*.

Excellent English language sources also are numerous. R. C. Anderson's two classics, *Naval Wars in the Levant* and *Naval Wars in the Baltic During the Sailing Ship Epoch: 1522–1850*, contain detailed accounts of Russian naval engagements prior to the Crimean War; these works in most cases have been taken as authority wherever discrepancies appeared in source material. Frederick T. Jane, *The Imperial Russian Navy*, and Nestor Monasterev, *Histoire de la Marine Russe*, were used as sources for this chapter also. Walter C. Hucul's Ph.D. dissertation, "The Evolution of Russian and Soviet Sea Power, 1853–1953," which actually begins with Peter the Great, was consulted. The most recent treatments are David Woodward, *The Russians at Sea: A History of the Russian Navy*, and Oliver Warner, *The Sea and the Sword: The Baltic,*

1630–1945. A somewhat limited but highly informative account published by the Navy Records Society of Great Britain is *The Russian Fleet Under Peter the Great.* Long considered anonymous, this work is now thought to have been written by John Deane, an English captain who served in Peter's navy before 1722. By far the best single-volume biography of Peter is Ian Grey, *Peter the Great: Emperor of All Russia.* Also consulted were Eugene Schuyler, *Peter the Great,* 2 vols.; Serge Terestchenko and Victor Llona, *Pierre le Grand,* 2 vols.; and B. H. Sumner, *Peter the Great and the Emergence of Russia.*

G. M. Trusov's *Podvodnye lodki v russkom i sovetskom flote* (Submarines in the Russian and Soviet Fleets) is the source of the submarine story, as well as of much of the material dealing with submarines in later chapters.

CHAPTER 3. *Successors to Peter (1725–62)*

A few general Russian naval histories are among the better sources for this none-too-well-documented period. Several volumes by the official Russian naval historian, F. F. Veselago, are pertinent here, especially *Kratkaia istoriia russkago flota: 1700–1801* (A Short History of the Russian Navy: 1700–1801). Others are S. I. Elagin, *Istoriia russkago flota* (History of the Russian Fleet), and A. S. Grishinsky and V. P. Nikolsky, eds., *Istoriia russkoi armii i flota* (A History of the Russian Army and Navy). *Materialy po istorii . . .* is an excellent general source. L. G. Beskrovny, *Russkaia voenno-teoreticheskaia mysl* (Concepts of Russian Military Theory), was used here; so were R. C. Anderson's two volumes, which are extremely good sources for detail on battles and naval movements. Alfred Stenzel continues to be good. Jane in English and Monasterev in French also were used. Oliver Warner, *The Sea and the Sword: The Baltic, 1630–1945,* and David Woodward, *The Russians at Sea: A History of the Russian Navy,* are recent additions.

CHAPTER 4. *Catherine the Great: The Turkish Wars*

Most of the references mentioned for chapter 3 also were used in preparing this chapter. In addition, the W. L. Blease biography *Suvorov;* R. N. Mordvinov, *Admiral Ushakov,* published under the auspices of the Soviet Main Archival Administration (Glavnoe arkhivnoe upravlenie); and Samuel E. Morison, *John Paul Jones: A Sailor's Biography,* are worthy of note. E. V. Tarle, one of the better Soviet historians, made a contribution in his *Chesmensky boi i pervaia russkaia ekspeditsiia v Arkhipelag, 1769–1774* (The Battle of Chesma and the First Russian Expedition to the Archipelago . . .).

CHAPTER 5. *Catherine the Great: War with Sweden*

Though this war developed a great deal of naval action, it has been obscured largely by the greater impact of the Napoleonic Wars. It is barely mentioned by Mahan and quite largely overlooked in general histories in English. R. C. Anderson, *Naval Wars in the Baltic During the Sailing Ship Epoch,* is by far the best English source. Jane and Monasterev are other less valuable sources. A comprehensive Russian account may be found in P. Ya. Chichagov, *Voennyia dieistviia rossiiskago flota protiv shvedskago v 1788, 1789, i 1790* (Military Actions of the Russian Fleet Against the Swedish . . .). Stenzel has an excellent 60-page account of this war in Volume IV of his *Seekriegsgeschichte. . . .* Charles G. Lahavary, *L'Admiral Tchitchagoff: Ses memoires et sa vie, 1769–1849,* is a good biography of one of the main characters in this war.

CHAPTER 6. *The Napoleonic Wars (1789–1815)*

The contents of the Russian naval archives have not been released for the years since 1801. Consequently, a definitive Russian naval history based on original documents is impossible beyond that date. Anderson's two volumes continue to be the best English sources for the Napoleonic Wars period; the best foreign language source is Stenzel's Volume IV. Some information is available in Alfred T. Mahan, *The Influence of Sea Power upon the French Revolution and Empire, 1793–1812*, 2 vols., in his *The Life of Nelson*, and in Jane's *The Imperial Russian Navy*. The general naval histories in Russian are better sources, especially those of Veselago and Tarle. Two other valuable works are A. I. Mikhailovsky-Danilevsky, *Istoriia voiny Rossii v tsarstvovanie Imperatora Pavla I v 1799 godu* (The History of Russia's War During the Reign of Emperor Paul I in 1799), and V. B. Bronevsky, *Zapiski Vitse Admirala D. N. Seniavina* (Notes of Vice Admiral D. N. Senyavin), 4 vols. Woodward and Warner cover this period, but only superficially. The general history background was found mainly in the Russian histories by Nicholas V. Riasanovsky and Andrei A. Lobanov-Rostovsky and in A. B. Rodger, *The War of the Second Coalition, 1799–1801: A Strategic Commentary*.

CHAPTER 7. *The Last Years of the Sailing Navy (1815–53)*

This period suffers from its in-between-the-wars character and is not well covered either in English or Russian. Anderson continues to be the best authority on naval battles. S. F. Ogorodnikov, *Istorichesky obzor razvitiia i deiatelnosti Morskago Ministerstva za sto let ego sushchestvovaniia: 1802–1902* (A Historical Review of the Development and Activities of the Naval Ministry During the Hundred Years of Its Existence . . .), is a good source on the internal history of the navy, and was used in compiling this and the two following chapters. Several of the volumes by F. F. Veselago were helpful; Hucul, Woodward, and Monasterev, as well as the general Russian naval histories, also were used. An extensive bibliography exists in both Russian and English concerning Russian explorations during the nineteenth century. This was not fully utilized because the topic is necessarily treated only briefly in a general history such as this. Probably the best account of the Battle of Navarino is in the book of that title by C. M. Woodhouse, published in 1965.

CHAPTER 8. *The Crimean War and Its Lessons (1853–77)*

Although books dealing with the Crimean War are numerous, unfortunately there is no single first-class one-volume treatment in English. E. H. Nolan's eight-volume *History of the War Against Russia* contains a great deal of detail but is rare and also difficult to use. British works edited by Alfred C. Dewar and David Bonner-Smith are of an official character and contain little analysis. Previously cited works by Stenzel (Volume V), Monasterev, Jane, and Hucul contain some useful information. Also worthy of note are the brief treatment of Sinope in R. C. Anderson, *Naval Wars in the Levant*; Rear Adm. Adolphus Slade, *Turkey and the Crimean War*; and the predominantly nonmilitary accounts by Vernon J. Puryear and Harold Temperley. Russian accounts, both better and more numerous, include E. V. Tarle, *Nakhimov*; the biography of Kornilov in A. Zhandr, *Materialy dlia istorii oborony Sevastopolia i dlia biografii V. A. Kornilova* (Materials for a History of the Defense of Sevastopol and for a Biography of Vice Admiral Kornilov); the fine two-volume *Krymskaia voina* (The Crimean War) by E. V. Tarle; E. I. Totleben (Todtleben), *Opisanie oborony Sevastopolia* (Description of the Defense of Sevastopol); I. P. Ziugenkov, *Morskoi flot Rossii v Krymskoi voine* (Russia's Fleet in the Crimean War); and works listed in the bibliography by Nikolai Fedorovich Dubrovin, Daniil Iosifovich Kornienko, F. F. Veselago, and Andrei Medardovich Zaionchkovsky. For the period of development following the Crimean War the documentation is far less complete; however, mention should be made of several of the Russian general naval histories, including Monasterev, Jane, and Ogorodnikov, the Hucul dissertation, and Woodward. The Russian naval magazine *Morskoi sbornik* started publication in 1848 and is a must reference for anyone researching Russian naval history after 1850, though its coverage does include some events prior to that date.

CHAPTER 9. *Naval Development (1877–1904)*

Documentation for this period is generally unimpressive, and more is to be found in magazines and annuals than in books. The two most useful annuals are *Jane's Fightng Ships* and *Brassey's Naval Annual*. Among periodicals two stand out: *Morskiia zapiski*, published by the Association of Russian Imperial Naval Officers in America (New York), covers the entire period of Russian naval history but is particularly good for the late nineteenth and early twentieth centuries; *Morskoi sbornik*, published in Leningrad, also was most useful. Among the numerous biographies of Makarov, the one by B. G. Ostrovsky and the account in the Russian Military Encyclopedia (*Voennaia entsiklopediia*) were most helpful. Other sources consulted were Hucul, Ogorodnikov, and the frequently cited *The Imperial Russian Navy* by Frederick T. Jane; in fact, Jane's data concerning ships, shore establishments, and personnel are probably the best in any single source for the entire period.

CHAPTERS 10, 11, and 12. *Russo-Japanese War: Life and Death of the Pacific Fleet; Voyage to Disaster;* and *The Battle of Tsushima*

Though neither the Russians nor the Japanese have released their official records of the Russo-Japanese War, there is no lack of good material on the subject. Comparatively little from the Japanese side has been published, but most of the more informative Russian works have been translated into English. Among the best sources, mention should be made of Cmdr. (later Capt.) Vladimir Semenoff's trilogy, *Rasplata (The Reckoning), The Battle of Tsu-Shima,* and *The Price of Blood;* Nicholas Klado, *The Russian Navy in the Russo-Japanese War* and *The Battle of the Sea of Japan;* Alexei S. Novikov-Priboi, *The Battle of Tsushima;* Eugene S. Politovsky, *From Libau to Tsushima;* Richard Hough, *The Fleet That Had to Die;* J. N. Westwood, *Witnesses to Tsushima;* Lt. Serge Terestchenko, *La Guerre Navale Russo-Japonnaise;* A. Stetchine, *La Guerre Russo-Japonnaise;* Frank Theiss, *The Voyage of Forgotten Men;* Maurice Larrouy, *Tsar et mikados: la bataille de Tsoushime,* collection entitled "Russo-Japanese War" in the U.S. Navy Department Library; Stenzel, Volume V; Herbert W. Wilson's excellent account in *Battleships in Action;* and various articles appearing in *Morskoi sbornik, Morskiia zapiski, Brassey's Naval Annual, Marine Rundschau* (Frankfurt), *United States Naval Institute Proceedings* (Annapolis), and other naval journals. Several previously unused accounts were made available to the author through the kindness of the Association of Russian Imperial Naval Officers in America.

CHAPTER 13. *Between Wars (1905–14)*

The period between wars never has received definitive study, though some treatment is available in general Russian naval histories, and in Woodward's history, the Hucul dissertation, standard naval publications, and the New York archives of the Association of Russian Imperial Naval Officers in America. All of these sources were used in compiling this chapter.

CHAPTERS 14 and 15. *World War I: Baltic, Pacific, and Arctic* and *World War I: Black Sea*

Until recently no first-rate source existed in English dealing with the Russian Navy in World War I. The publication in English of René Gregor's *The Russian Fleet in the First World War, 1914–17* in Great Britain has partly filled this gap. By far the best single work in Russian is a 1964 Soviet publication, *Flot v Pervoi Mirovoi voine*, edited by N. B. Pavlovich. Several excellent German sources are available, especially the volumes put out by the German naval archives dealing with activities in the Baltic and Black seas. Other sources are H. Graf, *The Russian Navy in War and Revolution from 1914 up to 1918*; Woodward's history; Nestor Monasterev, *La Marina Russa durante la Guerra Mondiale, 1914–1917*, and his general naval history and two lesser works, *Dans la Mer Noire* and *Sur Trois Mers*; M. A. Petrov, *Podgotovka Rossii k Mirovoi voine po more* (Russia's Preparedness at Sea for the World War); Hucul's dissertation; Henry Newbolt, *Naval Operations (World War I)*; D. Fedotoff White, *Survival Through War and Revolution in Russia*; and numerous articles in English, American, German, French, and Russian naval publications. The author also is grateful for the assistance of many former officers of the Russian Imperial Navy now resident in the United States. The availability of unpublished personal accounts from their archives has added substantially to these two chapters as well as to several other chapters of this volume.

CHAPTER 16. *Revolution, Intervention, and Civil War*

The best general source for the military and political history of the Soviet Union between 1917 and 1922 continues to be William H. Chamberlin, *The Russian Revolution, 1917–1921*. Soviet sources, however, are extremely numerous. Among those used were A. S. Bubnov, *et al.*, eds., *Grazhdanskaia voina; 1918–1921* (The Civil War . . .); A. P. Lukin, *Flot: Russkie moriaki vo vremia Velikoi voiny i revoliutsii* (The Navy: Russian Sailors During the Great War and the Revolution); and monographs by N. F. Izmailov and V. I. Sapozhnikov. John Erickson, *The Soviet High Command: A Military-Political History, 1918–1941*, yielded some important material. Writings by White Russian émigré officers published either in Paris or New York proved another valuable resource. Paul Avrich's *Kronstadt 1921* provided a definitive treatment of a limited topic. *Morskiia zapiski* and the New York archives of the Association of Russian Imperial Naval Officers in America probably were the most valuable combined source for naval history of the period. D. Fedotoff White's autobiography was useful if limited. H. Graf, *The Russian Navy in War and Revolution . . .*, was valuable for its coverage of the Baltic in 1917–18. Serge Terestchenko and L. Guichard, *Sous la Croix de Saint André*, is the source of the story of Admiral Shchastnyi's great feat and his subsequent execution, two episodes which Soviet writers commonly misrepresent. The British intervention is well covered in a number of volumes, perhaps the best being Geoffrey Benett, *Cowan's War: The Story of British Naval Operations in the Baltic, 1918–1920*. Richard Luckett's *The White Generals: An Account of the White Movement and the Russian Civil War* provides a good evaluation of the principal leaders involved and particularly of Admiral Kolchak. For reasons mentioned in the text of the chapter, it is unlikely that a complete and thoroughly reliable account of the naval history of this period ever will be written.

CHAPTER 17. *Rise of the Red Navy (1922–40)*

Because Soviet authorities are exceedingly close-mouthed concerning the first portion of the period covered in this chapter, reliable Russian sources are limited almost exclusively to *Morskoi sbornik*. *The Soviet Navy*, Cmdr. M. G. Saunders, ed., furnishes some additional information, as do a few of the Russian naval histories. John Erickson's study entitled *The Soviet High Command: A Military-Political History, 1918–1941* was of considerable value; so were the standard Western language naval annuals. Most other sources are scattered, limited in scope, and often unreliable.

CHAPTERS 18, 19, and 20. *World War II*

Unfortunately, the vast amount of naval writing of the Soviets since World War II does not contain a single scholarly and complete general history of the naval war that is comparable to the works of Adm. Samuel E. Morison in the United States or Capt. S. W. Roskill in Great Britain. The six-volume, 4,000-page, official Soviet World War II history (*Istoriia Velikoi Otechestvennoi voiny Sovetskogo Soiuza*), the last volume of which appeared in 1965, contains a great deal of information but also leaves much in obscurity. Not written by naval men, it tends to deal in generalities and at the same time to emphasize heroic individual performances, omits figures of Soviet losses, and asserts implausible and even impossible enemy losses. Some of these shortcomings are remedied in a recently published work edited by Adm. N. A. Pitersky, *Boevoi put Sovetskogo Voenno-morskogo Flota* (Battle Path of the Soviet Navy) which the author consulted in its German edition, *Die Sowjet-Flotte im Zweiten Weltkrieg*. More than 30 naval officers assisted in the preparation of this work, which is the first comprehensive Soviet account of the naval war. While it is a popular, propagandist presentation which exaggerates enemy losses and ignores Soviet failures, much can be learned from this volume.

So far as the total Soviet role in World War II is concerned, there are a number of good works. Possibly the best English language treatment is Alexander Werth's *Russia at War: 1941–1945*. Also good is Albert Seaton's *The Russo-German War, 1941–45*. Adm. I. S. Isakov's *The Red Fleet in the Second World War* was found to be almost worthless as history, but there are a number of reasonably good Soviet monographs—mostly in Russian—dealing with specific battles or campaigns. Among them may be mentioned Ivan I. Loktionov's two accounts of river flotillas on the Danube, the Pinsk, and the Dnieper; A. N. Mushnikov's accounts of the fighting for Leningrad and Vyborg; Capt. Grigory M. Gelfond, *Sovetsky flot v voine s Yaponiei* (The Soviet Fleet in the War with Japan); and Konstantin Vasilevich Penzin's story of the siege of Odessa.

These chapters are based largely on German sources, especially the works of Vice Adm. Friedrich Ruge (*Der Seekrieg . . .*), Adm. Otto Groos (*Was Jeder vom Seekrieg wissen Muss*), Jürgen Rohwer (*Die Sowjetische U-Boatwaffe in der Ostsee . . .*), and Jürgen Meister (*Die Seekrieg im Osteuropäischen Gewässern*). Two excellent monographs by former Russian Imperial Navy officers, published in *Morskiia zapiski*, were used by the author: Lt. Karl von Notbeck, "Soviet-German War on the Baltic Sea, 1941–45," was especially informative; also useful was P. A. Warneck's account of the Black Sea fighting. While a few good British and American sources are available dealing with special topics, a comprehensive English language account of the Soviet Navy in World War II has yet to be written. On the article level, Donald W. Mitchell, "The Soviets versus the Germans at Sea, 1941–45," *Journal of the Royal United Service Institution* (August 1968), may be noted. Cmdr. M. G. Saunders, ed., *The Soviet Navy*, is of some value; David Woodward's *The Russians at Sea . . .* is lively and readable but incomplete in its coverage. Raymond Garthoff's article on Soviet participation in the Pacific War in the *United States Naval Institute Proceedings* is particularly good. Even allowing for the fact that Soviet naval participation was less than impressive, this is probably the most inadequately reported phase of World War II.

CHAPTER 21. *The Fight for Sea Power*

This chapter is based almost wholly on contemporary naval works in Russian, English, German, and French. Articles dealing with various phases of the Soviet drive for sea power also have appeared with fair frequency in American, British, and French serial publications. Saunders, Woodward, and Hucul were used here to a minor degree. By far the best single volume dealing with the period is *Die Seerüstung der Sowjet Union* by Siegfried Breyer. Works dealing with general strategy by Thomas W. Wolfe, Anthony E. Sokol, H. S. Dinerstein, Bernard Brodie, and Raymond Garthoff were of some value in preparing this chapter and chapter 22.

CHAPTER 22. *The Achievement of Sea Power (1962–72)*

The sources for this chapter, all current newspaper and periodicals, were combined with background knowledge gained by the author in his studies of naval affairs in general, and by his first-hand observations in the Soviet Union and elsewhere in Europe and Asia.

CHAPTER 23. *Strategic Capabilities of Soviet Sea Power*

Most of this chapter is an analysis based on the author's eighteen years of research in the field of Russian sea power. Other contemporary analyses were consulted at certain points. These included Siegfried Breyer's *Guide to the Soviet Navy*, Fairhall's *Russian Sea Power*, Theberge's *Soviet Seapower in the Caribbean*, Eller's *The Soviet Naval Challenge*, Kintner and Pfalzgraff's *Soviet Military Trends*, and the excellent study on the Indian Ocean done by the Center for Strategic and International Studies of Georgetown University.

Bibliography

BOOKS AND MANUSCRIPTS

IN ENGLISH (*including translations*):

Agar, Capt. Augustus, *Footprints in the Sea*. London, 1959.

Anderson, R. C., *Naval Wars in the Baltic During the Sailing Ship Epoch: 1522–1850*. London, 1910.

———, *Naval Wars in the Levant*. Princeton, 1952.

Armstrong, Terence, *The Russians in the Arctic: Aspects of Soviet Exploration and Exploitation of the Far North*. London, 1958.

Avrich, Paul, *Kronstadt 1921*. Princeton, 1970.

Bacon, Reginald H., *The Life of Lord Fisher of Kilverstone*. Garden City, New York, 1929.

Baldwin, Hanson W., *The Great Arms Race*. New York, 1958.

Baxter, James Phinney, III. *The Introduction of the Ironclad Warship*. Cambridge, Mass., 1933.

Bennett, Geoffrey, *Cowan's War: The Story of British Naval Operations in the Baltic, 1918–1920*. London, 1964.

Bishop, Reginald, *Ships and Sailors of the Red Navy*. London, 1944.

Blease, Walter L., *Suvorov*. London, 1920.

Boles, Cmdr. Sheldon S., "Why Soviet Naval Power? The Role of the Soviet Navy in General War." Air University thesis 1708, Class of 1960. Maxwell Field, Alabama.

Bonner-Smith, David, ed., *Russian War 1856: Baltic*. London, 1944.

———, and A. C. Dewar, eds., *Russian War 1854: Baltic and Black Sea*. London, 1943.

Breyer, Siegfried, *Guide to the Soviet Navy*. Lt. Comdr. M. W. Henley, R. N., ret., tr. Annapolis, 1970.

Broomfield, Peter, *With the Red Fleet: The War Memoirs of Admiral Arseni Golovko*. London, 1965.

Bunyan, James, *Intervention, Civil War, and Communism in Russia 1918*. Baltimore, 1936.

Burrell, R. M., and Alvin J. Cottrell, eds., *The Indian Ocean: A Conference Report*. Center for Strategic and International Studies. Washington, 1971.

Campbell, Vice Adm. Sir Ian, and Capt. Donald Macintyre, *The Kola Run: A Record of Arctic Convoys, 1941–45*. London, 1958.

Chalmers, W. S., *The Life and Letters of David, Earl Beatty*. London, 1951.

Chamberlin, William H., *The Russian Revolution, 1917–1921.* 2 vols. New York, 1935.

Chew, Allen F., "The Russo-Finnish War, 1939–1940: The Facts and the Communists' Versions of Soviet Military Operations in Finland." Ph.D. dissertation, Georgetown University. Washington, 1960.

Clarkson, Jesse Dunsmore, *A History of Russia*, New York, 1961.

Clowes, Sir William L., Sir Clement Markham, Capt. A. T. Mahan, H. W. Wilson, Theodore Roosevelt, and E. Fraser, *The Royal Navy: A History.* 7 vols. Boston, 1897–1902.

Coates, William P. and Zelda K., *Armed Intervention in Russia, 1918–1922.* London, 1935.

Collingwood, G. L. N., *Life of Vice Admiral Lord Collingwood.* London, 1829.

Corbett, Sir Julian, *Naval Operations (World War I).* 3 vols. New York, 1920.

Corey, Herbert, *Submarine: The Autobiography of Simon Lake.* New York, 1938.

Cottrell, Alvin, ed., *Symposium on National Strategy in a Decade of Change.* Airlie House, 1971.

Cowie, Capt. J. S., *Mines, Minelayers, and Minelaying.* London, 1949.

Cressey, George, *How Strong Is Russia? A Geographical Appraisal.* Syracuse, 1954.

Curtis, John S., *The Russian Army Under Nicholas I.* Durham, N. C., 1965.

Dawson, Capt. Lionel, *Sound of the Guns; Being an Account of the Wars and Services of Sir Walter Cowan.* Oxford, 1949.

Debenham, Frank, ed., *The Voyages of Captain Bellingshausen to the Antarctic Sea, 1819–1821.* 2 vols. London, 1945. Hakluyt Society New Series, vols. 91, 92.

Dewar, Alfred C., ed., *Russian War, 1855: Black Sea.* London, 1945.

Dinerstein, H. S., *War and the Soviet Union: Nuclear Weapons and the Revolution in Soviet Military and Political Thinking.* New York, 1962.

Dix, Lt. C. C., *The World's Navies in the Boxer Rebellion (China 1900).* London, 1905.

Dominique, Maroger, ed., *The Memoirs of Catherine the Great.* New York, 1957.

Domville-Fife, Charles W., *Submarines and Seapower.* London, 1919.

Donin, George, *Navarin.* New York, 1927.

Dugan, James, *The Great Mutiny.* New York, 1965.

Edwards, Kenneth, *We Dive at Dawn.* London, 1939.

Eller, Rear Admiral Ernest M., *The Soviet Naval Challenge.* New York, 1971.

Ellis, C. H., *The British Intervention in Transcaspia, 1918–1919.* Berkeley, 1963.

Erickson, John, *The Soviet High Command: A Military-Political History, 1918–1941.* New York, 1962.

Fairhall, David, *Russian Sea Power.* Boston, 1971.

Falk, Edwin A., *Togo and the Rise of Japanese Seapower.* New York, 1956.

Fayle, C. Ernest, *Seaborne Trade.* Vol. III, *The Period of Unrestricted Submarine Warfare.* New York, 1924.

Fleming, Peter, *The Fate of Admiral Kolchak.* New York, 1963.

Foltz, Charles S., *Surgeon of the Sea: The Adventurous Life of Surgeon*

Jonathan N. Foltz in the Days of Wooden Ships and Iron Men. New York, 1931.

Footman, David, *Civil War in Russia.* New York, 1961.

———, ed., *St. Anthony's Papers No. 6: Soviet Affairs No. 2.* London, 1959.

Garthoff, Raymond L., *The Soviet Image of Future War.* Washington, 1959.

———, *Soviet Doctrine.* Santa Monica, 1953.

———, *The Soviet Military Policy: A Historical Analysis.* New York, 1966.

———, *Soviet Strategy in the Nuclear Age.* New York, 1958.

Golder, F. A., *Bering's Voyages.* New York, 1922.

———, *Russian Expansion in the Pacific, 1641–1859.* Cleveland, 1914.

Golovin, N., *The Problem of the Pacific in the Twentieth Century.* London, 1922.

Golovko, Adm. A. G., *With the Red Fleet: The War Memoirs of the Late Admiral Arseni G. Golovko.* Peter Bromfield, tr. London, 1965.

Gooch, G. P., *Catherine the Great and Other Studies.* New York, 1954.

Graf, H., *The Russian Navy in War and Revolution from 1914 up to 1918.* Munich, 1923.

Graham, Gerald S., *The Politics of Naval Supremacy: Studies in British Maritime Ascendancy.* Cambridge, 1965.

Grant, Capt. R., tr., *Before Port Arthur in a Destroyer: The Personal Diary of a Japanese Naval Officer.* London, 1907.

Gregor, René, *The Russian Fleet in the First World War, 1914–17.* Ian Allen, ed., Liverpool, 1972.

Grey, Edward, *Twenty-five Years, 1892–1916.* London, 1951.

Grey, Ian, *Catherine the Great: Autocrat and Empress of All Russia.* Philadelphia, 1962.

———, *Peter the Great: Emperor of All Russia.* Philadelphia, 1962.

Halsey, Francis W., *The Literary Digest History of the World War.* New York, 1915.

Harcave, Sidney S., *First Blood: The Russian Revolution of 1905.* New York, 1964.

Heath, Adm. Sir Leopold G., *Letters from the Black Sea During the Crimean War, 1854–55.* London, 1897.

Herrick, Cmdr. Robert W., *Soviet Naval Strategy: Fifty Years of Theory and Practice.* Annapolis, 1968.

Higgins, Trumbull, *Hitler and Russia. The Third Reich in a Two Front War.* New York, 1966.

Horelick, Arnold L., and Myron Rush, *Strategic Thinking and Soviet Foreign Policy.* Chicago, 1966.

Hough, Richard, *The Fleet That Had to Die.* New York, 1958.

———, *The Potemkin Mutiny.* London, 1960.

Hucul, Walter C., "The Evolution of Russian and Soviet Sea Power, 1855–1955." Ph.D. dissertation, University of California, Berkeley, 1954.

Isakov, Adm. I. S., *The Red Fleet in the Second World War.* New York, 1947.

James, Robert R., *Gallipoli.* London, 1965.

Jane, Frederick T., *Heresies of Seapower.* London, 1906.

———, *The Imperial Russian Navy.* London, 1904.

Jones, John Paul, *Life and Battles of John Paul Jones, the Greatest Naval Hero of Modern Times.* Janette Tylor, ed. Boston, 1855.

Kaus, Gina, *Catherine: The Portrait of an Empress*. New York, 1935.

Kerner, Robert J., *The Urge to the Sea: The Course of Russian History*. Berkeley, 1926.

Kintner, William R., and Robert L. Pfalzgraff, Jr., *Soviet Military Trends: Implications for U.S. Security*. Philadelphia, 1971.

Kintner, William R., and Harriet F. Scott, *The Nuclear Revolution in Soviet Military Affairs*. Norman, Oklahoma, 1968.

Klado, Nicholas, *The Battle of the Sea of Japan*. London, 1906.

————, *The Russian Navy in the Russo-Japanese War*. London, 1905.

Kolkowicz, Roman, *The Soviet Military and the Communist Party*. Princeton, 1967.

Kotzebue, Otto, *A Voyage of Discovery into the South Sea and Bering Straits, 1815–1818*. 3 vols. London, 1821.

Kruzhenstern, Adam J., *Voyage Around the World in the Years 1803, 1804, 1805, 1806*. 2 vols. London, 1813.

Lake, Simon, *The Submarine in War and Peace: Its Development and Its Possibilities*. Philadelphia, 1918.

Lantzeff, G. V., *Siberia in the Seventeenth Century*. Berkeley, 1943.

Lensen, George A., *Russia's Japan Expedition of 1852 to 1855*. Gainesville, Fla., 1955.

Lisiansky, Urey, *A Voyage Around the World in the Years 1803–4–5 and 6*. London, 1814.

Lobanov-Rostovsky, Andrei A., *Russia and Europe, 1789–1825*. Durham, N.C., 1947.

Longworth, Philip, *The Art of Victory: The Life and Achievements of Field Marshal Suvorov, 1729–1800*. New York, 1965.

Lorenz, Lincoln, *The Admiral and the Empress*. New York, 1954.

Luckett, Richard, *The White Generals: An Account of the White Movement and the Russian Civil War*. New York, 1971.

Lundin, L., *Finland in the Second World War*. Bloomington, Ind., 1957.

Mackintosh, Malcolm, *Juggernaut: A History of the Soviet Armed Forces*. New York, 1967.

Madariaga, Isabel de, *Britain, Russia, and the Armed Neutrality of 1780: Sir James Harris's Mission to St. Petersburg During the American Revolution*. London, 1962.

Mahan, Alfred T., *The Influence of Sea Power upon the French Revolution and Empire, 1793–1812*. 2 vols. Boston, 1892.

————, *The Life of Nelson: The Embodiment of the Sea Power of Great Britain*. Harmondsworth, Mx., England; New York, 1942.

Marder, Arthur, *Fear God and Dread Nought*. 3 vols. London, 1952, 1965 (two volumes published to date).

Maurice, Frederick, *Lessons of Allied Cooperation: Naval, Military, and Air*. London, 1942.

Mitchell, Mairin, *Maritime History of Russia*. London, 1949.

Morison, Samuel E., *History of U.S. Naval Operations in World War II*. Vol. I, *The Battle of the Atlantic, September 1939–May 1943*. Vol. X, *The Atlantic Battle Won, May 1943–May 1945*. Boston, 1947.

————, *John Paul Jones: A Sailor's Biography*. Boston, 1959.

Mottley, J., *The History of the Life of Peter I, Emperor of Russia*. 3 vols. London, 1739.

Navy Records Society, Vol. 19: *Letters and Papers of Admiral of the Fleet Sir Thomas Byam Martin*. London, 1941.

———, Vol. 101: *A Memoir of James Trevenen*. London, n.d.

———, Vol. 18: *The Russian Fleet Under Peter the Great*. London, n.d. (Probably written by John Deane before 1722.)

Nazikov, Nikolai A., *Russian Voyages Around the World*. London, 1945.

Newbolt, Henry, *Naval Operations (World War I)*. Vols. IV-V. New York, 1920.

Nolan, E. H., *History of the War Against Russia*. 8 vols. London, 1857.

Novikov-Priboi, Alexei S., *The Battle of Tsushima*. London, 1936.

O'Ballance, Edgar, *The Red Army of China*. New York, 1963.

Ogasawara, Vice Adm. Nagayo, *Life of Admiral Togo*. Tokyo, 1934.

Oldenbourg, Zoé, *Catherine the Great*. New York, 1965.

Onacewicz, Włodzimierz, and Robert Dickson Crane, eds., *Soviet Materials on Military Strategy: Inventory and Analysis for 1963*. Georgetown University, Center for Strategic Studies.

Pares, Sir Bernard, *A History of Russia*. 4th ed. London, 1955.

Peltier, Adm. M. A., *Soviet Encounter*. London, 1955.

Politovsky, Eugene S., *From Libau to Tsushima*. New York, 1906.

Possony, Stefan T., *A Century of Conflict*. Chicago, 1953.

Puryear, Vernon J., *England, Russia, and the Straits Question, 1844–56*. Berkeley, 1931.

Ravenstein, E. G., *The Russians on the Amur*. London, 1861.

Reed, Edward James, *Letters from Russia in 1875*. London, 1876.

Riasanovsky, Nicholas V., *A History of Russia*. New York, 1963.

Rodger, A. B., *The War of the Second Coalition, 1799–1801: A Strategic Commentary*. Oxford, 1964.

Roskill, S. W., *The Strategy of Seapower*. London, 1962.

———, *The War at Sea, 1939–1945*. 3 vols. London, 1954–61.

Ruge, Vice Adm. Friedrich, *Der Seekrieg: The German Navy's Story, 1939–1945*. Annapolis, 1957.

———, et al., "The Soviet Russians as Opponents at Sea: Analysis of German and Russian Naval Operations in the Second World War." 4 vols. This is an unclassified, typewritten manuscript of 1,200 pages written for the U.S. Army in 1955 by a team of German naval experts headed by Vice Admiral Ruge, and later translated by the U.S. Office of Naval Intelligence, Washington, D.C.

Saunders, Cmdr. M. G., ed., *The Soviet Navy*. New York, 1958.

Scheer, Vice Adm. Reinhardt von, *Germany's High Seas Fleet in the World War*. New York, 1934.

Schmitt, Bernadotte E., *The Coming of War, 1914*. New York, 1930.

Schofield, Vice Adm. Brian B., *The Russian Convoys*. London, 1964.

Schuyler, Eugene, *Peter the Great*. 2 vols. London, 1884.

Scott, Percy, *Fifty Years in the Royal Navy*. London, 1919.

Seaton, Albert, *The Russo-German War: 1941–45*. New York, 1971.

Semenoff, Capt. Vladimir, *The Battle of Tsu-Shima*. London, 1907.

———, *The Price of Blood*. London, 1910.

———, *Rasplata (The Reckoning)*. London, 1909.

Shapiro, Lt. Cmdr. Sumner, "The Kremlin Views the Sea." Paper written in the Foreign Area Specialized Training Program (Russian), U.S. Army Institute of Advanced Russian Studies, March 1, 1961.

Slade, Rear Adm. Adolphus, *Turkey and the Crimean War*. London, 1867.

Sleeman, C. W., *Torpedoes and Torpedo Warfare*. Portsmouth, England, 1880.

Smirnov, M. I., "Admiral Kolchak." *SEER*, vol. II (January, 1933), 373–387.

Smith, C. Jay, *The Russian Struggle for Power, 1914–1917: A Study of Foreign Policy During the First World War*. New York, 1956.

Sokol, Anthony E., *Seapower in the Nuclear Age*. Washington, 1961.

Sokolovsky, Marshal V. D., ed., *Military Strategy: Soviet Doctrine and Concepts*. Introduction by Raymond L. Garthoff. Translated by Air Force Systems Command. New York, 1963.

Soloveytchik, George, *Potemkin: Soldier, Statesman, Lover, Consort of Catherine of Russia*. New York, 1947.

Springhall, D. F., *The Soviet Navy and Its Fight Against Fascism*. London, 1943.

Steer, Lt. A. P., *The "Novik" and the Part She Played in the Russo-Japanese War, 1904*. London, 1913.

Sueter, Cmdr. Murray F., *The Evolution of the Submarine Boat, Mine, and Torpedo from the Sixteenth Century to the Present Time*. Portsmouth, England, 1907.

Sumner, B. H., *Peter the Great and the Emergence of Russia*. London, 1950.

———, *Peter the Great and the Ottoman Empire*. Oxford, 1949.

Takaev, Grigori, *Soviet Imperialism*. London, 1954.

Tanner, V., *The Winter War*. New York, 1955.

Taracouzio, T. A., *The Soviets in the Arctic*. New York, 1938.

Temperley, Harold, *England and the Near East: The Crimea*. London, 1936.

Theberge, James D., ed., *Soviet Seapower in the Caribbean: Political and Strategic Implications*. New York, 1972.

Theiss, Frank, *The Voyage of Forgotten Men*. Indianapolis, 1937.

Thomson, Gladys S., *Catherine the Great and the Expansion of Russia*. London, 1950.

The Times, London, *The Times Documentary History of the War*, vols. 3, 4, 7, & 11. 11 vols. London, 1917–1920.

Togo, Kichitaro, *The Naval Battles of the Russo-Japanese War*. J. Takakusu, tr. Tokyo, 1907.

Tupper, Harman, *To the Great Ocean: Siberia and the Trans-Siberian Railway*. Boston, 1965.

Ullmann, R. H., *British Intervention in Russia, November 1917 to February 1920: A Study in the Making of Foreign Policy*. Oxford, 1960.

Vernadsky, George, *History of Russia*, Vol. I: *Ancient Russia*. Introduction by Michael Karpovich. New Haven, 1929.

Von Tschischwitz, Lt. Gen., *The Army and Navy During the Conquest of the Baltic Islands in October 1917*. U.S. Army, Command and General Staff School, Ft. Leavenworth, Kan., 1933.

Voyetekhov, Boris, *The Last Days of Sevastopol*. New York, 1943.

Warner, Oliver, *The Sea and the Sword: The Baltic, 1630–1945*. New York, 1965.

Werth, Alexander, *Russia at War: 1941–1945*. London, 1964.

Westwood, J. N., *Witnesses to Tsushima*. Tallahassee, Fla., 1970.

White, D. Fedotoff, *Survival Through War and Revolution in Russia*. Philadelphia, 1939.

White, John A., *The Diplomacy of the Russo-Japanese War*. Princeton, 1964.

Wilson, Herbert W., *Battleships in Action*. 2 vols. Boston, 1926.

Wolfe, Thomas W., *Soviet Strategy at the Crossroads*. New York, 1965.

Woodhouse, C. M., *The Battle of Navarino*. London, 1965.

Woodward, David, *The Russians at Sea: A History of the Russian Navy*. New York, 1966.

IN OTHER LANGUAGES:

Achkasov, V. I., *Krasnoznamenny Baltiisky flot v Velikoi Otechestvennoi voine* (The Red Banner Baltic Fleet in the Great Patriotic War). Moscow, 1957.

Azarov, Vice Adm. Ilia Ilich, *Osazhdennaia Odessa* (Odessa under Siege). Moscow, 1962: 2d ed., 1966.

Barbashin, I. P., et al., *Bitva za Leningrad, 1941–1944* (Battle for Leningrad, 1941–1944). S. P. Platonov, ed. Moscow, 1964.

Bekker, Cajus, *Ostsee: Deutsches Schicksal 1944–1945*. (The Baltic: Germany's Fate 1944–1945). Oldenburg, 1959.

Beskrovny, L. G., *Russkaia armiia i flot v XVIII veke* (The Russian Army and Navy in the Eighteenth Century). Moscow, 1958.

———, ed., *Russkaia voenno-teoreticheskaia mysl XIX i nachala XX vekov* (Concepts of Russian Military Theory of the Nineteenth and Early Twentieth Centuries). Moscow, 1960.

Bestuzhev, Nikolai Aleksandrovich, *Opyt istorii rossiiskogo flota* (A Study of the History of the Russian Fleet). Leningrad, 1961.

Billevich, B. V., *Voenno-morskoe delo* (Naval Affairs). 2nd ed., Moscow, 1935.

Bogoslovsky, Mikhail Mikhailovich, *Petr I: materialy dlia biografii* (Peter I: Materials for a Biography). 5 vols. Moscow, 1940–48.

Boiko, F. F., *Tsitadel Chernomoria* (Black Sea Citadel). Moscow, 1963.

Breyer, Siegfried, *Die Seerüstung der Sowjet Union* (The Build-up of Soviet Seapower). Munich, 1964.

Bronevsky, V. B., *Zapiski morskago ofitsera v prodolzhenii kompanii na Sredizemnom more pod nachalstvom Vitse Admirala D. N. Seniavina* (Notes of a Navy Officer During the Campaign in the Mediterranean Sea Under the Command of Vice Admiral D. N. Seniavin). St. Petersburg, 1818–19.

Bubnov, A. S., S. S. Kamenev, and R. P. Eideman, eds., *Grazhdanskaia voina: 1918–1921* (The Civil War: 1918–1921). 3 vols. Moscow, 1928.

Bykhovsky, Izrail Adolfovich, *Atomnye podvodnye lodki* (Atomic Submarines). Leningrad, 1957.

Celona, Toti, *La Russia sul mare* (Russia on the Sea). Milan, 1968.

Chernyshev, V. F., *Nadvodnye korabli v sovremennoi voine* (Surface Warships in Modern Warfare). Moscow, 1945.

Chichagov, P. Ya., *Voennyia dieistviia rossiiskago flota protiv shvedskago v 1788, 1789 i 1790* (Military Actions of the Russian Fleet Against the Swedish in 1788, 1789 and 1790). St. Petersburg, 1826.

Danilov, Yuri, *La Russie dans la Guerre Mondiale* (Russia in the World War). Paris, 1927.

Delpeuch, Maurice, *La Navigation sous-marine à travers les siècles* (Submarine Navigation down through the Centuries). Paris, 1902.

Dubrovin, Nikolai Fedorovich, *Istoriia Krymskoi voiny i oborony Sevastopolia* (History of the Crimean War and the Defense of Sevastopol). 3 vols. St. Petersburg, 1900.

———, *Trekhsot-soroka-deviati dnevnaia zashchita Sevastopolia* (The 349-Day Defense of Sevastopol). St. Petersburg, 1872.

Egorev, Vsevolod, *Operatsii Vladivostokskikh v Russko-Yaponskoi voine: 1904–1905* (Operations of the Vladivostok Squadron in the Russo-Japanese War: 1904–1905). Moscow, 1939.

Elagin, S. I., *Istoriia russkago flota* (History of the Russian Fleet). St. Petersburg, 1875.

Firle, Rudolph, Heinrich Rollman, and Ernst von Gagern, *Der Kreig in der Ostsee.* (The War in the Baltic). 3 vols. Berlin and Frankfurt, 1921–67.

Gelfond, Capt. Grigory Mikhailovich, *Sovetsky flot v voine s Yaponiei* (The Soviet Fleet in the War with Japan). Moscow, 1958.

Giese, Fritz E., *Kleine Geschichte der Deutschen Flotte* (Little History of the German Navy). Berlin, 1965.

Glavnoe arkhivnoe upravlenie MVD SSSR. Tsentralny gosudarstvenny arkhiv Voenno-morskogo Flota. Institut istorii Akademii Nauk SSSR. *Materialy po istorii russkogo flota. Russkie flotovodtsy.* (Materials for a History of the Russian Fleet. Russian Naval Leaders); R. N. Mordvinov, ed., *Admiral Ushakov* (Admiral Ushakov); A. A. Samarov, ed., *P. S. Nakhimov: Dokumenty i materialy* (P. S. Nakhimov: Documents and Materials); V. S. Shlomin, ed., *S. O. Makarov: Dokumenty* (S. O. Makarov: Documents). Moscow, 19—.

Golikov, Ivan Ivanovich, *Dieianiia Petra Volikago mudrogo preobrazitelia Rossii* (The Deeds of Peter the Great, the Wise Reformer of Russia). 12 vols. Moscow, 1788–89.

Golovachev, Viktor Filippovich, *Istoriia Sevastopolia kak russkago porta* (History of Sevastopol as a Russian Port). St. Petersburg, 1872.

Gordeev, I., *Krasny morskoi flot* (The Red Navy). Moscow, 1925.

Grechaniuk, N., et al., *Baltiisky flot: Istorichesky ocherk* (The Baltic Fleet: A Historical Sketch). Moscow, 1960.

Grishinsky, A. S., and V. P. Nikolsky, eds., *Istoriia russkoi armii i flota* (A History of the Russian Army and Navy). 15 vols. Moscow, 1911—.

Groos, Adm. Otto, *Der Seekrieg* (The Sea War). Berlin, 1943.

———, *Was Jeder vom Seekrieg Wissen Muss* (What Everyone Must Know of Naval War). Berlin, 1940.

Guichard, Louis, and Dmitri Novik (pseud.), *Sous la Croix de Saint André* (Under the St. Andrew Cross). Paris, 1929.

Iagling, Boris, et al., *Severny flot v Velikoi Otechestvennoi voine* (The Northern Fleet in the Great Patriotic War). Moscow, 1949.

Istoriia russkoi armii i flota v epokhe Petra Velikago (History of the Russian Army and Navy in the Period of Peter the Great). Moscow, 1911.

Istoriia Velikoi Otechestvennoi voiny Sovetskogo Soiuza (History of the Great Patriotic War of the Soviet Union). 6 vols. Moscow, 1965.

618 Bibliography

Izmailov, N. F., *Baltiisky flot v oktiabrskie dni* (The Baltic Fleet During the October Days). Moscow, 1957.

Kamalov, Kh. Kh., *Morskaia pekhota v boiakh la Rodinu* (The Naval Infantry in Battles for the Fatherland). Moscow, 1966.

Kirin, Iosif Danilovich, *Chernomorsky flot v bitve za Kavkaz* (The Black Sea Fleet in the Battle for the Caucasus). Moscow, 1958.

Klado, Nikolai Lavrentevich, *Ocherki Mirovoi voiny* (Essays on the World War). Petrograd, 1915.

——, *Osnovy sovremennago voenno-morskago dela: Populiarnyia soobshcheniia, chitannyia v 1900–1901* (Fundamentals of Modern Naval Affairs: Reports Widely Read in 1900–1901). St. Petersburg, 1901.

Kolbasev, Sergei A., *Voenno-morskoi flot* (Naval Fleet). Leningrad, 1926.

Kondratev, N. D., *Sovetsky Voenno-morskoi flot* (The Soviet Navy). Moscow, 1957.

Kononov, Rear Adm. Ivan Anatolevich, *Puti k Golgofie russkago flota: Istorichesky ocherk i morskie razskazy* (The Russian Fleet's Paths to Golgotha: A Historical Sketch and Sea Stories). New York, 1961.

Kornatovsky, N. A., *Borba za krasnyi Petrograd 1919* (The Fight for Red Petrograd, 1919). Moscow, 1958.

Kornienko, Daniil Iosifovich, *Flot nashei rodiny* (Our Homeland's Fleet). Moscow, 1957.

——, *Geroicheskaia oborona Sevastopolia v Krymskoi voine 1853–1856 godov* (The Heroic Defense of Sevastopol During the Crimean War Years 1853–1856). Moscow, 1954.

——, *SSSR—Velikaia morskaia derzhava* (The USSR—A Great Sea Power). Moscow, 1950.

——, and N. Milgram, *Voenno-morskoi flot Sovetskoi sotsialisticheskoi derzhavy* (The Navy of the Soviet Socialist State). Moscow, 1949.

Lahavary, Charles G., ed., *L'Admiral Tchitchagoff: Ses mémoires et sa vie, 1769–1849* (Admiral Tchitchagoff: His Memories and His Life, 1769–1849). Leipzig, 1862.

Larrouy, Maurice, *Tzars et Mikados: La bataille de Tsoushima* (Tzars and Mikados: The Battle of Tsushima). Paris, 1935.

Loktionov, Ivan Ilich, *Dunaiskaia flotiliia v Velikoi Otechestvennoi voine* (The Danube Flotilla in the Great Patriotic War). Moscow, 1962.

——, *Pinskaia i Dneprovskaia flotilii v Velikoi Otechestvennoi voine* (The Pinsk and Dnieper Flotillas in the Great Patriotic War). Moscow, 1958.

Lorey, Hermann, *Der Krieg in den Turkischen Gewässern* (The War in Turkish Waters). 2 vols. Berlin and Frankfurt, 1928–38.

Makovsky, Aleksandr Alekseevich, and Boris Mikhailovich Radchenko, *Kaspiiskaia Krasnoznamennaia: Istorichesky ocherk* (The Red Banner Caspian Fleet: A Historical Sketch). Moscow, 1961.

Markov, I. I., *Kerchensko-Feodosiiskaia desantnaia operatsiia* (The Kerch-Feodosiya Landing Operation). Moscow, 1956.

Matveev, Aleksandr Ivanovich, *V boiakh za Moonzund* (In the Battles for Moonsund). Moscow, 1957.

Mauten, Vice Adm. G. von, *Der Krieg zur See: 1914–1918* (The War at Sea, 1914–1918). Berlin, 1921.

Meister, Jürgen, *Die Seekrieg im Osteuropäischen Gewässern* (The Sea War in East European Waters). Munich, 1958.

Mikhailovsky-Danilevsky, A. I., *Istoriia voiny Rossii v tsarstvovanie Imperatora Pavla I v 1799 godu* (The History of Russia's War During the Reign of Paul I in 1799). St. Petersburg, 1852.

Miliutin, Count Dmitrii Alekseevich, *Istoriia voiny 1799 goda mechdu Rossiei i Frantsiei v tsarstvovanie imperatora Pavla I* (A History of the War of 1799 between Russia and France During the Reign of Emperor Paul I). 2nd ed. 3 vols. St. Petersburg, 1857. Vol. I, pt. 1, written by A. I. Mikhailovsky-Danilevsky.

Moiseev, S. P., *Spisok korablei russkogo parovogo i bronenosnogo flota, s 1861 po 1917 g.* (List of Vessels in the Russian Steam and Armored Fleet from 1861 to 1917). Moscow, 1948.

Monasterev, Nestor, *Histoire de la Marine Russe* (History of the Russian Navy). Paris, 1932.

————, *La Marina Russa durante la Guerra Mondiale, 1914–1917* (The Russian Navy During the World War, 1914–1917). Florence, 1934.

————, *Sur Trois Mers* (On Three Seas). Tunis, 1932.

————, *Vom Untergang der Zarenflotten* (The Downfall of the Tsarist Navy). Berlin, 1930.

————, and Lieutenant Serge Terestchenko [Dmitrii Novik], *Dans la Mer Noire* (In the Black Sea). Paris, 1927.

Mordvinov, R. N., *Volzhskaia voennaia flotiliia v grazhdanskoi voine, 1918–1920* (The Volga Naval Flotilla in the Civil War, 1918–1920). Moscow, 1952.

Mushnikov, A. N., *Baltiitsy v boiakh za Leningrad 1941–1944* (Baltic Fleet Sailors in the Battles for Leningrad, 1941–1944). Moscow, 1955.

————, *V boiakh za Vyborg: Petrozavodsk* (In the Battles for Vyborg: Petrozavodsk). Moscow, 1961.

Naida, Sergei Fedorovich, *Revoliutsionnoe dvizhenie v tsarskom flote, 1825–1917* (Revolutionary Movement in the Tsarist Fleet: 1825–1917). Moscow, 1948.

Nevsky, N. A., *Voenno-morskoi flot* (The Navy). Moscow, 1959.

Novikov, Nikolai, *Operatsii flota protiv berega po Chernom more v 1914–1917 gg.* (Operations of the Fleet Against the Black Sea Coast During 1914–1917). Moscow, 1917.

Ogorodnikov, S. F., *Istorichesky obzor razvitiia i deiatelnosti Morskago Ministerstva za sto let ego sushchestvovaniia: 1802–1902* (A Historical Review of the Devolopment and Activities of the Naval Ministry During the Hundred Years of Its Existence: 1802–1902). St. Petersburg, 1902.

Ostrovsky, B. G., *Stepan Osipovich Makarov, 1848–1904*. Leningrad, 1951.

Padalka, G., *Krasnoznamennyi Baltiisky flot v Velikoi Otechestvennoi voine* (The Red Banner Baltic Fleet in the Great Patriotic War). Moscow, 1949.

Pavlov, D. V., *Leningrad v blokade* (Leningrad in the Blockade). Moscow, 1959.

Pavlovich, N. B., *Flot v Pervoi Mirovoi voine* (The Navy in the First World War). Moscow, 1964.

Penzin, Konstantin Vasilevich *Chernomorsky flot v oborone Odessy: 1941 god* (The Black Sea Fleet in the Defense of Odessa: 1941). Moscow, 1956.

Petrov, M. A., *Obzor glavneishikh kampanii i srazhenii parovogo flota v sviazi s evoliutsei voenno-morskogo iskusstva* (Review of the Major Campaigns and Battles of the Steam-powered Fleet in Connection with the Evolution of Naval Strategy). Leningrad, 1927.

———, *Podgotovka Rossii k Mirovoi voine po more* (Russia's Preparedness at Sea for the World War). Moscow, 1926.

Pickert, W., *Vom Kuban Brückenkopf bis Sevastopol* (From the Kuban Bridgehead to Sevastopol). Heidelberg, 1965.

Pitersky, Nikolai Alekseevich, ed., *Boevoi put Sovetskogo Voenno-morskogo Flota* (Battle Path of the Soviet Navy). Moscow, 1964. In German: *Die Sowjet-Flotte im Zweiten Weltkrieg*. Oldenburg, 1966.

Pukhov, A. S., *Baltiisky flot na zashchite Petrograda, 1919 g.* (The Baltic Fleet at the Defense of Petrograd, 1919). Moscow, 1958.

Rohwer, Jürgen, *Das Deutsche Bild der Russischen und Sowjetischen Marine* (The German Picture of the Russian and Soviet Navies). Frankfurt, 1962.

———, *Die Sowjetische U-Boatwaffe in der Ostsee: 1939–1945* (Soviet Submarine Warfare in the Baltic, 1939–1945). Frankfurt, 1956.

Rumiantsev, N. M., *Razgrom vraga v Zapoliare 1949–1944 gg.* (The Rout of the Enemy in the Sub-Polar Region, 1941–1944). Moscow, 1963.

Rybkin, E., *Voina i politika* (War and Politics). Moscow, 1959.

Sapozhnikov, V. I., *Podvig baltiitsev v 1918 godu* (The Baltic Fleet Sailors' Heroic Deed in 1918). Moscow, 1954.

Sergeev, Mikhail Alekseevich, *Oborona Petropavlovska na Kamchatke* (Defense of Petropavlovsk-on-the-Kamchatka). Moscow, 1954.

Sobolev, A. A., *Krasny flot v grazhdanskoi voine: 1918–1920* (The Red Fleet in the Civil War: 1918–1920). Leningrad, 1926.

Sokolov, A. V., and E. T. Kushnarev, *Tri krugosvetnykh plavaniia M. P. Lazareva* (M. P. Lazarev's Three Round-the-World Voyages). Moscow, 1951.

Stenzel, Alfred, *Seekriegsgeschichte in Ihren Wichtigsten Abschnitten mit Berücksichtigung der Seetaktik* (History of Naval Warfare). 5 vols. Hanover and Leipzig, 1907–11.

Stepanov, M. A., et al., eds., *Deistviia Voenno-morskogo flota v Velikoi Otechestvennoi voine* (Operations of the Navy in the Great Patriotic War). Moscow, 1956.

Stetchine, A., *La Guerre Russo-Japonnaise* (The Russo-Japanese War). Paris, 1913.

Svinin, Pavel R., *Vospominaniia flota Pavla Bunina* (Memoirs of Pavel Bunin's Fleet). St. Petersburg, 1819.

Tarle, Yevgeny Viktorovich, *Chesmensky boi i pervaia russkaia ekspeditsiia v Arkhipelag, 1769–1774* (The Battle of Chesma and the First Russian Expedition to the Archipelago, 1769–1774). Moscow and Leningrad, 1945.

———, *Krymskaia voina* (The Crimean War). 2 vols. Moscow, 1945; 2nd ed., 1950.

———, *Nakhimov*. Moscow, 1942.

——, *Russky flot i vneshniaia politika Petra I* (The Russian Navy and the Foreign Policy of Peter I). Moscow, 1949.

——, *Severnaia voina i shvedskoe nashestvie na Rossiiu* (The Northern War and the Swedish Invasion of Russia). Moscow, 1958.

——, *Tri ekspeditsii russkogo flota* (Three Expeditions of the Russian Fleet). Moscow, 1956.

Terestchenko, Lt. Serge, *La Guerro Navale Russo-Japonnaise* (The Russo-Japanese Naval War). Paris, 1930.

——, and Victor Llona, *Pierre le Grand* (Peter the Great). 2 vols. Paris, 1931.

——, and L. Guichard, *Sous la Croix de St. André* (Under St. Andrew's Cross). Paris, 1929.

Timirev, Sergei N., *Vospominaniia morskogo ofitsera: Baltiisky flot vo vremia voiny i revoliutsii, 1914–1918* (Memoirs of a Naval Officer: The Baltic Fleet During the War and Revolution, 1914–1918). New York, 1961.

Tomashevich, A. V., *Podvodnye lodki v operatsiiakh russkogo flota na Baltiiskom more v 1914–1915 gg.* (Submarines in Operations of the Russian Fleet on the Baltic During 1914–1915). Moscow, 1939.

Totleben (Todtleben), E. I., *Opisanie oborony Sevastopolia* (Description of the Defense of Sevastopol). St. Petersburg, 1863.

Trusov, G. M., *Podvodnye lodki v russkom i sovetskom flote* (Submarines in the Russian and Soviet Fleet). Leningrad, 1963.

Ustrialov, Nikolai Gerasimovich, *Istoriia tsarstvovaniia Petra Velikago* (History of the Reign of Peter the Great). 8 vols. St. Petersburg, 1858–63.

Vainer, B. A., *Severny flot v Velikoi Otechestvennoi voine* (The Northern Fleet in the Great Patriotic War). Moscow, 1964.

Veselago, F. F., *Istoriia russkoi armii i flota: Epokha Petra Velikago* (History of the Russian Army and Navy: The Period of Peter the Great). Moscow, 1911.

——, *Kratkaia istoriia russkago flota: 1700–1801* (A Short History of the Russian Navy: 1700–1801). St. Petersburg, 1893.

——, *Kratkiia svedeniia o russkikh morskikh srazheniiakh za dva stoletüa, s 1656 po 1856 god* (Short Accounts of Russian Naval Conflicts During Two Centuries from 1656 to 1856). St. Petersburg, 1871.

——, *Ocherk russkoi morskoi istorii* (A Sketch of Russian Naval History). St. Petersburg, 1875.

——, *Spisok russkikh voennykh sudov s 1686 po 1860 god* (A List of Russian War Vessels from 1686 to 1860). St. Petersburg, 1865.

Viunenko, Nikolai Petrovich, *Chernomorskii flot v Velikoi Otechestvennoi voine* (The Black Sea Fleet in the Great Patriotic War). Moscow, 1957.

Volkov, Yvgeny Zakharonovich, *Sredi moriakov i rechnikov torgovogo i voennogo flota* (Among the Sailors of the Sea and River Merchant Marine and Navy). Moscow, 1923.

Zaionchkovsky, Andrei Medardovich, *Podgotovka Rossii k imperialisticheskoi voine: Ocherki voennoi podgotovki i pervonachalnykh planov* (Russia's Preparations for the Imperialist War: Studies of Military Preparations and Original Plans). Moscow, 1926.

——, *Sbornik oborona Sevastopolia* (Record of the Siege of Sevastopol). St. Petersburg, 1904.

————, *Vostochnaia voina, 1853–1856 gg. Sviazi s sovremennoi ei politicheskoi obstanovkoi* (The Eastern War, 1853–1856, Its Connections with the Political Situation at the Time). 6 vols. St. Petersburg, 1900.

Zhandr, A., *Materialy dlia istorii oborony Sevastopolia i dlia biografii V. A. Kornilova* (Materials for a History of the Defense of Sevastopol and for the Biography of Vice Admiral Kornilov). St. Petersburg, 1859.

Zhukov, V. K., *Chernomorsky flot v revoliutsii: 1917–1918* (The Black Sea Fleet in the Revolution: 1917–1918). Moscow, 1932.

Ziugenkov, I. P., *Morskoi flot Rossii v Krymskoi voine* (Russia's Fleet in the Crimean War). Moscow, 1900.

PERIODICALS

(*Specific Issues*)

IN ENGLISH:

Airforce/Space Digest (Washington, D.C.), February 1966.

Airpower Historian (Washington, D.C.), Vol. X, no. 3, July 1963.

America (New York), Vol. 59, January 27, 1968.

American Heritage (New York), Vol. 11, June 1960.

American Historical Review (New York), Vol. 20, July 1915.

American Mercury (Los Angeles), Vol. 86, May 1958.

Atlantic Monthly (Boston), September 1964.

Blackwoods (Edinburgh), Vol. 167, April 1900.

Cassier (London), Vol. 19, April 1901.

Chambers Journal (Edinburgh), Vol. 24, 1855, and Vol. 72, 1904.

Christian Century (Chicago), Vol. 62, August 1, 1945.

Interavia (Geneva, Switzerland), November 1962.

Journal of Central European Affairs (Boulder, Colorado), April 1962.

Journal of Contemporary History (London), Vol. 4, 1966.

Journal of the American Society of Naval Engineers (Washington, D.C.) Vol. 63, 1951.

Life (Chicago), Vol. 53, December 21, 1962.

Metropolitan (New York), May 1904.

Missiles and Rockets (Washington, D.C.), Vol. 18, April 4, 1966.

Nation (New York), Vols. 79–80, 1904–05; Vol. 107, November 16, 1918.

National Review (New York), September 1948.

Naval War College Review (Newport, Rhode Island), Vol. 18, 1966–Vol. 23, 1971.

Navy (Washington, D.C.), June 1957–March 1968.

The Navy: The Magazine of Seapower (Washington, D.C.), May 1, 1958.

New York Times Magazine (New York), February 5, 1950.

Orbis (Philadelphia), Vol. 10, Spring 1966.

Ordnance (Washington, D.C.), March–April 1949.

Outlook (London), July 29, 1905.

Review of Reviews (New York), Vol. 31, June 1905.

Saturday Review (New York), November 14, 1936.

Shipmate (Annapolis, Maryland), May 1965.

Smithsonian Journal of History (Washington, D.C.), Vol. 1, 1966.
Soviet Military Review (Moscow), February 1967.
Soviet Review (New York), Winter 1964–65.
Soviet Studies (Glasgow), June 1, 1949.
Studies of the Soviet Union (New York), No. 2, 1965, and No. 3, 1966.
Vital Speeches of the Day (New York), June 1, 1968.

IN OTHER LANGUAGES:

Istoriia SSSR (History of the U.S.S.R.) (Moscow), 1957.
Kommunist (Moscow), No. 7, May 1962.
Journal des Débats (Paris), Vol. 32, January 30, 1925.
Morskoi flot (Moscow), 1941.
Novaia i noveishaia istoriia (Moscow), No. 1, 1964.
Revue des Deux Mondes (Paris), Vol. 49, January 15, 1949.
Revue Français (Paris), 1885.
Voennaia mysl (Military Thought) (Moscow), No. 7, July 1955.
Voprosy istorii (Questions of History) (Moscow), February 1963.

NEWSPAPERS:

London Times (London), April 27, 1961.
Los Angeles Times (Los Angeles), September 1939.
New York Evening Post (New York), April 9, 1904.

PERIODICALS

(General References)

Publications listed below are those used by the author repeatedly over a long period of time. Several are among the most important references used. It is almost impossible to conceive of a student doing serious work in Russian naval history without familiarity with *Morskoi sbornik*. *Morskiia zapiski* is perhaps less vital but still valuable. So to a lesser degree are many newspapers and foreign naval periodicals such as *Revue Maritime*. Of course, not all references listed in this section were of equal value in preparing this work.

IN ENGLISH:

American Neptune (Salem, Massachusetts), Vol. I, 1941–Vol. XXXI, 1971.
Aviation Week and Space Digest (New York), October 23, 1967–March 4, 1968.
Bulletin of the Institution for the Study of the U.S.S.R. (Munich, Germany), 1954–71.
Business Week (New York), Vol. 48, October 11, 1967–Vol. 49, March 2, 1968.
Colliers (New York), Vol. 112, July 24, 1903–Vol. 132, September 4, 1954.
Contemporary Affairs (Toronto, Canada), Vol. 88, August 1905–Vol. 93, April 1908.

Current History (Philadelphia), 1939–72.

Far Eastern Review (Canton, China), Vol. 6, September 1919–Vol. 35, November 1939.

Foreign Affairs (New York), Vol. 24, January 1946–Vol. 46, April 1972.

Fortnightly Review (London), Vol. 74, July 1900–Vol. 115, May 2, 1921.

Harpers Weekly (New York), Vols. 47 and 48, September 12, 1903–December 31, 1904.

Illustrated London News (London), Vol. 198, June 28, 1941–Vol. 225, October 2, 1954.

Journal of the Royal United Service Institution (London), Vol. 80, 1935–Vol. 113, 1968.

Literary Digest (New York), Vol. 56, February 4, 1918–Vol. 92, January 22, 1927.

Living Age (London), Vol. 222, 1894–Vol. 298, August 10, 1919.

Marine Corps Gazette (Quantico, Virginia), August 1955–October 1965.

Mariner's Mirror (London), Vol. 21, 1911–Vol. 57, 1971.

Military Affairs (Washington, D.C.), Vol. 1, 1937–Vol. 35, 1971.

Military Review (Ft. Leavenworth, Kansas), December 1965–January 1968.

Naval Review (Annapolis Maryland), 1964–72.

Navy (London), 1957–67.

Newsweek (Washington, D.C.), Vol. 30, July 2, 1947–-Vol. 80, July 17, 1972.

Reporter (New York), September 24, 1964–December 14, 1967.

Russian Review (Stanford, California), October 1962–April 1972.

Saturday Evening Post (Philadelphia), Vol. 153, April 9, 19 4–Vol. 230, November 2, 1957.

Scientific American (New York), Vol. 80, March 11, 1899–Vol. 94 May 1906.

Spectator (London), Vol. 102, January 16, 1909–Vol. 193, September 10, 1954.

Survival (London), March 1959–April 1967.

Time (New York), Vol. 61, March 30, 1953–Vol. 100, July 12, 1972.

United Service Magazine (London), March 1883–April 1906.

United States Naval Institute Proceedings (Annapolis, Maryland), Vol. 1, 1874–Vol. 98, 1972.

U.S. News and World Report (Washington, D.C.), Vol. 27, December 30, 1949–Vol. 73, July 12, 1972.

IN OTHER LANGUAGES:

Kommunist vooruzhennykh sil (Communist of the Armed Forces), 1963.

Krasnaia zvezda (Red Star) (Moscow), (Ministry of Defense), 1960–71.

Krasny flot (Red Navy) (Moscow), 1938–71.

Marine Rundschau (Frankfurt, Germany), August 1912–May 1962.

Morskoi sbornik (Sea Collection) (Leningrad), 1848–1971.
   This is by far the most important single source for the student of Russian naval history since 1850. Numerous articles appearing here were published later in book form. For three years during the revolution and civil war publication was suspended. For the early Soviet period this is very nearly the only source.

Morskiia zapiski (Naval Records) (New York), Vol. I, 1943–Vol. XXIV, 1966.

Revue de Défense Nationale (Paris), 1939–March 1966.
Revue Maritime (Paris), January 1963– December 1971.
Sovietsky flot (Soviet Navy) (Moscow), 1945–71.
Voenno-istorichesky zhurnal (Military History Journal) (Moscow), 1959–66.

ANNUALS:

Brassey's Naval and Shipping Annual (several titles) (London), 1892–1972.
Les Flottes de Combat (Paris), 1950–71.
Jane's Fighting Ships (London), 1878–1972.

ENCYCLOPEDIAS:

Bolshaia sovetskaia entsiklopediia (The Great Soviet Encyclopedia), 2nd ed.
    (Moscow), 1951–58.
Encyclopedia Americana (New York), 1948.
Encyclopedia Britannica (Chicago), 14th ed., 1967.
Voennaia entsiklopediia (Military Encyclopedia) (St. Petersburg), 1912–1916.
    Publication of this excellent but little known reference work ceased with
    the outbreak of World War I and was never resumed. The last reference
    is "Port Arthur."

NEWSPAPERS:

Christian Science Monitor (Boston), 1929–72.
Des Moines Register (Des Moines, Iowa), October 1965–October 1968.
Izvestiia (News) (Moscow), 1956–71.
Kansas City Star/Times (Kansas City, Missouri), March 1968–July 1972.
London Observer (London), 1791–1921.
New York Times (New York), 1938–72.
Pravda (Truth) (Moscow), 1932–71.
Washington Post (Washington, D.C.), 1950–72.
Washington Star (Washington, D.C.), 1950–56.

ARCHIVES AND SPECIAL SOURCES:

Association of Russian Imperial Naval Officers in America.
    This organization had published 86 volumes of material (principally
    in Russian) prior to its disbandment in 1965. Most of this material first
    appeared in *Morskiia zapiski*, the magazine of the organization, but a
    number of articles and studies were published separately.
Technical Museum of Munich, Germany.
United States National Archives, State and Navy department sections, Wash-
    ington, D.C.
University of Edinburgh, Edinburgh, Scotland.
Interview, Author with Honorable John L. Warner, Washington, D.C., June 23,
    1972.

The Gorshkov Papers. These consist of a series of articles under the general heading "Navies in War and in Peace" which appeared during 1972–73 in *Morskoi sbornik*. They were made available to the author in translation through the courtesy of the U.S. Navy Office of Naval Analyses.

Subject Index

Index of Persons

Abdul Hamid II (ruler of decadent Turkish Empire), dislike of in Europe, 185

Abramov, Rear Adm. N. O., 405

Agar, Lt. Augustus, 338

Alachev, led expedition against Turks, 9

Alafuzov, Adm. V. A., 566

Aleksandrov, A. P., critique of command of sea, 370–371; killed in purge, 373

Aleksandrovsky, I. F., 1866 submarine of, 181

Alekseev, Vice Adm. Yevgeny, character of, 210; May 5, 1904, assignment of fleet command to Vitheft, 221

Aleksianov, Lt., successful attack of on Barbary ships, 65

Alexander I (1801–25), education and background of, 113; reverses anti-British policy and cancels Indian project, 113; war with Persia and annexation of Georgia, 113; naval policies of, 111–114; disregard of advice of Kutuzov and defeat at Austerlitz, 114; sending of fleets into British waters in 1812, 113; failure to appreciate work of naval leaders, 134; naval policy of, 1815–25, 135–136; consents to circumnavigation of the globe, 141; hopes of extending American possessions discouraged by Monroe Doctrine, 145

Alexander II, character and views of, 183; role of in 1877 war with Turkey, 184; xvii, 8, 173

Alexander III, xvii; character of, 183; friendly to army and navy but not fully informed, 184; approval of 1881 twenty-six-year naval program, 192

Alexander-Sinclair, Adm. Sir Edwyn, 335–336

Alexis (1645–76), inability of to create navy, 14; defeat of Swedish galleys, 14; failure of attempt to build ships for the Caspian, 14–15, 16

Amelko, Adm. Nikolai N., 479

Andreev, Rear Adm., V. A., 46

Andrews, Baldwin, shipbuilder used by Peter I, 20

Anne I (1730–40), naval reforms of, 46–47; War of Polish Succession, 47; war with Turkey, 47, 48; 42

Antonov, Rear Adm. N. V., 446

Apraksin, Adm. Fedor M., direction of shipbuilding on White Sea, 18; background of and relations with Peter, 30; cuts off Swedish rear guard, 34; condemns murder of Dutch seamen, 36; capture of Viborg, 35; victory of at Gangut, 36; command of Revel and Kronstadt squadrons, 37; plunder raids of Swedish coast, 38; expedition against Persia, 40; non-naval concerns, 43;

637

Index of Ships

649